Deciphering Culture

Representation, subjectivity and sexuality continue to be central issues in the humanities and social sciences. *Deciphering Culture* explores their relationship, focusing on the way representations are used in practices and narratives of self formation. The authors develop the concept of 'curiosity' as a way of deciphering the working of distinct cultural formations, considering questions of knowledge and authority; reading and decipherment; and the ethics of critical and textual inquiry. Each author takes a distinct approach, using examples from the visual arts, literature, popular culture, and cultural history and examining questions of gender and cultural difference. They address a variety of topics including

- the historical formation of subjectivities, identities and differences
- everyday cultures and negotiation
- cultural conduct and habits of the self
- consumption and the body
- memory, history and autobiography

This fascinating book will appeal to students and academics from a variety of disciplinary backgrounds in the social sciences and cultural studies.

Jane Crisp is Adjunct Senior Lecturer in the School of Film, Media and Cultural Studies at Griffith University. **Kay Ferres** is Senior Lecturer in the School of Humanities at Griffith University. **Gillian Swanson** is Senior Lecturer in the School of Cultural Studies at the University of the West of England.

Deciphering Culture

Ordinary Curiosities and Subjective Narratives

Jane Crisp, Kay Ferres and Gillian Swanson

London and New York

First published 2000
by Routledge
11 New Fetter Lane, London EC4P 4EE

Simultaneously published in the USA and Canada
by Routledge
29 West 35th Street, New York, NY 10001

Routledge is an imprint of the Taylor & Francis Group

Typeset in Baskerville by Taylor & Francis Books Ltd

Printed and bound in Great Britain by Biddles Ltd, Guildford and King's
Lynn

British Library Cataloguing in Publication Data
A catalogue record for this book is available from the British Library

Library of Congress Cataloging in Publication Data
Crisp, Jane.
Deciphering culture: ordinary curiosities and subjective narratives/
Jane Crisp, Kay Ferres, and Gillian Swanson.
p. cm.
Includes bibliographical references and index.
1. Individuation (Psychology) in literature. 2. Individuation (Psychology)
3. Gender identity in literature. 4. Gender identity. I. Ferres, Kay,
II. Swanson, Gillian. III. Title.
PN56.I57 C75 2000
809'.93353–dc21

00–034473

ISBN 0 415–10837–3 (hbk)
ISBN 0 415–10838–1 (pbk)

Curiosity (kiuerĭp siti). ME [A.OF. *curioseté*, ad. L. *curiositatem*; see CURIOUS and –TY]

1. Carefulness – 1747; scrupulousness, accuracy – 1694; ingenuity – 1772; undue niceness or subtlety – 1766. 2. Desire to know or learn; inquisitiveness ME.; inquisitiveness about trifles or other people's affairs 1577. 3. Scientific or artistic interest; connoisseurship – 1781. 4. A hobby – 1661. 5. A fancy, a whim – 1718. 6. Careful or elaborate workmanship; nicety of construction – 1807. 7. Curiousness 1597. 8. A curious matter of investigation – 1700. 9. A vanity, refinement – 1705. 10. A curious detail or feature – 1747. 11. Anything curious, rare, or strange 1645.

2. A noble and solid c. of knowing things in their beginnings 1632. Curiositie, which I take to be a desire to know the faults and imperfections in other men HOLLAND. 7. Rotterdam, where the c. of the place detained us three days 1686. 11. Japanese goods, lacker ware and curiosities SEMMES

(*Oxford English Dictionary*)

A man possesses nothing certainly save a brief loan of his own body: and yet the body of man is capable of much curious pleasure.

(James Branch Cabell, *Jurgen*, 1919)

Contents

Figures

Preface
How to read this book

The idea for this book began in our teaching collaboration: we taught a course on the representation of gender together – in various combinations – between 1990 and 1998. Our students were drawn from a variety of disciplinary backgrounds – cultural studies, film and media studies, literature, history, visual arts and professional areas such as health and education – and we therefore devised a way of teaching that allowed us to address issues in gender and representation in an interdisciplinary context. We drew from a broad base of different models, presenting differing approaches, outlining their implications, and demonstrating their applications in a range of contexts.

Of course, many gender studies courses name their distinctiveness as 'interdisciplinarity'. What was different and challenging in this case was that we were teaching in an institutional context that was also successfully interdisciplinary. We could make no territorial claim on 'gender', either: it appeared in many other courses. Our students were not seeking refuge from traditional departments indifferent or hostile to 'gender'; they were coming to develop an expertise, whether 'theoretical' or 'applied' in its orientation.

We didn't, then, set ourselves or our project up as 'oppositional' or 'subversive'. We each were members of teaching teams in other subject areas: in film studies (Jane), cultural policy studies (Gillian) and Australian studies (Kay). What we sought to achieve was a productive convergence of gender studies with these fields. This pedagogic impulse inevitably influenced our research interests and directions as well.

From this beginning, we took our research and writing – as well as our teaching – in different directions, and we have developed a book that maintains the distinctiveness of our individual involvements and intellectual orientations. Each of our contributions, then, shows a different pathway through the common questions that addressing representation and gender raises.

The order in which each section's chapters are arranged allows for a progressive build from the more personal and accessible chapters by Jane to the denser explorations of each section's issues by Kay and Gillian. While Jane is concerned primarily with the textual, and the ways readers negotiate their meanings and use them in their everyday lives, Gillian is concerned with the configuration of knowledges and the way these constitute the 'environments' of subjectivity, as institutional definitions are disseminated to become part of popular cultural repertoires. Kay's chapters bridge these concerns – working from the practices of reading and writing, she considers the way representation functions as a practice of memory and history.

The book can therefore be read in two ways at least: 'down', taking each section and examining the different ways each author formulates the question of the relationship of representation and gender; or 'across', by following the thread of a particular author's analysis and argument, and moving through from one section to another to assemble a particular approach and discern its implications and productivity. Each author's contribution to the section is outlined in the section introduction, which identifies our common starting points and the different way we pursue them.

The sections of the book move from the general to the particular. In Chapter 2, we offer three introductory essays on curiosity as a way of thinking about culture, representation and subjectivity. In Part 2, we outline distinct approaches to representation, and in Part 3, we consider how the different frameworks we adopt lead to the analysis of different forms of representation and thereby reconfigure the object of representation. And finally, in Part 4, we each take up a particular case study, focusing on the blurred line between memory and history. Each of these chapters demonstrates the application of the models we describe in Part 2 and takes up one dimension of those forms of representation we identified in Part 3. And they show the implications of these approaches in a sustained way, based in our respective forms of research. In these final chapters, we see subjectivity being mobilised in ways that foreground the instability of the definitions and categories of gender, as representation is seen as a provisional process, open to competing versions and alternative readings.

Acknowledgements

Firstly we must thank those at Routledge who helped to bring this project to fruition: Chris Rojek for his early support; Mari Shullaw for putting her confidence in such a 'quirky book' and for constructive advice as we remodelled it over time; and the unknown readers, whose comments made us consider our 'threaded conversations' more closely, and allowed us to rethink our early conception of its form.

We owe a debt of gratitude to our colleagues within the former School of Humanities, now Faculty of Arts, at Griffith University for the stimulus that working with them provided and for their constructive interest in the various projects out of which our individual chapters have arisen. We are also indebted to the many students from different disciplinary backgrounds who attended our courses and whose enthusiasm and commitment provided the major inspiration for writing the present book.

We would also like to thank various people who gave advice or commented on earlier versions of particular chapters: Rachel Bowlby, the late Christian Metz, Francie Oppel, Helen Crowley. Thanks to Chris Barry for permission to use the images discussed in Chapter Seven. And special thanks to Janice Mitchell for her invaluable help in the conversion and formatting of our individual manuscripts into their final publishable form.

Personal thanks are also due to our families, for their patience and support throughout and especially during the hectic final stages of getting this book ready for publication: to Colin Crisp, to Ken and Allison Ferres, to Gwen and Ron Swanson, and to Colin Mercer, Taara and Joseph.

Part 1

Introduction

Curiosities

Introduction

A key feature of this book is that it contains three different approaches to 'deciphering culture'. Although it is a collaborative work, we have chosen to keep our voices distinct rather than melding them together into one collective editorial voice, except in the introductions to each section. The primary function of the first two chapters, therefore, is to provide a sense of the different backgrounds, interests, methodologies and styles that inform our individual contributions to the book.

Chapter 1, 'Curious Histories', directly introduces the three writers through autobiographical sketches characterising those intellectual engagements that inform our writing of this book. These histories chart our involvement with particular subject areas – literary studies, film and media studies, gender studies, cultural studies – and with the various evolving and competing methodologies associated with these fields. Because they are individual, they make clear what each of us is drawing on in the chapters that follow; but because they are also representative of the trajectories followed by so many of our contemporaries, they serve to give the reader a sense of the wider domain within which our work and this book are situated.

These three journeys are all, in a sense, 'through the looking glass'. Mirrors reflect what is behind the looker, as we reflect here on the routes we have taken. However, like Alice's journey through the looking glass, ours too have led to different ways of seeing and understanding the world we inhabit. The moment of passing through or beyond the looking glass is one in which alternatives are simultaneously in play; it is also an emblem of the 'between-ness' that is a key element of all our subsequent chapters. Between-ness is a condition of curiosity as it moves from arousal to satisfaction and back again.

In Chapter 2, each of us takes up this central motif of curiosity. Jane Crisp discusses curiosity in Rudyard Kipling's 'The Elephant's Child'; Kay Ferres, in the stories of Eve and Pandora; Gillian Swanson, in *Alice's Adventures in Wonderland* and *The Old Curiosity Shop*. Our treatment of the notion of curiosity and of our chosen texts makes fully visible the differences in approach already glimpsed in our curious histories. Jane Crisp concentrates on a playful analysis of her text, drawing on structuralist and psychoanalytic ideas in the process. Kay Ferres deciphers evidence of the workings of curiosity in both the production of representations and critical rereadings of them. Gillian Swanson shows how new spaces of consumption in the nineteenth-century city allowed new ways of exercising curiosity, bringing about an encounter with difference that '[unhinged] cultural certainty' and destabilised sexual categories.

Taken together, the two chapters in this section introduce the range of themes foregrounded in the title, *Deciphering Culture: Ordinary Curiosities and Subjective Narratives*. Curiosity, which is the linking motif of our individual contributions to Chapter 2, becomes visible as a motivating force not only in the activities and pleasures of daily life but also in academic investigations. It underpins the study of culture: subjected to a curious and inquiring gaze, the ordinary and everyday becomes curious, a subject for interrogation – to be read for clues that might help decipher the inner workings of distinct cultural formations. The inclusion of our curious histories in Chapter 1 introduces our interest in subjective narratives, providing an instance of the fact that the act of narration, whether of national or personal or fictional histories, is also inevitably an act of construction of the narrating subject, which draws on patterns already laid down within that subject's formation. The act of reading is also one of construction and negotiation, as evidenced by the different ways in which familiar texts and stories are read and used in Chapter 2. As we show in that chapter, these processes inevitably involve questions of gender. And finally, the treatment of subjective narratives in this section foreshadows our later engagements with questions of memory, narrative and the subjective in writing the past in the book's final section.

1 Curious histories

Jane Crisp, Kay Ferres and Gillian Swanson

Jane Crisp

My journeys to this point, both physical and intellectual, are fairly typical for someone of my background. Like the majority of Australians, I was born elsewhere – in my case, in England. My parents and I settled in New Zealand after the war. After completing a BA and a Master's degree, I married and spent some years in France while my husband was doing his doctorate. Many of our friends and contemporaries were doing much the same thing, studying overseas at British, European and American universities for higher degrees that would eventually earn us university jobs 'back home'. In 1965 my husband joined the French department of an Australian university; we had a child and I completed a doctorate. Since then we have been back to Europe regularly on the sabbatical leaves to which our employment as university teachers has entitled us, and are likely to continue to do so after retirement, since our son has reversed the trajectory of his mother and grandparents and is now living in England. This pattern of migrations and journeyings to and fro across the world for purposes of work, study and tourism reflects the mobility of his and our generations within postwar Western capitalist society.

Looking back on the parallel intellectual journey, as writing this section obliges me to do, I note that it, too, is one that many of my contemporaries have followed. My undergraduate studies were conventional enough – majors in English and in Latin language before the spread of literary theory – literary history and close reading of selected 'great authors' were the order of the day, and no one mentioned the New Critics or F.R. Leavis, despite their influence on the orientation of our studies. So naive was I that, later, when I was first tutoring in Australia and a colleague was pointed out to me as being 'a Leavisite', I assumed that he must practise some strange religion. However, this naive assumption was perhaps not so far from the mark after all, given the fervour with which the various competing approaches to literary and other studies have been espoused by their practitioners over the last few decades.

My doctoral thesis, which I worked on during the 1960s, involved a study of the relationship between the novels that Jane Austen read and those that she wrote. Although I didn't realise it at the time, this work tied in with several contemporary developments within the study of English. On the one hand, it related to a growing interest in popular genres and in writing by women that addressed female readers, which was leading to a broadening of the university curriculum to include women's or gender studies. On the other, it reflected a shift away from an emphasis on the unique work of art that embodied the vision of its author, towards questions of intertextuality – a text's place within a web of other texts on which depended its material, strategies and meanings. I had not heard of structuralism yet, but when I did I had no trouble recognising the implications of what I had been doing in my doctorate.

During the 1970s and 1980s, I extended my doctoral work to include a number of once popular, but since neglected, nineteenth-century women writers, among them Rosa Nouchette Carey; her critical reception provides one of the case studies for Chapter 6. During this period, however, my teaching and research interests were being influenced not only by the rise of gender studies but also by that of film and media studies, both of which developments typically occurred first within departments of English. I found myself spending progressively less time teaching in courses on 'seventeenth-century poetry' or 'the twentieth-century novel' and more and more time in newer subjects on the curriculum, such as 'language and communication' and 'rhetoric of the mass media'. The similar shift occurring within my research is evidenced by the titles of some articles and book chapters produced by me during this period: ' "Descriptive Syntagma" and ' "Descriptive Pauses" – A Problem in Film Analysis' (Crisp 1986), ' "No Message, No Sex, Just Good Fun": Dealing with Gender Representation in the Popular Cinema' (Crisp 1987), 'Past History, Present Concerns: The Bicentenary of the French Revolution' (Crisp 1992). Underpinning two of these items is an interest in theoretical questions around how the standard repertoire of narrative film practice engages the viewer; these questions provide another case study for Chapter 6.

Even more significant, though, was the growing influence of a range of theoretical frameworks which were radically altering the questions that informed much of our work. As a means of simplifying what was then a complex and fiercely contested terrain, and still is within many universities, one can divide up the competing frameworks and their followers into three broad groups. First, the traditionalists continued to regard the appreciation of individual texts and their authors as the central and most worthy object of study, and stoutly rejected as irrelevant the wider social, political and theoretical issues raised by members of the other two groups. Second, there were those who were drawing on various Marxist and sociological frameworks to introduce questions about the particular interests and values that were being served by the way English studies were currently constituted. Such questions made visible the implicit biases of culture, class and gender within the official curriculum and helped to promote the inclusion of such previously marginalised and devalued areas as Third World and colonial writing, gender studies, and the study of popular media. Third, there were those who were influenced by the ideas of structuralism and semiotics and focused not so much on individual texts as on the broader systems of language or narrative on which the production and making sense of texts depends. Orwell had asserted that 'good prose is like a window pane' (1970: 30) – a transparent medium through which an undistorted vision of the world could be conveyed; this view was challenged by an alternative view of language, not as a medium that we use but as the very means through which our world and our places within it are constructed. Just how contested this terrain was may be gauged by the struggles that I and some of my colleagues had during 1985 to persuade a 'Department of English' to accept the introduction of a first-year survey course of these contemporary theoretical issues. The course was finally accepted, but under the anodyne title of 'Approaches to Literature', in deference to more traditional colleagues' fears about the possible effects of the dreaded word 'theory'!

Despite the ongoing divisions and debates between these three broad approaches, in practice many academics draw on aspects of all of them. I am no exception. In the pleasure that I enjoyed while doing my close reading of 'The Elephant's Child' in Chapter 2, I recognise my earliest training in the more orthodox skills of close reading, even though these have now been augmented by insights from the theoretical frameworks that I have worked with since then. My most recent research draws on highly theoretical structuralist and semiotic ideas about how language systems work, yet uses these for the practical project of helping members of one of the most devalued groups within our society – people who have Alzheimer's disease. The questions that inform this research are typical of those posed by the more politically and sociologically oriented scholars: Who speaks for whom? What are the practical consequences of representing someone as lacking the capacity to reason or to speak intelligibly? Whose interests and values are served in the way we define and treat people with Alzheimer's (certainly not those of people with the condition)? Yet the strategies that I have been developing to help carers to listen to and make sense of someone with dementia arise directly out of structuralist and semiotic theories of language as a sense-making system. Meaning and sense are products of that system, not a result of matching words and things. People with Alzheimer's speak differently from 'normal' people; they lose the ability to distinguish between fact and fantasy and to give people and things the right name. However, because their language use still follows identifiable rules, from a semiotic perspective it is still meaningful – provided we know what those rules are. This project, which brings together all my previous interests, is touched on again in Chapter 3, when I consider the role of other people in the fashioning of our identities, and is covered in more detail in the final section as an example of how the ideas I discuss elsewhere in this book have been taken up in my own research.

I would never have guessed when I embarked on my intellectual journey that it would end with my working on and for people with Alzheimer's, nor that the baggage that I have acquired along the way would eventually prove of such practical help in this work. Yet my basic trajectory, from a Department of English to a School of Film, Media and Cultural Studies, and from work within English literature to a project that brings theory to bear on a lived contemporary issue, is one that many of my colleagues have followed.

Kay Ferres

When Jane proposed that we use biography as a means of discriminating our different voices and positions in the chapters that make up this book, this presented itself to me as a problem of writing: how to inscribe the personal, what were the uses of the autobiographical voice, how to evade the 'confessional' genre. This, of course, is a question that many scholars working in cultural studies and gender studies have addressed in their work: I think immediately of Valerie Walkerdine, Annette Kuhn, Nancy Miller and Jane Tompkins. When Jane Crisp and I have taught together, the shadow of Jane Tompkins is never far away. Gillian Swanson introduced me to the writing of Valerie Walkerdine when we arrived together at Griffith in 1988, and I remember her account of Carolyn Steedman's mother's longing for the New Look coat. But, temperamentally, disclosure is not something I am drawn to. And so I want to begin with a reference to Rachel Brownstein's essay, 'Interrupted Reading: Personal Criticism in the Present Time' (Brownstein 1996).

Preparing an introduction to a new edition of her book, *Becoming a Heroine*, Brownstein includes an anecdote. It describes an incident in the subway when a stranger interrupts her reading, and her annoyance at this unwelcome intrusion. She offers it as a 'story about the enormous gulf between compulsive readers like me and practical, militant nonreaders' like the strange young man in the subway and her mother (Brownstein 1996: 30).

In spite of her intention, 'the anecdote stubbornly refused to make that point', and was excised from her text. Her editor fretted that the story was about other kinds of difference that Brownstein didn't recognise and deconstruct – race, generational difference, sexual difference. 'Readers' and 'non-readers' – these categories perhaps recall a kind of class difference, focused on the high culture–popular culture distinction, which cultural studies has critiqued and dismantled. In 1932, Queenie Leavis (wife of the influential literary critic F.R. Leavis) published a book about taste and class, *Fiction and the Reading Public*, which marked out the differences between elite and mass culture in Britain. Brownstein draws a similar line in 1996 but the groups that fall out on either side of it do not correspond neatly to class, race or ethnic categories. Indeed, writing and reading were practices critical to the emergence of minority cultural politics in the late twentieth century.

The difference in my story might be named as 'cultural' rather than 'class'. In common with many Australian women, I am a reader with tastes formed by exposure to 'classic texts', newspapers and to public radio, the only form of mass culture whose networks extended to remote and rural areas until the 1970s. ABC radio and ABC-sponsored concerts broadcast an 'Englishness' among a diversifying Australian population in the 1950s and 1960s, when I grew up. The advent of television and popular music, on the other hand, brought a dangerous proximity with 'Americanness'. The difficulty of isolating elements of an Australian cultural identity against these dominant cultures has been critical in recent debates about the formation of intellectual identities in Australia. Those identities are shaped by that contact with the great 'elsewhere'; they are not formed in isolation from it.

Masculine intellectual formation has been much written about in biographical and autobiographical writing in Australia. For the generation who grew up under the regimes of the 'White Australia' immigration policy of the 1950s, it typically involves Irish Catholic schooling and, in early adulthood, expatriation. A postwar generation began to look to North America, rather than Great Britain, for this experience of 'elsewhere'. My impression of women's accounts is rather different. Institutions don't figure to the same extent: women were not eligible for the Rhodes scholarships that provided a colonial passage for many of the men who became prominent in public life. The transition from Australian country towns to the metropolitan centres of culture for women is often a story centred on romance; but it is a story that is difficult to tell in terms of starting points and destinations that are not 'personal'. Jill Ker Conway (1990) and Meaghan Morris (1998) have tried to tell it. Conway's is a narrative about leaving things behind; Morris, on the other hand, is a returner. I have never left, in any sense that could position me credibly as 'outside' my own culture.

I pondered the distance from my own and Meaghan Morris's Australian childhoods to the working-class rooms of Carolyn Steedman's and Annette Kuhn's family stories; the intellectual trajectories that take Morris to Paris and the US; and the glamour of expatriation compared to my own fixity. Would it ever make sense to ask of an Oxford or Cambridge intellectual (or one from Harvard or New York), 'Why have you never left?' I am a tourist in other cultures, especially intellectual cultures. I am a reader.

I wasn't 'schooled', though I went to school. But I learned to read, indiscriminately. My mother used to buy books from Americans who appeared on the doorstep selling Bible stories. These blue-bound volumes were divided between biblical narratives (in the back half of the book) and morality tales of contemporary family life; tales which, in the great elsewhere of the televisual world in the 1950s, were becoming the staples of this domestic medium. The clean-cut purveyors of this morality would appear on our back porch and my mother would emerge from the adjacent kitchen or laundry to pay them off. As far as I know, no other member of my family ever read these books – not my sisters who taught Sunday school, or my older brother. Collectively, we came together around contemporary music (the radiogram and the piano and the saxophone), the cinema and backyard cricket.

And we were all encouraged to be performers.

A memory: at 7, being Alice in the school concert in a blue dress; reappearing in the same dress as a doll in a toy shop in the Christmas play, bending stiffly as a boy (whose name I've forgotten) wound me up with a cardboard key.

A photograph: at 9 or 10, at another school; smaller even than the last and in North Queensland, in a settlement that is probably most accurately described as a hamlet. It boasted a beach, a cinema, a garage, a butcher's shop and a general store. There was a hairdresser who ran a business from under her house and a music teacher from Poland. In the photograph, my hair has been cropped to a helmet and I am in the midst of a group of kids who look thinner, less substantial. One is an Aboriginal girl, Jeannie, who always seemed to be slipping away. Here she is all angles, almost crouching. I recall how I always felt afraid for her because the teacher upbraided her mercilessly.

And on Sundays, when my father had a day off work, we would drive to the nearby town to Mrs Schelling's shop where, each time, I would choose a new book: *What Katy Did* or *Little Women*. My older sister, who lived in the city and was an amateur actress, would send books as birthday gifts: *Pollyanna*, which I went to see at the open-air picture theatre, where bougainvillea curled around the gap in the roof between the canvas seats and the screen, and where the salt breeze and the sound of the waves penetrated. Hayley Mills' Englishness overwhelmed any sense of Pollyanna's Americanness: a curious contamination of the 'Americanisation' of Australian culture in the 1960s.

At home my father read into the night, sitting at the dining table under the light. In the humidity of summer the light would attract clouds of small black beetles, which crawled over the pages and through his hair. He placed bowls of water on the table for them to fall into. When television finally glimmered into life, we often watched in a shop window, those same beetles falling from fluorescent tubes on to the pavement.

I read my way into a liminal existence between Anglo and American culture. When I went to university, I read literature (the canon) and psychology. Film studies were new and glamorous; Germaine Greer, Kate Millett and Mary Ellman shocking in their exposure of the academy's exclusion of women. Many of the scholars in the Australian university system came from the United Kingdom or North America; and many Australian writers, painters and performers became permanent expatriates. Although expatriates are often regarded in Australia as having left their culture behind, or even to have repudiated it (as, indeed, some have), it seems to me that they have contributed a doubled vision that is the other side of the 'cultural cringe'. 'Australia' is located against an international horizon. It is a threshold, rather than a liminal or marginal space. My contributions to this book reflect this way of being in the world. I do not know my 'place' except through its relation to these other alluring places. My beginnings in literary studies have not been left behind as I have made moves into cultural history and applied ethics. The 'itinerary' that connects my chapters with one another is an interest in the way people occupy the space 'in between' identities and cultures. In the chapters that follow I have read texts and practices together and against each other, deciphering the textual exchanges that are implicated in the transformation and reconfiguration of identities.

My own recent research has been concerned with an expatriate Australian writer, Rosa Praed, an exponent of the 'sensation novel' who published over a long and unevenly successful career spanning the 1870s to the 1930s. Her subject was often Australia and colonial race relations, but she also wrote about marriage reform and, from the 1890s, took up with what Rita Felski has called 'the popular sublime' – theosophy and psychic research. I've several times gone to Europe and the US to trace her engagements with political and literary cultures. I've followed the walk along the Thames that she describes in a book written with the Irish politician Justin McCarthy and the fellow Australian expatriate artist, Mortimer Menpes. I've visited the various places in Cornwall where she and her companion Nancy Harward found lodgings during the Second World War, when their usual French destinations were impossible to get to.

I have read my way into a familiarity with those places that shocked me when I actually saw them. I do not belong there, yet those landscapes and urban vistas are sedimented with meaning for me through the memory of countless readings and writings. My contributions to this book are about memory, history and belonging, about the transmission of culture through practices of reading and writing.

Gillian Swanson

How do I begin to trace an intellectual narrative that would make sense of my contributions to this book? I find the harnessing of the autobiographical mode to this task an awkward one, eliciting a different kind of thinking. I love those forms of autobiography which mess with its difference from academic writing, and have a powerful interest in the unstable boundaries between the actual and fictional – in the subjective narrative of figures like T.E. Lawrence, for example. And I have myself wandered between those genres. But, in my own writing, these days I like to keep them separate. Disclosure, for me, belongs in other compartments of my life, and exists in the more intimate exchanges of talk, and other forms of personal correspondence. There is a distinctive pleasure in the restraint, in the impersonality, of academic writing.

So it is with some trepidation that I attempt to retell the story of the way my intellectual interests develop, in a way that fits with my writing of these chapters. I can tell about my 'beginnings': nearing the end of my degree in French and English Literature in the mid-1970s. In those days, I meandered carelessly between the stark and defiant precision of modernist writing and the voluptuous and engulfing narrative of classic and popular novels; it didn't strike me as even worthy of comment that each of them excited me in quite different ways. To restate Kay's phrase, but with a different meaning, I too was a reader: my route into critical analysis was one dominated by this pattern of reading rather than by the established principles of academic inquiry. Yet this was a period in which differences in textual construction *were* critical, as textual innovation and transgression became the hallmark of intellectual inquiry and cultural work, and structural theory looked for its ultimate object. A serious concern with the engagement of the reader, with the way a text 'constructed' and 'signified' its reader, would only later lead – ironically perhaps, given the early dismissal of 'real' readers – to considering the extratextual formation of readers, or the way different modes of address were formed within literary genres or popular novels, different media forms, or a postcolonial frame. I would have to wait to discover these questions and their connection to cultural difference.

In a chance encounter within the newly developing field of film studies during a course on French critical theory, I found modes of analysis that allowed for the exchange between popular, classical and modernist forms. When I started teaching film, I explored with students the differences in pleasure that moving beyond conventional textual repertoires could bring, and the other kinds of meaning that new forms allowed. After we watched the films of Hitchcock and Douglas Sirk, traced the development of Clint Eastwood's star persona, or identified the conventions of *films noirs* for their syllabus, they stayed behind to help me with my own research on the way 'independent cinema' asked spectators to challenge their own viewing formations and recast the way classifications of taste intersected with social class and difference. So they became experts on films of the British avant-garde – based on the exploration of colour, movement and light, the film frame, and the passage of film through the projector – and independent film, which worked with narrativity, adopting Brechtian conventions or following the writings of Gertrude Stein.

This was, perhaps, an awkward way of negotiating the 'divide' in my own interests, adopting Bourdieu's schema of the relation of education, cultural capital and distinction 'against the grain'. I tortuously attempted to show that cultural subjects were able to negotiate differences between the popular and classical and the avant-garde, that taste communities were not so cut and dried as Bourdieu's hierarchical grids indicated. This seems less awkward now, when empirical or historical work has shown us something of the patterns of 'ordinary readers' less governed by literary canons and institutional protectionism: book clubs, libraries and letters tell us of more experimental readers than of those whose writing established regimes of literary value.

Here I pause. It's difficult to convey the ordinariness of this work: a series of incremental musings, learning to worry away at an idea, rather than a string of epiphanies. But also it is a difficult move to bring this narrative back to my work for this book. My route has been a more circuitous one than I could chart through a theoretical shift from texts and readers to cultural history; one that has to find its explanation in less deliberate moves.

My early family life was one of stories and talk, and it was there, as much as in fiction, that I discovered other lives. The attachments which overlay my intellectual interests were borne from the calm talk of women knitting in front of a quiet television, telling stories of the living of lives, of conversations held elsewhere, exchanging letters from people I knew well but never met.

My mother's stories of life in the war were a particular delight: ironing next to the French windows until the last minute before the doodlebugs went silent, then tearing down the garden and jumping headfirst through the door of the shelter on to the bed before they dropped; her mother packing up with her children and travelling up and down between London and Wales, my mother hating the schools where only she didn't speak the language (each one she started at just beginning to 'do Australia in geography'); going back into the London house after a near hit and finding in front of the piano her brother's birthday goldfish dead among the shattered shards of their glass bowl. My father told of his German grandparents, bricks thrown through their shop window before the First

World War, before they were driven to return to their homeland; his own father, with his English public-school education provided at the cost of staying in a country his family had left, never able to reconcile himself to the tensions of living as a foreigner; my father's own recollections of life on the move, as this reluctance to settle was translated into a restless and insecure family life. My grandfather told of a life more remote still: his large family living in a tiny cottage on the edge of a country estate; the expectation that the boys would go 'up to the house' as gardeners and the girls into service, but ambition and chance taking them to India, China, Egypt and Australia; his injury in Ireland; his 'chance' in life dashed by the lay-offs of the Depression. He told his stories – as, too, he recounted the poems he remembered for ever after learning them at the age of 6 – at the prompting of his daughter, who'd heard them for fifty years when he died. These were stories told by my family in communal recollection; told to let us all know 'what life was like'; told just to me, inciting my identification.

What I could never unravel in these stories was the 'interior' map of these foreigners – so unlike the people who told of these extraordinary events, their own past lives. I wondered how they thought and felt, what pattern of everyday life connected these events, what drove them to move the pattern of their lives in the direction they did, how it became possible to think beyond their own forma-tion and reinvent themselves in such different times. Though these may seem to be psychological questions, they are also historical ones. This was the compart-ment of my life in which I was able to exercise an historical attention, and it wasn't until much later that I could address similar questions in my intellectual work. Now, the questions about subjectivity that impel me more than any other are those about the formation of everyday cultures, of private life, of historical sensibilities, and the management of intimacy, of emotion. And I want to under-stand the repertoire of knowledges that are used in those ordinary environments, and how they derive from those authoritative disciplines which appear to address a different, more public, subject. What struck me then, as it does now, is the way subjectivity operates as a series of gestures, the impossibility of getting beyond the account, the futility of aiming for an essence. It is determining the limits of the known that excites me.

I moved, in the mode of a lone adventurer, to Australia. There I found I had no analytic tools for understanding a culture that hadn't already gripped me and seeped into my skin; one in which, moreover, I was addressed as a member of the seat of empire and positioned by the history of an encounter that I knew shamefully little about. I'm sure that was a critical moment in destabilising the political and intellectual certainties – habits, in the pejorative use of the word – that I'd become tired of, that had driven me to leave. But I can't tell any stories to show how it worked. All I know is that it manifested itself in a massive uncer-tainty for a long period about how to speak and write convincingly. I also know that I'm now more interested in understanding culture – and gender – in the particular than in the general; examining the environments of subjectivity, the logics of cultural repertoires, and the way they have evolved in specific times and places.

It was in Australia, a country with a more eclectic and experimental culture, that I found I could move beyond the political shibboleths of a tired intellectual formation, and reinstate some of the imaginative connections that I'd left alone in the name of moral and political certainties and intellectual modism. Being 'out of place', as I was in my early years in Australia – a most thrilling dislocation – made possible a less insular and pessimistic form of intellectual inquiry. At the university where this book was first conceived, I discovered a less rarefied arena for theoretical work, combining work on institutional knowledges, cultural tastes, urban resources, the government of populations, and practices of everyday life, while the attention to conduct and conduct management appeared to me to complement studies of the history of the formation of subjectivity. Here, a more practical engagement with institutions and public life developed, which allowed me to use this kind of historical work to fuel an involvement in the management of cultural resources, and in cultural policy formation.

But a ten-year period spent living in Australia can't be seen just in terms of adventure, though it may have started that way. I may have had dreams of leaving, but soon I was confronted with the less romantic event of the arrival. Arrivals – as now I relocate myself in an environment with deep-rooted connections and an older familiarity, but without the coordinates of being and living that I assembled over those ten years – are harder to narrativise. This is the work of intellectual reconfiguration: the ability to move beyond seeing that which is different as invisibility, as emptiness. It's the work of assembly, not individual vision; archaeology, not transcendent inspiration; audit, not epiphany. But it is perhaps in these more banal activities that we find the pleasures of the curious.

Bibliography

Brownstein, R.M. (1996) 'Interrupted Reading: Personal Criticism in the Present Time', in H. Aram Veeser (ed.) *Confessions of the Critics*, New York: Routledge, 29–39.

Conway, J.K. (1990) *The Road from Coorain*, New York: Vintage Books.

Crisp, J. (1986) ' "Descriptive Syntagma" and ' "Descriptive Pauses" – A Problem in Film Analysis', *Australian Journal of Cultural Studies* 4, 1: 115–21.

—— (1987) ' "No Message, No Sex, Just Good Fun": Dealing with Gender Representation in the Popular Cinema', *Hecate* 13, 1: 35–50.

—— (1992) 'Past History, Present Concerns: The Bicentenary of the French Revolution', in T. Bennett, P. Buckridge, D. Carter and C. Mercer (eds) *Celebrating the Nation*, St Leonards, Australia: Allen & Unwin.

Leavis, Q.D. (1932) *Fiction and the Reading Public*, London: Chatto and Windus.

Morris, M. (1998) *Too Soon, Too Late: History in Popular Culture*, Bloomington: Indiana University Press.

Orwell, G. (1970) 'Why I write', *Collected Essays, Journalism and Letters*, vol. 1, Harmondsworth: Penguin, 23–30.

2   Curious pleasures

Jane Crisp, Kay Ferres and Gillian Swanson

THE CURIOUS CASE OF 'THE ELEPHANT'S CHILD'

Jane Crisp

Curious pleasure – the pleasures of curiosity for me bring to mind a favourite story from my childhood, that of 'The Elephant's Child' and his 'satiable curtiosity' in Rudyard Kipling's *Just So Stories*. For those of you who are unfamiliar with this tale – a curious tale indeed – here is a summary of it:

> Originally the elephant had no trunk, 'only a blackish, bulgy nose, as big as a boot'. 'The Elephant's Child', however, 'was full of satiable curtiosity', and kept on asking questions even though the only response he got was a series of spankings (this is a very English story) from the other animals. His final question, 'What does the crocodile have for dinner?', earns him spankings from everyone. Undeterred, he sets out for 'the great grey-green, greasy, Limpopo River, all set about with fever trees' to find the answer. On his journey he receives another spanking from the 'Bi-Coloured-Python-Rock-Snake' for asking his question again. Finally, he meets the crocodile, who grabs him 'by his little nose' and tells him the answer – he is today's dinner. A tug-of-war ensues, which the elephant's child eventually wins (thanks to help from the 'Bi-Coloured-Python-Rock-Snake'), but not before his nose has been pulled into 'a really truly trunk'. He soon discovers the many advantages this new trunk has over the 'mere-smear nose' he had before. Best of all, though, is the fact that he can now spank all the members of 'his dear families'.
>
> (1950: 59–77)

Rereading 'The Elephant's Child' now, certain things struck me which never did before. This is a reverse castration story, in which the child's curiosity, despite being initially punished, is eventually rewarded. Instead of something being taken away, as the already castrated word 'satiable' might seem to foreshadow, something is added: the 'mere-smear' boot of a nose becomes the real thing, 'a really truly trunk' that gives its owner power over the other members of his animal family. The would-be castrator, the crocodile with its dangerous jaws lurking in the 'great grey-green, greasy, Limpopo River', perhaps stands for some predatory female principle – the teeth hidden in the waters of life; the help that frustrates the crocodile comes, appropriately enough, from the phallic python who also, Lacanians will be pleased to hear, has a particular fluency with words.

So the little boy elephant becomes a man. What puts an additional twist to this story, however, is its framing. The *Just So Stories* are all presented as being told by an avuncular narrator to a child, addressed as 'O Best Beloved'. My assumption all those years ago – that this child was, like me, a little girl – is confirmed in this case by the additional frame provided by the poem that follows each story and comments upon it. This is the poem accompanying 'The Elephant's Child':

> I keep six honest serving-men
> (They taught me all I knew);
> Their names are What and Why and When
> And How and Where and Who.
> I sent them over land and sea,
> I sent them east and west;
> But after they have worked for me,
> *I* give them all a rest.
>
> *I* let them rest from nine till five,
> For I am busy then,
> As well as breakfast, lunch, and tea,
> For they are hungry men:
> But different folk have different views;
> I know a person small –
> She keeps ten million serving-men,
> Who get no rest at all!
> She sends 'em abroad on her own affairs,
> From the second she opens her eyes –
> One million Hows, two million Wheres,
> And seven million Whys!
>
>   (Kipling 1950: 77)

Feminine excess of curiosity is contrasted here with masculine restraint. However, in showing that the story of an overly curious child might just as well apply to a girl, the poem opens up the text it accompanies to an alternative reading. We little girls with our smaller 'noses' may none the less, if we refuse to be discouraged and persist in exercising our own excessive curiosity, gain a larger organ and the power it represents. That this power is a matter of language is suggested by the linguistic games played by the story's narrator. Thus, the child addressee's incomplete command of language is marked by the misspelt and mispronounced words that supposedly echo hers, and also by the simple speech of the elephant's child; the 'Bi-Coloured-Python-Rock-Snake' (the phallic helper) and the narrator are alike in the range, fluency and sophistication of their language use.

Interestingly, the link that I have suggested is implied here between language and power, and the possibility of women's access to that power, is affirmed in two other stories later in the book: 'How the First Letter Was Written' and 'How the Alphabet Was Made'. Their protagonist is Taffy, a little girl who is the 'Best Beloved' of her cave-dwelling parents. In the first story Taffy identifies the 'awful nuisance' it is not to be able to write. As an alternative, she sends her mother a message in a series of pictures, which get comically misinterpreted. However, all ends well, with Taffy being praised by the Head Chief for her invention, which will eventually lead to the written word with its more precise meanings. In the second story, Taffy sets about developing a phonetic alphabet. Her father soon joins in and they finish the task together; none the less, it is Taffy who has the idea first. The energy and ingenuity of a little girl are represented as being the source of written language – so much for binary oppositions, which construct the power of language as 'phallic' by relegating the feminine to the prelinguistic realm.

To conclude, the curious tale of how the elephant got its trunk suggests that the curious pleasures of curiosity may indeed be empowering. So, all you little girls out there, keep asking questions.

DECIPHERING PANDORA

Kay Ferres

Forensic pleasures

Jane's retelling of Kipling's story involves a pleasure in omnipotence, derived from dexterity in language. The little girl who read or listened to the story engaged with both the 'satiable curtiosity' of the little elephant and the relentless questioning of the 'small person' in the poem. As a child reader, her identifications are not bound by the framing poem's binarisms of masculine restraint and feminine excess. Her adult pleasure is constructed rather differently. That pleasure involves both a recognition of those binarisms, and a deconstruction and reversal of them. She reads this story of sexual difference as a reverse castration story; that is, one in which the threat or fear of castration is dissolved by the materialisation of phallic power, in the growth of the trunk, and through the python's intervention. Her narrative is a knowing one in another respect: it invokes a professional persona as well as a merely 'adult' one. Her interpretation is informed by Freudian psychoanalysis, while her performance acknowledges Lacanian accounts of the subject in language.

I want to defer one pleasure that the occasion of this reading offers me: the pleasure of entering into an exchange of interpretation, to highlight instead some further dimensions of the pleasures of the text that Jane has performed here. These pleasures involve both restraint and excess: on the one hand, the engagement with psychoanalytic knowledges instances the powerful pleasure of authorised knowing; on the other, the insertion of the gendered self of the reader into the text authorises experience, and subjective ways of knowing. In turning to my own discussion of curiosity, I want to keep the following considerations in view: that decipherment (the moment when a possible meaning becomes apparent) is crucial to the pleasure of such encounters with a text or with another reader; and that pleasure oscillates between a close-up sense of being *in* the experience, which might involve a range of bodily or sensory connections, and a more distanced and restrained mediation of the experience through other knowledges. As the little elephant found, the pleasure of knowing involves both plenitude and loss; and that pleasure materialises as a kind of transitivity, a capacity to move between and across the positions of subject and object of knowledge. For feminist writers of the last few decades, finding ways to speak about the gendered character of the relations of knowledge production has come to entail a renegotiation of those relations.

An aesthetics of curiosity

As a noun, curiosity refers to a (small) object, valued as exotic or strange. It is a remnant, there to be known for itself rather than in terms of its use value, but paradoxically it cannot be known, because it is out of place, other, excessive. Pleasure in the object derives from its proximity, its survival in the here and now, and its distance from the original relations of its production, use or exchange. The curiosity is a particular kind of commodity.

Used to describe an object, 'curious' can mean strange or rare, intricately worked, delicate. Those associations also attach to the work that produces the object: it is skilful, painstaking and subtle. In this context, 'curious' is a term that addresses itself to detail, to the craft of the worker rather than to the design or vision characterising the grander enterprises of classical art and philosophy. Intricate work and attention to detail mark other traditions, particularly seventeenth-century Dutch painting, which requires of its viewers attention to the detail of its visual surfaces (Jay 1988: 12). Martin Jay uses Svetlana Alpers' term, the 'art of describing', to differentiate this visual culture's dependence on detail and close attention from the Cartesian perspectivalism, which characterises art of the Italian Renaissance and which has come to dominate theories of the 'gaze'. Those theories have cemented the associations of the look with masculinity.

In contrast, as Naomi Schor's commentary on nineteenth-century aesthetics has shown, the detail itself may be feminine. In *Reading in Detail: Aesthetics and the Feminine*, Schor surveys the influence of Sir Joshua Reynolds' *Discourses* and of the principle 'that the great style in painting consists in avoiding the details, and peculiarities of particular objects', as well as the 'logic of the discourse marshalled *against* the detail' (Schor 1987: 12). The nineteenth-century taste for the Italian sublime was founded on such principles, and very much at odds with the appeal of Flemish vulgarity. The unmediated, abundant detail of narrative art appealed to the devout, rather than those who knew about art. According to Michelangelo, 'It will appeal to women, especially to the very old and the very young, also to monks and nuns and certain noblemen who have no sense of true harmony' (Schor 1987: 20). Although greater value might be attached in the classical canon to the sublime dimensions of a Turner than to a finely worked miniature, new technologies transformed taste as the nineteenth century unfolded. Art nouveau 'raised the small *objet* – the jewelled brooch, the table lamp, the figurine – to the status of a serious artwork', a value in keeping with the movement's celebration of the female form, its preference for undulating, feminine lines and its adoption of a smaller, 'feminine' scale (Garelick 1995: 318, fn 10).

The nineteenth-century high-cultural disdain of detail was linked to a distaste for middle-class excess. The experience of the sublime depended on two attributes: grandeur and uniformity, 'as when in a vast and uniform Heaven there is nothing to stop the Eye, or limit the Imagination' (John Baillie 1747, *Essay on the Sublime*, in Schor 1987: 18). This pleasure also depended on the distanced view: it was visual, and of the mind. The taste for the small and the detailed is of a different order: it is an experience of proximity, drawing the eye closer, and engaging with other senses as well. But it need not be an experience of excess: as the preceding discussion has indicated, the pleasure taken in the curiosity may be related to the object's status as something left, a remainder.

Writing about Victorian photographs, objects at once familiar, domestic and curious,[1] Carol Mavor describes the pleasure of 'part-objects' as imbricated with loss, the 'embrace of a certain privation':

> I pursue small things, dislodged from the whole, like buttons popped. The buttons, or a thread, or a bead, or a piece of satin lining, are the remainders left over from the plots of the big stories (histories, theories); but they make a text(ure) that I can wear, one that houses, rustles, and touches my own privation.
>
> (Mavor 1995: 121)

This statement engages with the aesthetic in an altogether different register than Michelangelo, Baillie or Reynolds on the sublime. Instead of the appeal to abstract visualisation, these sentences invoke sound, touch, movement – their point of reference is the body. The body is also central to Roland Barthes' taste for 'the detail, the fragment, the *rush*', and to the discourse that might account for it:

> What shall we call such discourse? *erotic*, no doubt, for it has to do with pleasure; or even perhaps: *aesthetic*, if we foresee subjecting this old category to a gradual torsion which will alienate it from its regressive, idealist background and bring it closer to the body, to the *drift*.
>
> (quoted in Schor 1987: 79)

I started out by speaking of curiosity as an experience of transitivity: of immersion or closeness *and* of distance and negotiation; of a movement across the positions of object and subject of knowledge. In bringing the detail into the foreground of this discussion of curiosity and its pleasures, I have tried to suggest that we need to take account not only of the manifest content of an experience or image, but also of the technologies of its production. Most importantly, and this is to take up with the direction of a great deal of feminist discussion of how the shift from feminine object to subject of representation might occur, we need to engage with how the body is implicated in these negotiations. That discussion will be joined and extended in many of the essays in this book, in an inquiry that construes the problem as ethical as well as aesthetic.

I borrowed the term 'transitivity' from Carol Mavor, who glosses it as a negotiation across the spaces of desire, a negotiation driven, I would argue, by curiosity and by an impulse to decipherment, but yet carefully respectful of its object and the distance between them. Mavor indexes the pleasure of her own intellectual inquiry to Emmanuel Levinas' description of a loving touch: 'In a caress what is there is sought as though it were not there, as though the skin were a trace of its own withdrawal, a languor still seeking, like an absence which, however, could not be more there' (*Otherwise Than Being or Beyond Existence*, quoted in Mavor 1995: 80). This trope figures knowing as a relation of intimacy, an encounter of self and other that reconstitutes both, but preserves difference.

Gendering curiosity

In Kipling's story, excessive (that is, childish and feminine) curiosity is a nuisance at best, life-threatening at worst. The desire to know is transgressive, but also indispensable to a mastery of oneself and the world, to becoming a subject. That mastery, however, also requires restraint, initially externalised through deferral to adult (and masculine) authority, ultimately internalised through symbolic participation in that authority. The desire to know has been organised in this story and in many myths of Christian and classical cultures, along hierarchical lines of gender, race and age. Feminine curiosity is figured as excessive or inappropriate, and as heedless of consequences, whether in the everyday person of the gossip or in stories like those of Eve and Pandora.

Knowing is also indexed to the knower here. Curious women are represented as overinvested in their wish to uncover forbidden secrets, too immersed in their desire, having no capacity for disinterested inquiry or ethical judgment, let alone proper deference to authority. In the case of Eve and Pandora, the destructiveness of their wishes is not limited to themselves; humanity suffers the consequences of their transgression. The little boy elephant gets to know the answer to his question about the crocodile's dinner without actually becoming its meal, and is redeemed as part of the natural order of things. His experience is a rite of passage; his reward, a symbolic and bodily plenitude. The childish question that provided the pretext for Kipling's story is both curtailed and indulged by the tale of how the elephant got its trunk.

The stories of Eve and Pandora have come to be read as object lessons about feminine excess and lack. In both cases, a remnant – the apple, the box – have come to stand in for the woman and her offence. In both cases, this remainder has obscured the contextual detail of the stories. I want here to take up with some recent retellings of the Pandora myth which decipher and reconstruct a feminist narrative. Two of these readers, Janet Malcolm and Laura Mulvey, locate their retellings within and against a psychoanalytic frame. Interpreted within this frame, the box stands in for femininity as a sign of 'lack'.

The Pandora story told to child readers elaborates her transgression and its consequences: by opening the forbidden box, she releases all kinds of disaster into the world; closing it, she is able only to guarantee hope. This abbreviation of her story fixes her as a conduit of the wrath of the gods, which everyone must suffer; she and human misery are hinged together, objectified in the box. But Pandora was created to exact retribution against a particular transgressor: Prometheus, whose theft of fire struck directly at the source of the gods' power. Fire transmutes matter from one state to another, simulating the gods' powers of creation and metamorphosis.

While the children's version of the story focuses on Pandora's inability to resist the allure of the forbidden, its abbreviation diverts attention from the fact that Pandora herself is a lure. She is at once artefact and artifice, 'a most subtle, complex, and revealing symbol of the feminine, of its contradictory compulsion, peril and loveliness' (Warner 1985: 214). Feminine beauty is a trick, an enticement that conceals fearful dangers – so fearful, indeed, that it must be repudiated. Janet Malcolm's reading of Freud's case study of hysteria, 'Dora', indicates why.

Malcolm, like other commentators and Freud himself, is fascinated by the pseudonym Freud chooses for this patient: Dora is the name of his sister's nurse. In assigning this name to Ida Bauer, Freud is said to put her in her subordinated place: like a servant, Ida gave him two weeks' notice of her intention to quit the analysis. But Malcolm extends the chain of association and undoes the manifest content of the name by tracing it back to Pandora, appropriately in a case study that 'rattles with boxes'. This association goes some way to explaining Freud's hostility to Dora, whom he treats as a 'deadly adversary' (Malcolm 1982: 97).

Like Malcolm, other commentators have recognised that Freud gets too personally involved in Dora's case. He is affronted by her decision to discontinue the analysis and not at all professional in his reaction to her dismissal of him, unable to discriminate what is inside and outside the analytic context. The association with Pandora illuminates this lack of judgment, at the same time as Freud's overinvestment indicates why he does not make the connection himself.

Malcolm undertakes a sceptical investigation of psychoanalysis, 'the impossible profession', turning its techniques against itself. In particular, she probes the concept of the counter-transference, a concept crucial to the definition and the ethical limitation of the analyst's participation in the process of the analysand's self-disclosure. The analysis depends on the ethical participation of both parties in the contract: the free-associating patient and the abstemious analyst. But ultimately the analyst's training and professionalism entail an obligation to preserve the contract that binds both parties. The danger that Malcolm sees here refers to the analyst's failure to recognise the line distinguishing what is inside and outside the analysis, to their trespass into the space of the analysand's experience. In the terms of my discussion, this is the (feminised) problem of lack and excess. It is a problem Freud explicitly analyses in his notes on Dora; though, as Malcolm puts it, Freud is in danger of taking Dora too personally, not because of her sexual allure, but because she is in a position 'to trash his therapeutic ambitions' (Malcolm 1982: 93).

Dora never appears as a 'messed up teenager' to Freud: she is a woman, and a seductive and alluring one at that. Like Pandora, she is also an object of exchange in a masculine economy. Pandora did not entice Prometheus; instead, she is married to his brother. Dora is similarly intricated in the circuits of sexual intrigue: she has rejected (inexplicably!) the advances of the husband of her father's lover. Like Pandora, she is set up as a *femme fatale* to serve more powerful interests (the gods, Dora's father). But the *femme fatale's* seductive allure cuts two ways, involving both attraction and anxiety.

Laura Mulvey sees Pandora as one of a succession of *femmes fatale* who figure femininity as a riddle to be known. Pandora is a signifier of 'the anxieties installed in the patriarchal psyche in its rendering of the symbolisation of sexual difference' (Mulvey 1992: 60). The box is a fetish object, which signifies the disavowal of the knowledge of castration: 'I know very well, but all the same ...' (Mulvey 1996: 8). The identification of Pandora with the box installs her as the object to be known. Psychoanalytic accounts of the fetish position the subject who disavows knowledge as masculine. In *Fetishism and Curiosity*, Mulvey supplements the image of Pandora and the box with a fuller account of the myth and a history of the iconography of the box. And she supplements the Freudian account of the fetish with Marx's account of commodity culture. Her purpose is to show how sexualised objects and images have figured in that culture of the spectacle, and specifically in the cinema, 'soaking up semiotic significance' (Mulvey 1996: 5).

Mulvey opposes curiosity ('a compulsive desire to see and to know, to investigate what is secret and to reveal the contents of a concealed space') and fetishism ('born out of a refusal to see, a refusal to know, and a refusal to accept the difference that the female body symbolises'), noting the temptation to gender the difference (Mulvey 1992: 70). She comments on her initial interest in Pandora, that the myth about feminine curiosity 'can only be decoded by *feminist* curiosity, transforming and translating her iconography and attributes into the segments of a puzzle, riddle or enigma'. Her aesthetic of curiosity, with its emphasis on active looking and decipherment, a 'merging' of intellectual analysis with 'the pleasure of curiosity and seeing with the mind's eye' (Mulvey 1996: 54) might usefully be supplemented by attention to the detail. Mulvey's analysis takes the box to be both a signifier of femininity and a device which destabilises distinctions between inside and outside: hence her spatial metaphor is about surfaces and screens – 'topographies'.

Mulvey's earlier conference paper 'Pandora: Topographies of the Mask and Curiosity', works over 'the phantasmagoric space to be conjured out of the image of woman as mystery' (1992: 57). In it, Mulvey works from the representation of femininity as a mask or a chest concealing secrets, the female body as a screen on to which masculine desire and anxieties are projected. But her essay goes further, to raise the question of how a shift might be effected in the aesthetic imperatives and ideological constraints that this iconography propels: how the property of active looking might be transposed to a female subject. To find an answer, Mulvey looks to a logic of curiosity, and a topography of cinematic space that includes the space of the frame on the screen. Moving outside the spaces of narrative to include a phantasmatic (see page 24) dimension involves Mulvey with psychoanalysis, as an instrument to plumb interiority. Mulvey's way of knowing thus assumes that there are depths to be probed, meanings concealed beneath the surface of the screen there to be deciphered.

Her own practice as a knowing subject turns on three themes: 'first, an active look, associated with the feminine; second, the drive of decipherment, directed towards riddles or enigmas; third, a topography of concealment and investigation, the space of secrets'. The drive to decipherment: this signifies the completion of the look (or the lack) of femininity. Mulvey figures this drive in Pandora. Yet it seems to me that Pandora figures less in Mulvey's argument as actively curious than she does as the object of the voyeuristic gaze, and that this is the limitation of the use of psychoanalysis as the decoder of apparitional femininity.

The space of the subjective

To pursue this point, I want to disengage the psychoanalytic drive to decipherment and to prise apart one of Mulvey's key propositions about the cinema as a technology of gender with a particular history. Discussing the aesthetic imperatives and ideological constraints that are encoded in the conventional representation of the *femme fatale* in *film noir*, Mulvey observes:

> It has been … argued that the cinema has, through specific properties, enhanced the image of feminine seductiveness as a surface that conceals. That is to say, the codes and conventions of Hollywood cinema refined the representation of femininity, heightened by the star system, to the point where the spectator's entrancement with the effects of the cinema itself became almost indistinguishable from the draw exerted by an eroticised image of woman. It is as though the scopophilic draw of the cinema, the flickering shadows, the contrasts between light and dark became concentrated in and around the female form … . The luminous surface of the screen reinforces the sense of surface radiated by the mask of femininity, flattening the image, so that its usual transparency, its simulation of a window on the world, becomes opaque.
>
> (Mulvey 1992: 59)

Here, the surfaces of femininity and of the screen are conflated and, as Mulvey's discussion proceeds, the projections – of image on to the screen, and of desire and anxiety on to the female body – are almost indistinguishable. This carries over into the use of the terms 'phantasmatic' and 'phantasmagoric'. These terms are used more or less interchangeably, but this substitution conceals a historical shift in signification. The nineteenth-century phantasmagoria referred to a technological spectacle involving the projection of light on to a screen. As interest in psychology developed, the mass appeal of fantastic images came to be explained as a projection of the workings of the mind (understood as a function of the nervous system, and rather differently to how 'psychology' is understood today). Thus 'phantasmagoric' referred not primarily to a similarity of the content of the images on the screen and the images produced – for example, in dreams – but to a similarity in the technology or process by which those images were produced. The phantasmagoria's place as a precursor of the cinema encourages another conflation, of projection and the screen, caught in Mulvey's spatial term 'topography'. Mulvey's frame of reference for her decipherment – the language of the unconscious – constrains her to the workings of condensation, displacement, substitution. Given her interest in 'socially constructed' fantasy, the two terms' different and separable referential fields might usefully have been kept in view.

Terry Castle and Max Milner have uncovered what Margaret Cohen describes as the phantasmagoria's 'lively nineteenth century life' in both England and France (Cohen 1993: 228). Though the phantasmagoria initially referred to an artificially produced, publicly experienced illusion (first produced in Paris by Étienne-Gaspard Robertson), it has come to refer to something internal and subjective (Castle 1988: 29). In Castle's view, the shift in meaning is indicative of 'a very significant transformation in human consciousness … the spectralization or "ghostifying" of mental space'. Milner's work also focuses on the convergences of the technology with a way of describing and understanding mental activity:

> a new form of imagination starts to gain prominence, which assumes the opening of an interior space, an 'other stage,' in which images are projected, undergo metamorphoses, and follow one another with the violation of logic found in dreams, and which constitutes both a route of access towards the depths where interior and exterior being, desire and reality, have relations other than in everyday life, and a fearful power.
>
> (Milner 1982, *La Fantasmagorie*, quoted in Cohen 1993: 243)

In shading in the history of the term and the technological transformations of the instrument that produced this popular mass spectacle, both Castle and Milner fix on the way the experience of the phantasmagoria at once derives from Enlightenment notions of the transcendent human subject, and challenges both the rational nature of that subject and the divide that Enlightenment thought draws between the subject and the objective world (Cohen 1993: 243–4).

The phantasmagoria was a nineteenth-century antecedent of cinema, a 'profane illumination' which Walter Benjamin, in his 1939 revision of the

Passagen-Werk, proposed as a concept corresponding to the image that commodity-producing society 'produces of itself, and that it is wont to label its culture' (Cohen 1993: 229). Margaret Cohen has discussed Benjamin's theorising of the phantasmagoria and its work of ideological transformation in impressive detail; that discussion takes as its starting point Benjamin's abandonment of the dream theory, which had figured in the earlier (1935) version of the text. I will not reproduce that discussion here; rather, I want to emphasise the shift of attention that follows from this abandonment of dream theory: a shift from the image projected to the instrument that projects it.

The magic lantern producing the spectral illuminations of the phantasmagoria was a box containing an arrangement of lens, mirror, candle and glass slides. Unlike the camera obscura, it did not simply reflect an external reality; instead, it conjured up images that the audience found difficult and, when it achieved its most thrilling effects impossible, to distinguish from reality. As Castle argues, its figuring of ghosts has been displaced by the absorption of ghosts into the world of thought: we are 'haunted' by our thoughts (Castle 1988: 29). Tracing the etymology of the phantasmagoria, however, brings us always back to the box, to the technology that opened up an 'other stage' and a new form of imagination, and which required, as Milner points out, an other aesthetic than an imagination of reproduction, or a romantic, creative imagination.[2]

REGIMES OF TRUTH AND THE FASHIONING OF THE SELF

Gillian Swanson

Knowledge and culture: environments of the self

In the previous sections of this chapter, Jane and Kay have identified the two main dimensions of the concept of curiosity. The first is a condition of the subject, consisting in the will to know, as the subject becomes caught up in the pursuit of knowledge and attracted to the promise and pleasure of mastery, which is associated with occupying a position of knowledge. The second dimension is a property of the object, which is *perceived by* the subject, and is thus separate from it. This concerns the intriguing quality of that which is curious – unfamiliar, and inciting the desire to know more. Those 'curiosities' exercise our attention, stimulate our interest and entice us. In this section, I want to take up Kay's emphasis on that second dimension, looking at how cultural objects, practices or identities become seen as 'curious', how they appear as 'curiosities' and to ask what challenges to a stable concept of subjectivity these hold. What I hope to show in this introduction to the way I take up the concept of curiosity in my chapters in the book, is that there are different kinds of knowledge and subjectivity and that those implied by 'curiosity' are of a particularly problematic sort.

The concept of 'curiosity', therefore, refers to more than just a state of mind, or an object. It is even more than just a condition of subjectivity – in fact I will be concerned to address the *environments* within which subjectivities can be formed, included in which are objects of curiosity. The concept of curious pleasures also focuses our attention, therefore, on a cultural habit we have developed: the 'habit' of establishing a difference between the 'self' and that which lies beyond. This is a difference created through those conceptual boundaries drawn between the self and its environment – which we mark through routines of everyday life, through practices of the body, through habits of thinking, etc. This approach to studying culture suggests that we should be attentive to the environments within which identities are composed and enacted, the practices that establish distinctive models of the self, and their connections to specific times and places. This has been the subject of sociological inquiry, in the adoption of Pierre Bourdieu's concept of 'habitus': a 'unifying, generative principle' of practices that comprise a particular demeanour and disposition in relation to the varied dimensions of lifestyle and repertoires of taste, body management, language, etc. and which form 'classifying practices' as a systematic 'expression of a particular class of conditions of existence' (Bourdieu 1984: 175). Bourdieu shows the separation and connection between the different 'departments' of these practices in his discussion of practices of 'taste' or 'distinction':

> In the ordinary situations of bourgeois life, banalities about art, literature or cinema are inseparable from the steady tone, the slow, casual distinction, the distant or self-assured smile, the measured gesture, the well-tailored suit and the bourgeois salon of the person who pronounces them.
>
> (Bourdieu 1984: 174)

One consequence of an attention to those 'habits' of subjectivity is that we understand the self as a 'cultural category', one that is defined through cultural representations and practices. It may be strange to think of the self as a *definitional* achievement rather than as an organic and unified entity which just 'is', or which we just 'live'. But if we look at the concepts of the self that are current within different periods, we can see that it has undergone significant change – the 'self' has, in fact, a history, as I show in Chapter 5. Because they are interdependent, this indicates that the *environments* of the self change historically also, and hence the analysis of such changes is critical to understanding the cultural processes of the formation and enactment of subjectivity. How do we focus on those historically specific environments within which the varied concepts of the 'self' have been forged? And how do we unravel the ways these concepts of the self have been imprinted with the markers of those relations of difference operating within such environments?

A key point in this book is that such definitions are made through representations. In my chapters, a further argument is that representations can themselves be seen as part of a field of knowledge which is brought to bear on the organisation of social life. For they are documents of their own time, which contribute to those 'regimes of truth' concerning the way individuals behave, interact, arrange their lives, think and feel – in other words, the way they govern themselves. This approach allows us to examine the way representations 'order' and 'classify' by establishing regimes of knowledge about the world, the individuals populating it, and the social frameworks by which their lives are governed. It also allows us to propose that cultural knowledges exist in dialogue with cultural practices – that knowledge is made within specific environments too, and that it bears their imprint. And, finally, it suggests we look at the application of cultural knowledges in specific times and specific places, to understand the conditions that made those knowledges and their applications possible.

This is the force of an interest with the environments of subjectivity – that it looks at the self as a product of culture and knowledge as well as of individual action. It is these relationships that I will look at in my chapters – how the social identities and attributes that an individual takes on are negotiated through and by means of a complex of environments, and how a particular understanding of subjectivity – specifically one that is marked by sexual difference – becomes an intelligible way of articulating a sense of individual coherence and identity.

Governmentality and privacy

One dimension of these regimes of knowledge is that concerning the relationship between the body, sexuality, private life and the self. In fact, rather than seeing the practices of these domains as a testimony to one's essential and inner self, we can see that those regimes of knowledge produce an historically specific understanding of what a 'self' is, or should be – an understanding that situates the self as a private, unique and internalised dimension of one's being. Michel Foucault has shown that the development of the concept of an 'inner' self went hand in hand with a particular attitude to sex (Foucault 1976/1981). As we see in the work of Norbert Elias, outlined in Chapter 5, by the nineteenth century, sex had become something to be kept hidden from public view, as part of a new sense of personal privacy. But Foucault stresses that this did not mean that sex was ruled out as a practice of managing the self. In contrast, the individual's attitude to sex was a critical component of self-management, part of the process of fashioning a self with a modest demeanour, with a knowledge of propriety and, above all, a *conscience*. Rather than seeing this period as repressing talk of sex or sexual activity, Foucault identifies a 'proliferation of discourses concerned with sex … an institutional incitement to speak about it, and to do so more and more', which provided those conditions of knowledge that allowed the individual to develop a particular kind of sexual disposition (Foucault 1976/1981: 18).

It is this paradox which Foucault identifies so well: how is the sexual body made a matter of public concern just as sex becomes identified as a private matter; how does it present itself as at once something that is a component of an inner, private self, and at the same time something made central to questions of modern government? His contention is that 'the sexual conduct of the population was taken both as an object of analysis and as a target of intervention'

(Foucault 1976/1981: 26). In my chapters for this book, I aim to show that this project of government provided the conditions of intelligibility for an array of writings – from medical, sociological and criminological documents to fictional texts. These proposed both a particular attitude to sex, but also, more subtly, they supported the development of a whole array of attitudes to the self: a sense of privacy and a relationship to private life; a concept of a unique, inner, *individual* self; a relationship to the sexualised body; the sexual differentiation of character, and so on.

Knowledge is no less pressing in these intimate arenas of self-management, although perhaps discourses concerning sexuality are more disparate and diffuse, and their impact more difficult to discern, than those that emanate from some other dimensions of government. Certainly, from this period onwards, we can see that practices of government are oriented towards a more intimate level of analysis and intervention, and those knowledges that constitute part of that project are developed to address subjects in the most intimate domains of their lives. This is, in effect, a new kind of environment for subjectivity, and has partic- ular outcomes in terms of the way individuals are oriented by a distinctive sense of their own unique capacities and potential, their tastes, desires, and the whole array of activity and thought which was taken to constitute the conduct of an 'inner' life.

Subjectivity and consumption: managing the self

The historical development of these 'attitudes' to the self established the envi- ronment within which a modern self could be fashioned – the distinctively modern coordinates of subjectivity. And one of the facets of that environment, which is significant in defining a modern sexual self, is the way that the practices of consumption became recast by modern commerce, realigning the orientation towards the body, and offering a domain for the enactment of sexual character. For one significant way in which the management of sexuality becomes repre- sented as a distinctively modern problematic is through the negotiation of public and private life that urban commerce (and its provision of public entertainments) demands. 'Public women', and women in city streets, represented a particular problem for sexual definitions, as the coordinates of female character were estab- lished through the environments of private life and the family. But the new environments of the modern city gave plentiful opportunities for women to take up new dimensions of the self, which could be fashioned through an involvement in practices of urban consumption – public entertainments and the perambula- tions associated with shopping, among others. How could these be reconciled with those dimensions of femininity which were established within the more contained environments of domesticity?

Of course, practices of consumption did not 'escape' the establishment of regimes that shape conduct and provide the coordinates by which the self is formed. In fact, regimes of consumption provide a critical dimension to the development of an 'attitude to' female deportment which is disciplined, moderate and contained. These are forms of emotional, as well as physical, management, and depend upon an invocation of the dangers of female 'appetite' as an 'inner' force which must be controlled, and the need to regulate its expression.

In this context, the mobilisation of an interest in 'curiosity' takes on a particular force. It refers to those commodified 'curiosities' which were presented for the pleasure of the shopper, or the cinema spectator, for example, as they made available sights, objects, images and narratives that lay outside common experience, often drawing on the exoticism of 'other' lives, past times, or unfamiliar places and events. It also refers to the apprehension of these curiosities: associated with an expansion of commerce that gave access to new commodities, to products from unknown places only travellers had hitherto seen, curiosity could now be exercised in the increasingly familiar public domains of personal consumption. The concern with which such new experiences were met indicates that curiosity was seen as a feature of modern subjectivity, a distinctive and contemporary disposition which bore the imprint of those difficulties and conflicts involved in managing the self in new environments. Where we may understand the exercise of curiosity as a *practice of attention* – in other words, a cultural activity – it is more usually represented in nineteenth-century writings in terms of an *exercise of appetite* – situated as an expression of a biological, elemental drive, which the individual should master according to a regime of social constraint.

Alice's Adventures in Wonderland provides a useful illustration of the convergence of consumption, the fashioning of the self, and anxieties concerning the changed conditions of modern life. The curious nature of Wonderland is established in Alice's first encounter with the White Rabbit, who takes a watch out of his waistcoat-pocket and worries aloud about being late as he runs by. Later, he is seen 'splendidly dressed, with a pair of white kid gloves in one hand and a large fan in another'. Alice is 'burning with curiosity', and her fascination with this anomalous creature brings her to fall down the rabbit hole, and thus to encounter a new world (Carroll 1865: 2, 15).

These casual intrusions of the banal world of industry, commerce and consumption into a tale of fantastic encounters and creatures who yet talk and act within – and against – the rituals of middle-class gentility, is distinctive of a period in which the availability of fine goods and Oriental artefacts were part of a common repertoire of middle-class social life.

This connection makes Alice's 'Wonderland' something more than an Other Land, instead showing its 'curiosities' to be part of the changing texture of everyday family and social life. As Nancy Armstrong (1990) argues, Alice's dream worked over the principles of consumption that were part of a middle-class girl's training in social deportment – her predilection to eat and drink whatever she encountered has dire consequences for her ability to negotiate the new spaces she travels to, as her body grows and shrinks in response to her careless disregard for proper constraint and self-denial. Her unruly curiosity, then, is linked to the dangers of unconstrained appetite. As she carefully works through those rules of self-preservation she has been taught, her eventual conclusion – that, since the bottle marked 'DRINK ME' is not marked 'poison' there can be no harm – shows her ability to curb both curiosity and appetite has only been partly internalised (Carroll 1865: 9–11). It is her own contemplation of her stretched-out body after drinking from the bottle, and eating the cake marked 'EAT ME' that stimulates her most well-known comment: 'Curiouser and curiouser!' (Carroll 1865: 13). The outcomes of an imperfect mastery of regimes of consumption are marked at the level of the female body, whose curious transformations indicate her accession to a world of sexually specific and familial subjectivities. The possibility of failed accession is embodied in the female grotesques who populate her Wonderland.

Commerce and commodification

That 'curiosities' are seen as part of the experience of the modern world – and a part of the transition from the less elaborated order of a child's work to the adult world of civility, custom and manners, is reinforced by the curiosity that Alice's own body becomes to her. She is thus caught up herself in the transformations that become part of her accession to a socially formed world of consumption, self-presentation and the cultural styling of the self. Alice's observation elsewhere, that the curious happenings she had started to encounter made it seem 'quite dull and stupid for life to go on in the common way' (Carroll 1865: 12), indicates something of the everyday thrills that consumption held. For part of the promise of consumption lay in the possibility of encountering difference in the framework of the ordinary.

Commerce was of course the engine for such everyday thrills and sensations, and showed the link between the accumulation of 'curiosities' and an expanded sense of knowledge of the world, as the elaboration of a mercantile order both allowed contact with new goods, fabrics, foods but also ideas. As Lisa Jardine's study of cultures of commodification and consumption in the Renaissance shows, the 'discovery' of new lands and the opening up of international trade routes, new overseas markets and access to exotic foreign goods also implied an encounter with new and challenging intellectual traditions, an ongoing and 'sometimes tense' dialogue between the civilisations of East and West, and the 'percolation' of political instabilities from one culture to another (Jardine 1996: 3–34, 56, 77). The dynamics of the modern world are inseparable from the transformations wrought by commercial enterprise: '[the] imperatives of trade, and the practicalities of the pursuit of commerce shape the beginnings of the world we recognise' (Jardine 1996: 90). However, while anxieties concerning the expansion of commercial culture were voiced as if it were new to the nineteenth century (and often to the twentieth and twenty-first), these are processes which had their roots much earlier, and which have much more heterogeneous effects than is often suggested. In fact, it may be that the heterogeneity of identities and practices is one of the major outcomes of this transformation, and that in fact it is a problematic relationship to difference which underlies the reaction against commerce. Could the anxiety concerning the expansion of consumption upon which texts like *Alice's Adventures in Wonderland* rest, be brought about by the collisions of meaning, identity and everyday cultural practices brought by an encounter with difference?

The grotesque figures in *Alice's Adventures in Wonderland*, such as the Duchess, are modelled on physiological signs drawn from the taxonomies of cultural difference, both racial (in the encounters brought by contact with the colonial populations of the Empire) and social (as anthropological methods were applied to those unknown quarters of the new cities in which were found the 'primitive tribes' of the poor). But they are everyday grotesques and, while they embody the difficulties for cultural meaning that social, racial and sexual difference represents, they also render these conflicts less dangerous, more manageable, even comic. In a similar manner, in *The Old Curiosity Shop*. Charles Dickens uses the trade in curiosities as a context for a more ethnographically based concern, drawing on the models made available by contemporary sociological inquiry to catalogue the features of those curious and grotesque figures – both criminal and benign – with whom he populates the world of the lower social strata of the city, depicting their everyday eating, dressing and speaking habits, and showing the dominance of cultural habits such as racing, drinking, gambling, etc. The distorted morality of one of his central characters, Mr Quilp, is shown through his deformed and dwarfish body, his excessive and horrific explosions of laughter, his cruel expression and delight in torturing his obedient wife, and his love of money. He drives his counterpoint, the heroine Nell, whose only wish is for a poor and simple life that will bring her to a serene awareness of God's love, from her grandfather's curiosity shop. Homeless, and travelling with her grandfather, she is now exposed to the more everyday and varied curiosities of the social worlds they encounter before settling in the country, in the shadow of a church. It is only here, among the kindness of country folk connected through religious affiliation, that Nell can move beyond the cares of the world and, through death, reach the peace that raises her above the world of commercial culture and unconstrained appetite. Dickens' commentary shows the thrills of popular culture to be without redeeming force, in this novel, as the Old Curiosity Shop of metropolitan life becomes simply a random collection of tawdry characters who find cheap amusement in worthless pursuits. The novel can thus be taken as another warning about the correct forms of self-management, of a disposition that must be created out of the division between commerce and urban cultural involvements, and a supposedly 'natural', traditional disposition towards inner contemplation, spiritual insight and material self-denial that implies a rejection of modern urban life and its associated forms of subjectivity.

Representation, classification and instability

In the two examples of *Alice's Adventures in Wonderland* and *The Old Curiosity Shop*, we can see distinctions made between forms of conduct and dispositions of the self; the emergence of a 'regime of truth'; and the foregrounding of boundaries between what is known, normal, expected, endorsed, and that which eludes conventional frames of reference, classification and sanction. Their narratives operate through both emotional and moral registers. But they are not the models of disciplinary authority we would find if we turned to medical, sociological, psychological or criminological sources on similar topics relating to the effects of urban life and practices of consumption on individual character. For fictional texts operate on a symbolic level. And, as Franco Moretti argues in his study of the *Bildungsroman*, they show more readily the uncertainty and openness of models of classification: the truly central ideologies of our world are not in the least … intolerant, normative, monologic, to be wholly submitted to or rejected. Quite the opposite: they are pliant and precarious, 'weak' and 'impure' (Moretti 1987: 10).

This is a useful observation for our consideration of the way gender features within the 'regimes of truth' that inform the fashioning of the self. For, rather than seizing on those moments of closure in which systems of classification appear with most clarity, we can perhaps form a more complex view if we focus on the process of building such systems, systems that rely on the exchange between both terms in a system of difference, without which individual categories would be meaningless. This is certainly a more precarious project, a more unstable system, and a less totalising view, which allows 'impurity', moments of fissure or weakness. As I aim to show in the following chapters, in their identification of the feminine as a reciprocal term, regimes of truth concerning sexual difference give to those edifices which are built around masculinity a form of instability that perpetually undermines its centrality, its unity and its apparent dominance.

For, just as the contemplation of 'curiosities' brings about a heightening of the signs of difference, there is also assumed to be in that act a pleasure in such differences. This is a pleasure that derives from finding oneself in the presence of the instabilities involved in moving beyond that which is known and classifiable. Perhaps what is at stake here is a fragile delight: the pleasures of contemplating the *unknown* without the means of incorporating it into established systems of meaning. And if that creates delight, it must surely be bound up with the delight of finding oneself outside those established systems of positioning through which the knowing self is made coherent, anchored in meaning, stabilised through the manufacture of a unified perspective with known coordinates and precedents. Here are two further aspects to this concept of curiosity, then. First it assumes the existence of that which is outside intelligibility, and hence beyond secure knowledge and the forms of perception and identity that creates a shared sense of 'reality'. And second, it gestures to those systems by which we both incorporate the unknown, the different, that which is other to that shared knowledge of the world and experience, bringing it *into coherence*. And it highlights those adaptations that such incorporations compel us to make to those systems of intelligibility and the logics that underpin them. Systems of knowledge, classification and meaning are therefore never absolute or fixed, and their positioning of the self is never entirely secure.

Stephen Greenblatt considers something of this dimension to the process of

meaning-making in his account of the encounters with difference – 'radically unfamiliar human and natural objects' (Greenblatt 1991: 7) – brought about by colonial
voyages of discovery from Europe to the New World. Even though these travels
were driven by the will to possess that which is encountered, and a fierce – violent,
even – sense of the alien nature of these 'marvels', the 'wonder' that accompanies
the moment of such encounters brings about a 'marvelous dispossession', a loss of
secure positioning and thus a 'self-estrangement'. This contemplation of the
boundaries of cultural meaning and identity, of distinct cultural worlds – the absolute inability of applying culturally specific modes of recognition and classification
across those boundaries of encounter, yet the unavailability of any *other* system for
comprehending these distinct worlds – brought about an 'immobilised' moment of
absorption and identification. In this moment, the distinctions between the self and
other were confounded, bringing about a 'dissolving of the self as a point of knowledge', which required a further move to anchor the self outside of such 'radical
alterity' (Greenblatt 1991: 135, 150).

This unhinging of cultural certainty provides a connection between
Greenblatt's concept of culture and that expressed by the twinning of curiosity
with pleasure, as he alludes to 'a world which is always rolling, turning, slipping
away, a world of perennial, inescapable circulation', a world in which 'we are
incomplete and unsteady, we are go-betweens' (Greenblatt 1991: 150). In a world
in which wonder exists, there can be no absolute meaning, no immutable forms
of knowledge or classification, and so there can be no stable and coherent positioning of the self. So, too, in the possibility of curiosity, we find a radical
absence of knowledge, and therefore also the absence of a stance of possession.
This can only point to an instability of positioning that challenges stable,
coherent and whole depictions of self.

Categorial instability, the subjective perspective and the feminine disposition

It is no mistake that many of the representations I have chosen in the chapters
I have contributed to this book have been drawn from a phase in the late nineteenth century when a certain cultural undecidability – and an attentiveness to
the curious – was linked to the new importance that had been given to individual
experience and perspective. Nor less that this configuration of uncertainty gave
rise to a question concerning the endurability of sexual definitions which was
realised as a problem of knowledge. This is not to say that the nineteenth
century was any more – or less – certain of its terms of reference than any other
period, but that the way the movement of culture was manifested in that period
in many parts of Europe, and particularly Britain, was critically bound up with a
realignment of the coordinates by which sexuality, the body, private life, could be
known, and the encounters that could occur in a newly described and commodified public life. In that process, a capacity for curiosity was not simply an event,
but a cultural disposition, as described in Chapter 5. The new forms of knowledge that were generated by the attempt to provide a taxonomy of cultural

difference, and the categories of person they give rise to, are outlined in Chapter 8, while the force that cultural undecidability has in generating narratives of masculine self-estrangement, and the knowledges we draw upon to determine the particular coordinates of such categorial instability as we read narratives of T.E. Lawrence, are the subject of Chapter 11.

In summary, then, the import of the concept of 'the curious', and curiosity as its realisation in a subjective orientation, is something of a marker of the unhinging of cultural certainty that I referred to earlier. In our examination of the way sexual difference is connected to such uncertainty, it is not just through the challenge of difference to categorial stability that this occurs, but by the way sexual difference is implicated in the status of knowledge and in the stability of cultural meaning. Steven Shapin argues that civility in seventeenth-century England was critically shaped by the relation between honour and truthfulness, as truth-telling became established as a prerequisite of membership of gentlemanly society and the reliability of a gentleman's word was based on the 'understood relationship between birth, wealth and virtue' (Shapin 1994: 65). He goes on to show that 'the cultural practices attending the English gentleman fit him for the role of being a reliable spokesman for reality', an authority which was transferred to scientific practice and experimental philosophy, centralising the gentleman scholar as a personage who guaranteed the veracity of scientific observation and thus underpinned scientific testimony: 'who could speak for empirical realities inaccessible to other practitioners, and whose representations might be accepted as corresponding to things themselves' (Shapin 1994: xxvii–xxviii). Credible knowledge was the basis of scientific testimony and thus of objective meaning. But *curiosity* implies a quite different relationship to meaning, one which centralises the subjective perspective and will to know. It thus stands in contradistinction to scientific objectivity, as the curious, and that knowledge derived from a relationship to it, is positioned as insufficiently anchored by the empirical base of objective knowledge.

It is not only that the domain of consumption has been imbued with associations of the feminine, therefore, but those forms of knowledge which can be developed through the subjective perspective, and the forms of attention elicited by commercial cultures (characterised in terms of 'distractions'), cannot attain the credibility – the claim to represent reality through a perspective of objectivity – that are bestowed upon such realms associated with the masculine, such as scientific knowledge. Curiosity is thus firmly established as a feminine pleasure and form of attention, those knowledges that derive from curiosity are not stabilised by the reality claims of gentlemanly scholarship or empirical science, but open to the imputation of mendacity, inaccuracy, misinterpretation and alternative accounts. Curiosity thus constitutes an unstable domain of knowledge and classification, one which invites controversy and contestation, which challenges the categorial certainty of disciplinary knowledge, which introduces the messy dimension of subjective perspective, and which thereby allows the dynamics of difference to be played out.

Notes

1   Among the subjects Mavor discusses are the little girls who found favour with Lewis Carroll.
2   W.B. Yeats refers to the phantasmagoria as a form of imagination, a structure or technology recombining the elements of experience. Discussing the way experience – tragedy, loss of love, loneliness – is transformed in poetry, he says: '[a poet] never speaks directly as to someone at the breakfast table, there is always a phantasmagoria' (c. 1937/1968: 509). Thanks to Francie Oppel for drawing this to my attention.

Bibliography

Armstrong, N. (1990) 'The Occidental Alice', *differences* 2, 2, 3–40.

Bourdieu, P. (1984) *Distinction: A Social Critique of the Judgement of Taste*, London: Routledge & Kegan Paul.

Carroll, L. (1865) *Alice's Adventures in Wonderland*, London: Macmillan and Co.

Castle, T. (1988) 'Phantasmagoria: Spectral Technology and the Metaphorics of Modern Reverie', *Critical Inquiry*, 15 (Autumn), 26–61.

Cohen, M. (1993) *Profane Illumination: Walter Benjamin and the Paris of Surrealist Revolution*, Berkeley and Los Angeles: University of California Press.

Foucault, M. (1976/1981) *The History of Sexuality*, vol. 1, *An Introduction*, Harmondsworth: Penguin.

Garelick, R. (1995) '*Bayaderes, Stereorama*, and *Vahat-Loukoum*: Technological Realism in the Age of Empire', in M. Cohen and C. Prendergast (eds) *Spectacles of Realism: Gender, Body, Genre*, Minneapolis: University of Minnesota Press, 294–319.

Greenblatt, S. (1991) *Marvelous Possessions: The Wonder of the New World*, Oxford: Clarendon Press.

Jardine, L. (1996) *Worldly Goods*, London and Basingstoke: Macmillan.

Jay, M. (1988) 'Scopic Regimes of Modernity', in H. Foster (ed.) *Vision and Visuality*, Seattle: Bay Press, 3–23.

Kipling, R. (1950) *Just So Stories*, London: Macmillan, 59–77; originally published 1902.

Malcolm, J. (1982) *Psychoanalysis: The Impossible Profession*, London: Picador.

Mavor, C. (1995) *Pleasures Taken: Performances of Sexuality and Loss in Victorian Photographs*, Durham and London: Duke University Press.

Moretti, F. (1987) *The Way of the World: The Bildungsroman in European Culture*, London: Verso.

Mulvey, L. (1992) 'Pandora: Topographies of the Mask and Curiosity', in B. Colomina (ed.) *Sexuality and Space*, New York: Princeton Architectural Press, 53–71.

—— (1996) 'Introduction' in *Fetishism and Curiosity*, Bloomington: Indiana University Press, 1–15.

—— (1996) 'Pandora's Box: Topographies of Curiosity', in *Fetishism and Curiosity*, Bloomington: Indiana University Press, 53–64.

Schor, N. (1987) *Reading in Detail: Aesthetics and the Feminine*, New York: Methuen.

Shapin, S. (1994) *A Social History of Truth: Civility and Science in Seventeenth-Century England*, London and Chicago: University of Chicago Press.

Warner, M. (1985) *Monuments and Maidens*, London: Weidenfeld and Nicolson.

Yeats, W.B. (c. 1937/1968) 'A General Introduction to my Work', in *Essays and Introductions*, New York: Collier Books, 509.

Part 2

Gender and representation

Introduction

The chapters in this section ask what is meant by the term 'representation' and its relationship to gender, taking up the way 'identity' or 'the self' is framed in and through representation, and examining how meanings are produced within those institutional and cultural practices that operate in specific times and places. Each chapter demonstrates how the features and capacities of femininity and masculinity have been represented, and how these intersect with everyday cultural practices to contribute to the formation of subjectivity. Understanding the way representations work to establish – or, indeed, unsettle – concepts of femininity and masculinity underpins all three authors' contributions, yet this common concern has given rise to different emphases. Each demonstrates an alternative way of thinking about representation, allowing us to address different issues and formulate different questions.

In Chapter 3, Jane uses the example of fashion to show that representations propose a whole repertoire of femininities within which the female reader/viewer may situate herself. Hence we should move from a singular concept of identity as essence to a pluralised model of identities, which are contingent on time, place and occasion. Although the discourse of fashion 'appeal[s] to an essential, unified, true self which the choice of clothing and perfume serves merely to express and enhance', we can by contrast consider femininity as a 'range of possibilities'. This allows fashion to be seen as a means by which multiple, competing and often contradictory feminine identities can be negotiated. The use of masquerade and curiosity provides for movement across boundaries of meaning and the playful adoption of alternative identities. Jane demonstrates that identities are fashioned in an ongoing process, arguing that categories such as 'women' and 'men' are not given, but are the work of cultural processes; thus individuals constitute 'unstable sites on which and through which the competing femininities and/or masculinities of our culture interact and are acted out'.

Questions of negotiation are central also to Kay's chapter on the interrelationship of practices of reading and writing. She outlines the development of feminist approaches that focused on the 'exclusion', 'invisibility' and 'silences' of women writers, artists and composers, and the 'relegation of female cultural practices and tastes to the popular and the domestic, and the alliance of masculinity with high culture and public life'. But, as Kay notes, these approaches stopped short of addressing the distribution of power that allowed such divisions to occur, or the agents of that distribution, such as the practices of reviewing, criticism and the 'canonisation' of texts and authors that contribute to the literary 'tradition'. Hence early feminist approaches 'left those institutions and practices which [they] critiqued largely untouched'.

Kay argues that seeing women as the subjects of culture means developing an understanding of the practices of reading and writing. She discusses the public nature of an Irish literary cultural tradition, and its place in Irish nationalism, noting that the 'very publicness' of this tradition 'accounts for its permissiveness, its accommodation of clamouring voices', which allowed women writers to engage tactically with it. But this is not the space in which women writers can develop a tradition of their own, formed from the conversation and everyday relations between women. To identify this, Kay turns to discuss the encounters of three women writers, 'staged in correspondence, in reading, in occasional visits, in the exchange of gifts'. She shows how these women's reading of one another's works has effects in their own writing. Moving beyond the text, and the trope of the woman silenced in culture, she chooses to read 'across and between [texts], broadening the contexts in which they emerge, and the practices and institutions with which they engage', not deepening but expanding 'across practices'. Thus, while she argues that 'relations of gender and writing may be read as constitutive of the (woman) subject in culture', her analysis also considers the social relations within which texts circulate and proposes a model of subjectivity that evolves within a network of social relationships.

Finally, Gillian pursues this 'extratextual' dimension to representation and subjectivity, examining the relationship of cultural knowledges, institutions and social practices to 'individual' identity. She traces the historical formation of our modern concept of the self within an emerging cultural repertoire of 'civility', which sees practices of social life, family habits and bodily behaviours increasingly governed by principles of moderation, restraint, modesty and privacy. Self-definition and an 'authoritative *way of being*', which maintained a division between public and private behaviours, became central to the sexual differentiation of the modern individual. This allows Gillian to argue that personal identity – dependent on a culturally specific notion of an 'inner self' – is a 'cultural achievement', as is the 'historically specific process of imagining the self as sexually differentiated'. Thus 'culturally divergent' systems should not be seen as 'backdrops to original and essential individuals, but as formative of particular intellectual and emotional dispositions [and] types of character'.

Gillian's emphasis on the way texts are given authority allows her to examine the 'logics' of cultural systems of knowledge, and the way representations 'order and classify the social'. But the bestowal of authority in itself presumes the existence of competing representations and problematic forms of subjectivity, which provide the space for alternative meanings and the revision of established definitions. To this extent, representation is never a closed process, and definitions of

gender are never final or fixed. Gillian stresses the 'instability' that 'derives …
from the way that the cultural motifs of the private self which are associated
with "the individual" … act to align this notion of subjectivity with the feminine'. As the 'subjective' self becomes associated with intimate realms of activity
and with a moral disposition rather than with the principles of rational self-
government, it is thus counterposed to the motifs of masculine self-definition.
This opposition introduces a constitutive instability to concepts of masculinity,
which must maintain a divide between the subjective and the rational self.
Gillian shows how the instabilities of masculinity are represented in the nineteenth-century genre of the sensation novel, as masculinity becomes 'overwritten
with the *problems* of subjectivity and the association of individuality with private
life', and subjectivity itself becomes defined as 'dangerously feminine'.

3 Fashioning gendered identities

Jane Crisp

> Vain trifles as they seem, clothes have, they say, more important offices than merely to keep us warm. They change our view of the world and the world's view of us. … there is much to support the view that it is clothes that wear us and not we them; we may make them take the mould of arm or breast, but they mould our hearts, our brains, our tongues to their liking.
>
> (Virginia Woolf, *Orlando*: 1928: 170–1)

In everyday terms, we tend to think of our identity as a central core or essence which we reveal or mask depending on the constraints of the moment. This is the 'true' or 'real self' which we express by 'doing our own thing', which we want time off to find, and which we betray through those activities that we disavow by saying, 'I wasn't myself when I did/said that'. However, rather than regarding our identity as a fixed essence at our centre, acted on, but separate from, the forces around us, we might better understand it as something constructed from the start through a complex and ongoing series of negotiations between us and our society. Indeed, rather than thinking of our identity as singular, it would be more appropriate to think in terms of a number of constructed identities that relate to the different periods and different occasions within our lives.

Gendered identities: from nappies to high fashion

The process of construction of our various identities begins at our birth – before it, even, in these days of prenatal scans – with the labelling of us as male or female on the basis of our genital configuration. I still remember the gynaecologist's first words on the delivery of my child: 'It's a boy, Mrs Crisp – look at your son', and how he brandished the infant's crotch area for my immediate inspection. Yet how curious it is that this should be the first thing most of us care to know and that we should take its primacy so completely for granted. After all, alternatives can be imagined: in a society in which skill at playing the piano was the determinant of the highest status, the first question might relate to the length of the newborn baby's fingers; in one in which pollution or nuclear fallout was causing a high percentage of mutations, conformity to pre-Apocalypse norms might have the priority, as it does in the future depicted by Margaret Atwood in

The Handmaid's Tale (1986). However, one particular anatomical distinction rather than some other imaginable possibility provides the basis for the construction of our subsequent cultural identities; these are therefore implicated from the very start in a founding opposition of male to female which can always be naturalised by an appeal to bodily difference.

Our earliest garments play their part in constructing a gendered identity for us. Nappies were once simply squares of towelling, but today's disposable varieties are marketed in two different shapes, one for boy babies and the other for girl babies, and the packages that they come in may well be coded in blue and in pink; one brand that I noticed on sale in Australia even had a macho little belt and buckle depicted on the blue box and a cute little ribbon tied in a bow on the pink one. Moreover, a television advertisement for Pampers widely shown in Australia some years ago illustrated the depressing tendency for that founding distinction to be perceived not as a matter of difference between two otherwise equal sexes, but as male possession versus female lack. Two toddlers stand holding out the front of their nappies and peering inside: 'I've got one,' says the little 'boy'; 'I haven't got one,' says the little 'girl'. Nappies, in fact, demonstrate in microcosm the construction of our identities as gendered, and as gendered on the basis of a simple binary opposition marked by outward signs of difference and legitimised as reflecting a biological presence or lack.

Once we move from nappies to fashion, our gendered identities become more complex: we move beyond simple difference into a realm of fluid and multiple differences, with the possibility even of playful transgressions across the bounds of masculinity and femininity. In September 1989, the well-known French fashion magazine *Elle* offered the woman of the 1990s seven possible styles. Browsing through the March 2000 issue of *Vogue Australia*, I am intrigued to note how well *Elle's* predictions have stood the test of time. I propose to discuss this example in some detail because such fashion texts (together with the ways we read and use them) provide a simple model of how we fashion gendered identities for ourselves from the materials our culture makes available, and also a model of the possibilities and the problems of that fashioning.

Each of the seven styles that the 18 September 1989 edition of *Elle* presented was not just a style but a whole identity as well, as I hope my account of them makes clear. First, 'ecological', represented by the 'natural elegance' of wood and cashmere in earthy tones, worn with wood and leather accessories. Second, 'theatrical' – solid black with touches of gold, and associated with evening and mystery. The third identity is that of the city action girl, sporty, zany, and 'switched on', with her backpack, tights, shorts, pullover and roller skates (the one dated note – today it would be Rollerblades). The fourth is 'beyond fashion', a 'Zen minimalism' of simple shapes and contrasts in shades of white, black and grey. The fifth is the 'classic' look, a 'refined simplicity' of everyday good taste in soft pinks and blue greys. The sixth is an 'authentic' and 'traditional' 'country style', based on English tweeds and Irish knits worn with horsey accessories. The final identity is a 'baroque' one of 'romantic eccentricity', expressed through richly decorated velvets, silks and tulles in odd colour and texture combinations.

The pictures of each of these styles, moreover, show that they are capable of a number of inflections to suit the needs of public and private, work and leisure selves. The new millennium identities proposed by *Vogue Australia* are not so neatly tabulated, but cover a remarkably similar range: 'cool' and 'ladylike' glamour, 'urban safari gear' and 'biker-style suits', 'new conservative chic', 'horsy chic', 'retro' looks, and a number of baroque and fantasy possibilities including 'snake charmers' in simulated python skin and 'warrior woman' in 'blanket wraps, strong knits, tribal jewellery'.

The first thing that this example demonstrates is that femininity is not a single option, but a range of possibilities. A woman can opt for any of these feminine iden-tities depending on whim, occasion, taste and means; she is not bound to choose one only and reject all the others. Second, these identities are not only multiple, but also competing and, in many cases, contradictory ones: the theatrical and action-girl styles are clearly incompatible, as are the Zen and baroque, or even the public and private inflections of the classic look, but none the less one person can adopt any or all of these. Thus, however much the discourses of fashion, like many other discourses within our culture, appeal to an essential, unified, true self, which the choice of clothing and perfume serves merely to express and enhance, those very same discourses simultaneously make visible how constructed, multiple and divided the fashion – and human – subject is.

Faced with this multitude of competing identities, we engage in a process of negotiating our self-representations from the range on offer. We read a fashion magazine or browse in a department store and comment on the looks on offer and, later, we may or may not allow these looks to influence our own style of clothing. When I flip through *Elle* or *Vogue* with a woman friend, we say to each other such things as: 'This style I like, but these colours don't suit me'; 'This one is ridiculous – fancy anyone appearing in public in such an outrageous outfit'; 'This one, though, I love – I think I can achieve something like that effect ...' The process of self-representation continues in what we elect to buy or make for ourselves, and what we decide is suitable for us to put on for work, for a party or for a job interview. This process is usually a double one: it involves reading various fashion texts, be they magazines, shop windows or other people's outfits, and then drawing on these in our own performances, when we dress up and play the Zen minimalist or romantic baroque role or our own version of it. We are consumers of fashion, but we can and do actively produce a 'look' for ourselves, too.

As the example of fashion makes clear, though, the identities we are working with here may be individual but they are also very much culturally determined. We can give a highly personal inflection to a current style, assemble our own outfit from old and new items of clothing, but what is available to us is provided by our culture or cultural group. This applies not only to the physical materials – the garments on sale or the types, styles and colours of fabric if we make our own clothes – but also to the meanings they bear. What counts as wearable, let alone fashionable, depends very much on that cultural context. In the early 1960s, when I was living in France, I can remember buying myself a black leather jacket, which was considered at that time and place the height of bourgeois chic; a month later I wore the jacket on a visit to London, only to find to my embarrassment that black leather was associated there with a much less respectable set of values. Within a culture, too, as my London experience suggests, some identities are more sanctioned than others. The models in *Elle* and *Vogue* present styles acceptable to the dominant socioeconomic group; and this applies to their body styles, too. None of them are elderly or fat; tattoos or piercings, if present at all, are discrete – or fake; 'ethno-chic' fashion ideas may come from Peru, Morocco, Ghana or Hungary, but only a very few of the models displaying them do. Not all identities are equally acceptable or even visible in the fashion pages, although they may be seen readily enough in the street.

In the differential visibility and valuing of identities in these magazines, fashion intersects with politics in both the broader and narrower senses of the term. Similarly, the work we do as consumers here, of products and of images, implicates us willy-nilly in the capitalist system within which they are made and circulated; indeed, we owe it to the influences of humanist individualism and consumer capitalism that there are so many identities on offer, so strong an illusion of abundance and freedom of choice. The limits to our apparent freedom become visible if we should deliberately choose to opt for none of the styles or identities *Elle* proposes, for it is the dominant fashion itself which implicitly sets the rules of what can count as rejection or opposition to itself. Indeed, it may even go so far as to appropriate any systematic form of opposition as a new fashion – the bomber jacket, once emblem of rebellious lower-class youth, is a case in point. Even extremes of counter-style such as grunge and punk are capable of appropriation: the French *Elle* for 3 January 1994 announced with some degree of humour the advent of 'cringe', the new 'non-style' following on from 'le grunge' in which anything goes, except good taste, and the only worry is 'not confusing good bad taste and bad good taste'; *Glamour* for the same period shows supermodel Christy Turlington in 'punk' makeup and explains to its readers precisely how to reproduce this for themselves. Similarly, *Vogue Australia* for March 2000 offers its 'horsy chic' with 'a punk edge'. The feminist movement has found itself in a similar bind, in its search for alternative models of womanhood to those offered within patriarchy; and has seen the incorporation of apparently liberated ideals into advertisements for cigarettes and tampons with far from liberated subtexts.[1]

On a more positive note, however, the example of fashion reminds us that identities are indeed *fashioned*. They are not static or stable selves with which we are stuck once and for all, but processes of dressing up and playing roles. Note how carefully even the look that is to reveal 'the real you' has to be constructed; all the art and artifice needed to conceal art. Moreover, not only are there many identities that a woman can assume – daughter, mother, student, environmentally aware liberal, action girl, theatrical – but these, like fashion, change over time. The bustles and incredible skirts that so impeded Virginia Woolf's Orlando during part of her life as a woman are long gone, to be replaced by unisex bikey leathers, as the Sally Potter film (1993) so graphically illustrates; flared trousers have been in and out and in again – for years I wouldn't have been seen dead in mine, but in 1993 I was able to give them a brief airing. We do not occupy a static position throughout our lives, our masculine or feminine identities having once been constructed definitively; instead we can, and indeed must, continually reconstruct and renegotiate them in an ongoing process that lasts throughout our lives. Our bodies change, too, to compound this process. We are not so much women or men as unstable sites on which and through which the competing femininities and/or masculinities of our culture interact and are acted out.

Dressing up: the pleasures of fantasy

The climate, social and meteorological, in which we live obliges us to wear clothing, and helps determine both what that clothing consists of and the meanings it bears. However, putting on clothing and its attendant identities often goes beyond matters of climatic or cultural necessity, to become 'dressing up'. Mainstream fashion itself frequently offers the possibility of adopting various ethnic and historical identities. *Elle* for 3 January 1994, for example, proposed a 'harmonious' blend of Scottish, Peruvian, Tibetan, Mongolian and Afghan ethnicities; at the same time the Christmas/New Year issue of *Glamour* added the options of British looks from the 1940s and the Edwardian periods, as well as self-conscious imitations of figures from Renaissance paintings. *Vogue Australia* for March 2000 offers its sophisticated urban readers the dramatic alternative of the 'warrior woman', all tousled hair, roughly textured fabrics and barbaric accessories shot against a desolate landscape and available for a substantial price at an exclusive boutique near you.

Dressing up can allow one to indulge in the pleasures of fantasy, and to give rein to one's curiosity about alternative and even taboo identities through masquerade – acting out a whole range of subversive and transgressive possibilities. The various public personae that Madonna has developed, and the way some of these have been taken up by adolescent girls, is a highly visible case in point.[2] Feminine modesty and good taste could be flouted in favour of an attention-getting display of overcharged and conflicting symbols and sexualities – crucifixes, exaggeratedly pointy brassières, tarty tights. The arguments both in the popular arena and within cultural studies over what Madonna represents – hard-nosed maker and exploiter of an image or genuine free spirit; whore or heroine; subverter or reinforcer of the gendered identities with which she plays – add to this pleasure by freeing her and her imitators from the tyranny of fixed meanings. Similarly, Madonna's recent adoption of a softer maternal image demonstrates that the more outrageous possibilities do not preclude one from identities at the other end of the spectrum – much as one can dress up as 'warrior woman' one day and wear 'the new conservative chic' the next.

Even without dressing up, we can try on the alternative identities represented by someone like Madonna through our engagement with the character they perform. As Ien Ang has suggested, popular forms of entertainment such as soap operas, films and novels 'offer a private and unconstrained space in which socially impossible or unacceptable subject positions, or those which are in some way too dangerous or too risky to be acted out in real life, can be adopted' (Ang 1990: 85–6). One of the pleasures of watching soap opera, for instance, may well be the range of characters with whom viewers can identify. Consider, for instance, the satisfying escape from the daily round that man-eating superbitch characters such as Lexie and Amanda in *Melrose Place* may provide for women who spend most of their time being supportive and self-effacing.

Among the pleasurable fantasies that fashion offers both women and men – and, in so doing, sanctions – are those of playing with and across the polarities of the standard gender opposition through various 'masculine' and 'feminine' styles. The tailored suits for women promoted by *Elle* for 3 January 1994 and more recently in *Vogue Australia* could either be 'feminised' through the addition of such accessories as a fluffy stole in Tibetan lamb or have their masculinity further enhanced by close-cropped hair and solid-looking boots. For men, there have opened up the feminine, but now respectable possibilities of frilly shirts, neck chains and bracelets, or a 'soft and flowing' outfit in gentle shades of green and mauve from Versace, as promoted in the special style directory for men sold with *Vogue Australia*. Even perfumes are acceptable, albeit sold as 'aftershave' in some Anglo-Saxon countries to protect male sensibilities. The Christmas/New Year issue of *Glamour* discussed the 'semantics of scent' of thirteen new perfumes for women and twelve for men – among the names given the latter are 'Egoist', 'XS', 'Heritage', 'Sultan' and 'Eternity'. The images associated with perfumes (or aftershave) for men in advertisements for these products are by no means uniformly macho or sexually aggressive (lean, muscular hands grasping phallic bottles), but include tweedy, intellectual-looking men and sensitive nudes with head on arms, eyes hidden. Less respectable, perhaps, but openly advertised in mainstream British papers like the *Observer* is 'lingerie for men … from camisoles to stockings' – a black-and-white photograph in one such advertisement shows a man wearing distinctly feminine undies – he is shaving, perhaps thereby simulta-neously asserting his masculinity and removing the evidence of it the better to enjoy the alternative identity he has just put on. Even that all-important signifier of masculine difference and presence, the penis, has a range of identities avail-able to it through condoms, with such names as 'nuform', 'elite', 'new gold', 'rough', 'tight-fit', and 'fruit-flavoured'.

These examples show the extent to which the simple identification of us at birth as male or female gives way to competing and often contradictory feminini-ties and masculinities available to both women and men. Indeed, gender is itself in a sense a role composed of clothes, gestures and a way of walking and talking, which anyone can play regardless of their sexed body. This possibility has been demonstrated in a number of films, including *Some Like It Hot*, *Victor/Victoria*, *Tootsie*, *The Crying Game*, *Orlando* and *Priscilla, Queen of the Desert*. In such cases, though, the body under the clothes may be out of sight but it is rarely out of mind. Male and female roles take on different values depending on the body acting them; masculinity embodied by a man has a different significance from masculinity embodied by a woman (Kuhn 1985: 48–73). The meanings already imposed upon our particular body from the moment of birth onwards interfere with the otherwise free assumption of the fashionable and/or gendered identities of our desires – too bad, for instance, if one has a fat, aged body, the 'wrong' colour of skin or the 'wrong' genital form.

The body and its meanings

Such is the weight of meaning with which the body itself is invested, we may feel obliged to refashion it more or less radically through anti-wrinkle creams, corsets, padded bras, 'hip and bottom shapers', diet, exercise and surgery, and even (so great is the tyranny of that founding, fleshly distinction over our identity) through changing our genital configuration itself as the only means of authenticating the desired gender identity. Alternatively, we can work at refashioning the social meanings of bodily forms and functions into ones more enabling for us and our group. Indeed, this has necessarily been central to the agenda of the feminist movement, given the extent to which patriarchal perceptions of the female body and its weaknesses have been used to control and limit women's role in society. Germaine Greer's attempt to convert the menopause from a negatively to a positively valued 'change' is one of the more recent endeavours in this tradition.

The body, then, is not simply a neutral frame over which we drape the clothes that go with a role that we wish to play. It is already inescapably invested with cultural meanings. As Moira Gatens (1982/1991) has argued, the commonly made distinction between biological 'sex' and social 'gender' has tended to obscure this point by implying that our sexed body is a separate, material given to which a set of cultural ideas are attached. However, as she points out, the body at issue here is not 'the anatomical body, the neutral, dead body, but the body as lived, the animate body – the *situated* body' (1982/1991: 147). The body we are aware of, as human subjects, is 'an imaginary body', imagined and experienced through the eyes and minds of our culture, and hence inseparable from the meanings and values with which it is endowed. The notion of a neutral, separate body is a specifically cultural representation, which functions to naturalise certain cultural assumptions about gender.

Annette Kuhn's discussion of cross-dressing in some of the films mentioned above provides an illustration of the work done by this 'fundamentalism of the body' within our culture. She notes how such films are able:

> to offer, at least momentarily, a vision of fluidity of gender options; to provide a glimpse of 'a world outside the order normally seen or thought about' – an utopian prospect of release from the ties of sexual difference that bind us into meaning, discourse, culture.
>
> (Kuhn 1985: 50)

Yet, at the same time, that very 'fluidity of options' is undercut by being construed as depending on an 'essential' truth of the body:

In its performance aspect, clothing sets up a play between visible outward
appearance – in this case, gender as signified by dress – and an essence
which may not be visible but is nonetheless held to be more 'real' than
appearance – here the gender of the person whose true nature may be
concealed, both literally and metaphorically, beneath the clothes. What is at
stake in this expression of the dualism of appearance and essence is a
fundamentalism of the body, an appeal to bodily attributes as final arbiter of
a basic truth.

(Kuhn 1985: 53–4)

Thus, freedom from the tyranny of gendered identity at one level is undercut at
another. The hero's attraction for Victor, for example, is sanitised by our knowledge that Victor is really Victoria; similarly, the potential subversiveness of the
outrageous drag performances in *Priscilla* is offset by discourses circulating
around this film which reassure us that we are not watching 'real drag queens'
but resolutely heterosexual stars playing these characters.

The possibilities and contradictions Kuhn discusses and, indeed, the way our
curiosity is aroused by tales of changed or ambiguous sexual identities, find
particularly striking expression in the real-life story of the French diplomatic
employee and the Chinese opera star, which was announced on the cover of
Marie Claire (January 1994) – appropriately enough, a fashion magazine – as the
story of 'the man who did not know that his wife was a man'. To satisfy the
curiosity this headline was presumably designed to arouse in its readers, here are
the main details.

Bernard Boursicot, a minor employee in the French Embassy in Beijing,
develops a close friendship with Shi Pei Pu, a young Chinese playwright, 'slight,
small, no bigger than a girl', who used to play female roles in Chinese opera.
One evening Shi tells Bernard the story of his best operatic role, one in which he
plays a beautiful girl who changes identity with her brother to gain access to a
formal education, and in the process meets a handsome boy who 'does not
understand the strange attraction he feels for another boy'. Later, Shi confesses a
closely guarded secret: 'he' is really the third daughter of a family ruled by a
mother-in-law desperate for a grandson, and was brought up from birth as a boy.
Bernard believes this story, despite realising its incredibility – 'he was not even
really surprised; at heart it was as if he had always known'. He is determined to
help Shi to 're-become a woman'. To this end, he insists that they should 'make
love'; their relationship is consummated, albeit in a fairly perfunctory manner,
and Bernard, returning from the bathroom, sees the confirmatory marks of
blood between Shi's thighs. Just before Bernard leaves China, Shi tells him that
she is pregnant. Four years later, Bernard returns, and learns that they have a
son. Being together is difficult because of the Cultural Revolution, but lessons on
the thoughts of Chairman Mao provide an excuse; Bernard passes on embassy
documents about Russia which might be of interest to the Chinese, and also

makes use of the diplomatic bag to bring in various consumer goods demanded by his now wife and her mother. Sexual relations between the couple happen spasmodically during this period, and gradually peter out. Finally, after two more years, Bernard meets his son – it is, he says, 'the most wonderful day of his life'. On his return to France, he organises visitor's visas for his son and Shi. Shi, as always, is dressed as a man, and presented to Bernard's friends as his son's uncle. Shi is well received as an artist who has survived the Cultural Revolution, but later he and Bernard are arrested on the charge of being spies. Bernard learns via the radio in his cell that a medical examination has proved that Shi is not a woman, but a man with normal male organs; blood tests confirm that the 'son' is no relation of either. Devastated by these revelations, Bernard attempts suicide. Shi and Bernard are both condemned to prison, but separately pardoned within the year. The magazine article saves for last the answer to the 'central enigma of this affair' – how Shi managed to create with his male body the illusion of being a woman.

This story suggests more than I can begin to cover here. One thing it reminds us of, though, is the centrality of heterosexuality in our society; our identity is not only gendered in respect to our own body but also that of the bodies of those with whom we enter into close relationships. Not only is there a difference of cultural meaning between a man embodying masculinity and a woman embodying it, but there is a difference too between a man loving and 'making love to' a woman and to another man; between a woman loving a man or another woman. And these differences are capable of being further complicated by the masculinity or femininity of the roles taken on by the respective partners.

The story also plays out a dazzling complexity of masquerades, of endlessly mirrored gendered identities. A man masquerades as a woman masquerading as a man, both in opera and in his private life; the same man acts out being a woman, not by wearing a woman's clothes (this he does only on the stage), but by the material evidences of the body – the blood of defloration, a female genital form, pregnancy, a child – all of which prove able to be no more than an illusion; another man is married to a woman whom the rest of the world takes to be a man, or is he married to a man masquerading as a woman, or does he perhaps need to believe that his partner is really a woman for the relationship to happen? Does the medical evidence that reveals the 'truth' really clear up the mysteriousness of the whole affair? And, although no mention is made of Bernard having a medical examination, we accept his and the magazine's presumption about his identity.

The power of others in determining our identity

Before concluding this chapter I want to give attention to something that the example of fashion, which I have been using so far, may obscure; that is, the power of others in determining our identity, and the grave consequences that this can and does have for people who are defined by the dominant group within their society as having an inferior identity or no identity at all. Negotiating an identity within the constraints imposed by our culture depends upon having something to bring to the negotiating table that others are prepared to recognise.

Psychoanalytic ideas about the original formation of our sense of self, of having a distinct identity, evoke the notion of the gaze of the Other. At the so-called mirror stage, the infant becomes first aware of itself as seen from the outside, as a separate unit. This sense of how we seem from the outside, how the eyes of our culture sees us, becomes a determining force in our ongoing social identity. A very simple incident illustrates this process. I recall glancing at myself in a mirror before heading off to the shops, and deciding to change what I was wearing because 'I don't want to be seen looking like this'. Most readers have probably had a similar experience. It is a fairly safe bet that nobody at the shops would have taken much notice of my shabby attire, but my sense of how I might appear to that gaze of some generalised Other person was enough to make me change into something more businesslike and respectable.

Throughout our lives, the various social identities that we assume depend for their existence on the cooperation of other people. My identity as a university lecturer, for example, depends on the authorising power of the institution that employs me and the wider community that accepts this authorising power; it is supported by the physical layout of lecture theatres and tutorial rooms, which represent my position as the central, controlling one; and it is supported, too, through the way in which colleagues and students adopt roles that complement mine. Without such supports, we risk having no identity at all.

This is what happens to people diagnosed as having Alzheimer's disease. Textbooks actually refer to the condition as a 'living death' and the 'loss of self'[3] – terms which openly confirm the view that people with Alzheimer's cease to have a valid identity and effectively become non-persons. This view, however, is contradicted by the experience of many carers, who have been able to maintain warm and supportive relationships even with someone in the advanced stages of dementia. As Sabat and Harré (1992) have demonstrated, it is not the direct effect of dementia in itself, but the negative reactions of other people that brings about this so-called 'loss of self'.

People with Alzheimer's, like anyone else, cannot construct a valid social identity unless those around them cooperate in the process by recognising and responding appropriately to the identity to which they are laying claim. Unfortunately, though, their claims are all too often ignored. People stop listening to them, talk about them as if they are no longer there, and in so doing deny them any status as a fellow human being.

However, social identities, whether negative or positive, are contingent, held in place by the historically and geographically located institutions and practices that authorise them. Over time, the once-dominant paradigms within a society become subject to challenge and renegotiation, as witness both changing attitudes towards homosexuality and the recent rewriting of colonial history to incorporate the experiences and perspective of colonised peoples. A shift is happening also within the medical and caring professions in how dementia is understood, allowing for the subjectivity and personal identity of someone with the condition to be recognised. My own work on understanding people with Alzheimer's disease, which I discuss in Chapter 9, is representative of that shift.

Notes

1   See, for example, Ann Treneman (1988) 'Cashing in on the Curse', in L. Gamman and M. Marshment (eds) *The Female Gaze*, London: The Women's Press.
2   See, for example, Lisa L. Lewis (1990) 'Consumer Girl Culture: How Music Video Appeals to Girls', in M.E. Brown (ed.) *Television and Women's Culture*, Sydney: Currency Press.
3   These terms are used in the titles of well-known books for carers by Robert Woods (1989) and by Donna Cohen and Carl Eisdorfer (1986).

Bibliography

Ang, I. (1990) 'Melodramatic Identifications: Television Fiction and Women's Fantasy', in M.E. Brown (ed.) *Television and Women's Culture*, Sydney: Currency Press.

Atwood, M. (1986) *The Handmaid's Tale*, London: Cape.

Cohen, D. and Eisdorfer, C. (1986) *Loss of Self, a Family Resource for the Care of Alzheimer's Disease*, New York: New American Library.

Gatens, M. (1991) 'A Critique of the Sex/Gender Distinction', in S. Gunew (ed.) *A Reader in Feminist Knowledge*, London and New York: Routledge.

Kuhn, A. (1985) *The Power of the Image*, London: Routledge & Kegan Paul.

Sabat, S.R. and Harré, R. (1992) 'The Construction and Deconstruction of Self in Alzheimer's Disease', *Ageing and Society* 12: 443–61.

Woods, R. (1989) *Alzheimer's Disease: Coping with a Living Death*, London: Souvenir Press.

Woolf, V. (1928) *Orlando*, London: Hogarth Press.

4 Fleshed by the pen
Writing and reading gender

Kay Ferres

Life has no words;
Life has but cries;
Love, hate and pain,
As these arise.

But words have life,
They stand like men,
Linked or alone,
Fleshed by the pen.
(Mary Gilmore, 'Words', *Fourteen Men: Verses*: 62)

> Once I began to live my own life – a life with a husband, a home, and small children –
> I could see firsthand how remote it was from the life of the poet as I had understood
> it. … But increasingly I came to regard each poem not as a series of technical strate-
> gies, but as a forceful engagement between a life and a language …
>
> [Occasionally] – … the life beckoned to the language and the language
> followed.
>
> (Eavan Boland, 'Preface', *An Origin Like Water: Collected Poems 1967–1987*: 14)

In 'Words', Mary Gilmore (1865–1962) invokes a series of oppositions which
have become commonplace in discussions of gender and culture: culture (words)
is set against nature (cries); experience and life, against the symbolic realm of
writing; the world of the (feminine) emotions, contrasted with the social order of
words, which 'stand like men'. But one term intervenes to unsettle these oppositions: 'fleshed'. The body, which, in its rawest materiality, produces cries of 'love,
hate and pain', is transformed by culture and language. A comparison of writing
with maternity and childbearing is implicit in this gesture. Writing is a kind of
cultural reproduction. In setting these two enterprises against each other here,
the text enacts an understanding of the position of the woman poet which
provided the impetus for a feminist scholarship that mapped the 'anxieties' of
female authorship.

Commemorated in Australian cultural history as a poet, despite a long career
as a journalist at the Sydney *Worker*, Gilmore here draws upon the resonances of
Christian tradition and a romantic understanding of authorship to valorise the

process of literary creation and to stake a claim in it. 'Words' addresses a set of issues about the gendered dimensions of the production of culture which preoccupied feminist critics who undertook the recovery of the work of lost and neglected women writers and artists in the early 1970s and 1980s. Those scholars might have perceived here the delimitation of separate spheres – the feminine world of love and domestic ritual, the masculine world of reason and the abstract intellect – in the psychoanalytic frame evoked by the fashionable French feminisms of the 1970s, the Kristevan semiotic and the Lacanian symbolic. In these terms, the poem poses the problem (and represents the allure) of the feminine desire to cross those boundaries as a question of the flesh, the sexed body. This poem underwrites the tensions implicit in the cultural separation of public and private spheres. The words which 'stand like men' recall Wordsworth's description of poetry as the 'sensuous incarnation' of thought.

In the preface to her *Collected Poems*, published in 1996, Eavan Boland represents her career as a poet as a negotiation of the claims her identities as 'woman' and 'poet' made on each other. She discusses this in terms of movement between public and private spheres, from the 'safe and well lighted circle' of Irish literary culture to the 'shadow' of ordinary life. Boland's poetry strives for a connectedness of these spheres which Mary Gilmore's poem cannot contemplate. The identities of 'woman' and 'poet' are both produced through the struggle with the skills particular to poetic language: rhyme, metre tapped out on a kitchen table; and through an engagement with the institutions of Irish culture: the persona of the bard; the nationalist tradition; the public, political uses of poetry.

Early feminist criticism turned its attention to the apparent exclusion of women writers from the Western canon, to the virtual invisibility of women as artists, and to their mute musical compositions. This work uncovered a seemingly sexual division of labour in cultural production. As Dorothy Smith (1988: 17–43) described it: 'men create culture, women transmit it'. Men were at the centre of public life, creating its monuments and institutions; women were at home creating the conditions for such production and training the children who would maintain it. Women were the objects and the inspiration of culture; men, its subjects. Men, in Western cultures at least, were the bearers of what Pierre Bourdieu has termed 'symbolic capital': the 'power to consecrate objects (with a trademark or signature) or persons (through publication, exhibition etc) and therefore to give value, and to appropriate the profits from this operation' (Bourdieu 1986: 132). The initial feminist concern with authorship, then, was a concern about the distribution of power, the power to engage in the production of meaning and value, and to participate in the institutions of culture. Feminist critics' concerns, and female writers' anxieties, about authorship were linked to the way value is assigned to literature. Indeed, as Michel Foucault (1977: 113–38) has pointed out, the designation of an 'author' to a text is crucial to the assignation of literary value. Power flows from and through this designation of value, via the practices of reviewing and criticism, and the academic study of 'authors' and the 'canon'.

This orientation to authorship as the critical factor in the production of meaning went along with an acceptance (though not an unquestioning one) of the divide between popular and high culture. The strategic challenge to gendered relations of cultural production was directed to the relegation of feminine cultural practices and tastes to the popular and the domestic, and the alliance of masculinity with high culture and public life. Virginia Woolf's materialist analysis of the conditions of cultural production in Britain at the beginning of the twentieth century in many respects still held in Anglophone societies. Her demands for economic independence, for education and training that attended to the needs of the body and the spirit as well as the intellect (wine and fine-spun puddings rather than water and prunes), and for the brute strength to overcome that self-effacing femininity so powerfully embodied in the 'Angel in the House', struck a chord with the many women readers who took up her texts in the 1970s, looking for ways to account for women writers' and artists' exclusion from the canon.[1]

Cultural authority was assumed to be bound up with the status of authorship because what Michel de Certeau describes as the 'scriptural model' of culture still held. In that model, the 'writing economy' shapes cultural institutions and the circulation of texts (de Certeau 1974, 1984).[2] Consequently, contemporary developments in critical theory – principally in the work of Roland Barthes and Michel Foucault – which drew attention away from authors, was viewed with some suspicion. The female author seemed to be silenced just as there were readers gathered to hear her speak. Indeed, the trope of the silenced storyteller was reiterated in many key feminist texts: in discussions of Isak Dinesen's story 'The Blank Page',[3] in Nancy Miller's 'Arachnologies', a parable of the woman artist (1986: 270–95), in the essays of Tillie Olsen (1980) and Adrienne Rich (1979). Commentaries on Dinesen's story emphasised its appeal to a female tradition of storytelling, and its identification of that tradition with the subversion of heterosexual marriage. Silence and other tactical evasions of speech – lies, secrets, inventiveness – were valorised in this criticism as practices that gave the weak and marginalised access to power. The object of this analysis was to gain access to the institutions that were the subject of the critique.

More recently, attention to the histories of authorship and the ways it is organised and regulated has been better able to account for women's various historical appearances as authors – for example, as writers of particular genres of domestic fiction in the nineteenth century[4] – as well as for the ascendancy of men in other movements.[5] This work is underwritten by a different and more pluralist understanding of the field of culture. It locates the institutions of the writing economy – the canon, the academy, literary criticism – in a more heterogeneous and diversified field. In particular, it does not understand the 'popular' in a limited way, as simply the excluded 'other', held apart from the 'high' culture represented by writing. Authors of domestic fiction, for example, cannot be treated as part of an 'elite', culturally productive minority writing for an audience of passive readers, when there is an indelible historical trace of the interactions of those audiences with the texts that circulated among them. Similarly, the diverse products of authors who write poetry, popular journalism, political speeches, and even new variants on marriage vows for a utopian community in South America (as Mary Gilmore did), cannot be captured by the high cultural notion of 'authorship'.

The shifting historical and social circumstances which differentiate Mary Gilmore's engagements in the field of culture from those of Eavan Boland can be characterised by de Certeau's description of the shift from a universalising 'scriptural' model that valorises a writing economy and the text, to a pluralist and differentiated model that pays attention to the overlooked practices of reading. This is to understand writers as readers, and writing as a practice that incorporates reading. It also treats readers as active users of texts, rather than as abstractions constructed by or interpellated in the text.

In this chapter, I want to look again at the idea of a feminine tradition, but in a different frame from those scholars who sought to extend the canon. Like those scholars, I am returning to *A Room of One's Own*, and Woolf's claim that women writers found in the novel a set of as-yet-unfixed conventions, a pliable form, 'soft in her hands' (1974: 77). While Woolf's attention is directed to writing, and the development of a feminine sentence, the point I want to pick up here is her recognition that traditions are invented and sedimented by a process of continual renegotiation to serve the interests of particular groups. By contrast with the way the term 'canon' is used to signify a set of texts that represent 'universal' and 'unchanging' aesthetic values, which are an alibi for undeclared political interests, 'tradition' is understood to be invented. By attending to this process of invention, rather than proceeding with a notion of a set of texts that exist to be discovered and revalued, it is possible to explore the way cultural production and transmission involves a wide array of cultural practices and social relations. I do not mean simply to shift attention from author to reader as the site where meaning is produced; rather, I want to argue that an understanding of women as the subjects of culture needs to take account of particular practices of reading and writing. My approach takes up Teresa de Lauretis' understanding of experience as a process through which subjectivity is constructed:

> Through that process one places oneself or is placed in a social reality, and so perceives and comprehends as subjective (referring to, even originating in, oneself) those relations – material, economic, and interpersonal – which are in fact social and, in a larger perspective, historical. The process is continuous, its achievement unending or daily renewed. For each person, therefore, subjectivity is an ongoing construction, not a fixed point of departure or arrival from which one then interacts with the world. On the contrary, it is the effect of that interaction – which I call experience; and thus it is produced not by external ideas, values or material causes, but by one's personal, subjective, engagement in the practices, discourses and institutions that lend significance (value, meaning and affect) to the events of the world.
>
> (de Lauretis 1984: 159)

In the discussion that follows, I want to trace the way a particular group of women participate in the production of meaning, and in the process become provisional subjects of culture, through interaction in the circuits of reading and writing. Although my emphasis is not on the interpretation of texts, the discussion will demonstrate how reading and writing have been central to the achievement of the sense of 'placement' in the social reality Lauretis refers to. Returning to de Certeau, that sense of placement involves both 'the tactical and joyful dexterity involved in the mastery of a technique' and 'a pleasure in getting around the rules of a constraining space' (Ahearne 1995: 160). Those pleasures are produced not just through textual relations, but through the insinuation of texts in social inter-actions. The text and the positions it offers to readers do not solely determine reading. Rather, readers import elements of their experience and social context into the text as they enter into an interpretive exchange with other readers.

The following discussion describes a reading economy, as opposed to a writing economy. Instead of emphasising 'exclusion' from institutions, it exposes the tactics and interactions involved in getting around the 'constraining space' of the writing economy, shifting its boundaries, re-employing its objects in new texts and interpre-tive exchanges. The first part focuses on Eavan Boland's account of her excursions in Irish culture; the second, on a reconstruction of a series of textual and social exchanges among a group of women writers. My case studies take up first with the way the term 'poet' is taken over by Eavan Boland to describe what she is and what she does. Second, I explore the ways a 'community of readers' transform the mean-ings of texts through time – that is, make claims of texts which produce not 'universal' meanings and truths (the basis of claims to traditional 'literary' value), but make the texts meaningful in new and contingent ways.

Eavan Boland, an Irish poet who grew up in the 1950s, restates Mary Gilmore's dilemma in *Object Lessons*:

> There were times when I sat down at that table, or came up the stairs, my key in my hand, to open the door well after midnight, when I missed some-thing. I wanted a story. I wanted to read or hear the narrative of someone else – a woman and a poet – who had gone here, and been there. Who had lifted a kettle to a gas stove. Who had set her skirt over a chair, near to the clothes dryer, to have it without creases for the morning. Who had made the life meet the work and set it down.
>
> (Boland 1996: xvi)

This demand (or longing) for representation was answered in the 1970s by the establishment of publishing houses and programmes whose remit was 'women's writing'. New work flourished and forgotten writers were rediscovered. A 'new' feminist criticism, which theorised the authority of the woman writer within a masculinist tradition, contributed to this discursive formation. This enterprise uncovered the stories that Boland wanted to hear: stories that made her own experience intelligible and offered women readers a subject position within the text.

The voice Boland longs to hear is the voice of a woman *and* a poet; the two identities are no longer assumed to conflict, though how they might productively coexist is still in question. Coming to her profession in the 1960s, from a university training, Boland understands that critical practice still depends on and reproduces its own authority through a denial of poetry's particularity, of its embeddedness in social relations:

> I ought to have felt that my experiences, even my half-formed impressions at this time, connected well with my training as a poet. But I did not. As each morning came around, with its fresh insights and senses, I felt increasingly the distance between my own life, my lived experience and conventional interpretations of both poetry and the poet's life. It was not exactly or even chiefly that the recurrences of my world – a child's face, the dial of a washing machine – were absent from the tradition, although they were. It was not even so much that I was a woman. It was that, being a woman, I had entered into a life for which poetry had no name.
>
> (Boland 1996: 18)

Boland enters into that life in Ireland, where poetry (and the poet) has a privileged place in a nationalist tradition. Yet as Boland argues, 'flawed permissions' (1996: 204) surround this tradition; those permissions authorise certain voices and utterances, but position women poets as a 'species of insubordination' (1996: 191). Kathleen ni Houlihan can represent Ireland, and figures like Maud Gonne and Lady Constance Gregory enter the mythology of nationalism, but the poet/singer of that tradition was resolutely male. Boland responds to this as a problem, a test, rather than as an outright exclusion. The Irish woman poet has to struggle with a dragon, the image of Irish womanhood which has sustained this tradition, in much the same way as Woolf fought to overcome the 'Angel in the House'. Inside the poem, however, the woman poet encounters opportunities as well as interdictions. She sees her opportunity in the way the tradition admits a personal and politicised voice. By theorising a space between public and political poetry, between the locale of the present and historicised place, by 'disassembling' poetic relations as social and thoroughly politicised, Boland finds a voice within an Irish tradition.

Traditions, she asserts, are made 'in downright ways' (1996: 215) by a series of textual exchanges, poets reading poets reading other poets. In the case of Irish poetry, this is a conflictual but public process. The bard's authority is challenged in pubs, cafés and on the streets. The very publicness of Irish tradition accounts for its permissiveness, its accommodation of clamouring voices. Texts are objects to be used, re-employed, not artefacts to be preserved intact. Occupying that contemporary urban space, Boland finds herself in the midst of endlessly renewable talk, talk and poetry which is experienced bodily in the space of the pub and the suburban garden, in the air of the streets and the hills. Because this cultural field is not rigidly hierarchical and because 'poetry' enters into and emerges from these social spaces, there are openings for the tactic de Certeau calls 'insinuation'. 'Insinuation' is derived from a French legal term, which denotes the 'inscription of a private act upon a public register' (Ahearne 1995: 163). It does not simply mean 'insertion', because the element that is insinuated transforms the received text or meaning – or, in this case, tradition. Insinuation is the 'introduction of a supplementary element, bearing the mark of the individual subject, into a structured composition of other elements in such a way as to alter the composition and hence the signification of these elements' (1995: 174).

Boland's poetry does insinuate domestic experience, particularly that which relates to mothering and the dailiness of life with children, into a recognisably 'Irish' cultural tradition. Boland's volume of collected poems, *An Origin like Water* (1997), exposes the traces of this negotiation, and shows up some of the limits of the tactic of insinuation. The early poems from 1967 engage the Irish nationalist tradition, but from 1975 the woman who figures in the poems takes her bearings from the present as much as the past. The discourse of suburbia – of domestic life, marriage and children – is joined to a politics of the Irish diaspora through tropes of displacement and substitution. Boland experiences her 'Irishness' as a child at school in England in the 1950s. Private life does not concede to politics; rather, the poems expose the workings of political power through the domestic:

> It was never predictable. … The language remained partially inherited: resistant and engrossing. But the life at least was wholly mine. It took place in a house, in a garden, with a child in my arms, on summer afternoons, in winter dusks, and with eventual confidence that however formidable the poetic tradition might be, however assured its inherited language, its ethical survival still depended on the allowance it provided for a single life to make … a new name for itself and commend it to all the old ones.
>
> (Boland 1997: 14)

Writing about that experience, she uncovers another space, which is more difficult to negotiate: the space of the erotic and the sexual. Boland ends *Object Lessons* with a discussion of some women poets whose situation in many ways speaks to her own. This is a discussion without the resolution of her exchange with the Irish tradition: reading it, one senses that these issues are not yet incorporated in endless, nuanced talk. The erotic is encountered in an uncertain, ageing body as a perilous territory whose contours are indistinctly drawn. Boland's tactic is to map the space through poetic reference points, taking on the experience of women poets who are her contemporaries, and re-employing their texts to her own ends. She invokes Sylvia Plath, writing a 'pre-erotic' poem about her children's Christmas balloons five days before her death, on the same day as Plath also wrote 'Edge'; Carol Anne Duffy, evoking the pleasure and power of one woman's desire for another in 'Warming Her Pearls'; and Louise Glück, disassembling the elements of the sexual and the erotic in 'Mock Orange'. Alongside these, Boland sets down her own poem, written 'away from' the traditional erotic object: 'The Black Lace Fan My Mother Gave Me'.

Boland reads through these poems to find her way to a writing practice which shadows and disrupts the circuits of power reproduced in the traditions of love poetry. Her purpose is not simply to invert the relations of power inscribed in relations of desire understood in terms of a subject and object. Instead she sets out to restore the object of desire, to reimagine and reinfuse desire with the erotic. Here Boland finds her feminist commitments unhelpful, and so her efforts to theorise a still tentative practice founder on lack – the lack of a tradition, and of the conversation and everyday talk that Virginia Woolf lamented, but which gave Boland an entry into the Irish tradition.

I want to turn to a discussion of that kind of conversation now, to uncover a set of everyday relations among women, which might underpin an account of the shift from a 'writing economy': 'New meanings are not there to be discovered, but are produced by a community of readers in creative dialogue with texts, producers and each other' (Betterton 1996: 2).

First, let me figure this group of three women: two (Marjorie Barnard and Jean Devanny) are contemporaries, writers and friends both; and one (Beverley Farmer) is from the next generation of writers and readers. They are linked through degrees of acquaintance and intimacy, through friendship and through professional regard; they are readers of one another's work, and share other acquaintances with women writers and their work. These relations are not lived out in face-to-face encounters: they are staged in correspondence, in reading, in occasional visits, in the exchange of gifts. Yet they are intimate encounters, however mediated. In part, that intimacy comes from a shared experience; in part it comes from a particular infusion of private and professional life with what Boland calls the sexualised erotic.

I am constituting Barnard, Devanny and Farmer (and myself) as a 'community of readers', in order to show how new gendered meanings of the term 'writer' are produced through their exchanges and practices. These exchanges involve both objects and texts which traverse the spaces of public and private consumption. Our point of entry into this 'community' is another notebook. In *A Body of Water: A Year's Notebook*, published in 1990, Beverley Farmer locates her published writing in a web of experience: journals, letters, meditations, conversations, readings and remembrances. Embedded in this text are stories she has published elsewhere: *A Body of Water* represents the *work* of cultural production, which is usually concealed and disavowed by the finished object.

Let me introduce this group of readers/writers:

Marjorie Barnard (1897–1987) A graduate of Sydney University, awarded the University Medal in History in 1918. Her father refused to allow her to take up a scholarship to Oxford. She worked as a librarian, and took up a career as a writer in collaboration with Flora Eldershaw, producing novels (*A House is Built, Tomorrow and Tomorrow and Tomorrow*), criticism and historical works. Barnard was also active in the Fellowship of Australian Writers, especially in the period when the Menzies government sought to outlaw the Australian Communist Party. She lived at home until her mother's death, nursing her through a long illness. A relationship with the writer Frank Dalby Davison ended in 1942, after eight years. Just before her death, Barnard sent Beverley Farmer a signed first edition of 'The Persimmon Tree', a gesture Farmer returned by writing 'Black Genoa' after Barnard's death.

Jean Devanny (1894–1962) Born in New Zealand, Devanny moved to Sydney in 1929 with her husband Hal and two children, following the death of her 4-year-old daughter. Already a published writer with five books to her credit, she attracted notoriety rather than a literary reputation. Her work took up sexual and political themes, but even so it existed in an often unresolvable tension with her commitment to the Communist Party of Australia. She was a Party organiser and a formidable public speaker, as well as an active campaigner for sex education and birth control. Her expulsion from the Party, ostensibly for promiscuous conduct in 1942, also precipitated the end of a long relationship with a key Party figure, J.B. Miles, who refused to intervene on her behalf. She was one of a group of women writers who corresponded regularly with Marjorie Barnard, and with each other. Devanny and Barnard were especially sympathetic. Each suffered debilitating illness and experienced disappointment in love affairs with men who were committed elsewhere. Barnard disclosed details of her relationship with Davison in a series of letters to Devanny in January 1947. In Jean, who had 'taken bitter blows and remained steadfast', she found the understanding that allowed her to 'take off my armour for a moment' (Ferrier 1992: 157, 162). Jean sent Marjorie a coral and shell necklace she had made herself, still in Barnard's possession at the time of her death.

Beverley Farmer (1941–) A writer of fiction, educated at the University of Melbourne, she spent three years in Greece. Her life there with her partner, his family and their child has been worked over in her fiction. Loss, loneliness and failed relationships recur in her narratives. She came to know Marjorie Barnard through a mutual friend, who knew that Beverley admired Marjorie's story, 'The Persimmon Tree'.

Although Devanny and Farmer are not directly connected in this circuit of exchange, this exchange of gifts – material and symbolic – is crucial to my reading of Farmer's account of how she takes on the identities of 'woman' and 'writer'. My extension of the circuit to include Devanny, and later Katherine Mansfield, is in keeping with Farmer's sentiment: 'It matters very much to me, the invisible network of women reading each other's work and cherishing it' (Farmer 1990: 27). This 'invisible network' of readers is not easily mapped on to the institutions which shape 'literature': the publishing industry, reviewing and academic criticism. Their uses of texts as objects that stand in for intimate interaction and personal disclosure might be understood through an analogy with the exchange of gifts. In de Certeau's terms, the exchange of gifts and letters which is insinuated into this cultural field extends the series of operations involved in 'reading'. The 'literal' readings of a text sanctioned by institutionalised interpreters – academics, critics – limit this field. De Certeau's 'impertinent reader' does not identify so closely with the text. Readers are more like travellers than they are like writers. As he puts it in *The Practice of Everyday Life*, they move across the text like nomads (de Certeau 1984). Jeremy Ahearne comments, 'This movement – gleaning, poaching, making do – ought to make any cultural history based (inevitably) on writings and representations appear merely as the tip of an iceberg, a drop in the ocean' (Ahearne 1995: 171). The reader as traveller does not stick to the itineraries of the text; she turns, detours, diverts and manoeuvres. Fragments of the text prompt meditation, flights of fancy, the insinuation of new elements from an already established repertoire.

Beverley Farmer's homage to Barnard, 'Black Genoa', enacts such a reading. It figures friendship between women as the surety that underwrites grief and pain. In this story, two women share experiences of loss and redemption. Both have lost a father: one in the present time of the narrative, a slow death from cancer; and for the other, estrangement preceded actual death. For both, loss is experienced separately from dying, though the event itself precipitates the need to make sense of what has happened. The story participates in this groping towards meaning, but finds only a partial redemption in the gesture of planting a fig tree, a Black Genoa: 'Green hands would reach out of it one day, loose on spread arms; and a thousand pouches, purpling, oozing, burst apart' (Farmer 1990: 139). The purpling figs are directly related to Joanna, who has taken refuge with her friend following her father's death. Joanna brings 'bruise-purple figs, with a red crack in each one, a glow of seeds', as a gift. She herself is like a fig, according to her friend: 'Opulent. Purple. Abundant, syrupy and gritty, bursting …' (1990: 135). The tree, the figs and the woman – an idea of consolation works its way through the gaps and displacements of metonymy.

'Black Genoa' ends in an echo of 'The Persimmon Tree'. The spread arms of the tree recall the woman who appears in the window at the end of Barnard's story. The anticipation of the ripening figs chimes with the eroticism of woman's gesture, raising her arms as her robe falls. In *A Body of Water*, Farmer tells us she had planted a fig tree just before news came of Marjorie Barnard's death.

'The Persimmon Tree', first published in 1941, is a much-anthologised story in Australian cultural history, included on the basis of its difference from the dominant radical realist tradition of bush stories. In an economy of writing, it is difficult to place. It is taken to represent a weaker modernist strain, at odds with the realist tradition; and, within Barnard's work, as a departure from her more overtly political writing. Barnard's politics, though of the Left, also sit oddly with the masculine egalitarianism of radical nationalism. 'The Persimmon Tree' would be more at home in the company of the stories of Katherine Mansfield or Jean Rhys than in its usual institutional location in the 'Australian' canon. It is a story of recovery and loss, a lonely monologue whose intensity of feeling is displaced on to a carefully detailed domestic interior. In its attention to the division of inside and outside, it has a great deal in common with the work of women artists of the period, like Stella Bowen, Grace Crowley, Grace Cossington Smith and Vida Lahey.

The narrative exposes the still raw pain of the convalescent narrator through its attention to the minimalist detail of the space she occupies. The bare walls of the room are as sensitive to the imprint of shadows as her own nerves are to a touch upon her skin. The shadows prompt reflections on the fragility of human happiness. The narration turns on the coming of spring, and the simultaneous appearance of a second woman in a flat opposite. The swelling tenderness of the buds of spring blossom is initially too painful to behold directly; instead, it becomes apparent in the shadowed branches on the wall. When the narrator does look outward, it is to be aware of a yet more poignant sight: the voluptuousness of out-of-season persimmons, carefully placed on a windowsill in the woman's flat, to ripen in the sun. At the story's end, the narrator looks outward to see the other woman standing in the window, stretching her arms upward like the branches of a tree, letting her wrap drop in a gesture of graceful sensuality. In this moment, the narrative fulfils its promise: 'I saw the spring come once'. The inarticulate recognition of the erotic is expressed in a sensation ('My blood ticked like a clock') and a cry ('I thought my heart would break') (Barnard 1986: 112).

In Barnard's story, the appearance of the persimmons marks sensuality as a point of difference in the two women's subjectivity; in Farmer's, the figs are a point of convergence. There is no direct eroticism in Farmer's story. As in 'The Persimmon Tree', the women whose consciousness is exposed here are vulnerable: the death of the father and the recognition of their ambivalence about him threatens disintegration and despair. The fig, like the persimmons, figures another experience that lies beyond loss and signifies recovery.

In reading these two stories side by side, I had found a point of connection in the tree. To return to de Certeau, my own reading practice performed an operation of 'metaphorisation', an operation in which one thing – the image of the tree – came to stand for something other than the text allowed. The tree seemed to be the point at the centre, around which the women's relationships were configured. And it wasn't until I read Beverley Farmer's account of her joy in reading it that I realised that there was no actual persimmon tree – rather the memory of one – in the story:

> I read 'The Persimmon Tree' for the first time three or four years ago and was puzzled, when my joy in it died down enough for thought, to realise that the story in fact contained *no persimmon tree*. There was a row of persimmons put to ripen on a window sill, autumn persimmons although it was spring in the story. But there was no tree; and at last I decided that the tree of the title was the shadowy solitary woman behind the curtain in the flat across the road, holding her bare arms up to the sun, the spring.
>
> (Barnard 1986: 26)

I insinuated Beverley Farmer's reading into my own. I had substituted the woman for the tree, but had not thought about what the absent presence of the tree might signify. Reading about the publication of the story, I happened upon Barnard's correspondence with Jean Devanny. The tree's absence and the narrator's loneliness resonate with Marjorie Barnard's own experience, as she tells it to Devanny, in an exchange of letters after the story's publication.

Barnard reveals her own grief at the end of her relationship with Frank Dalby Davison. Her disclosures illuminate the story, but do not reduce it to 'autobiography'. Her narrator has 'put her life on a shelf' and retreated to the shell of a room 'that fitted without touching me', her mind 'as transparent and as tender as new skin'. The freshness of the wound, and the mingled pain and joy of erotic longing, is brought home to her by the other woman's sensuous display. Barnard's pain is experienced differently: her heart does not break, and instead she learns courage and trust. 'I've been hurt too much to imagine a wound where there is none', she tells Devanny, who had been concerned that, in her ignorance of Marjorie's relationship with Frank, she might have trespassed on a private grief. Though she speaks of Davison without malice, there is no prospect of a reprise: 'I'd have died in vain if there is to be any more dabbling' (Ferrier 1992: 162, 163). The narrator of her story may be inarticulate, but Marjorie Barnard is not. And, where the story could only affirm the separation of its women characters, the exchange between Barnard and Devanny redraws the line between public and private life. Barnard's story passes between herself and her friend as a disclosure that reorients their relationship. For the reader of 'The Persimmon Tree', who enters into another community as a reader of Barnard and Devanny's published correspondence, the story's meanings are expanded. It passes from one context – the public context of the literary object – to another, as a confidence, a gift between intimates. Devanny's response to Barnard's disclosure indicates that she recognises the meaning of the exchange.

Insinuating the tree, and reconfiguring relationships around it, introduces a fourth figure to this circuit of exchange, another absent presence: Katherine Mansfield. Mansfield is memorably incarnated for Farmer in Anne Estelle Rice's portrait:

> After sketching for two hours, Anne painted Katherine in a scheme of vivid reds … Her closely fitting yoke-collared persimmon dress reveals the contours of her thin chest and body, and sets her solid form against the floral painted background. Oh, Katherine. Her *persimmon* dress.
>
> (Farmer 1990: 26)

Here is a modernist epiphany recalling a similar inarticulate moment of sexual tension in Mansfield's story 'Bliss' (1920), where the thoroughly modern Bertha Young stands before her flowering pear tree in the company of the thrillingly sophisticated Pearl Fulton:

> The windows of the drawing room opened onto a balcony overlooking the garden. At the far end, against the wall, there was a tall, slender pear tree in fullest, richest bloom; it stood perfect, as though becalmed against the jade-green sky. … Although it was so still it seemed, like the flame of a candle, to stretch up, to point, to quiver in the bright air, to grow taller and taller as they gazed – almost to touch the rim of the round, silver moon.
>
> (Mansfield 1980: 96, 102)

The two women – Bertha in white and jade, Pearl all in silver – have a surface brilliance which deflects any probing of emotional depths. Like the two women in Barnard's story, they are side by side yet entirely separate; and Bertha's mistaken sense of a connection, her 'bliss', is cruelly undercut when, in a later scene, she is a silent witness to her husband arranging an assignation with Pearl. In both stories, their prospects of happiness and of fulfilled erotic longing marks the difference between women.

Eavan Boland's discussion of Louise Glück's poem 'Mock Orange' opens another window on 'The Persimmon Tree'. Here, too, it is a remembered sensation that is brought vividly into the present, to reopen a wound. The voice of this poem is steeped in sexual antagonism, hostility so immediate that the remembrance of sex is at the same time the act experienced in the present. Yet no sexual act is taking place. Instead, it is the scent of the mock orange which drifts through the window to awaken a memory, to stir unwelcome desires:

> How can I rest?
> How can I be content
> when there is still
> that odour in the world?
> (Boland 1996: 229)

With Louise Glück's transference of grief on to the scent of the mock orange, I want to bring this circuit of reading/writing exchange to a (provisional) close. Her cry brings forcefully back to mind the notion that, where gender is organised as an asymmetrical relation, women are the objects of exchange between men. Yet, in my discussion of the way the subject comes to be in culture, I have described subjectivity as a relation among women, privately acknowledged in the letters of Marjorie Barnard and Jean Devanny, and inscribed publicly, and not surreptitiously or tactically, in Beverley Farmer's 'Black Genoa'.

In moving beyond the trope of the woman silenced in culture, I have opted not to look deeply into the meanings of texts, but rather have mapped an itinerary across and between them, broadening the contexts in which they emerge, and the practices and institutions with which they engage. This is a practice of reading differently, not to interpret or penetrate, or to place text

> within a continually deepening context but as an attempt to place it within a perpetually broadening one … not to go underneath it, into a meaning covert within it, but to connect it to other texts and to their authors, to see what texts have made [it] possible, and what texts it, in turn, has made possible itself.
>
> (Nahemas 1987: 278, 287)

This practice, as Alexander Nahemas describes it, involves less a delving beneath surfaces than an endless expansion across them. I have extended this idea to an expansion across practices, linking the exchanges of meaning to the exchange of gifts, a practice that finely nuances social relationships. The practice of gift-giving here is seen both as a substitute for, and a supplement to, the processes of subject formation which materialise in the practices of writing and reading. The exchange of gifts, as the anthropologist Nicholas Thomas describes it in *Entangled Objects*, can represent both (though not only) the mutability of things in recontex-tualisation and the subtle mutations of transactions between friends (Thomas 1991: 28, 33). Tracing the re-employment of a sign of the erotic – the image of the tree – and by describing the exchanges – of gifts and meanings – among a community of readers, offers a 'non-literal'[6] account of the way relations of gender and writing may be read as constitutive of the (woman) subject in culture.

In *Object Lessons*, Eavan Boland quotes T.S. Eliot: 'No poet, no artist of any kind has his complete meaning alone'. Boland comments: 'The woman poet is more alone with her meaning than most' (1996: 242). How is meaning shared, made 'communal'? To answer this, we have to go beyond the economy of writing, as Certeau suggests, to explore the overlooked practices of reading; beyond the universalising, scriptural model of culture to one that recognises its plurality.

Notes

1   See, in particular, Virginia Woolf (first published 1928, Penguin, 1974) *A Room of One's Own* and 'Professions for Women', in Virginia Woolf, *The Death of the Moth*, London: Hogarth Press, 1932.
2   See also the discussion of de Certeau's work in J. Aherne (1995) *Michel de Certeau: Interpretation and its Other*, Cambridge: Polity Press.
3   See Gayle Greene and Coppelia Kahn (1985) 'Feminist Scholarship and the Social Construction of Woman', in *Making a Difference: Feminist Literary Criticism*, London: Methuen, 1–36, and Susan Gubar (1981) '"The Blank Page" and the Issues of Female Creativity', in *Critical Inquiry* 8: 243–63.
4   See Nancy Armstrong (1989) *Desire and Domestic Fiction: A Political History of the Novel*, New York: Oxford University Press.
5   See Gaye Tuchman (1989) *Edging Women Out: Victorian Novelists, Publishers, and Social Change*, London: Routledge; and James Eli Adams (1995) *Dandies and Desert Saints: Styles of Victorian Manhood*, Ithaca: Cornell University Press.
6   See de Certeau's account of 'literal' meaning as the product of a social elite in *The Practice of Everyday Life* (1980), trans Steven Rendall, Berkeley: University of California Press, 171–2.

Bibliography

Ahearne, J. (1995) *Michel de Certeau: Interpretation and its Other*, Cambridge: Polity Press.
Barnard, M. (1986) 'The Persimmon Tree' (1st published 1941), in L. Hergenhan (ed.) *The Australian Short Story: A Collection 1890s–1990s*, St Lucia: University of Queensland Press.
Betterton, R. (1996) *An Intimate Distance: Women, Artists and the Body*, London: Routledge.
Boland, E. (1996) *Object Lessons: The Life of the Woman and the Poet in Our Time*, London: Vintage.
—— (1997) 'Preface', *An Origin Like Water: Collected Poems 1967–1987*, New York: W.W. Norton.

Bourdieu, P. (1986) 'The Production of Belief: Contribution to an Economy of Symbolic Goods', in Richard Collins, James Curran, Nicholas Garnham, Paddy Scannell, Philip Schlesinger and Colin Sparks (eds) *Media, Culture and Society: A Critical Reader*, London: Sage.

de Certeau, M. (1974) *La Culture au Pluriel*, Paris: Seuil.

—— (1984) *The Practice of Everyday Life*, trans. Steven Rendall, Berkeley: University of California Press.

de Lauretis, T. (1984) *Alice Doesn't: Feminism, Semiotics, Cinema*, London: Macmillan.

Farmer, B. (1990) *A Body of Water: A Year's Notebook*, St Lucia: University of Queensland Press.

Ferrier, C. (ed.) (1992) *As Good as a Yarn with You: Letters Between Miles Franklin, Katherine Susannah Pritchard, Jean Devanny, Marjorie Barnard, Flora Eldershaw and Eleanor Dark*, Sydney: Cambridge University Press.

Foucault, M. (1977) 'What is an Author?', in D. Bouchard (ed.) *Language, Counter-Memory, Practice: Selected Essays and Interviews*, Ithaca: Cornell University Press.

Gilmore, M. (1954) 'Words', in *Fourteen Men: Verses*, Sydney: Angus and Robertson.

Mansfield, K. (1980) *Collected Stories*, London: Constable.

Miller, N. (1986) 'Arachnologies: The Woman, The Text and the Critic' in N.K. Miller (ed.) *The Poetics of Gender*, New York: Columbia University Press, 270–95.

Nahemas, A. (1987) 'Writer, Text, Work, Author', in A. Cascardi (ed.) *Literature and the Question of Philosophy*, Baltimore: Johns Hopkins University Press.

Olsen, T. (1980) *Silences*, London: Virago.

Rich, A. (1979) *On Lies, Secrets and Silence: Selected Prose, 1966–1978*, New York: W.W. Norton.

Smith, D. (1988) 'A Peculiar Eclipsing: Women's Exclusion from Men's Culture', in *The Everyday World as Problematic: A Feminist Sociology*, Milton Keynes: Open University Press.

Thomas, N. (1991) *Entangled Objects: Exchange, Material Culture, and Colonialism in the Pacific*, Cambridge, MA: Harvard University Press.

Woolf, V. (1974) *A Room of One's Own*, Harmondsworth: Penguin.

5 Subjectivity, the individual and the gendering of the modern self

Gillian Swanson

> When it studies groups' representations of themselves or of others ... cultural history is able to reflect usefully on social questions, since it focuses its attention on the strategies that determine positions and relations and that assign to each class, group, or milieu a perceived being which constitutes its identity.
>
> (Chartier 1988: 9)

Cultural approaches to the relationship between subjectivity and sexuality have shown the importance of the historical construction of concepts of the self, individuality and identity: they have stressed that these concepts are, in fact, historically and culturally specific, and that we can trace their histories in representations. This implies that 'subjectivity' – the social identities and attributes that an individual takes on – is formed by the social environment within which he or she operates. It also suggests that 'sexual subjectivity' – the way those characteristics and attributes, ways of feeling and behaving, are framed by a particular system of sexual differences – is also an *historical*, rather than solely a personal, achievement.

I will suggest in this chapter that to analyse this process fully, we need to trace the ways that a particular understanding of subjectivity becomes an intelligible way of articulating a sense of individual coherence and identity, and how this can be seen as part of an historically specific process of imagining the self as sexually differentiated. The interrelationship of subjectivity and sexual classification acts to define individuals according to specific and distinct sexual identities. One of the intriguing things about the development of this model of subjectivity and its constitutive link to sexual difference, however, is that as it becomes consolidated from the mid-eighteenth to the end of the nineteenth century, it simultaneously becomes marked by a form of instability. This derives, I will argue, from the way that the cultural motifs of the private self, which are associated with 'the individual' – as opposed to those of the public self of 'the citizen', which are associated with masculinity – act to align this notion of subjectivity with the feminine.

The approach I am taking is a particular one within cultural studies; one which prioritises cultural history. It looks at the 'logics' of cultural systems of knowledge that circulate and become accepted as intelligible ways of defining sexual difference and identity. It does so by taking the documents that become generated within various social institutions and by various groups in particular spaces and times, as representations which can be interrogated and analysed for the systems of meaning and the cultural frameworks they draw upon and generate. Roger Chartier outlines this approach to cultural history as follows:

> On the one hand it must be conceived as the analysis of the *process of representation* – that is of the production of classifications and exclusions that constitute the social and conceptual configurations proper to one time or one place. ... [On the other] this history must also be understood as the study of the process by which meaning is constructed ... *practices that give meaning to the world* in plural and even contradictory ways.
>
> (Chartier 1988: 13–14, my emphasis)

While Chartier stresses that a cultural approach to history should be concerned with the way representations order and classify the social, he also stresses that these representations are themselves 'anchored' to the social practices and institutions whereby those systems of classification and ordering become intelligible and accepted. It is this dual process that he posits as necessary to analyse the field of cultural representations. What his approach also implies is that there is a process of selection at stake in the representations which can be taken as exemplary of a culture's 'intellectual tools', those 'classifications, divisions and groupings that serve as the basis for our apprehension of the social world as fundamental categories of the perception and evaluation of reality' (Chartier 1998: 4–5). For an emphasis on analysing the 'proper' knowledges and definitions that become available in any particular time or place recognises that some texts are given authority – are generated, disseminated and read as authoritative ways of categorising reality.

This is to take a different approach to studying representations from those approaches to popular culture which explore the way that popular texts operate to establish and reinforce cultural meanings and identities, or the extent to which they allow the possibility of alternative meanings to those of 'dominant culture'. Instead it focuses on the way that commonly held definitions are established through disciplinary systems of knowledge production, and their application in specific social realms, and to trace the way certain – sometimes elite – texts become accepted *in practice* as authoritative and intelligible ways of seeing the world. As a complementary approach, we may also trace the reasons why certain texts become popular, why popular texts take the form they do, how they come to mobilise the particular representations of social reality that they do – sexual difference among them.

Such differences between types of text and their circulation set in play a series of social dynamics, or 'rivalries', between representations and those groups that generate them, which we will explore to the extent that they attempt to define and set into play the terms of sexual difference:

the representations of the social world that are constructed ... are always a product of the interests of the group that forged them. This means that for each motif, what is said must be related to the social position of whoever says it ... [and how they] have understood and presented a fragment of the reality in which they lived ... [These representations] engender social, educational, or political strategies that tend to impose one authority at the expense of others that are discredited. ... A study of representations thus sees them as always captive within a context of rivalries and competition, the stakes of which are couched in terms of power and domination. Rival representations are just as important as economic struggles for under-standing the mechanisms by means of which a group imposes (or attempts to impose) its conception of the social world, its values and its dominion.

(Chartier 1988: 5)

The emphasis on this process suggests we should examine the interplay between representations, social practices (or various forms of social interaction and thereby self-definition), and the way institutions operate to endorse and appro-priate various kinds of knowledges in the ways they govern social life. One further important feature is that this approach restores an importance to the minutiae of daily life – and those practices, rituals, cultural habits and represen-tations which are a part of a communicative culture – and allows us to investigate how difference is constructed in our perceptions and enactments of the social (see Bourdieu 1984; Chartier 1988: 44).

The modern subject: discipline and self-fashioning

When we refer to 'the subject' we call upon a social category of the person with a particular history and significance, one which, even though it is not often pref-aced by the words, is more specifically a modern Western subject. In other words 'the' subject within our contemporary cultural understanding is a social category of the person as it has been thought and practised within modern Western culture. Norbert Elias' interest in charting the development of the modern Western subject leads him to identify a series of critical shifts in the way this category of the person is conceived, as the formation of a new set of social circumstances between the twelfth and nineteenth centuries were accompanied by distinctive changes in ways of feeling and behaving. It is this process that he refers to as 'the civilizing process', a process which brought into being a new conception of the 'civilized' subject: 'the civilizing process is a change of *human conduct and sentiment* in a quite specific direction', a change upon which modern forms of subjectivity are based (Elias 1982: 229). There are two phases to this development: one that follows the decline of a dispersed network of medieval warrior societies, and that instigates the foundation of centralised court societies throughout Europe, within which elite groups positioned themselves in favourable positions of prestige and status; and a later one, in which a bourgeois system of civility modelled on the systems of etiquette and codes of social interaction established in court societies permeated into a wider cultural and social realm, and became organised within distinctive national groupings.

Court societies: prestige, etiquette and moderation of the affects

First, as the warrior (or chivalric, medieval) societies gave way to courtly societies, which invested their power in an absolute sovereign, they instigated a set of changes in social organisation. One was the monopolisation of violence by the State – in the establishment of public institutions such as the military – rather than its use by warring lords for the control of land and wealth. Another was the unification of society through state powers which regulated socially interdependent (though sometimes rival) networks rather than being composed of fragmented, self-standing and militarily competitive estates (Elias 1982: 3–5; Chartier 1988: 85). While court society brought about a new centralising of power and a new and more elaborately organised social arena, which now comprised different groupings, it also brought about a new set of social customs. Social interdependencies instigated the need for more disciplined and differentiated patterns of conduct, and social stability depended upon the adoption of 'self-restraint' and norms of etiquette, or 'courtoisie'. In court societies, power was invested in and disseminated through the sovereign, and different elite groups competed for the king's – and therefore also the court's – recognition of their privilege and status as the basis of their position within the social hierarchy, and their personal dignity and value: 'in [the royal court] the threads of society ran together, from it the rank, reputation and even, to an extent, the income of court people continued to depend' (Elias 1983: 79).

The social existence of court people, therefore, was 'enmeshed in' and 'bound to' etiquette – through it, they were bound to the king and to each other – as the nuances of court rituals and manners allowed them to perform, enact and gain recognition of their status, within a highly differentiated and fluctuating order of rank (Elias 1983: 87–91). This competitive struggle for position was thus based on a continual 'measured calculation of one's position in relation to others … [and a] characteristic restraint of the affects': social intercourse implied a 'constant, precisely calculated adjustment of behaviour' (Elias 1983: 90–96). The 'intensive elaboration of etiquette, ceremony, taste, dress, manners and even conversation' (Elias 1983: 111) provided a register which adjusted modes of feeling, gesture and expression so that they would be attuned to the particular configurations of position and prestige that were necessitated by the combination of two reciprocal processes – on one hand, those of social interdependence and alliance and, on the other, those of competition and distinction. Both of these processes, or 'pressures', in the establishment of an individual's or a group's standing, were implicated in the 'formative and controlling instrument' of nuanced behaviour and attitude: in the emulation of those habits associated with greater prestige and in the adoption of customs that distinguished oneself and one's group or rank from others of lower status.

Court society took different forms in different parts of Europe: the Parisian court of the *ancien régime* (court society before 1789) was the most pure example of a centrally unified court society, while in England a network of integrated aristocracies in the seventeenth and eighteenth centuries formed a series of political and social centres, and in Germany there was no central social elite but a set of regionally based noble groups (Elias 1983: 96–7). What is common to these centres of elite society, however, is the way that prestige and social power were regulated by a 'code' of social behaviour and interaction – producing 'distinction through dependence' (Chartier 1988: 87) – rather than, for example, the transferable and mobile forms of power accorded in (bourgeois) systems of hierarchy, in which social position is tied to wealth or professional standing. The interdependences and distinctions between the members of these societies were thus created and adjusted by a system of disciplined behaviour, a form of self-fashioning based on restraint and adherence to custom and the manufacturing of a fine-grained and socially attuned sensibility: 'refinement'.

Bourgeois civility: private life and the formation of national cultures

These are the components of civility: in contrast to the 'coarser habits, the wilder, more uninhibited customs' of medieval societies, whose elites consisted of its warriors, habits were ' "softened", "polished", and "civilised" ' (Elias 1982: 7). Manners and forms of social behaviour were choreographed around the principle of diplomacy rather than force, an 'internalisation' of prohibitions and constraints that was developed into a code of disciplined self-control and restraint oriented by 'long-term reality-oriented considerations' rather than motivated by 'momentary affects' (Elias 1983: 92). This was the claim to a 'rational' basis for civility, as controlling behaviour according to the vicissitudes of the distribution of power was translated into a distinctive style of life that stood as a key component of 'civilisation'. In the eighteenth century, courtly societies gradually became decentralised and heterogeneous, allowing a more open social formation that was eventually dominated by a bourgeoisie dependent for its status on economic and professional activities and their influence on attitudes and relationships (Elias 1983: 114). One of the claims Elias makes for this system is that those cultivated codes of behaviour, which in court societies were given a role in the social distribution of power – the intersection of public affairs and private interests – were now relegated to a newly distinct private sphere separated from public life, so they became transformed, and robbed of a certain power and centrality:

> For those making up the *bonne compagnie* of the *ancien régime*, the tasteful arrangement of house and park, the more elegant or more intimate decoration of rooms according to fashion and social convention, or the refined cultivation of relations between men and women, were not only amusements enjoyed by individuals, but vital necessities of social life. Competence

in these fields was a prerequisite for social esteem, which professional success brings today. ... Almost everything that shaped court society in the seventeenth and eighteenth centuries, whether it be dance, the nuances of greeting, the forms of conviviality, the pictures decorating the houses, the greetings of courtship or the *lever* of a lady, all this moved more and more into the sphere of private life. It thereby ceased to be at the centre of the tendencies shaping society.

(Elias 1983: 114–15)

Elias claims that it was 'the forms of behaviour imposed by *professional* life [which] ... were now moulded, cultivated and calculated' (Elias 1983: 115, my emphasis). But, while he stresses the continuity between the importance given to those habits and styles of living of the court aristocracies and the bourgeois elites which came to precedence from the mid-eighteenth centuries, Elias underestimates the extent to which the formation of private and social life acted as an essential underpinning and logic of professional and public life in bourgeois society, and the extent to which a new attentiveness to a *national* style of life and character was brought about by the disintegration of the connections between different European court societies and their replacement by a 'national form of integration' (Elias 1982: 7). To this extent, the management of the customs and habits of nationally distinctive cultures was a mechanism for securing national integration – unifying the members of different social groupings. The 'reform' of social life and family habits – the behaviours now constituted as occupying a newly conceived private realm – was an essential element in specifying national character and stabilising social relations in the interests of professional and economic success. The very definition of privacy, in fact, depended on the existence of a complementary and effectively regulated social and public life. This 'public' world would operate in the interests of, but without interfering in, a separate domestic realm, while the principles governing social institutions – such as the concept of the 'public good' – were established on the basis of their protection and value of an increasingly privatised family life. From this point of view, we have to regard the ascending definition of a distinct arena of 'private life' as a phenomenon which was intricately connected to, and which deeply influenced, 'the tendencies shaping society'.

This relationship gives a particularly important role to the formation of a 'moderate' and 'civilised' private life in the consolidation of common national cultures. One of the means whereby this was established was in the reform of popular culture and manners. The spread of literacy and the development of print culture up to the beginning of the nineteenth century becomes an important means by which a national culture could encompass those different environments, occupational groups and regional ways of life that had previously allowed separate cultural systems to remain intact (Burke 1978: 245). As popular culture moved from a performative culture, based on presence and thus locality, to a literate culture, based on a greater dissemination to a wider range of social and geographical groups, print became an important technical means of regularising everyday life, initiating 'the civilising process' on a more extensive scale. For a new and broader range of elite groups, this allowed the cultivation of 'distinction' as they learned the rules of dignified behaviour, decorum, language, everyday routines and manners from a proliferating number of conduct manuals. In a similar fashion, the instigation of such habits as the attentive reading of the Bible cultivated disciplined approaches to private and moral life, a pious reflection and the searching of one's own conscience, which crossed social classes (Burke 1978: 244–73; Ariès 1989: 4).

Civility: the body, gesture and styling the self

One of the features common to both courtly and bourgeois systems of civility is the modernisation of bodily habits, involving a stricter bodily control. This implies a distinction between 'gesture' and 'gesticulation', or between 'disci-plined' bodily behaviours and those contrasting gestural systems that now came to be seen as 'flamboyant' (Burke 1991: 79). The demonstrably deliberate, or 'mannered', gesture – functioning within a system of significant and meaningful bodily behaviours – stands as the ultimate demonstration of a civility based on the development of an appropriate repertoire of social conduct and moderated corporeal codes as the central basis of social interaction. This is an uneven process – as an element of civility, gesture is designed to reflect those same processes of interdependence and distinction. Gestural systems can therefore be seen as the product of social and cultural differences (Thomas 1991: 3). Gesture became one means by which national differences began to be marked, for example, as the 'reform of gesture' and the establishment of codes of decorum, order, moderation, prudence and sobriety, gained a more widespread purchase in their movement beyond ecclesiastical contexts and personnel from the sixteenth century. Seventeenth-century British and Spanish writers commented on the excessive gestures of the Italians, French and Greeks – in this period the stereotype of the gesticulating Italian was established, while Italians noted the 'stiffness' and the 'arrogance' of the Spanish. Each of these distinct repertoires was taken to embody something of the differences in national styles and cultures, and to an extent the more successful consolidation of the reform of gesture in the Protestant parts of northern Europe compared to the southern Catholic countries is testimony to the cultural specificity of systems of gesture and their contribution to changes in the formation of conduct and sentiment (Burke 1991: 76–81).

Alongside the reform of gesture, Elias charts the advance of a threshold of shame and modesty. From table manners, spitting and blowing one's nose, to sleeping or relieving oneself, a new care over the precise ways in which bodily behaviour should be rendered non-intrusive, and incivilities curbed, is evident in conduct books containing instructions concerning the manners appropriate to particular situations. A greater withdrawal for the exercise of bodily functions is evident from the sixteenth century – retiring to a private place for toilet purposes, for example – while the cultivation of a feeling of shame concerning references to these activities themselves increases up to the nineteenth century. This difference between the two periods is particularly evident in relation to sexual conduct. The education of boys in sexual habits was the subject of school texts from the sixteenth to the eighteenth century. Erasmus's *Colloquies* was a standard educational text for this period, taking the form of exemplary conversations, including one of a woman discussing her husband's behaviour and another between a young man and a prostitute. Yet, by the nineteenth century, this text – seen previously as inculcating a sense of self-regulation and the restraint of instinctual urges in its instruction regarding the correct practices of wooing, ideal forms of sexual speech and sexual manners, and its commentary of the undesirability of the dishonourable life – was regarded as 'base' in its direct references to sexual matters and its absence of a moral framework suited to nineteenth-century standards of modesty and sexual discretion (Elias 1978: 169–71).

One of the explanations Elias gives for this transition in the threshold of shame regarding sexual writings, and especially the writing of texts on sexual habits for children, points to the changes that occurred in the way the sexual life of adults was conducted: until the eighteenth to nineteenth centuries, 'adults did not impose upon themselves either in action or in words the same restraint with regard to the sexual life as later ... the idea of strictly concealing these drives in secrecy and intimacy was largely alien' (Elias 1978: 175). The shift to removing sexual behaviour from public life occurred within aristocratic court societies, but only later does a more general shift towards concealment, or modesty, link it to a moral system of appraisal for sexual relations, including a stricter system of monogamous marriage and the definition of sexual character according to the degree of self-discipline and self-restraint that one exerted (Elias 1978: 179–80). At this point, one's personal identity became bound up with, and defined by, one's attitude towards sex and sexual behaviour.

In both the reform of gesture and of sexual relations, the transition from courtly to bourgeois codes of gentility sees restraint become imbued with a *moral* sense: the 'undisciplined' behaviour of 'unruly' working-class 'mobs' (and their 'indelicate' language and frankness concerning sexual activity) was taken as a sign of their social and moral degradation; modesty in relation to sexual matters became the template of a refined sensibility that indicated a spiritual attentiveness and denoted a virtuous character, but it was a modesty demonstrated and assured by a demeanour whose lapses were as much to do with comportment and physical styling as with actual sexual behaviour. Those public spaces which were the subject of vehement reform in the eighteenth century included the Restoration theatre, in which bustle, talking, the indecorous appearance of shirt sleeves and the throwing of orange peel were part of a problem that also included the passing of urine and a 'market of sexual liaison' (Stallybrass and White 1986: 84–93). The recasting of bodily gesture, physical modesty and sexual continence in such a space produces a new set of proscriptions and exclusions. But it also sets out the terms of sobriety and decency within which 'civil' behaviour could be delineated, and attentive citizens given a structure of personality which translated bodily comportment and social conduct into a particular social type. This established the attentive and vigilant citizen as a type modelled on the codes of civility. By these means an orderly, disciplined and authoritative principle of social organisation and regulation was translated into an authoritative *way of being*, reflective of the self-regulation of manners that maintained an internal division between public and private behaviour and self-definition. This division between public and private 'selves' also meant that the 'civil subject' – that is, one who adopted the codes of civil conduct – was a sexually specific one; this period also saw women segregated from the spaces of public life. The eighteenth-century coffee house (a place where women were not permitted) became the principal public site for sociable exchange for such citizens – a place to read a play rather than see one, it was linked to reflectiveness, sobriety, rational and intellectual discussion, quietness and a strict control of the body (Stallybrass and White 1986: 95–100). Its sense of *containment* offered, on the one hand, an ordering of the physical according to the rational demands of the intellect and, on the other, a sense of enclosure – both from the intrusions of the unruly crowd and in a space apart from the private concerns and sexual interactions of family and personal life. It thus drew on the habits of solitary reflection established in print culture, translating these into a public context of rational intellectual debate and discussion that fed into the organisation of political and social life as the realm of *male* subjectivity.

What is evident in the second phase of the development of civility, then, is first a 'moralising' of the relationship between conduct and feeling in a way which is translated into a particular and modern concept of the person, cast according to a division between public and private. This division is created according to a standard of decency, played out according to public modesty and private intimacy. Sexual and physical manners move from being a matter of knowing the right way to behave according to social rank and *politesse*, to actions that reveal a person's moral demeanour and private moral self. This produces a structure of evaluation in which modesty – now understood as an appropriate sense of one's own privacy and a respect for that of others – becomes seen as a 'natural' disposition, a 'natural' and inherent component of the inner being, or 'self'. The adherence to conventions of behaviour now becomes oriented towards a demonstration of the integrity of the self, a moral consciousness played out through social behaviour and the disciplined deployment of the body. Hence the reform of bodily habits becomes a way of marking out the dimensions of the self according to a new sense of privacy: in this way a new sense of the essential 'inner self', separate from its contact with all that exists outside of it, is established (see Elias 1978: 245–63, for example). As we have seen, however, this is an effect of particular *representations* of the relationship between bodily behaviours, self-discipline and the organisation of feeling, including new levels of shame. It is also an effect of newly introduced *practices* of the self, the designation of the public and private self, and the claim to a moral composure, as they can be articulated through bodily regimes. It therefore should not be seen as a process of taming and hiding a more 'natural' form of bodily expression, but as a transition from one system of bodily behaviour to another; the proliferation of different forms of bodily practice and gestural conventions oriented around the new *perception* that there existed a private, inner self. This shift introduces a bodily repertoire of 'self-containment', continually to draw the attention to – and claim the existence of – a conception of a private inner self.

Civility, gender and the female body: private life

During the nineteenth century in particular, the consolidation of a separation between public and private life, and the differences in conduct and self-definition associated with each of these spheres, brought about an important intensification of the function of modesty in relation to women, and the female body became the site where refinement was to be marked. While men's public demeanour was defined according to the conventions attached to professional status and social situations and spaces, the appearance and demeanour of women were oriented by their association with the 'natural virtues' of domesticity, the family and private life. The boundaries between public and private, civil and personal life, masculine and feminine, were evident within the domestic sphere as well as in the split between the public 'civil' world and that of the private sphere of the home. Women were responsible for the effective segregation of living spaces in the home into public and private zones, so that functions concerning family and physical concerns – eating, cooking, washing, sleeping – were separated from areas where entertainment and social intercourse would occur, and the maintenance of hygienic and visual barriers between the home and the dirt and crowded bustle of the city outside was a task that denoted a family's sense of order – and a woman's virtuous respectability. This quality was definitive of middle-class women, contrasting them to the disorderly working-class women who worked in public or whose family life was conducted in the street rather than in the home (Davidoff and Hall 1987: 380–88). One aspect of this was the establishment of the 'moral' effects of a home with 'order' in nineteenth-century England; that is, an order that separates male and female activities and involvements by segregating them to different spaces. The moral self-improvement of the middle-class woman could not be achieved by public routes to self-advancement or intellectual distinction: hers lay in developing an orderly home of 'proper' places that served to cultivate ways of behaving, thinking and expressing oneself. The function of the domestic realm was to cultivate forms of taste and familial feeling which were appropriate to the personae of middle-class men and women and which equipped the members of the middle-class family for the moderate forms of behaviour that were attuned to social interaction and, for men, a moral sense which contributed to the responsible execution of public office. As such, the organisation of (and women's shaping of) the spaces of private life can be seen to undergird the constitution of both the civil sphere and the citizen. Women were defined not only as antipathetic to public life, but also as the linchpin of its effective functioning and definition.

Above all, though, female virtue was associated with a code of appearance and behaviour that was based on refinement, good taste, 'grace' and moderation in language, dress and movement. In the same way as their arrangement of the space of the home, the space of the body – its conduct, gesture and appearance – was fashioned to externalise personal values and inner disposition. Women's required form of restraint was oriented by cultivating a spirituality and a distaste for 'worldly' subjects, and a physical frailty and delicacy that demonstrated a heightened moral sensibility. It implied a retiring nature, in such a way that, even in public, her demeanour should indicate a withdrawal from the 'strains' and 'shocks' of modern public life, and the incompatibility between public and private sensibilities. Codes of civility and gesture therefore establish gender distinctions – forming our understanding of a distinctive female subjectivity – rather than simply 'reflecting' women's association with private life in bourgeois culture.

Private life and the 'inner self': the domain of the individual

As the concept of the individual became refined and extended in the nineteenth century, the space of a modern 'individuality' became that of privacy, and its governing principle that of morality. The 'subjective self' came to be regarded as one associated with an 'inner self' defined by a moral disposition, in contrast to the 'rational self' governed by objective social principles, laws and procedures. The 'subjective self', then, was seen less as a *social* self – despite, as we have seen, being modelled on a set of social examples and governed indirectly through social customs – and was seen more in terms of *persona*, individual characteristics that were formed in a realm 'outside' social governance and control. This perception of a space of a 'private' self – which sees subjectivity separated from social regulation – was only possible because of the distinctions being made between public and private realms, and the customs that now accrued to private life, in middle-class culture. As a way of enacting lifestyle and subjectivity, therefore, 'the individual' was a highly class-specific concept: the movement to a more privatised arrangement of family life, and the adoption of middle-class regimes of hygiene and modesty, especially among women, did not occur in working-class cultures until the beginning of the twentieth century, and then they were largely the result of programmes of middle-class philanthropy and 'motherhood education' (see Walkowitz 1992).

In contrast to seventeenth-century individuality, which was pursued in the 'convivial' spaces of social life (Ariès 1989: 8), the nineteenth century saw a newly elaborated concept of 'the individual' associated with the now distinct spaces of private life. The spaces of private life – constituted in relation to home, family and personal bonds – functioned as a refuge from the public world, maintaining the boundaries of individual 'nature'. Thus, the notion of the *subjective* self – and its translation into individual 'identity' or 'character' – became associated in the nineteenth century with intimate realms of activity.

Private life became a domain in which individuals could lay claim to a right to determine their patterns of life in ways that departed from previous traditions of family standards and emphasised a solitary and unique pattern of development. Partly this depended on the conception of 'inner space' and the need for the contemplative cultivation of this precious space of the unique individual and personal inclination:

> More and more people rebelled against communal and family discipline and declared that they needed more time and space of their own. Individuals wanted to sleep alone, to be allowed to read books and newspapers in peace and quiet, to dress as they pleased, to come and go as they wished, to eat or drink whatever they liked, and to see and love whomever they chose.
>
> (Perrot 1990: 454)

Rather than an essential human desire, this set of changes in mentality and social interaction derives from the introduction of a new attentiveness to the practice of private life. Those representations that are formed as part of the practices of everyday privacy help to make sense of individuality as an intelligible way of perceiving subjects and their social definition.

The sense of an individual self was enhanced by the use of an extended and more various range of names, which acted to mark out a distinctive self and emphasise individual 'personality' rather than to reflect family heredity in the tradition of repeating the names of previous generations. Similarly, individuals were able to contemplate their own image with the increased availability of mirrors, and photography allowed the portrait to become common across different social classes. Postcards with photographic portraits allowed people to distribute images of themselves, individual epitaphs and photographs on headstones perpetuated the sense of self as an enduring entity, and the portrait was given a newly intimate form and circulation in the miniature (Corbin 1990: 457–67). These technologies of self-representation and self-definition were influential in creating a heightened awareness of the personality as a motif of the self – delineated according to a unique set of personal characteristics.[1] Such representations proliferated across a range of different forms, using new techniques and ways of circulating images of the self in ways which, while they originated at the point of the individual defined in relation to a personal and familial situation, formed a new culture that 'publicised' private life and the identity of the individual (see Colomina 1994: 6–8).

The documentation of private life became an essential component of the intimate histories of individuals and their attachments. Diaries, photograph albums, relics, souvenirs – all recorded familial and personal bonds and significant events, and thereby became saturated with sentimental meaning of an individual's emotional and subjective life (Martin-Fugier 1990: 262–5). The memorialisation of everyday life was to refashion it according to an emotional economy and a diminutive scale ('fleeting happy moments') that rendered it feminine; the collection of everyday objects was referred to by one writer as the formation of 'feminine chronologies' (Martin-Fugier 1990: 262–3). As such, they became recast according to a different temporality and centre of meaning. Framed according to their individual or family significance, they became relics of a subjective history set within a relational zone of the personal and private, of intimacy and emotion, of attachment and nostalgia.

The intensified link between a conception of the 'inner' self and privacy gives a particular emphasis to the concept of the individual as the subject of private life – the world of personal attachments, subjective emotions and sentiment, spiritual vigilance and moral discretion – rather than the 'disinterested' and rational public citizen. Subjective identity, which now constituted a fundamental component of individuality, was thus both personalised and positioned within a private sphere which by the end of the nineteenth century had become conceptually solidified by its association with the 'world of women' and its various activities and states of being.

Albeit that men constituted part of this private realm, its definitive features – those distinguishing it from the principles of public life – were categorised according to the attributes of femininity. As a more intense relationship to the body was formed through such habits as grooming and hygiene, the adoption of more complex undergarments – including the corset – functioned to recast the body as both a potentially erotic and yet a technically, or functionally, modest object (Corbin 1990: 482–9). The connection between the hygienic body and a refined eroticism allowed individual allure to be created in modern practices of fashioning the body in sexually distinctive ways. These practices, and their re-presentation of the body according to modern conventions, therefore made a significant contribution to emphasising sexuality as a central component of individual personality.

Subjectivity and sexual difference: associations and instabilities

The concepts of subjectivity and individual identity thereby come into being as ways of imagining the self that act against the way public masculinity is conceived as a fundamentally unified and rational entity. With a new intensified interest in private life in the nineteenth century, the public fashioning of the self came to assume a particular set of meanings about the private individual, and subjectivity *per se* thereby became associated with femininity. In the assumption that private life was the primary domain of individuality – and the space of an 'inner self' – its connection with the 'feminine' introduces an instability, or dissonance, in concepts of masculinity. How is masculinity positioned by this alliance between private life, individual subjectivity and femininity?

Two examples will suffice to illustrate the tension between masculinity and concepts of individual subjectivity, and the way their incompatibility – or the 'instability' I alluded to at the beginning of this chapter – instigates an ambivalence concerning the public representation of the subjective *per se*, a kind of suspicion of those dimensions of human experience which were not subjected to the principles by which public life is organised and those authoritative disciplinary principles embodied in institutionally validated and 'objective' forms of knowledge. First is the anxiety that accompanied the appearance of the sensation novel in the second half of the nineteenth century. The sensation novel was a genre of writing whose narratives were based on sexual and psychological maladies – instabilities of personal and private life. Such maladies were understood to derive from a dangerous overemphasis on the subjective aspects of the self – the emotions, the instincts, the 'nerves', the senses and the passions – in ways which hampered the disciplinary influence of the intellect, or moral consciousness. Commentators prescribed the exercise of 'sense' over 'sensibility' in ways that inculcated 'self-control' and 'self-management' rather than self-interest or the exploration of self. In this example, then, we see the way a recommended regime of moral management also acts as a sign of constitutive frailty. Bourne-Taylor argues that the concept

> 'moral management', itself … might promote the belief that a stable, sane identity could be built up by proper training and self-regulation, yet at the same time it could also tacitly suggest the very fragility of the identity that it aimed to sustain.
>
> (Bourne-Taylor 1988: 31)

This is evident in the instabilities of character in the sensation novel itself, with the appearance of characters whose failures of discipline are clear by their departure from the conventions of appropriate demeanour established in nineteenth-century sexual definition. In this genre, narratives of the 'inner self' are given priority over the moral regimes of public convention and constraint. The 'female malady' of mental derangement or madness shows how attributes of femininity are seen as pathological – a sign of an inherent weakness in women, and a sign of perversity in men. For example, in Wilkie Collins' novel *The Woman in White*, first published in 1860, the madness of the central female character, Laura Fairlie, occurs because she is subjected to her uncle and guardian, Mr Fairlie's, negligent discharge of family responsibilities and its sexual consequences in her marriage to an unsuitable and morally dissolute imposter. She is the victim of abnormal circumstances and, while she becomes unhinged – and then homeless, wandering the nighttime streets after she escapes the asylum her husband places her in – she can also be saved by the 'civilised' influences of the proper ordering of family and personal matters. This is not the case for Mr Fairlie, the head of the family, whose weakness and self-indulgences are the cause of the family's fall. His is the constitutional failure of a masculinity insufficiently grounded in public life and the mechanisms of moderation and self-restraint. Unnaturally attached to his own corporeal symptoms as a raging hypochondriac, as well as being drawn in terms of over-refinement and excessively feminine physical features and behaviours, he is depicted according to the 'drained' and bloodless features which contemporary medical literature describes as characteristic of that other nineteenth-century figure whose overattachment to his bodily functions has not been 'mastered' by a disciplined moral attentiveness – the masturbator (see Chapter 8). Fairlie's moral failure, his degenerate and unnatural masculinity, and his inappropriately disciplined and ill-managed subjectivity, are evident from his personal comportment and languorous demeanour. As he is first introduced to the narrator, Walter Hartright, we are drawn to note his frail, drained and feminised physique; his overadorned and dandy-esque appearance; his solitary habits; and his effete taste. He is located within an interiorised space battened down against the intrusions of the world outside that of the privatised self:

> At the lower end of the room, opposite to me, the windows were concealed and the sunlight was tempered by large blinds of the same pale sea-green colour as the curtains over the door. The light thus produced was deliciously soft, mysterious, and subdued; it fell equally upon all the objects in the room; it helped to intensify the deep silence, and the air of profound seclusion that possessed the place; and it surrounded, with an appropriate halo of repose, the solitary figure of the master of the house, leaning back, listlessly composed, in a large easy chair, with a reading-easel fastened on one of its arms, and a little table on the other.
>
> If a man's personal appearance, when he is out of his dressing-room, and when he has passed forty, can be accepted as a safe guide to his time of life – which is more than doubtful – Mr Fairlie's age, when I saw him, might have been reasonably computed at over fifty and under sixty years. His beardless face was thin, worn, and transparently pale, but not wrinkled; his nose was high and hooked; his eyes were of a dim greyish blue, large, prominent, and rather red round the rims of the eyelids; his hair was scanty, soft to look at, and of that light sandy colour which is the last to disclose its own changes towards grey. He was dressed in a dark frock-coat, of some substance much thinner than cloth, and in waistcoat and trousers of spotless white. His feet were effeminately small, and were clad in buff-coloured silk stockings, and little womanish bronze-leather slippers. Two rings adorned his white delicate hands, the value of which even my inexperienced observation detected to be all but priceless. Upon the whole, he had a frail, languidly-fretful, over-refined look – something singularly and unpleasantly delicate in its association with a man, and, at the same time, something which could by no possibility have looked natural and appropriate if it had been transferred to the personal appearance of a woman. My morning's experience of Miss Halcombe had predisposed me to be pleased with everybody in the house; but my sympathies shut themselves up resolutely at the first sight of Mr Fairlie.
>
> (Collins 1860/1974: 65–6)

This is an image of masculinity overwritten with the *problems* of subjectivity and the association of individuality with private life. Mr Fairlie confounds social and sexual categories, representing not an 'achieved' and appropriate balanced form of civility, but its negative manifestation in a form of over-refinement, as the pursuit of privacy and the overemphasis of sensibility as the template of the self are left to run riot, unmediated by the disciplines of a 'disinterested' or rational, public, constitution of the person. He becomes the antipathy of a 'natural' order of public masculinity counterposed to a distinct and separate femininity that is 'properly' placed in relation to the private sphere. Mr Fairlie's subjective lapses show the need for masculinity to embrace the exigencies and disciplines of a 'selfless' form of citizenship. Like the masturbator's channelling of sexual drives away from its accepted social aim in the form of familial reproduction, Fairlie's abdication of his public presence as civic head of his family is based on a perverse self-absorption that locks him into an internalised and solitary erotic relation to his own body. Mr Fairlie thus becomes defined in contrast to the norms of sexual definition that a concentration on the 'inner self' of the individual, realised within private life, threatens to erode. He embodies a pathological sexual definition – a sign of an instability in systems of sexual difference – established in the interplay of the conception of the subjective self, the practices of private life, and the intensification of the body as a privileged site of the representation of individuality.

The second, more brief, illustration indicates the suspicion with which the concept of 'subjective' interpretation was met by scientific discourse in the same period, whose quest for 'mechanical objectivity' attempted to eliminate human intervention in recording scientific states and processes in medical texts by devising such technologies of mechanical registration as the X-ray, the lithograph and photography for use as illustrations in the place of drawings by great artists (Daston and Galison 1992). The subjective – and its associations with interpretation, individual perspective and personal bias introduced by the mediation of human senses – was considered 'dangerous' to a true depiction of reality in the 'image of nature' (Daston and Galison 1992: 82, see also Chapter 11). This demonstrates an ambivalence concerning the incursion of the 'unruly' subjective into a realm of knowledge supposedly free from the intervention of undisciplined human consciousness: to be true to scientific objectivity was a moral objective, which implied 'taming' or eradicating the personal as it occupied a realm beyond rational principles and regulation. While this debate does not explicitly address the sexual definition that subjectivity by now implies, a definition which in other representations of the subjectivity allies it with a dangerously *feminine* or feminised sensibility, it replays these same antagonisms in terms of a *validated* public consciousness (scientific thought and method) and a *derogated* private consciousness (human intervention and individualised 'perspective'). It also addresses the 'problems' of subjectivity when they interfere in the masculine public domain of science, showing the instabilities that the overvaluation of the subjective creates for public masculinity. We can see how far definitions of masculinity are marked by a fragility in this era of the subjective individual, both through its association with an enhanced private realm defined by its association with feminine attributes and activities, and yet also in their tentative guardianship of a public realm which is culturally defined in opposition to the realm of the 'inner self'.

The cultural formation of the self

In its emphasis on the historical formation of a conception of self, the approach I am suggesting we take to the issue of subjectivity and representation questions the assumption that there is an 'inner self' beyond the formative influences of cultural convention and custom. Even the definition of the most intimate realms of the self takes place through the regulation of customs and manners, and, just as behaviour is shaped by its harnessing to a socially legible, communicable, system, so too are ways of feeling made habitual and depend upon those established 'ways of being' that are offered within specific social environments. The differences between such environments have long been the subject of representations of various sorts. They were of particular interest in that period I am identifying as that which consolidated distinctions between public and private, and the sense of an inner and personal realm of individuality formed in the intimate, everyday habits of self-fashioning. Edith Wharton's fictional writings explored the difference between the 'old' European order of tradition and its combination of grandeur with an inflexible delineation of social rank, and the 'new' and brasher American culture, both unfettered by its lack of an established and ingrained way of being, but also less grounded and less secure. These culturally divergent systems were not seen as mere backdrops to original and essential individuals, but as formative of particular intellectual and emotional dispositions, types of character with particular needs, interests, aims, and ways of relating to the world and each other.

In Wharton's short story, *Madame de Treymes*, first published in 1907, John Durham falls in love with Fanny de Malrive during a visit to Paris. Fanny de Malrive is an American woman who had married a French nobleman from whom she has now separated, and he attempts to persuade Fanny to seek a divorce and marry him. Her devotion to her son binds her to the family of her husband: despite the unhappiness of her marriage, her husband's moral disreputability and her lack of sympathy with the family to whom she is now attached, she is conscious of this family's overwhelming power to control its destiny and that of those who become part of it. Her fear of losing her son, and her knowledge that he is inescapably bound to this family, prevents her acting according to the independence of will that an American could normally contemplate adopting – instead of seeking a divorce, she fears the terms by which it could be obtained, resisting seeking advice and help from the only member of the family whom she trusts. This is the obstacle to Durham's marriage to Fanny: Fanny's consciousness of being for ever changed by her experience of European culture, and Durham's inability to change her environment so that her desire to be with him can be realised as more than a sense of impossibility and loss. The gulf between her former life as Fanny Frisbee and her new identity as Fanny de Malrive prevents her from embracing her chance of happiness with Durham's offer by soliciting the opinion or aid of her sister-in-law:

'Oh – *you!*' broke from her in mingled terror and admiration; and pausing on her doorstep to lay her hand in his before she touched the bell, she added with a half-whimsical flash of regret: 'Why didn't this happen to Fanny Frisbee?'.

(Wharton 1907/1995: 19)

Durham sees her difference from the Fanny Frisbee he knew in his college days – when she embodied the 'showiest national attributes' of 'dash' and a 'native grace of softness' – when he meets her again for the first time: 'She was the same, but so mysteriously changed! And it was the mystery, the sense of *unprobed depths of initiation*, which drew him to her ...' (Wharton 1907/1995: 21, my emphasis).

Paradoxically, her difference is most clearly written in her joyous engagement in talk of America when she visits his mother and sisters. For, while she talks animatedly of how 'dear and strange and familiar' their talk was to her, her very embrace of its pleasures emphasises the new form she now takes, expressed in Durham's sister's response to their first meeting: '"Well, I never saw anything so *French*."'

Yes, it was the finish, the modelling which Madame de Malrive's experience had given her that set her apart from the fresh uncomplicated personalities of which she had once been simply the most charming type. The influences that had lowered her voice, regulated her gestures, toned her down to harmony with the warm dim background of a long social past. ... And it gave him a sense of the tremendous strength of the organisation into which she had been absorbed, that in spite of her horror, her moral revolt, she had not reacted against its external forms. She might abhor her husband, her marriage, and the world to which it had introduced her, but she had become a product of that world in its outward expression, and no better proof of the fact was needed than her exotic enjoyment of Americanism.

(Wharton 1907/1995: 21–2)

Fanny is the embodiment of a cultural gulf: her Americanness has taught her a moral perspective that revolts against the French culture of family tradition to which she nevertheless now shows obedience. The cultural formation of her son's personality and sense of the world becomes the terrain on which this conflict is to be fought. As she reveals to Durham the mechanics of this foreign 'civilisation' – which as a 'good' American she nevertheless still fights, especially in its influence on her son – she also acknowledges the inevitability that he will be moulded in its image:

'There is nothing in your experience – in any American experience – to correspond with that far-reaching family organization, which is itself a part of the larger system, and which encloses a young man of my son's position in a network of accepted prejudices and opinions. Everything is prepared in advance – his political and religious convictions, his judgments of people, his sense of honour, his ideas of women, his whole view of life. He is taught to see vileness and corruption in every one not of his own way of thinking, and in every idea that does not directly serve the religious and political purposes of his class. The truth isn't a fixed thing: it's not used to test actions by, it's tested by them, and made to fit with them. And this forming of the mind begins with the child's first consciousness; it's in his nursery stories, his baby prayers, his very games with his playmates! Already he is only half mine, because the church has the other half, and will be reaching out for my share as soon as his education begins. But that other half is still mine, and I mean to make it the strongest and most living half of the two, so that, when the inevitable conflict begins, the energy and the truth and the endurance shall be on my side and not on theirs!'.

(Wharton 1907/1995: 11–12)

It is this change, and the 'transmitted force of her resolve', that attracts Durham to Fanny. As he wonders why he had not been drawn to her in earlier days, he realises that it was because 'there were, with minor modifications, many other Fanny Frisbees; whereas never before, within his ken, had there been a Fanny de Malrive' (Wharton 1907/1995: 20). Yet it is also this difference that prevents her being able to give herself freely; she is for ever changed by her reluctant embodiment of this culture.

'I don't know why I brought you here,' she said gently, 'except from the wish to prolong a little the illusion of being once more an American amongst Americans … But it was no use – they were waiting for me here … ' 'They are a part of me – I belong to them. I must go back to them!' she sighed.

(Wharton 1907/1995: 17)

She is reluctantly changed, between cultural repertoires: outwardly French, having incorporated Europeanism into her way of thinking and behaving, but yet inwardly American, having retained an American moral sense. Fanny de Malrive is not a transcendent individual personality but an exile, the product of the distance between each culture as she battles for the psychological custody and cultural affiliation of her son through her resolve to remain consistent with her bifurcated formation.

Gender and the cultural technologies of the self

As we see from *Madame de Treymes*, the cultural formation of the self is a dispersed and subtle process, operating at a level of intimacy shown by a moment of Fanny's discomposure – the 'heat' of her parting with Durham's mother and sisters results in her failing to draw on her white gloves before leaving their hotel. Durham becomes absorbed in her confusion: as she distractedly finishes buttoning the gloves prior to calling for her carriage, he latches on to this action as a privileged sign of an interior state which offers him a longed-for intimacy with her. However, the assembly of those conventions by which we mark a legitimate or lapsed command of the self are sometimes more prosaically marshalled.

Lesley Johnson has shown how the 'building' of the modern self in a distinctively modern postwar world corresponded to other modernisation projects, but the selves to be formed were understood differently for young women and young men. Dams and power stations were defined in masculine terms: the Snowy Mountains Hydro-Electric Scheme initiated in 1949, for example, offered the chance for a 'colossal game with nature …' whose heroes were 'men of the outdoors, engineers dedicated to grand concepts and achievements', who would produce Australia in the image of a 'lusty youth' (Johnson 1993: 49–50). But modern Australia and modern Australians were also to be 'made' by – among other things – the operations of the newly expanded consumption industries, which offered another image of national progress and industrial efficiency, this time geared towards producing a modern femininity.

The rhetoric of educational, psychological, legal, medical and industrial agencies showed how modern femininity was to be appropriately composed and directed, how young women could constitute themselves as choosing, self-defining selves. Yet paradoxically, these forms of fashioning female identities were offered to young women as a route to discovering an essential sexuality, rather than defining themselves in social terms. This was achieved by the introduction of a marital 'destiny'. Girls should access the rewards of prosperity indirectly, by becoming the 'loved individual' (Johnson 1993: 116). Training in deportment and the correct angle to hold one's head was the appropriate form of work for young girls. Newspaper articles instructed girls in how to remain attractive from any angle – 'The Man Higher Up', 'The Man Beside You', 'The Man Behind You' – and how to select a strategy to 'sit pretty' – from the 'short girl look' or the 'tall girl party look' or 'the sophisticate' – but above all to avoid the 'leg-entwined sit' or the 'arms akimbo sprawl' (Johnson 1993: 127–30).

> The purpose of this … [was not] to pursue the tasks of making a self, the tasks of the modern individual; it was a space in which the young woman was supposed to discover in herself heterosexual desires, to be troubled by those desires, but to learn that they were to be managed, kept under control. … Modern young women had to learn to find in themselves the desire for marriage and to learn the rules of conducting their relations with men so as to ensure they achieved this end.
>
> (Johnson 1993: 136)

The achievement of 'maturity' meant the young woman would invest her pleasure in that of others, and playing her part in a modern citizenry meant choosing to perform her duties as a mother and wife (Johnson 1993: 146). It was by this process that the 'discovery' of an 'essential' self was defined by contemporary disciplines and formed by social agencies towards the political futures being drawn for Australia's youth, and by this process that the coordinates of a modern and youthful female identity could be claimed as inherent components of a female 'inner self' or subjectivity. These are the technologies of cultural training that simultaneously propose a natural process of development and self-realisation, and yet integrate the formation of 'appropriate' subjectivities with those conventions of gender that define individual identity according to a distinctive and historically specific modern system of sexual difference.

This brings us back to Roger Chartier's argument that it is necessary to look at the historical formation of our often specifically national-cultural systems of classifying reality. To understand the way subjectivity and the concept of the self is formed, as much as those features of social life whose cultural origins may on the surface seem more empirically transparent and verifiable, we need to disentangle the threads of these conceptions and see them as the result of particular processes of historical development – as 'cultural achievements' rather than inevitable ways of being. Chartier's argument, that there are 'rival', or competing, representations, will be taken up more explicitly in other chapters, but it is clear that the representations of subjectivity that we have considered here have social claims built into them, and that even the most intimate realms of our experience and self-definition are influenced by these social dynamics and formed according to how representations make our subjective identities thinkable.

Notes

1   Celia Lury shows how, as the individual becomes more and more important, so the uniqueness of individual attributes allows techniques of individuation to merge, through technologies of surveillance and classification – such as the use of the photographic portrait in medical and criminological sciences – and in the adoption of techniques of self-surveillance (Lury 1998: 9–12).

Bibliography

Ariès, P. (1989) 'Introduction', in R. Chartier (ed.) *A History of Private Life*, vol. 3, *Passions of the Renaissance*, trans. Arthur Goldhammer, Cambridge, MA and London: The Belknap Press of Harvard University Press.

Bourdieu, P. (1984) *Distinction: A Social Critique of the Judgement of Taste*, trans. R. Nice, London and New York: Routledge & Kegan Paul.

Bourne-Taylor, J. (1988) *In the Secret Theatre of Home: Wilkie Collins, Sensation Narrative and Nineteenth-Century Psychology*, London: Routledge.

Burke, P. (1978) *Popular Culture in Early Modern Europe*, Aldershot, Hants: Wildwood House.

——— (1991) 'The Language of Gesture in Early Modern Italy', in J. Bremmer and H. Roodenburg (eds) *A Cultural History of Gesture*, Cambridge: Polity Press.

Chartier, R. (1988) *Cultural History: Between Practices and Representations*, Oxford and Cambridge: Polity Press.

Collins, W. (1860/1974) *The Woman in White*, Harmondsworth: Penguin.

Colomina, B. (1994) *Privacy and Publicity: Modern Architecture as Mass Media*, Cambridge, MA and London: MIT Press.

Corbin, A. (1990) 'The Secret of the Individual', in M. Perrot (ed.) *A History of Private Life*, vol. 4, *From the Fires of Revolution to the Great War*, trans. A. Goldhammer, Cambridge, MA and London: The Belknap Press of Harvard University Press.

Daston, L. and Galison, P. (1992) 'The Image of Objectivity', *Representations* 40 (Fall): 81–128.

Davidoff, L. and Hall, C. (1987) *Family Fortunes: Men and Women of the English Middle Class 1780–1850*, Chicago: Chicago University Press.

Elias, N. (1978) *The Civilizing Process: The History of Manners*, Oxford: Basil Blackwell.

—— (1982) *The Civilizing Process: State Formation and Civilization*, Oxford: Basil Blackwell.

—— (1983) *The Court Society*, Oxford: Basil Blackwell.

Johnson, L. (1993) *The Modern Girl: Girlhood and Growing Up*, Sydney: Allen and Unwin.

Lury, C. (1998) *Prosthetic Culture: Photography, Memory and Identity*, London and New York: Routledge.

Martin-Fugier, A. (1990) 'Bourgeois Rituals', in M. Perrot (ed.) *A History of Private Life*, vol. 4, *From the Fires of Revolution to the Great War*, trans. Arthur Goldhammer, Cambridge, MA and London: The Belknap Press of Harvard University Press.

Perrot, M. (1990) 'Introduction' to 'Backstage', in M. Perrot (ed.) *A History of Private Life*, vol. 4, *From the Fires of Revolution to the Great War*, trans. Arthur Goldhammer, Cambridge, MA and London: The Belknap Press of Harvard University Press.

Stallybrass, P. and White, A. (1986) *The Politics and Poetics of Transgression*, London: Methuen.

Thomas, K. (1991) 'Introduction', in J. Bremmer and H. Roodenburg (eds), *A Cultural History of Gesture*, Cambridge: Polity Press.

Walkowitz, J.R. (1992) *City of Dreadful Delight: Narratives of Sexual Danger in Late-Victorian London*, London: Virago.

Wharton, E. (1907/1995) *Madame de Treymes*, Harmondsworth: Penguin.

Part 3

Reconfiguring the object of representation

Introduction

In Part 2, we looked at how subjectivity and identity are formed by specific cultural and institutional practices. In this section we take the discussion further by exploring how representations are configured by the frameworks that are brought to bear upon them and, hence, how the employment of different frameworks reconfigures the objects of representation, altering their meanings, uses and social functions. Jane considers how the practices of writing, reading and spectatorship have been represented by mainstream critical discourses in ways that are problematic for women's engagement with, and pleasure in, these activities, and canvases some alternative models of these practices that subvert the more conventional hierarchies of cultural value. Kay takes up photography, considering how it works both as an archive of the past and a practice of remembrance, as photographs become used as objects of commemoration. Gillian examines the exchange between fictional narratives and sociological, psychological and criminological texts in configuring a new repertoire of pathological types as a means of understanding and regulating the growing urban population of nineteenth-century Britain.

The objects of representation analysed in these chapters cover a wide range: popular fiction, forms of mass entertainment, visual arts, documentary images and narratives, critical and theoretical discourses, and public and institutional documents. The methods brought to bear on these objects also cover a wide interdisciplinary range drawn from literary theory, film and media studies, cultural studies, art history, psychoanalytical theory, history, and communication studies. This range of objects and methods shows the necessity for a diversified model of cultural subjectivity: one that is attentive to the space between different readings and reading populations; histories and regimes of knowledge; identifications and emotional affiliations at both a national and personal level.

The arguments developed within each chapter carry a distinct set of implications for understanding representation. For Jane, the 'feminine' styles of reading, writing, talking and film viewing, which have conventionally been accorded a low status in the hierarchy of discourses, merit reconsideration for the alternative experiences and perspectives that they offer both women and men. The concept of a woman reader, for example, is relevant whatever our sex, because it 'changes our apprehension of a given text, awakening us to the significance of its sexual codes'; in the same way, the culturally 'feminine' 'sensitivity to detail' might with justice be understood as one among the range of skills that any genre of text or activity demands of its reader or viewer. For Kay, photography is a 'technology of memory' that preserves, restores and transforms its objects of representation; the repertoires of emotion that the use of photographs of the past elicits (dispositions of loss, mourning and nostalgia) contribute to understanding history in the present. More specifically, this technology of memory affords the opportunity to capture an object or feeling, 'to hold something in the here and now, to make it persist'. Yet it can also elicit the tensions of the 'almost': suspended 'between disappointment and hope, between loss and longing, between memory and history'. For Gillian, the relationship between cultural knowledges and practices is dialogic, producing definitions of the gendered individual that serve to make urban populations both knowable and manageable. She shows, for instance, how Mayhew's charting of the characteristic features and behaviour of 'urban types' leads him to pathologise the female costermonger's 'incorrigibly public, commercial and sexualised femininity', summing up her nomadic and consuming existence in the compelling image of 'a locomotive stomach'. Her voracious, degenerative and 'unnaturally "virile" ' public femininity is complemented by its obverse: the enfeebled, sickly, weakened male body subject to urban 'strains' and 'moral drain'. The basis of social ills is seen as lying in this 'loss of sexual distinctiveness', which is an outcome of an irregular kind of sexual behaviour and character.

In all three chapters, reconfiguring the object of representation involves processes of negotiation: within a range of often contradictory viewing (and subject) positions in Jane's chapter; as part of attempts to move beyond the dislocation that exile brings to diasporic cultures in Kay's chapter; or in the way we engage with those definitions which 'become … part of the texture of our everyday patterns of living and thinking', as outlined in Gillian's chapter. Curiosity is a useful concept here, bringing us back to the 'between-ness' implicit in an awareness both of cultural differences and of the awkward alignment between personal identity and definitions of gender. Reconfiguration is at work, too, in Kaja Silverman's argument that 'what passes for "femininity" is actually an inevitable part of human subjectivity', and Jane's use of this to emphasise that subjectivity involves negotiating a range of contradictory possibilities. It is at work in Kay's use of Edward Said's observation that 'exile has emerged as a *topos* of human experience' to explore how photography works both to commemorate and transform the loss that exile implies, in order to imagine new futures and to reconstitute identities. And Gillian shows how the institutional definitions of a moderate sexual character simultaneously offer the coordinates for imagining those 'unruly' and 'destabilising' forms of identity that help to create and perpetuate a state of 'categorial uncertainty'.

6 Problematic pleasures

The position of women as writers, readers and film viewers

Jane Crisp

Introduction

A glance at the cartoon strips in the daily newspaper serves to confirm that certain activities tend to be represented in stereotypically gendered terms. Hagar the Horrible drinks and riots with his band of men while Helga stays at home doing the cooking and housework. On that rare occasion when Hagar is actually shown in the kitchen preparing dinner, it is scarcely a surprise to discover that the pot he is stirring contains rum punch! Similarly, we 'know' that men read the newspaper, watch the football on television and read spy and war stories whereas women watch soap operas and read Mills and Boon romances. Another cartoon that I recall from several years ago shows a middle-aged man sheltering behind a newspaper, while his wife, novel laid temporarily aside, proclaims rapturously, 'Just think, Rodney. For every romance published, how many trees, how many tall, dark, silent sentinels of nature, mute keepers of who-knows-what deep secrets, gave their all?' In practice, of course, we know very well that many husbands do cook and even read romances, and many women enjoy football and read newspapers, but popular representations suggest that this is untypical.

What is at issue here is not so much these stereotypical images of men and women in themselves as their political and social implications. The belief that certain types of activity, practice or language are 'natural' to a certain group effectively works to control and limit what members of that group can do. The practical consequences of this for groups that are defined as naturally inferior by reason of their gender, sexual preference, class or racial origin can be extremely serious, as the all-too-numerous victims the last century of policies of ethnic 'purification' and 'cleansing' bore witness.

In this chapter I will be exploring the issue of representations and their consequences in more detail. My first major case study looks at how women have been represented as writers and readers of what was labelled 'feminine fiction'. I draw upon the reception of the work of the highly popular nineteenth-century novelist, Rosa Nouchette Carey, to demonstrate the double bind imposed upon women writers and, by implication, their readers. Women were seen as different from men, and accordingly expected to produce an appropriately feminine style of novel; however, when they did produce work that conformed to the gendered ideals of the times, this was all too likely to be dismissed as unworthy of serious attention.

Operating here is a hierarchy of discourses in which a higher, more prestigious style is effectively maintained as the prerogative of members of a dominant cultural group, and thus serves both to mark and confirm their privileged status. Such hierarchies and the institutions that perpetuate, and are served by them, have been under challenge in recent decades. One example of this has been recent attempts by feminists to gain greater recognition for the social, informal and personal dimensions of language use, which have tended to be excluded from the supposedly more rational discourses of science, medicine and academic disciplines. My own work on the language of people with Alzheimer's belongs here, since it essentially involves restoring meaning and value to a linguistic practice that breaks with rational norms. Especially relevant to the case study of feminine fiction, however, is the broadening out of literary studies in ways that allow the voices of women writers and their readers to be heard and their pleasures – and displeasures – to be turned to critical account.

My second major case study focuses on a popular form developed in the twentieth century. Mainstream narrative cinema provides the complementary

Figure 1   Rosa Nouchette Carey

Source: The Key of the Unknown (Nouchette Carey 1909)

instance of a type of text that has been represented as masculine, and the implications that this has had for female viewers and their pleasures. Its form has been represented within film theory as implicitly masculine, positioning its viewers to share in a 'male gaze'. This hypothesis has been extremely useful to feminist critics concerned with making visible the misogyny implicit in many mainstream films. However – not surprisingly – women viewers of masculine texts are represented in terms as problematic as those used for women readers of feminine texts. Their pleasures this time become sexually aberrant inflections of the male position on offer, a transvestite taking up of the masculine perspective and/or a masochistic identification with the fetishised objects of this 'male gaze'. Equally problematic, too, is the way this theoretical model draws upon and thus helps to perpetuate a set of skewed binaries that align the masculine with power, looking and agency, and the feminine with their opposite. However, these over-neat binaries can be unsettled through appealing both to a range of well-known films and to alternative theories about how the film medium engages its viewers. The discussion here intersects with the earlier case study, in arguing against a simple two-term hierarchy of powerful masculine looking at its powerless opposite, and for alternative and more inclusive models of spectatorship and its pleasures. These latter suggest that mainstream film offers a complementary set of positionings, active and passive, powerful and powerless, masculine and feminine, which interact with the subjectivities and desires of socially situated viewers.

The case of 'feminine fiction'

Do women write – and read – differently from men? Some of the implications of believing that there is or should be such a difference are demonstrated by the case of a Victorian novelist, Rosa Nouchette Carey. In all probability, few readers will have heard of her, despite the forty-one novels to her name, and their considerable popularity. This is because Carey wrote domestic or 'feminine' fiction, which was very much seen as written by a woman for women readers. Hence, although her novels have been read with pleasure by three generations of women in my family, none of our menfolk have ever bothered to sample them (although my father did once buy his mother a set in matching bindings for her birthday).

During the second half of the nineteenth century, mainstream critics had a very clear idea of the sort of novel that it was appropriate for women to write. An article on 'women's novels' in the *Broadway Annual* of 1867/8, for instance, explicitly subscribes to the contemporary belief that a woman's different nature, experience and perspective made it appropriate for her to write (and, by implication, to read) an alternative, more 'feminine' style of fiction. Typically, this 'feminine fiction' would deal with situation rather than being strongly oriented towards plot. Its proper subject matter would be the domestic and everyday, rather than the broad range covered in novels by men; indeed, there were some subjects about which 'educated women' were expected to 'display a pleasing ignorance'. Women writers should not venture into the realm of philosophy and ideas, either, but should stay where their peculiar strengths were believed to lie, in the field of sentiment and detailed observation. Their novels could not be expected to aspire to the status of art, but at their best would 'resemble gossiping letters on an extended scale'. This neat gender opposition could not be upset by an appeal to the example of George Eliot, for 'her genius is so exceptional, and so different in quality from that of any of her compeers, that we scarcely reckon her as a representative female novelist' (Anon 1867/8: 504–11).

The feminine style of fiction outlined in the *Broadway Annual* represented an ideal, as the article's disapproval of much contemporary practice makes plain. Later in the century, too, Charles Dickens lamented that the high example of 'fine observation' and 'pure moral feeling' set by earlier writers such as Jane Austen had been so little followed, judging by the 'flood of unwholesome and pestilent novels' written, read and 'applauded' by 'the New Woman' (Dickens 1894: 537–40).

Dickens' charge of 'unwholesomeness' is a particularly significant one. Given the belief that woman's primary role was that of nurturer, it was only appropriate that her writings should be 'wholesome' – that is, actively nourishing for her readers. 'Wholesome' is the adjective that was most frequently applied to Rosa Nouchette Carey's own novels, and 'sound and wholesome' was the phrase used to sum up her oeuvre in her brief obituary notice in *The Times* (20 July 1909). Similarly, articles on her in magazines of the time stressed the author's womanly sense of priority, which made her ready to put aside her pen in response to any 'higher' claims made upon her time. Her companion, Helen Marion Burnside is quoted as saying:

> I do not think that I have known any author who has to make her writing – the real work of her life – so secondary a matter as has Rosa Carey. She has so consistently *lived* her religion, so to speak, that family duty and devotion to its many members have always come first. She never hesitates for a moment to give up the most important professional work if she can do anything in the way of nursing or comforting any of them, and she is *the* one to whom each of the family turns in any crisis of life.
>
> (Black 1906: 155–6)

Rosa Nouchette Carey, then, was clearly regarded as conforming to the recommended criteria for writing by women, but the reception of her novels by many mainstream critics shows the double bind that women writers of her time found themselves in. If they did not conform to these criteria, they were likely to be condemned; but even when they did conform to them they were equally condemned, since 'feminine' novels were frequently dismissed as inferior and trivial, and the readers who enjoyed them as feeble-minded. This, for instance, is what one critic had to say about Carey's first novel, *Nellie's Memories*, on its publication in 1868:

No designation could be more appropriate than that of 'domestic' as applied to this book. The simple good faith with which the most minute incidents of family life are dwelt upon will no doubt be justified by the interest and sympathy of impressionable persons of the novel-reading sex. For the rest of us, affectionate demonstrations which would be offensive in reality are not interesting when they form the staple incidents of a voluminous work.

(Pall Mall Gazette, 3 December 1868: 12)

Not all of Carey's reviewers were so ungenerous; indeed, many showed an appreciation of 'domestic' fiction and acknowledged her skill as a practitioner of it. However, dismissive reviews of her novels continued to appear even when her reputation as a popular and wholesome novelist was well established. *Rue with a Difference*, published in 1900, is an extremely interesting work, given Victorian pieties about marriage, since its heroine has been rescued by widowhood from the stifling effects of life with the clergyman husband whom she has intellectually and spiritually outgrown. Yet one reviewer commented that it is 'full of nothings – mild, inoffensive, inexpressibly tedious. It is so negligible that in the very act of perusal you scarcely know whether you are reading it or not' (*Academy*, 3 November 1900: 413).

Many other examples of the unfavourable reception given writers of feminine fiction are recorded by Elaine Showalter in her account of the alternative tradition of women novelists, *A Literature of Their Own* (1977). I have concentrated on Rosa Nouchette Carey because she is a favourite of mine and one of the neglected Victorian women novelists of whom I have made a particular study. Showalter's book and my own work on Carey (Crisp 1989) are examples of the efforts that are being made by feminists to reassess that alternative tradition of novels written by women for women in more positive terms. With this in mind, let us take a second look at the often pejorative equation of novels like Carey's with 'gossiping letters'.

'Gossip' is a term with highly gendered and negative connotations. As has often been noted, it is women who 'gossip', whereas men engage in 'discussion' or 'debate'. However, as Patricia Meyer Spacks has stressed, gossip can be highly functional for women, providing a means of getting to know others, of exploring attitudes and of affirming group solidarity. The gossipy style of the realistic, domestic novel may be one of its special pleasures for the reader, celebrating and reinforcing a specifically 'feminine' identity (Spacks 1985: 10, 19–20, 168). Similarly, Ellen Moers, in discussing the letters written by women novelists of the period to one another notes that their informal, friendly tone and habit of making something out of the daily incidents of a woman's life are qualities that flow on into the novels written by their authors, too (Moers 1979: 163–4). Thus, a novel that reads like a gossiping letter might be seen as one that addressed its predominantly female readers in intimate, friendly, 'feminine' terms.

The apparent 'lack' of style in a novel such as *Rue with a Difference* can be seen as contributing to this more feminine mode of address. You 'scarcely know whether you are reading it or not' precisely because of its difference from the highly self-conscious aesthetic and educated style practised by many mainstream male writers – a style which, in a period of unequal educational opportunity and expectations, placed the majority of women readers in the position of an inferior, being spoken down to by a more educated male authority.

The 'lack' of action such novels supposedly suffered from is also a question of perspective. From a woman's point of view, a great deal actually happens in them: their heroines move house; grapple with changed financial and social circumstances; establish a place for themselves within a new community network and in the process form the relationships that will influence their future life; they work within and outside the home; strive to reconcile personal and family needs; and struggle on limited incomes or in a hostile emotional climate to provide a decent life for themselves and those for whom they are responsible. The emotional incidents that get dwelt on are not the 'non-events' that some reviews accuse them of being, but moments of some psychological importance in the characters' lives, such as the first Christmas celebrated by the young family in *Nellie's Memories* after the deaths of their much-loved parents. These are very much female-centred narratives, which cover areas of experience often neglected in other types of fiction, and take women's activities and women's concerns of their period seriously.

The excess of minute detail that was recognised as being a major characteristic of these novels can also be seen positively as an appeal to what was believed to be a peculiarly female ability to notice and make sense of such details. As Naomi Schor points out, 'the detail does not occupy a conceptual space beyond the laws of sexual difference: the detail is gendered and doubly gendered as feminine' (Schor 1987: 4). The ability of women to interpret signs that their menfolk overlook is the subject of a Glaspell story, 'A Jury of Her Peers', discussed by Annette Kolodny (1986: 55–8). While the men of the community hunt around for clues that will reveal the motives for a murder, their wives take in the details provided by the accused woman's house, coming to understand what had really been happening from 'evidence which the men, at any rate, cannot recognise as such' (Kolodny 1986: 56). Carey herself appears to have believed that women had this superior sensitivity to detail, as the following comment on a husband's failure to notice that his wife is suffering from overwork shows:

> but men are so dense. … They take in vast vistas of landscape, and never see the little nettles that are choking up the field path. Women would have noticed the nettles at once, and spied out the gap in the hedge besides.
>
> (Carey, *Merle's Crusade*, 1889: 99)

The abundance of detail in Carey's novels can be seen as a key feature of their address to a female reader. Descriptions of appearance and personal environment are used to introduce and develop characters. Arrangement of one's private room or of one's home is presented as a means of self-expression, available even to those with limited resources. And a responsiveness to details of body language, behaviour and environment is crucial to a heroine's ability to fulfil her role of establishing and maintaining harmony within the household or social group. It is this which enables her to spot what the male head of the household has missed; namely, the often subtle signs that indicate that a weaker member is being bullied or exploited, that another one is feeling neglected, or that an apparently strong or indifferent one may be trying to come to terms with a secret grief or some difficult problem. The reader, too, through her identification with character and situation, might be thought of as having the opportunity to learn and exercise such feminine skills, which she could then apply in her own life. Indeed, there is a wealth of practical ideas that can be gleaned from these novels, thanks to the particularity of the description of events and activities, whether about cleaning a sickroom or staining a floor, disciplining a young child or taking a job outside the home.

Overall, then, there is nothing inherently trivial about such novels. They may subscribe to traditional values, but they in no way underestimate the problems of living up to these amid the strains, imperfections and trials of domestic life; they also, as is very much the case in novels such as *Lover or Friend* or *Cousin Mona*, recognise the extent to which women risk being trapped and depleted through their compulsion to nurture others. They actively attempt to nourish their intended female readers by valorising their interests and concerns, by providing practical strategies for coping with problems of the sort many of them might well be facing and, not least, by fostering through their sympathetic mode of address a potentially enabling sense of female capacity and worth.

A little incident from one of Rosa Nouchette Carey's novels serves as a closing comment on the Peters of this world, who insist on dismissing their sisters' taste for such novels (in this instance, being chosen to lend to a woman the family has befriended):

> with all his reliance on Ranee's common-sense and cleverness, he would not have been Peter if he had not sneered a little over the girl's choice of books.
>
> '*Heir of Redcliffe – Daisy Chain* – very good and pious and charming, no doubt. But Miss Burke was not a school-girl; a woman of her age needed strong meat. Miss Austen – humph – that was better ...'
>
> Ranee listened to these remarks with outward meekness, but Vera noticed that *The Heir of Redcliffe* was not returned to the book-case; when Peter left the room it was popped into the parcel and safely wedged in between *Emma* and *The Story of a Short Life*.
>
> (Carey, *The Household of Peter*, 1905: 67)

There are no prizes for guessing whether Miss Burke enjoyed Ranee's choice of novels.

To return to our original question – Do women write differently from men?

As the case of Rosa Nouchette Carey demonstrates, certain women writers did indeed write differently, but this was very much in accordance with the cultural ideals of the time as to what was proper for them. That these ideals served to limit and control women's production is betrayed both by the condemnation of those writers who ventured outside the prescribed limits, and by the frequent belittling of those who kept within them as being practitioners of a minor genre, attractive only to 'impressionable persons of the novel-reading sex'. Thus, the differences of the 'feminine' novel from mainstream (i.e. 'masculine') fiction, such as its more friendly, informal style, its emphasis on situation, and its strategic use of abundant detail, rather than being valued as a specific and highly functional mode of address were all too often represented in negatively gendered terms as a typically feminine 'lack' or 'excess'. That these attempts at control were not absolute is shown by the number of women who did write successfully in less feminine genres – some of them, like George Eliot or George Sand, to considerable critical acclaim. However, as with cross-dressing discussed in Chapter 3, the body of the author is far from neutral in its effects. The sex of the owner of the hand that once held the pen, like that of the body hidden under the clothes, becomes inescapably part of the meaning attributed to the text.

Hierarchies of discourse making a case for the banished 'mother tongue'

In recent decades feminists have directly challenged such established hierarchies of discourse, in which intellectual, rational, scientific – and hence, implicitly, 'masculine' – modes of speaking and writing are privileged over their more emotional and personal 'feminine' counterparts. A representative instance of this with particular relevance to the current discussion is an essay by the distinguished feminist scholar Jane Tompkins, 'Me and My Shadow'. In this essay Tompkins tackles the problem of the split that she and other women academics are required to make between their professional self and another, more private self – the 'shadow' of her title, with all its personal feelings, attitudes and concerns. As she notes, she is expected to exclude this shadow self on the pretext that her public intellectual work is 'more exalted, more important, because it (supposedly) transcends the personal'. However, she rejects the need for this exclusion:

> The public–private dichotomy, which is to say, the public–private hierarchy, is a founding condition of female repression. I say to hell with it. The reason I feel embarrassed at my own attempts to speak personally in a professional context is that I have been conditioned to feel that way. That's all there is to it.
>
> (Tompkins 1989: 123)

Rather than criticise this impersonal, professional discourse in the same academic style, which would implicitly reinforce its authority, Tompkins attempts to speak in another voice. But, as she notes, this is not easy:

I find that when I try to write in my 'other' voice, I am immediately critical of it. It wobbles, vacillates back and forth, is neither this nor that. The voice in which I write about epistemology is familiar, I know how it ought to sound. This voice, though, I hardly know. I don't even know if it has anything to say. But if I never write in it, it never will. So I have to try.

(Tompkins 1989: 126)

This 'other' voice is identified by Tompkins as being the 'mother tongue' that Ursula LeGuin sets up in opposition to the rational and objective 'father tongue' of expository and scientific discourse. The distinction, as LeGuin makes it, is a valuable one, for it not only makes clear that these varieties of language are used by both men and women, but also that they implicitly serve very different purposes:

The essential gesture of the father tongue is not reasoning, but distancing – making a gap, a space, between the subject or self and the object or other. … Everywhere now everybody speaks [this] language in laboratories and government buildings and headquarters and offices of business. … The father tongue is spoken from above. It goes one way. No answer is expected, or heard.

… The mother tongue, spoken or written, expects an answer. It is conversation, a word the root of which means 'turning together.' The mother tongue is language not as mere communication, but as relation, relationship. It connects. … Its power is not in dividing but in binding. … We all know it by heart. John have you got your umbrella I think it's going to rain. Can you come play with me? If I told you once I told you a hundred times. … O what am I going to do? … Pass the soy sauce please. Oh, shit. … You look like what the cat dragged in.

(Tompkins 1989: 127)

Both men and women speak these different tongues, then, as they do the subversive, 'semiotic' language of metaphor and poetry, which Julia Kristeva sees as disruptive of the rational 'symbolic' (Kristeva 1986). However, as the examples that LeGuin gives, and as cases like that of Rosa Nouchette Carey make clear, these discourses have different cultural values according to whether they are gendered as 'masculine' or 'feminine'. At issue here are the institutions that regulate these languages, and determine their place in a cultural hierarchy of values.

The consequences of speaking the wrong language: people with Alzheimer's

The institutional regulation of language and privileging of some discourses above others is dramatically illustrated in another case study, which I want to mention briefly here. The case study this time concerns not women writers or academics but people whose use of language is being affected by Alzheimer's disease. I include it here to stress two important points: first, that the issues we have been exploring in relation to writing have a much wider social relevance and, second, that the valuing of one type of discourse over another has serious, real-life consequences.

People with Alzheimer's typically have trouble finding the right word to refer to things: they may start using the word 'dog' for a whole range of other animals, including cats and lambs, for instance. They have problems with short-term memory, too, so forget recent events and information, often not knowing where they are, what time of day or even year it is, or what they have just said or done. My mother assumed she was in England although she had been living on the other side of the world since 1947, referred to her father as though he were still alive, and thought that her stiff leg must be due to a kick from a horse or a car accident (since she had forgotten the rheumatism from which she has long suffered). People like her also lose the ability to distinguish between fact and fantasy, between what they have actually done or only heard or read or dreamed about. My mother would tell me wonderful tales about running up to the top of a nearby mountain during the night or about killing thousands of the enemy on top of it during the war. She did, however, like many other people with her condition, still enjoy chatting with people and, even when in an advanced stage of dementia, could still cope reasonably well with routine social exchanges. She also had no trouble communicating her feelings to us.

Any readers who consult the official literature on Alzheimer's disease may well be struck, as I was, by the very different estimates of people like my mother, provided on the one hand by medical research papers and textbooks and on the other by accounts from care-givers. The picture painted by the former is bleak indeed, whereas many of the latter see these people as attempting to communicate and using language to do so to the best of their ability well into the dementing condition (Crisp 1993, 1995). The difference is explicable in terms of the aspects of thought and language use which are given priority. The discourse of scientific and medical research speaks what LeGuin calls the 'father tongue': it places greatest value on the more rational, objective and instrumental uses of language that we employ in the accurate description and successful management of our world – that is, precisely on those functions that are soonest and most profoundly disturbed by the dementing process. The practitioners of this discourse, therefore, are principally aware of what these people cannot do, judging what they can still say to be 'confused' and 'empty' and of interest only as a symptom of their condition. The continued ability to carry on a conversation is either ignored or dismissed as routine and 'trivial'. Those who are engaged in the daily care of people with dementia , however, tend to place much greater value on the more social, interactive functions of language overlooked by their colleagues. They notice and value any attempt at a social exchange and tend to regard emotion as a meaningful content which even confused, disoriented and fragmentary vocalisations can express if we 'hear the underlying message … what the person is telling you beneath the words' (Sherman 1991: 109). Relationship, connectedness – the qualities of LeGuin's 'mother tongue' – matter to them.

The gendered implications of these two discourses are reinforced by the predominance of men in medicine and science, and of women in the significantly labelled 'caring professions'. To put it simplistically, the discourse that is least favourable in its representations of people with Alzheimer's is higher in the cultural hierarchy, thanks to a triple conjunction of privileged terms – scientists, doctors, men. It is worth noting, too, that the social skills that survive in people like my mother, and which are so often dismissed by the dominant discourse on Alzheimer's, are precisely those culturally 'feminine' skills which women are socialised into practising – the same skills that we have already seen dismissed as inferior and gossipy earlier in this chapter. Furthermore, scientific or medical discourse necessarily objectifies and depersonalises its subject of study. If that subject is considered unable to think or use language, it becomes an object in real earnest, no longer a person but a mere shell of a body, a problem to be dealt with. However, if we think of someone with Alzheimer's as still interacting with others and still having emotions to communicate, they remain a person, despite the effects of their dementia. Given that one in five of us are likely to be affected by dementia, we have a real stake in which of these opposing views prevails, since this will influence not only the degree of funding and attention given to people in care, but also the attitudes and behaviour of care-givers towards them.

Marginalised readers speak back

I will be discussing my work on Alzheimer's disease in more detail in the last section of this book. Now I want to return to the discourse that has been responsible for devaluing feminine fiction and LeGuin's 'mother tongue': the dominant discourse of literary criticism. This discourse, like the dominant medical and scientific ones, is implicitly masculine. As Nina Baym neatly puts it in her own exercise in reassessing women's fiction:

> I cannot avoid the belief that 'purely' literary criteria, as they have been employed to identify the best American works, have inevitably had a bias in favor of things male – in favor, say, of whaling ships rather than the sewing circle as a symbol of the human community; in favor of satires on domineering mothers, shrewish wives, or betraying mistresses rather than tyrannical fathers, abusive husbands, or philandering suitors; displaying an exquisite compassion for the crises of the adolescent male, but altogether impatient with the parallel crises of the female.
>
> (Bayn 1978: 14)

In recent decades feminist criticism has drawn attention to the situation within mainstream literary studies of students who have a pen but not a penis. Sydney Janet Kaplan describes how she and other women students felt 'alienated' and 'excluded':

> Not only did many of us feel alienated by the content of the canon we were expected to 'master', but we also felt excluded by the assumed objectivity of the critical jargon we were expected to use, with its accompanying assumption of the generically masculine 'reader', its implied universality, as well as its estrangement from our lived experience.
>
> (Kaplan 1985: 39)

An important aspect of that sense of exclusion for many women students was the absence from the canon of works for 'serious' study of their 'secret loves' – the novels by 'a favourite woman author' eagerly devoured by an earlier self 'who read with a flashlight to finish a book long after she was supposed to be asleep' (Kaplan 1985: 38).

I suspect that many readers, both men and women, will recognise something of an earlier self in that engrossed reader with the flashlight. However, it is women readers in particular whose taste in reading matter and manner of reading have tended to receive the most critical scorn. As the reviews of Rosa Nouchette Carey quoted earlier show, the reader of feminine fiction tended to be represented as credulous and uncritical, identifying over-closely with what she read; in effect, her 'lack' of discrimination complemented the female writer's 'lack' of style, and her 'excess' of identification the 'excess' of social and affective detail on which it fed. Hence the reassessing and rehabilitating of fictions written for women has necessarily entailed doing the same for their readers. Exemplary here is Janice Radway's *Reading the Romance*, a detailed study of a population of frequent readers of Harlequin romances. By bothering to question these women about their reading, Radway discovered how discriminating in their own way they actually were, with distinct likes and dislikes, about which they were very articulate. Their comments reveal that they were well aware of the escapism involved, but also that such reading gave them recuperative moments of time for themselves in the midst of a busy week attending to the needs of other people. Radway does give critical attention to the ways in which such romantic novels reinforce the very gender ideology that causes so many women to turn to them in the first place, but at the same time she neither underestimates nor belittles the importance of the pleasure they give, nor the intelligence of their readers (Radway 1987).

Empirical research, such as that undertaken by Radway into what their reading means for the women who engage in it, is complemented at the level of textual criticism by the critical practice of 'reading as a woman' (see Culler 1983: 43–64). The conscious adoption of this alternative perspective challenges the objectivity claimed for traditional literary criticism by highlighting the gender politics of a particular text and of the reading the dominant critical discourses invite us to make. The result may be a new and unapologetic appreciation of the achievements of a neglected writer of 'feminine fiction' or, equally, a revised assessment of works in the approved canon of 'great literature'. If I reread the much-praised and -studied *Heart of Darkness* by Joseph Conrad, for instance, forgetting what I was taught as an undergraduate and deliberately allowing myself to judge it 'as a woman', I notice certain elements to which my attention had not previously been drawn. Despite its promotion as a book that takes us into a supposedly universal realm – the 'inexpressible, terrifying reality of the heart'[1] – its biases are very much turn-of-the-century, white, London-centred … and male. Both its narrators are men, with the predominant one, Marlow, being explicitly represented as telling his story to other men. The male characters all have names or are labelled by their profession, whereas the women are referred to exclusively in terms of their relationship to men – Marlow's aunt, Kurtz's Intended. The lie Marlow believes it necessary to tell to the latter confirms a gendered opposition around which the whole book is structured; namely, women's impractical idealism and need to be protected from a truth, the knowledge of which only men are capable of enduring. The silences and omissions of the novel become visible, too: the lack of comment on the women of the Congo and their sexual exploitation by the white male colonisers; and the failure to represent the life of the Intended, waiting in Brussels for the return of Kurtz, as anything but a sterile entombment. The story of Nellie, as told by Rosa Nouchette Carey, fills out one of these gaps, in its portrayal of the activities and personal growth which could enrich such a period of 'waiting' for the woman back home.

Significantly, reading as a woman is a strategy that men can adopt as well as women, although their different status and conditioning will tend to give the activity a particular inflection for them. This is one of the points we need to keep in mind, to avoid an essentialism of reading related to one's sex alone and disregarding the influences of a culture and of the gendered identities acquired within it. Otherwise this alternative reading strategy becomes self-defeating, reinforcing a simple binary opposition based on gender and duplicating the assumptions of orthodox criticism about a universal and unproblematic meaning that a text will have for all women readers. In 'reading for the other woman', as Nancy Miller notes (1988: 110–11), we need to be conscious of the risk of collapsing the differences between groups of women, forgetting the hierarchies of class, race, religion, education and individual circumstances that will also be operating within a particular society and upsetting the over-neat formulation of a two-term hierarchy of oppressive men/oppressed women. We also need to bear in mind Showalter's point that the concept of a woman reader is a hypothesis that 'changes our apprehension of a given text, awakening us to the significance of its sexual codes' (1986: 128). It is not a claim to know how all or any women might respond to a given text, but rather a strategy of imagining how a woman might read this particular text which serves to destabilise the meanings that dominant critical discourses have attributed to that text and to make visible the gender implications of those meanings.

Given the extent to which women have been positioned by mainstream critical discourses and the texts that these privilege to 'read as men', the strategy of reading as a woman is very much one of resistance to preferred or dominant meanings and values. Such a practice of resisting reading or counter-reception has been useful in explaining how women and other culturally 'disenfranchised' groups, such as blacks, lesbians and gays, are able to gain 'curious pleasures' of their own from mainstream novels and films, despite the often uncompromising espousal by these of white, middle-class and heterosexual norms, by selectively reworking them in the interests of an alternative set of interests (Zimmerman 1985). It also helps free up monolithic and over-deterministic models of reading and viewing in favour of a set of more flexible understandings incorporating notions of fantasy and negotiation, which allow for a more dynamic relationship between reader and text (as I discuss later in this chapter in relation to theories of film spectatorship).

Counter-reception, though, is not just a matter of resistance to dominant norms: it involves a double process, which Bonnie Zimmerman felicitously calls 'double vision' (Zimmerman 1985: 203). Double vision allows us to take up and enjoy a text from the dominant perspective and at the same time to criticise or rework it from some alternative position; to go along with mainstream academic practice, yet be aware of the perceptions of that other, shadow self to which Jane Tompkins wants us to give a voice. It has allowed me to appreciate a novelist like Rosa Nouchette Carey, despite her old-fashioned values and lack of status with 'masculine' critics; to look beyond the obvious changes and deterioration produced by dementia in someone like my mother and recognise the ways in which they are still functioning as a person.

This process of double vision is assisted by the degree of complicity that mainstream texts may have with their own counter-reception, counterbalancing or even subverting the values to which they subscribe. Even as resolutely wholesome a novelist as Rosa Nouchette Carey, for instance, makes abundantly plain to her readers the effort, risks and psychological costs of living up to the traditional ideals of womanhood that her novels uphold. Indeed, as Sandra Gilbert and Susan Gubar (1979) argue, certain nineteenth-century women novelists such as Charlotte Brontë, may well have been compensating their heroines (and readers) for having to stick to certain rules of conduct through the activities of some surrogate double, 'the mad woman in the attic' who is free to run amok in their stead and bring the patriarchal house tumbling down. In such cases, the double vision of women writing as women, in effect, speaks to the complementary double vision of women reading as women. Writers like Rosa Nouchette Carey may be excluded from 'the great tradition' of novelists identified by the influential critic, F.R. Leavis, as worthy of study, but she is very much part of another tradition – read and unashamedly enjoyed by several generations of women readers.

Film and the case of 'the male gaze'

My second major case study deals with a different but complementary situation: the position of women in relation not to 'feminine' but to 'masculine texts'.

As Laura Mulvey argued in a highly influential article (published in 1975) that mainstream cinema organises the experience of looking and its narrative dynamic in such a way that the viewer is positioned as male. This theory of 'the male gaze' has subsequently been refined and modified by Mulvey, but the original thesis became a given of film theory, providing the basis for much feminist film analysis and the obligatory starting point for theoretical exploration and debate around issues of spectatorship over the next decade.

Film texts, according to Mulvey, invite their viewer to engage in an extended and concentrated looking from the powerful position once occupied by the camera. This position is also a privileged voyeuristic one, since what is looked at appears to be unaware of being watched. Typically, the object of this voyeuristic cinematic gaze is the image of a woman, offered up to be looked at in ways that tie in with masculine ideals, as in close-ups and glamour shots. The woman is typically the object of the action or its reward, rather than its agent; when she does take the initiative, she is usually punished and then either destroyed or returned to her 'proper' role. As spectacle she interrupts the forward momentum of narrative action; camera, viewer and male characters take time off, as it were, to gaze upon her. Thus the position – both literal and in terms of implied perspective and values – which is offered the viewer is a masculine one, leaving those viewers who happen to be female with the option of either a masochistic identification with the object of that male gaze or the adoption of a transvestite position.

Mulvey's thesis also considers the question of why the image of the woman should be so fascinating, why it is so glamourised, why it tends to disrupt the narrative. The answer is that the sight of the woman risks evoking a fear of 'castration', but that this fear is suppressed through a compensatory process of fetishisation: her 'lack' is disguised by an overvaluing of other areas of her anatomy.

Mulvey is drawing here on psychoanalytic theories about the early formation of our psychic and social identities. To put these ideas as simply as possible – and at the risk, therefore, of oversimplifying them – a child's access to language and culture is seen as involving a necessary shift from a maternal to a paternal realm. The earliest state of existence is one of abundance, instant gratification, and fusion with the all-powerful mother – this is the plenitude of the imaginary, a fantasised ideal state that one can become aware of only after one has already lost access to it. And lose it one must, learning to accept the renunciation, deferral and lack on which the paternal symbolic depends. The process being hypothesised here is the psychic dimension to more concrete aspects of moving away from infancy: losing access to the mother's breast, being forced to defer the evacuation of bladder and bowels, learning to deal with words and images that operate in the absence of that to which they refer. These lacks and losses are a symbolic castration, which becomes associated with the mother and the now perceived limits to her power – her lack of the phallus, emblem of the law of the Father. Theoretically speaking, the phallus is not the penis, the woman's lack not a literal castration, but phallus and penis, sexual difference and castration readily become conflated in a patriarchal world in which power is associated with maleness. There are two complementary methods of compensating for the lack the woman represents: by identification with a powerful male; and by diverting attention away from the woman's lack on to other attributes, such as her face and breasts, which are invested with a compensatory overabundance of value.

Both Mulvey's thesis and the psychoanalytic theories upon which it draws implement and reinforce a particular set of strongly gendered oppositions, in which agency and power are yet again firmly aligned with masculinity:

gazer	object of the gaze
camera	image
male character/s}	landscape, fetishised woman
viewer }	
narrative	spectacle
action, forward impetus	stasis
movement	closure
agent of action	its reward
to see, know, master	seen, known, mastered
phallic power	castration, fetishisation
language, culture	instinct, the body
adult, paternal realm	infancy, maternal realm

Mulvey's thesis of the male gaze has proved extremely useful to feminist film critics as a means of explaining and exposing the misogynist bias of many popular films and, moreover, suggesting how this bias might be underpinned by the basic mechanisms of mainstream film practice. The well-known film *Crocodile Dundee* provides a neat demonstration of this, not least because its female protagonist 'tests the rule' by usurping the 'masculine' role of narrative agent and active looker.[2] We are first introduced to Sue Carlton, a photojournalist whose desire to see and know is what initially drives the action. When she attempts to demonstrate her independence in the outback, however, she becomes the object of the voyeuristic gaze of Mike Dundee and of the viewer who is positioned to share his look; this gaze may be legitimised as a necessarily protective one, exercised for her good, but it is still a highly voyeuristic one, as the dwelling on female flesh revealed by her scanty bathing suit makes clear. Punished by the attacking crocodile, re-castrated by the attack on the water bottle hanging conveniently low on her body, this would-be phallic woman reverts to her role as object to be rescued, admirer of the exploits of the hero and his eventual reward. The maleness of the gaze is affirmed shortly after the crocodile attack. When Sue takes on the voyeuristic role in her turn, spying on an all-male gathering, her gaze is returned and she is forced to retreat; the viewer, however, is allowed to look a little longer.

A more drastic breaking of the rules, with even more drastic consequences for the breaker, is represented by another well-known film, *Fatal Attraction*. Alex – note her masculine name – is an even more resolutely phallic woman than Sue, insisting on the fulfilment of her own desires; on to her is projected all the film's active female sexuality, not only her own but also that of the male protagonist's wife and daughter, both of whom are represented as being rather too suspiciously sweet and pure. As embodied by Alex, female initiative, agency and desire become truly monstrous – malevolent forces that must be kept away from the family, lest they destroy it. The cheers with which some cinema audiences, according to reports by my students, greeted the destruction of Alex suggests the level of psychic engagement that this film offers. Linda Williams, in an article significantly titled 'When the Woman Looks' (1984: 83–99), suggests that the bond established between woman and monster in certain horror films might well be read as founded on the monster's capacity for representing the distortion woman's image undergoes within patriarchy. What is monstrous about Alex, then, is that she should be represented as such. Monstrous, too, and ripe for unsettling, are the gendered oppositions at work in the examples discussed above.

Taking another look

As many feminist film critics have noted, the 'power to explain' of Mulvey's thesis is offset by its 'largely negative accounts of female spectatorship, suggesting colonised, alienated or masochistic positions of identification' (Gledhill 1988: 66). Indeed, the terms of this thesis help to perpetuate the very oppositions that it was designed to critique: masculine rationality and control versus feminine instincts and excess; masculine looking versus its powerless feminine object; masculine power versus feminine lack. Hence it is worth taking a second look, in the interests both of upsetting this over-neat gender alignment and of proposing some less obviously masculinised models of the pleasures offered by mainstream film.

First, we might consider the extent to which this privileged alignment of masculinity and power depends on the status that we, whether as feminists or theorists, give theory itself. Once we stop treating any theory, however convincing, as a working hypothesis and come to regard it as a truism – a law of the Father, in effect – it may well rebound on us by perpetuating the very tendencies that it was originally intended to expose and subvert. In the present case, the emphasis on the male as owner of the gaze reinforces the centrality of maleness and its association with agency and power, and thus continues to render women's access to these problematic and even 'unnatural'. The 'bachelor machines' of psychoanalytic and sociopolitical theory – to use Penley's (1985) apt phrase – are capable of endlessly reproducing their own image and values. One way of counteracting this tendency is to restore theory to its role of working hypothesis so that it opens up the possibility of fresh understandings rather than keeping us prisoners of earlier speculations that have been allowed to harden into received 'truths'.

Another general strategy for undermining the orthodox alignment of looking, masculinity and power within film theory is to bring into the equation the complementary case of television. Instead of the concentrated, masculine gaze of film, television is theorised as catering for a distracted, feminine glance (Ellis 1982; Houston 1984). However, the idea of a monolithic feminine positioning is equally problematic, not least in perpetuating a negative association between the lower-status activity of television viewing, the domestic and the feminine. Rather than fostering yet another unequal opposition, this time between a powerful male cinematic gaze and a powerless, feminine televisual glance, we might argue instead that gaze and glance are different modes of viewing, employable by either sex and with respect to either medium. In practice, we can and do often behave socially in the cinema or, conversely, give our undivided attention to a favourite television show, duplicating in our home the privileged viewing circumstances of the cinema. VCRs and the new generation of larger and higher-definition television sets have further increased the potential both for such home duplication of the cinematic gaze and, for its obverse, the domestication of the viewing of film texts. Gaze and glance, therefore, may be privileged by the mediums with which they are associated in screen theory but are not exclusively linked to them; particular texts, occasions, viewing circumstances and viewer interests work together to foster the adoption of either or both modes, as appropriate.

Indeed, we can take the argument about modes of viewing even further and state that the overall process of making sense of a film or television text depends on a combination of culturally 'masculine' and 'feminine' ways of seeing and understanding. As noted in the previous case study on feminine fiction, there is an established distinction between the supposedly masculine ability to 'take in large vistas' and the feminine sensitivity to the telling detail. Hence we might argue for the fundamental relevance to any viewing activity of both these inter-pretative competences. If mainstream film texts often position their viewer as masculine, they also depend for their understanding and appreciation on not only a sense of 'the big picture' but also a culturally feminine responsiveness to the significance of details of the story world and of the various marks of filmic narration.

Returning to the more specific formulations of film theory, as outlined earlier, what are the arguments for unsettling the hypothesis of a gendered alignment of looking, masculinity and power? The central point on which this alignment depends – the positioning of the spectator to share the camera's look – is a good place to start.

The mechanics of the medium and of film projection do indeed position the viewer, male or female, at the point from which the camera once 'looked' at what is now represented on the screen. However, this positioning is a contradictory one, capable both of bestowing power and denying it. Sometimes the viewer does share in the camera's omniscient perspective. In both *Tootsie* and *Mrs Doubtfire*, for example, we know what is going on right from the start: we see the male hero putting on the body and clothing of a woman and so are never at risk of being fooled, as the other characters are, by his cross-gender masquerade. However, at other times the limits to sight or knowledge are made all too clear – the first-time viewer sees and hears only what they are allowed to. *The Crying Game* lets us share its protagonist's assumption that the attractive young woman with whom he is becoming involved is what she seems; as a result, we also share with him the shock of the unsettling discovery later in the film of 'her' hitherto hidden male genitalia. Nor does knowing more than the characters necessarily give the viewer an impression of power, as another example, Hitchcock's *Frenzy*, demonstrates. We know the identity of the serial killer, having seen him brutally strangle a previous female victim, but must watch helplessly while he leads the unsuspecting heroine into the room, where we know she will be murdered in her turn. Our very lack of power to see what is happening or to intervene is under-lined by means of a long, slow tracking shot away from the closed door behind which the action is taking place.

Similarly, the characteristically voyeuristic look offered the viewer is not neces-sarily one of power. At the level of individual texts, one can cite Hitchcock's *Rear Window*, in which the parallel between viewing and voyeurism is overtly drawn. Yet its peeping Tom hero has already been rendered inactive, castrated – 'feminised' even – confined to his apartment with one leg in plaster and obliged to delegate all agency other than that of looking to others. By the end of the narrative, his gaze has been returned by the suspected murderer who is its object, and he narrowly escapes being the next victim. More generally, one might ques-tion whether the position film usually offers its viewers is truly voyeuristic. As Mulvey acknowledges in her original article, the case for voyeurism has to be made against the fact that '[What] is seen on the screen is so manifestly shown' (Mulvey 1975: 9). The power associated with voyeurism proper surely depends on the look being an unsolicited and transgressive one, invading the private sphere of an unknowing object – the very opposite of the looking that spectacle and performance invite, and for which film is so obviously made. Given this, it might be more appropriate to think of cinematic voyeurism in terms of Metz's proposition that there is a double spectator in each viewer: a 'credulous' one, who accepts the illusion of spying on a pre-existing reality at face value; and an 'incredulous' one, who knows all along that this is indeed just an illusion staged for our benefit (Metz 1982: 72).

Another theoretical argument for associating the sharing of the camera's look with power is that its look duplicates the gaze of the Other. As pointed out in Chapter 3, on fashioning gendered identities, the gaze of the Other is the eyes (as it were) of a culture upon its members – that sense we have of how we seem to other members of our society which both affirms our individual identity and controls our behaviour. However, the gaze of the Other is the basis of all iden-tity, from the founding moment when, as Lacan puts it, we first 'recognise' our self from the outside via our reflection in a mirror (Lacan 1966: 89–97). All members of society, both men and women, are subject to this gaze. Hence, as Kaja Silverman for one has argued, film can be seen as simultaneously offering two contradictory positions: a pleasurable sharing in the powerful, controlling look of the Other, doubled with the look at the cinematic spectacle, which is a constant reminder of our own state of looked-at-ness, of being under the surveil-lance of that gaze (Silverman 1988b).

The gendering of these two contradictory positions through alignment with a masculine agency of looking and its feminine object is problematised even further by Silverman's critique of the complementary association of woman and 'lack'. For men and women alike, entry into the world of language, representation, culture, is an entry into a world of deferred pleasures, of limits to individual power; into a world of signs operating in the absence or lack of what they refer to:

> since no one assumes identity except by being separated from the mother, losing access to the real, and entering into a field of pre-existing meaning, and since no identity can be sustained in the absence of the gaze of the Other ... what passes for 'femininity' is actually an inevitable part of human subjectivity. Women have nothing to gain by denying this legacy. On the contrary, what is needed here is not so much a 'masculinisation' of the female subject as a 'feminisation' of the male subject – a much more generalized acknowledgement, in other words, of the necessary terms of cultural identity.
>
> (Silverman 1988a: 149)

The gender oppositions we have been considering in this section, therefore, are produced by the appropriation as masculine of whatever is positive and powerful, complemented by the projection of negative qualities on to the feminine, thereby allowing the masculine share in these to be disavowed. This skewed attribution is further secured by being construed as a 'natural' consequence of women's biological difference from men, which, as we saw in Chapter 3, on fashioning gendered identities, is all too often represented as a female 'lack'.

Silverman's model of the basic mechanism of film as a double positioning, both with the controlling look of the Other and the object of its control, complements a similar model proposed by the French film theorist Oudart. According to him, film engages the viewer in an endless replaying of the process involved in our original formation as human subjects. He calls this filmic engagement 'suture', on an analogy with the joining together of two sides of a wound. Each fresh image appears to offer so much that it provides a pleasurable sensation of completeness and plenitude. This is rapidly eroded by a growing and inevitable awareness of the something beyond the limits of the frame, the more to see and know that is necessarily still lacking and withheld – an awareness that converts pleasure into desire. The next image momentarily satisfies that desire, restoring a plenitude that is eroded in its turn, and so it goes on throughout the film, catching up the viewer in an endless oscillation between abundance and lack, pleasure and desire, presence and absence, which duplicates the original shift between the imaginary and the symbolic. Through this process the viewer is repeatedly 'stitched' into an involvement with the ongoing narrative – at the same time, presence and absence are repeatedly 'sutured' together, but the division between them never disappears (Oudart 1977–8: 35–55).

The orthodox one-way, masculine model of how film positions its viewer is also challenged by various fantasy models that propose a more complex set of complementary identifications for viewers of either sex. Freud's original ideas about voyeurism are relevant here since he saw it as coexisting with exhibitionism in the one subjectivity: 'Every active perversion is ... accompanied by its passive counterpart: anyone who is an exhibitionist in his unconscious is at the same time a voyeur' (Freud 1977: 81). This notion allows for a much wider range of androgynous, bisexual, oscillating and contradictory positions of identification.[3] As both Cowie (1984) and Penley (1985) have stressed, the basic psychic fantasies and the film narratives that embody them offer a range of positions, masculine and feminine, active and passive, all or any of which are available to the fantasizer or viewer, irrespective of their sex or sexual alignment – even though these will necessarily have some effect on how the positions are taken up:

> all the possible roles in the narrative are available to the subject: he [*sic*] can be either subject or object and can even occupy a position 'outside' the scene, looking on from the spectator's point of view. Again, it is only the formal positions themselves that are fixed (there are 'masculine' and 'feminine' positions of desire); the subject can and does adopt these positions in relation to a variety of complex scenarios, and in accordance with the mobile patterns of his or her own desire.
>
> (Penley 1985: 54)

A similar freeing up of the pleasures offered by film to the 'patterns' of the individual viewer's 'own desire' is also allowed for by Christine Gledhill's concept of 'pleasurable negotiations' (Gledhill 1988). Negotiation proposes a dynamic interaction between the positions offered at various levels by the film medium and specific film texts, and the already formed social and psychic subjects who engage with these positions. The term 'negotiation' is itself especially apt, since it implies a process that, like the fashioning of identities discussed in Chapter 3, is neither entirely bound nor entirely free; a process through which competing interests, both obvious and hidden, strive for the maximum of satisfaction with the minimum of compromise or risk. Negotiation allows, too, for the possibility of a pleasurable engagement with mainstream, white, masculinist film texts from feminine, black, feminist, lesbian and gay perspectives through processes of 'rereading' and 'counter-reception' similar to those engaged in by women readers of canonical literary texts.

The concept of negotiation, in referring to the attempt to reconcile opposite positions, also allows for the extent to which any positioning of the film spectator involves conflict and contradiction. Not only do particular films compromise the association between looking, masculinity and power, but the basic mechanisms of the film medium itself and of the subject formation which they replay are founded upon presence *and* absence, abundance *and* lack, subject *and* object, power *and* its opposite, culturally masculine *and* feminine positions.

Linda Williams has argued that female spectatorship may need rethinking in terms of a multiple identification with contradictory positions; indeed, that the female spectator may 'identify with contradiction itself' (Williams 1987: 314). However, one can go further and argue that all viewers, irrespective of sex, are regularly positioned to identify with narrative contradiction. Since our patriarchal system is also a competitive, capitalist one, feelings of contradiction and alienation are far from being exclusive to women; as Mulvey herself notes, the 'pent-up emotion, bitterness and disillusion' and the suffering under paternal despotism which are characteristic of Sirkian melodrama, for instance, can speak strongly to men and women alike (Mulvey 1977–8: 77). Thus any general model of spectatorship needs to recognise that masculine positioning can be fluctuating, unstable and contradictory, too – not least to avoid relocking the feminine position into another disabling binary opposition to a stable, unified masculine one.

A final, much simpler model, which I have saved to end this chapter, replaces the problematic adult, masculine, voyeuristic pleasures of the male gaze with those of an earlier type of looking, which we experienced in our infancy. As Baudry notes, the literal position we are expected to adopt in a cinema is an infantile one of relative immobility and silence; the screen before us with its possibilities of identification and its plenitude of images and sounds becomes a surrogate maternal breast (Baudry 1974/1986: 294). In such a position, the maleness or femaleness of the viewer seems scarcely relevant! However, the key point that I want to make here for challenging the voyeuristic model is that film offers us a stare at other people and their activities, including private ones, which is both uninhibited and licensed. We are allowed to indulge freely in such a stare as very small children; as we grow older though bodies become covered in our presence, and bathroom, toilet and bedroom doors become closed against us; we start to be told that we mustn't stare at people. Curiosity, and the desire to satisfy it, arise from such withdrawal of an earlier permission to look. Hence a great deal of the pleasure that film – and television – give their viewers may be through indulging to the full that earlier, frustrated desire to see and know. Unlike Pandora, we can look into the box without fear of consequences; unlike the elephant's child, we can be curious without getting spanked for it (see Chapter 2).

Notes

1   As described in the back cover blurb of the 1983 Penguin edition.
2   For a more detailed discussion, see J. Crisp (1994) 'Desiring the Real Dundee', in P. Fuery (ed.) *Representation, Discourse and Desire*, Melbourne: Longman Cheshire, 163–83.
3   See P. Adams, (1988) 'Per Os(cillation)', *Camera Obscura* 17: 17–29. See also *Camera Obscura* (1989) 20–21, special issue 'The Spectatrix', for a range of statements by feminist film theorists on this issue.

Bibliography

Anon (1867/8) 'Women's Novels', *Broadway Annual*, 504–11.
Baudry, J.-L. (1974/1986) 'Ideological Effects of the Basic Cinematographic Apparatus', in P. Rosen (ed.) (1986) *Narrative, Apparatus, Ideology*, New York: Columbia University Press, 286–9.
Bayn, N. (1978) *Woman's Fiction*, Ithaca, NY and London: Cornell University Press.
Black, H. (1906) *Notable Women Authors of the Day*, London: Maclaren.
Carey, Rosa Nouchette (1889) *Merle's Crusade*, London: Religious Tract Society.
—— (1905) *The Household of Peter*, London: Macmillan & Co.
Cowie, E. (1984) 'Fantasia' *m/f* 9, 71–105.

Crisp, J. (1989) *Rosa Nouchette Carey*, St Lucia (Australia): Victorian Fiction Research Unit, University of Queensland.

—— (1993) 'Enhancing Communication with People with Alzheimer's', *Australian Journal of Communication* 20, 1: 63–70.

—— (1995) 'Les Conceptions de la démence: différents modàles de discours sur les déments', *Psychologie Médicale*, 27, 3: 180–83.

Culler, J. (1983) *On Deconstruction*, London: Routledge & Kegan Paul.

Dickens, C. (1894) 'A Century of Feminine Fiction', *All the Year Round* 3, 12: 537–40.

Ellis, J. (1982) *Visible Fictions*, London: Routledge & Kegan Paul.

Freud, S. (1977) *Three Essays on the Theory of Sexuality*, Harmondsworth: Penguin.

Gilbert, S. and Gubar, S. (1979) *The Madwoman in the Attic: the Woman Writer and the Nineteenth Century Literary Imagination*, New Haven and London: Yale University Press.

Gledhill, C. (1988) 'Pleasurable Negotiations', in E.D. Pribram (ed.) *Female Spectators*, London: Verso, 64–89.

Houston, B. (1984) 'Viewing Television: The Metapsychology of Endless Consumption', *Quarterly Review of Film Studies* 9, 3: 183–95.

Kaplan, S.J. (1985) 'Varieties of Feminist Criticism', in G. Greene and C. Kahn (eds) *Making a Difference: Feminist Literary Criticism*, London and New York: Routledge: 37–58.

Kolodny, A. (1986) 'A Map for Rereading', in E. Showalter (ed.) *The New Feminist Criticism*, London: Virago, 46–62.

Kristeva, J. (1986) 'Revolution in Poetic Language', in T. Moi (ed.) *The Kristeva Reader*, Oxford: Basil Blackwell, 90–136.

Lacan, J. (1966) 'Le Stade du miroir comme formateur de la fonction du Je', *Écrits*, vol. 1, Paris: Seuil, 89–97.

Metz, C. (1982) *The Imaginary Signifier: Psychoanalysis and Cinema*, London: Macmillan.

Miller, N. (1988) *Subject to Change*, New York: Columbia University Press.

Moers, E. (1979) *Literary Women*, London: Women's Press.

Mulvey, L. (1975) 'Visual Pleasure and Narrative Cinema', *Screen* 16, 3: 6–18.

—— (1977–8) 'Notes on Sirk and Melodrama', in C. Gledhill (ed.) *Home is Where the Heart Is*, London: British Film Institute, 1987, 75–9.

Oudart, J.-P. (1977–8) 'Cinema and Suture', *Screen* 18, 4: 35–47.

Penley, C. (1985) 'Feminism, Film Theory and the Bachelor Machines', *m/f* 10: 39-59.

Radway, J. (1987) *Reading the Romance*, London: Verso.

Schor, N. (1987) *Reading in Detail*, London: Methuen.

Sherman, B. (1991) *Dementia with Dignity*, Sydney: McGraw-Hill.

Showalter, E. (1977) *A Literature of Their Own*, London: Virago.

——(1986) 'Towards a Feminist Poetics', in *The New Feminist Criticism*, London: Virago, 125–43.

Silverman, K. (1988a) *The Acoustic Mirror: The Female Voice in Psychoanalysis and Cinema*, Bloomington: Indiana University Press.

—— (1988b) 'Masochism and Male Subjectivity', *Camera Obscura* 17: 31–66.

Spacks, P.M. (1985) *Gossip*, New York: Knopf.

Tompkins, J. (1989) 'Me and My Shadow', in L. Kauffman (ed.) *Gender and Theory*, Oxford: Basil Blackwell, 121–39.

Williams, L. (1984) 'When the Woman Looks', in M. Doane, P. Mellencamp and L. Williams (eds) *Re-vision*, Los Angeles: University Press of America/AFI, 83–99.

—— (1987) 'Something Else Besides a Mother: Stella Dallas and the Maternal Melodrama', in C. Gledhill (ed.) *Home is Where the Heart Is*, London: British Film Institute, 299–325.

Zimmerman, B. (1985) 'What Has Never Been: An Overview of Lesbian Feminist Criticism', in G. Greene and C. Kahn (eds) *Making a Difference: Feminist Literary Criticism*, London and New York, Routledge, 177–210.

7 'A sentiment as certain as remembrance'

Photography, loss and belonging

Kay Ferres

In a caress what is sought is sought as though it were not there, as though the skin were a trace of its own withdrawal

> (Emmanuel Levinas,*Otherwise Than Being or Beyond Existence, 1981*)

She, so belov'd, that from a single lyre

more mourning rose than from all women-mourners, –

that a whole world of mourning rose, wherein

all things were once more present

> (Rainer Maria Rilke, 'Orpheus. Eurydice. Hermes', 1967)

I keep two relics of my childhood home stored away: a pair of china bookends and a studio photograph. The bookends remind me of my father reading. They were a birthday gift to him from my mother. Though I still find them beautiful, they are not tasteful objects. Fashioned as horses' heads, their glaze resembles the iridescence of carnival glass. The photograph is of my mother, in black crepe, supporting my older brother, whose head is slumped forward in the way babies' heads do. His age and her clothes indicate that the photograph was taken early in 1944, when my father was away from home on army service. The three people associated with these objects are all dead, yet for me their presence can still be felt, if no longer known, through these things. In his study of the photograph, *Camera Lucida*, Roland Barthes tells how, after his mother's death, he sought to restore her to memory, to find her again, in photographs:

> Photography thereby compelled me to perform a painful labour; straining toward the essence of her identity, I was struggling among images partially true, and therefore totally false. To say, confronted with a certain photograph, 'That's the way she was!' was more distressing than to say, confronted with another, 'That's not the way she was at all.' The *almost*: love's dreadful regime, but also the dream's disappointing status ...

> (Barthes 1984: 66)

One photograph, found for the first time after her death, answers his need for a 'just image' and supplies his grief with 'a sentiment as certain as remembrance'. The 'Winter Garden Photograph' shows his mother as a child, posed with her brother in a conservatory. In it he finds unmistakable traces of her looks and character, in a figure he has never seen.

The possibilities of reproduction offered by photographic technology, and the rapid refinement which saw the camera become widely available, has made the photograph central to the constitution of the family and domestic life. Photography democratised access to culture and made the production of personal artefacts and histories possible. The circulation of photographs has played a part in binding family relationships across space and time. Photographic evidence supplements oral testimony and failing recollections to lay down memory and family history as populations have dispersed across the globe.

To take a photograph is to attempt to capture an object or feeling, to hold something in the here and now, to make it persist. The photograph is both icon and narrative. Like the caress, it seeks 'an absence that could not be more there', an other that is an 'alterer' of the subject who looks at it (Mavor 1995: 48–9). The photograph's arrested moment is a stay against the passage of time. In the photograph as *memento mori*, lost things are once more present. Or *almost* present, *almost* recognisable. The space of the 'almost' is a space of hesitation between disappointment and hope, between loss and longing, between memory and history. It is the space of narratives of return and belonging and of new beginnings and new futures.

Nineteenth-century European imperial expansion produced a class of émigrés, colonial officials who settled and established new societies while still looking backward to the home they had left. During the twentieth century, particularly the years after the Second World War, political refugees comprised a distinct category of displaced persons. Significant diasporas now exist in the former empires as well as in the New World. As Edward Said has observed, exile has emerged as a *topos* of human experience in the literature of the twentieth century, alongside the literature of adventure, education and discovery which accompanied urbanisation, industrialisation and imperialist expansion in the nineteenth (Said 1990: 364).

Homelessness, dislocation and migration are experiences widely shared; re-establishing a sense of belonging has become a project not only for displaced and marginalised groups but also for public-policy makers. Cultural production is critical to the task of reassembling identities and to remaking a habitus. This chapter will review the ways photography is used to commemorate loss and to transform it, whether through the 'indefinitely postponed drama of return' (Said 1990: 361) or through imagining new places of belonging.

Lingering glances: looking at photographs

In *Camera Lucida* Barthes discusses two genres of documentary photographs: 'family snaps' and news photographs. He finds in both a common structure.

These signs have two components, which he names the 'studium' and the 'punctum'. These components exist in a kind of tension. The studium puts us in the picture, supplying a context of interpretation. The punctum makes us look again, or look deeper. It 'pierces' or reorders relations among elements of the image and unsettles the distance between object and viewer. The photograph that interests Barthes is the one which interpellates its viewer in an immediate and emotional way, inviting a lingering glance. It answers this look with uncertainty and doubt. His own experience of uncertainty and privation – his habitation of the space of the *almost* – is most poignant in Barthes' discussion of photographs of his mother.

The 'triumphant mimesis' of the photograph, however, has evoked ambivalence from the outset. In *A Short History of the Shadow*, Victor Stoichita describes a history of representation from the earliest attempts to reproduce the image of the human body by tracing an outline from a projected shadow. A persistent feature of these representations is that they bear the imprint of their maker: a hand, an implement, later a signature. Photographic processes erased this mark. The image was produced by mechanically mimicking the workings of perception and by a chemical process. An engraving produced in Paris in 1839 caricatured this miraculous process. Stoichita comments on this split image, which juxtaposes a black illegible print with a drawing representing the technical process of its production:

> What it expresses is without a doubt the ironic and sceptical viewpoint of an academically trained draughtsman of this new technique of reproducing reality. Through the medium of caricature, Cham discourses on the illusions of the triumphant mimesis to reveal its other side: the nothingness of the image produced by the indiscriminate recording of optical perception.
>
> (Stoichita 1997: 189)

Stoichita argues that the photograph recapitulates Platonic uncertainties about how images relate to the 'real' or material world (Stoichita 1997: 192). Like Barthes, he notes how the world of objects and the world of images appear to merge in the photograph. The way Barthes describes this is to say that the referent 'adheres', closing over the space between signifier and signified that was opened out in the theories of semioticians working with language. In his analysis the punctum serves to reintroduce that space of uncertainty or indeterminacy. Barthes' discussion has been widely taken up within cultural studies, where semiotics has driven textual interpretation. His association of the photograph with death and loss has also appealed to scholars interested in the formation of sexual identities, for example Carol Mavor (1995) and D.A. Miller (1992). Working within the discipline of art history, Stoichita sees it differently. Though the photograph appears to re-produce the object, in fact it 'redoubles' everything: it opens up 'the infinite sequence of all possible reproductions' (Stoichita 1997: 195).

These different 'takes' on the photograph show how different disciplinary formations produce different objects of representation. Where Barthes tries to distinguish between the look of the cinema and the look of the photograph, between the camera obscura and the camera lucida, Stoichita locates the photograph in a different field of visual culture. Discussion of visual cultures has been dominated by film theorists and by a now well-established critique of Cartesian perspectivalism. However, as Martin Jay has shown, visual culture is more heterogeneous than this critique allows. Jay suggests that looking had been organised in at least three ways in visual arts traditions: he associates Cartesian perspectivalism with the Italian Renaissance; the 'art of describing', with Dutch painting; and identifies the Baroque as a third system (Jay 1988). Because the photograph is so identified with mass culture, its participation in these visual arts regimes may be overlooked. Although commentators have looked beyond the text, to the 'diversity of practices, institutions and historical conjunctures in which [it] is produced, circulated and deployed' (Hall 1991: 152), its history is somewhat foreshortened by its association with mass culture and the cinema.

The discussion of the production, circulation and deployment of photographic texts that follows takes its point of departure from Barthes. Its focus, however, is less on loss and privation than on the way photographs are deployed in reconstituting relationships and futures: 'Such is the power of the photograph, of the image, that it can give back and take away, that it can bind' (hooks 1995: 56). I want to examine the way photographs circulate, not only in the private context of the family but within groups of displaced people, immigrants and refugees, not only to reinforce ethnic identities but to produce new configurations of identity and belonging as well as new relationships to the past.

Keepsakes

Photographs leave a poignant and sometimes painful trace of the negotiation of new identities. bell hooks and Stuart Hall argue that the images of black people that circulate in cultures still marked by slavery, segregation and colonial power cannot be read simply in terms of the imposition of a white ideology or aesthetic. Analysis of the meanings attaching to texts, practices and institutions needs to be attentive to common historical and political contexts differentially occupied and stratified. hooks speaks of an aesthetic space between the image and herself; Hall constructs a social and political itinerary through which the infinite sequence of reproductions travel.

bell hooks examines the place of photography and representation in black life and politics in the segregated society in which she lives. She articulates an oppositional aesthetic which celebrates black culture 'in its glory'. Although she rejects the 'stereotyped and colonising imagery' that circulates in mass culture and advertising, the contemporary culture she celebrates is very much a hybrid and contested one.

Her discussion is structured around the problem of loss, the gaps and absences in official histories as well as personal ones. What does it mean *not to have* a photographic record of a black history of slavery? What does it mean to have lost photographs which represent important attachments to others and to oneself? Within domestic space, collections of photographs compose partial genealogies, and the arrangement of family portraits form altars to commemorate the dead and to provide a locus of ritual observance. The lack of photographic technology when slavery ended has meant that African Americans are without a means of recognising lost family members and of restoring familial links.

This privation is brought closer to home in hooks' longing for a missing photograph of her father. She feels a particular attachment to this photograph, which shows her father 'in his glory'. He has posed in a pool hall, dressed in a white T-shirt. His body and his boldness are open to the camera and to the photographer, clearly someone he 'cared for – deeply'. hooks' pleasure in it derives from this: she interposes herself into the space of intimacy 'between the image and myself', which Barthes also occupies. She does not own the photograph or know its history. It was given to the daughter he was closest to, 'daddy's girl'. hooks asks for a copy but is not given one. Finally, a third sister, who recoils from its evident signs of class and sexuality, hands the photograph on. She has no taste for it or for the father with no class, who displays himself in his undershirt. The circuits of power and desire inscribed by these exchanges shape social and sexual identifications within a family and society where segregation, though broken down, has yet to disappear.

In 'Reconstruction Work', Stuart Hall explores a historiographical problem and develops a politics of reading. Examining a rich and varied archive of photographs (news shots, studio portraits, posters and advertising), he reconstructs a history of immigration. An historical, as opposed to historicist, account of the circulation and deployment of these images produces readings that subtly expose the transformations of identity that immigration entails. History leaves behind 'cultural signposts and multiaccented traces'. What is lost from the perspective of the present is the 'inventory' (Hall 1991: 157). Hall sets out to supply the inventory, locating these texts in a complex field of representation.

The archive provides a photographic record of a 'passage' from Jamaica to Britain. The stages of this passage are marked by the arrival halls where immigrants are processed and redirected by the new contexts of work and family life, more or less successfully negotiated, and by the imaginary return to the places and families left behind. Each of these stages is marked by different photographic genres. The passage is not a straightforward narrative of exchanging one kind of colonialism for another. 'Slavery, colonisation and colonialism locked us all – them (you) and us (them) – into a common but unequal, uneven, history, into the same symbolic and representational frames' (Hall 1991: 157). Hall describes the complexities of positioning us all – not just immigrants – in this frame.

In the liminal space of 'arrival', Hall deciphers the 'innocence' that is constructed through the expectation and anticipation of the moment, and by the formality and respectability of the travellers' dress and appearance. This formality is referenced to the urban culture from which most Jamaican migrants came. Their formality is a sign of self-respect, as well as style. It does not connote abject or 'primitive' innocence in its 'Sunday best'. The decision to come to Britain entailed the immense sacrifice of tearing up roots and leaving family, as well as risky financial investment in a new life. Their 'innocence' is about what this new identity will mean in a racist Britain. The photojournalistic frame is indexed to a social democratic realism that produces immigrants as a social problem – they present as a population to be managed. Realism, however, is not only or simply organised around a fixed scrutinising gaze classifying its objects. It needs to be understood as capable of moving among positions, and able to incorporate repositionings.

The 'high-street' photo-portrait marks a different stage of 'arrival' and offers an alternative tradition to 'social problem' documentary. This tradition can do little with the problems and issues it exposes, apart from 'summon[ing] up a concern which made powerful claims on our humanism'. By contrast, the 'high-street' portraits display a newly adopted persona. They exist as 'evidence', to be sent back home, of 'arriving' and prospering. To read these images as evidence of a simple-minded complicity with 'white' codes is to ignore immigrants' invest-ments in the signs of successful passage: 'the codes of respectability and of respect were every bit as powerful, and as complex, amongst black people in post-Victorian colonial Jamaica as they were in post-Victorian colonising Britain' (Hall 1991: 157).

Mourning and nostalgia

Photographs bring back the past in ways that re-engage our emotional attach-ments to lost objects and to the larger abstractions – community, 'nation' – in which they are embedded. We look back to shared times and places. Conjuring the past in this way accentuates an absence in the present, and in a future we project. This absence may evoke nostalgia or mourning. Here I want to consider these two dispositions to loss and to the uses of memory in the present.

Barthes sees a 'rather terrible thing' in every photograph: 'the return of the dead' (Barthes 1984: 9). Technology has made this terror both more immediate and more banal. At the level of the personal, backward looks are morbid or self-indulgent at worst and futile at best. Nostalgia stages this return not as redemption but as misrecognition or misrepresentation. Things are no longer as they were, but they never were as we remember them.

The story of Orpheus' grief for Eurydice captures the exquisite agonies of grief-work, as Orpheus' impulse to 'hold on' betrays him. This myth has taken many forms, from medieval 'lays' or songs to the earliest appearance of opera. The story celebrates the powers of art. Orpheus' music is so sublime that the gods agree to release his wife from death, on the condition that Orpheus goes ahead of her and does not look back. But he turns, and Eurydice is lost.

In 'Orpheus. Eurydice. Hermes'(1967), Rainer Maria Rilke imagines those fraught moments, as Orpheus' trust wavers. Walking ahead of his wife and her escort Hermes, Orpheus is nervous. His gaze, like a wandering dog, anxiously searches the path before him and returns to his feet. His sense of smell casts backward, seeking the two who walk silently behind. In Rilke's version, Eurydice is already lost, even before his fateful backward look. Death has absorbed her, and she, like a pregnant woman, is 'wrapt in herself, like one whose time is near'. Orpheus' backward look is fatal not simply because it defies the gods' prohibition, but because it breaches the distance that love requires. Gillian Rose expresses this idea with illuminating clarity: 'The Lovers must leave a distance, a boundary, for love' (Rose 1995: 133). The object of mourning is to restore that distance, whereas nostalgia aims to dissolve it.

In Freud's account, mourning is a 'passionate or hyper-remembering … a dizzying phantasmagoria of memory' (Kuhn 1995: 105). Annette Kuhn returns to Freud's account of dreamwork to analyse the operations (displacement, substitution and condensation) she performs on the texts she reads together: a photograph of St Paul's taken during the Blitz, the Ministry of Information's documentary, *Listen to Britain* (1942), Derek Jarman's *The Last of England* (1987) and the painting of the same title by Ford Madox Brown (c. 1852–5). Each of these texts calls up a lost object – 'England' or the 'nation' – in order to offer new identifications and to reorient habitus: the reactions they evoke are about the loss not of a loved one but of 'some abstraction which has taken the place of one'. According to Kuhn, memory work connects private and public worlds – crosses over between the personal and the historical, social and political.

Kuhn demonstrates this in a discussion of the way her own sense of 'belonging' is evoked by representations of 'England' and a lost past. Although she consciously resists the pull of nostalgia, nevertheless her recognition of landmarks and icons elicits an emotional response. Her 'take' on the phantasmagoria emphasises the emotional state these projections evoke – a kind of reverie, rather than a 'fevered condition' – and the 'illusory' quality of the images projected, rather than their 'historical' referentiality. Her 'acts of memory' are performed to tease out the different interpellations assumed by nostalgic longing and a sense of belonging.

Screen images of familiar places call up her own sense of place, and the way her itineraries map out that part of central London where she works and lives. In turn, her images of these places – the steps of the British Museum, the passageway through Senate House, the plane trees in Great Russell Street – work their way into her viewing. Familiar objects are displaced from their actual location to the texts, so that, for example, the steps of the museum substitute for the National Gallery in her rememberings of the film text. 'Her' view momentarily dislodges the camera's position. Like bell hooks, she interposes herself in the space between the image and the camera. Kuhn's focus is on the way these images interpellate her – on their affects as well as their meanings. Her emotional engagement and the sense of 'recognition' they inspire is imported into her present experience as she walks the streets, mapping that part of London she regards as her 'territory'.

Memory, she suggests, is better understood as a point of view in the present than as nostalgic immersion in the past. 'Perhaps it is only when we look back that we make a certain kind of sense of what we see?' (Kuhn 1995: 108). The familiar is constructed out of images and experiences (of which we have no direct knowledge) as much as out of our immediate surroundings. A sense of belonging arises out of the way those images are drawn in to our itineraries in the present.

Histories and futures

Memory has particular work to do in diasporic cultures, where 'ethnic' identities are grafted on to new locations, and where belonging exists in a tension with displacement:

> And just beyond the frontier between 'us' and the 'outsiders' is the perilous territory of not-belonging: this is to where in a primitive time peoples were banished, and where in the modern era immense aggregates of humanity loiter as refugees and displaced persons.
>
> (Said 1990: 359)

For the generation who are born into the new place, this territory takes on other contours. They negotiate their parents' memories as well as their own. This discussion introduces a series of such negotiations, taking up with three different kinds of memoir: Eva Hoffman's autobiography *Lost in Translation* (1989/1998), Mark Baker's documentary history *A Journey through Memory: The Fiftieth Gate* (1997) and two series of photographs by Chris Barry, 'Displaced Objects' and 'Lost in Translation' (1992).

Eva Hoffman left Cracow at 13, for Canada. In 1957, the ban on emigration from Poland was lifted for Jews. These migrations were departures 'neither entirely chosen nor entirely forced and that are chosen and forced at the same time' (Hoffman 1989/1998: 83). The family went to Vancouver rather than Israel, and from there Eva was educated in the United States. Her family's stories of the people taken away to the camps, and of their own narrow escapes, populated her childhood with ghosts. Her younger sister is named for one of them, Alina, the sister whom their mother 'can't stop thinking about'. Alina exists as 'my mother's most alive pain' (Hoffman 1989/1998: 6). 'The man who saw her go into the gas chamber said that she was among those who had to dig their own graves, and that her hair turned gray before her death' (Hoffman 1989/1998: 6–7). By contrast, Hoffman's father's memories do not become part of this family story. It is not until she is an adult and has left their new home in Vancouver that she becomes aware of her father's lost brother. A rift is introduced here, cutting through the consolations of memory work.

Lost in Translation commemorates Hoffman's attachment to Cracow:

> the country of my childhood lives within me with a primacy that is a form of love. … Insofar as we retain the capacity for attachment, the energy of desire that draws us towards the world and makes us want to live within it, we're always returning.
>
> (1989/1998: 74–5)

The first part of the book reconstructs this world as a 'Paradise', a place one is banished from. The backward look here is filled with longing. Hoffman's word for it is 'tęsknota', 'a word that adds to nostalgia the tonalities of sadness and longing' (Hoffman 1989/1998: 4). This meaning and the old existence are 'lost' in translation: 'lost' in its two senses of 'missing' and 'absorbed in' (Zournazi 1998: 20). Hoffman's exile is a kind of 'loitering' in between languages – a perilous territory where reactions are always delayed as meaning sinks in; where 'lack' is signified by the laugh that comes too late, responses that don't chime; or where attempts to convey the texture of experience are met with blank indifference.

Those losses are partially redeemed by a return visit, and by the appearance of remainders of Poland in everyday life. One such event is a meeting with a childhood friend, now a concert violinist. A photograph unearthed from a small cache of memory reconstitutes the old familiarity. The two girls are posed with Alinka, all three wearing daisy wreaths in their hair, on a day that Hoffman remembers 'quite distinctly'. Zofia, the violinist and Eva, the writer, search for the past in the photograph.

A new generation of descendants of Holocaust survivors has no bodily memories of ancestors – no physical points of identification (voice, gesture, gait, expression) between those people in the past and themselves. In many cases, the only remainders are the widely circulated images of the camp inmates, dressed in the awful garb of stripes, with hollow faces and fixed looks. All the markers of identity – except as Jews – are removed. There are no graves; not even dates of death. At what remains of Treblinka, the field has markers of place of origin:

> Where once stood flower beds, barbed wire fences, residential barracks and a concrete temple whose doors beckoned almost one million Jews, there is grass, there are trees and there are stones. Boulders are scattered throughout the field, hundreds of them, human forms in stony relief, each bearing the name of a village or a city whose residents once visited this location. It is now a commemorative site, no longer the place where men and women and children and grandparents huddled before the gates of the temple whose entrance mocked its visitors with the biblical inscription: 'This is the gate of God through which the righteous shall enter.'
>
> (Baker 1997: 11–12)

These markers evoke the scale of loss for future generations, but do not identify the individuals who met dreadful deaths here. Jewish people use stones as markers of grief on graves, not flowers. But these boulders don't have bones beneath them and, in any case, these martyred people are 'expelled into the borderless cemetery of the air, for the soil of the death camps is cursed not consecrated ground' (Rose 1995: 10). Some survivors, like Mark Baker's father, see no reason to visit: 'No one who was there returns' (Baker 1997: 13). In *Facing the Extreme*, Tzvetan Todorov discusses the enduring guilt of survivors, distinguishing the different kinds of shame that result from the humiliation and abjection experienced in the camps. There is shame in remembering that abjection and guilt because of the belief, as Primo Levi puts it, 'that the others died in your place, that you're alive gratis' (Todorov 1991/1999: 264). Yossl Bekiermaszyns resists his son Mark Baker's disturbance of his memories and forgettings.

For Baker, born in Melbourne and growing up in its Jewish community in Caulfield and Carlton, both personal and professional impulses drive him to excavate the archives and to record his parents' experience. As a historian, he pursues the 'fecks' his father has little time for. He recovers the personal histories of incarceration and death that the countless undifferentiated photographs of inmates obscure. As a son of survivors, he collects documents to supplement albums of family photographs. The few remaining images of his parents' prewar existence are black and white, and this monochrome becomes the colour of childhood memory too:

> I first appear in a red album. … My mother is throwing me into the sky, smiling at me. I don't know why I should think of that memory as a colourless moment. I presume the sky was deep blue, my hair blonder than that shade of grey, my mother's lips polished in red hues applied with the aid of a hand mirror. When I walk along the beachfront suburb of my childhood, the orange-brick flats and the tree-lined streets still lose their colour. All that remains is a landscape of shadows. I sometimes see my children this way, observing them at play in black and white fragments as if they were photographs of myself resurrected from a forgotten flash. When my father revisited Auschwitz, the wintry sky and the foggy air seemed to conspire with death's past, burying his tour beneath a mist of greyness.
>
> (Baker 1997: 32–3)

Baker's remembering is a kind of expiation. He takes a Jewish name, adding 'Raphael' to his historian's persona. His journey into memory reaches the 'fiftieth gate': the gate to the highest understanding (memory or oblivion? blessing or curse?). His object is to integrate identities, his Australian present and his parents' past. His father's past can be retrieved from the historical record and is more intact, as an artefact of the archive, than his mother's. Even so, Baker's training as a historian makes something of the dismal 'fecks' his father would prefer to forget.

Chris Barry, another Australian born child of Polish immigrants, also goes to Poland to 'make a claim, to reckon with the concrete shadows of my history'. Barry was born Krystyna Marczak in Melbourne in 1954. Her work is a multi-layered assemblage of photographs, found objects, text, paint and other elements, rephotographed to produce a glossy surface. The two series that concern me here, 'Displaced Objects' (1986 and 1996) and 'Lost in Translation' (1992), represent her personal and family history and the cultural dislocation central to migrant experience. These sequences have something of the character of bell hooks' family altars, creating personal genealogies as a means of ensuring against losses of the past (hooks 1995: 62). But they are not purely personal. The extended family is located in a political, not merely a cultural, context. The dislocations figured in these photographs are very specific. Though they partially evoke the sense of exile Edward Said describes as 'the unhealable rift between a human being and a native place, between the self and its true home: its essential sadness can never be surmounted' (Said 1990: 357), they also register ambivalence.

The photographs refer not only to this 'true home' and to the tęsknota that is so powerful in Hoffman's text, but they also take account of the present state of the homeland and of the political contexts of Australia in the postwar period of mass immigration. Barry's parents arrived in Australia in 1950. Immigrants coming to Australia in this period of the 'White Australia' policy were drawn from Europe and included significant numbers of displaced persons as well as large groups from Greece and Italy. By 1949, more 'aliens' than British migrants were being admitted. At the same time, the Immigration Restriction Act, which remained in force until the late 1960s, excluded non-Europeans. 'Assimilation' was the objective of immigration policy at this time, and public opinion favoured British migrants. Identification with Britain was still strong: the Nationality and Citizenship Act (1948) defined 'aliens' as those who were not British subjects, Irish citizens or protected persons. Australian citizens were still also British subjects until 1973.

'New Australians' contributed to postwar reconstruction, working on vast projects like the Snowy River scheme. Various forms of discrimination worked against the publicly proclaimed doctrine of 'assimilation'. There was overt discrimination in the provision of public housing and there were restrictions on private land ownership. Labour unions feared that immigrant workers would tolerate poorer pay and conditions than Australian workers. Opposition to immigration was strong in left-dominated unions like the Miners' Federation, which had attempted to ban Poles from working in mines in 1948. Fears that immigrant labour would diminish conditions were one dimension of hostility; another was suspicion of fascism. Since the 1970s, 'multiculturalism' has replaced 'assimilation' as a policy objective. Cultural and ethnic differences are now officially recognised, to the extent that those differences consist in such things as customs, dress, dance and food. Chris Barry's work recognises the limits of this definition of 'difference'.

Barry's works feature family photographs, found objects, newspaper clippings, representing the family's history in Australia. Their 'ethnic' identity is evident in their appearance and in the domestic objects. But 'ethnicity' is not only indexed to the past and to the place they have left: the markers of difference are also constructed from Australian culture and politics. 'Half Life' incorporates the genre of the family portrait, superimposed with strands of barbed wire and with Australian flags in the lower corners. A framed portrait of old men emerges from the centre of a torn outline of Australia in 'Epitaph'. The torn edges of newspaper employment columns and human skulls suggest the trajectory of refugee history.

Figure 2 'Half Life'

Source: Taken from the series 'Displaced Objects' (1986/1996), by Chris Barry

During an extended visit to Poland, Barry also sees what it is to be an Australian of Polish extraction. The series 'Lost in Translation' reverses Eva Hoffman's migration. It makes an elegiac gesture towards the old culture, destroyed first by the war, then by Russian occupation, and finally by the massive inflow of capital that followed the collapse of the Soviet Union. 'Nocturne' recreates this location and comments on the homogenisation of Polish cities, standing behind the signs of consumer culture. Where does this new Poland leave the memories and the past that migrants had left behind, imported with them to Australia? Where does it leave the 'ethnic' identifications of the generation of Polish Australians? 'Puppet' poses just these questions. A small girl in richly coloured 'ethnic' costume, wearing a wreath in her hair just like the young Eva, is posed against a background of crumbling buildings and rubble, suspended by puppets' strings. The question of whether these strings refer to attachments to the old or the new culture remains open. The buildings signify the decay of the past and the rupture of war; the awkwardly posed child signifies the kind of ethnicity demanded by the new culture.

Figure 3 'Puppet'

Source: Taken from the series 'Lost in Translation' (1992), by Chris Barry

Barry's images do not represent the position of the migrant simply as marginal or alienated. 'Cargo' features a young woman in a swimsuit, posed on a beach, surrounded by left-over party streamers. Small black-and-white family portraits in the centre gesture to history and the past; a postcard and palm trees, to the sybaritic new life. The beach is the essential Australian locale, a point acknowledged by the watery outline of the map in the sand. Just as Annette Kuhn substitutes her own perceptions for images in Jarman's film, so I find myself making a similar substitution whenever I see this image. The young woman's dark features mark her European origins, but the style of her costume and her hair distinctly reminds me of Ava Gardner. This resemblance cautions against a too-optimistic reading of the image as an embrace of Australian culture. Gardner's comment, when in Melbourne to film *On the Beach*, that this was the perfect location to make a movie about the end of the world, has been engraved on popular memory.

Figure 4   'Cargo'

Source: Taken from the series 'Displaced Objects' (1986/1996), by Chris Barry

Commemoration and public culture

The importance of commemoration has become a compelling trope in contemporary culture. Public memorials and ceremonies perform an expiation and have become the catalysts of public debate about history. The Truth and Reconciliation Commission in South Africa, the Vietnam memorial in Washington DC, and the sites of the concentration camps in Poland – all these have generated a discussion of the uses of history in the present. These memorials do not sublimate grief: they call it forth for the people whose names are engraved on their polished surfaces, from the people who stand reflected before them. Mourning, unlike nostalgia, is a process which achieves separation. It brings us, rather than the lost object, into the present. It is a process which requires artefacts – photographs, graves, memorials, elegies and rituals.

Public memorialisation has been called upon to incite a kind of grief-work and to achieve reconciliation. In Washington, the Vietnam memorial is a gash in the soil. The black-granite wall lining one side records the name of every one of that war's dead. Visitors cannot avoid seeing their own shadows reflected back to them from the surface. Other museums have devised strategies to incorporate the visitor into their narratives, using ordinary objects as curiosities in their exhibitions. These images 'pierce' in the manner of Barthes' punctum, inviting the glance to linger.

I have lingered over this series of snapshots – for other people's photographs are every bit as fascinating as our own. We are not only captivated by our personal histories, or caught up in nostalgic longing. I first became interested in photographs when I picked up Carol Mavor's *Pleasures Taken* (1995), and read there of her childish performances as Alice. Her discussion of Levinas' observation about the caress stayed with me. Like the caress, the lingering glance enacts an attempt to cross the boundary between self and other, even as it acknowledges that the boundary exists. 'No human being possesses *sureness of self*: this can only mean being bounded and unbounded, selved and unselved, "sure" only of this untiring exercise' (Rose 1995: 125).

Bibliography

Baker, M.R. (1997) *A Journey through Memory: The Fiftieth Gate*, Sydney: Flamingo.

Barry, C. (1992) 'Lost in Translation', exhibition catalogue, Centre of Contemporary Art, Warsaw.

Barthes, R. (1984) *Camera Lucida*, London, Fontana.

Hall, S. (1991) 'Reconstruction Work: Images of Post-War Black Settlement', in J. Spence and P. Holland (eds) *Family Snaps: The Meanings of Domestic Photography*, London: Virago, 152–64.

Hoffman, E. (1989/1998) *Lost in Translation: A Life in a New Language*, London: Vintage.

hooks, b. (1995) 'In Our Glory: Photography and Black Life', *Art on My Mind: Visual Politics*, New York: The New Press, 54–64.

Jay, M. (1988) 'Scopic Regimes of Modernity', in H. Foster (ed.) *Vision and Visuality*, Seattle: Bay Press, 3–23.

Kuhn, A. (1995) *Family Secrets: Acts of Memory and Imagination*, London: Verso.

Levinas, E. (1981) *Otherwise Than Being or Beyond Existence*, trans. Alphonso Lingis, The Hague: Martinus Nijhoff.

Mavor, C. (1995) *Pleasures Taken: Performances of Sexuality and Loss in Victorian Photographs*, Durham and London: Duke University Press.

Miller, D.A. (1992) *Bringing Out Roland Barthes*, Berkeley: University of California Press.

Rilke, R.M. (1967) *Selected Works* vol 2, *Poetry*, trans. J.B. Leishman, London: Hogarth Press.

Rose, G. (1995) *Love's Work*, London: Chatto and Windus.

Said, E. (1990) 'Reflections on Exile', in R. Ferguson, M. Gever, T. T. Minh-ha and C. West (eds) *Out There: Marginalisation and Contemporary Cultures*, Cambridge, MA: MIT Press, 357–66.

Stoichita, V.I. (1997) *A Short History of the Shadow*, London: Reaktion Books.

Todorov, T. (1991/1999) *Facing the Extreme: Moral Life in the Concentration Camps*, London: Weidenfeld and Nicolson.

Zournazi, M. (1998) 'Life in a New Language – Eva Hoffman', *Foreign Dialogues: Memories, Translations, Conversations*, Sydney: Pluto Press, 17–26.

8 Locomotive stomachs and downcast looks

Urban pathology and the destabilised body

Gillian Swanson

Competing representations: knowledge, classification and legibility

In Chapter 5, I examined the historical formation of the concept of the individual self, and how this intersected with systems of sexual difference, looking at the way cultural subjectivity became defined and read in culturally specific styles of living, habits, taste and feeling. This showed that our contemporary notions of subjectivity developed in association with a particular form of social organisation consolidated from the end of the eighteenth century – that which aligned femininity with private life and masculinity with the public world of the citizen. The concepts of subjectivity that are articulated in these everyday cultures, however, are also produced in texts which circulate within particular institutional contexts: as such, they endow certain definitions of social and sexual difference with a particular *authority* through their association with the validated disciplines of knowledge. It is these disciplines – including medicine, the law and the social sciences, among others – which are deployed in the government of populations, and which develop definitions of the gendered individual as a way of making this population knowable and hence manageable. You will remember Chartier's argument that representations 'order' and 'classify' reality, and that to understand how this process of ordering occurs, we have also to examine the ways that they become 'anchored' to the social practices and institutions which adopt their systems of order and classification. Representations and their systems of *intellectual* ordering, in other words, are part of a larger system of *social* ordering, in which conceptual frameworks and definitions are put into play and have material effects.

This chapter will look at the way that cultural *knowledges* – and the way they are drawn upon by various institutions, such as medicine and the law – intersect with cultural *practices*: how forms of sexual knowledge are used as frameworks that govern the activities and practices of our everyday interactions and activities, and the way that this allows a space for sexual relations and identities to be enacted. How do definitions of sexual difference become produced, and how are they given legitimacy in a range of representational forms?

Representations have material effects – functioning as ways of knowing the world – and therefore act as templates for social interaction. The forms of knowledge that we think by are in turn part of the 'environment' of subjectivity that I discussed in Chapter 5. How are these made systematic, and how do frameworks of meaning become legitimated? If cultural practices take on meanings according to the way they develop a certain pattern in the historical organisation and hierarchising of social life, so too is there a pattern to the forms by which representation and communication between social subjects take place. One important way this pattern can be analysed is by tracing the way social institutions employ certain bodies of knowledge in order to construct definitions and classifications which help in 'ordering' the social world. As Paula Treichler argues, some definitions of childbirth are given social authority – within the law, within medical knowledge and practice, within government policy – but these are changeable, and competing (or 'rival') representations may exist. However, we need to understand how authoritative definitions work:

> Childbirth in the United States takes place in hospitals because a definition of childbirth as a medical event is powerful enough to determine its physical location for nearly three million women a year. Thus it is of interest to ask how some meanings come to function as official definitions within a culture, with considerable power to influence material conditions. And what is the relationship of existing social arrangements – including cultural authority, scientific expertise, political activism and economic incentives – to the construction and deployment of these definitions?
>
> (Treichler 1990: 115–16)

This is a particular approach to understanding how meaning is produced, by locating it in an institutional network of power which shapes knowledge in systematic ways. Dugald Williamson gives a definition of 'discourse', and its reference to the way knowledge is shaped by its social uses, as follows: 'A discourse may be defined as a group of statements (about objects, persons, situations, even texts) which display a certain regularity that is traceable to some public or institutional deployment of knowledge' (Williamson 1989: 34).

This explains how some meanings become legitimated over others: the regularity of discourse comes about through the weight of *precedent*, the way certain statements have been given prior institutional endorsement in their previous, authorised, uses. Treichler expresses this difference between discursive statements and other non-legitimated statements, in her distinction between 'definition' and 'meaning'. As she argues, there are possibly infinite *meanings* which can be given to childbirth, but only some have institutional validity, have a precedent in those bodies of knowledge which are endorsed, legitimated and circulated – by and within the institutions which govern social life – as accepted *definitions*.

> Multiple meanings may coexist in a culture … . But a *definition* … sets limits, determines boundaries, distinguishes … definitions claim to state what *is* …

the distinction enables us to look at the construction of definitions as a complex cultural process in which there occurs, at some point, legislation among existing meanings that shapes their official entry into discourse in the form of a constructed definition.

(Treichler 1990: 123–4)

Dialogue and 'becoming': from 'many voices' to classification

This 'complex cultural process' takes us to the shaping of the 'official entry into discourse' of particular definitions, by the institutional deployment of disciplinary knowledges in particular social circumstances. It is not a uniform process, as Chartier argues, and for this reason, although we will see the coincidence, complementarity and continuity of bodies of knowledge that establish definitions as part of a cultural system of intellectual and social ordering, we will also see that these apparently coherent bodies of knowledge are marked by 'variety, nonrecurrence, and discorrespondence' (Clark and Holquist 1984: 1, 9).

This diversity and discordance is a feature which has been illuminated by Mikhail Bakhtin in his concept of 'heteroglossia'. This refers to the diverse forces which make up the precise set of conditions within which any language use occurs. These conditions ensure that any statement has a particularity, which is dependent upon the way conditions are balanced in specific times and spaces. So, while institutional processes may authorise certain definitions and hence regularise and secure the meanings that are authorised concerning any subject, the way knowledges develop is also dependent upon the circumstances in which these knowledges are applied, and the ways it is possible to think and speak about those circumstances or the events, practices or phenomena that occur in those times and spaces, under those very conditions.

Bakhtin's argument emphasises the dialogic nature of discourse, existing as a series of social interactions (Bakhtin 1981: 275). He shows that any given utterance has to be given shape by its interaction with all the potential and actual social uses of language:

> no living word relates to its object in a *singular* way: between the word and the speaking subject, there exists an elastic environment of other, alien words about the same object, the same theme … . It is precisely in the process of living interaction with this specific environment that the word may be individualised and given stylistic shape.
>
> (Bakhtin 1981: 276)

Discourse, then, is subject to its own 'uninterrupted process of historical becoming' (Bakhtin 1981: 288). All the forms of discourse we adopt – what he refers to as 'languages' – bear the histories of the previous uses to which they have been put:

> Languages … may all be taken as particular points of view on the world …
> there are no 'neutral' words and forms – words and forms that can belong to
> 'no one'; language has been completely taken over, shot through with inten-
> tions and accents … . *Each word tastes of the context and contexts in which it has
> lived its socially charged life*; all words and forms are populated by intentions … .
> Language is not a neutral medium that passes freely and easily into the
> private property of the speaker's intentions; it is populated – overpopulated
> – with the intentions of others.
>
> (Bakhtin 1981: 293–4, my emphasis)

It is perhaps in the social interactivity of discourse, more than any other feature,
that the practical application of knowledge can be seen. Institutional forms of
knowledge do not develop as remote disciplines with their own internal logics,
but bear the imprint of the world that makes them necessary, the interests they
are designed to serve, and the specific applications to which they are put over
time. Cultural knowledges, in other words, exist *in dialogue with* cultural practices
– we can only see how they work if we examine their applications in specific
times and in specific places, and can understand the conditions which made
those knowledges and their applications possible.

The dialogue between different institutional knowledges put to work in
specific circumstances, and the dialogue between cultural knowledges and
cultural practices, is the subject of this chapter. We will trace the ways in which
this process of constructing definitions occurs in a particular social circumstance
(the expansion of the modern city) and in relation to a particular governmental
objective (the management of spaces and bodies in the modern city) in order to
see how representations function historically, *discursively*, and become part of a
process of social interaction and dialogue. How do definitions of sexual difference come to play a part in this social process, and how are institutional
deployments of knowledge consolidated, revised and contested by rival groups,
in the form of public representations?

Cities: spaces, bodies, knowledges

Let us now consider one particular area where the cacophony of voices and
dialogues was becoming deafening in the nineteenth century. The nineteenth-
century city provides an interesting case study of the way institutional
knowledges are put to practical use, in the management of the social changes
which were occuring during a period of urban consolidation in which new kinds
of populations were emerging and gaining visibility. If we look at the new environments of the modern city as indicative of not only the new forms of persona
that emerged in modern Western culture, but also of the new spatial locations
within which individuals enacted subjectivity and were addressed by the developing disciplines of social management, we can see the influence of those
knowledges which are applied to the problem of managing spaces and bodies.

First, what were the context and incentives for regimes of mass population and citizen management? The city brought together new social groupings in new kinds of social spaces. People from different classes and races were drawn to the new opportunities for work which were centred in the new metropolis, and women of all classes became visible in the public spaces of the city through philanthropy, activities of consumption and entertainment. Working-class women were employed in new manufacturing and consumption industries and, as a result of working outside the conventional and local pastoral occupations of agricultural and domestic work, they were separated from their families and became more mobile.

The development and adoption of new forms of mass travel, such as the train, and the organisation of metropolitan cities around a centre of large streets or boulevards also led to a new *aggregate* of people becoming identified – the crowd. For the first time, nineteenth-century cities brought together in public places a mass of individuals, undifferentiated by the forms of spatial or social segregation that had existed in villages and small towns. It made visible a new urban 'population', the manifestation of a new social phenomenon whose features needed to be known, and whose activities and ways of living planned and managed, just as new mechanisms of differentiation and hierarchy were developed. Disciplines of social management needed to be developed, applied and revised to plan the organisation of city *spaces* and the movement of *bodies* within them.

How did institutionally recognised discourses represent metropolitan life and urban populations and 'types'; what kinds of texts were generated around these problems of knowledge and management; and how did sexual difference feature as a motif of the city as a new environment for the development of modern subjectivities? To answer these questions, we will need to examine the way representation intersects with the practices of everyday life in a specific historical context: how texts were developed to classify, define and evaluate certain types of behaviour and character, how particular images of social types were composed and collected, how particular kinds of writing about city life and city people emerged. At a moment when everyday life seemed to have changed drastically, how were the features of this new style of life represented in different kinds of texts of the period? Part of the reason cultural studies now finds it has the intellectual tools to address or analyse 'everyday life' at all is because of the techniques of social investigation which were developed in the context of nineteenth-century city life, in texts which formed the precedents for the development of social science as a discipline. How did these texts help to prescribe particular models of the normal healthy type of person against which others could be measured as abnormal and needing to be regulated by juridical or medical interventions? And how did these implicitly address popular cultures of sociability and self-definition and link them to certain forms of urban pathology and sexual behaviour?

Cities became objects of investigation partly because they were signs of achievement, symbols of growth and progress, but also because they were expanding so rapidly that new ways of living were demanded. Hence they became also a focus of some social concern about how those new patterns would be managed or governed and organised effectively: an enterprise which required new techniques of analysis and new forms and mechanisms of knowledge. The cultural process of understanding and writing about city life was also a way of assessing the ways that city life, and the lives of its inhabitants, could be conducted according to a defined and acceptable regular pattern. However, in doing so it also became evident that urban life was in fact lived according to a number of diverse styles, many of which did not concur with those being established as legitimate or desirable.

Geographical dislocations: the destabilised body

City life presented a collected population. Populations in the nineteenth century could be observed and described in a new way precisely because they were collected together en masse in urban environments. The newly developing statistical sciences were oriented by the need to know a new object, the urban population: to create a statistical profile of how many people lived in cities, how many lived in each district, their social background, their levels of poverty, levels of infant mortality, and so on, to offer a statistical representation of the spatial arrangement and conditions of city life, so that urban planning and management could be conducted effectively. However, this profile was also used to develop a picture of the characteristic patterns of individuals' lives, providing a social and moral map of the city, as well as a range of city 'types' – of life and of person.

The geographical organisation of urban populations was understood to bring about a loss of moorings, as it became arranged not through kinship, but in a way which was oriented to the patterns of industrial production, centralised in major cities that were manufacturing or distribution centres. In other words, while cities were composed of collected populations, these were populations of individuals who were now redistributed and dispersed within a new industrial environment, rather than being located in space in a continuous way over centuries. Urban culture was presented by many commentators as a 'machine culture' and a 'man-made' environment which disturbed the conventional rhythms of a pastoral life attuned to natural cycles, a closer connection to the land, and the secure locatedness of family and community. In particular, the train – as a technology of distribution and travel between industrial metropolitan centres – was given a negative taint. The speed of train travel – as opposed to travel by horse in pre-industrial periods – gave a visual and psychological dislocation: the traveller lost an immediate relationship to the land travelled through, and lost the close view of those features in the foreground as they 'dissolved' or became blurred by the rapid sideways movement of the train (Schivelbusch 1979: 65). There was much writing about the 'shocks' and dislocations to the internal organs and brain that derived from being shot through the landscape like a bullet (Schivelbusch 1979: 118–26) and the artifice arising from new creations of space and time in both travel and the reorganisation of everyday living in urban work and home life. As a result of these changes – the lack of an 'authentic' relation to the land, the erosion of 'natural' ties of family, and the 'instability' of spatial location and time compared to pastoral attachments and rhythms – the conventional and tested coordinates of emotion and personality seemed to be under threat as railways were said to have 'completely changed our habits':

> one's affections tend to go out to a greater number of objects and individuals, and consequently become less intense or durable in each case. This encourages inconstancy and creates excitement over variety; life and affections are seen to lose in depth what they gain in range; the social and general sentiments, on the other hand, find this to be a most pleasing state, while *the private sentiments, the familial ones, would seem to suffer from it.*
>
> (Schivelbusch 1979: 71, my emphasis)

As we see in this response to the railway as a component of modern life and a new form of travel based on the existence and needs of urban populations brought together in new social networks, an opposition and conflict between the 'social' and the 'familial' (or the 'private') sentiments is understood to flow from these new social phenomena arising from the functioning of cities. The city, and train travel, brought about a new relationship to spaces and objects. They were characterised by 'commotion', a disorderly and chaotic array of stimuli and activity which brought about continual movement, a 'jostling' of the individual so that powers of reflection and, above all, of *discrimination* – a process in which the individual exerted a judgement borne from the apprehension of conventional boundaries, hierarchies and perspectives – were eroded.

The effects of these changes were charted at the level of individual sentiment, as an orientation towards other people and things was seen to bring about less discriminating affections and an unwelcome 'promiscuity' of contact, stimulation and movement, threatening to undermine those family sentiments which had previously acted as the basis of the coherence and self-discipline that assured the stability of social groupings. Since structures of sexual difference were anchored by those conventional positions accorded by family, these changes – and their description as 'promiscuous' – were greeted with some concern over the effects they would have on sexual relations and behaviour and the integrity of sexual identities. The new forms of social contact that train travel afforded women, in particular, were understood in terms of a dangerous public mobility – shooting through the landscape surrounded by strangers – which endangered their moral security as well as potentially disturbing their delicate nervous system, whose stability could only be ensured by a security of domestic confines and relationships. Appropriate middle-class femininity was threatened *both* by the lack of distinctions between classes (as they came upon others of lower social status who may not act according to the codes which confirmed their gentility) *and* by an unregulated contact between men and women, which failed to reflect a privatised and restrained femininity. These new patterns of living – as cultural practices which formed part of a repertoire of motifs for representing urban life

– were therefore being read according to the concerns over these new environments of subjectivity and the potential they had to distort conventional distinctions between social groupings and sexual identities. Train travel thereby became a focus for debates about the 'shocks' that were incurred by alien experiences on individual psyches, threatening to bring about not only new physical and emotional states but also new kinds of identity and personality: these were linked to the 'shocks' of modern life and the city and the changes they wrought to the conventional anchors for systems of sexual differences.

Codes of legibility: urban types and public femininity

In the attempts to know and manage the collected populations of the nineteenth-century city, it was the urban poor – created by the overcrowded and unsanitary nature of those districts in which they lived – who constituted the most pressing object of social investigation and commentary. From the 1840s in Britain, a series of Royal Commissions and Select Committee reports charted the 'unknown country' occupied by the labouring poor. Edwin Chadwick, in his *Report on the Sanitary Condition of the Labouring Population of Great Britain in 1842* (cited in Himmelfarb 1984), revealed the 'foul odors of open cesspools, the garbage, the excrement, and dead rats rotting in the streets, the filth and scum floating in the river, the sewage that passed as drinking water', which caused to emanate a poisonous 'miasma' that was 'the source of the physical, moral and mental deterioration of the poor' and threatened to invade and contaminate (physically and figuratively) middle-class districts and their inhabitants (Himmelfarb 1984: 357). That this moral and mental state could be attributed to physical conditions showed how far it was taken as read that the poor constituted a characterological weakness in the British condition.

The social commentator and journalist Henry Mayhew, however, was concerned to chart the characterological features and patterns of behaviour and living of these urban 'types'. In his *London Labour and the London Poor*, published originally as a series of journalistic exposés in 1850–52, Mayhew made poverty 'a form of pathology, a cultural rather than an economic condition' (Himmelfarb 1984: 366). He set out to compose 'a cyclopaedia of the industry, the want, and the vice of the great Metropolis' through a series of portraits of 'London street folk' – street sellers, street buyers, street performers, street artisans, street labourers, prostitutes, thieves, swindlers and beggars, which he named as 'Wandering Tribes' (cited in Himmelfarb 1984: 323–4). The 'costermongers', wandering street sellers, were taken as emblematic of street folk in general, as they formed the largest group and embodied their characteristics in a form so exaggerated that they almost constituted a distinct race. One of the defining characteristics of the costermonger is an overvaluation of 'amusement' and an undervaluation of 'home':

> Home has few attractions to a man whose life is a street-life. Even those who are influenced by family ties and affections, prefer to 'home' – indeed that

word is rarely mentioned among them – the conversation, warmth, and merriment of the beer-shop, where they can take their ease among their 'mates'. Excitement or amusement are indispensable to uneducated men.

(Mayhew 1985: 17)

Female costermongers, too, were understood to have an aversion to the 'confinement' of home: 'to the mother the house is only a better kind of *tent*' (Mayhew 1985: 43–6). Indeed, talking of the coster-girls in particular, Mayhew goes so far as to associate their 'notions of morality' with 'those of many savage tribes', seeing these as blighted by their inattention to domestic values: 'The hearth, which is so sacred a symbol to all civilized races as being the spot where the virtues of each succeeding generation are taught and encouraged, has no charms for them' (Mayhew 1985: 43).

The moral concomitant of this is a lax sexual code: coster-girls live with, rather than marry, men and 'entertain the most imperfect idea of the sanctity of marriage', understanding it instead only in terms of a commercial contract of shared gains and failing to accord any importance to a church ceremony (Mayhew 1985: 42). This derogated view of femininity is particularly evident in Mayhew's description of the 'penny gaffs' – shops which become makeshift theatres at night, and which are largely patronised by women and girls. Mayhew is largely concerned with the deleterious effects of these kinds of urban entertainments on the character of the girls, which he sees confirmed both in the nature of the show and the behaviour of the audience:

> What notions can the young female form of marriage and chastity, when the penny theatre rings with applause at the performance of a scene whose sole point turns upon the pantomimic imitation of the unrestrained indulgence of the most corrupt appetites of our nature. …

> Some of the girls – though their figures showed them to be mere children – were dressed in showy cotton-velvet polkas, and wore dowdy feathers in their crushed bonnets. They stood laughing and joking with the lads, in an unconcerned, impudent manner, that was almost appalling. Some of them, when tired of waiting, chose their partners, and commenced dancing grotesquely, to the admiration of the lookers-on, who expressed their approbation in obscene terms, that, far from disgusting the poor little women, were received as compliments, and acknowledged with smiles and coarse repartees.

(Mayhew 1985: 37, 38)

In Mayhew's depiction, urban streetlife is characterised by a precocity and licentiousness, a 'disregard of female honour' that leads to 'a greater development of the animal than of the intellectual or moral nature' (Mayhew, cited in Himmelfarb 1984: 325). Yet the addiction of the life of the coster-girl is such that when 'a girl has once grown accustomed to a street-life, it is almost impossible to wean her from it' ((Mayhew 1985: 46). While retelling the story of a coster-woman who explains that she became a costermonger as a chaste escape from the sexual perils of domestic service, Mayhew comments that a virtuous English girl would rather 'have struggled on and striven to obtain any domestic labour in the preference of a street occupation', indicating that he draws on a framework of knowledge equating public femininity with vice, even in the absence of actual sexual behaviour (Gallagher 1987: 101).

This incorrigibly public, commercial and sexualised femininity is the antithesis to a virtuous middle-class femininity based on domestic enclosure, and shares many of the features of another public and urban female figure – the prostitute. However, these are images of femininity characterised as much by inappropriate forms of consumption and love of 'amusement', and improvident habits of dress and demeanour, as they are by sexual behaviour. As the public woman's failures of morality, sentiment and behaviour are identified, the causes of her fall are laid at the door of the contours of urban vice and misery and unregulated develop-ment of patterns of urban culture. The female vices which are characteristic of the urban poor are consolidated in an image of voracious and undisciplined *appetite* which eclipses any human moral, emotional or intellectual capacity. As Mayhew asserts that the coster-girl's 'mind, heart, soul, are all absorbed in the belly', she becomes an exemplar of the dehumanising effects of metropolitan existence, depicted in an image which condenses the disruptions incurred by new technologies of train travel, the indiscipline of untrammelled consumption seen to be characteristic of urban streetlife, and a bodily existence separated from civilised and refined human capacities and thus said to be 'the rudest form of animal life'. The sacrifices of those higher faculties that the coster-girl performs in order merely to live allow her to become simply 'a locomotive stomach' (Mayhew 1985: 44).

Urban pathology, the female body and medical knowledges

Statistical surveys and early forms of sociological inquiry represented the patho-logical elements of city life, but, while they indicated the social problems that needed to be treated through parliamentary and legislative reform, urban plan-ning, philanthropy, and other forms of intervention, they also became aligned with medical discourse, used both as a diagnostic technique and as a means of identifying forms of treatment. In this way, the urban problem could be posed in terms of physiological processes, as the 'urban body' came to be represented as an organism needing regulation for its component features to be rendered more healthy. This deployment of medical knowledges beyond clinical research and practice first occurred at the level of the city as a whole – seen as a *social body* whose health is threatened by distinctive urban ills or diseases, and whose patho-logical conditions needed to be eradicated to eliminate or prevent social sicknesses such as poverty or crime. But it also occurred at the level of *individual 'types'*, which were seen either as a threat to the integrity of the social body through their 'contagious' qualities, or as the products or victims of the social

pathologies characteristic of city life. The coordinates of medical and anatomical knowledges as they were applied to practical contexts of documenting,
diagnosing or treating 'urban ills' in both these ways, were influential in generating texts across a range of different domains, both institutional and popular,
including social commentary, public and parliamentary debates, economic policy,
criminology, urban planning, more general uses (such as novels, press reports and
investigations), and informal representations (such as songs and broadsheets).

The body of the woman featured both in representations of a weakened or
diseased social body, and as a motif of those pathological types who threatened
to infect the population, primarily in the figure of the prostitute, but by extension
in the figure of any other type of 'public woman'. In the first case, the image of
the social body became identified from the 1830s and 1840s as an anatomical
metaphor used to address social problems by scientific means, using a 'nerve-
centered model of the body' to identify appropriate mechanisms for the
physiological and economic self-regulation of the social organism (Poovey 1993:
4). Malthus' influential economic writings (first published in the late eighteenth
century, but made more central to nineteenth-century social discourses –
Malthus was a source upon which Mayhew depended, for example), developed a
picture of the social body by referring explicitly to the features of the physical
body, as he commented on the new economic systems that were developing to
accompany industrial production (Gallagher 1987: 84). Malthus' model of the
social body developed in response to a series of changes in economic and industrial organisation. Instead of a household producing what it needed by working
the land, in an industrialised economy production was based in metropolitan
centres and needed to anticipate a different end-point, a newly aggregated body
of anonymous consumers commensurate with 'the population' or 'the crowd'
rather than constituted at the intimate level of the family. The production and
consumption process were now seen to be separated, no longer having an
organic connection, and the consumer was brought into view for the first time as
the driving point of processes of production (Birken 1988: 25–30). As such, 'the
consumer' was seen as a parasitical, voracious figure satisfying its bodily cravings
in a similar way to the activities of those figures characterised in Mayhew's
survey of the urban poor. Malthus thus configured the population in an image of
an indulgent, idle, consuming body, in contrast to the noble image of a vigorous
body sacrificing its energy as it gave itself to productive labour. The consuming
population became the physical body to whom goods were distributed through
routes likened to the 'arteries' and channels of the physical body, distributing
sources of energy to the various parts of the population but also dissipating and
dispersing the fruits of productive labour (Gallagher 1987).

The Malthusian image of the body, reflecting the new conditions of industrial
production and reproduction of the population manifested in the incrementally
expanding and crowded urban centres, was of one which was continually
becoming fatter and larger and more unhealthy, distending and growing beyond
the capacity of its own circulatory system and thus becoming unbalanced and
providing a threat to social well-being, as systems of production (in Malthus'

view) would eventually fail to feed its population properly. However, this social body was represented not only as a consuming body but also as a *female reproductive body*, which 'doubled' itself. Such a body might seem fertile and healthy, but the consequence and product of its reproduction was an eventual degeneration, as its ability to 'populate' shifted beyond its ability to provide the means of its own subsistence, thus inducing misery and vice as organic counter-mechanisms to the vitality of an ever-expanding population and leading to drastic decline. Malthus' message is that prosperity which is promised by expanding industry and metropolis would end in degeneration: 'the blooming body is only a body about to divide into two feebler bodies that are always on the verge of becoming four starving bodies' (Gallagher 1987: 84–5). In his view, the social body is always an 'old woman', even during the appearance of youth. The eventual demise of the social body was equally figured in terms of a female physiology characterised by its reproductive processes – one who starts as a fertile body in the bloom of youth ends as an enfeebled and shrivelled old woman without further issue (Gallagher 1987: 86).

A degenerative female body is also the model for those female figures who threaten the health of the social body through their actual appearance in the city – as 'types' – rather than through their metaphorical embodiment of the social. From the 1830s and 1840s onwards, the phenomenon of prostitution became an important object of social investigation, as a feature of the contaminated moral environment of the city which paralleled the sanitary contamination of those areas of the city afflicted by 'miasma'. Prostitution was likened to both putrefaction and the sewer, as it was seen as a means of flushing out those characteristic evils that city life brought to the social body, but also as a service which was rendered at the cost of the prostitute's own moral and physical integrity – her body becoming rotted by the waste she carried. The prostitute was therefore characterised in physical, as well as moral, terms as *she herself* became waste: diseased, foul and degenerate (Corbin 1987: 210–12). Just as her voracious sexual appetite and her overpowering will to attain the means to consume and indulge her appetite for 'vanities' and adornment were understood to bring her to prostitution, so they bring about her eventual decline: her 'idle' body (given to a non-productive form of exertion, unlike productive 'physical' labour) becomes a barren body with no further value, brought to a state of degeneration that becomes a further metaphorical elaboration of Malthus' envisaged misery- and vice-ridden social body. It is in the moral domain, however, that the image of the woman's body is used with most prescience, in an image of a woman not only 'disfigured by the expression of sexual desire' (Armstrong 1990: 5) but especially one which had become so by separating sexual expression from reproductivity and, further, by allowing this to pervade the public domain of the city.

The putrefied, rotting body of the prostitute threatens to infect the social body populated by the bourgeoisie, as syphilis manifests in physical disease the moral contagion that her activity represents to conventional social mores and organisation. The municipal inspection and flushing of a clogged sewer to avoid the spread of disease by contaminated water is paralleled by the medical examination and treatment of the infected vagina of the prostitute advocated for effective regulation of the prostitute's contagion (Poovey 1993: 21). Both imply a medical dimension to the technologies demanded by urban planning and the management of the presence of actual bodies in actual spaces, in their attempt to govern the metaphorical social body.

Medicine worked in alliance with the law to address the problem of the prostitute: the Contagious Diseases Acts of 1864–9 (which were repealed in 1886) permitted women on the streets of garrison towns to be detained and forcibly inspected by physicians for signs of venereal disease and, if those signs were present, to be confined in 'Lock Hospitals' until treatment had been administered (see Walkowitz 1980). Medicine thereby became deployed as a technology of social management within a logic of public health, in addition to constituting a powerful domain for the representation of women's sexuality and the prostitute's sexual pathology. The sexual physician Dr William Acton, for example, published an extensive study of prostitution, its causes, and the characteristics of prostitutes, mounting an argument for the prevention of conditions understood to allow prostitution to develop, an approach that, like Parent-Duchatelet's work upon which he draws, positioned it as a public-health issue, or one to be addressed 'on sanitary grounds' (Acton 1857: 2). Acton's work stands not only as a form of advocacy for an 'authoritative', medico-legal, understanding of prostitution and prostitutes as social types, but also as a text which positions and represents women as sexual beings of particular types, and which in particular situates prostitutes as beings created by the circumstances of modern city life. Just as Mayhew states that prostitution is 'an inevitable attendant upon extended civilization and increased population' (Mayhew 1985: 476), so the emphasis on the 'sanitary conditions of prostitutes' (Acton 1857: 3) renders the prostitute an artificial being, created from the unnatural conditions of city life rather than the natural affections of her role in middle-class family life. She is thus potentially monstrous: in fact, she becomes a voracious and devouring figure, her activity 'eating into the heart of society' (Acton 1857: v). Acton has a reformist end in mind, and argues against prostitutes being seen as beyond redemption. In fact he stresses their suffering, describing their 'calling' as 'an epilepsy of punishment', and he cites Mayhew's study of the London poor to stress the hardship that drives poor women to prostitution (Acton 1857: 5, 21). However, in his adoption of the view of W.R. Greg, another influential commentator on prostitution, we can also see that he assumes a constitutional weakness in women's moral make-up, which allows him to suggest that those women who resort to prostitution

> fall in the first instance from a mere exaggeration and perversion of one of the best qualities of a woman's heart. They yield to desires in which they do not share, from a weak generosity which cannot refuse anything to the passionate entreaties of the man they love. There is in the warm fond heart of woman a strange and sublime selfishness … a positive love of self-sacrifice – an active, so to speak, an *aggressive* desire to show their affection.
>
> (Greg 1850, cited in Acton 1857: 20)

The prostitute is drawn to the first stage of her fall, therefore, not by sexual passions – which 'as little disturb the economy of the human as they do that of the animal female' (Acton 1857: 20) – but by a perverted and 'aggressive' distortion of those capacities for generosity and self-sacrifice that characterise 'womanly nature'. To this, Acton adds his own view that another critical cause is 'vanity, vanity, and then vanity – for what but this are love of dress and admiration' (Acton 1857: 21). Hence the potential or capacity for prostitution is embodied in the various guises of womanliness – in both her virtues and her weaknesses and follies.

Physiognomy and sexual sickness: medicine and criminology

Medical and sociological commentators are unified on the various 'types' of prostitute. Acton, like others, adopts Mayhew's classification of the prostitute along the stages of a continuum – from the kept woman, who is closest to the state of matrimony, to the 'criminal' prostitute, whose career has stamped itself on to her physiognomy:

> Two women, both well-known prostitutes, were confined in the cells, one of whom had been there before no less than *fourteen times*, and had only a few hours before been brought up charged with nearly murdering a man with a poker. Her face was bad, heavy and repulsive; her forehead, as well as I could distinguish by the scanty light thrown into the place by the bullseye of the policeman, was low; her nose was short and what is called pudgy, having the nostrils dilated.
>
> (Mayhew 1985: 480)

The fact that Mayhew contents himself with describing the companion of the above woman as 'much better looking', without further detail, suggests that there is something telling about these facial features in his understanding of the defining characteristics of those extreme types of prostitute he outlines with such attention above. The features he identifies coincide with those physiognomies which were interpreted as indicating a kind of appearance that translated into a pattern of pathology; a pathology of character which manifested itself in pathological behaviour and could thus also be addressed as a social pathology as it became a problem of population management. One of the most widespread uses of photography as an instrument of social science in the nineteenth century, for example, was to compile a catalogue of 'problem types', types who could be defined as abnormal or deviant and therefore identified as the object of disciplinary inquiry and treatment – whether by criminology or the law, medicine or psychology, or by those forms of social administration which were concerned with the conditions of the neighbourhoods and families of the urban poor (see Lury 1998: 42–7). Photography allowed various 'types' (classified according to those practical disciplines of urban management which might address them: the criminal, the delinquent, the sick, the retarded, the mad) to be identified from their visual features. It therefore functioned not only as a means by which vast archives recording the features of abnormality might be compiled, but also as an instrument to classify the features of those particular states or conditions of abnormality which were the subject of disciplinary inquiry or treatment. These technologies of classification thereby represented 'the abnormal' in the image of those knowledges which were directed towards the problems of urban manage-ment and the effects of modern life on the character of the population.

One study that carries particular interest for the way texts emerging from these disciplinary inquiries generate definitions concerning sexual difference within the framework of urban pathologies is Caesar Lombroso and William Ferrero's *The Female Offender* (1959), first published in Britain in 1895. This proposed itself as an 'anatomico-pathological investigation', measuring the anomalies present in the skulls, skeletons, brains and facial features of prostitutes and other criminal subjects (Lombroso and Ferrero 1895/1959: 2–3). Lombroso and Ferrero not only claim that women are 'naturally' less inclined to criminal behaviour so that those who are criminal represent a particularly deviant section of the population, but they also record a 'very much larger number of anomalies in prostitutes than in criminals' (Lombroso and Ferrero 1895/1959: 32). Those features they assemble in their patterns of criminal features include: heavy or 'virile' lower jaw; deep frontal sinuses; narrow or receding sinuses; abnormal nasal bones, abnormal teeth, prominent cheekbones. That all these were charac-teristic of female criminals, but even more so of prostitutes, gives the prostitute a particular defining role in the determination of female abnormality. It also gives female crime and abnormality a sexual meaning, as criminal behaviour in women comes to be understood as deriving from some foundational sexual abnormality which is evidenced in a virility or manliness that indicates a 'degen-eration' occurring to the degree that there is also a loss of sexual specificity and distinctiveness. For example, in their assembly of anomalies, Lombroso and Ferrero include those of the larynx, finding that in prostitutes there was a char-acteristic proliferation of deep and masculine voices: 'in each case the larynx resembled a man, thus showing once again the virility of face and cranium char-acteristic of the prostitute class' (Lombroso and Ferrero 1895/1959: 84–5). When they add to this their claim that prostitutes more frequently have 'moles, hairiness, prehensile feet, the virile larynx, large jaws and cheekbones, and above all anomalous teeth … [thus] are marked by more of the signs of degeneration', we see a form of sexual representation that equates prostitution with an atavistic and uncivilised form of sexual non-specificity. This sexual instability threatens those forms of sexual convention, character, sensibility and habits which main-tain a coherent system of sexual difference as a feature of modern subjectivity and its dependence on the maintenance of secure boundaries between public and private life. When we recall the argument made that those women who succumb to prostitution do so as a result of their feminine characteristics and natural capacities, we see that a polarisation emerges between femininity and the stability of modern subjectivity – just as it has done between urban conditions and stable subjectivity – which points to a sense of alignment between the pathologies of femininity and the pathologies of the city. The image of the 'unruly woman' is, therefore, not one who simply steps out of her conventional place, but who (by so doing) alters the balance of sexual difference and definition as a stable system of coordinates for the modern manifestation of sexual subjectivity. She therefore carried a danger that went beyond her own disordered corporeality and pathological character.

Masculine pathologies: the downcast look

The correlate of the diseased body of the prostitute, both voracious and degenerative according to the dual properties of Malthus' model of the doomed and vice-ridden social body, but also unnaturally 'virile' according to the pathologies of public femininity, was the weakened male body, which no longer had those traditional means of subsistence available in more 'noble' occupations of productive labour or traditional familial connections to landed property. Commerce and business weakened the physical constitution of men as they grappled with the 'strains' of business life and succumbed to the 'moral drain' of new and routine occupations, which made them susceptible to sexual vices such as masturbation (McQueen 1991: 12). The sexual sicknesses attributed to the altered conditions of modern life were vastly documented in terms of physiological afflictions, as medical texts represented the outcome of those dissolute practices of masturbation, satyriasis and other forms of sexual incontinence, in a wasted physique, sickly constitution and nervous debility that was instantly recognisable. Almost twenty years later, the same William Acton who had paid such attention to the pathological features of prostitutes describes the features indicative of masturbation in his *Functions and Disorders of the Reproductive Organs ...*, by quoting Lallemand's description:

> However young the children may be, they become thin, pale, and irritable, and their features assume a haggard appearance. We notice the sunken eye, the long, cadaverous-looking countenance, the down-cast look ... . Habitual masturbators have a dank, moist, cold hand, very characteristic of great vital exhaustion ... they may gradually waste away if the evil passion is not got the better of; nervous symptoms set in ...
>
> (Lallemand, cited in Acton 1875: 39)

Acton attributes these afflictions to a new set of perverse sexual habits stimulated by an increased exposure to sexual sights and encounters, and the strains of abstinence during prolonged engagements arising from insecure economic relations. These are conditions particular to 'a state so artificial as that of our modern civilisation' (Acton 1875: 8). The enfeebled and sickly male body, then, becomes a complementary motif to those female images which embody the ills of urban life: a loss of sexual distinctiveness, which manifests itself in this case as a *loss* of vitality, just as it manifests itself in the over-vigorous female body characteristic of the prostitute and costermonger. Acton's response to the sexual disorders of men was similar to his earlier invocation that moral training was necessary so that men would cease to be the cause of prostitution (women's 'weakness' prevented them from being the object of this kind of moral regime of public-health management, which depended on self-discipline). The use of medico-management as a mechanism of urban regulation identified the basis of social ills in an irregular kind of sexual behaviour that needed to be disciplined. Acton was one of the first to outline how particular sexual behaviours (practices of continence) could be used as a way of disciplining the body, guarding it against the dangers of too much excitement. If overstimulation was one of the key conditions of urban life, and could lead to sexual disease, so the dangerous conditions of city life could be guarded against by the development of a *moderate* sexual character. Again, women were not addressed in this scenario: Acton simply indicates that women's whole being is 'built up around her womb', consigning her to an unruly physical constitution beyond processes of management that depend upon will (Acton 1875). The extent to which a sexual origin could be identified as the cause of all nervous diseases is evident in the similarity of the description of the masturbator above, and that of Mr Fairlie (outlined in Chapter 5). The feminisation of Mr Fairlie produces an implicit reference to the sexual effects of modern urban life, its refinements (or artifices) and its excitements. The relationship of masculinity to urban life was a feature not only of the medical texts and diagnostic practices that were part of British cultural life in the nineteenth century, but became consolidated in motifs of character that feed into and inform popular representations in the period.

Nerves, psychology and lost women

While medicine, social sciences and criminology attempted to provide a picture of urban life and its social problems, 'mental medicine' or psychology provided a particularly important view of how individuals could be managed as a way of solving these problems and preventing social ills. Theories of madness focused on changes in social relations brought about by the growth of cities: the development of modern urban life, it was argued, would lead to the breakdown of social cohesion and social stability, and the social ills would manifest themselves in a series of mental illnesses. Cities, in other words, were destructive of previously secure social frameworks and the result of that destructiveness on modern subjectivity was evident in an increasing visibility of nervous diseases and mental instability.

   In a serial which was the outcome of a collaboration between two popular novelists, Charles Dickens and Wilkie Collins, a character records a visit to a county lunatic asylum, which he describes as 'a society of human creatures who have nothing in common but that *they have all lost the power of being humanly social with one another*' (cited in Bourne-Taylor 1988: 27, my emphasis). In this formulation, the condition of madness is proposed as the very antithesis of humanness; a sign of the very opposite of human characteristics is their lack of being able to be social with one another and recognise themselves as part of a society of human creatures. This is a common theme in assessments of madness, that city life and the loss of traditional community structures and their connection to national life afflicted populations in dangerous ways, so that their behaviour fails to obey normal social dictates and places individuals outside normal conventions and social rules. The character quoted in Dickens' and Collins' fiction goes on to a disturbing recognition of something like himself in one of the mad individuals he observes, and Bourne-Taylor suggests that the social and medical observation of the mad was so compelling in this period because it was a point at which, instead of locking them up and treating them as lost causes, medicine (like Mayhew with the poor) was attempting to find ways to restore the nervously deranged to health. The recognition that environmental influences such as the changing social circumstances and evils of city life could make a potentially healthy individual mad presented the ever-present possibility of breakdown in the midst of normality. Bourne-Taylor quotes a view published in a *Times* article of the same period: 'In strictness, we are all mad when we give way to passion, to prejudice, to vice, to vanity' (Bourne-Taylor 1988: 27). It was on the basis that individuals were at risk of giving way to vices, vanities and passions that, in the new environment of the city, psychology could be seen as insulating the healthy through the development of appropriate regimes of moral training, and could be used to diagnose those who did give way so that they could be prevented from communicating their madness to others.

The nervous illnesses attributed to women in the nineteenth century were characterised by symptoms demonstrating their lack of maternal disposition or domestic orientation, their 'uncontained' physical demeanour (laughing, crying, moving uncontrollably) or their lethargy (and concomitant retirement from family life). The causes were variously a disturbance of uterine functioning, a disturbance of sexual appetite, and a general 'overstimulation' and excitability of the brain and nerves brought about by exposure to the fast pace of modern living, especially in the urban context. Walter Hartwright, the narrator, first encounters the 'Woman in White' alone, in flight from the enclosure of the asylum, lost on the streets of London at night.

> What sort of a woman she was, and how she came to be out alone in the high-road, an hour after midnight, I altogether failed to guess. The one thing of which I felt certain was, that the grossest of mankind could not have misconstrued her motive in speaking, even at that suspiciously late hour and in that suspiciously lonely place.
>
> (Collins 1860/1974: 48)

These circumstances give some sense of the motifs of female nervous illness and its antipathy to authorised and prescribed forms of feminine subjectivity and its domestic locatedness. The novel presents her thus, however, in a counter-move – to show that her form of nervous agitation follows from a perverse marriage into which she was pushed by her morally negligent and physically enfeebled hypochondriac guardian, Mr Fairlie. The dilemma posed, of how to 'know' the 'Woman in White', is evident in Walter's immediate reaction to the news that he had aided this woman to evade the men who sought to capture and return her to the asylum

> What had I done? Assisted the victim of the most horrible of all false imprisonments to escape; or cast loose on the wide world of London an unfortunate creature, whose actions it was my duty, and every man's duty, mercifully to control? I turned sick at heart when the question occurred to me, and when I felt self-reproachfully that it was asked too late.
>
> (Collins 1860/1974: 55)

Is this 'lost' woman a victim, or a curse for the city and its population? Madness is represented as part of the 'condition of being female' (Miller 1987: 121) – just as Greg and Acton had supposed prostitution to be – with the city as a stimulus to those unruly tendencies being made public and *manifested*, psychologically or figuratively.

In the case of *The Woman in White*, Miller points out that 'Laura ... takes a nightmarish detour through the carceral ghetto on her way *home*, to the domestic haven where she is always felt to belong' (Miller 1987: 122). But other figures remain 'lost'. The artificial life of the city which created a distorted and unnatural character in individuals led them away from pure habits and created its own 'vices'. These included that of suicide, which was seen as one of the dangers of modernity and urban life but one which particularly threatened men as a result of their greater involvement in the mechanics of public life. Suicide was defined in psychological terms as an illness of moral insanity rather than nervous disease, and middle-class women were considered to be more insulated from this derangement as a result of the boundaries of family and home (Kushner 1993).[1] Female suicides could therefore only be understood as having breached the boundaries of this moral insulation, so that the female suicide became frozen in an ambivalent moment of public escape and abandonment that became the subject of popular and press repetition (Gates 1988). In a similar move to that evident in representations of female costermongers, criminals and prostitutes, 'experts ... labelled women who killed themselves as entering the male sphere' (Kushner 1993: 462), while also suggesting that they were 'lost to love' (Lombroso and Ferrero 1895/1959). The female suicide was therefore pathologised while simultaneously being seen as 'a "threat" to the moral fabric', as she was associated with those urban working women who left the home and undermined the traditional values that safeguarded men from the moral and psychological breakdown that brought temptations of suicide (Kushner 1993: 462). In both male and female suicides, then, the threatening forces of modernity and urban anomie are finally traced back to a destructive and unruly femininity that refuses to be contained by the traditional boundaries of sexual difference.

We have seen that the city functions as an example of the way in which cultural knowledges and their connection to cultural practices produce representations of sexual difference that intersect with other questions of social management. As those representations which are generated by authoritative institutional disciplines are disseminated into popular domains, and are taken up in popular forms of representation, they become part of an archive of common knowledge and part of the texture of our everyday patterns of living and thinking. These are the patterns of classification and definition through which we identify the coordinates of sexual difference and identity. Texts can be read according to the logics of different institutions and disciplines of knowledge, and through this process we can discern the investments of those groups for whom they speak and the way they function as products of a specific configuration of cultural circumstances and environments. The 'becoming' of discourse, then, and the different ways in which knowledges are adopted and deployed, is a fundamental feature of the process of representation as a cultural practice.

Note

1   Although some, like the eminent psychiatrist Henry Maudsley, saw those who took on the extremes of nervous symptomology such as hysteria, as embodying moral insanity or perversion: ' "believing or pretending that they cannot stand or walk, lie in bed … all day … objects of attentive sympathy on the part of their anxious relatives, when all the while their only paralysis is a paralysis of will." The "immoral vagaries" and the "moral degeneration" of some of these women, he thought, would make them perfect case studies of systematic moral insanity' (Showalter 1985: 133).

Bibliography

Acton, W. (1857) *Prostitution Considered in Its Moral, Social, and Sanitary Aspects in London and Other Large Cities; with Proposals for the Mitigation and Prevention of Its Attendant Evil*, London: John Churchill.
—— (1875) *The Functions and Disorders of the Reproductive Organs in Childhood, Youth, Adult Age, and Advanced Life Considered in their Physiological, Social and Moral Relations*, London: J.A. Churchill.
Armstrong, N. (1990) 'The Occidental Alice', *differences* 2, 2: 3–40.
Bakhtin, M.M. (1981) *The Dialogic Imagination: Four Essays by M.M. Bakhtin*, ed. M. Holquist, Austin: University of Texas Press.
Birken, L. (1988) *Sexual Science and the Emergence of a Culture of Abundance, 1871–1914*, Ithaca and London: Cornell University Press.
Bourne-Taylor, J. (1988) *In the Secret Theatre of Home: Wilkie Collins, Sensation Narrative and Nineteenth-Century Psychology*, London: Routledge.
Clark, K. and Holquist, M. (1984) *Mikhail Bakhtin*, Cambridge, MA and London: The Belknap Press of Harvard University Press.
Collins, W. (1860/1974) *The Woman in White*, Harmondsworth: Penguin.
Corbin, A. (1987) 'Commercial Sexuality in Nineteenth-Century France: A System of Images and Regulations', in C. Gallagher and T. Laqueur (eds) *The Making of the Modern Body: Sexuality and Society in the Nineteenth Century*, Berkeley and Los Angeles: California University Press, 209–19.

Gallagher, C. (1987) 'The Body Versus the Social Body in the Works of Thomas Malthus and Henry Mayhew', in C. Gallagher and T. Laqueur (eds) *The Making of the Modern Body: Sexuality and Society in the Nineteenth Century*, Berkeley and Los Angeles: California University Press, 83–106.

Gates, B. (1988) *Victorian Suicide: Mad Crimes and Sad Histories*, Princeton, NJ: Princeton University Press.

Himmelfarb, G. (1984) *The Idea of Poverty: England in the Early Industrial Age*, London: Faber and Faber.

Kushner, H.I. (1993) 'Suicide, Gender and the Fear of Modernity in Nineteenth-Century Medical and Social Thought', *Journal of Social History* 26, 3 (Spring): 461–90.

Lombroso, C. and Ferrero, W. (1895/1959) *The Female Offender*, London: Peter Owen Limited.

Lury, C. (1998) *Prosthetic Culture: Photography, Memory and Identity*, London and New York: Routledge.

McQueen, R. (1991) 'Mortified and Punished: The Businessman and His Body in the Victorian Age', paper presented at the Tenth Annual Law in History Conference, Melbourne.

Mayhew, H. (1985) *London Labour and the London Poor*, Harmondsworth: Penguin.

Miller, D.A. (1987) '*Cage aux folles*: Sensation and Gender in W. Collins's *The Woman in White*', in C. Gallagher and T. Laqueur (eds) *The Making of the Modern Body: Sexuality and Society in the Nineteenth Century*, Berkeley and Los Angeles: California University Press, 107–36.

Poovey, M. (1993) 'Anatomical Realism and Social Investigation in Early Nineteenth-Century Manchester', *differences* 5, 3: 1–30.

Schivelbusch, W. (1979) *The Railway Journey: Trains and Travel in the Nineteenth Century*, New York: Urizen Books, 1–30.

Showalter, E. (1985) *The Female Malady: Women, Madness and English Culture, 1830–1980*, London: Virago.

Treichler, P.A. (1990) 'Feminism, Medicine, and the Meaning of Childbirth', in M. Jacobus, E. Fox Keller and S. Shuttleworth (eds), *Body/Politics, Women and the Discourses of Science*, London and New York: Routledge, 113–38.

Walkowitz, J.R. (1980) *Prostitution and Victorian Society: Women, Class and the State*, Cambridge: Cambridge University Press.

Williamson, D. (1989) *Authorship and Criticism*, Sydney: Local Consumption Publications.

Part 4

Subjective narratives

Writing the past

Introduction

Part 4 considers how the subjective is implicated in attempts at narrating or writing the past. In particular, it considers how the subjective 'voice' is represented, in both autobiography and biography, in the telling of a life story, in the narrativising of the events of the past. It shows how this voice undermines or challenges the authority of those accounts which are given the status of history, and of those versions of subjectivity which are established by disciplinary knowledges and their professional application.

Focusing on the subjective voice allows us to reinstate the concept of memory in studies of representation, and to consider its value for rethinking the writing of history. It suggests that, if there are narratives of the past which are invested with the authority of 'history', there are also counter-narratives. The concept of memory here functions to highlight this plurality, as it 'operates under the pressure of challenges and alternatives', and works against the critical distance of singular, unified and impermeable accounts of historical continuity. This approach upholds the claim that 'if there is a gap between memory and history there are also ways of negotiating it' (Zemon Davis and Starn, 1989: 2). The chapters in Part 4 each demonstrate an approach to that enterprise of negotiation.

One significant point of connection between these chapters is an attention to the relationship of time and place, in accounting for the historical character of memory. The foregrounding of subjectivity in cultural narratives suggests that the activity of narration has a finite and specific location. Here this allows us to prise apart the gaps between past and present in the accumulated stories of a life; between the different circumstances of the event and its narration, whether as history or as fiction; and between varying accounts and those frameworks of knowledge upon which they draw. Jane's chapter, on the stories her mother told after she developed Alzheimer's, shows the importance of 'confabulation' to the fashioning of identity. Her mother made her own 'negotiation of a lifetime' outside the conventions of meaning that others around her ascribed to the past, and in so doing was able to make sense of her present surroundings. By merging fiction and reality, she resituated the fragments of memory that she still held, reworking them to create her own meanings. Her mother movingly tells us of the importance of place and memory to identity (giving another understanding of *les lieux de mémoire*) as she struggles to find a place for her self to cohere. Her words give some intimation of the dislocation that loss of memory brings: 'I don't know who I am and why I'm here'; 'When I'm here, it feels as if I'm nowhere.'

Other chapters show the way that foregrounding place and time relativises the accounts which may otherwise claim closure, showing the specific cultural contexts within which a particular sense is given to historical events, or figures. Kay's discussion of the different ways that the events of Hornet Bank are (or could be) retold suggests the importance of attending to 'the sites in which such memories are evoked, both in the telling and the hearing', showing the divergence between official histories and other understandings of the events which derive from indigenous cultures. Gillian charts the shifts that occur in stories of T.E. Lawrence between the 1920s (in his own autobiography and other contemporary accounts) and the 1950s, as a new configuration of sexual knowledges recasts his persona according to the pathologies of homosexuality, demonstrating how changing repertoires of knowledge shape popular understandings of masculinity and its relationship to national identity in a period of colonial decline.

The chapters also show that the subjective perspective in cultural narratives offers a point of instability which throws into relief models of subjectivity and sexual difference, and even reveals a crisis of authority in cultural knowledge – in particular those concerning the hierarchies endemic to sexual difference and colonial power. Jane's analysis indicates that the 'confusions' in her mother's 'disorderly ramblings' – as she took on the achievements of male members of her family and dramatised the events of her past – may be understood as a critique of the sexual hierarchies that had determined the pattern of her own life. Kay's reading of Rosa Praed's accounts of her Australian girlhood allows her to identify moments of excess, or ' "textualised" … remainders of the past' in which the 'particular anxieties of British colonial authority are exposed', and 'identities shaped through sex, gender and race are … destabilised and fractured across the lines of sexuality'. And Gillian's situating of narratives of Lawrence shows how the integration of the subjective into public narratives of masculine achievement provides a 'categorial instability' which challenges 'the intelligibility of apparently authoritative systems of cultural – or sexual – classification'. She reads the second wave of accounts, and the film *Lawrence of Arabia*, against the differences 'which clustered around a fragmented national masculinity and its declining hold on a position of cultural centrality'. This allows her to conclude that the 'unravelling of masculinity' is signalled by the exchanges that overwrite the figure of Lawrence as the colonial subject enters the space of indeterminacy and by 'those traits of instability that Lawrence exhibits'.

Awareness of these mechanisms of instability allows each author to analyse figures caught between different cultural repertoires. Medical discourses empty Jane's mother's stories of meaning and deprive her of identity, while an alternative reading that recognises the social and subjective significance of her narrative strategies restores to her the fragments of a familial and individual identity constructed over the course of her lifetime and reinvoked in the 'ritualised constructions of a past' through which she could continue to communicate meaningfully with her daughter. In the narratives that surround Lawrence, he is positioned as 'between', wandering in the space of 'elsewhere'; in the absence of a regime of knowledge that can take account of subjectivity as a series of practices, the figure of Lawrence disorganises the boundaries of sexual identity. Rosa Praed's life was constructed across those boundaries of domestic and political life, as she refused to ascribe to a femininity relegated to the private sphere and her writing crossed the borders into politics and history. Kay looks beneath the veil of concealment that official histories have drawn, to find evidence of two further figures who do not cohere to the tropes of femininity: Martha Fraser, whose 'voice survives as a helpless cry' against white male sexuality; and the figure of Jenny, a 'half-caste' positioned between indigenous and European cultures, whose excessive presence in Praed's writing signals the disavowal of white masculine promiscuity and the sexualised male body, even as – and precisely because – she is constructed as a cipher of sexual promiscuity attributed to the female. These figures undermine the 'crucial dichotomy which underpins colonial power'. They are the signs of colonial anxiety that can be found in sites of memory.

The examples discussed in Part 4 indicate the political significance of work on cultural narratives, and their ability to 'write the past' in different ways. At the end of her chapter, Jane argues that history should be understood in terms of our ability to confabulate, to devise stories which make sense of our past, and that the attention to such stories is not just an analytic enterprise but a political and ethical practice. This political and ethical dimension to work on cultural narratives is clear throughout her chapter: as she restores her mother's voice in the face of a medical discourse which 'silences' those with Alzheimer's by robbing their narratives of sense and them of identity, she continues a tradition which gives value to alternative voices and thus constructs a 'competing' discourse of femininity that challenges the authority of scientific and medical discourses. Kay takes this up in her chapter, arguing for an approach that works with the inconsistencies of narrative voices – notably those of Praed as she struggles to invent a place within those discursive lines of race and sexuality. Kay shows how in Praed's autobiographical writing, the self is 'at once being destabilised and reworked', and thus how those discursive lines may become rearticulated. This is a critical practice which itself contributes to such processes of rearticulation.

Gillian adopts a different strategy. By assembling the knowledges through which sexualities are understood in the narratives of a particular time and place, she reveals that those models of subjectivity through which sexual and colonial authority is established are themselves fragmentary constructions, fictions by which individual subjects take their bearings, reinvent a 'self', and which in moments of transition or crisis create the possibility of alternative gestures – of alternative narratives which unseat the centrality and disturb the functioning of colonial power – as occurred in the aftermath of Suez.

Each of these strategies has different implications. In Jane's chapter, an ethical approach is aimed at restoring the feminine voice and, in the process, destabilising authoritative narratives. In Kay's chapter, we find that restoring the feminine works alongside another process – setting it within the lines of power that situate subjectivities within hierarchies of race, sex and gender, and put them into play along the axes of 'racial conflict and colonial power'. And Gillian's undermines the apparent coherence of 'proud masculinity', showing the permeability of the subjective voice and its ability to narrativise the instability of cultural categories, as the relationship between public life, subjectivity and the body is unsettled. To this extent, the narratives of Lawrence show the impossibility of achieving a unified masculinity, and this instability of sexual classifications exposes a space for alternative definitions of sexual difference. In different ways, then, both Kay and Gillian reinstate the sexualised male body, thus threatening those dichotomies which underpin sexual hierarchies.

Kay perhaps most clearly articulates an ethics of critical practice when she shows how Praed, held in the spell of her own curiosity, unable to speak of her forbidden knowledge of the rituals of Aboriginal ceremony, struggles to write outside a position of European authority. Praed's ambivalent relation to European authority, and her attempt to 'establish an alliance with subordinated Aboriginality which is not absolutely complicit with imperialism' – recalls bell hooks' call for the coloniser to enter the space of the margin. But there is a corresponding move in hooks' call to cultural critics to bring the marginal voices to the centre, and speak of 'the path of their resistance'. This is a complex path; one which suggests that feminist critics, biographers and cultural historians should scrutinise the coordinates of their own practice, exposing the work of memory to an archaeological gaze which '[displaces] the dichotomies which hold those positions apart', raking over the remains and reconstructing the world that these remains imply so that they, too, 'trace the struggle to possess meaning'.

Bibliography

Zemon Davis, N. and Starn, R. (1989) 'Introduction', *Representations* 26, Special issue, 'Memory and Counter Memory', Berkeley: University of California Press.

9　Disorderly ramblings

Alzheimer's and narratives of subjectivity

Jane Crisp

Remembering my mother

There is a certain fitness to beginning a chapter about disorderly ramblings and narratives of subjectivity by breaking the rules of academic discourse and indulging in some personal reminiscences about my mother. She was born on 8 June 1906 at Landaff in Wales and was christened Bettie because, as she often told me, her father said that 'there had to be a Bettie Caple'. One of the stories about her early childhood I particularly enjoyed had as its setting their Georgian terrace house in Bath. Bettie removed the rods that held the carpet in place on the hall stairs, pulled the carpet tight, then came swooping down it on a tea-tray into the hallway. Stories of such childhood naughtinesses, both hers and mine, were always told with a distinct relish, suggestive of their special appeal for someone who as an adult was much more self-effacing than this earlier self appears to have been.

Bettie had an older brother, Howard. They were very close during her childhood, despite their six-year age difference, and were to remain so throughout their lives. (He was eventually to marry my father's sister and followed us to New Zealand when we migrated there after the war.) Howard used regularly to buy cork dolls for Bettie – not because she liked such dolls, but because their stuffing was needed to refurbish Growler, her much-loved teddy bear; together they used to carry out the important restuffing operation. When Bettie was grown up and living away from home, Growler was thrown out in the rubbish by their newly acquired stepmother – a crime that Bettie never forgave. There was special significance, therefore, in the fact that, when my uncle received the news of my birth, he went immediately to Hamley's, the well-known London toy shop, and bought me a teddy bear. It was wartime, he was in uniform, and his purchase, because of wartime shortages, was given to him unwrapped. Thus it was that my uncle walked through London exchanging salutes with fellow officers while carrying a teddy bear under his arm. The incident was to become a favourite story at family reunions. I still have the bear in question, rather dilapidated, but with his paws carefully patched by my mother.

Both my maternal grandparents died before I was born. My mother's memories of her mother tended to be centred on her skill at embroidery; this was

Figure 5   Jane and her mother, 1941

indeed great, judging by pieces that we still have, including two panels of a four-fold screen which she was working on before she died. Certain flowers are also associated with my grandmother: Solomon's seal and hellebores were always grown by my mother because they had been her favourites, and I have kept up the tradition. Bettie's relationship with her father appears to have been somewhat unusual for the period, in that he wanted her rather than her brother to join him in his profession as an architect. He involved her in his work, obliging her – despite her fear of heights, which he obviously neither shared nor understood – to climb with him about buildings he was restoring. My mother often told me with appropriate shudderings about how he sent her up church steeples. However, Bettie resisted the pressure from her father to study Architecture, taking a degree in History instead and eventually becoming a librarian. 'We would never have got on', she used to tell me. I often think of another story about Bettie and her father. When they were living near the sea, he used to insist on her coming swimming in the early mornings. My mother used to describe how much she disliked the walk back in a wet swimsuit and how rapidly he would stride along while she had to run to keep up.

All these details about my mother's life before I knew her come from stories she told me many times during my childhood and adolescence. One story about that earlier period, however, stands out in my memory as different from the others. It describes an incident that was so magical and yet so dreadful that my mother could only bring herself to tell me about it once or, at most twice, when I was nearly grown up. She was out walking in the countryside and saw in a ditch a medieval helmet with flames coming out of the visor. When and where did this happen? Was it a hallucination? Was it an interpretation of something else – a charcoal-burner's brazier or some burning rubbish? Did Bettie actually see a flaming helmet? All I do know is that it was a special moment in her life, and one about which I dared not question her.

Bettie was 32 when she married in 1939, and I was born nine months later in the first year of the war. With my father away for long periods and only home briefly on leave, it is perhaps hardly surprising that my mother and I became very close. I was a spoilt and adored only child, and accepted my mother's devotion with the unselfconscious egotism of childhood. An emblematic memory from wartime is of a rare teatime treat – a pot of strawberry jam that actually contained some whole strawberries, which my mother encouraged me to fish out and put on my piece of bread and butter. I honestly cannot remember my mother ever being cross or impatient with me, either then or after the war during my school and university days in New Zealand. By now I was calling her Bettie, for she was as much a friend as a mother. For as far back as I can remember she was unfailingly supportive, lavishing care and affection upon me and sharing my enthusiasms, yet making no demands in return. I used to tease her by suggesting that if I told her I had just murdered somebody, she would simply reply 'Jane, you are naughty' (the closest she ever got to reprimanding me, and always said in an indulgent voice), and set about whatever was necessary to protect me from being found out. Together we read and discussed the eighteenth- and nineteenth-century novels that were a major research interest of mine; many of the books in my collection today I owe to her diligent searching through junk and second-hand bookshops on my behalf. Throughout the long periods of absence that my marriage and subsequent living overseas necessarily entailed, Bettie continued to manifest her loving support. The news that we had found a picturesque cottage to rent in the south of France, rather than the dingy attic which we had thought would be our lot as students, received a characteristic reply by return mail. Alas, I no longer have the letter, but I remember Bettie describing herself as literally dancing with joy in the garden on learning of our good fortune. All my letters to my parents from that time still survive, thanks to Bettie's careful hoarding of them – I am glad to see that there were so many of them. Preserved, too, is the manuscript of *Laura, or Filial Obedience*, a pastiche of our favourite reading written to amuse her, and dedicated to her in suitably flowery terms. Her thoughts of me during my absences found physical expression in the clothes that she continued to make for me – as she had always done and continued to do until the task was beyond her. The last item, a blouse, was made when she was over 80 years old and I was nearly 50.

Threats to memory and identity: the effects of Alzheimer's disease

My mother had difficulties completing this last blouse, because she was becoming more and more forgetful. The coordination of a task that took several days or even several hours was getting beyond her, as the weeds now flourishing in her favourite rockeries also showed. By December 1990, when we visited my parents for Christmas, the diagnosis that had been made earlier of probable Alzheimer's disease was already being confirmed by my mother's obvious and frequent failures of short-term memory, her disorientation as to time and place, and her increasing inability to distinguish fact from fantasy. My parents were by then living in sheltered accommodation in the grounds of the hospital to which my mother would soon be admitted for the full-time care her condition would render inevitable.

At times that Christmas, my mother was painfully aware that something was wrong. In particular she was frightened by the way even deep-rooted memories of her past were becoming eroded, and with them her sense of identity. 'I don't know who I am, or why I'm here', she said in an anguished voice one morning, refusing to be comforted. Suddenly, I had an idea. 'Listen, Bettie – I'm going to tell you a story. Once upon a time, a dear little girl was born at Landaff in Wales …' and I proceeded to tell her the story of her own life, stringing together the various incidents that she had so often told me (including the one about sliding down the stairs on a tea-tray) and in much the same words as she had always used. Her attention was caught, and she began to smile: 'That little girl was me,' she announced triumphantly.

At other times, however, she appeared confident and sure of herself, finding her own patterns for weaving together fragments of past memories and present stimuli into satisfyingly coherent wholes. On one electrifying occasion, she stood peering intently out of the window at the distant hills – hills which she had never visited and, given her problems with walking, never would. Here's what she said, written down by me shortly after:

> All those different things – yet one doesn't notice how they fit together – I've walked up there looking for pieces of my mother's tapestry – if you look closely you can see pieces of tapestry, some of them whole – I've gone for long walks across those hills looking for pieces because they were worth a great deal to me.

Often that Christmas, and on later visits, she told me new versions of stories about her childhood. 'You see that hill over there – my father sent me up that.' Repeatedly, too, she boasted to me of various past and present exploits, many of them boldly appropriated from the menfolk whom she had so self-effacingly supported in the past. Always a poor swimmer, she now borrowed her father's skill and claimed to swim regularly across the nearby lake. The war, which she had spent largely looking after me while her husband and brother were away fighting, had, I now learned, been won by her thanks to 'a gift of guns from the people at Buckingham Palace'; 'Tom may think he is a great rifle shot' (my father indeed was, having represented the British Army in international competitions) '*but I* …' Other stories borrowed heavily from her reading. The details of the 'many treasures' her friends at Buckingham Palace had shown her when she visited them seemed based on a picture book about the royal collection in the hospital library. And the deathbed scene attributed to Willy, a pet sheep she had indeed once had, reminded me strongly of certain edifying incidents in the Victorian novels we had once enjoyed together. Her accounts of what she had done recently tended also to depart significantly from the known, and even the probable. The fact that she could now walk only with the aid of elbow crutches did not prevent her telling me that she had slipped out of bed during the night when no one was watching and rearranged the rocks in the hospital garden or had ran up to the top of the nearby mountain and back. Yet these, and all such stories about herself, were told with absolute conviction. 'Are you calling me a liar?' she proclaimed indignantly when someone dared to query her version of events.

Such stories – confabulations or pseudo-reminiscences, as they are called in the medical literature – are typical of people who are dementing. Usually they are regarded merely as symptomatic of the condition and meaningless in themselves, but it seemed to me then, and still does after some years both researching the question and listening to my mother, that her stories made perfectly good sense.

Learning to listen to another language

In Chapters 3 and 6, I have touched on the manner in which women, women writers and certain other groups have been marginalised and controlled by the ways in which they, and what they do, are represented. People with Alzheimer's disease provide a particularly telling example of how dominant discourses can not only silence but even deny the personhood of whoever fails to meet the criteria privileged by these dominant discourses. The mental and linguistic disorder shown by someone who is dementing disrupts precisely those aspects of language use most valued by the scientific, rational and objective discourses of the 'father tongue' (to use Ursula LeGuin's label for them; cited in Tompkins 1989: 127). Hence, medical textbooks on dementia routinely define what people with Alzheimer's say in terms of a lack or absence of meaning; their words are 'confused', 'meaningless', 'empty'. However, many nurses and family carers value the more social and subjective aspects of everyday language use (LeGuin's 'mother tongue'), and thus are more ready to accept what their charges say as valid and potentially meaningful attempts to communicate. These different estimates of the discourse produced by people with Alzheimer's have serious implications for care. Seeing such people without reason, without meaningful language, reduces them to something less than human – mere bodies to be kept fed and clean – whereas believing that what they say still has a sense upholds their continued status as human beings with social and emotional needs, as well as physical ones.

In my own case, my closeness to my mother and the survival of the rapport between us, despite the obviously limiting effects of her condition, inclined me to subscribe to that alternative, more positive estimation of people like her. She forgot what year it was and her own age ('I think I must be over 20', she replied when questioned on her 89th birthday); and she could no longer discuss with me the novels of Rosa Nouchette Carey, or even those of Jane Austen, after whom I am named; but we were still able to enjoy each other's company for all that. My familiarity with my mother's past obviously helped me to make sense of some of the things she said to me, but was a potential hindrance as well, since this personal knowledge made all too obvious how often and how far her current stories about herself deviated from what I knew about her life. What helped me most, I realised during that traumatic Christmas of 1990, was a set of professional knowledges, which gave me the means to perceive the order in my mother's apparently disorderly utterances and to devise strategies for understanding them. Thus began my research into the discourses on (and of) people who are dementing. This project brought together all the diverse interests of my previous academic work – interests in Victorian fiction, in narrative and narrative theory, in language and communication, in feminist work on revaluing those alternative voices which have been suppressed and silenced by the dominant, rational and scientific discourses. And it has involved my mother, too, even more closely and centrally than those earlier projects and interests to which she loved to contribute.

Let me explain briefly some of the professional knowledges on which this project draws – knowledges which allow for a more positive reworking and renegotiation of the apparently nonsensical ramblings produced by someone with Alzheimer's.

First, ideas about the different functions that language serves can be used to explain the conflicting estimates of the capacity of people who are dementing to use language meaningfully. According to linguists, there are six general purposes served by language, each one related to a key component in any act of communication.[1] The two most obviously instrumental functions are the informational one, which stresses giving information about the subject matter to which the communication refers, and the directive one, in which the emphasis is on directing or influencing the actions or thoughts of others. The problems with memory and with distinguishing fact from fantasy (which are characteristic symptoms of Alzheimer's disease) have an early and drastic effect on someone's ability to use language effectively to perform these functions (which are also those to which the medical discourse on Alzheimer's gives priority). However, the other functions of language – aesthetic, metalinguistic, expressive and phatic – are much less affected.

The aesthetic function predominates when the form of a communication becomes of particular interest, as happens not only in literary texts but also in more everyday cases, when an image or turn of phrase intrigues us for its own sake. Even someone who is dementing may sometimes speak poetically. My mother's search for pieces of her mother's tapestry is an example, as was her telling comment about life in a well-run and caring institution: 'When I'm here, it feels as if I'm nowhere.' Similarly, her obvious pleasure in repeating poetry she learned by heart at school, and, later, in chanting familiar nursery rhymes, suggested that her lifelong aesthetic delight in the patterns of language stayed with her to the end of her life.

The metalinguistic function is served by those aspects of a communication that provide us with whatever information we may need about its frame of reference to ensure that we respond to it appropriately. Given their problems with memory and the fact that the past often seems very much present to them, someone who is dementing may well not realise that their listener may need orienting towards the time, place or topic that they are talking about. However, when my mother put on a growly voice to show that it was her teddy bear, Growler the Second, speaking, or brought me back to the subject of one of her confabulations after a frivolous interruption on my part with the remark, 'but seriously now …', she was using language metalinguistically.

The expressive function of language places the emphasis on the feelings and emotions of the communicator. People who are dementing continue to have feelings and can still make them clear. 'Oh what a beautiful morning,' my mother would sing over and over when she was feeling happy. 'Appalling, that's appalling,' she would shout when she was in a bad mood, pointing at whatever had become an outlet for expressing her displeasure. Tone of voice and body language obviously make an important contribution here, and help carers to grasp the emotional tenor of utterances that might otherwise be unintelligible. If my mother was propelling her wheelchair about aggressively, for example, my father and I knew we were in for a hard time this visit.

The phatic function of language is also less dependent on the content of what is said: what counts most is the fact of communicating in itself as a means of establishing and maintaining contact between members of a community. Again, this function, too, survives the effects of the dementing process, not least because of the resilience of procedural memory, our deeply learned memory for routines which we have repeated so often that they become virtually automatic. Hence my mother, like so many other people in her situation, was able to establish friendships with particular nurses and residents and to carry on polite social chit-chat for some years after being admitted to full-time institutional care. 'I hope I got that right, Jane; it's so important to be pleasant to people,' she said to me after a polite exchange with a passer-by. She may have carried out the exchange itself on autopilot, as indeed most of us do, but she was still aware of having done so and of it being worth doing.

Whatever functions of language we give priority to, then, will determine our assessment of the capacity of people who are dementing. If we take into account the whole range of general language functions, we can look beyond the symptoms of someone's dementia and recognise what they can still do. The survival of the social and expressive functions is especially valuable, because on them depends our continued interaction with those around us and our participation in the life of our community. Soft toys and pets are known to help people who are dementing to maintain contact with others, both by turning their attention outwards and providing a ready-made topic of conversation. With this in mind, I bought my mother the old-fashioned teddy bear mentioned earlier. He was instantly named by her Growler the Second, and became her inseparable companion; he was always there for her, ready to be stroked and spoken to, and to act as reinforcement if called upon. 'Why don't you sleep with me any more?' she demanded of my father soon after her admission to full-time care. 'You like sleeping with me, don't you Growler?' 'Yes I do, very much,' Growler agreed in his growly voice.

Another set of professional knowledges which were crucial to my continuing to make sense of what my mother was saying concern theories about what language is and how it works.[2] The commonsense, everyday way of thinking about language is that it is meaningful because of what it refers to – words are labels that point to particular objects and concepts which are attached to (yet exist separately from) them. Dictionaries, and the cards one sees at kindergarten saying 'table' and 'window' attached to the items in question, confirm this label model. According to this model, when we communicate with someone, we use words as a vehicle for conveying our thoughts to them; our reader or listener receives our verbal package and unpacks from it the meaning we intended. If the package appears to have nothing in it, as may happen when the person speaking to us is affected by Alzheimer's, we assume this is due to a breakdown at the sending end of the process. The speaker had nothing to put in the package in the first place, and has lost the ability to use words meaningfully.

However, a semiotic approach conceptualises how language works rather differently. Instead of words being labels that derive their meaning from what they refer to, they are elements within a language system; and it is that system itself on which their meaningfulness depends. Indeed, rather than our world determining our language, it is our language that determines our world, providing us with the categories and distinctions that we use to make sense of our experience. To give a simple example, the meaning the word 'river' has for us depends less on the bodies of moving water to which it refers than on the set of words for such bodies of water within our language system and the distinctions represented by that set – 'river', 'brook', 'stream', etc. There is no exact equivalent of 'river' in French, because this different language system makes a different set of distinctions; our category 'river' covers both 'fleuve' and 'rivière' – rivers that flow into the sea and those that are tributaries of another river.

This alternative, semiotic approach, which sees meaning as dependent on the language system itself, has obvious advantages for dealing with the utterances of someone who is dementing. Their inability to refer accurately to the world around them or to past events is no longer the major impediment that it is if we keep to the commonsense, referential model of how language works; all that is necessary for what they say to be meaningful is that their language should still operate systematically. Even though their system may differ from our own, if we know its underlying rules we can make sense of the utterances produced by it, just as we can the utterances of someone speaking French, German or Chinese if we have learned these languages. The semiotic approach has an added advantage, too, in stressing the role of the listener in producing meaning. Meaning is not simply transferred from one person to another, but is the responsibility of both parties involved. Our failure to make sense of what we hear or read, there-fore, is not necessarily the fault of the originator of the message but of our own lack of appropriate sense-making strategies. The point is obvious if we are being spoken to in Chinese or in some regional dialect of English with which we are unfamiliar. It is less obvious, but perhaps just as valid, when someone is speaking to us in the language of Alzheimer's.

The alterations in the language of people who are dementing have already been well documented in the medical research literature, but the emphasis has tended to be on what these people get wrong, and how this knowledge can be used to diagnose their condition and its stages. Rereading this evidence from a semiotic perspective, however, one becomes aware of all the ways in which their language is indeed still functioning as a system (Crisp 1999: 112–16). The rules of normal grammar continue to operate, so what they are saying is usually well formed, however odd their choice of actual words may be. And that choice of words itself is usually far from random. Indeed, at least 65 per cent of the char-acteristic 'naming errors' made by people like my mother actually manifest a strong connection with the 'correct' word. To illustrate the two major types of link, consider the following greeting which my mother gave to one of her favourite nurses, Robyn Thomas: 'Hello redbreast!' As most readers will already have spotted, the word 'robin' frequently occurs with 'redbreast'; both are closely associated in our mental word-store. This semantic link was reinforced in the present case by a perceptual link. Robyn usually wore a red cardigan as part of her uniform, so the two robins also resembled each other – both of them were red. Strictly speaking, my mother had given Robyn the 'wrong' name, but there is still a recognisable system underlying her production of an appropriate alter-native name. The frequency with which these semantic and perceptual links occurs provides the basis for two simple interpretative strategies. Does what this person is saying make better sense to us if we relate the 'wrong word' to other words commonly used with this one? Is there a link of likeness operating here?

Another well-known feature of the language of people with Alzheimer's is the over-extended use of a specific word to refer to a broader category. In one example, studied in some detail, the word 'dog' was regularly being applied to a larger range of animals including cats, rabbits and squirrels, but not, however, to 'birds, fish, horses, cows and elephants' (Schwartz *et al* 1979). Again, these misnamings do seem to conform to some underlying logic: 'dog' now means something like 'small, furry, dog-like animal'. This suggests another strategy for interpreting an apparent misnaming – does the name being given make sense if we mentally add 'like this in some way'? Asking this question may also suggest to us some emotion being expressed through that likeness. My mother, for instance, frequently over-extended 'bear', applying it to all her favourite animals: dogs, sheep and cats. Her usual expression – 'look at the dear little bear' – confirmed that the broader category so designated was 'animals of which I am especially fond, like my Growler bear'. Similarly, her calling my father 'Howard' as she sometimes did, instead of his correct name, 'Tom', showed that she still recognised him as belonging to the broader category of men who have been important in her life.

From 'disorderly ramblings' to narratives of subjectivity

As these examples suggest, an alternative understanding of how language functions allowed me to look beyond the obvious errors in my mother's use of language and recognise that she was still saying something that made sense. A third set of professional knowledges about narrative allowed me to recognise the purposes and value of her confabulatory storytelling, too.

Confabulations are especially hard for family and care-givers to cope with, not only because of the way fact and fantasy are indiscriminately intertwined in them and yet presented as autobiographical fact, but also because they tend to be repeated over and over again. This perseveration, as it is called, is typical of someone who is dementing; my mother could keep going for a whole morning on one of her favourites, ignoring all of my attempts to change the subject. It is hardly surprising, therefore, that such stories are readily dismissed as nothing more than the disorderly and empty ramblings of a deteriorating mind. However, just as the general grammatical structure of language survives well into the dementing process, so too does the basic grammar of narrative. As I have demonstrated at length elsewhere (Crisp 1995b), my mother's stories follow the patterns around which all narratives are organised – a basic movement from problem to solution, from the upsetting of a status quo to the restoration of a new order. Like all stories, too, they resemble the patchwork my aunt used to make, stitching together fragments from a range of recognisable sources into a pre-established pattern.

In form, then, my mother's confabulations are little different from any other stories. What set them apart from the memoirs that my father was writing at this time was that she was no longer able to distinguish what actually happened to her from what she had fantasised or read about – all the mental fragments she was drawing on seemed equally real to her. However, research into the life stories told by non-dementing people suggests that the distinction between lying and truth may not be as centrally relevant to these stories as we might believe. Considered in the light of the alternative approach to language already mentioned, the stories that we tell about ourselves are not so much reportings of past events to be evaluated in terms of their accuracy or distortion, but rather active re-constructions of those events made to serve the needs of a specific interaction in the present. Think, for example, of the different versions of your earlier life that you may have given to a friend, a colleague, a prospective employer, a much younger member of your family, or a person you have just met at a party. In each instance you will have been highly selective both of the incidents you are going to cover and how you will cover them; events will be reshaped and rearranged to make them more worth telling; and in the process you will have been presenting yourself as a particular sort of person. Indeed, it is through such acts of turning our memories of our past into a narrative that we make sense of that past for ourselves and for others – that we construct and affirm our identity. This work of fashioning an identity is, as I noted in Chapter 3, a process that is never completed but ongoing throughout one's life. The reminiscences of the institutionalised elderly are a continuation of that work, 'the negotiation of a lifetime' in which the claim to be someone of worth is asserted to counteract the stigma associated with old age and loss of independence (Tarman 1988: 171–91). For someone like my mother, the task becomes even more urgent, as gaps appear in their memory and their grasp of when, where, and even *who*, they are becomes increasingly tenuous. Without the ability to weave together the remaining fragments of her mental tapestry into a coherent narrative, my mother would have been lost indeed.

Thus, however fantastic my mother's stories about herself became, I could make sense of them as serving much the same general purposes that her earlier stories did. Like them, they were ritualised constructions of a past, which provided the basis for a pleasurable interaction between us. They affirmed the bond between her and me by appealing to knowledges and tastes which we shared, and they presented my mother as someone interesting and still deserving of attention and respect. This more positive perspective also allowed me to recognise the additional, more personal value that certain of her stories had for her. Relocating her father's act of sending her up a church steeple from the other side of the world to her present environment, or claiming, after a lifetime of gardening, that she was responsible for the attractive arrangement of rocks in the hospital garden, helped convert her present surroundings into something familiar and supportive of an ongoing sense of identity. Some of her stories had a strong element of compensation for present restrictions, much as I suspect the narratives of her childhood naughtinesses had. As she said to me after claiming to have performed the impossible feat of running up to the top of the nearby mountain and back, 'It's nice to know that there are some things I can still do.' Other stories seemed to be fantasies of wish-fulfilment, making good some past lack or injustice by bestowing upon herself the extra children she would have so dearly liked to have, for example, or appropriating the achievements of her menfolk after a lifetime of providing daughterly and wifely support. Yet others seemed to offer a concrete way of dealing with some current preoccupation or fear – her search for pieces of her mother's tapestry providing a metaphor for her own attempt to find and hold together the rapidly disappearing fragments of past memories; the elaborate description of the peaceful death of her much-loved pet sheep serving as a meditation upon the 'good death' which we would all prefer for ourselves and those we love.

To conclude, dementia of the Alzheimer's type is frequently described in terms very different from those I have used here. It is represented both in popular journalism and in official medical discourse as a terrible 'plague', a sickness that 'ravages' the brain, a 'living death', the 'loss of self' (Crisp 1995a). People with this condition readily become objects of contempt and fear; they carry the burden of our collective sickness, that fear of an inevitable decline and death which they appear to play out in a lingering and nightmarish form

(Maisondieu 1989). Hence it is easier to see them as alien, other than ourselves, no longer human, than to recognise and accept their continuing likeness to us; easier to regard what they say as meaningless than to continue to listen to them. Even the kindlier, therapeutic approach to dementia care which has come to be practised in better nursing homes and hospitals carries the legacy of this negative attitude. Its emphasis on restoring or maintaining 'normal' functioning all too readily keeps the focus of attention on what people with dementia can't do, defining them in terms of the lacks, losses and deficits that differentiate them from 'normal people' like us.

Work such as mine, then, that takes a more positive attitude towards people with dementia has to contend with a vast body of both medical and popular opinion which takes a very different position. However, in the decade during which I have been engaged in my current project, a new paradigm has started to emerge. Having begun on the margins, speaking against what was then the orthodox position on Alzheimer's disease, I now find myself named in a recent study of tendencies within dementia care as a proponent of 'a new ethics of relating to elderly patients with dementia' (Rigaux 1998: 22), based on acceptance, respect and a willingness to 'bet on there being a sense' to whatever such people say and do.

You will understand now why I chose to begin this chapter as I did. It was not just to subvert the rules of academic discourse by introducing a more subjective and intimate note, but also to make Bettie visible to you as the person that she was, not only before the onset of Alzheimer's disease, but as she continued to be despite her dementia. As another, more famous teller of stories puts it:

> History isn't what happened. History is just what historians tell us … it is a tapestry, a flow of events, a complex narrative, connected, explicable. One good story leads to another. … The history of the world? Just voices echoing in the dark; images that burn for a few centuries and then fade; stories, old stories that sometimes seem to overlap; strange links, impertinent connections. We lie here in our hospital bed of the present (what nice clean sheets we get nowadays) with a bubble of daily news drip-fed into our arm. We think we know who we are, though we don't quite know why we're here, or how long we shall be forced to stay. And while we fret and writhe in bandaged uncertainty – are we a voluntary patient? – we fabulate. We make up a story to cover the facts we don't know or can't accept; we keep a few true facts and spin a new story round them. Our panic and our pain are only eased by soothing fabulation; we call it history.
>
> (Barnes 1990: 242)

Bettie, you, me – we all engage in confabulation; it is not so much a symptom of dementia as of being human.

Notes

1 For accounts of the functions of language, see R. Jakobson (1960) 'Closing Statement: Linguistics and Poetics', in R. Innis (ed.) *Semiotics*, Bloomington: Indiana University Press, 147–75; and G. Leech (1974) *Semantics*, Harmondsworth: Penguin, 47–94.
2 For a fuller discussion of these ideas, see J. Fiske (1982) *Introduction to Communication Studies*, London: Methuen; and R. Penman (1988) 'Communication Reconstructed', *Journal of the Theory of Social Behaviour* 18, 4: 391–410.

Bibliography

Barnes, J. (1990) *A History of the World in 10 1/2 Chapters*, London: Picador.

Crisp, J. (1995a) "She has Alzheimer's and They All Suffer from it", in K. Ferres (ed.) *Coastscripts*, Brisbane: Australian Institute for Women's Research And Policy (AIWRAP).

—— (1995b) 'The Stories That People with Alzheimer's Tell: A Journey with My Mother', *Nursing Inquiry* 2, 3: 133–40.

—— (1999) 'Towards a Partnership in Maintaining Personhood', in T. Adams and C. Clarke (eds) *Dementia Care*, London: Baillière Tindall, 95–119.

Maisondieu, J. (1989) *Le Crépuscule de la raison*, Paris: Centurion.

Rigaux, N. (1998) *Le Pari du sens*, Le Plessis-Robinson: Institut Synthèlabo.

Schwartz, M., Marin, O.S.M. and Saffran, E.M. (1979) 'Dissociation of Language Function in Dementia: A Case Study', *Brain and Language* 7: 277–306.

Tarman, V.I. (1988) 'Autobiography: The Negotiation of a Lifetime', *International Journal of Aging and Human Development* 27: 171–91.

Tompkins, J. (1989) 'Me and My Shadow', in L. Kauffman (ed.) *Gender and Theory*, Oxford: Basil Blackwell, 121–39.

10 Sites of history and memory
Hornet Bank 1857

Kay Ferres

Our interest in *lieux de memoire* where memory crystallises and secretes itself has occurred at a particular historical moment, a turning point where consciousness of a break with the past is bound up with the sense that memory has been torn – but torn in such a way as to pose the problem of the embodiment of memory in certain sites where a sense of historical continuity persists. There are *lieux de memoire*, sites of memory, because there are no longer *milieux de memoire*, real environments of memory.

(Pierre Nora, 'Between Memory and History: *Les Lieux de Memoire*', 1995: 635)

For the historian, the very reconstruction of a 'context' or a 'reality' takes place on the basis of 'textualised' remainders of the past.

(Dominick La Capra, *Rethinking Intellectual History*, 1983: 85)

In October 1857, Aborigines of the Jiman group carried out a carefully planned attack on Hornet Bank station in the Dawson Valley in what was then the colony of New South Wales. In the hour or so before daybreak, they killed all the white inhabitants, the Fraser family and employees, with the exception of 14-year-old Sylvester. The men sleeping on the verandah were killed first, then Sylvester was knocked unconscious, but lay out of sight in the darkness between his bed and a slab wall. From there, he heard his widowed mother pleading for her own life and that of her daughters, before they were raped and killed. Later, he found his way to the next station to report what had happened. Two men, William Miles and Thomas Boulton, went to Hornet Bank and buried the bodies. Their report of what they saw marked the women's bodies thereafter as 'violated in their persons and frightfully mangled'. Depositions made by all three were later published in the press, so the offence was widely known to Europeans. White reprisals were swift and indiscriminate. One of the Fraser sons, William, absent at the time of the attack, undertook a vendetta which (he claimed) resulted in the deaths of some eighty Aborigines in the remainder of his lifetime. Both the attack and the retribution fuelled public debate about the inadequacies of the Native Police, detachments of indigenous men under the command of a European officer, who were used to patrol settled areas and to 'disperse' Aborigines.

The narrative I have outlined here is the story that has been told from the official records of Europeans. It already exists in some tension with another story which might be told, constructed not only from the textualised remainders of European experience, but from an oral history and an indigenous history which has been transmitted through story and performance. Any European history, however 'inclusive', will not approximate an indigenous history of these events. Indigenous histories do not merely reproduce and recirculate a narrative; they map stories on to 'country'.

As bell hooks says of the distribution of authority across discursive positions, it is the marginalised who traverse the space of enunciation. The Other meets the coloniser at the centre. hooks calls for the coloniser to enter the space of the margin, to speak of 'the path of their resistance, of how it came to be that they were able to surrender the power to act as colonisers'; her message comes 'from that space in the margin that is a site of creativity and power, that inclusive space where we recover ourselves, where we move in solidarity to erase the category colonised/coloniser' (hooks 1990: 343).

Recent revisionist and postcolonial histories have taken account of relations of domination on racialised lines, emphasising the erasure of indigenous cultures and the Eurocentric constructions of Aboriginality that ensured the invisibility of those cultures. Aboriginality is included in contemporary histories as a representation of the other side of the frontier, the underside of a domination unevenly exercised by the white representatives of imperial power. While histories of contact have now taken into view indigenous people's interactions and negotiations with Europeans (Reynolds 1981; Goodall 1996; Rowse 1998), less attention has been given to the doubts and uncertainties Europeans expressed about the treatment of indigenous people. Marginality is no longer read simply as exclusion, but as potentially a site of *Aboriginal* resistance. Gordon Reid's account of Hornet Bank (Reid 1982), for example, reinstates the Jiman as strategically reacting to their dispossession, successfully overpowering an otherwise superior force with the tactics of stealth and cunning. This view of history as a political and ethical practice has also recently been supplemented by the publication of contemporary documents that express the hesitations and whisperings of conscience in the public writings of churchmen, journalists and citizens (Reynolds 1998). Further, new practices are beginning to emerge: Jackie Huggins, Rita Huggins and Jane M. Jacobs, for example, writing about Jackie and Rita's country, perform the ethical and epistemological encounters involved in collaboration (Huggins *et al.* 1995).

For as long as they continue with a narrative of marginalisation, feminist recoveries of 'women's history' also run the risk of preserving the binary categories of race and gender. This narrative reproduces the normative association of women with the domestic sphere, and admits only as exceptional women's negotiations of the public, political sphere. As Carolyn Steedman has observed of her own project on the contribution of Margaret McMillan to working-class culture and politics in Britain:

> One legacy [of the work being done in the field of women's history] is an
> altered sense of the historical meaning and importance of female *insignificance*.
> The absence of women from conventional historical accounts' discussion of
> this absence (and of the real archival difficulties that lie in the way of presenting
> their lives in a historical context) are at the same time a massive assertion of
> the littleness of what lies hidden.
>
> (Steedman 1990: 248)

Women fit uneasily in the conventional narratives of power – of class struggles, of racial subjugation – which continue to shape our understanding of
'politics'. White women are reductively represented in colonial narratives as
complicit in and legitimating an imperialist project. Their motives and interests
are differentiated in terms of the domain in which they are deployed: men serve
imperialism through the economy, the bureaucracy or the army; women's sphere
is the family, and here their part in the subordination of colonised peoples is seen
to betray an essentialist, nurturing femininity. This construction of the private is
part of the project of imperialism and industrialisation; it cannot take account of
the position of Aboriginal women in colonial or contemporary culture.

My subject is the Australian expatriate author Rosa Campbell Praed, who (in
1885) published *Australian Life: Black and White*, which recalls her early childhood
at Naraigin station, also in the Dawson Valley. She was 6 years old at the time of
the Hornet Bank massacre. This event becomes a defining moment in Praed's
autobiographical and fictional accounts of her 'wild bush' girlhood, and her
version of events was for a time incorporated in the historical record. This incorporation is dependent upon an understanding of the presence of the self in
autobiographical narrative as a guarantor of truth, of the eyewitness account as
confession. Praed's insertion of herself into the events at Hornet Bank, however,
needs to be understood not in terms that assume that she was telling, or even
wanting to tell, a truth about herself; not as a confession, but as a way of delim-
iting a space from which to speak. As a textual remainder, it should be situated in
a reconstructed context, in a narrative sensitive to the enmeshment of racialised
and gendered subjectivities.

Cultural theory and commentary have recently been preoccupied with the
notion of self-fashioning. In addressing autobiography, critics have also privileged self, partly in keeping with this broader trend, but also as a means of
identifying a generic point of difference from biography. Here, I am less
concerned to distinguish the two genres than to consider the uses of the self in
autobiography, both for its author and for the biographer who turns to autobiographical evidence in reconstructing her subject. My concerns, then, are not
limited to an understanding of self-fashioning as congruent with subject formation, and my attention to it is not primarily directed to the disclosure of a truth
of the subject. Rather, this chapter explores self-fashioning in autobiographical
writing and considers how the biographer's reconstruction of her subject can
take account of the ways that self and identity are caught in the webs of history

and memory, and how the historical and political circumstances of the present in which that self is fashioned shapes the possibilities of its enunciation.

As Elspeth Probyn has argued, the self is never simply put forward in discourse, 'but rather it is reworked in its enunciation' (Probyn 1993: 2). In my reconstruction of Praed's Australian girlhood, her account of that episode figures as a puzzle in the workings of memory and as a moment of excess in which particular anxieties of British colonial authority are exposed. My interest here is with the ways ideologies of sex, gender and race are reworked and re-membered in Praed's representation of herself and in her concern to represent Aborigines as both subjected to British law and as subjects of history. I am using the concept of self to designate, in Probyn's terms, 'a *combinatoire*, a discursive arrangement that holds together in tension the different lines of race and sexu-ality', lines which are rearticulated when the self is spoken in various contexts. In Praed's case, I argue, those lines are rearticulated in the political, historical and literary conjunctures of the early 1880s, when issues of colonial authority surfaced in British parliamentary debates about Home Rule and, more particu-larly for my purposes, the Ilbert Bill.[1] Rosa Praed lived in London during this period, and was to become a regular visitor to the Ladies' Gallery of the House of Commons as the guest of the Irish politician Justin McCarthy.

Toni Morrison has explored the oral and textual transmission of Afro-American histories and identities, excavating sites of memory at the intersections of autobiography and fiction (Morrison 1990). As Pierre Nora noted, literary and historical narratives come into a curious alignment as *lieux de memoire* (Nora 1995). Morrison locates her own fiction in a narrative tradition which encom-passes written slave narratives and oral storytelling, and which also takes account of the sites in which such memories are evoked, both in the telling and the hearing. The sites of memory are the loci of connection, the points at which identities and identification are forged and remade. Here, I treat Hornet Bank as a site of memory, where identities shaped through sex, gender and race are formed, principally along the lines of colonial power, and also destabilised and fractured across the lines of sexuality. I am concerned to unravel the ways that a contemporary feminist biographer and historian can understand how gender, sex and race work as intersecting webs of power to constitute colonial subjects, rather than to consider these categories as impinging in some hierarchical way on an already formed subject. Hornet Bank becomes a site of memory which is not just a personal nightmare, but a racial memory which has played a part in sedi-menting the meanings of 'whiteness' and 'Aboriginality' in Queensland history.

In the colonial press Hornet Bank was constituted as a site where relations of power were disrupted and reasserted by repeated comparisons with the uprising at Cawnpore, earlier in the same year. Rosa Praed's return to this site compli-cates racialised analyses of power through the figuring of sexuality, using her self to enunciate a gendered viewpoint on the maintenance of colonial authority. She continues to return to this site in fictional texts published over a period of several decades, as well as in a later autobiography, *My Australian Girlhood* (1902). The structure of the *Bildungsroman* shapes a narrative of self-fashioning in *My Australian Girlhood*, where *Australian Life* contains a mixture of genres: melodrama, documentary and memoir. Self-fashioning is not its object. Rather, it is a text which stakes a claim to a public, political voice. The self is used here as a tactic to open up a space of enunciation, not only to function as an expression of personal experience but also as a *mise en abyme* (Morris 1988: 7). Praed's first return to the site of memory is staged as a drug-induced projection, a phantasmagoria. But the historical circumstances of this first attempt to speak are telling. It occurs at a time when colonial politics and questions of authority were again a subject of public debate and contestation. The Ilbert Bill to amend the Indian Penal Code was introduced in February 1883, but before it was passed in January 1884 its provisions for 'native' officials to have limited criminal jurisdiction over European British subjects in India had aroused controversy in the British Parliament as much as in India. It is in the context of that debate that Praed's return to Hornet Bank, and to issues of colonial authority, might usefully be read. 'Hornet Bank' is wrenched out of its marginal colonial context and inserted into imperial politics at the metropolitan centre, for a British as well as Australian readership.

Although in describing the events of the massacre Praed draws upon a romantic notion of direct access to consciousness through mind-altering narcotics to conjure up an event from thiry years before, the veils that she sets aside are drawn back by a much more conscious process: 'We go on groping after lost clues and tormenting ourselves till we become exasperated by the very vividness of those early impressions that are like flashes in the darkness, and cause even later experiences to seem vague and unreal' (Praed 1885: 26).

She aligns memory with trance and dream; it is retrieved from 'the grey matter folds' of the brain not as the record of what actually happened in childhood, but as an experience constituted by, and constitutive of, the person we have later become. Memories are not unmediated: they are not recalled intact and unalloyed to consciousness, and they do not transparently lay bare the 'truth'. Remembering is an experience very much about the present as well as the past.

Praed's memories are not only retrieved from 'grey matter folds'. In writing *Australian Life: Black and White*, she drew heavily on her father's unpublished memoir of Hornet Bank, and of a later 'massacre' at Cullinlaringo. Thomas Murray Prior's recollections of the Fraser killings are spare, perhaps partly because they were transcribed by his second wife, Nora Barton, specifically for his daughter's literary purposes. He diminishes his considerable role in reprisals, as a member of a vigilante group, emphasising instead the inadequacies of Native Police protection of European settlers. In his role as a Justice of the Peace, Murray Prior had also been a signatory to a petition for an inquiry into the operations of the Native Police. It seems likely, then, that in the context of the renewed controversy about the limits and efficacy of authority vested in 'natives', his own uses of the self are directed by the concerns of the present as much as the past.

As narrator, Praed situates herself as a commentator on Australian life and politics and, by extension, on colonial politics in Britain. *Australian Life: Black and White* is a memoir whose subject (the author) is at once curiously absent and contentiously present as an actor in historical events. And her voice, as narrator of this history, is also interestingly uneven. As author, she takes on an explicitly political persona, narrating a history which exposes a particular crisis in colonial authority. This narrative voice is not confident or consistent, and often its liberalism collapses into prejudice. The lack of confidence is contingent upon the marginality of her position: the narrator is not unambiguously aligned with European authority; she refuses, at least to some extent, the position of vulnerable, pure femininity and she attempts to establish an alliance with subordinated Aboriginality which is not absolutely complicit with imperialism.[2]

The author's self-presence in the narrative functions as a prism through which events are refracted, sometimes in a very tremulous way. The instabilities and ambivalences of this 'self' are apparent, even as it is asserted as a locus of judgement and perspective. That perspective does not always correspond with her father's. Praed's text explicitly inserts itself into a discourse of colonial history, as well as autobiography:

> There was treachery on both sides, and the Blacks had as good a right as the Whites to claim retribution for their wrongs. Does not the history of colonisation tell over and over again the same story? Justice has hardly been awarded by their historians to the Australian Aboriginals.
>
> (Praed 1885: 41)

My attention to this account of Praed's Australian origins, then, is directed to what it discloses of the child who was formed through the political conjunctions of Australian life and to the expatriate author's construction of herself as an historian of colonial and nationalist politics in the 1880s. The autobiography which can be read between the lines here was reworked in the later *My Australian Girlhood* as a narrative patterned more obviously on the notion of *Bildung*. *Bildung* plots, when enacted in the feminine, typically contain the self in a domestic, romance narrative. While attention to the private self has counteracted women's invisibility, it does not necessarily disturb the gendered distinction of domestic and political life which secured that invisibility. In *Australian Life: Black and White*, Praed's self is constructed across those boundaries, and through the intersections of gender and race. In the 1885 version, ideas of self and origins are subsumed by the elaboration of a commentary on contemporary events. I am drawn to this earlier version because it seems to offer a perspective on self and life which does not relegate the feminine to the private sphere, but crosses the borders into politics and history and opens out questions of the way women embodied their civil personalities.

Praed enters the debate about the status of Aborigines as subjects of British law and colonial authority that had preoccupied the colonial press in the middle decades of the nineteenth century. The parameters of this debate were set by two episodes in the frontier wars that frame Praed's narrative: the Myall Creek massacre of 1838, as well as the Hornet Bank massacre of 1857. These events posed the problem of the 'nature' and legal status of the Aborigines in stark terms: at Myall Creek, white men were brought to trial and sentenced to hang for the murder of Aborigines; at Hornet Bank, more than a hundred Aboriginal men and women were killed in revenge. At issue in the outcry in both cases was the Aborigines' status as rational subjects. If they were to be understood as 'primitive', then they could neither be answerable for crimes nor be seen as victims. The prosecution of white offenders against them, and of Aborigines for offences against whites, required that they be recognised as rational subjects of law.

Although Praed's juxtaposition of Myall Creek and Hornet Bank acknowledges this dilemma, her narration is shot through with ambivalence and contradiction. *Australian Life: Black and White* does not draw back the veil and restore justice to the Aborigines, but it does allow some insight into the ways racial and sexual anxieties impinged on the exercise of colonial authority, and into the way white women figured as the guarantors of that authority. This reading of the text, however, requires that notions of 'crime' should also be reconstrued. As Greta Bird points out, for Aborigines crime has traditionally centred around 'the breaking of marriage taboos, the telling of secrets and the making of magic' (Bird 1987: 8). As well, Aboriginal culture was predicated upon an understanding of propriety and obligation in which sexual exchange was significant. Such understandings were frequently explicated in Praed's fiction. Additionally, she often returns to the issue of marriage law, contrasting Aboriginal and European systems. The existence of such ethical systems among indigenous people is a detail that some contemporary historians, as well as the colonial press, find difficult to deal with. Yet rape is the key trope in Praed's text, as it is in her father's – and it fuels the press's vituperative outrage.

Praed's account of Hornet Bank survived in Queensland historiography because of its appearance as a personal, eyewitness account. In one sense, this is hardly surprising: very few first-hand documents of frontier life have survived, apart from newspaper and 'official' sources, and those that have survived have been largely written by men. Aboriginal memory has had no place in the record until recent revisionist history. Yet it seems that those who have taken Praed's account at face value have paid little regard to the status of literary 'evidence', nor have they taken account of Praed's capacities as a witness. At the time of the massacre, she was six years old; and the family's 'run' at Naraigin was some distance from Hornet Bank. Her family had had little contact with the Frasers, and had no direct knowledge of events until some time afterwards. Her father, however, had been among those settlers agitating for more adequate policing of the Aborigines, and after the massacre he and some neighbours had formed a vigilante group, known as the Browns, to keep the peace in their part of the Dawson Valley. Subsequently, he and other magistrates on the Dawson successfully petitioned for the suspension of Lieutenant Nicol, the commander of the local Native Police. Thomas Murray Prior's memoir of Hornet Bank is largely concerned with his role in this group, and with his concern to maintain good working relations with local Aborigines (he sees little contradiction, since he differentiates [tame] 'station blacks' from [wild] 'myalls'). His references to the killings are brief: 'It is better to draw a veil over a scene which cannot be described' (Praed papers, OM64–1). Yet his horror is apparent in the detail of the women's 'horribly abused' and the men's 'mutilated' bodies, and in the mention of a 'hideous travesty' which was reported to have been perpetrated on their corpses. In Murray Prior's memoir, then, both male and female bodies are sexualised, but in the press it is the bodies of the women that are so marked. The disappearance of the sexualised male body is necessary to maintain the crucial dichotomy which underpins colonial power. This dichotomy differentiates the rational subject of European law from the natural or 'primitive' other who is subject to that law. Where the mind–body split is crucial to the construction of that rational subjectivity as masculine, it is imperative to the structure of hier-archy within the category of masculinity itself (see Bordo 1987; Hekman 1992). The true manliness of the European is disembodied and desexualised, the inferi-ority of the 'native' is made apparent in the representation of his uncontrolled urges.[3] So the polarisation of race and sexuality opposes white (feminine) purity with rapacious black (masculine) sexuality *and* with promiscuous black (feminine) sexuality.

Reports of the 'massacre' in the colonial press were little concerned with the details of personal tragedy – their indignation at the killings installed the figure of the raped white woman as an icon of the crisis in colonial authority it signi-fied. On the local level, an ongoing debate between authorities in Moreton Bay and more liberal Sydney officials about the exercise of power and the mainte-nance of the Native Police was again enjoined. At the level of British imperialist power, the figures of Martha Fraser and her soon-to-be married daughter Elizabeth merged with the British women raped at Cawnpore:

> Little did we imagine when reading the horrible indecencies inflicted upon, and the subsequent butchery of, one hundred and seventy women and chil-dren at Cawnpore, that a tragedy of similar nature was being enacted at our very doors – that while we were hurling our anathemas at that consummate fiend, Nana Sahib, who presided over the barbarous atrocities, a tribe of hostile blacks were attacking an almost defenceless station, and ruthlessly murdering eleven men, women and children.
>
> (*Moreton Bay Free Press*, 18 November 1857)

This comparison with Cawnpore transforms the meaning of the violence: the innocence of the victims is never in question, while the Aborigines are charac-terised as savages and criminals, but never as sovereign people. There is a further point: not only is any notion of the workings of Aboriginal justice unthinkable, but the political significance of the attack is read in terms of insurrection against properly constituted authority. There is no acknowledgement of alternative systems of criminality and justice at work here, and the Aboriginal peoples are reduced to the figure of the bestial (male) criminal. There are no 'innocent' Aborigines; much less 'wronged' Aboriginal women.

Jenny Sharpe's study of the ways femininity figures in the allegories of empire fixes on the trope of the raped white woman (Sharpe 1993). Her function is to provide an image of innocence and vulnerability which justifies the exercise of power and retributive justice. Black and white are absolutely differentiated in the figures of the white woman and the black rapist – thus white power is legitimated. Black innocence and vulnerability, as well as legal responsibility, are not in the frame. Nor can white abuses of power be acknowledged.

From the evidence of *Australian Life: Black and White* and of Praed's novels, where the vulnerability to and fear of attack is a recurrent trope, there can be little doubt that the veil drawn by Murray Prior and by the pressmen had some other function than protection of white women's sensibilities, and that it served as an incitement to fear. In Praed's case, its significance materialises in the nightmare of vulnerability and guilt:

> I have not ceased to dream that I am on an out-station besieged by Blacks; and during many a night do I fly through the endless forests, and hide in stony gullies, pursued by an Aboriginal as ruthlessly as was de Quincy by his Malay.
>
> (Praed 1885: 27–8)[4]

In *Australian Life: Black and White*, the dream precedes the reality. Praed claims to have witnessed a corroboree in which the Fraser massacre was rehearsed:

> Four or five rude effigies of women, made of saplings and clothed in red blankets, were brought forward. Screams of demoniacal laughter echoed among the gum trees. A series of hideous gestures were gone through. The figures were mocked with yells of derision: they were thrown down, stomped upon, set up again, and at last dragged to the central pyre. The dance went on again, wilder than ever, but I felt faint and sick. I was convinced that a human sacrifice was about to be offered. I turned and fled towards the river. Tombo and Ringo followed, and led me back to the house. I crept into my bed and lay shuddering. I did not dare go for comfort to my parents, who, believing me asleep, were on the verandah watching the red illumination. Alas! had I described to them the horrible travesty I had witnessed, it is just possible that the tragedy might have been averted.
>
> (Praed 1885: 69–70)

Here is Murray Prior's 'travesty', though his chronology is reversed. Here it figures as a rehearsal for a premeditated attack, rather than as a sign of the Aborigines' bestiality. There are possibly temptations here of the psychologising kind. Why did Praed take upon herself the guilty knowledge of a premeditated attack in the 'little war' which raged in the Dawson during her childhood? I want to set that question aside, however, to consider what it is she describes so luridly, and to draw attention to the work of lurid in this deployment of the phantasmagoria. She describes the rape of the women, the climax of the attack, thus drawing back the veil (at least partially) on these 'events which cannot be described'. Though the language of melodrama, deployed in these circumstances, makes the twenty-first-century reader cringe, it is just the language of the colonial press and of Thomas Murray Prior, and it owes something as well to the sensationalism of the illustrated press in the 1880s. Those papers juxtaposed murder, misadventure and all manner of sexual misalliance on their graphic front pages. It is Praed's placement of herself, at once on the edge and at the centre of these events, which appals and perplexes a postcolonial critic, but which might be better understood in terms of the convergence of the historical and the fantastic that characterised the earliest stagings of the phantasmagoria. Étienne Gaspard Robertson's experiments with this spectacular technology in the 1790s called up before the citizens of Paris a crowd of shades whose part in Revolutionary struggle is fresh in his audience's memory:

> And Robertson performs on this history a transformation exemplifying the ideological transposition of material reality. ... Robertson turns the bloody events of class warfare into aesthetic apparitions, fantastic nightmares of an evening's entertainment. ... Divested of their material reality, these historical figures are more than entertaining. Robertson helps them to *entrer dans la légende*, integrating them into the pantheon of the phantasmagoria of 'cultural history'. ... Robertson's representation thus seeks to exorcise the demonic power of the revolutionary memories haunting the Parisian imagination ...
>
> (Cohen 1993: 234)

Recovering this convergence of history and memory in the technology of the phantasmagoria goes some way to deciphering this particular puzzle at the site of memory. The corroboree scene is reiterated in *My Australian Girlhood*, reproduced in the work of amateur historians, and repudiated angrily by Gordon Reid, who denounces Praed for her lack of interest in truth (Reid 1982: 154), as if her account were a transparent representation of real events, rather than a transformation of them and, in part at least, polemical. The workings of that transformation are revealed through the recontextualisation of this remainder.

Praed recontextualises her father's memory. Where he draws a veil over the depredations suffered by the Fraser women, rape is at the centre of her account. But she represents herself in a particular relation to it; she is a privileged witness to the meaning of the ceremony, having been taken to view it by the 'first object of my childish affections', the Aboriginal boy, Ringo. This ceremony is some kind of childish initiation, signifying an affiliation which Praed later, to her shame, repudiates when she fails to recognise her childhood friends. But as a white woman – and it is her whiteness which is so present to the reader here – the meaning of the massacre was interpreted for her by the colonial press: the rape of white women testified to the inhumanity of the Aborigines, and to the legitimacy of white colonial authority. At the time of the text's composition, the dangers posed to European women by native men were again reiterated, as objections to the Ilbert Bill raised the spectre of the white woman forced 'to submit to the jurisdiction of the Calibans lusting after the Mirandas of Anglo-India' (Sinha 1992: 99).

Praed's imagined presence at the corroboree suggests that, from a different position in colonial power relations, another meaning which cannot be spoken (or cannot be heard, because unauthorised) is possible. Praed pictures herself, creeping home, unable to reveal to her parents (who are sitting on the verandah taking in the picturesque glow of the corroboree fires, hearing the high-pitched yells) her guilty knowledge. The *faire*[5] of the image of self, the work that it is doing here, is to materialise the space of the enunciation, to divide itself (Probyn 1993: 88–92). Praed locates herself on the margins, looking on at the image of vulnerability and powerlessness which figures colonial femininity. She returns home, unable to speak what she saw. Explanation of her absence would involve disclosure of her alliance with Ringo and the others, and such alliances are only legitimated through the discourse of the 'civilising mission'. If Praed's position is not congruent with that discourse, not complicit with the objectives of imperialism, then she cannot produce a reasonable excuse. And this assumes that she can make her motives intelligible. As Ian Reid has commented on narration, 'the enunciative aspect [of a narrative] is better understood as a struggle to possess the meanings of what is told than as the mere capacity to impart a tale' (Reid 1992: 14). The unevennesses and inconsistencies of Praed's attempt to do justice to the Aborigines in *Australian Life: Black and White* are produced by the struggle to possess the meanings of what is told. Those meanings are not transparent, or even now readily articulated. Perhaps I should say especially now, when within feminism and postcolonial discourse the problems of white appropriations of otherness and the difficulties of assuming the existence of an undifferentiated category 'woman' are compelling. Yet the very excessiveness and visibility of Praed's whiteness here seems to me to allow a strategy along the lines of Nancy Miller's 'overreading' (Miller 1986) or Gayatri Spivak's 'scrupulous and plausible misreadings' (Spivak 1990: 389). Miller and Spivak use these strategies to bring the margins to the centre and to displace the dichotomies that hold those positions apart.

In drawing a veil over the fate of the Fraser women, Thomas Murray Prior also concealed a narrative which makes a different kind of sense of their rape. That narrative sees the rape as a form of Aboriginal justice, rather than criminality. At Hornet Bank, the young Fraser men had a reputation for their dealings with Aboriginal women that alarmed their mother. Martha Fraser had feared the consequences of their habit of 'forcibly taking the young maidens' and had appealed to Mr Nicol of the Native Police to intervene when her own influence was unavailing (cited in Reynolds 1982: 67).

Martha Fraser's voice survives as a helpless cry in the official records, and one heard by few historians, though Henry Reynolds (Reynolds 1982) and Ray Evans (Evans 1992) have given conjugality and its obligations serious attention. Gordon Reid, who has written the only book-length account of Hornet Bank (Reid 1992), specifically excludes sexual motives as a 'cause' of the massacre, arguing instead that dispossession of land and resources was the primary consideration. Reid's account shows, through the trope of the dispossession of land, how 'whiteness' is a politically constructed category parasitic upon Aboriginality/blackness (compare West 1990: 29). My intention has been to show how the alignment of whiteness with femininity, through the trope of the vulnerable white woman, reduces the axes along which racial conflict and colonial power are played out. Sexuality is a site where power relations are embodied; white power materialised through the possession of Aboriginal women as well as the dispossession of Aboriginal land. There was no public discourse available to Rosa Campbell Praed through which she could speak of this site of struggle, except the discourse of myth.

In this discourse, women's woes are still ancillary to men's battles, their virtues (and vices) active in a minor key. Jenny, a 'half-caste' whose 'adoption' had occupied a considerable part of Thomas Murray Prior's memoir, left Naraigin with the Murray Priors and lived with them in Brisbane until 1863. Then, apparently at his wife Matilda's urging, Thomas sent her to Port Denison, hundreds of kilometres to the north, as an apprentice:

> I was afraid that taking her at all was a mistake and I did not like to let her go. She was so incorrigibly lazy, so dirty – the animal predominating. She would be quite happy lolling like a black gin in the dirt all day. Poor thing did not at all like leaving the children, but it would not do keeping her any longer. I only hope I have not done her harm instead of good by giving her the tastes and habits of civilisation.
>
> (Murray Prior papers, MSS 3117/2, 3)

Murray Prior's journal entry reveals how the 'half-caste' was read as dangerous, a sign of the precariousness of the 'civilised' values which underpinned the imperialist mission. The sense of this danger was brought home to the young Rosa in the presence and absence of Jenny. The journal entry ends: 'I shall not lose sight of her.' I want to suggest that Praed does not lose sight of her either, but neither can she bring this recollection clearly into view.

Jenny figures in Rosa's memory as Hebe, a cup-bearer who displeases the gods when she falls and inadvertently exposes her genitalia. Once again, a veil is drawn back to disclose that which cannot be spoken and that which mutely speaks itself. Hebe's story has some connections with the Christian story of the Fall, in that sin is sexualised and mapped on to the female body. As Hebe, Jenny is a cipher of sexual promiscuity attributed to the female, as it is with Eve. In this scheme, white masculine promiscuity is disavowed and the sexualised male body is disavowed.

Toni Morrison thinks of the site of memory as a place where 'the two crafts [of memoir or self-recollection and fiction] embrace and where that embrace is symbiotic' (Morrison 1990: 299). While it has become commonplace to speak of the self as an invention, and to read autobiography in these terms, we are still uncomfortable with trespassing across the boundaries of fiction and autobiography. When women writers blur those boundaries, their trespass is often held against them; in Praed's case, the suspicion of an expatriate writer's appeal to a home she had left behind has also had an effect. That effect is to diminish the self which is written in both the autobiography and the fiction, to cast it into the shadows of the central debates in Australian cultural history. The 'glamour of the bush', so often invoked in Praed's writing, has an allure at once seductive and distracting, its romances irreconcilable with the realism of the dominant tradition. But if that allure is taken as the sign of excess, as a sign that self here is at once being destabilised and reworked, then the strategies of over-reading or scrupulous misreading at the sites of memory might disclose the possibilities of another self, a rearticulation of the lines of race and sexuality in its discursive arrangement. Toni Morrison describes her own strategic embrace of autobiography in fiction:

> It's a kind of literary archaeology: on the basis of some information and a little bit of guesswork you journey to a site to see what remains were left behind and to reconstruct the world that these remains imply. What makes it fiction is the nature of the imaginative act: my reliance on the image – on the remains – in addition to recollection, to yield up a kind of truth.
>
> (Morrison 1990: 302)

In this chapter, I have journeyed to such a site. The remains are few, and the found objects have been well worked over by the keepers of official histories. The image of Jenny and the woman who tried to speak need not be lost sight of. Recalcitrant histories can work with the tension between stories that have been told and stories that might be told, in the convergences and divergences of narratives of memory – history, autobiography and fiction – to trace the struggle to possess meaning, rather than to uncover 'truth'.

Notes

1   For a discussion of the bill and the intersections of feminist and colonialist politics, see Sinha (1992).
2   On the conjunctions of feminism and imperialism, see Burton (1992).
3   Compare Mrinalina Sinha's discussion of the construction of Bengali masculinity in imperialist texts in Sinha (1987).
4   In *Confessions of an English Opium Eater* (1822), de Quincy recounts his haunting by the figure of a Malay, which transports him nightly to the 'unimaginable horror' of the Orient.
5   This term is Michele Le Doeuff's, quoted and elaborated in Probyn (1993: 88–92).

Bibliography

Bird, G. (1987) *The 'Civilising Mission': Race and the Construction of Crime*, Contemporary Legal Issues, 4, Melbourne Faculty of Law, Monash University.
Bordo, S. (1987) 'The Cartesian Masculinisation of Thought', in S. Harding and J.F. O'Barr (eds) *Sex and Scientific Inquiry*, Chicago: University of Chicago Press, 233–64.

Burton, A.M. (1992) 'The White Woman's Burden: British Feminists and "The Indian Woman" 1865–1915', in N. Chaudhuri and M. Strobel (eds) *Western Women and Imperialism: Complicity and Resistance*, Bloomington: Indiana University Press, 137–57.

Cohen, M. (1993) *Profane Illumination: Walter Benjamin and the Paris of the Surrealist Revolution*, Berkeley: University of California Press.

Evans, R. (1992) 'A Gun in the Oven: Masculinism and Gendered Violence', in K. Saunders and R. Evans (eds) *Gender Relations in Australia: Domination and Resistance*, Sydney: Harcourt, Brace, Jovanovich.

Goodall, H. (1996) *Invasion to Embassy: Land in Aboriginal Politics in New South Wales*, Sydney: Allen and Unwin.

Hekman, S.J. (1992) *Gender and Knowledge: Elements of a Postmodern Feminism*, Boston: Northeastern University Press.

hooks, b. (1990) 'Marginality as a Site of Resistance', in R. Ferguson, M. Gever, T.T. Minh-ha and C. West (eds) *Out There: Marginalisation and Contemporary Cultures*, Cambridge, MA: MIT Press, 341–3.

Huggins, J., Huggins, R. and Jacobs, J.M. (1995) 'Kooramindanjie: Place and the Postcolonial', *History Workshop Journal* 39 (Spring): 165–81.

La Capra, D. (1983) *Rethinking Intellectual History: Texts, Contexts, Language*, Ithaca, NY: Cornell University Press.

Miller, N.K. (1986) 'Arachnologies: The Woman, The Text and The Critic', *The Poetics of Gender*, New York: Columbia University Press, 270–95.

Morris, M. (1988) *The Pirate's Fiancée: Feminism, Reading, Postmodernism*, London: Verso.

Morrison, T. (1990) 'The Site of Memory', in R. Ferguson, M. Gever, T.T. Minh-ha and C. West (eds) *Out There: Marginalisation and Contemporary Cultures*, Cambridge, MA: MIT Press, 299–305.

Murray Prior papers, Mitchell Library, State Library of New South Wales, ML MSS 3117.

Nora, P. (1995.1984) 'Between Memory and History: *Les Lieux de Memoire*', in J. Revel and L. Hunt (eds) *Histories: French Construction of the Past*, New York: The New Press, 631–42.

Praed papers, John Oxley Library, State Library of Queensland, OM-64.

Praed, R.C. (1885) *Australian Life: Black and White*, London: Chapman and Hall.

—— (1902) *My Australian Girlhood*, London: T. Fisher Unwin.

Probyn, E. (1993) *Sexing the Self: Gendered Positions in Cultural Studies*, London: Routledge.

Reid, G. (1982) *A Nest of Hornets*, Melbourne: Oxford University Press.

Reid, I. (1992) *Narrative Exchanges*, London: Routledge.

Reynolds, H. (1982) *The Other Side of the Frontier*, Ringwood: Penguin.

—— (1998) *This Whispering in Our Hearts*, Sydney: Allen and Unwin.

Rowse, T. (1998) *White Flour, White Power: From Rations to Citizenship in Central Australia*, Sydney: Cambridge University Press.

Sharpe, J. (1993) *Allegories of Empire: The Figure of Woman in the Colonial Text*, University of Minnesota Press.

Sinha, M. (1987) 'Gender and Imperialism: Colonial Policy and the Ideology of Moral Imperialism in Late Nineteenth-Century Bengal', in M.S. Kimmel (ed.) *Changing Men: New Directions in Research on Men and Masculinity*, London: Sage.

—— (1992) ' "Chathams, Pitts and Gladstones in Petticoats": The Politics of Gender and Race in the Ilbert Bill Controversy, 1883–84', in N. Chaudhuri and M. Strobel (eds) *Western Women and Imperialism: Complicity and Resistance*, Bloomington: Indiana University Press, 98–116.

Spivak, G.C. (1990) 'Explanation and Culture: Marginalia', in R. Ferguson, M. Gever, T.T. Minh-ha and C. West (eds) *Out There: Marginalisation and Contemporary Cultures*, Cambridge, MA: MIT Press, 377–93.

Steedman, C. (1990) *Childhood, Culture and Class in Britain: Margaret McMillan 1860–1931*, London: Virago.

West, C. (1990) 'The New Cultural Politics of Difference', in R. Ferguson, M. Gever, T.T. Minh-ha and C. West (eds) *Out There: Marginalisation and Contemporary Cultures*, Cambridge, MA: MIT Press, 19–36.

11 'Flying or drowning'

Sexual instability, subjective narrative and 'Lawrence of Arabia'

Gillian Swanson

> The daydream transports the dreamer outside the immediate world ... it flees the object nearby and right away it is far off, elsewhere, in the space of elsewhere.
>
> (Bachelard 1964: 183)

> In the desert ... identity, like direction, was dispersed; the subject himself immersed in a greater medium, hidden, invisible. Yet this delicious sensation of being curled up in the pocket of the night could not be separated from terror of the immensity. In this world of streaming winds, to travel was never to walk or ride: it was to fly or drown.
>
> (Carter 1987: 290)

Imagining a self

In this chapter, I want to focus on the way cultural knowledges, developed in particular times and places, contribute to the way that subjectivity can be written in narratives of masculinity. In Chapter 8, I drew on Bakhtin's argument to stress the dialogic nature of discourse, which works as a series of social interactions: as such it is always in process, interactive, subject to revision and contestation. To that extent, representations – however authoritative – hold within them the possibility of alternative knowledges, and, as I indicated in the introduction, this may give rise to a 'categorial instability'.

In the case of sexuality, this is particularly evident for two reasons. First, because sexual difference is premised upon the existence of two distinct and *incommensurate* categories and yet this distinction is built upon two interdependent and *reciprocal* terms; and second, because notions of the individual and subjectivity and the model of an 'inner' self have a conceptual association with private life and those intimate dimensions of the person that are associated with the feminine. This provides an instability of definition – especially for masculinity – which ensures that difference is always in play in any representation of subjectivity or sexuality, and suggests that there is always the possibility of encountering the limits of coherence and stable subject positioning. The concept of 'categorial instability' signals the possibility that representations of subjectivity may challenge the intelligibility of apparently authoritative systems of cultural – or sexual – classification. It is this possibility that I wish to explore in this chapter.

The subject I will take for this exploration is the figure of 'Lawrence of Arabia', as an assembly of the cultural narratives that surround the historical character of T.E. Lawrence. Many accounts of colonial adventure epics suggest that they assert heroes of the British Empire just as its power contracts and that these stories shore up and bolster a myth of British greatness with an image of 'idealised masculinity' which is contrasted to 'other and subordinated, "non-white" masculinities' (Dawson 1991: 119). Accounts such as these assume a causal interpretation, in which representations have a discernible function: the coalescence of images into stable forms which reassure or reassert, offering 'wish-fulfilling fantasies' as a kind of ideological therapy for insecure subjects whose preoccupation is the coherence of identity and absolute power (Dawson 1991: 119). Graham Dawson argues that, even in its 'fascination with and fear of the colonised "other" ', imperialist military adventure still offers an example of the 'exercise of imperial authority', as the encounter with 'peripheral and colonised others' is used to secure the 'idealised, omnipotent masculinity of the central hero' (Dawson 1991: 125–7). Dawson sees the 1920s 'heroic' biographies' evocations of a Lawrence who identifies with the Arabs as a way of 'repossessing' the other, producing a legendary 'new kind of ideal unity and coherence' (Dawson 1991: 136). And he argues that even the feminisation of descriptions of Lawrence offers a masculinity whose power is simply *sustained* by the dissolving of gender difference, as the 'imagined integration' of 'passive', contemplative and 'feminine' or 'effeminate' characteristics with traditional images of the military man of action 'suggests … an alternative and superior mode of being a man' (Dawson 1991: 124, 137). Such an argument forecloses analysis of the effects of those fractures to masculinity which Lawrence's particular narrative may create, by giving greater weight to the generic characteristics of military adventure. If, instead, we move beyond the analysis of their narrative strategies, we may find that the 'dilemma of identity' which is foregrounded in all narratives of Lawrence poses greater difficulties for the representation of a triumphant colonial masculinity. The challenges his figure poses to conventions of masculinity become more intelligible if we examine how it is crossed by contemporary knowledges of sexuality – which, rather than replaying fantasies of coherence, foreground the ambivalence of sexual and colonial relations and their *fragmentations* of the relations between national identity and masculinity.[1] This asks us to chart a more complex series of exchanges between masculine achievement, sexual ambivalence and subjective incoherence.

The narratives that are generated around Lawrence can be divided into two phases. The first is that of his autobiographical account of his role in the Arab revolt, *Seven Pillars of Wisdom: A Triumph*, which was printed privately in 1926 and given its first public release after his death in 1935. This is accompanied by contemporary biographical accounts, beginning with the slide-show presentations of his exploits in Britain's 'desert campaign' during the First World War made by the popular journalist Lowell Thomas in 1919, which generated immediate public acclaim for Lawrence and were followed by the celebratory accounts of Robert Graves (1927) and Sir Basil Liddell Hart (1934). The second period includes the reassessments of Lawrence made by biographies and newspaper reports appearing through the 1950s – most notably, a biography by Richard Aldington, published in 1955, offered a damning appraisal of his military achievements, his character and his sexuality. Lawrence's autobiographical account of his time as an enlisted member of the RAF, *The Mint*, was released posthumously in 1955, and *Seven Pillars of Wisdom* was republished in a Penguin edition in 1959, to be followed by the film based on his role in the Arab revolt, *Lawrence of Arabia* (directed by David Lean) in 1962. Lawrence's sexual ambiguity – and a concern over whether his recoil from women, love of the company of men and involvement in flagellation testifies to a homosexuality – is a critical part of this second wave of accounts, and the 'revival' of interest in Lawrence in this second period is undoubtedly connected to a pervasive public interest, during the 1950s, in identifying the features of homosexuality.

There are two reasons why the narratives surrounding Lawrence offer a compelling case for examining the relationship of cultural knowledges to representation and sexual difference. First, they centralise a 'problem of identity' – in his Arab identifications, his sexual ambiguity and talk of his 'breakdown' after returning from Arabia – in ways that show something of the disturbance that the subjective brings to narratives of masculinity, and the consequent fragility of systems of classification and their ability to offer categorial stability. Second, they bring into focus a series of shifts in knowledges of subjectivity and sexual difference between the 1920s and 1950s, as a series of homosexual scandals throughout the 1950s, and the preparation of the Report of the Committee on Homosexual Offences and Prostitution (HMSO 1957), referred to as the Wolfenden Report, from 1954 to 1957, create the conditions for the development of a more elaborated range of homosexual features and types.

Subjectivity and narrative[2]

First, I want to examine the relationship of the subjective to modern forms of narrative and the implications of the introduction of the subjective into narratives organised around individual perspective. As a result of the perspectival nature of subjective perception, cultural narratives with the subjective at their centre came to be seen as problematic sources of knowledge about 'the world' rather than 'a self'. How does a 'subjective narrative' act to undermine the stability of public masculinity?

In his account of the development of the modern novel, Mikhail Bakhtin argues that the development of novelistic form is intimately connected to modern ways of conceiving of time and space, history and memory, and the sense of the present (Bakhtin 1981). As the premodern epic writes an 'absolute' past – complete, unchangeable and closed – as the achievement of revered ancestors and founding fathers, it has recourse to a concept of hierarchical meaning outside human intervention or familiarity, and is thus constructed in the absence of relativity and human perspective (Bakhtin 1981: 11–17).

> The epic world is constructed in the zone of an absolute distanced image, beyond the sphere of possible contact with the developing, incomplete and therefore re-thinking and re-evaluating present. ... In the world of (epic) memory, a phenomenon exists in its own particular context, with its own special rules, subject to conditions quite different from those we meet in the world we see with our own eyes, the world of practice and familiar contact.
>
> (Bakhtin 1981: 17–18)

Epic memory, as a way of writing the past, is thus impersonal, immutable, unquestionable and absolute. The modern novel, on the other hand, operates on the same 'time-and-value plane' as that of contemporary reality: 'the zone of "my time", from the zone of familiar contact with me' (Bakhtin 1981: 14). It builds in the sense of a present, and the contemporary viewpoint, thereby incorporating openendedness, perspectival relativity, indeterminacy, continuation. While his intention is to analyse the development of modern narrative form, therefore, Bakhtin also outlines the introduction of the subject, and the subjective perspective, into representation, demonstrating the conditions of possibility for subjective knowledge. In this schema, the novelistic image is left open to a new kind of 'problematicalness ... an eternal rethinking and re-evaluating' deriving from the (multiple) perspective of the subject (Bakhtin 1981: 31). In short, this is a field which we may associate with forms of subjective narrative.

However, a further effect of the introduction of the subjective into representation is that the subjective itself becomes formed in the image of the inconclusiveness and relativity which perspective and recognition brings to the novel. What Bakhtin actually describes when he notes the incorporation of perspective and human interjection into the novelistic field of representation is, in fact, a new way of thinking of the subject. It is actually the beginning of the formation of the concept of 'the subjective' in all its relativity and openendedness, in all its indeterminacy and its intimacy. The concept of the 'individual', therefore, is thereby characterised by a lack of wholeness and completedness, and thus a new *instability*, which renders it historical. As he claims that the novel 'is the genre of becoming', we can read in Bakhtin's account an absolutely constitutive link between a new historical consciousness and a new conception of subjectivity, not as essence, but *as itself historical*, caught up in the process of 'becoming'. Subjectivity should also, therefore, be understood in the light of what Bakhtin has referred to as that relative field of 'knowledge', incorporating difference as well as familiarity. As it takes on the relativity of historical knowledge, subjectivity (and those forms of narrative formed in its perspective) also becomes ongoing, inconclusive and processual.[3]

The introduction of the subjective into narrative comes at some cost to the authority of such representations, however. With the limits of knowledge which were attributed to the private – the world of secrets, personal intimacy and individual moral discretion – the subjective began to occupy an epistemologically derogated field. In scientific discourse in the last quarter of the nineteenth century, for example, a higher, *non*-subjective standard – that of 'mechanical objectivity' – was sought. Thus, science attempted to eliminate human intervention between its own standard of reality – nature – and scientific representation, drawing on the technologies of mechanical registration such as photography, the X-ray, the lithograph in place of the drawings of great artists (Daston and Galison 1992). This, it was hoped, would avoid the exercise of interpretation, individual judgement, artistry, which were 'subjective temptations requiring mechanical or procedural safeguards' (Daston and Galison 1992: 98).

Perspective, bias, and a dependence on the inexact, suspect and 'tempting' mediation of human senses, was to be eliminated, to free scientific endeavour from human interference or will, as the mechanically registered image was seen to guarantee a 'truth' that was firmly contrasted to the individual or subjective viewpoint. This 'disciplining' of subjectivity was not simply a scientific or technical matter, but also a moral task, and scientific representations were only one aspect of the new ways in which the imperfections of individual interest – enshrined in the subjective model of the observer as mediator – could be overcome: 'the machine ... embodied a positive ideal of the observer: patient, indefatigable, ever alert, probing *beyond the limits of the human senses*' (Daston and Galison 1992: 119, my emphasis).

The scientific debates centring on those human interferences which put objectivity at risk, then, show one area in which a sense of the 'dangerously subjective' became a template for the contaminating force of wilful individual intervention (Daston and Galison 1992: 82).

The subjective, as a constitutive element in the functioning of the modern subject, was understood to put at risk the disciplined, attentive, impersonal functioning of moral consciousness, triumphing over the limits and wilful temptations of the senses. Even in fiction, attempts were made to distinguish narrative with claims to a greater 'truth' than the subjective, from derogated forms like the sensation novel. An aesthetic enterprise, which Laqueur refers to as the 'humanitarian narrative', was directed towards the development of literary techniques that would allow the realist novel to make a claim to represent the social world in ways that moved beyond the limits of the 'individual view' and its imbrication in the sensual, the particular, the personal (see Laqueur 1989a).

Drawing on those repertoires of cultural knowledge that establish sexual difference within the frame of a public–private divide, the frailties of the subjective are connected to a 'feminine sensibility' that is managed by its spatial and psychological removal from public life and masculine character. Public domains of knowledge became opposed to individualised and subjective narratives, and the status of subjective knowledge was rendered questionable. By its association with the feminine, then, the subjective, the individual and the private came to be seen as antipathetic to the knowledges that are appropriate for the effective conduct of public life. Hence, subjective narrative, with its connection to the private and intimate realms of the self, could only be seen as a problematic form for representing masculinity.

The subjective in narratives of Lawrence

How are the instabilities associated with the subjective mapped on to the narratives of Lawrence? T.E. Lawrence has been the subject of sustained biographical attention ever since the popular celebratory accounts begun by Lowell Thomas in 1919. His own autobiographical account of his role in the Arab revolt was withheld from publication for a general readership until after his death in 1935. Such a delay also occurred with his second autobiographical volume, *The Mint* (Lawrence 1955): written from 1922 to 1928, and published in a subscribers' edition in 1936, Lawrence made a note in his will that this volume should not be published until after 1950, and it finally appeared in 1955.

What are the difficulties in his writings, and why is there a hesitancy about making them available publicly? It is not, I would argue, just their preoccupation with sexual ambivalence which is at stake, although clearly this has some role to play. For there is a deeper problem in the imbrication of the public narratives of history with those personal narratives of psychological development, cultural identification, moral introspection. The introduction of the subjective viewpoint – particularly in *Seven Pillars of Wisdom* – disturbs the conventions of military histories, and renders his public persona (based on his heroic role in the desert campaign) questionable. But the introduction of the subjective may also disturb the conventions of masculinity. Gilles Deleuze concludes of Lawrence that his is not merely a 'personal difference', but the difference that is created by a subjective disposition, which undermines unified constructions of masculinity and the self:

> Lawrence's undertaking is a cold and concerted destruction of the ego, carried to its limit. Every mine he plants also explodes within himself, he is himself the bomb he detonates. It is an infinitely secret *subjective disposition*, which must not be confused with a national or personal character, and which leads him far from his own country, under the ruins of his devastated ego ... a profound desire, a tendency to project – into things, into reality, into the future, and even into the sky – an image of himself and others so intense that *it has a life of its own*: an image that is always stitched together, patched up, continually growing on the way, to the point where it becomes fabulous.
>
> (Deleuze 1998: 117–18)

This is a quality of writing *in the subjective*, rather than *as an individual*, as the writer becomes caught up in the process of subjectivity, absorbed in the 'force through which the images are projected'. Deleuze aligns this projection with 'an "absence of being", an emptiness that bears witness to a dissolved ego' (Deleuze 1998: 119) and so indicates the damage to a unified conception of being that the subjective narrative brings to public masculinity, as it empties it of meaning.

The derogated form of the 'subjective narrative' of *Seven Pillars of Wisdom* thereby invites a focus on his 'troubled persona', allowing Lawrence's military role to recede in favour of his sexual ambivalence as a problem of subjectivity.

Lawrence's statement of his aim in writing *Seven Pillars* incorporates both public and private dimensions, and shows a curiously split intention. In the 'suppressed' introductory chapter to the book, he states that

> the book is just a designed procession of Arab freedom from Mecca to Damascus. It is intended to rationalise the campaign, that everyone may see how natural the success was, how little dependent on direction or brain, how much less on the outside assistance of the few British. It was an Arab war waged and led by Arabs for an Arab aim in Arabia.
>
> (Lawrence 1939: 140)

However, he goes on to refute the claim to historical documentation and authoritative overview, in his acknowledgement of the 'failures' of the subjective and his inability to move beyond the actual, in a statement that carries very strong echoes of Greenblatt's classification of history as anecdote (see note 3):

> In these pages the history is not of the Arab movement, but of me in it. It is a narrative of daily life, mean happenings, little people. Here are no lessons for the world, no disclosures to shock peoples. It is filled with trivial things, partly that no one mistake for history the bones from which some day a man may make history, and partly for the pleasure it gave me to recall the fellowship of the revolt. We were fond together, because of the sweep of the open places, the taste of wide winds, the sunlight, and the hopes in which we worked. The morning freshness of the world-to-be intoxicated us. We were wrought up with ideas inexpressible and vaporous, but to be fought for. We lived many lives in those whirling campaigns, never sparing ourselves.
>
> (Lawrence 1939: 142)

In centralising his individual role in the campaign and embracing the subjective, Lawrence introduces into his narrative a repertoire that is at once 'reduced' to the everyday and the trivial – the 'discontinuous wonders' of his encounter with difference[4] – but which also operates in terms of the sensual, the emotional and the dimension of fantasy. This repertoire allows him to focus on the 'fellowship of the revolt', and the effect of the desert landscape, both sustained themes involving his pleasure in the proximity to and admiration of the bodies of other men, and his identification with the Arab cause. It is this absorption in the play of recognition and difference that brings him to express the pleasure in 'living many lives' and yet which simultaneously exposes him to accusations of inauthenticity, of lack of truthfulness, of instability.

In particular, the rhetoric of the personal and the subjective – in the emotional and moral self-questioning concerning his military role – undermines his public persona as military strategist and national hero, as his revelation of personal duplicity allows him to mount a critique of the British government's role, promising the Arabs self-government as a reward for aid in the desert campaign. His dilemma is posed in terms of a personal shame, which pitches him against national affiliation, and in the 'Suppressed Introductory Chapter' to *Seven Pillars of Wisdom* he complicates the claim of his subtitle, 'A Triumph', by questioning the morality of his own actions and the role of leadership per se, in a way which renders heroism problematic:

> instead of being proud of what we did together, I was continually and bitterly ashamed. ... It was evident from the beginning that if we won the war these promises would be dead paper, and had I been an honest adviser of the Arabs I would have advised them to go home and not risk their lives fighting for such stuff.
>
> (Lawrence 1939: 145)

Lawrence's own complication of his involvement with the Arabs invited system-atic interrogation and interpretation from other commentators, as proliferating accounts speculated on and quarrelled over his character and background, his military and diplomatic career, his psychological and sexual instability. His char-acter itself became the subject of these narratives, despite the fact that they were legitimised by being woven around a figure who had been elevated to a public hero. One of his first biographers, Robert Graves, makes it clear that history is less important to him than the figure of 'Lawrence':

> This is not the method of history ... I have attempted a critical study of 'Lawrence' – the popular verdict that he is the most remarkable living Englishman, though I dislike such verdicts, I am inclined to accept – rather than a general view of the Arab freedom movement and the part played by England and France in regard to it.
>
> (Graves 1927: 6)

Pronouncements on the power of this figure indicate that his fascination could not be limited to his military, diplomatic or political roles, and he came to occupy a position outside social convention. As Churchill indicated, on the announce-ment of Lawrence's abdication of his diplomatic and political career to enter the ordinary ranks of the RAF:

> The world looks with some awe upon a man who appears unconcernedly indifferent to home, money, comfort, rank, or even power and fame. The world feels not without a certain apprehension, that here is some one outside its jurisdiction; some one before whom its allurements may be spread in vain; some one strangely enfranchised, untamed, untrammelled by conven-tion, moving independently of the ordinary currents of human action.
>
> (cited in Wilson 1989: 4)

The inefficacy of social incentives and the lack of conventional motivations in Lawrence give him a particular kind of romantic allure, but also generated the 'apprehension' that Churchill notes, as they erode the persuasiveness of models of public masculinity. His 'indifference' challenges the mechanisms of social management and creates a flaw in the relation of masculinity, public life and national identity, a point of weakness in the maintenance of those boundaries which mark individual passions off from the 'ordinary currents of human action'. In a frequently quoted passage, John Buchan conveys something of the irrational influence the figure of Lawrence exerted over men, as well as its lethal potential:

> I am not a very tractable person or much of a hero-worshipper, but I could have followed Lawrence over the edge of the world. I loved him for himself, and also because there seemed to be reborn in him all the lost friends of my youth.
>
> (cited in Mack 1976/1990: 460)

While some have been concerned to analyse *Seven Pillars* as an 'introspection epic' (Meyers 1973/1989: 131), and thereby to gain further understanding of Lawrence as a figure, it is precisely this emphasis on the self – and its perceived dichotomy with the objective 'truth' of 'history' – which others have found so problematic. Richard Aldington's 1955 biography mounted a savage critique of what he referred to as 'the Lawrence legend', proposing that *Seven Pillars* was 'rather a work of quasi-fiction than of history', that Lawrence was guilty of 'a systematic falsification and over-valuing of himself and his achievements' through a desire for 'self-advertisement', and that his major achievement was simply his capacity 'to convince others that he was a remarkable man' (Aldington 1955: 12–13).

> [T]here was 'a real self' … an unhappy, wistful, tortured, hag-ridden self … Yet he had the courage, the skill – the cunning, if you like – and the force of will and character to impose on the world his over-valued persona as reality, and to receive world-wide acclaim – for what? For the clever patter and pictures of a glib showman untroubled by the majesty of truth.
>
> (Aldington 1955: 350)

It is partly the refutation of the subjective that appears to be at stake for writers such as Aldington, as he questions the legitimacy of Lawrence centralising his own thoughts, feelings and impressions:

> May it be questioned whether a style so mannered, so literary and so inexact was really the most suitable for an honest war narrative? True, every personal war narrative is autobiography; but War is action, whatever it may involve of plans and preparations, and however much the neurotic intellectual who is writing may have been plagued by mental conflict and divided aims. Action does not ask a too sophisticated style, but rather a speech which is vigorous, direct, and unaffected, where the very existence of the sayer is

forgotten in the vividness and meaning of the thing said. Is there a page of *Seven Pillars* in which we are allowed to forget Lawrence of Arabia?

(Aldington 1955: 330)

But while he is questioning the legitimacy of the subjective in a public narrative of military action, Aldington is also questioning the subjective as a legitimate dimension of a masculine narrative, or a narrative of masculinity. He creates a popular and enduring pathology for Lawrence that connects his 'Guilty Secret' – the effect of his discovery of his illegitimacy and his parents' guilt at their 'adultery' – with an 'arrested mental development' and 'mental fixation in adolescence', as well as 'in later life, the bitter antagonism to women as a sex, [and] a puritanical horror of normal sexual intercourse'. Aldington finds a pathological homosexual identity unconsciously inscribed into his writings, alongside 'a downright, if not defiant, statement of Lawrence's disdain for heterosexual and sympathy with homosexual relations', which he argues constitutes a sexual disorder lying at the root of his alleged overvaluation of self (Aldington 1955: 332–5). Aldington proposes that this 'over-valued self' is the counterpoint of an 'impulse of refusal, of rejection, of wilful courting of plebeian degradation', and therefore a fiction created by pathological tendencies (Aldington 1955: 346–7). Here we have the implication of the introduction of the subjective: its connection to a disturbance of personality that is ultimately one of sexual disorder, in Aldington's invocation of an underlying homosexual impulse.

Sexual instability and subjective incoherence: from T.E. Lawrence to 'Lawrence of Arabia'

There is a connection, then, between writing in the subjective, Lawrence's narrative of sexual indeterminacy (and interpretations of his 'sexual disorder') and claims of his homosexuality. The foregrounding of the subjective is translated into an 'unreliability' which compromises the truth of his account, his authenticity of self, and his masculinity. Even Deleuze claims that Lawrence's 'subjective disposition', though it is not coincident with it, *includes* homosexuality. Why is this such a natural connection, and how is Lawrence's sexuality explained, and linked to the other features of his writing?

There is a continuity of two propositions in the first wave of accounts of Lawrence from 1919, and those from the 1950s; first, that his movement between cultures either was propelled by, or induced, a radical split in Lawrence's psyche that contributed to a breakdown, and a recurring nervous or depressive condition. The intimations of Lawrence's instability include his courting of danger and his preoccupation with his ability to suffer pain, his over-attachment to the male community of the army and his eschewing of officer protocols, his perilously close involvement with the Bedouins, his absorption in the wild expanses of the desert and, above all, his insufficiently grounded national identification as he becomes an ambiguous figure who 'passes between' cultures, adopting Arab costume and the Arabs' military strategies, and making himself and his military success dependent on Arab aid.

This indeterminacy is connected to the second proposition, that his was a subjectivity that could not be reconciled to conventional heterosexuality, one that is discussed in terms of a dislike of bodily contact, a hostility to sex and an inability to come to terms with the existence of women. Lawrence himself claims a revulsion to physical matters and a practice of sexual continence while declaring his delight in the proximity to the bodies of other men, and admitting to feeling a 'delicious warmth, probably sexual' during his beating and rape by Turkish guards (Lawrence 1926/1935: 445).

The coordinates of the appraisals of Lawrence's subjectivity are to be found in the connection of sexuality with pathology in psychological inquiry from the First World War to the 1950s, as Freudian theories were adopted to bring a new understanding of the psychosexual aetiology of 'shell shock'.[5] Karl Abraham, speaking about the war neuroses in 1918, suggested it was the pressing narcissism of the war neurotic that prevented him sacrificing his ego for the benefit of the general good of the mass.[6] While it may have been a model designed around men's withdrawal from – or failure in – military encounter, the claim that narcissism introduces a conflict between individual aim and community goal contributes to the evaluation of a figure who, though heroic, stands apart from the mass, and is more 'individual' than military representative. It also underwrites the distaste with the 'over-valuation' of self which feeds into the pathologising of Lawrence's 'courting of danger', his recoil from 'normal sexual relations' and physical contact, and his introspection in *Seven Pillars*. And it provides an explanation for the poles of daring and mental breakdown in Lawrence, as his apparent bravery also becomes a sign of pathological narcissism and renders him vulnerable to psychic disturbance. In contrast to the healthy person's suppression of narcissism, the 'inferior' war neurotic,

> up to the moment when the trauma upsets them have supported themselves only through an illusion connected with their narcissism, namely, through the belief in their immortality and invulnerability.
>
> (Abraham 1921: 25–6)

The theory that the susceptibility to war neurosis had its root in a homosexual disposition infused the discussion of shell shock. Abraham reiterated psychoanalysis' claim of an absolute connection between narcissism and homosexuality, allowing him to describe war neurotics as 'female-passive in the surrender to their suffering' (Abraham 1921: 25). This gave a framework for Lawrence's instability to be positioned within a matrix of masochistic female identification (as his problematic relationship with his mother was identified as the origin of his flight into military adventure and his sexual recoil and also of his ambivalent response to the Deraa episode, and his later involvement in flagellation). But these coordinates of a feminised, passive and narcissistic masculinity of fragile stability were not only used as a reference point for pathological definitions of masculinity.

They also fed into a strain of celebratory representations of damaged and with-drawn, wandering and elusive male figures. Both 'inferior' and heroic, 'dangerous' and a source of erotic contemplation and pleasure, the dispositions used to explain Lawrence were almost directly continuous with Isherwood's cele-bration of the 'truly weak man' of the 1920s and are evident in the attention given to him by Isherwood and Auden in their play *The Ascent of F6*. The disposi-tion of homosexuality – connected to his famous 'breakdown' as a result of war experiences – came to inform an understanding of Lawrence's evasion of the norms of social life, sexual convention and masculine identity.

But, while the psychic dispositions of homosexuality underlie contemporary assessments of a 'weakness' in masculinity that allows the war neurotic to succumb to nervous breakdown, Lawrence does not write his experiences or identity in terms of homosexuality. The question of whether Lawrence was 'actively' homosexual or not is immaterial – it is of greater significance that his private letters and his public writings consistently confirm his distaste for sexual contact and his practice of continence. The lack of specification concerning Lawrence's sexual definition in *Seven Pillars* and contemporary accounts may not so much be evidence of a confusion over Lawrence's sexuality or of a reluctance to speak of homosexuality in direct terms, as has been assumed, but rather of the combination of his sexual indeterminacy with the unresolved nature of the male homosexual as a category of masculinity in this period. This can be seen by examining those motifs by which his sexuality is written, and charting the changing cultural frameworks within which his sexual indeterminacy features from the 1920s to the 1950s.

Celibacy and continence: virile autoeroticism

In his own, and early biographical accounts, Lawrence is figured as celibate, soli-tary and ascetic. He writes in *Seven Pillars* that his personality prevented him from allowing sexual contact: 'To put my hand on a living thing was defilement ... This was an atomic repulsion, like the intact course of a snowflake' (cited in Mack 1976/1990: 419). And, in *The Mint*, he makes a more elaborate statement in which his lack of sexual knowledge corresponds to that of his fellow airmen:

> I fear and shun touch most, of my senses. ... Of direct experience I cannot speak, never having been tempted to so peril my mortal soul. ... Shyness and a wish to be clean have imposed chastity on so many of the younger airmen, whose life spends itself and is spent in the enforced celibacy of their blankets' harsh embrace.
>
> (cited in Mack 1976/1990: 421–2)

But most of these statements of sexual disinclination are made in the context of reflections on sex with women, and he makes clear his greater pleasure in the sight of male bodies than those of women:

I take no pleasure in women. I have never thought twice or even once of the shape of a woman: but men's bodies, in repose or in movement – especially the former, appeal to me directly and very generally.

(cited in Mack 1976/1990: 425)

In *Seven Pillars*, Lawrence's observations of the Arab youths' sexuality gives rise to some poetic passages, creating an ideal model of 'sexless and even pure' relations, as they would 'slake one another's few needs in their own clean bodies'. And he relays without judgement the Arab perspective that 'quivering together in the yielding sand with intimate hot limbs in supreme embrace, [they] found there hidden in the darkness a sensual co-efficient of the mental passion, which was welding our souls and spirits in one flaming effort' (Lawrence 1926/1935: 30). The 'tease' of Lawrence's narrative, in this respect, is in the exchange between the sympathetic yet distanced account of the young Arab's relations – as, for example, he describes the '[Eastern] boy and boy affection which the segregation of women made inevitable' (Lawrence 1926/1935: 237) – and his attempt to account for this through a psychic disposition within which he too is absorbed:

Some of the evil of my tale may have been inherent in our circumstances. For years we lived anyhow with one another in the naked desert … At night we were stained by dew, and shamed into pettiness by the innumerable silences of stars … The men were young and sturdy; and hot flesh and blood unconsciously claimed a right in them and tormented their bellies with strange longings. Our privations and dangers fanned this virile heat, in a climate as racking as can be conceived. We had no shut places to be alone in, no thick clothes to hide our nature. Man in all things lived candidly with man.

(Lawrence 1926/1935: 29–30)

But his valuation of celibacy is clear, as his comments on 'boy and boy affection' show:

Such friendships often led to manly loves of a depth and force beyond our flesh-steeped conceit. When innocent they were hot and unashamed. If sexuality entered, they passed into a give and take, unspiritual relation, like marriage.

(Lawrence 1926/1935: 237)

This is no simple renunciation of the sexual, then: in addition to translating the cultural differences in this model of sexuality, Lawrence draws on a model of homoerotic formation that renders accounts of the relations between men at the front in the First World War according to a sentimental and sublimated 'homoerotic tenderness' (Fussell 1975: 277), one which mobilises an intensified contemplation of the male body and comes to heighten, rather than erase, corporeality, even in the case of celibacy. The concept of a 'chaste' male sexuality, articulated around the body but one in which genital contact had not the central defining force that is claimed for it in more recent models, reiterates a more ancient version of homoerotic exchange. Lawrence mobilises this older model of homoerotic formation, which allows a range of models of sexual love between men without categorising them in terms of 'homosexuality' *per se*.

From this perspective, it is possible to argue that his and other contemporary accounts do not simply repress Lawrence's 'actual' homosexuality, but rather that the pathway from an attachment to the bodies of men to 'homosexual acts' was not a given outcome in this period, and that such a move was therefore simply less of a pressing question in his sexual definition. In early twentieth-century models of masculine homoeroticism, male bodies were available for a variety of forms of erotic contemplation, and 'crushes' could be separated from an impulse towards corporeal exchange. In such a model, the defining force of sexual deployments of the body is not their genital nature. Hence they could be directed towards a form of celibacy which took on a positive sexual meaning as the exercising of certain focused constraints constituted a virile autoeroticism rather than being simply seen as an absence of sexual activity.[7]

Lawrence's 'celibate' body was thereby made available to a very specific form of masculine eroticism. This drew on nineteenth-century exhortations to discipline the body towards sexual continence, initially directed towards intensifying a limited set of corporeal energies towards a reproductive sexual future, with masturbation at the centre of a series of sexual pathologies. Medical advocations of continence were given their own autoerotic force: the 'virile struggle' necessary for the mastering of 'a spirited horse' would eventually give rise to 'splendid energy' (Hall 1992: 372).

But there is a mechanism in narratives of Lawrence that connects a 'clean', 'chaste' form of autoerotic or homoerotic pleasure to a capacity for degradation, and to the terrors of 'filth' (Lawrence 1926/1935: 30). As the solitary male body took on the project of continence, it was rendered susceptible to 'strains' and failures as much as to glories (Hall 1992: 374–5). But the path of development for masturbators was understood to be as likely to lead to sexual contact with prostitutes as towards homosexuality, as it indicated an overinvestment in sensual pleasure and a preoccupation with the body which could manifest in several deleterious sexual outcomes.

Breaching the barriers of effective sexual economies, the 'social evil' of prostitution directed masculine sexual desire 'outward', away from the family, while the 'solitary vice' of masturbation was identified as directing it 'inward', allowing 'the channelling of perfectly healthy desire back onto itself' as the circuit of sexual activity is held within the same body (Laqueur 1989b: 339). Male homosexuality came to occupy the space between these two 'disorders' – channelling desire outward yet towards a 'like' body. As such, it began a process of condensing both sets of meanings: anti-familial, narcissistic and antisocial.

As masturbation becomes associated with homosexuality in warnings against masturbation with 'evil companions' (Hall 1992: 374–5), the potential for sexual vice solidifies around the figure of the homosexual and yet simultaneously invokes the meanings of prostitution. This can be seen in the way debates and legislation of male homosexuality from the 1880s centre the act of sodomy; two 'like' bodies become linked, as masculinity is channelled back on to itself in an exchange which is no longer solitary, but produced through a disordered sociality. Here, the inscription of homosexuality on to the male body brings the anus into visibility. Read as a gap, a tear or a wound – in other words as a disfigurement – it draws on the motif of the diseased vagina of the prostitute. Denoting filth, waste, and figured as a sewer, in nineteenth-century Britain this motif represented the threat syphilis posed to the healthy body of the middle-class mother as guarantor of the imperial race (see Armstrong 1990). Through its association with prostitution and masturbation, the 'likeness' which now distinguishes the body of the homosexual brings the anus to represent an unsecured, feminised, zone, which must be repudiated and erased for the male body to guarantee a socially meaningful masculine subjectivity.

In fact, as Hocquenghem's elaboration of the anus as a cultural sign of male homosexual desire shows, the narrative of masculine sexuality positions the anus as both *necessary* to the socialisation of sexual subjectivities, in the sublimation of its eroticism, and *antipathetic* to it, in its constitution as a regressive organ, 'private' and evacuated of social meaning (Hocquenghem 1978: 82).

> The anus only exists as something which is socially elevated and individually debased; it is torn between faeces and poetry, between the shameful little secret and the sublimated
>
> (Hocquenghem 1978: 82).

The sexualised anus thus disorders the processes by which identity and sexuality are secured in difference and creates a loss of coherence for masculinity. It holds out what Bersani calls the 'nightmare of ontological obscenity … the prospect of a breakdown of the human itself into *sexual intensities* as … proud subjectivity is buried' (Bersani 1988: 222).

Deraa

The event which is regarded as the key to Lawrence's character – and one which shows the connection between the destruction of the integrity of the male body through the experience of anality, with the destruction of the subjective integrity of 'proud masculinity' – is the 'Deraa incident', where Lawrence was captured by the Turks while in Arab disguise, then tortured and subjected to anal rape by soldiers under the instruction of Hajim Bey, the Governor of Deraa. Lawrence's experience of anality is universally seen as the cause of a recurring nervous condition and a continuing sexual ambivalence, and thereby contributes to understanding him as a fragmented personality of sexual instability and subjective incoherence. Lawrence's letters frequently document his nervous attacks, and in the opening chapter of *The Mint* he writes of his assessment at the recruiting office, as the medical examiner stated he had 'nerves like a rabbit', which, upon Lawrence's ashamed explanation of the scars on his buttocks as 'persuasion', the medical examiner attributes to the flogging at Deraa (Lawrence 1926/1935: 35; see also Wilson 1989: 667–8).

But the imprint of the floggings did not only testify to their physical damage. Lawrence's shame is created rather by his submission within the scenario of sexual encounter. His description of this pivotal experience in *Seven Pillars of Wisdom* is sexually detailed and explicit – lyrical, even, in parts – as he documents the bey trembling and sweating in sexual anticipation, his 'fawning' admiration of Lawrence's 'white' and 'fresh' body and 'fine' hands and feet, his flailing attempts to drag Lawrence down on to the bed in his arms and his words of supplication, inviting Lawrence's love. He goes on to write of how the bey bit him, kissed him and slit his skin to 'dabble' the blood over his stomach 'with his finger-tips' after Lawrence rejected him (Lawrence 1926/1935: 442–3). After the guards beat and rape him, Lawrence's description of his momentary recovery is oddly pleasant: 'I snuggled down, dazed, panting for breath, but vaguely comfortable'. And he recalls 'smiling idly' at the corporal kicking him, 'for a delicious warmth, probably sexual, was swelling through me' (Lawrence 1926/1935: 445). Despite being 'broken' by the rape and floggings – 'They splashed water in my face, wiped off some of the filth, and lifted me between them, retching and sobbing for mercy, to where he lay' – it is this pleasure that creates a simultaneous damage to subjective coherence: 'in Deraa that night the citadel of my integrity had been irrevocably lost' (Lawrence 1926/1935: 447).

In *Seven Pillars*, Lawrence writes that the bey 'rejected him in haste, as a thing too torn and bloody for his bed … the fault [resting] upon my indoor skin, which gave way more than an Arab's' (Lawrence 1926/1935: 445). However, subsequently, Lawrence's letters revise this published account by admitting that, in his attempt to avoid the excruciating pain of further beatings, he had in fact submitted to the bey, a fact which gave him a further sense of the degradation of his integrity:

> I'm always afraid of being hurt: and to me, while I live, the force of that night will lie in the agony which broke me and made me surrender. It's the individual view. You can't share it. … For fear of being hurt, or rather to earn five minutes respite from a pain which drove me mad, I gave away the only possession we are born into the world with – our bodily integrity. It's an unforgiveable matter, an irrecoverable position.
>
> (cited in Mack 1976/1990: 419–20)

Lawrence's body is marked with the experience of anality and his passivity is read as humiliation, but this reading of his sexuality is also crossed by that of his identification with the Arabs, whose conventional featuring in sexual cultures has been drawn in terms of an 'uncivilised' anality that spans both homosexual and heterosexual practices, and so disorganises sexual categories. As anality becomes consolidated around the body of the homosexual in nineteenth-century British culture, so Lawrence's Arab identification becomes a sign of his inability to form an alliance between sexual and social modes of masculinity, and to withstand the disrupting effects of a feminised disposition of passivity on his masculinity. Within the context of these challenges to sexual categories, Deraa represents the imposition of a foreign and primitive anality on to a cultivated British male body, which becomes torn and bloodied, covered in 'filth'. The consequence of this was Lawrence's corporeal, moral and psychic disfigurement; the destruction of the citadel of his integrity.

The effect of his submission at Deraa – whether through his sexual response to his flogging and rape, or his subjection to the bey – becomes the core of narratives of Lawrence, as the reliving of his experience is seen to cause recurrent episodes of depression, his further sexual recoil, and his staging of further beating episodes later in life for both a form of gratification and penance, replaying 'the fusion of intimacy and simultaneous desecration' (Wilson 1989: 666; Mack 1976/1990: 427–41). The explanation for the severity and endurance of the psychological torture Lawrence suffers on account of Deraa has been found in the stylistic similarity of his expression of the fear that his feelings would be 'violated' by his mother, if she knew of them, and had got 'inside the circle of my integrity' (letter to Charlotte Shaw, 1928, cited in Meyers, 1973/1989: 119; and Mack 1976/1990: 420), or in its revival of the earlier conflicts associated with his mother's childhood beatings (Mack 1976/1990). The wider significance of his sense of the destruction of his integrity has been found in a connection to his feeling that he betrayed the Arab cause (Wilson 1989: 668) or in his horror at his own savagery in the massacre of the Deraa police battalion at the Battle of Tafas, where 'by Lawrence's order and for the only time in the war, the Arabs take no prisoners ... as if only Turkish "death and running blood could slake our agony" ', both of which contribute to an 'increasingly grim' mood through the remaining parts of *Seven Pillars* (Meyers 1973/1989: 119–20, 134–5).

But, however this event was invested with further meanings, its key significance lies in calling up a masochism that imprints itself on his sexual consciousness. Jeremy Wilson cites Lawrence's reflection on the version of *Seven Pillars* that he finished in 1922:

> Probably it had been the breaking of the spirit by that frenzied nerve-shattering pain which had degraded me to beast level when it made me grovel to it, and which had journeyed with me since, a fascination and terror and morbid desire, lascivious and vicious, perhaps, but like the striving of a moth towards its flame.

> (cited in Wilson, 1989: 668)

Deraa, and the meanings of anality, thus stand as the consolidation of those traits of instability that Lawrence exhibits, and the stimulation of his capacity for 'perversion', marking his body and subjectivity in ways that signal the unravelling of masculinity.

Lawrence of Arabia: wandering in the space of elsewhere

By 1962, Lawrence's sexuality had been definitively linked to the pathologies of male homosexuality: albeit that his 'homosexuality' remains contested and speculative even to the present, writers such as Aldington claimed to reveal that in his letters and writings he had 'unconsciously left a record of his sexual sympathies … [and] a good deal of evidence as to what sexually repelled him, what he tolerated, and what excited his preference and sympathy' (Aldington 1955: 333).

The release of *Lawrence of Arabia* followed a string of homosexual scandals in the 1950s, including the defections to the Soviet Union of Guy Burgess and Donald Maclean in 1951, the trial of Lord Montagu and Peter Wildeblood for homosexual offences in 1954, and ongoing cases of prosecution of public figures arising from newly targeted police operations in Britain's metropolitan centres (Hyde 1970: 212; Weeks 1981: 240–41). *Lawrence of Arabia* was made in the four years following the publication of the Wolfenden Report and released two months after the trial of John Vassall for espionage amidst claims that he was recruited by the threat of blackmail for homosexual practices.

These circumstances allow a more elaborated range of features to become part of the popular classification of the homosexual, as a pathway is established between 'homosexual propensities' (involving a psychic disposition, including narcissism, as much as a sexual inclination) and homosexual activity. From the 1920s to the 1950s, masculine sexual pathologies see masturbation *per se* fade away and become incorporated into a phase of normal male adolescent sexual development, while homosexuality as pathology becomes consolidated in terms of psychic instability and ungrounded sexual intensities. Homosexuality thereby *incorporates* the dangers of masturbation – the Wolfenden Report notes that 'solitary masturbation with homosexual fantasies' was probably the most common *homosexual* act – while its association with prostitution is integrated into repertoires of social regulation (HMSO 1957: 12). While the Wolfenden Report attempted to decriminalise male homosexuality in private and proposed that homosexual 'urges' were not confined to practising homosexuals, it nevertheless pathologised the homosexual through his lack of a disciplined control of rational will, the masculine faculty that should overcome the bodily urges deriving from homosexual 'propensities'. Wolfenden's address to sexual offences thus posed a corporeality which constituted a disorderly realm within the construction of masculinity (Swanson 1994).

In Wolfenden's re-zoning of the 'problem' of male homosexuality to a private domain, there to become a matter of self-management rather than of public regulation, the homosexual became opposed to public masculinity, antipathetic to the public realm. While women's associations have a 'natural' location in the family, there is *no place* for associations between men in private that is not understood to have an origin in the public domain. This concern was articulated in the Commons debate:

[In the Report] … statutory authority is given to all adults to approach other adults and attempt by invitation or otherwise to get them to go to a private place for homosexual behaviour. … Adult males can get other adult males to go to some private place. They can set up as lovebirds anywhere.

(Mann 1958: 455)

This indicates the emphasis now placed on the dangers of sublimated homosexuality: the redirecting of a homosexual drive towards socially valuable work suggests a public danger related to the presence of men with homosexual propensities. And the more subtle repertoire of indeterminacy mobilised in the period in which the earlier narratives of Lawrence appear is surpassed by a new repertoire: of seduction.

The homosexual male body was seen to move across the boundaries of public and private. Moving between, inscribed with the attributes of femininity, it became dislocated and placeless, wandering in the space of elsewhere. The motifs generated by such disturbances are clear in a depiction of John Vassall by Rebecca West – writing in 1965, but reflecting on the impact of the events surrounding his trial in 1962. Here we find a feminised figure, 'doe-eyed, soft-voiced, hesitant and ephebic', 'a much sought-after "queen", playful and girlish' (West 1965: 361–2). Vassall is represented as wandering in an interim space between worlds:

the public imagination was haunted by visions of the slender figure in sweater and tight jeans who lurks in the shadow by the wall, just outside the circle of the lamplight, whisks down the steps of the tube-station lavatory, and with a backward glance under the long lashes offers pleasure and danger.

(West 1965: 382)

Nomadic subjectivity and panoramic space

The figure of Lawrence in the film is situated by this debate: his exhibitionistic delight in disguise and cross-dressing, his feminised appearance, his gestural and linguistic hesitancy, all – while contributing to the pleasures in Lawrence's difference – correspond to the motifs of homosexuality in the late 1950s.

Lawrence of Arabia does not draw on the model of contemporary British films in representing male homosexual pleasure. A film such as *Victim* (1961, directed by Basil Dierden), whose narrative concerns homosexual blackmail, uses a landscape of private, dark, hidden spaces, backrooms, passages and corridors, secret packages, the passing over of sexual evidence. The film takes up a liberal position on legislative debates over homosexuality, identifying the 'problem' of homosexual blackmail not in homosexual activity but in ignorance and prejudice against homosexual men. But, even as it represents the victim of blackmail, the tortured image of the loyal husband struggling to overcome his homosexual inclinations, in the restrained but emotional performance of Dirk Bogarde,

Victim's constitution of homosexuality is undoubtedly one of the closet – the confinement of private shame, a secret, an interruption of the constitution of public masculinity within British national identity.[8] In contemporary films addressing the 'social problem' of homosexuality, the forms of rhetoric for male homosexual desire foreclose its attraction.

But in *Lawrence of Arabia* we find a relocation of the generic framing of sexual departures in British films of this period, towards the fullness of a spectacular, cinemascope and technicolour, epic of travel. This plenitude of visibility and the swelling waves of the orchestral score figure Lawrence's unresolved subjectivity not through negation and interruption – a gap, a flaw – but through *immensity*. Lawrence's movement across the desert escapes the meanings of lineage, location and masculine embodiment, the everyday.[9] Elusive and permeable in the billowing folds of his Arab costume, his figure is constantly resituated as the changing terrain of the desert and the shifting sands transform the contours of a landscape across which corporeal relations are enacted. Boundary-less, infinite and continually in a process of transformation, the situating of a refigured male body of contradictory sexual inscriptions in the desert is one of the most striking differences of *Lawrence* from contemporary masculine images.[10]

This figuration of Lawrence's body disrupts not only the coordinates of contained corporeality, but also the organisation of geographic and cinematic space, as the sublime landscape of the desert is associated with a subjectivity cut loose from its conventional coordinates.[11] As the urban panoramic gaze of the nineteenth-century *flâneur* is endlessly displaced by new and ever-proliferating views, the alliance of a panoramic gaze with the landscape of the desert blocks the positioning and sociality of commanding vision, which depends on an elevated and distant, fixed viewpoint that links vision and knowledge in an assertion of absolute space (Harvey 1989: 224, 260). As it moves across the spaces of the desert, then, the panoramic gaze and its cinemascope image in *Lawrence* replaces the authority of commanding height with an assertion of horizontality; the aesthetics of abandonment and the dream of the unbroken vista that dissolves boundaries and secure classifications (Burns 1991).

As the expanse of the desert opens out the vista, it simultaneously prevents the visibility of one's own position by reference to landmarks, through the 'vertical deprivation' of endless desert and a receding horizon (Carter 1987: 285). The *cost* of excessive visualisation, then, is placelessness, the dispersal of self. As Paul Carter has noted in his study of the Australian desert experience, the immensity of space suggests to the traveller 'the tenuousness of his balance and stability in the world' (Carter 1987: 289). At the other end of the freedom of the open expanse of the desert is a terrain where space fails to cohere into place around the stable perspective of the subject, one that threatens a dissolution of subjectivity.

From sublimation to psychosis: the dynamics of seduction

The fascination of Lawrence's escape from the conventional coordinates of masculinity – based on *Seven Pillars*, but informed by the debates of the 1950s –

allows the film to draw on two regimes of knowledge to approach his masculinity. The first relies upon his own account of continent homoeroticism, to allow a voluptuous pleasure in his abandonment, while the second regime invokes the figure of the 'invert', originating in a dissonance between masculine physiology and feminine psychology, and depicted in terms of a 'weakness' or passivity which is here given a positive inflection. The common element in these two models is that they are not dependent upon the existence of homosexual activity. In fact, most of the sociological and medical accounts of male homosexuality from the 1920s to the 1960s make a distinction between 'homosexual propensities' which could be sublimated in socially valuable work, and an involvement in homosexual activity (for example, see Anomaly 1927: xii, 117–28; Allen 1962: 196). And, like the earlier models of homoeroticism that Lawrence himself invokes, sublimation offers the space for a continent form of homosexual pleasure which is not pathologised, while Clifford Allen's distinction, in which '[homosexual] behaviour should not be regarded as perverse unless it leads to ejaculation through stimulation from the other partner' (Allen 1962: 166), shows us the elasticity of such definitions of continence.

But Deraa disturbs the pleasure in abandonment and an absorption in erotic delight, and provides the mechanism for homosexual propensities to develop into something more lethal, investing Lawrence's 'instability' with murderous consequences. The film's omission of the period of Lawrence's life which is documented in *The Mint*, and allowing Deraa to be followed by the climax of the Tafas massacre, and the film to end with his fatal motorbike ride, gives a particular inflection to his temperament and connects him to contemporary pathologies of homosexuality.

As the male homosexual becomes delineated in ever-greater sociological, as well as psychopathological, detail in the 1950s, there were attempts to surpass the classic conception of homosexuality as sexual inversion. The most prevalent model – resting on a distinction between the tragic invert and evil pervert – is evident in the Church of England's influential 1954 advisory paper to the Wolfenden Committee, 'The Problem of Homosexuality': 'an invert is a man who from accident or birth has unnatural desires … whereas a pervert is a man who either from lust or wickedness will get desires from either natural or unnatural functions' (cited in Allen 1962: 172).[12]

But the key innovation to this dichotomy in contemporary models of homosexuality lay in the argument that homosexuality was not an 'inborn' condition and yet did not arise from a 'perverse wish to behave differently from others', either. Instead, it was argued, the 'tragedies of inversion' result from an 'immaturity' or a lack of development formed from dysfunctional family patterns which are as unwilled as 'dwarfism' (Berg and Allen 1958: 35). These arguments proposed that a homosexual disposition was created by early influences and hence was neither 'inborn' nor a sign of individual corruption. However, they also claimed that, if left untreated, homosexuality would be more likely to lead to psychoses than the other sexual perversions (Allen 1962: 181–8). What comes to replace the dichotomy of inversion and perversion, then, is a developmental model of subjective disintegration.

This gave a particular inflection to the debate concerning the legislative and medical regulation of male homosexuality. While sociologists advocated 'sympathy' for the predicament of individual homosexual men, they also proposed that the prevalence of male homosexuals in the community constituted a 'social infection' (Hauser 1962: 24). Most of the calls for a replacement of juridical with medical treatment were motivated by the understanding that homosexuality could be 'cured' through psychiatric treatment (insulating those with propensities), while prison would 'spread' homosexuality (with the presence of homosexuals in prison endangering those with unrealised propensities).

The prominent psychopathologist Clifford Allen[13] – himself opposed to the imprisonment of homosexuals, and instead supporting treatment and affirming the possibility of 'cure' – went further. He claimed that homosexuals were fixated in an incestuous stage of infantile development, which meant that 'the average invert has strong ambivalency in his emotional relations which make his affections a source of danger to the loved one', giving him a predilection to suicide and making homosexual murder common (Allen 1962: 186).

The breakdown of 'proud masculinity' is brought about by surrendering to corporeal intensities. It is this dangerous outcome that the distinction between disposition and act signals. And the pathway between homosexual disposition and homosexual activity is provided in the exchange between 'seduction' and initiation. Here, rape and other forms of sexual initiation are elided in the assumption that physical penetration had the capacity to unleash a suppressed homosexuality. A 'corrupted' sexual character is shown to have lethal consequences, dispersing subjectivity into an incoherence which renders it as nothing more than an immoderate absorption into 'intensities'.

It was precisely the foregrounding of seduction which characterises the public trials and sociological investigations of homosexuality with a corresponding preoccupation with 'susceptibilities' within psychological disciplines. While contemporary commentary on Vassall and others in cases throughout the 1950s and 1960s was largely condemnatory, newspaper reports simultaneously centred on their attention to elegant style, and luxurious and urbane forms of living; they nevertheless offered figures of glamour. But the forms of fascination invoked by the category of the homosexual – the ability to move into another space beyond the limits, to offer infinite and unknown gratifications – simultaneously place those who succumb to their charms outside the coordinates of 'ordinary human action' and initiate them into the practices that lead to psychosis. As the *Sunday Pictorial* series on 'Evil Men', published in 1952, stated; '[So] many *normal* people have been corrupted and in turn corrupt others … once a callow youth has become enmeshed in the practices of the pervert … it is hard to win him back to normal life' (*Sunday Pictorial*, 25 May 1952: 6). As the homosexual represented a realm of unlicensed corporeal pleasures in a hidden world of secret sexualities, the fascination, or seduction, of the spaces outside 'normal life' constituted the space of elsewhere as site of lethal pleasures.

Flying or drowning: the dangers of unbecoming

It is this context of knowledge which allows accounts of Lawrence to move from an elusive indeterminacy, or ambivalence – a less than perfect mastery of the 'spirited horse' of corporeal drives – to become an embodiment of a divergent model of vulnerability and perversion. The passage from one to the other, from homosexual propensities to homosexual activities, and its consequences for masculinity, is what preoccupies the film of *Lawrence of Arabia*. While Lawrence's 'fascination' offers the pleasure of wandering, abandonment and the sublime, crosscultural identification and sensual pleasure in the first part of the film, *Lawrence of Arabia* also works from the instability attributed to homosexual consciousness and the homosexual body.

The second half of the film shows Lawrence's descent into brutality, murder and corporeal debasement as his involvement with the Arab revolt sees him acting outside Anglo-French military strategy and ceding the rational embrace of military discipline to an emotional identification with the Arab cause, which brings him to enact the massacre at Tafas as an act of revenge. But the event that provides a route from the earlier 'Lawrence' to the later one is that of Deraa, a pathway premised on the relationship between seduction and initiation, and its destructive consequences for masculine self-definition – for it is this event which brings him to grovel in the blood of the Turks at Tafas.

Caught between drowning and flying, faeces and poetry, the desert figure wanders between the fear of the void and the fantasy of the sublime. Although the film's aesthetic offers the pleasures of abandonment, even the repertoire of horizontality and panoramic space invokes the 'other' side of the anal scenario. The fascination implied by breaking free of sexual and cultural categories is linked to the 'repulsion' such a disordering of systems of difference will bring. In discourses of homosexuality, that repulsion is associated with the meanings of anality, the descent into psychosis, and the breakdown of proud subjectivity, as masculinity loses coherence.

As his Arab identification disorders masculinity itself as the proposition of cultures, the awkwardness of his mastery of the processes of survival and accomplishment in the desert exposes Lawrence's existence between the domains of classification. As the bey touches his body and comments on the fairness of his skin, we see his is an incomplete mimicry. He justifies his attempt to recoil from the Arab revolt by showing Ali the same piece of skin caressed by the bey: 'A man can do whatever he wants ... but he can't *want* what he wants; this is the stuff that decides what he wants.' A mark of his different constitution, this irreducible bodily-ness renders masculine identification incomplete; its failures are to be read from his body's surfaces. In the spaces of masculine exchange, Lawrence remains 'between'.

The negative meanings of the anus in this cultural repertoire are evident in the depiction of the events of Deraa in *Lawrence of Arabia* as Hajim Bey examines Lawrence's body, touching his skin and ordering him to be beaten. As Lawrence is pushed down to lie face down on to a bench, the bey looks from the doorway, gazing directly between Lawrence's splayed legs. When Lawrence is finally released, he falls, exhausted, into the mud. Implications of buggery are as inseparable from the beating here as they are in the controversies over his accounts of what happened at Deraa. However, they have none of the delicate alliance of pleasure and pain that exist in his own renderings, and lack the ambiguity in Abraham's comment on war neurotics, that 'the damaged part of the body receives from them a significance as an erotogenic zone which did not previously belong to it' (Abraham 1921: 27). Thus they validate only one side of the double meaning of the anal scenario, moving beyond the moment of seduction to its consequences for masculine self-definition. Thrown out like waste, Lawrence's beaten body represents homosexual desire itself; the breaching of corporeal boundaries and the possibility of passive pleasure and its dangers to masculine subjectivity.[14] To T.E. Lawrence in *Seven Pillars of Wisdom*, the Arab is like water – elemental, fluid, liminal, without boundary or edge. 'And like water', he says, they 'would probably prevail' (Lawrence 1926/1935: 43). So they do, but for 'Lawrence of Arabia', for whom there is now 'only the desert', the anal body is marked under the sign of absence, emptiness, meaninglessness.

Unravelling colonial masculinity

This film wrote in its own way a sexuality that was posed as problematic in this period, one that was used to play out a series of concerns over British national identity and cultural authority. As the possibilities and dangers of 'passing between' are mapped on to the unstable figure of Lawrence in the desert, we can read its representations of differences back on to those which clustered around a fragmented national masculinity and its declining hold on a position of cultural centrality.

But why, in 1958, would David Lean and Sam Spiegel, set on a film about Gandhi, switch to finding an intelligible project in the narratives of Lawrence? The nationalisation of the Suez Canal – the event that precipitated Britain's 'Suez crisis' – represented a weakening of Britain's colonial hold on the Middle East. By fostering and supporting the Arab revolt against Turkish domination in the First World War, Britain had helped ensure that the Allied forces gained control of Arab territories. If 'the potentially explosive power of Arab nationalism thus became a key to Britain's plans for imperial expansion in the Middle East' after the First World War (Spurr 1993: 129), in the 1950s that same power was turned against Britain, exploding its own sense of imperial power and centrality. Britain's 'Suez failure' therefore directly undid and reversed the very achievement and 'triumph' created by Lawrence's support and betrayal of the Arab cause, rendering his figure as a hero as problematic as that of British imperial masculinity itself.

The fact that there was an overlap in systems of knowledge shared by those surrounding the Suez affair and the film is signalled by the appointment of Anthony Nutting (who resigned from Eden's government on the sailing of the British expeditionary force) as the film's Director of Public and Political

Relations, and in his authorship of a connected biography of Lawrence (Nutting 1961). But there is a further chain of association, between the events of Suez and public debates over male homosexuality. It was Sir David Maxwell-Fyffe who, as Home Secretary, had announced that 'Homosexuals, in general, are exhibitionists and proselytisers and a danger to others, especially the young'; had overseen the escalation of homosexual prosecutions in London from the mid-1940s, which led to the proliferation of trials of public figures for homosexual acts (Weeks 1981: 241); and had set up the Wolfenden Committee – arguing against its recommendations to decriminalise male homosexuality in private. In 1956, now restyled Lord Chancellor Kilmuir, it was his sanction that allowed the British expeditionary force to sail. These interconnections of personnel and their involvement in events surrounding Wolfenden, Suez and 'Lawrence of Arabia' suggest individual incidents do not proceed according to an autonomous and segregated set of principles, but are related through common cultural repertoires concerning masculinity and national identity, and the unhinging of their certainties. Peter Rawlinson, in his autobiography, talks of the Suez crisis as that which brought the House of Commons to '[erupt] into a madhouse', as the conventions governing public masculinity were 'swept away' to reveal the 'naked partisanship' of a corporeal exchange beyond rational control:

> For a government backbencher it was rather like being a spectator with a ring-side seat at a particularly bloody prize fight, in which one's own man was often on the ropes, sometimes driven to the floor but somehow always climbing back on to his feet to carry on the fight, acquiring thereby a dignity which his attackers singularly lacked. ... The passion and the fever swept away all judgement. We were all naked partisans.
>
> (Rawlinson 1989: 69–70)

In the exchange between masculinity and national identity, an overlapping range of knowledges of masculinity (specifically those concerning male homosexuality) informed the figuration of the male body in a film whose immediate landscape was one of British colonialism. As the spaces of empire contracted from the late 1940s, so too national spaces became re-zoned as immigration, the changing sexual profile of labour relations and the recasting of class boundaries exercised the formulation of legislation and government policy in 1950s Britain (Hall 1980). International relations became strained as British public services submitted to United States pressure to 'purge' homosexuals who were held to corrupt the integrity of social institutions. Espionage scandals showed the extent to which concerns over the alteration of the 'natural' patterns of British social life, the permeability of not just social and national boundaries but the contours of British national identity, could be mobilised in an address to questions of sexual definition and exchange.

Following Britain's disastrous attempt at military intervention after the Suez Canal was nationalised in 1956, colonial dynamics took on a problematic recognition of failure. Yet, while the 1950s biographies of Lawrence may have foregrounded the 'darker' side of the Desert Campaign and made the selection of this particular subject relevant in the aftermath of Suez, *Lawrence of Arabia* recasts the discourses of colonial erosion as they also offer a *pleasurable* engagement with scenarios of dispersal, of fragmentation and loss. This is achieved in the figuration of Lawrence's body within a space of extended horizontality through the alliance of desert landscape, a panoramic gaze and its cinematic correlative in the cinemascope image. The pleasures *and* torments of Lawrence's corporeal instability are based on his mobility in an unsecured landscape.

The conventions of colonial geometry are 'not only literal descriptions of the physical settlement patterns of the European community, but also vivid testimonies to the culture's obsession with naming, with demarcation, and with segregation' (Ching-Liang Low 1989: 84). This spatial order offers a unified position of colonial authority and coherence, maintaining a separation, a difference, from a culture where 'private and public spaces are not delineated', which threatens to 'run riot, spilling and intermixing' and so lies 'out-of-bounds' for colonial subjectivity (Ching-Liang Low 1989: 87). But these demarcations also provide the conditions whereby centrality becomes destabilised. For Greenblatt, 'the colonial impulse is a desire to know one's own culture by the encounter of, the knowledge of, that which is alien' (Greenblatt 1991: 124). In its pursuit of the possession of the Other as an *alien* object, the constitution of self within the colonial dynamic moves from radical alterity to an identification that risks self-estrangement as military encounter is read in terms of attachment and differentiation (Greenblatt 1991: 128). This is the tension endemic to colonial encounter – that the exchange between attachment and difference ruins the claim to unified subjectivity.

In the context of colonial decline, there are further spatial disruptions, as reterritorialisations bring into view those spaces 'in-between' which have no place in the colonial accounting of cultural difference, and the hybrid identifications that are part of colonial presence are displaced back on to the places of 'home'. For, as the shift towards Arab nationalism is consolidated through the nationalisation of the Suez Canal, this gesture does more than cut loose from a colonial power and reverse colonial dynamics – bringing about 'Britain's final military and diplomatic humiliation' (Bohne 1990: 3–4) – it re-zones the territories of the Middle East, shifting the centre of meaning to a Pan-Arab position that could not be conceived of within a colonial rhetoric of national identification. The gesture of nationalising the canal not only exposes the specific spatiality of colonial discourse, but also brings the colonial subject within its gaze.

As Arab nationalism presses its own designations of otherness into colonial dynamics, systems of cultural difference are confounded. The subject who embodies colonial power is now seen to enter a space of indeterminacy, whose only form of management is an incomplete identification that leaves open the gates to cultural exchange. After Suez, then, the canal becomes the mark of another passage between. As the territories of Europe's other shift, such a gesture renders British colonial discourse meaningless; a gap, or tear, in the figuration of British identity whose distinctive intelligibility is formulated around an irreducible difference designated in space and ultimately marked upon the male body. This exchange is the precondition for the existence of a hybrid third term, one that testifies to a loss – of certainty, of cultural authority, of the centrality whereby colonial identity can be secured. It simultaneously undermines the fiction of a self-sufficient masculinity whose coordinates are of difference rather than dependency as it allows the pleasures of absorption, the pleasures of other worlds and hybridising exchanges.

As his 'lawlessness' draws on the psychopathological models of male homosexuality circulating in the 1950s, the figure of Lawrence in the desert accomplishes a double task. It designates a cultural and sexual instability that now shows the impossible fiction of British masculinity, and its relation to cultural achievement and colonial authority. While *Lawrence of Arabia* draws on the debates surrounding the 1950s homosexual scandals and the Wolfenden Report, it connects sexual exchange and cultural difference, and captures both the seductions and the dangers of cultural and sexual hybridisation, through an indeterminacy which fragments masculinity and subjective coherence.

Notes

1   This is a broader task than that of reading Lawrence's autobiography in order to chart those patterns of fantasy which manifest his psychic conflicts, as we find in Kaya Silverman's account (1992). Her analysis promotes a reading of *Seven Pillars* in terms that 'reveal' a reflexive masochism that both acts 'as a defense against the castrating consequences of feminine masochism' to sanction a retreat from heroic masculinity, and also sustains and promotes virility and authority as components of masculine identity. For Silverman, Lawrence's 'identity' is thus discoverable through a psychoanalytic analysis of the text alongside other supporting evidence of its textual 'tropes', such as his letters.

2   The argument outlined in this section was developed more fully in an earlier essay (Swanson 2000).

3   Stephen Greenblatt has charted the effects of the introduction of the subjective in narratives of colonial discovery in the early modern period, arguing that forms of travel narrative that emerge in the context of the discovery of the 'New World' come to embody a distinctively modern Western experience. Their driving force is the experience of difference rather than confirmation of self, chronicled as a series of 'local excitement[s]' provoked by 'discontinuous wonders' (Greenblatt 1991: 2–3). This presents the subjective perspective as a series of views: 'not in stately and harmonious order but in a succession of brief encounters, random experiences, isolated anecdotes of the unanticipated' (Greenblatt 1991: 2). History is understood by Greenblatt in terms of 'anecdote', then, as this kind of narrative has perspective – or subjectivity – built in as part of the fabric of its claim to representation.

4   This is Greenblatt's term: see note 3 above, Chapter 2 and Greenblatt (1991: 2).

5   The attempt to understand and treat 'shell shock' provided the most significant contribution to the adoption of Freudian theories of the psychosexual (as an alternative to the organic) origin of neuroses and pathologies in Britain (Showalter 1987: 189–90).

6   This text was published in Britain in 1921 by one of the 'popularisers' of Freudian approaches to the treatment of shell shock, Ernest Jones.

7 As it did in nineteenth-century feminist campaigns, which saw this as a strategy of *taking charge of* sexual availability and used it as a key to redefining female sexuality.

8 Even the moment of a representation of passionate longing that Andy Medhurst uses to retrieve in *Victim* the articulation of homosexual desire – Bogarde's passionate delivery of a speech where he talks of 'wanting' the boy Barrett (Medhurst 1984: 31–2) – derives its effect from a break in his voice, an aural *interruption*, a strangulated disordering of speech.

9 Advocating caution against critical practices that romanticise or mystify 'marginal' regions or figures which therefore continue to represent them through the lens of colonial discourse, Caren Kaplan notes the way the figure of the nomad has been celebrated as 'the one who can track a path through a seemingly illogical space without succumbing to nation-state and/or bourgeois organisation and mastery. The desert symbolizes the site of critical and individual emancipation in Euro-American modernity; the nomad represents a subject position that offers an idealized model of movement based on perpetual displacement' (Kaplan 1996: 66).

10 However, Marjorie Garber notes a connection to the 'fantasy of abduction-turned-to-passionate-love in the desert' – and to that of masochism – in the robed figure of Rudolph Valentino, in films of the 1920s, which provides a contextualising reference point for the later filmic representation of T.E. Lawrence (Garber 1992: 309). See below for my argument that *Lawrence of Arabia* situates Lawrence in the desert according to an aesthetics of seduction.

11 A barren and uncultured landscape has long been associated with the sublime as a solitary experience in which sensibilities are extended and visionary capacities and physical powers are enhanced in the escape from the visual contours of the everyday (see Horne 1991: 87).

12 This dual definition – homosexuality as unwilled condition or as willed perversion – was used by the defence counsel in the trial of Lord Montague and Peter Wildeblood for homosexual acts, and informed the distribution of blame in the Burgess and Maclean case, as Burgess's homosexuality comes to be seen as the sign of a monstrously perverted character who preys on the weakness of Maclean's suppressed homosexual propensities to entice him away from his family and into national betrayal, espionage and treason (see West 1965).

13 Clifford Allen was called to give expert testimony by the Wolfenden Committee.

14 As D.A. Miller shows in his account of Hitchcock's *Rope* (1990).

Bibliography

Abraham, K. (1921) in S. Ferenczi, K. Abraham, E. Simmel and E. Jones with an introduction by S. Freud (1921) (eds), *Psycho-analysis and the War Neuroses*, London, Vienna and New York: The International Psycho-analytical Press, 22–30.

Aldington, R. (1955) *Lawrence of Arabia: A Biographical Enquiry*, London: Collins.

Allen, C. (1962) *A Textbook of Psychosexual Disorders*, London: Oxford University Press.

Anomaly (1927) *The Invert and His Social Adjustment*, London: Ballière, Tindall and Cox.

Armstrong, N. (1990) 'The Occidental Alice', *differences* 2, 2: 3–40.

Bachelard, G. (1964) *The Poetics of Space*, Boston: Beacon Press.

Bakhtin, M.M. (1981) *The Dialogic Imagination: Four Essays by M.M. Bakhtin*, ed. M. Holquist, Austin, TX: University of Texas Press.

Berg, C. and Allen, C. (1958) *The Problem of Homosexuality*, New York: Citadel Press.

Bersani, L. (1988) 'Is the Rectum a Grave?', *October*, 43: 197–222.

Bohne, L. (1990) 'Leaning Toward the Past: Pressures of Vision and Narrative in *Lawrence of Arabia*', *Film Criticism* 15, 1: 2–16.

Burns, K. (1993) 'Beating the System: Systems, Genres and the Topos of Place', in J. MacArthur (ed.), *Knowledge on/or/of Experience*, Brisbane: Institute of Modern Art, 41–62.

Carter, P. (1987) *The Road to Botany Bay: An Essay in Spatial History*, London and Boston: Faber and Faber.

Ching-Liang Low, G. (1989) 'White Skins/Black Masks: The Pleasures and Politics of Imperialism', *New Formations* 9: 83–104.

Daston, L. and Galison, P. (1992) 'The Image of Objectivity', *Representations* 40 (Fall): 81–128.

Dawson, G. (1991) 'The Blond Bedouin: Lawrence of Arabia, Imperial Adventure and the Imagining of English-British Masculinity', in M. Roper and J. Tosh (eds) *Manful Assertions. Masculinities in Britain since 1800*, London and New York: Routledge, 113–44.

Deleuze, G. (1998) 'The Shame and the Glory: T.E. Lawrence', in *Essays Critical and Clinical*, London and New York: Verso, 115–25.

Fussell, P. (1975) *The Great War and Modern Memory*, New York and London: Oxford University Press.

Garber, M. (1992) 'The Chic of Araby: Transvestism and the Erotics of Cultural Appropriation', in *Vested Interests: Cross Dressing and Cultural Anxiety*, London and New York: Routledge, 304–52.

Graves, R. (1927) *Lawrence and the Arabs*, London: Jonathan Cape.

Greenblatt, S. (1991) *Marvelous Possessions: The Wonder of the New World*, Oxford: Clarendon Press.

Hall, L.A. (1992) 'Forbidden by God, Despised by Men: Masturbation, Medical Warnings, Moral Panic, and Manhood in Great Britain, 1850–1950', *Journal of the History of Sexuality* 2, 3: 365–87.

Hall, S. (1980) 'Reformism and the Legislation of Consent', in National Deviancy Council (ed.) *Permissiveness and Control: The Fate of Sixties Legislation*, New York: Barnes & Noble, 1–43.

Harvey, D. (1989) *The Condition of Postmodernity*, Oxford: Oxford University Press.

Hauser, R. (1962) *The Homosexual Society*, London: The Bodley Head.

HMSO (1957) *Report of the Committee on Homosexual Offences and Prostitution*, London: HMSO, Cmnd Paper 247.

Hocquenghem, G. (1978) *Homosexual Desire*, London: Allison & Busby.

Horne, J. (1991) 'Travelling through the Romantic Landscapes of the Blue Mountains', *Australian Cultural History* 10: 84–98.

Hyde, H.M. (1970) *The Love That Dared Not Speak Its Name*, Boston and Toronto: Little, Brown & Co (published in the United Kingdom as *The Other Love*).

Kaplan, C. (1996) *Questions of Travel: Postmodern Discourses of Displacement*, Durham and London: Duke University Press.

Laqueur, T. (1989a) 'Bodies, Details, and the Humanitarian Narrative', in L. Hunt (ed.) *The New Cultural History*, Berkeley, Los Angeles, London: University of California Press, 176–204.

—— (1989b) 'The Social Evil, the Solitary Vice and Pouring Tea', in Michel Feher with Ramona Naddaff and Nadia Tazi (eds) *Fragments for a History of the Human Body Part III*, New York: Zone, 334–43.

Lawrence, T.E. (1926/1935) *Seven Pillars of Wisdom: A Triumph*, London: Jonathan Cape (reprinted 2000, Harmondsworth: Penguin Classics, with the 'suppressed introductory chapter' restored).

—— (1939) 'The Suppressed Introductory Chapter for *Seven Pillars of Wisdom*', in *Oriental Assembly*, London: Williams and Norgate Ltd, 139–46.

—— (1955) *The Mint: A day book of the RAF Depot between August and December 1922 with later notes, by 352087 A/C Ross*, Harmondsworth: Penguin.

Liddell Hart, B. (1934) *'T. E. Lawrence' in Arabia and Others*, London and Toronto: Jonathan Cape.

Mack, J.E. (1976/1990) *A Prince of Our Disorder: The Life of T.E. Lawrence*, Oxford: Oxford University Press.

Mann, J. (1958) Debate on 'Homosexual Offences and Prostitution (Report)', 25 November, *Hansard House of Commons Debates* vol. 596: 365–507, London: HMSO.

Medhurst, Andy (1984) '*Victim*: Text as Context', *Screen* 25: 4–5: 22–35.

Meyers, J. (1973/1989) *The Wounded Spirit: T.E. Lawrence's Seven Pillars of Wisdom*, London: Macmillan.

Miller, D.A. (1990) 'Anal *Rope*', *Representations* 32: 107–36.

Nutting, A. (1961) *Lawrence of Arabia: The Man and the Motive*, London: Hollis and Carter.

Rawlinson, P. (1989) *A Price Too High: An Autobiography*, London: Weidenfeld and Nicolson.

Showalter, E. (1987) *The Female Malady: Women, Madness and English Culture 1830–1980*, London: Virago.

Silverman, K. (1992) 'White Skins, Brown Masks: The Double Mimesis, or with Lawrence in Arabia', in *Male Subjectivity at the Margins*, New York and London: Routledge, 299–338.

Spurr, D. (1993) *The Rhetoric of Empire: Colonial Discourse in Journalism, Travel Writing and Imperial Administration*, Durham and London: Duke University Press.

Sunday Pictorial (1952) 25 May: 6.

Swanson, G. (1994) 'Good-Time Girls and a Thoroughly Filthy Fellow: Sexual Pathology and National Character in the Profumo Affair', *New Formations* 24, London: Lawrence and Wishart, 122–54.

—— (2000) 'Memory, Subjectivity and Intimacy: the Historical Formation of the Modern Self and the Writing of Female Autobiography', in S. Radstone (ed.) *Memory and Method*, Providence, Rhode Island and Oxford: Berg, 111–32.

Weeks, J. (1981) *Sex, Politics and Society: The Regulation of Sexuality since 1800*, Harlow: Longman.

West, R. (1965) *The Meaning of Treason*, Harmondsworth: Penguin.

Wilson, J. (1989) *Lawrence of Arabia: The Authorised Biography of T.E. Lawrence*, London: Heinemann.

Index

ESSAYS
CATHOLIC AND CRITICAL

ESSAYS
CATHOLIC & CRITICAL

BY MEMBERS OF
THE ANGLICAN COMMUNION

EDITED BY

EDWARD GORDON SELWYN

Third Edition

Essay Index Reprint Series

 BOOKS FOR LIBRARIES PRESS
FREEPORT, NEW YORK

First Published 1926
Third Edition First Published 1929
Reprinted 1971

INTERNATIONAL STANDARD BOOK NUMBER:
0-8369-2075-9

LIBRARY OF CONGRESS CATALOG CARD NUMBER:
75-142695

PRINTED IN THE UNITED STATES OF AMERICA

PREFACE TO THE THIRD EDITION

I

THE contributors to this collection of essays have every reason to be grateful for the welcome extended to the volume as a whole during the past three years, and for the thoroughness with which it has been criticised by theologians of the most diverse standpoints, both at home and abroad ; and the publication of a third edition appears to offer an opportunity for considering some of these criticisms, and endeavouring in some sort to meet them. Of many of the book's deficiencies the writers were well aware at the outset ; others have been brought home to them in the course of discussion and review. It is impossible to attempt to deal with all of them, and it has been decided to leave the text of each essay as it stands. But certain points of detail raised in regard to particular essays are considered in a series of Additional Notes now appended to the volume ; and major issues of principle, as these have been presented both from the Catholic and from the Protestant side, form the subject of this Preface.

It has been urged that this book " attempts the impossible " in trying " to bring into synthesis the Catholic and critical movements." [1] The criticism contains a just expression of what was in fact the purpose of its writers, and they believe that the task was both practicable and necessary. They are convinced, moreover, that this belief is part and parcel of the principles to which Anglican theology is committed and by which it stands or falls. At the same time, Liberal Catholicism (to give these principles a name) has undoubtedly a very difficult task to perform. It appears to be at one and the same time trying to hunt with the hounds and to run with the hare—to uphold reason and freedom on the one hand and

---

[1] By Dr. Selbie in *The British Weekly*. Similarly Professor Bulgakoff maintains that it is not a question of a synthesis, but of a choice, " between two authorities ; the Church and criticism."

tradition and authority on the other.   It is exposed to attack, accordingly, from the stalwarts of either camp.   The conflict centres especially in its conception of authority.

Now, it is significant that the conception of religious authority outlined in the two essays here devoted to that subject has elicited almost identical criticisms from representative writers of the most diverse schools of thought.   Lutheran or Roman Catholic, Evangelical or believer in the Inner Light, each makes the same complaint, viz., that no satisfying answer is provided as to what and where religious authority is.   On further analysis it is found, however, that behind each of these complaints lies a very definite, though in each case, different, idea of what the true answer is— an infallible Pope, or an infallible Bible, or an infallible conscience. Judged from the standpoint of any of these, the Liberal Catholic conception must appear vague.   But what if the answer be really complex ?   If the truth lies not in any simple or single formula, but in a critical synthesis of all these other, so confident, answers ? What if those answers themselves spring from, and unwittingly appeal to, a vast volume of religious experience which calls for some larger theory to account for it than any one of them alone provides ?   Such a theory, it must be admitted—and especially if it were incomplete—would certainly appear to the votaries of those earlier theories as vague and unsatisfying : but it might none the less contain the truth.   In the Preface to the first edition of this volume we admitted that its doctrine of authority was as yet incomplete.   It may be worth while, therefore, to try to develop it further.

But first a preliminary question may be answered, which is not the less important because it takes the form of an *argumentum ad hominem*.   The learned and kindly reviewer in "The Expository Times" writes : " If authority rests on Christian experience, surely those great Churches (Free, Lutheran, etc.) have some authority to plead.   But if the Christian experience of these bodies is to count in assessing the authority of any truth, what becomes of the Anglo-Catholic contention ? "   Now, so far as the religious experience of the great Protestant bodies is concerned, its signific- ance for a Catholic doctrine of authority is by no means overlooked (*cf.* pp. 118, 119).   The reviewer's question, however, betrays a misunderstanding of the Anglo-Catholic claim.   That claim is not that Anglo-Catholicism gives a final and exclusive expression of the truth, but that it represents the best expression at present available, in thought, worship, and life, of the principles necessary to an ultimate synthesis. That this is no merely insular prejudice is indicated by the interest and respect which Anglo-Catholicism commands in circles unconnected with England or with the Church of England. Dr. Brilioth in Sweden, Dr. Heiler in Germany, and Professor H. L. Stewart in Canada are none of them either English or Anglican ; but all agree in seeing in Anglo-Catholicism an attitude towards the principles and practice of Christianity which is of moment to the whole Church of Christ. That attitude is what underlies the work of the essayists in this volume. They aim, as a sympathetic Roman Catholic critic has put it, " at the restoration of order in the truth." Inevitably, they must endeavour to conserve all elements of such order that exist already ; and their apologetic, if it is successful at all, will vindicate the Christian faith far outside the borders of the Anglo-Catholic movement or even of the Anglican Communion itself.

II

The standpoint of this book will perhaps be best exhibited by a consideration of a very weighty and thorough criticism of Catholicism which has appeared since it was first published, viz., Dr. Cadoux's " Catholicism and Christianity." Dr. Cadoux's Protestantism is of a very radical kind. He is a Congregationalist who believes that Congregationalism really affords a basis for the reunion of Christendom ; he is not afraid to jettison the Creeds as well as the Pope ; and he has the strength which comes from the desire to be fair, and even generous, to the best in his adversaries' position. Further, his book moves through many fields, theological, historical, and ethical, and each is made to add its quota to the case against Catholicism. It is a great thing to have the case thus presented within the covers of one volume. If Dr. Cadoux fails to establish it, probably no other attempt will succeed. Our contention is, not only that Dr. Cadoux fails, but that his failure reveals the need of precisely such an alternative to Protestantism as Liberal Catholicism provides.

What is Catholicism ? The Roman Catholic answers easily enough that it is identical with the Roman Church. But Dr. Cadoux is under no such delusion ; and, though much of his most effective controversy is directed against what is distinctively Roman, he regards Anglicanism as being in principle more Catholic than Protestant. It is significant, for example, how frequently his footnotes contain references to Roman and to Anglican authorities side by side as exemplifying the same points. Not that the distinction is blurred : far from it. Full justice is done, for instance, to the type of Anglo-Catholic theology represented by the present volume, which, indeed, Dr. Cadoux regards (together with the writings of Bishop Gore) as forming a kind of textbook for non-Roman Western Catholicism. The point is of paramount importance, and determines most of what will be said in this Preface. If Roman Catholicism is the only kind there is, then in the last resort the *gravamen* against Catholicism must be admitted. The verdict of history may not, indeed, be so simple as Dr. Cadoux maintains, nor the ethical issue so clear ; and a fuller allowance needs to be made than is made here for the fact that the dogma of Papal Infallibility is an unfinished product. But, when all is said and done, if Catholicism stands or falls with that dogma, then *cadit quaestio.* We are tied up to a conception of authority which, both in theory and in practice, cannot in our view be defended.

Fortunately, however, an Anglican finds himself pressed to no such *impasse* ; and we are free to defend Catholicism on a non-Roman basis, without Dr. Cadoux calling in our hand. And it is characteristic of Anglican and Anglo-Catholic apologetic, not only that it does this, but that in doing so it provides a rival interpretation of Roman Catholicism itself. By Catholicism we mean, that is to say, a presentation of Christian thought, worship, and life to which no one Church—Anglican, Roman, or Eastern—has any exclusive title ; and which yet does permeate all those bodies with a thoroughness and tenacity sufficiently marked to distinguish them from all those bodies which call themselves, and are known to history as, Protestant. Many different accounts have been given of what is the essence of this presentation. Some have pointed to its emphasis on the social and historical elements in religion as compared with its individual aspects ; others to its insistence on the objectivity of truth as against the subjectivity of feeling ; others again to its note of corporate authority and discipline. But we shall probably not be wrong if we say that all these can be summed up in the claim, so often made by Baron von Hügel, that Catholicism gives to the institutional element in Christianity a place not less fundamental than that given to its mystical and intellectual elements.

For it is in relation to this institutional element, and as expressions and safeguards of it, that creeds, sacraments, ministry, the liturgy and its ceremonial, have their significance. They are the structure and arteries of the *Corpus Christi*, guaranteeing to us the concrete reality and prevenience of the social organism which derives its life from the incarnate Lord, now both ascended and indwelling. And this same prevenience of the Church, as transcendent over and anterior to the individual (who yet gives to it as well as receives from it) is the visible manifestation of all those other preveniences which belong to Christianity as a supernatural Gospel—the prevenience of God's Word in revelation, of His grace in redemption, of His light in faith, of His Spirit in worship, of His power in right living. " He that cometh to God must believe that *he is* "—that is the inscription over the portals of the Catholic Church. This objectivity and priority of God in every moment of genuine religion are what constitute Catholicism and its emphasis on the institution. And, judged from that standpoint, it is plain that the Anglican and Orthodox Communions are Catholic no less than the Roman.

A further question arises as to the character of this non-Roman Catholicism ; for it is something far more than Catholicism *minus* the Pope. It was not the Papacy only which the Church of England rejected at the Reformation ; but also the whole temper of those rules and ordinances, mostly enshrined in Canon Law, which had reduced Christianity almost to the level of a legalistic religion. What was the origin of this feature of the Roman system ? Many, no doubt, would say that it was simply a case of mediaeval corruption, brought about by the hierarchy in the interests of their own sacerdotal caste. A corruption, perhaps : but a corruption of what ? Was it the introduction into Christianity of something essentially foreign to it, or was it the distortion and exaggeration of something legitimate and native ? Various considerations suggest that the second alternative is the true one. The amazing efflorescence of art and architecture, of philosophy and mysticism, in the Middle Ages, not to speak of the expansion of discovery and commerce in the fifteenth century, do not look like symptoms of a corruption which had gone to the very roots of religion—or at

least not to all of them.   On the other hand, Rome's great contribution to Christendom was in the realm of law ; and legalism is
simply law growing cancerously.   Many different facts—the
inclusion of the Old Testament in the Christian Scriptures, the
Sermon on the Mount, the Apostolic decree recorded in Acts xv—
indicate that Christianity came into the world as an institutional
religion, incorporating and fulfilling the law no less than the
prophets ; and it was not difficult for this element to become
overgrown when the Church passed into the Roman world.
If we find Roman theology bearing from early times a markedly
forensic character, strong enough in some cases to determine the
whole form in which a doctrine is cast, we cannot be surprised
at the growth of legalism in the sphere of Christian practice and
institutions.

Or the matter may be approached from another angle.
Catholic Christianity represents the confluence of three mighty
streams—the Hebraic, the Roman, and the Hellenic—which first
met in the personality of St. Paul, and have blended in different
proportions ever since.   The dominant stream is the Hebraic,
since it is charged in a unique sense with revelation.   But that
tradition is no less liable than the others to degeneration : it may
decay into a Christian legalism, as it did in the Middle Ages,
corrupting the tradition of law ; or it may swell until it has
absorbed both the other traditions and made the whole conception
of God revert to an Old Testament type, as has been the case with
some forms of Protestantism.   The real prophylactic against such
degeneracy is the vitality of the Greek tradition in the Church.
It was the loss of that tradition in the West which accounted for
the rigidity and narrowness in the mediaeval outlook on religion ;
just as it was the recovery of it which was the fine fruit of the
Renaissance, and which passed by way of Grocyn and Erasmus
into the Anglican Reformation.   The great achievement of the
English Reformation, as it has been the peculiar glory of Anglicanism since, was that it represented once more a real synthesis of the
three traditions.   It maintained all the essentials of the Christian
law and institution, without the cramping fetters of legalism ;
through a revived knowledge of the Scriptures in their original
tongues it brought into fresh prominence the Hebraic element, but
without giving it any monopoly ; and it fused these two into
living unity by the alchemy of Greek thought, feeling, and pro-

portion. The result was a Church where, in an age of religious license, law was maintained, where revelation was mated with reason, and where criticism—the characteristic product of the Greek genius—was steeped in the spirit of reverence.

III

One of the problems which Protestant no less than Catholic apologetic must face is that of the nature and seat of religious authority ; and Dr. Cadoux's treatment of this issue occupies an important section of his book. After an effective criticism of the presumption that a divine revelation inevitably implies an oracular authority, he proceeds to enumerate those " things, institutions or persons" which Christian people have, in fact, regarded as authoritative. They are (1) Nature, (2) the Church, (3) the Bible, (4) the historical Jesus, (5) the Christ within, (6) the Conscience, (7) Reason. These seven, again, are brought under two categories, the first four being classified as " objective " authorities, and the last three as " subjective." For this second category Dr. Cadoux considers that the most comprehensive title is the Inner Light, which, he says, " includes (besides reason in the narrow sense) both conscience and the indwelling Christ, and is in fact simply a modern name for the work of the Holy Spirit within mind and heart." It is to the Inner Light so conceived that ultimacy of authority belongs, in the sense that, where there is conflict between the other authorities, it is the final arbiter. Dr. Cadoux comes forward, in short, as a champion of private judgment ; and it is from that standpoint that he criticises the more " objective" conceptions of Catholicism. Now, one of the immediate and most serious consequences of this principle is to isolate truth in religion so sharply from all other kinds of truth as to make it doubtful whether religious truth exists at all.[1] Dr. Cadoux makes much of the contention that the " danger " of a tolerant attitude in controversy " besets our Catholic fellow-Christians more than it besets Protestants, for whom toleration in religious belief is a settled and avowed tenet." Unfortunately there is confusion here between

---

[1] Professor Taylor draws my attention to some words of Bacon in this connexion : " per mentis multam agitationem spiritum suum proprium sollicit[an]t et quasi invoc[an]t ut sibi oracula pandat, quae res omnino sine fundamento est et in opinionibus tantum volvitur " (*N.O.* i. 82).

two words which had far better be kept distinct, namely, tolerance and toleration. The principle of toleration asserts the civil liberty of the individual to teach and practise his religion without hindrance or duress ; and it would be endorsed by a large number of Catholics as well as by Protestants. The principle of tolerance, on the other hand—not least as Dr. Cadoux defends it—asserts that religious truth is at best so subjective, vague, and relative a thing that we can none of us be sure of it and had better admit that contrary views are equally likely to be right. Now that is simply to put religion in a watertight compartment—or rather in as many watertight compartments as there are individual opinions—and to treat it as truth is treated in no other branch of life or knowledge. For it is of the essence of truth to be intolerant. We do not mean by this, of course, that truth can justify that kind of cocksure or impatient or hasty spirit which is often found—and not where religion only is concerned—in those who expound or defend it, and which has gained for the word " intolerance " its unenviable meaning. What we wish to emphasise is the fact that scientific truth of every kind is engaged in perpetual warfare with error ; and the presupposition of all its processes of thought is that the truth does exist, is worth reaching, and can be reached. Some words of Karl Barth are in point here : " What the people want to find out and thoroughly understand is, *Is it true ?* . . . they want to find out and thoroughly understand the answer to this one question, *Is it true ?*—and not some other answer which beats about the bush. . . . Let us not be deceived by their silence. Blood and tears, deepest despair and highest hope, a passionate longing to lay hold of *that* which, or rather of *him* who, overcomes the world because he is its Creator and Redeemer, its beginning and ending and Lord, a passionate longing to have the *word* spoken, *the* word which promises grace in *judgment*, life in *death*, and the beyond in the *here and now*, *God's* word—this it is which animates our church-goers, however, lazy, bourgeois, or commonplace may be the manner in which they express their want in so-called real life." [1] We are back again at the principle already quoted from the Epistle to the Hebrews : " He that cometh to God must believe that he is " ; and no one who has hold of that faith can have room in his mind for the belief that its opposite, atheism, may be equally true. The attitude of mind which corresponds to tolerance in this sense is not

[1] *The Word of God and the Word of Man* (English translation, pp. 108 ff.).

faith, but suspense of judgment ; and, unless that suspense be ended, sooner or later it becomes indistinguishable from scepticism.

A similar doubt as to the existence of truth in religion is aroused by Dr. Cadoux's attitude to dogma and the Creeds. Dr. Cadoux makes a distinction, which is not very easy to understand, between the use of the Creeds as tests and their use in other ways. It is not clear what he means, for example, when he speaks of the " application of a credal test to candidates for Church-membership." The writer of " Robert Elsmere " used sometimes to say that she regarded the use of the Nicene Creed in the liturgy as a barrier which kept her from Communion, but such an interpretation of it is obviously individual. The use of the Apostles' Creed in adult Baptism might perhaps be impleaded, but that cannot be said to amount to " subscription." The truth is that Dr. Cadoux dislikes the Creeds. In his judgment, " the domain of reason is cut down . . . by the cold unpassable stream of dogma." It involves a " check " on reason's activity. The Creed " adds considerably to the simple profession of faith in Christ " ; the use of it as authoritative means that " genuine and thoughtful Christian men have to be shut up to a dire choice between remaining outside the Church and playing fast and loose with truth."

Now, the outstanding feature of this kind of criticism of the Creeds is its failure to realise what they primarily are. The Creeds are first and foremost expressions and safeguards of the worship of Christ. That worship, which was " to the Jews a stumbling-block and to the Greeks foolishness," is what underlies the whole development of the Christological issue in the past ; and the Christological issue is still right at the centre of Christianity. And it is because Catholicism is credal that it has been able to safeguard the worship of Christ in the modern world in a way in which Liberal Protestantism does not. There is a real danger to-day, especially in the Protestant churches in America, of a religious outlook and trend of thought, blended of Liberal Judaism and Liberal Protestantism, which, if its dogmatic implications were worked out, would be simply a species of Unitarianism. Against any such desertion of the Gospel as proclaimed in the New Testament Catholicism is the great bulwark and it is this which gives it its evangelical character. In Catholicism, as in Protestantism, the tide of faith ebbs and flows, and sometimes ebbs very low ; but where the Creeds are believed and used, there the Church is committed without reserve to the worship of Christ as God.

Once more Dr. Cadoux is aware that Catholic theologians allow for a symbolic and figurative element in the Creeds, and that this goes back to such early authorities as St. Jerome ; but he maintains that this concession " opens the door to an extremely dangerous tampering with truthfulness and sincerity of speech." Here it surely seems as though prejudice were warping judgment ; for equity always demands that theological statements shall be taken in their best, and not their worst, construction.   And, for that matter, what are we to say of the Lord's Prayer ?   " Our Father, which art in heaven . . ." is there nothing symbolic about " Father " ?   Or about " heaven "?   Is God really " in " heaven, as in a place ?   We cannot believe that Dr. Cadoux would maintain this, or that he is too much of a purist ever to use the Lord's Prayer.   The truth is that in all religious language there is bound to be an element of symbolism.   We can but figure out the deep things of God : human language is based on sense-perception, and cannot rid itself of its origin when it comes to speak of the things beyond the senses.

But there is another kind of symbolism, too, which attaches to dogma as it does to scientific statements of truth.   This aspect of dogma was first suggested by the French Modernists a generation ago, and popularised in England by Father Tyrrell ; it was further developed and given more precise form by the present Master of Corpus in his " Belief and Practice " (1915) ; and it has lately been endorsed by one of the weightiest of modern philosophers, Dr. Whitehead.   In " Religion in the Making," especially in the chapter entitled " Religion and Dogma," Dr. Whitehead expounds with rare power the necessity, functions, and limitations of dogma.   Dogma is necessary, because religion has " its own contribution of immediate experience " to make to knowledge, and dogma is its expression.   But its function is not only to express and interpret such experience : it is also creative, and elicits it.   At the same time a dogma can never be " final " ; for it is relative to a certain system of thought, and " can only be adequate in its adjustment of certain abstract concepts," *i.e.* its truth is schematic or symbolic.   None the less, it cannot be dispensed with until the experience thus expressed and made transmissible is taken up into some other formulation.   The attempt to reduce religion to " a few simple notions," natural as it may be as a reaction from the horrors of bigotry, is " shipwrecked on the rock of the problem of evil," and involves the arbitrary substitution of intuition for genuine (even if faulty) rationalisations of experience ; and intuition tends to become " a private psychological habit," which is without general evidential force.

The importance of Dr. Whitehead's defence of dogma lies not only in the high authority of the writer, but also in the fact that it is presented as part of a philosophical system in which Catholic theology to-day is deeply interested.[1] It affords the best possible example of the synthetic meaning and aim of dogma. So far, in fact, from being intellectually dead, dogma represents the continuous attempt of the Church as a body to relate its own devotional experience to all other experience of reality. I say " of the Church as a body," because it is precisely the *common* experience of Christ's grace—that which is shared in, or at least may be shared in, by all members of the Christian social organism —which is thus represented and expressed. Dr. Cadoux complains, and underlines the complaint, that " the Catholic view of the determination of authoritative doctrine makes no allowance whatever " for " the personal factor in all human thinking." If he means that the Church regards the consensus of the whole *Corpus Christi*, in many lands and ages, as of more consequence than the private judgment of isolated individuals, he is right. But if he means that there was in the early centuries some kind of ecclesiastical machine which ground out dogma for the Church's consumption, without regard to the personal needs and beliefs of the faithful, then there is no shadow of historical support for the contention. What the Church does by its dogmatic formulations is to preserve and re-transmit, for the common good, a common heritage of religious experience derived from Christ and His Apostles.

And, after all, that is the most liberal way in which authority can operate. It affords ample scope for the Inner Light, though not for the dogmatic Modernism which often seeks shelter under that principle. Dr. Cadoux himself does full justice to Catholic recognition of the sacredness of conscience. Newman's case is perhaps peculiar ; but the same cannot be said of the well-established principle that *conscientia semper sequenda*. Indeed,

---

[1] *Cf.* Fr. Thornton's recent book, *The Incarnate Lord.*

when Dr. Cadoux says that " the only ultimate ground is . . .
the witness of God's Holy Spirit operating in the will, heart, and
mind of the teachable believer," he is only voicing in his own words
the Catholic principle that faith is a grace of God to the individual.
Had he developed that point and its bearing upon the " objective "
elements in religious authority, instead of trying to drive these off
the field, he would have laid us all in his debt. Different minds
will certainly emphasise different elements in the complex system
of authority : Origen, Jerome, Aquinas, Catherine of Genoa,
Hooker, Law, Newman, Tyrrell—these are a few of the names
which illustrate the diversity of approach to the problem. But
there is not one of them who would not have gladly joined in the
singing of the Creed as the great battle-song of the Church's
spiritual warfare.

We may therefore attempt now to answer the question as to
the source, seat, and organ of authority in the Church of Christ.
Its source is in the Spirit of God, who revealed and still reveals the
unsearchable riches of Christ. It is He who inspired, within and
for the Church, the writing of the Scriptures, and their selection
and acceptance by the Church ; who has preserved the unity and
guided the development of Christian doctrine amid the conflicting
currents of human opinions ; and who in every age brings home
to the hearts and minds of believers the supernatural claims of the
Gospel. The seat of this authority is in the common mind of the
Church. If this common mind is not to be found in any one
single mode, it is none the less accessible and real. Its normative
expression is in the Scriptures, and especially in the revelations of
the Apostles and of those who knew our Lord personally. But
the Scriptures are not the only expression of the Church's mind.
Its creeds, its dogmatic formularies, its liturgical forms and phrases
—whatever in short has nourished and borne fruit in the lives of
the Saints—all these are also authoritative for our understanding
of Christian truth. This or that expression of it may not be final
or irreformable ; but at least it has been the symbol of a genuine
element of religious experience, and whatever formulation of the
truth may supersede it must account for, and conserve, that
experience. The chief weakness of Modernism and of Liberal
Protestantism lies in their failure to do this.

The question of the organ of Catholic authority presents a
more difficult problem, owing to the divided state of the Church.

The Roman theory evades the difficulty by accrediting one of the parts with the authority of the whole, and regarding the visible head of that part as the infallible spokesman of God. Those who in East or West, while retaining the faith, ministry, and sacraments of the undivided Church, reject the Papal theory are bound, no doubt, to speak rather of organs than of " the organ " of authority, so long as the collective episcopate cannot meet. That does not mean, however, that they are left without adequate guidance for practical needs. What it does mean is that the pronouncements of these authorities are incomplete, since they rest upon, and apply to, a part only of the whole field of Christian experience. The position is not a final one, and its limitations supply a powerful motive for Catholic reunion. But meanwhile it is strong enough to rest in, until such fresh illumination is given as can alone make the solution of the difficulties possible.

IV

In what sense can the term " Modernism " be applied to the theological position represented in this volume ? The question has been recently brought to the fore in a work by Professor H. L. Stewart, of Halifax, N.S., entitled " A Century of Anglo-Catholicism." In the very appreciative chapter which he devotes to a discussion of " Essays Catholic and Critical," Professor Stewart speaks of it as having " an unmistakable Modernist ring " ; it means " Modernism . . . in the sense in which Modernism is the name for a *method* rather than for a *creed* " ; its " writers are Modernists," though not Modernists of the Liberal Protestant persuasion. We could wish that all our critics from the conservative standpoint had been so discerning as Professor Stewart [1] ; for his reservations rob the title of its sting. It is certainly true that what we have sought is " a real reconciliation between religious faith and advancing secular knowledge " ; and we should readily acknowledge our debt to the methods and results of modern critical scholarship. But we should none the less claim that this is not properly called Modernism, except in the sense in which that term can also be applied to the work of Athanasius, Aquinas, and Westcott in their several generations. For better or worse, at least in English-speaking countries, Modernism has become in

---

[1] On certain errors of detail, however, see Additional Note C.

recent years as much a creed as a method ; it stands for a form of Liberal Protestantism which shades off almost imperceptibly into Unitarianism ; and it may be of service to distinguish it from our position.

The root of the distinction between the two schools of thought will be found to lie in the underlying assumptions of their theology. Modernism is the child of Biblical Criticism ; and the critical movement has always been governed by the search for uniformities and the belief that the discovery of such uniformities offered a royal road to truth in religion no less than in science. On this principle the Bible must be treated like any other historical book, the literary relations of its parts analysed and its historical narratives subjected to the same criteria of evidence and probability as any others ; the beliefs and customs of Christianity must be set alongside their parallels in other religions ; and all idea of uniqueness in divine revelation must be scrupulously excluded. As the presupposition of a strictly historical inquiry, and within those limits, the principle has been fruitful in yielding a richer and more sympathetic understanding of the origins and development of Christianity. But it may easily become a very dangerous weapon when its limits are forgotten, and when what was forged as a guide to a particular field of study is expanded into a dogma governing the whole field of religious knowledge. The *gravamen* against Modernism is not that it seeks for uniformities, but that it postulates for the explanation of Christianity as a whole uniformities which apply only to a particular part of it, and so reduces it to the level of natural religion.

The history of science during the last century offers an instructive parallel to what has happened in the case of theology. The rapid strides in physics and chemistry which had resulted from the work of Sir Isaac Newton led to the confident prediction that the single principle of the Uniformity of Nature would suffice to open all the doors of knowledge and give sufficient insight into every field of reality. In the middle of the century Darwin seemed to offer at once a criticism and an endorsement of this principle—a criticism because his work showed that the development of living species follows laws of its own, in addition to those which had been found adequate for lifeless matter, an endorsement because he summed these up under a new uniformity, that of Evolution. There are still those who believe that the underlying assumptions of physics and biology will suffice for the whole purposes of knowledge ; but they are increasingly in a minority. For, broadly speaking, the progress of science in the last generation has been towards increasing emancipation of its different departments. Neither History nor Comparative Religion will fit into the strait waistcoat of categories of thought which belong to the sciences beneath them ; and indeed even physical science itself has rebelled against its former tutelage. In each case a theory of uniformity has had to make way for new, or newly realised, facts which could not be brought under the formulae which were supposed to explain them ; and fresh fields have been opened to science in consequence.

Now, a process not unlike this has taken place in theology. Anglican theology of the last half of the nineteenth century, as seen in " Essays and Reviews," or in " Lux Mundi," was largely concerned with the attempt to come to terms with current scientific conceptions, and to see how far they could be accepted without danger to the Christian faith. What is called Modernism to-day results from hanging on too long to the concepts then current, and forcing them further than they will go, and its upshot is to reduce Christianity as a living religion to a mere shadow of itself. We might say that Modernism bears the same relation to the theology of to-day as Haeckel's " monism " bore to the science even of a generation ago. Liberal Catholicism, on the other hand, stands for the new, or newly realised, facts which give to theology its autonomy as a science. It appeals to these facts of religious experience as facts which, though embedded in history, cannot be adequately accounted for by historical science alone. As against the evolutionary immanentism characteristic of Modernist thought, it emphasises the facts of human freedom and account-ability, and the experiences of guilt and non-attainment, which cry aloud for the otherness of God and for a redemption that shall come from above ; and it points to the Christian experience as the experience of such a redemption centred in Christ.

Such a position inevitably involves, as Baron von Hügel used to point out, a peculiar tension and conflict for Christian theology. In so far as Christianity is a historical religion, the facts which it proposes as *credenda* must be subject to the ordinary canons of historical criticism ; and yet, in so far as it is supernatural, these canons will not apply. Is the faith, then, to be at the mercy of

the latest study of Christian origins ?   Or is the Church to make
a citadel of certain facts and say to Criticism, " Thus far and no
farther " ?   Neither policy is tolerable to the mind that combines
devotion with candour.   The solution lies in refusing the dilemma.
The historical science to which appeal is made is in part an abstraction ;   it proceeds—quite rightly, for its own purposes—by
postulating certain uniformities in human motive and action, and
by ruling out all exceptions to these as facts to be explained away
rather than explained.   Theology, on the other hand, insists that
the normal human experience which is the historian's guide is not
the whole of experience, and that other facts—the facts commonly
summed up under the phrase " religious experience "—must be
taken into account if the whole truth is to be reached.

The position may be illustrated from the case of miracle.
Nothing is more common in Modernist literature than the assumption that " miracles do not happen," and the consequent attempt to
discover for all narratives containing miracle a naturalistic explanation.   The Catholic apologist, on the other hand, can be content
with no such facile solution.   In the first place, his conception of
the nature of God, and of His relation to the universe, is such as to
preclude any *a priori* assumption that miracles cannot happen.
Secondly, he cannot disguise from himself the fact that miracle is
so integral a feature of the portraits of Christ contained in the
Gospels that it cannot be jettisoned without both destroying the
unity of each Gospel and also radically altering the profile of each
portrait :   and he is bound to conclude that it represents something
ultimate and indispensable in Jesus.   This conclusion, moreover, is
endorsed by the attitude which our Lord Himself appears to have
adopted towards His mighty works, as the proper signs, fulfilling
what the Scriptures had foretold, of the Messianic office.   And,
thirdly, he finds that, throughout Christian history, well-attested
cases of miracle have tended to occur in connexion with exceptional
manifestations of divine grace in human life.   He argues, therefore,
that miracle must be regarded as the symbol and safeguard of
supernatural religion, and that that context must not be forgotten.
He agrees with the Modernist that every narrative of miracle
must be judged on its merits ;   but he disagrees with him about
the merits, insisting that these must include the congruity of the
miracle with the whole dispensation of which it forms part.   It is
true, as Professor Stewart says, that the writers of this volume argue

to miracle rather than *from* it, but that does not mean that they regard it as an optional and detachable appendage of the faith.

The difference noted above in the underlying assumptions of Catholicism and Modernism respectively may be further illustrated by the importance attached by the former to the institutional side of religion. The oil and wine of the Christian life can only be preserved in vessels ; and if creed and dogma provide the intellectual vessels, the Church's pastoral and worshipping system provides those needed for more common and day-to-day uses. Professor Stewart both sees, and does not see, this point. On the one hand, he is severe upon those who, from the Protestant standpoint, object to the statement [1] that Protestantism tends to regard the sacraments as " optional appendages " to religion. So far as the teaching standards of the Protestant Churches are concerned, he regards the objection as well founded ; but he says that their practice belies their principles. " Will anyone who knows the Free Churches dispute it ? " he says. " Can one discover in their practice any such recognition of the solemn and unique import of the Eucharist as their formal acknowledgments should render imperative ? " These are strong words coming from a Presbyterian ; and the answer would not be uniformly negative. Yet the danger is real, and it is strange that Professor Stewart should not see that it is just this against which Catholicism is guarding by its careful use of symbol and ceremony in worship. The " queer ritualism," which more than once provokes Professor Stewart to an almost ribald mockery, does no doubt sometimes run to excess ; but he is greatly mistaken if he supposes that there is any real cleavage, so far as Anglo-Catholicism is concerned, between the theologians in their studies and the worshippers in their churches. The reverse is, in fact, the case. Among the writers of this volume there would probably be differences of opinion as to what symbols and ceremonies were desirable or otherwise : there would be none as to the desirability, or indeed necessity, of symbol and ceremony *in itself*. For symbolism in worship is an expression of a common faith and feeling, representing often more powerfully than words the religious experience and the mental attitude characteristic of the Christian revelation. It is thus a great safeguard against eccentricity of opinion and sentiment on the one hand and against a worldly and secularised worship on the other.

[1] See the essay on " The Origins of the Sacraments," p. 369.

It is one of the arteries of the *Corpus Christi*, by which the blood of the regenerate life circulates to all the members. It thus embodies and transmits in definite form that body of religious experience which provides Catholic theology with its subject-matter.

V

There remains one further issue of a broader kind on which something must be said before we close. It underlies some of the criticisms passed upon the treatment of the Reformation in this volume, and it is raised in an acute form in the section of Dr. Cadoux's book devoted to an indictment of Catholic Christianity on historical and moral grounds ; but what is of more moment is that this indictment represents a philosophy of Christian history which is widely popular and which has a far directer influence on public opinion than any issue of a more theological kind. It was claimed above that Liberal Catholicism offered to provide a rival interpretation of Roman Catholicism itself, not justifying indeed the Roman Church as it stands, but at least vindicating a very large part of the religious life and thought within its borders ; and the like is true of the great Churches of Eastern Europe. It may fairly be argued that such a claim cannot stop there ; that those who do not disown the Catholic title on theological grounds must be prepared to defend it on the ground also of its practical fruits ; and that they must convince the world that the progress of Catholicism, of whatever sort it be, will not mean a reaction to principles of public and private morality which Christian civilization is supposed to have decisively rejected.

The first and best-known count in the indictment is concerned with persecution. Few prejudices are more firmly established than the view that the Catholic religion is in its very nature a religion of persecution. Now, it must be at once admitted that certain Roman Catholic divines, including even Aquinas, have, by their teaching on the use of force to restrain error and propagate the faith, given a handle for this charge. It is also undeniable that in the sixteenth and seventeenth centuries the Roman hierarchy—through the Inquisition and otherwise—aided and abetted ruthless persecution both of Protestants, and of Jews who had relapsed from Christianity to Judaism, in many European countries ; that force has frequently been resorted to by the Church in Russia in the interests of the Orthodox faith ; and that the Church of England's hands have not been clean in its dealings either with Roman Catholics or with Puritans.   These facts, if they stood alone, might be taken to justify the kind of impression which has been stamped on the public mind by such books as Kingsley's " Westward Ho ! " or Foxe's " Book of Martyrs."   The truth is, however, that they do not stand alone, and that other facts, equally ugly and no less significant, have to be faced on the other side.   One of the inevitable results of the critical reconstruction of history which is now proceeding is that it brings these facts into prominence and insists on their being given due weight.

Nearly seventy years have passed since Lord Acton first published in " The Rambler " his remarkable essay on " The Protestant Theory of Persecution " ;   and, whether we regard the theory or the practice of persecution, that essay remains a work of classical importance, marshalling the relevant facts in compact and deadly array.   The upshot of the essay is twofold :   first, that the leading Continental Reformers—Luther, Melancthon, Calvin—while in some cases making profession of toleration, were all of them active defenders and promoters of persecution ;   and secondly, that the grounds on which they justified the policy of intolerance differed *toto coelo* from those advanced by Roman Catholics.[1]   Catholic intolerance was " handed down from an age when unity subsisted, and when its preservation, being essential for that of society, became a necessity of state as well as a result of circumstances."   For the Romanist, heresy was a form of apostasy from a settled ecclesiastico-political order, in the maintenance of which either the spiritual or the civil authority might fairly call upon the other for support. Protestant intolerance, on the other hand, was based—professedly, at least—solely upon doctrinal grounds ;   it was justifiable (so its defenders argued) only against error and in defence of Scriptural truth ;   but in that cause persecution was permissible, and might often be a duty.   The result was to substitute for a policy which could plead practical civic necessity one which was purely subjective and was far more the immediate offspring of religious bigotry. The cold discussion of the pros and cons of a sentence to the stake, as mirrored in Mr. Shaw's " Saint Joan," strikes us as belonging to another age than our own :   but at least it cannot be said that the blind bigotry of religion was the only power at work in the counsels of the Inquisition.

[1] *History of Freedom*, p. 165 ff.

The truth is that the Reformation period was essentially an age of persecution. Its root was that which has so often been the root of war ; it was fear—fear lest the old order or the new-won liberties, civil as much as religious, might be endangered. Even in the case of the persecution of witches, which reached in Presbyterian Scotland and in other countries affected by the Reformation such appalling dimensions, genuine fear played a leading part. Authority, when it feels itself secure, can afford to be liberal ; it is when that security is thought to be challenged that intolerance enters to defend it. No doubt Catholic intolerance was more widespread and more highly organised than that of Protestantism; but so was the authority that felt itself threatened, and indeed Catholicism with its belief in social solidarity and the corporate life will always be the more tempted to adopt the weapon of persecution. In the sense that it shattered the foundations of a civilised order which governed Western Europe for several centuries, the age of the Reformation was a decisive crisis in the history of Christendom. But constructively it failed. The minds of the Reformers were too deeply steeped in mediaevalism, and too close to the vortex of change, for them to know " what spirit they were of " ; and a just philosophy of history will tend rather to regard the eighteenth century, when a growing sense of security in the new order, particularly in England, gave occasion for the birth of toleration, as an age not less pregnant than the sixteenth with the true destiny of the Christian Church.

Closely allied with the memories of persecution lies another count in the charge against Catholicism, according to which it has been the persistent foe of all progress towards kinder and more humane standards of life. In one matter—the treatment of animals —the charge appears undeniable, until we realise that the ground of the different standards which undoubtedly exist is racial rather than religious ; the Latins, in sharp contrast to the Germanic and Anglo-Saxon peoples, sharing the Oriental insensibility to animal suffering. But when we pass to the relations of men to their fellowmen less fortunately placed, the indictment is far wide of the truth. Few higher tributes could be paid, for instance, to the Catholic Church's care for the sick than the description of what was done for them in Constantinople at the end of the eleventh century contained in the charming diary of Anna Comnena. The splendid hospitals of St. Paul or of the Pantocrator, with their separate wards for the different sexes and diseases, lady doctors for the women, careful precautions against sepsis, full equipment for the comfort of the patients, staffs of nurses provided by the Religious Orders—these things constitute a magnificent testimony to what the Church was doing out of its own generosity and sympathy five centuries before the Reformation.

Or turn again to the treatment of subject races. Popular opinion has it that the Spanish empire was one of uniform cruelty, and that it was left for Protestantism to combine national expansion with the precepts of the Gospel. The meed of praise we rightly give, however, to many leaders in our own history—to Robert Nelson, or Wilberforce, or the Lawrences, or Gordon— is no excuse for being blind to similar efforts by Catholic leaders in similar causes. The lamp of humanitarianism never burned, for example, more brightly than in the Spanish Dominican, Fray Bartolomé de Las Casas, the friend and companion and critic of Cortés. Long before the world listened to the resounding rhetoric of the Declaration of Independence, this Catholic priest had asserted before emperors and governments and conquerors in the field the equality of all men in the sight of God ; and he brought to bear upon Spanish colonial expansion principles and methods of treating subject races which are not a whit behind those aimed at to-day in our own African Protectorates or in the mandated territories of the League of Nations. Nor does he stand alone. Throughout the eighteenth and nineteenth centuries the Indians of North America had no more devoted friends and protectors from the ruthless white explorers and settlers than the priests of the Jesuit and Franciscan missions in the Western territories. If " Uncle Tom's Cabin " brought home to thousands of Englishmen what the Evangelical Churches were doing for the slaves in America, Helen Hunt Jackson's " Ramona " is no less a testimony to the solicitude of the Roman Catholic Church for the dispossessed natives of the same area. Even as to slavery, it is significant that the one Eastern state of America where slavery was never permitted was the Roman Catholic foundation of Maryland.

The third count in the indictment may be more briefly disposed of. There is a certain type of Protestantism which is never tired of proclaiming that the private morality of Protestant countries is of a far higher order than that found in countries mainly Catholic, and that the moral leadership of the world has now passed in consequence to Protestantism. Sweeping statements of this kind carry their own condemnation, and are only serious because they appeal to a large mass of ignorant and self-complacent prejudice. So far as statistics of crime or of divorce are concerned, the United States of America, which would vigorously claim the title of a Protestant country, cuts a sorry figure compared with any other civilised country, whether Catholic or Protestant ; and where statistics are unavailable it is obvious that generalisations are very treacherous. It is no doubt true that a different importance is attached in different countries to particular aspects of morality ; but when we find that these differences correspond with well-marked racial differences, it is reasonable to assume that race rather than religion is the ground of them. What is even more certain is that charges of this kind commonly arise from little more than a crude and arrogant nationalism ; and that such a spirit is totally at variance with the ideals not only of Catholicism but of Christianity. If we mention them here, it is because they illustrate an important aspect of the need of Liberal Catholicism in the world to-day, namely, the fact that it carries within it the germs of a patriotism which looks beyond the borders of its own nationality, and conceives of Christ's Church as international just as His Kingdom is super-national. In an age which believes that the forces of disruption and disintegration have had their day, and feels itself engaged upon the reconstruction of a new world-order, the importance of such an outlook is manifest.

It has seemed desirable to deal at such length with criticisms both of this volume and of the principles which underlie it, because the position which we represent is no transient phenomenon, but has had a long history and shows every sign of appealing more widely than heretofore. Just as in theology our aim is less to promote orthodoxy as an end in itself than to foster the desire to learn what orthodoxy has to teach, so in our general outlook we aim less at criticising others than at creating conditions in which mutual understanding between men of different allegiances may grow. " It was not more *toleration*," writes Professor Stewart, " but rather *sympathy* that was required—not the toleration which, as Coleridge said, is an herb of easy growth on the soil of indifference, but the sympathy by which different schools may be knit rather than frozen together." The promotion of such a sympathy has often been described as the historic task of Anglican theology.

Michaelmas, 1929.   E. G. S.

PREFACE TO THE FIRST EDITION

THE contributors to this volume have been drawn together by a common desire to attempt a fresh exposition and defence of the Catholic faith. They have nearly all been engaged in University teaching during recent years, and have thus been brought into close touch with the vigorous currents and cross-currents of thought and feeling amid which Christianity has to render its own life and truth explicit ; and they have been compelled, both for themselves and for others, to think out afresh the content and the grounds of their religion. This book is the result of their endeavour.

Among precursors in the same field, the essayists owe pre-eminent acknowledgment to the authors of "Lux Mundi," a book which exercised upon many of them a formative influence and still has a living message. But by two forces especially, both of them operating with great intensity, theology has been constrained both to lengthen its cords and to strengthen its stakes during the generation which has elapsed since that work was first published. On the one hand many thoughtful men have been led by the spectacle of a disordered and impoverished Christendom to a keener discernment of the supernatural element in religion, and to a renewed interest in the expressions of it which are seen in Catholic unity and authority, in whatever form these come ; so that solidarity has taken its true rank at the side of continuity, as a necessary "note" of the Church. On the other hand, the critical movement, which was already in "Lux Mundi" allowed to effect a significant lodgment in the citadel of faith, has continued with unabated vigour to analyse and bring to light the origins and foundations of the Gospel. As the title of this volume implies, it is the writers' belief that these two movements can be and must be brought into synthesis ; and we believe further that, in the task of effecting it, in thought, in devotion, and finally in the visible achievement of the Church's unity, the Anglican

Communion and its theologians have a part of peculiar importance to play.

For the two terms Catholic and critical represent principles, habits, and tempers of the religious mind which only reach their maturity in combination. To the first belongs everything in us that acknowledges and adores the one abiding, transcendent, and supremely given Reality, God ; believes in Jesus Christ, as the unique revelation in true personal form of His mystery ; and recognises His Spirit embodied in the Church as the authoritative and ever-living witness of His will, word, and work. To the second belongs the exercise of that divinely implanted gift of reason by which we measure, sift, examine, and judge whatever is proposed for our belief, whether it be a theological doctrine or a statement of historical fact, and so establish, deepen, and purify our understanding of the truth of the Gospel. The proportion in which these two activities are blended will vary in different individuals and in relation to different parts of our subject-matter : but there is no point at which they do not interact, and we are convinced that this interaction is necessary to any presentment of Christianity which is to claim the allegiance of the world to-day.

The scope and arrangement of the essays call for little explanation. The first three essays are concerned with the presuppositions of faith—with its rudimentary origins and development, with its justification in reason and experience, and with the claims of the Catholic Church to provide for it a rational basis of authority ; though there is a sense in which no doctrine of authority can claim to be more than a kind of torso, so long as the divisions of Christendom hinder its concrete expression and operation. The second and central section of the book aims at unfolding the revelation of God and the redemption of man which centre in, and derive from, the Person of Christ, incarnate, crucified, and risen ; and the historical evidence for these facts is considered with some fulness in face of modern criticism. The concluding section embraces the institutional expression and vital application of the redemptive resources of Christianity in the Church and the sacraments, particular heed being given to certain aspects of these which are much in men's minds at the present time. It will be clear that many problems have had to be left untouched ; but some omissions were necessary, if the book were not to assume an inconvenient bulk. Our purpose, however, has not been to be exhaustive, but rather to bear witness to the faith we have received and commend it, so far as may be, to others.

In a work of this kind the measure of collective responsibility is not easy to define. Nor perhaps is it necessary. Domiciled as we are in different places, and not all of us even in England, we have found it impossible to meet together for discussion. On the other hand, each author has seen and been encouraged to criticise every essay, and all criticisms have been considered before any essay assumed its final form. In some cases care has been taken by the use of the first person to show that an expression of opinion is markedly the writer's own. These cases, however, though not unimportant, are few ; and while none of the authors should be held responsible for more than his own contribution, it may be legitimately said that the volume represents a common faith, temper, and desire.

E. G. S.

Eastertide, 1926.

NOTE TO THE SECOND EDITION

The alterations in this edition are almost all only verbal or orthographical; but they provide an opportunity for expressing thanks to those readers who have been kind enough to send corrections, and also to the printer whose care and skill in the first instance have caused the total number of corrections to be so small. I should also like to express our gratitude to my friend, Mrs. Beardall, for her valuable secretarial help in the preparation of the volume.

E. G. S.

November, 1926.

CONTENTS

THE EMERGENCE OF RELIGION
BY EDWIN OLIVER JAMES

B

CONTENTS

I

INTRODUCTORY

THE progress of scientific research in recent years has not only changed our view of the universe, but it has also materially altered our conception of human and religious origins. In the old days when it was thought that the world was brought into being in a short space of time by a series of special creative acts culminating in man, the whole scheme of creation and redemption seemed to fit together into one composite whole. Now, for those who are acquainted with contemporary thought, religion, like all other attributes of the universe, is known to be a product of evolution, inasmuch as it has proceeded from simple beginnings to complex conceptions of man and his relation to the supernatural order. But since this fact was first demonstrated in the latter part of the nineteenth century, further evidence has thrown much new light on the early history of religion. Nevertheless, anthropology is still a young and somewhat speculative science, and it becomes anthropologists to be very modest in their assertions. At present we know only in part, and with the completion of knowledge (if indeed such is attainable) doubtless many of our provisional hypotheses will have to be abandoned or at least modified. Therefore, in venturing upon an account of the emergence of religion, it should be made clear to the general reader at the outset that we are dealing with tentative propositions based upon evidence that is in process of accumulation. But provisional formulation according to the data available at a given time and the use of the scientific imagination are part of the scientific method and not to be despised in the great quest of truth. Moreover, it is impossible for a writer who is himself engaged in specialised research to be entirely free from a mental bias resulting from his own investigations. It is the business of the scientist to collect and classify the data at his disposal and to form judgments upon the basis of this classification, but always claiming the right, of course, to adjust his conclusions, or, if need be, change them, in the light of new and additional evidence. Therefore, while he is concerned primarily with facts, he cannot altogether escape from theories.

It is now becoming clear that the view concerning the origin of religion which the late Sir Edward Tylor put forth in 1872 in his great work, " Primitive Culture," is too specialised to be a "minimum definition," as he described it. Religion, he thought, originated in animism, a term used to signify a " belief in the existence of spiritual beings," [1] that is to say, of " spirits " in the wide sense that includes " souls." Man is supposed to have arrived at this conception by the realisation that within him dwells a kind of phantasm or ghost which is capable of leaving the body during sleep, trance, or sickness, and finally going away altogether at death. This doctrine is thought to have been extended to the rest of creation, so that the entire scene of his existence was pervaded by these " spiritual beings." That such a view is held to-day by many people living in a primitive state of culture is beyond dispute ; but does it follow, therefore, that this was the case when man first emerged from his mammalian forbears ?

II

LIFE, DEATH, AND IMMORTALITY IN EARLY CULT

1. *Beliefs in Survival after Death*

When we turn from modern native races to the evidence revealed by the pick and spade of the archæologist—and after all it is this that is of supreme importance, since the savage can never be anything but a " modern man," however arrested his development may be—the first indication of religion occurs in what is known as the Middle Palæolithic period (the Old Stone Age), when, shivering under the effects of the great Ice Age, man was driven to seek shelter and warmth in the caves of France and Spain. The inference is based upon the manner of burial adopted by the prehistoric race named *Neanderthal* (after the place where the first example of the type was found), which inhabited these caves and rock-shelters perhaps a quarter of a million years ago. Though brutish-looking fellows, the Neanderthalers not only made beautifully worked flint tools, but also laid their dead to

[1] *Primitive Culture* (London, 1891), 3rd ed., i. 424.

rest with great care and ceremony. Thus at Le Moustier the skeleton of a youth about sixteen years of age was found carefully placed in the attitude of sleep, with the right forearm under the head. A bed of flint chips formed his pillow, and close by the hand was a splendid implement. Other flints of the pattern characteristic of this period were discovered in the grave, together with the bones of the wild ox. Since the latter were charred and split, it is generally thought that they were the relics of a funeral feast. Similar ceremonial burials have been found elsewhere, notably at La Chapelle-aux-Saints.[1]

These interments prove beyond doubt that Neanderthal man had some conception of a life after death. Professor Macalister, in his recent "Text-Book of European Archæology," has summed up the situation by saying that Neanderthal man, degenerate though he may have been, " was conscious of something more than merely animal within him : already he had begun to look forward to a life beyond the grave—a life like that to which he was accustomed, for he could conceive of none other, where he would need food and clothing, and the instruments for procuring them. As his comrades passed, each in his turn, into the silent land, he laid beside their bodies such things as he imagined would minister to their necessities in the mysterious otherworld." [2]

Neanderthal man, however, does not represent the earliest stages of human development. At least one example of a much older and probably far superior type of man has been found, taking us back to a very remote period, before the Ice Age, perhaps half a million years ago. This remarkable discovery was made in 1912 in a narrow stratum of river-gravel on Piltdown Common, near Uckfield, in Sussex. Although the precise date of the skull is a matter of dispute among scholars, all are agreed that the lady of Piltdown—for the skeleton was apparently that of a woman — is the oldest inhabitant of Great Britain, if not of the world, so far discovered.[3] Contemporary with, or perhaps rather earlier than, *Eoanthropus*, as the Piltdown woman is called, " a being human in stature, human in gait, human in all its parts, save its brain," and therefore named *Pithecanthropus erectus* (the ape-man

[1] *Arch. für Anthrop.* (1909), vii. 287 ff. ; *L'Anthropologie* (1913), xxiv , 609–634 ; H. Obermaier, *Fossil Man in Spain* (New Haven, 1924), pp. 95 ff., 132 ff.

[2] (Cambridge, 1921), p. 343.

[3] *Quart. Journal Geol. Soc.*, March 1913, xix. 117.

who stands erect), was found in Java in 1894.[1]   While some
authorities regard the Javan fossil as the most primitive member of
the human family, others think that it is most satisfactorily explained as a degeneration on lines of its own.   The size of a
man's head, of course, is no precise criterion of his intellectual
powers, but nevertheless a brain must reach a certain weight—
950 grammes, or 1000 cubic centimetres in volume—before it
can become the seat of human intelligence.   *Pithecanthropus*, with
a cranial capacity of 850 cubic centimetres, is therefore well
below the human level, whereas his contemporary (or successor)
in Sussex had a thoroughly human-shaped skull with a large
capacity variously estimated at from 1100 to 1397 cubic centimetres, and resembling in many ways the head-form of modern
man.   Moreover, as Professor Keith has shown, the front part of
the brain—the pre-frontal region, as it is called—with which all
the higher mental faculties are associated, was well developed.
This suggests that the ancient lady was a person of some intelligence, infinitely superior intellectually either to *Pithecanthropus*
or to Neanderthal man.[2]   Therefore, if the Cave people had some
conception of religion, although we have no direct evidence that
the same is true of the earlier Piltdown race, yet there is certainly
no adequate reason to deny it.   On the contrary, if we are compelled to grant a religious sense to Neanderthal man, it would
be illogical to suppose that his intellectually superior predecessor
was inferior in this respect.   It is, therefore, not improbable, if
the Piltdown remains are at all typical of the earliest human
beings, that religion emerged at a very early period in the history
of mankind.

Can we go a step further, and determine the nature of the
earliest strivings after things unseen ?   With regard to the theological doctrine of a primitive revelation and a state of original
righteousness having at one time prevailed, the anthropological
evidence, of course, is silent, the question being one for the
theologian to decide and not for the scientist.   Since we are here
concerned primarily with the scientific evidence, suffice it to say
that there is no *prima facie* reason for rejecting the possibility

---

[1] Keith, *Antiquity of Man* (London, 1916), pp. 257 ff.
[2] The pre-frontal region of Neanderthal man is by no means fully
developed, and has a protuberance as in the brain of the anthropoid apes.
Cf. Elliot Smith, *Evolution of Man* (Oxford, 1924), p. 41.

of a primitive revelation having been vouchsafed to man, since a person with a head like that of the Piltdown woman would not have been incapable of conscious communion with the Deity, but on the other hand there is nothing in the available evidence to suggest this having occurred. Again, there is no innate tendency in man to be progressive,[1] and apparently degeneration manifested itself in prehistoric times in the Cave period. These facts are certainly not inconsistent with the view that man started his career in a higher state than that in which he is to-day known to the archæologist. But, so far as the anthropological evidence is concerned, nothing is known of religion, if it existed, before the middle of the Palæolithic period, when the Neanderthal folk apparently asked the eternal question, " If a man die shall he live again ? "

To the primitive mind death doubtless appeared as a sleep that knows no waking, and therefore the Cave men laid their dead in a position of rest surrounded by implements, shells,[2] etc., in the belief that the grave was not the ultimate and absolute end of human existence. It is scarcely likely that his eschatological speculations went beyond this, though it has been suggested that burial in the contracted position had reference to the idea of rebirth—a conclusion presupposing a degree of anatomical and embryological knowledge, to say nothing of mystical interpretation, which early man could hardly have possessed. There is reason to think, however, that he may have been led by his observations as a hunter to associate the heart with the centre of vitality, since this organ figures prominently in some of the hunting scenes depicted on the walls of the later Palæolithic caves in France and Spain.[3] Life and death were facts of experience, and the obvious inference to be drawn from a dead body is that something has left it. Moreover, hunters would know that loss of blood produced loss of vitality, faintness, and death. It would therefore not require much speculation to associate the blood with the life ; and their experience in the chase again would lead them to the knowledge that the heart was the vital spot, as is proved by the

[1] *Cf.* Elliot Smith, *op. cit.*, p. 118.
[2] It is possible that these shells were used as amulets to give life to the dead. *Cf.* J. W. Jackson, *Shells as Evidence of the Migration of Early Culture* (Manchester, 1917), pp. 135 ff.
[3] E. A. Parkyn, *Prehistoric Art* (London, 1915), pp. 89, 107 ff. ; Sollas, *Ancient Hunters*, 2nd ed. (London, 1915), pp. 326, 333, 361.

Palæolithic drawings of animals in which this organ is represented with arrows in it.[1]

This belief in the blood as the vitalising essence doubtless led to the heart being regarded as the seat of the vital principle, and the blood as a vital fluid. Thus arose also the practice of painting the bones of the dead red, as in the case of the skeleton found in a Palæolithic cave at Paviland in Wales,[2] and in the later kurgans or Neolithic (New Stone Age) and Bronze Age tumuli of Russia.[3] The purpose of the rite is clear, for, as Macalister says, " red is the colour of living health. The dead man was to live again in his own body, of which the bones were the framework. To paint it with the colour of life was the nearest thing to mummification that the Palæolithic people knew ; it was an attempt to make the body again serviceable for its owner's use."[4]

2. *Response to the Mystery of Nature and Life*

Although it is not in the least likely that the primitive mind was concerned with problems of theology, yet it is not unreasonable to surmise, that when the knowledge of natural law was so limited, the overpowering awesomeness of Nature found a religious expression at a very early period. As the lightning shivered the trees, and the thunder crashed amid torrential rains, the cave-dwellers may have felt themselves in the presence of a Power that they did not understand, and which therefore terrified and mystified them. In all ages the sense of wonder in the presence of Nature has been one of the primary impulses of religion, and it may well be that it played a prominent part in the earliest stages of religious evolution. Thus Otto says, " all ostensible explanations of the origin of religion in terms of animism or magic or folk psychology are doomed from the outset to wander astray and miss the real goal of their inquiry, unless they recognise this fact of our nature—primary, unique, underivable from anything else—to be the basic factor and the basic impulse underlying the entire process of religious evolution." [5] This is more or less the view put forth by Marett. In his opinion, religion manifested itself on its emotional side when ideation was vague, as an attitude of mind

---

[1] *Cf. supra*, p. 7, n. 3.   [2] *Journ. Anthrop. Institute*, xlviii. (1913), p. 325.
[3] *K. Russ. Arch. Gesellschaft*, xi. 1.
[4] *Text-book of Europ. Archæol.*, p. 502.
[5] *The Idea of the Holy* (Oxford, 1923), p. 15.

dictated by awe of the mysterious, which provided religion with its raw material apart from animism.[1] This "pre-animistic" phase at the threshold of religion he terms *animatism*, and connects it with a mystic impersonal force, called by the Melanesians *mana*, which "works to effect everything which is beyond the power of men, outside the common process of nature."[2] It should be remembered, however, that while *mana* is largely impersonal in the Banks and Torres Islands, elsewhere in the Pacific its ultimate source is personal beings, and is "out and out spiritualistic."[3]

Nevertheless, apart from the precise significance of the Melanesian conception of *mana*, it would seem that something akin to the idea of "power" at a very early period was attached to objects that showed signs of "activity," life and mystery— "a primal numinous awe"[4]—which may represent "the beginning of the notion, however vague, of a transcendent Something, a real operative entity of a numinous kind, which later, as the development proceeds, assumes concrete form as a 'numen loci,' a dæmon, an 'El, a Baal, or the like."[5] It is this which lies behind the notion of "sacredness," tabu, and worship, producing that attitude of mind which finds expression in the cry, "How dreadful is this place!" Thus the concept of the eerie and awful passes into that of the "numen," a divine power associated with an object or place. "This is none other than the house of Elohim." On this hypothesis, the religious attitude of early man may not have been far removed from that of the author of the 29th Psalm to whom the thunderstorm that passed over the country was a revelation of God.

But if Neanderthal man felt himself in the presence of powers that mystified and terrified him, his successors the *Aurignacians*, as they are called, sought their god in the mysterious life-giving power that appears to animate Nature. The two great interests of primitive people everywhere and at all times are food and children. "To live and to cause to live, to eat food and to beget children, these were the primary wants of man in the past, and they will be the primary wants of man in the future so

[1] *Threshold of Religion* (London, 1914), pp. 3 ff.
[2] Codrington, *The Melanesians* (Oxford, 1891), pp. 119 ff.
[3] Hocart, *Man* (1914), p. 46.
[4] Otto coins the word "numinous" to express the apprehension of supernatural power producing the idea of non-moral holiness.
[5] *Idea of the Holy*, p. 130.

long as the world lasts."[1]   They have been described as the foundation-stones of magic and religion,[2] and as early as the Aurignacian culture phase Palæolithic man made female figures with the maternal organs grossly emphasised, identical with the statues found in Crete, the Ægean, Malta, Egypt and Western Asia, known to have been associated with the cult of the Mother Goddess.[3]   To the Aurignacians the Great Mother may have been little more than a life-giving amulet—the "push of life" from within and the struggle for existence from without directing the religious impulse to the conservation and promotion of life by magical devices.   But as life-giving amulets developed, the "numinous consciousness" was doubtless stirred, and gradually there arose the conception of the Great Mother, the giver of life and health.   Elliot Smith thinks that "this Great Mother, at first with only vaguely defined traits, was probably the first deity that the wit of man devised to console him with her watchful care over his welfare in this life, and to give him assurance as to his fate in the future."[4]   This perhaps is true, inasmuch as the religious sense in man was awakened largely through the practical problems of life and death calling forth the "numinous quality" of religious awe.   Ideas invariably originate not in speculation but in facts, and in the case of religions, it would seem that God led man on to a knowledge of Himself chiefly through natural means.   Nature proved a stern school in early days, and when man reached the end of his ordinary practical and emotional tether, he became conscious of his own limitations and of the vastness and mysteriousness of the world.   Thus the fear of Nature led him to the fear of the Lord, just as to-day the religious impulse is stimulated when a person reaches the limit of his own resources.   While, on the one hand, this may have led him to the notion of a "transcendent Something" akin to an external Creator, a real operative entity of a numinous kind, a personification of the concept of *mana;* on the other, the purely practical side, it is not improbable that the Great Mother represents the earliest expression of the creative principle in terms of deity, and therefore she may be the first concrete deity the wit of man devised.   Be

---

[1] *Golden Bough*, 3rd ed., pt. iv. ("Adonis, etc," I.), p. 5.

[2] J. Harrison, *Epilegomena to the Study of Greek Religion* (Cambridge, 1921), p. 1.

[3] Déchelette, *Manuel d'archéologie* (Paris, 1908), pp. 217, 428 ff., 584, 594.

[4] *Evolution of the Dragon* (Manchester, 1919), pp. 151, 143, 150.

this as it may, there can be little doubt that it was through the practical problems of life, coupled with an emotional attitude towards natural phenomena, that man was first made to seek God and feel after Him if haply he might find Him.

3. *Ideas of Body and Soul*

From these simple beginnings the history of religion pursues an even course for thousands of years along the lines indicated above until revolutionary and far-reaching changes appear in the Eastern Mediterranean about the middle of the fourth millennium B.C. In Mesopotamia the existence of a Sumerian civilisation has been revealed preceding the first Semitic kingdom founded in that region by Sargon of Akkad (*c.* 2800 B.C.), while at Anau in Russian Turkestan, and at Susa in Elam, the remains of an early copper culture occur having affinities with the 6th "city" at Hissarlik (Troy).[1] In the Ægean, the ancient civilisation of Crete has been divided into an early, middle, and late Minoan age, each in its turn split up into three sub-periods. Evans places the beginning of the Minoan age at 3400 B.C., and considers that the Neolithic deposits in Crete probably go back to 8000 B.C.[2] In Egypt the Dynastic period begins about the same time (3400 B.C.), and it has lying behind it a pre-Dynastic period, certainly going back to 8000 B.C., divided into early, middle, and late, according to the age of the graves found in prehistoric cemeteries scattered over Egypt and Nubia.[3] Thus the close of the Palæolithic age in Europe serves as the pedestal for the beginning of the history of the oldest civilisations.

While the majority of scholars look to Babylonia for the cradle land of civilisation, Elliot Smith argues in favour of the original broadcasting of culture from the Nile Valley.[4] The discovery that the bodies of the dead were desiccated by natural forces as a result of their having been deposited in the hot desert sand, turned the thoughts of the pre-dynastic Egyptians, he thinks, to the preservation of the body to eternal life. Around the

---

[1] R. Pumpelly, *Explorations in Turkestan* (Washington, 1908); De Morgan, *Délégation en Perse*, Mémoires xiii.; *Prehistoric Man* (London, 1924), pp. 105, 208 ff.; H. Frankfort, *Royal Anthrop. Inst. Occas. Papers*, No. 6, 1924, pp. 78 ff.

[2] *Palace of Minos* (London, 1921), i. 25, 35.

[3] Petrie, *Journal Anthrop. Institute*, xxix. 295.

[4] *Ancient Egyptians* (London, 1923).

practice of mummification there grew up, on this hypothesis, the complex system of ritual and belief which contributed to a considerable degree to the wonderful civilisation that subsequently developed in Egypt and Western Asia and finally spread throughout the world.[1]   Apart from this theory of the initiative of Egypt in the creation of civilisation, it is beyond dispute that in the Nile Valley at the beginning of the Dynastic period there arose a complex idea of immortality centred in the literal restoration to life of the dead body.[2]   Having freed themselves from the precarious and absorbing life of the chase by the discovery of agriculture, men turned their attention to the problem of the essential nature and destiny of man.   The notion of a vital principle in the body was elaborated in the doctrine of the *ka* or guardian genius, which was born with the man, and resided in his body during the whole of his terrestrial life except when it went on a journey during sleep.   It gave all the attributes of life to the human organism, but the actual personality consisted of the visible body and the invisible intelligence (*khu*), which was situated in the heart (*ab*) or abdomen.   The breath, as distinct from the intelligence, was the actual vital essence, and after the Twelfth Dynasty the two were symbolised by the *ba*, or human-headed bird with human arms, hovering over the mummy, extending to its nostrils in the one hand the figure of a swelling sail, the hieroglyph for wind or breath, and in the other the *crux ansata*, or symbol of life.[3]   The *ba* was the disembodied soul or ghost which came into existence for the first time at death.   It was represented as flying down the tomb-shaft to the mummy in the chamber below, and wandering about the cemetery.   The *ba* was therefore connected with the mummy (*sahu*), just as the *ka* was associated with the *khat* or body.   The *ka* was said to go to Osiris, the god of the dead, or to the boat of the Sun, or to the company of the gods who gave it, and it was separated from its protégé by more than the mere distance of the cemetery, for in one passage in the Pyramid Texts the deceased " goes to his *ka*, to the sky." [4]   It was always the protecting genius, and seems to have combined the function of a guardian spirit and an animating essence.   But it was always distinct from the conception of the soul (*i.e.* the ghost)

---

[1] *Proc. Royal Philos. Soc.* (Glasgow, 1910), xli. pp. 59 ff.

[2] Breasted, *Development of Religion and Thought in Ancient Egypt* (London, 1912), p. 56.

[3] Breasted, *op. cit.*, 52 ff.   [4] *Op. cit.*, p. 55.

as expressed in the doctrine of the *ba*. To ensure physical restoration to the dead the personality had to be reconstituted, and if the corpse was to be resuscitated, the missing "substance" or vitality must be restored. To this end elaborate ceremonies were devised which aimed at reconstituting the individual by processes external to him, under the control of the survivors and the mortuary priest. First the body had to be resuscitated, and the faculties were restored one by one, till at length the deceased became a "living soul" (*ba*), in which capacity he again existed as a person, possessing all the powers that would enable him to survive hereafter. A human being therefore did not become a *ba* merely by dying, but through the renewal of his vitality and personality. First the tissues of the physical body had to be preserved, and the individual features and natural form maintained so far as possible in the mummy itself. Then it had to be animated. But the technical difficulties in the way of making the mummy the *simulacrum* of the deceased were so great that, notwithstanding the measure of success achieved by the Egyptians of the Pyramid Age, the practice was never wholly successful, and the custom of making images of the dead in stone and wood and transferring the *ka* to them was adopted at an early period. These portrait statues seem to have been regarded not merely as abodes or vehicles of the life of the deceased, but as the man himself in his entire nature—that is to say, they were in all respects identical with the resuscitated mummy. Thus the sculptor was called "he who makes to live" (*s'nh*), and the ceremony of the animation of the statue—"opening the mouth," as it was termed—was looked upon as a creative act.[1] In Mexico and elsewhere images of the dead were brought into physical contact with the actual body, or a life-giving substance, to transform them into live men. Either the ashes of the cremated remains were transferred to the effigy, or blood (identified with the life) of human or animal victims was smeared upon them, a practice that very probably represents the beginning of sacrifice.[2]

This transference of the life of man to his portrait statue or effigy tended, however, to magnify the importance of the vital principle at the expense of the body ; and although the Egyptians

[1] Breasted, *op. cit.*, pp. 52 ff. ; A. H. Gardiner, *Encycl. Rel. and Ethics*, viii. 23.
[2] Oviedo, *Historia General de las Indias* (Madrid, 1855), iv. 48 ff. Cf. *American Anthropologist* (1914), p. 61.

never dissociated a person from the body, elsewhere the external embodiment—be it either the mortal remains or their surrogate—gradually lost its significance in the process of securing immortality for the soul. In Egypt, however, since the conception of the continuation of life beyond the grave was bound up with the imperishability of the body, cremation was never adopted. Nevertheless, as will be explained later, from the Fifth Dynasty onwards the Pharaohs began to turn their gaze skywards as the solar theology became predominant. In consequence the ritual of mummification gradually became celestialised, the mummy eventually being conveyed to the sky by Hathor, the divine cow, and other vehicles.

The Egyptian conception of the soul, while in many respects clearly an extension of the prehistoric notion of the indwelling vital principle concentrated in certain parts or attributes of the body, is a very specialised doctrine, in which all the various theories found elsewhere are contained. Thus in many parts of the world—*e.g.* Indonesia, China, New Guinea, the Pacific, North America, etc.—the belief that man has two souls is widespread.[1] The life or vital principle is invariably (but not always) distinguished from the kind of double of the deceased (the ghost) that came into existence at the moment of death as a new and independent entity. Even when the life was thought to become the ghost instead of returning to the sky whence it proceeded, it took over a rather different guise after death.

In Babylonia the spiritual double corresponding to the Egyptian *ka* was designated the *Zi* or "life," and was symbolised in the cuneiform script by a flowering plant. It was the *Zi* that made man a living soul in this world, and beyond the grave it continued to represent his personality. But in addition to this at death man became an *edimmu* or *lila*, *i.e.* a ghost.[2] The body was not essential to the attainment of immortality, as no attempt was made to preserve it, and cremation seems to have been practised in certain parts of Sumer and Akkad from very early times.[3] In the Ægean, on the other hand, great care was taken in the disposal of the body. The kings of Knossos and Mycenæ were buried in

---

[1] *Encycl. Rel. and Ethics*, vii. 233 ff. ; De Groot, *The Religious System of China*, iv. bk. ii. (Leiden, 1901), pp. 3, 57, 396 ; *Folk-lore*, xxxi. (1920), pp. 53 ff.
[2] Sayce, *Religion of Ancient Egypt and Babylonia* (ed. 1903), pp. 276 ff.
[3] Koldewey, *Zeitschrift für Assyriologie*, ii. (1887), pp. 403 ff.

elaborately furnished, chambered and domed tombs,[1] and although
the dwellings of the dead passed through many changes of form
during the Minoan age, they all agreed in testifying that soul and
body were not dissociated, till, in the Homeric period, there arose
a new conception of the soul as the last breath distinct from the
vital principle. While relics of preservation of the body remained
in the preparation of the corpse immediately after death, cremation
was adopted as the means of freeing the soul from its fleshly
entanglement.[2] The doctrine of transmigration added later by
the Orphics to the Dionysiac cult, and taught by Pythagoras,
developed this conception of the soul as an immaterial entity.

Thus in the great religions of antiquity in the Near East we
can observe the gradual dissociation of body and soul, which,
outside Egypt, found expression in such practices as cremation,
and possibly in the doctrine of reincarnation and transmigration.
From crude notions concerning the revivification of the physical
body with all its attributes, there arose apparently a belief in the
life of the spirit as a new entity carrying on the life of the individual
either in another body or in the disembodied state, but independent
of the mortal remains. Moreover, the same tendency may be
observed in the phenomena of nature as in man. The whole
universe, according to primitive philosophy, belongs to one great
system of interrelated and inherent life—probably the unconscious
expression of the religious emotion itself. But as the individual
object becomes associated with the religious emotion it takes on
an individuality of its own, and the inherent vitality becomes more
and more specialised and independent of its external embodiment.
By some such process as this the belief in spiritual beings, phantasms,
and all that is comprised by the term animism, used in its Tylorian
sense, may have arisen. Thus in North America, the Iroquois
of the Eastern States suppose that in every object there is an
inherent power called *orenda*, analogous to will and intelligence
rather than to purely mechanical force.[3] This is the equivalent
of the Melanesian concept of *mana*. On the Plains to the west
of the Iroquois, the Omaha address prayers and ascribe certain
anthropomorphic attributes to a kind of vital essence called *wakonda*

---

[1] A. Evans, *Prehistoric Tombs of Knossos* (London, 1906), p. 5 ; cf. *Journal of
Hellenic Studies*, xxii. 393 ; cf. Ridgeway, *Early Age of Greece* (Camb., 1901), i. 7.
[2] *Iliad*, xxii. 151, xiii. 763, xviii. 345 ff., 315 ff., xxiii. 106.
[3] Hewitt, *Handbook of Amer. Indians* (Washington, 1907–10), ii. 147.

(" the power that moves ").[1] It would seem that here we have the impersonal energy on its way to becoming a separate spiritual being with a cult of its own. To the north, the Eastern Algonquins apply the term *manitu* to any spirit or *genius loci*, but these spirits were not necessarily definite in shape. An arrow, for example, was *manitu* because a spirit had either transformed itself into the arrow, or dwelt in it.[2]

III

EARLY DEVELOPMENTS OF THEISM

1. *The Divine King and Culture-hero*

Once the doctrine of spirits became established their form and number were limitless. They appeared as human beings, animals, " mythological " creatures, rocks, trees, phantasies, etc., according to the predominance of the image in the mind of the individual. Some spirits were indeterminate in shape because the object with which they were associated had no definite form, as in the case of such spirits as wind, fire, water, etc. As spirits of definitely circumscribed type developed, one of the first and most natural reactions seems to have been that the people elevated to the supernatural order those chiefs and heroes so dear to the popular mind. Thus Seligman has shown that the Shilluk of the White Nile reverence their king because they regard him as a reincarnation of the spirit of Nyakang, the semi-divine hero who founded the Dynasty and settled the tribe in their present territory. The pedigree of the kings from Nyakang to the present day has been preserved. These monarchs number twenty, distributed over twelve generations, though probably many more have reigned.[3] The natives think of Nyakang as having been a real man in appearance and physical qualities, though, unlike his royal descendants of more recent times, he did not die but simply disappeared. His holiness is manifested especially by his relation to Juok, the Supreme Creator of the Shilluk who sends down rain at the intercession of Nyakang. The latter appears to have been a real man who led the tribe to their present home on the Nile, and he is therefore regarded by Frazer as the modern counterpart of the

[1] *27th Report Bureau Amer. Ethnol.* (1911), pp. 134, 597.
[2] *Journal Amer. Folk-lore*, xxvii. (1914), pp. 349 f.
[3] *Cult of Nyakang and the Divine Kings of the Shilluk* (Khartoum, 1911), pp. 216 ff.

ancient Egyptian Osiris whom Elliot Smith describes as "the prototype of all gods." [1]

The origin of Osiris is still a matter of controversy. Petrie thinks that he was a civilising king of Egypt who was murdered by his brother Set and seventy-two conspirators,[2] and Frazer concludes that " though in the main a god of vegetation and of the dead," originally Osiris was a real man who " by his personal qualities excited a larger measure of devotion than usual during his life and was remembered with fond affection and deeper reverence after his death ; till in time his beloved memory, dimmed, transfigured, and encircled with a halo of glory by the mists of time, grew into the dominant religion of his people." [3] Further he suggests the possibility " that Osiris was no other than the historical king Khent of the First Dynasty, that the skull found in the tomb is the skull of Osiris himself." [4] But what Frazer fails to show is how Osiris the divine king and Osiris the vegetation god are to be reconciled.

An examination of the early Texts reveals scanty evidence of Osiris as the source of all vegetable life, for in the Old Kingdom it is his royal character that is emphasised, especially in the sculptures and hieroglyphs. Furthermore, " it is always as a dead king that he appears, the rôle of the living king being invariably played by Horus, his son and heir." [5] Thus in the Sed festival, which appears to have been normally celebrated every thirty years, and is usually supposed to have been on the occasion of the king being deified as Osiris,[6] Gardiner has given reasons for believing that the king there played the part of Horus and not of Osiris, and that " it is only in death that the monarch's transformation from Horus to Osiris was effected," [7] on the twenty-fifth day of the fourth month during the embalmment ceremonies. In this case a complete identity existed between the king and the gods both in life and after death.

[1] *Golden Bough*, pt. iv. ("Adonis," etc., II.), pp. 160 ff. ; Elliot Smith, *Evolution of the Dragon*, p. 32. While it cannot be maintained, as the philosopher Euhemeros supposed, that all myths are of historical origin, and all gods merely deified men, it is nevertheless true that historical facts have been preserved in tribal traditions, and some culture-heroes have been deified after death.

[2] *Religion of Ancient Egypt* (London, 1906), pp. 38 f.
[3] *Golden Bough, op. cit.*, p. 160. [4] *Op. cit.*, p. 198.
[5] *Journal of Egyptian Archæology*, ii. (1915), p. 122.
[6] Petrie, *Researches in Sinai* (London, 1906), p. 185.
[7] *Journal Egypt. Archæol., op. cit.*, p. 124.

c

Nevertheless, that Osiris was connected with vegetation is shown by the unmistakable relation which exists between the dates of the Osirian festivals and the seasons of the agricultural year. The representation of a king on a very early mace using a hoe to inaugurate the making of an irrigation canal [1] has led Elliot Smith to conclude that there was a close connection between the earliest kings and irrigation. Civilisation, he thinks, began when the Egyptians first devised methods of agriculture and invented a system of irrigation. The irrigation engineer, on this hypothesis, became the ruler of the whole community—the king—whose beneficence was apotheosised after his death, so that he became the god Osiris, who was identified with the river, the life-giving powers of which he controlled. Thus he was at once a dead king and connected with agriculture, and regarded as the controller of life-giving powers to the dead as well as to the living.[2]   But as the originator of civilisation he was also, it is claimed, the prototype of all gods ; " his ritual was the basis of all religious ceremonial ; his priests who conducted the animating ceremonies were the pioneers of a long series of ministers who for more than fifty centuries, in spite of endless variety of details of their ritual and the character of their temples, have continued to perform ceremonies that have undergone remarkably little essential change." [3]

On this hypothesis the creative function of sky-gods is explained as the result of the deification of the Sun in the Fifth Dynasty when the king regarded himself as the physical son of Re, the Sun-god. Henceforth every Pharaoh ascended to the sky at death, and all life-giving powers were attributed to the sky-gods. The Sun was the source of life to the earth, and the realm whence life proceeded and whither it returned. Thus the Sun and the sky-beings came to be regarded as Creators.[4]   It is undoubtedly true that in the Pyramid texts and funerary literature in Egypt the sky-god is represented as the source of life and death, of rain and heavenly fire. Among his names that of Horu (symbolised by the hawk) has given rise to the so-called " hawk names " which appear among the most ancient forms of royal names—those of the Thinite period of the First and Second Dynasties. These show, when set in order, that the king was regarded as an

---

[1] Quibell, *Hierakonpolis* (London, 1900), i. pl. xxvi. chap. 4.   *Cf.* p. 9.
[2] *Evolution of the Dragon*, pp. 29 f.   [3] *Op. cit.*, p. 32.
[4] W. J. Perry, *The Children of the Sun* (London, 1923), pp. 201 ff., 440 ff.

emanation upon the earth of the Supreme Being. Thus in Egypt the conception of the monarch appears to have been based solely upon the assimilation of the king to the gods. But did the notion of a heavenly Creator arise as the result of the elaboration of the Sun-cult in the valley of the Nile at the beginning of the Dynastic period ?

The gods associated with creation in Egyptian theology are many. The genesis of the sun (Re) is variously attributed to Seb and Nuit, the First Dynasty sky-goddess who produced the earth, and gave the king the name of " Son of Nuit." This prepared the way for the assimilation of the king to Re and Osiris, according as these successive theologies connected these deities with Nuit. The Sun-god therefore was not the first sky deity to be assigned creative functions, and the conception of an external Supreme Creator is probably independent in origin of that of the divine culture-hero, the fusion of the two cults having been effected perhaps from the king being regarded as either the incarnation or the son of the Creator. Thus in Babylonia the Sumerian city-kings claimed to have been begotten by the gods and born of the goddesses, but they were not deified,[1] while in Greece the Homeric king was descended from gods (*diotrephes*) and had *supernatural* powers.[2] It is even possible that such phrases as " the Spirit of the Lord came upon him," used of Othniel, Jephthah, and Samson (Jud. iii. 10, xi. 29, xiii. 25) may have had originally a similar significance. The story of the birth of Samson is singularly like that of the birth of the solar deity Mithra,[3] and, as in the case of the other judges, he was certainly a vicar of God

2. *The Beneficent Creator*

It would seem, then, that the divinity of kings was intimately related with the early developments of theism, and one of the germs of monotheism may lie in this doctrine of divine kingship. If Osiris was the first king of Egypt, and if the Dynastic period in the Nile Valley predated the rise of other ancient monarchies, he may be regarded as a prototype of the gods who began life as

[1] Langdon, *The Museum Journal*, viii. (Philadelphia, 1917), p. 166.
[2] *Golden Bough*, 3rd ed., pt. i. p. 366. *Cf.* Hocart, *Man*, xxv. (February 2, 1925), pp. 31 f. *Cf. Od.* iv. 692 ; ii. 409 ; xix. 109-114. *Il.* ii. 335; xvii. 464.
[3] Cumont, *Mysteries of Mithra* (1913), pp. 124, 130

chiefs, kings, or popular heroes. Thus may be explained the striking resemblances between Nyakang and Osiris. Both died violent deaths, the graves of both were pointed out in various parts of the country; both were deemed great sources of fertility, and both were associated with certain sacred trees and animals, especially with bulls. Moreover, just as Egyptian kings identified them-selves both in life and death with Osiris, so Shilluk kings are still believed to be animated by the spirit of Nyakang and to share his divinity. But behind the figure of Nyakang there stands the shadowy form of the High God Juok, and although his worship has been eclipsed by that of the divine king and ancestor, yet he remains the Creator and Supreme God.

This is typical of the All-Father belief among primitive people. Beside the culture-hero there is the Creator, beneficent and ethical, who dwells in the heavens in dignified seclusion from the affairs of man. The Uitoto of Colombia, South America, for example, in addition to the deified ancestors, recognise Nainema, " He-who-is-appearance only," as the Creator,[1] while among the Dakota in North America the Supreme Deity is comprehended as Wakan Tanka, the Great Mystery, made up of four eternal essences to be regarded as one—the Chief God, the Great Spirit, the Creator, and the Executive.[2] In Australia the All-Fathers seem to be a combination of deified culture-heroes and beneficent Creators, since they are usually regarded as highly ethical gods who have had their abode on earth like Osiris, and retired to their present abode in the sky, whence they sent down "everything that the blackfellow has."[3] Therefore primitive monotheism is apparently a dual concept, one aspect of which is based on a custom which may be traced as far back as early Egypt and Sumer—the custom of worshipping kings in their own name—the other, the notion of the beneficent Creator, going back probably to a much earlier period of religious development.

In the determination of the evolution of theism it is important to remember the part played by these two concepts in the origin of the idea of God. It has often been suggested that ethical

[1] K. T. Preuss, *Rel. und Mythologie der Uitoto*, i. 166 ff.

[2] J. R. Walker, *Anthrop. Papers Mus. Nat. Hist.*, vol. xvi. pt. ii. pp. 78 ff., 152 ff.

[3] Spencer and Gillen, *Northern Tribes of Central Australia* (London, 1904), pp. 498 ff. ; Howitt, *Native Tribes of S.E. Australia* (London, 1904), p. 488 ; A. Lang, *Making of Religion* (London, 1898), pp. 187 ff.

monotheism is the result of successive transformations of some particular deity or lesser being. Thus while the religion of the Semites consisted of a complex system of polytheism and dæmonism,[1] there arose in Babylonia about 2000 B.C. a tendency towards henotheistic monolatry (belief in and worship of one God together with the recognition of other gods and spirits) when Marduk, the personification of the Sun and the early city god of Babylon, became the principal god of Babylonia and the head of the pantheon, when Babylon was made the capital, and all the attributes of the other gods were absorbed by him.[2] Again, in Egypt in the Eighteenth Dynasty (*c.* 1400 B.C., Amenhotep III and IV) the elaboration of the Sun-cult led to a belief in the universal and life-giving power of the Sun-god, who was the author of his own being as well as the Creator of all things visible and invisible. The Aton or solar disk was worshipped as the living manifestation of the one God behind the Sun. At Akhetaton (horizon of Aton), now called Tell-el-Amarna, between Thebes and the sea, Amenhotep, the brother or half-brother of Tutankhamen, who had changed his name to Ikhnaton, built a new capital which was evidently intended as a centre of the dissemination of solar monotheism, since the name of the Sun-god is the only divine name found there.[3] Here several sanctuaries of Aton were erected, and similar cities were founded in Nubia, and probably another in Asia. The recognition of the fatherly solicitude of Aton above all creatures—"thou art the father and mother of all that thou hast made "—raised this remarkable development of monotheism above anything that had been attained before in Egypt or elsewhere. The beauty of the eternal and universal light was identified with love as the visible evidence of the presence of God who is the author of the beneficence of the natural order.[4]

But why should the Sun-god become an ethical, intelligent, and benevolent Creator ? The magic word evolution does not really explain such a development of monotheism because there is no obvious reason why there should be one god rather than many, and such an intelligent people as the Greeks found that polytheism

---

[1] W. R. Smith, *Religion of the Semites* (London, 1907), pp. 84 ff.

[2] Jastrow, *Religious Belief and Practice in Babylonia and Assyria* (New York, 1911), pp. 100 ff.

[3] Breasted, *Development of Religion and Thought in Ancient Egypt*, pp. 322 ff.

[4] Weigall, *Akhnaton, Pharaoh of Egypt* (Edinburgh and London), pp. 115 ff.

solved their theological problems more easily than monotheism.[1] It is by no means clear why a centralised government or the political predominance of one city over another should cause the gods of a nation to become one. Thus in Babylonia henotheism which centred in Marduk passed into polytheism again because the people failed to regard each and every god as the highest deity, without conflicting with the claims of any other god, just as in Egypt a reaction in favour of the traditional gods took effect after the death of Amenhotep IV, and swept away the short-lived cult of Aton.

Once man had come to believe in gods, polytheism fitted in with the primitive conception of the universe much better than monotheism. Having no conception of the universality and continuity of natural causation, early man attributed every event which arrested his attention or demanded an explanation to supernatural agencies. Cause and effect, and even agent and act, were not clearly differentiated. Any extraordinary event that called for the help of an intervening agent provided an impetus to penetrate more deeply into the nature of the supernatural powers and to establish a more intimate alliance with them. But as knowledge of cause and effect in nature increased, it became apparent that the hitherto inexplicable events depended upon natural causes rather than on the intervention of departmental deities. Thus in the sixth century B.C., Thales, the earliest of the Greek philosophers, explained the universe as the result of a " primitive substance " which he identified with water, out of which all things were evolved ; but Socrates inferred from the presence of design in the world that a benevolent Creator existed behind the universe, to whom alone the term God is applicable.[2] Therefore the monotheism of the Greek philosophers defined God as the source and guiding principle of the world. But this is a very different conception both of the Deity and of the universe from that which found expression in the earlier developments of monotheism.

---

[1] The few passages in Homeric literature that seem to assert the principle of monotheism, as, for example, the use of θεός in the abstract as the equivalent of Zeus [*Il.* xiii. 730 ; *Od.* iv. 236], are more easily explained as the expressions of a special kind of religious thought and emotion than as a general trend towards monotheism, since the doctrine never affected the popular religion. *Cf.* Farnell, *The Cult of the Greek States* (Oxford, 1896), i. p. 84 ff.

[2] Aristotle, *Met.* i. 3, 983B. *Cf.* Burnet, *Early Greek Philosophy* (London, 1908), pp. 47 ff., 141, 314.

The benevolent Creators among primitive peoples are certainly not the product of philosophical thinking, nor the triumph of the unifying principle over the disruptive, of abstract over concrete thought. They would seem rather to represent the purposive functioning of an inherent type of thought and emotion,[1] rather than the elaboration of a certain kind of knowledge concerning the universe. Hence the recurrence of monotheism in all states of culture and in every stage of religious development. There is reason to think, as has been explained above, that in Palæolithic times there arose a notion akin to the idea of God as a " transcendent Something, a real operative entity of a numinous kind." The concept of supernatural power (*i.e. mana*) and the belief in Supreme Beings represent psychological tendencies rather than stages in an evolutionary system. The remote High God or beneficent Creator, as distinct from the deified culture-hero, is apparently the climax of primitive religious thought. Although the savage has hardly any relations with this All-Father in practice, yet he attaches to him a value superior to that of all other mythological beings, a value which may well accord with the divine in the highest sense.[2] Men probably did not search for this conception of the Deity in the beginning, since when the primitive mind did reflect upon the universe it was invariably led to a polytheistic interpretation of nature. But certain individuals were led to it spontaneously. In every community there are always a few people to whom religion makes a ready appeal, but in the case of the majority it is only at certain times—at crises such as birth, marriage, death, harvest, etc.—that the religious emotion is aroused to any appreciable extent.[3] To the intermittently and indifferently religious ethical monotheism seldom makes an appeal, and therefore it is the lesser deities, spirits, totems, or ancestors that men of this type usually approach. The High God thus tends to become remote unless he is brought into relation with a popular culture-hero or spirit. This doubtless explains why monotheism invariably gave place to polytheism in the religions of antiquity. Nevertheless, the recurrence of monotheistic notions in Babylonia and Egypt, to say nothing of savage Supreme Beings, and the ease with

[1] P. Radin. Cf. *Monotheism among Primitive Peoples* (London, 1924), p. 67.

[2] Otto, *op. cit.*, p. 134.

[3] Cf. *Journal of American Folk-lore*, xxvii. (1914), pp. 338 f. *Cf.* Farnell, *Cults of the Greek States* (Oxford, 1896), i. p. 86.

which primitive people identify the Christian idea of God with their own, show that this aspect of theism is an innate disposition rather than a later product of evolution or a mere survival of a primitive revelation.

3. *Towards Monotheism in Greece and Israel*

The emergence of this "instinct for unification," as James Adam called it, is clearly discernible in the literature of ancient Greece as well as in that of Israel. It runs there in two streams, the one poetical and popular, the other philosophical, which find their confluence in the mind of Plato, at once philosopher and poet, and derives from him through Aristotle to Cleanthes and the Stoics. It would be rash, perhaps, as we have seen, to trace it back to Homer's notion of the supremacy of Zeus as the father of the Olympian divinities. Pindar represents an advance upon the Homeric notion in that he abjures all idea of struggles and conflicts among the gods, as also does Sophocles ; yet in both the current polytheism is accepted rather than renounced. Aeschylus, on the contrary, marks a real step forward. It is true that he recognises a number of gods. But apart from particular phrases, like that poignant utterance of the Chorus in the *Agamemnon* [1]— Ζεὺς, ὅστις ποτ' ἐστὶν, κ.τ.λ.—there are whole passages, like the choric odes in the *Suppliants*, and at least one whole play, the *Prometheus*, which presuppose a belief that has crossed the border of monotheism. In these cases, if other gods are named, they are little more than such "principalities and powers" as St. Paul was to speak of later : the central issue lies between God and man.

But a far more serious inroad on popular polytheism had already been made a generation earlier by Xenophanes, who wrote with all the dogmatic certainty, the moral ardour, and even the poetical form of a Hebrew prophet. Aristotle says of him that " he throws his glance upon the whole heaven and says that God is unity !" [2] Despite occasional dissent, as from Gomperz, modern scholarship has not tended to revise that verdict. For Xenophanes God is one, uncreated, righteous, and without resemblance to man : the only prayer which we may address to Him is for " power to do what is right." In this he is nearer to the theism of Jew

---

[1] Aesch., *Ag.* 160, *cf.* Eur., *H.F.* 1263.　　　[2] Aristotle, *Metaph.* I. v.

and Christian than is Heraclitus ; for, though like Heraclitus he conceives of God as wholly immanent in the universe, he does not follow the logic of Pantheism to the point of denying the ultimate validity of ethical distinctions. For Heraclitus, on the contrary, God is beyond good and evil ; " to God all things are beautiful and good and right, but men consider some things wrong and others right." [1] The truth is that Xenophanes came to far closer grips with popular religion than either Aeschylus among the poets or Heraclitus among the philosophers ; and his protest against the traditional conceptions of deity was to receive classical expression a century later in the *Republic* of Plato.

Meanwhile philosophy was pursuing a path which more and more prepared the way for the break-up of polytheism as a possible belief for thoughtful men. The material unity—water, air, fire —proclaimed by the Ionian scientists, the logical unity asserted by Parmenides the pupil of Xenophanes, the deistic unity asserted by Anaxagoras all alike attest an instinct or innate disposition which could not rest content with pluralism, and either ignored the evidence of the Many or else relegated it to the sphere of unreality and opinion. In this atmosphere we are of course far removed from the theology proper to the Olympian deities : the problem of Being has ousted the problem of the gods : even in Anaxagoras the Mind which ordered Chaos in the beginning has no other rôle in things to play. Nevertheless we cannot regard this development as without significance for Greek theology. The abrupt dogmatic form which marks the surviving fragments of these philosophers points to its having some other source in the mind than either observation or dialectic, and suggests that human reason carries somehow within it the affirmation of unity.

It was reserved for the genius of Plato to give expression, first in the *Republic* and its correlative dialogues, later and with greater precision and critical analysis in the *Timaeus* and the *Laws*, to a thoroughly Greek monotheism, and to gather up into it all that the poetical imagination, moral earnestness, and metaphysical subtlety of his predecessors had portended. Into the Platonic conception of God it is impossible here to enter ; nor can we trace the criticism of it through which Aristotle passed to his pregnant conception of the Unmoved Mover. It will be clear from the next essay in this volume how much Western theology owes to

[1] Ritter and Preller, 436.

these two great lamps of antiquity. But if evidence be needed that the monotheism of ancient Hellas was not only a philosophical, but a religious belief, it may be found in a few lines of the Hymn of Cleanthes, the Stoic :

> O King of kings,
> Through ceaseless ages, God, whose purpose brings
> To birth, whate'er on land or in the sea
> Is wrought, or in high heaven's immensity ;
> Save what the sinner works infatuate.
> Nay, but thou knowest to make crooked straight :
> Chaos to thee is order : in thine eyes
> The unloved is lovely, who didst harmonise
> Things evil with things good, that there should be
> One Word through all things everlastingly.[1]

There are few believers in revelation who would not say that we hear its accents in these lines.

But of course it is in Israel that the note of revelation sounds most clearly. The Hebrew prophets certainly did not arrive at their remarkable conception of ethical monotheism through a process of observation and reflection upon causation, as they held in company with the rest of Israel that supernatural beings intervened in natural events. But they saw behind all the phenomena of nature one creative and sustaining, omniscient and omnipotent will—that of Yahweh, the righteous Ruler of the universe, the Doer of justice, whose law is holy and whose power is infinite. That such a Deity should intervene in the course of nature from time to time was not to them extraordinary, since He sends forth the wind, the ice, and the snow, and speaks in the thunder, and smites His enemies in the hinder parts. The prophets, therefore, combined a primitive theory of the universe and of causation with a pure ethical monotheism.[2] Thus they constitute a unique development in the history of revelation.

Whence did they obtain this knowledge ? Clearly they did not derive it from the observation of the facts of nature, especially as righteousness and not mere benevolence was for them the characteristic feature of Yahweh. They give no evidence of

[1] James Adam's translation in *The Vitality of Platonism*, Essay IV.
[2] H. F. Hamilton, *Discovery and Revelation* (London, 1915), pp. 98 ff.

possessing a knowledge superior to that of their age and environment, as in the case of the ancient philosophers. They were just ordinary men distinguished only by their religious experience and spiritual insight (Amos vii. 14). They were conscious, in fact, of the contrast between their own feelings and ideas, on the one hand, and of the purpose and mind of God who constrained them, on the other (Amos vii. 2 ff., 15 ; Is. vi. 5 ff.). They spoke that they did know and testified that they had seen and heard ; in other words, they were the recipients of a self-revelation given directly by God and not mediated through reflection on the natural universe. Each prophet's message bears the stamp of originality, of opposition to contemporary thought, of a word of God forcing itself to find expression through the human instrument. Surely here we may reasonably claim to have a revelation from God to man independent of human reflection and discovery—" a downrush from the super-conscious," rather than " an uprush from the sub-conscious." [1]

That truly religious men from the beginning by reason of their innate disposition were made to " seek God and feel after Him if haply they might find Him," seems clear. In this way He was not left without witnesses in any age or community, but, nevertheless, it was in Israel that the purest form of monotheism developed to the exclusion of all other theistic and animistic systems. If the view here advanced concerning the emergence of religion is correct, there is no adequate reason to deny the existence of Hebrew monotheists prior to the rise of the prophets in the eighth century B.C. In fact, it would be remarkable if believers in a Supreme Deity did not arise from time to time as elsewhere. There is nothing improbable, for example, in supposing that Abraham, who is generally thought to have lived at Ur of the Chaldees about 2000 B.C., developed the monolatrous and henotheistic tendency in Babylonian cult at this time in a monotheistic direction by assigning to one God all those attributes which hitherto had been distributed among many deities. The traditional history of Israel as it is set forth in the Old Testament represents a prolonged struggle between a mono-Yahwist minority of religious leaders against a polytheistic majority ending in the final triumph of the monotheists. This seems to be a very likely situation in view of the evidence from other sources which we have here

[1] Gore, *Belief in God* (London, 1921), pp. 102 ff.

briefly examined. Thus while there is no reason to suppose with Renan that the Semites, more than any other people, had a racial tendency to monotheism, they unquestionably produced men who were capable of transforming a system of nature-worship and polytheism into the lofty ethical monotheistic ideals of Amos, Hosea, and Isaiah, and thereby prepared the way for our Lord and His Church. The ethical teaching of the prophets emphasised the moral purity of God ; their Messianic expectations became more spiritualised and complex, until the supreme manifestation was vouchsafed in Him in whom dwelt the fulness of God. The main light thus shone more purely and powerfully till all shadows of lesser deities had fled away, and the conceptions of Israel were fulfilled by Him who was at once the light to lighten the Gentiles and the glory of His people Israel. By the Eternal Son assuming conditions of time the religious impulse was satisfied that led primitive man to bring himself into union with the Divine by sacrifice and prayer to lesser supernatural beings. Thus Catholic Christianity, with its doctrine of the Trinity in unity of the Godhead, and its sacramental system, meets the entire need of man and thereby supplies that which was wanting in the earlier conceptions both of monotheism and polytheism. The Incarnation and its extension in the Church, therefore, fulfilled the dumb, dim expectations of mankind throughout the ages.

THE VINDICATION OF RELIGION
BY ALFRED EDWARD TAYLOR

CONTENTS

INTRODUCTORY

" Being ready always to give answer to every man that asketh you
a reason concerning the hope that is in you, yet with meekness
and fear."—1 Peter iii. 15.

IT might fairly be said that these few words, written in the infancy
of the Christian Church, sufficiently indicate for all time the
scope of Christian " apologetics " and the temper in which they
should be conducted. The Christian is eminently a hopeful
being ; he has hopes for himself and for his kind which surprise
the non-Christian society around him. Since, as his neighbours
can readily satisfy themselves, he is not a mere lunatic, he presumably has good grounds for his hopefulness which he can make
intelligible to others, and it is his duty to produce them when they
are asked for. But he is to do so courteously and carefully.
His faith is not to be a blind faith for which he can give no better
reason than that it makes him comfortable to hold it, or that he
has been ordered to hold it by some authority into whose trustworthiness it is forbidden to inquire. Those who ask the reason
of his hope are asking a fair question and are entitled to a candid
and mannerly answer. They are not to be met, as they too often
have been by imperfect Christians, with revilings and anger
at their presumption in daring to put the question. The answer
is to be given not merely courteously but " with fear," with
a scrupulous anxiety not to exaggerate the strength of his case,
to push an argument further than it will legitimately reach, or
to cover up the difficulties of his position. Above all, there
is no suggestion that the Christian believer should expect to
be able to demonstrate the truth of his convictions as one may
demonstrate a proposition in the mathematics. No doubt we
should all like to show that it would be as absurd in a rational
being to deny the truths upon which we base our highest hopes
for ourselves and for the world as it would be to deny the statements of the multiplication table, or of an accurately calculated set
of logarithms. But just in so far as a man could succeed in doing

this he would be converting " faith " into knowledge and hope
into vision.[1]   The apostolic writer makes no such demand as this
on the believers whom he is addressing.   It may be that none of the
considerations on which their hopes are founded can be proved to
demonstration, in a way which must compel the assent of every
rational man ;   it is certain that not all of them can be so demonstrated.   If they could be, faith would have lost all its value as a
test of a man's spiritual condition ;   as the theologians put it, faith
would no longer be a response of the soul called out by " grace "
and could consequently have no " merit " towards salvation.
Where demonstration is forthcoming, assent, just so far as a man
is reasonable, is not free but necessitated ;   the worth of a faith
in anything at all as a revelation of a man's inmost self depends
on the fact that it is a free assent to the drawings of a dimly descried
high and noble object which cannot be *demonstrated* not to be an
illusion.   It is because this logical possibility of illusion is never
simply closed, where faith is in question, as it is in matters of
demonstration, that the exercise of faith ennobles the man who
has it—in fact, that faith " justifies."   We can readily see that
this is so when we compare the attitude of the religious man who
lives by his faith in God with similar attitudes to which we give
the same name.   We speak of a man's " noble " confidence in
the loyalty of his friend, or the fidelity of his wife, in the face of all
appearances to the contrary ;   there would be nothing " noble "
in being convinced of your wife's fidelity, if you had locked her up
in a high tower and carried the key away in your pocket.   The
moral nobility of trust is only possible when a man is trusting where
he cannot demonstrate, or, at any rate, has not demonstrated and
does not know that he ever will.   (The Vatican Council, it is
true, decreed that " the existence of God can be demonstrated by
natural reason."   But its decree was not meant to legitimate
suspense of assent until the demonstration has been produced and
found satisfactory.)

It may even be worth while to remark that this attitude
of trust and faith, where demonstration is impossible, is just as
characteristic of science, as the word is commonly understood,
as it is of religion.   Outside the sphere of mathematics how far
can we say that any of the propositions which make up the

[1] In medieval language, he would be exchanging the *lumen gratiae* for the
lumen gloriae, a thing impossible, except by a miracle, for Christians still in the
state of " pilgrimage."

" scientific view of the world " are strictly and rigidly proved ? It is at least certain that most of them have never received and do not seem capable of receiving anything like demonstration. Thus it is a commonplace that all natural science is bound up with a belief in the principle that " nature " is in some way " uniform." Without this conviction it would be quite impossible to argue from the handful of facts we have learned, by observation or active experiment, about the little region of space and time open for our direct examination to the structural laws of events in vastly remote spaces and distant times. Yet it is quite certain both that this fundamental principle cannot be demonstrated, since all reasoning in the sciences depends on assuming it, and that it cannot even be definitely expressed by any formula which does not appear highly questionable.[1] Or, to take a rather different instance, no scientific man to-day doubts that the enormous variety of vegetable and animal species have been developed in the course of a long history from a few simpler types, perhaps a 'single simpler type. The precise factors which have contributed to this development, the precise steps in the process, may be and are the subjects of controversy, but the general conception seems to have established itself permanently. But if we are to speak of proof or demonstration in the matter, it is plain that we are using the words in a very lax sense. It has been said of Darwin that the actual basis of fact on which his gigantic edifice of speculation was raised amounts to little more than the experiences of a small number of breeders of animals, and it might equally well be said of the later formidable theory which directly contravenes the peculiar Darwinian conception of the process of " evolution " as due to the accumulation in successive generations of imperceptible differences, that it too has for its foundation in observed fact only a relatively few experiences of gardeners and observational botanists. In both cases the superstructure of theory is quite incommensurable with the narrow basis of fact on which it is reared. Little indeed would be left of " evolutionary science " if we cut away everything which a cautious logician would pronounce not proved by the evidence. To take a third illustration. The late Philip Gosse was at once a keen naturalist and a firm believer in the literal inerrancy of the Book of Genesis. As a naturalist he could not deny the genuineness

[1] See particularly the thorough discussion by Professor C. D. Broad, " Relation between Induction and Probability," in MIND, N.S., Nos. 108, 113 (October 1918, January 1920).

of the discoveries of fossil remains which suggest that life on our planet had its beginnings at an era immensely more remote than any honest interpretation of the Book of Genesis will allow. As an amateur theologian he felt unable to deny the inerrancy of Genesis.   Accordingly, he reconciled his theology with his natural science by the theory that the earth was indeed created out of nothing a few thousand years ago, but created with fossil deposits ready-made under its surface.   It is not surprising that the men of science would have nothing to say to Mr. Gosse's theory ; yet it is equally clear that there is not and cannot be any means of demonstrating its falsity.   What led to the ignoring of the specu- lation was not, as would be the case with a claim to have "squared the circle," knowledge of its falsity, but sound scientific instinct.

Speaking quite generally, I suppose we may say that no great and far-reaching scientific theory is ever adopted because it has been demonstrated.   It is not believed because it can be shown by stringent logic that all other accounts of facts involve self- contradiction.   The real reason for belief is that the theory pro- vides a key for the interpretation of the facts on which it is said to be founded, that on further investigation it is found also to provide a key to the interpretation of numerous groups of often very dissimilar facts, which were either uninterpretable or actually unknown when the theory was first put forward, and that even where at first sight there are facts which seem refractory to the proposed interpretation, the general theory can be made to fit them by some modification which does not interfere with its continued use for the interpretation of the facts by which it was first suggested.   In this respect the interpretation of the " book of Nature " is exactly similar to the process of deciphering a cryptogram or an inscription in a hitherto unknown language. The decipherer has first to be in possession of a " key " of promising make.   Thus, the inscription may be bilingual and one language may be a known one ; there may be good reasons for believing that the cipher message is in English, and this enables the reader to make a probable conjecture from the relative frequency of certain signs alone or in combination.   The original identifications will usually be in part erroneous, but even where they are so, if enough of them are correct, the partial decipherment will make the words of the text sufficiently intelligible to lead to subsequent correction of initial mistakes ; though, when all our ingenuity has been expended, it may still remain the case that some of the signs we are trying to decipher have to be left uninterpreted owing to the insufficiency of our data. If our inscription were interminable, we might readily have to acknowledge that, though successive scrutiny made each new reading more nearly correct than those which went before, a final and definitive transcription was beyond our reach, and that all we could do was to make the tentative and provisional element in our readings steadily smaller. It is hardly necessary to mention the way in which this tentative process of decipherment of symbols, applied to the hieroglyphs of Egypt and the cuneiform of Babylon, has already enriched our historical knowledge of the early civilisations by making real to us the politics and social life of people who, a few generations ago, were little but names to us, or the still greater flood of light on the past of our race which may yet come from the successful reading of Cretan and Hittite records.

Consider for a moment the assumption which lies behind such an attempt at the reading of a cipher. It is taken for granted that the marks we are examining convey a message or statement which someone was meant to understand. They must have been read and understood by someone and therefore presumably may be read and understood by us, if we will have patience. Commonly, no doubt, we should say that the very fact that an intelligible statement has been extracted from the marks proves both that this general assumption was correct and that the meaning the decipherer has extracted is the meaning intended by the composer. But, strictly speaking, we have no right to call this demonstration. If the series of marks is a very short one it is quite a reasonable suggestion that there is *no* meaning behind them. There is a fair chance that in some cases they were not made by man at all, and that in others they were made in mere idleness and are quite insignificant. Even if the series is a tolerably long one, there is an appreciable chance that the various symbols may succeed one another in the very order which would yield an intelligible sense without any such sense being in the mind of the inscriber. Yet if a proposed decipherment yields a satisfactory sense, a sound instinct will lead to its acceptance long before the point is reached at which the probability that it was unintended becomes mathematically negligible. We may make the same point in a rather different way. Why do sober scholars refuse to believe in the existence of a " Baconian " cipher in the works of Shakespeare ? Not because the thing is an impossibility. Indeed, it might be argued that the very fact that an ingenious " Baconian," by applying his " key " to such an enormous mass of writing, can extract a narrative with any sort of coherence supplies a high mathematical probability that there really is a narrative to be extracted and that the " Baconian " is, at any rate, largely right in his proposed reading of the " cipher." The real reason why sober scholars refuse to believe in such a cipher, and would still refuse were the " Baconians " more able than they are to make the " key " work, without a host of subsidiary hypotheses to explain its apparent failures, is their unproved and unprovable conviction of the inherent craziness of the whole thing. It is " not in human nature " that a sane man should have conceived the idea of embodying a secret narrative in a series of plays produced over an interval of many years for the entertainment of the public, nor, if he had done so, that the seventeenth-century printers of a posthumous volume of such magnitude should have been so scrupulously exact in their typography as to leave the key to the narrative unobliterated. These are convictions which we cannot demonstrate by an appeal to the mathematical calculus of Probability ; they rest simply on our conviction of the sanity of the parties concerned. " Men do not do such things."

Now, let us apply these considerations to the closely parallel case of the whole body of scientific workers who are engaged in the decipherment of the book of Nature. Here too we shall find that the whole interpretation presupposes convictions which are neither self-evident nor *demonstrably* true. No great scientific theory is accepted because it accounts for all the facts of Nature without a remainder. There always are facts which are recalcitrant to explanation by the theory and remain over as " difficulties," and, for this very reason, it is idle to reject a great scientific theory, as a certain type of apologist often proposes to do, because there are difficulties which it cannot explain. It would, for example, be silly to reject the theory of " evolution "—I mean here the theory of the derivation of living species from a smaller number of original types—on the plea that the theory has its unexplained " difficulties," or that there are grave differences between eminent men of science about the particular process which leads to the appearance of a new permanent " kind." Even the greatest of all modern scientific theories, the Newtonian gravitational astronomy, all along had its difficulties, as Newton himself was well aware. To mention only the most far-reaching and obvious of these difficulties, in the gravitational astronomy it appears as an outstanding and unexplained oddity that we have to assume the " law of gravity " side by side with the general laws of motion : the " laws " of themselves indicate no reason why there should be this universal attraction between material particles or why it should follow the law of the "inverse square " rather than any other. This was the reason why Newton himself was careful to hint that there must be some as yet undiscovered " cause of gravity," and one principal attraction offered by the Theory of Relativity is that it removes this particular difficulty by making gravitation itself a direct consequence of its revised version of the laws of motion. Yet it is notorious that the Theory of Relativity has its own difficulties too, and that at present some of these are so grave as to prevent many eminent physicists from accepting it.

Perhaps I may be pardoned if I take still a third illustration. One of the first principles of the science of Thermodynamics is the so-called " principle of Carnot " or " law of the dissipation of energy." In virtue of this principle, heat always tends to pass from a body of higher temperature to bodies of lower. The hotter body tends to impart heat to colder bodies in its vicinity, so that it becomes cooler and they warmer. It follows that at the end of a period of time which, however long, must be finite, the heat of our stellar universe must ultimately be distributed uniformly over its whole extent ; change, variety, and life must thus be lost in one dreary monotony. But if we ask why these dismal consequences have not as yet occurred, we are driven to assume that at a remote, but still finite, distance of past time the distribution of heat through the stellar universe must have been one which, on mathematical principles, is infinitely improbable. The difficulty is a recognised one, and attempts have been made to meet it, though apparently without success. In fact, there seems to be ample justification for the thesis of a brilliant writer on the philosophy of science, that all a scientific theory ever does in the way of explanation is to remove the inexplicable a few steps farther back.[1]

[1] E. Meyerson, *L'explication dans les sciences* (1921). For the particular difficulty here specified see bk. ii. chap. 6 (vol. i. pp. 181–225) and appendix iv. (vol. ii. p. 405).

Yet, in face of all the difficulties which beset every great scientific theory and are much more familiar to the scientific man himself than they can be to outsiders, there is one attitude towards Nature which no scientific man ever thinks of taking up.   He never says, as the pessimistic man of letters sometimes does, " since all scientific theory of Nature whatever has its difficulties, we may infer that the whole attempt at the construction of a scientific theory of Nature has been a mistake.   Nature is radically unknowable and irrational ; there is no sort of coherence between our notions of intelligibility and the reality in which we are immersed.   Let us have done with this secular nightmare and interest ourselves in something else."   No one who has the scientific spirit in him ever dreams of the possibility that Nature is like one of those riddles to which there is no answer.   The progress of science absolutely depends on the conviction that our difficulties arise from the fragmentary character of our know- ledge, not from the inherent incoherence of Nature.   Even as concerns our acquaintance with what we call the " bare facts," it holds good that what we are looking for determines what we see.   If men ever convinced themselves that Nature is in her own structure incoherent, not only should we have no more scientific " theories," we should cease, except occasionally and accidentally, to discover the " facts " which suggest theories.   Yet it is not demonstrable that Nature is not incoherent, and it is not self-evident that the sceptic's assertion that we have no right to expect her to conform to our " human " standards of coherence is absurd.   Scientific progress is only made possible by an act of faith—faith that there really is coherence in Nature and that the more we look for it, the more of it we shall find.   The words in which Newman describes his own attitude to the " difficulties " of theology might equally well be used by men of science with reference to the no less real " difficulties " of natural science : " ten thousand difficulties do not make one doubt." [1]

If all this is so, we cannot be fairly asked to justify religion by producing a different kind of vindication, or a fuller degree of vindication, of the " religious view " of the world than the man of science would think adequate if he were called on to " vindicate "

[1] *Apologia*, Pt. VII.   The parallel would not apply in the case of a theologian who regards the whole of theological knowledge, or at any rate of its principal propositions, as revealed together once for all in a definitive form.   It holds of Newman precisely in virtue of his doctrine of " development."

the " scientific view " of the world. In either case the most that can be demanded of us is to show that there are real and undeniable facts which call for explanation and must not be explained *away* ; that the interpretation supplied brings coherence and " sense " into them, where they would, without it, be an unintelligible puzzle ; that the more steadily and systematically the principles we fall back on are employed, the less puzzling does the reality we are trying to interpret become. In a word, we need to show that there is the same solid ground for holding that religion cannot be dismissed as a passing illusion incident to a particular stage in the mental growth of humanity as there is for holding the same view about science. If we cannot *demonstrate* that religion is not temporary illusion, neither can we *demonstrate* that science is in any better position. And it may be worth while to observe in express words that the real weight of the " evidence " which is accepted as sufficient ground for assurance can only be judged by a mind of the right kind and with the right training. This holds good without exception in all branches of " secular " learning. An experiment which the trained chemist or physicist sees to be " crucial " as deciding for or against a speculation will often seem of no particular significance to a layman ; it requires another and a different type of mind and a different training to appreciate the sort of considerations which a trained palæographer will regard as decisive for the authenticity of a document, the soundness of a reading, the worth of a speculation about the relations between the various extant manuscripts of an ancient author.[1]

---

[1] This is why even men of high intellectual power so often make themselves merely ridiculous when they venture into fields of knowledge where they are amateurs. Their training has not prepared them to be sound judges of the kind of considerations which are decisive in dealing with the unfamiliar matter. It is notorious that some of the very worst Biblical and Shakespearian " criticism " has been produced by lawyers who are very sound judges of evidence within their own sphere. The trouble is that their training disposes them to assume that what cannot be " proved " under the rules of the English or some other law of evidence cannot be adequately established in history or in literary criticism, or that what would be regarded as sufficient evidence for a British jury must always be sufficient evidence for the historian or the critic. Both assumptions are mistaken. Thus a " lawyer turned apologist " will argue that the critical analysis of the Pentateuch must be rejected because no one can " produce to the court " copies of the earlier documents into which it is analysed, or again that he has proved the correctness of the traditional ascription of a work like the Fourth Gospel to a particular author by merely showing that the tradition is ancient, as though some sort of law of " prescription " held good in questions of authorship.

In secular matters men of sound sense are pretty quick to recognise the truth of this principle. No one would think of regarding the verdict of an archæologist or a chemist on a moot point in law as deriving any particular value from the eminence of the archæologist or the chemist in his own subject ; no one would attach any weight to a Lord Chancellor's opinion about the genuineness of an alleged Rembrandt, or a disputed fragment of Simonides, because the opinion was that of the best Lord Chancellor the country had ever possessed. We all understand that the sort of consensus of " authorities " which makes it proper for the man who is not an " authority " to dispense with his own private judgment is the consensus of " authorities " in a particular subject, who derive their claim to authority from native aptitude and long training. But we ought to be equally ready to recognise that in the same way the only consensus which is of weight in matters of religion is the consensus of deeply religious men. Religion is not shown to be an " illusion " because worldly-minded men, who have never felt the sense of personal sin or the need of adoration, can see nothing in it, any more than, for example, the Theory of Relativity is shown to be " moonshine," because it seems unintelligible to the type of man whom R. L. S. used to speak of as " the common banker," or disinterested devotion to be an illusion, because a clever cynical diplomatist assures one that he has never felt such devotion himself and sees no evidence of it in the behaviour of others. If the diplomatist sees no disinterestedness in human life, it is because he is not looking for it, and the reason why he does not look for it in other men is probably that he has never felt it within himself. The evidence which a Talleyrand finds non-existent may be overwhelming to a plain man who has friendliness in his own heart and consequently finds it in his fellows, just because he goes half-way to meet them by showing that he expects it. In the same way the " evidences of religion," whatever they may turn out to be, must not be expected to produce much conviction in the man of thoroughly irreligious temper who has done nothing to counteract that temper, the merely sensual or ambitious or proud or inquisitive ; it is sufficient that they should be found adequate by those who have within them at least the making of " holy and humble men of heart," who feel the need of something they can love and adore without any of the reservations which clear insight sets to all our devotion to friend

or wife or child or country, the need of deliverance from their own
ingrained sinfulness and self-centredness, support and guidance
in their own creaturely helplessness and ignorance, abiding peace
in a world where things are mutable. If, among all their differences, such men are agreed that what they are seeking with their
whole hearts is really to be found, it is no detraction from the
weight of such evidence to say that others who are looking for
nothing of the kind have, very naturally, not found what they
never troubled to seek. It is as though one should say that there
can be no gold in a certain district because I, who know little or
nothing of the signs of the presence of this metal, and care less,
have traversed the district from end to end, without discovering
what I made no attempt to find.[1]

So far we have been speaking of the similarity of the religious
man's quest with that of the student of science, a similarity which
may be briefly expressed by saying that both are seeking a clearer
and more coherent explanation of something which they find
obscurely and confusedly " given " as part of our human experience, or, if you prefer to put it so, " suggested " by that
experience. The common problem of both is to find the presuppositions of the facts of life. But it may be necessary to add
a remark on an important difference in the kind of facts with which
the two quests deal. Perhaps we do not commonly recognise
as clearly as is desirable that " science " in the current sense of the

---

[1] These considerations ought to make us careful in not being too eager to
get the blessing of scientific men on our religion. If both our religion and our
science rest on truth, they cannot, of course, come into conflict. And it is our
duty as religious men to see that we do not confuse religion with science by
asserting or denying, *e.g.*, biological theories on grounds which have nothing
to do with the kind of evidence which is available and relevant in biology.
But equally there is the same obligation on the men of science not to judge of
matters which belong to religion on irrelevant evidence. I incline to think
that though both theologians and students of natural science have sinned in
this way in the past, at the present moment it is the men of science who have the
greater sin. In every branch of the Christian Church theologians are at
present only too eager to snatch at what they take to be the " latest results "
in the natural sciences and work them into the fabric of their creed. Usually
they commit the two inevitable errors of the amateur : they misunderstand the
precise meaning of the scientific speculation and they often take a brilliant but
disputed hypothesis, which a few years may see abandoned or gravely modified
in the light of newer knowledge, for a fully established theory. But the " man
of science " is often as bad if not worse, (worse, I mean, because his vaunted
intellectual training ought to have borne fruit in the production of the judicious
mind).

word is not the whole of knowledge but a special kind of knowledge which makes up by its one-sidedness and limitation of scope
for the precision and exactitude of its vision, just as the field of
view under the microscope compensates its definition and wealth
of detail by the narrowness of its limits.   The natural sciences,
in the first place, if we take the view of their range which is perhaps commonest among their votaries, are exclusively concerned
with physical reality, what is outside and around us.   Of ourselves as movers and agents they have nothing to say.   They
can indeed tell us much about the human brain, but always about
the human brain as it is for the physiological or anatomical
observer who is looking at it from the outside.   Even if we take,
as I for one think we must, a rather more generous view and
admit that psychology has established its right to count as an
independent natural science, and that anthropology, in its various
branches, is at least a natural science *in fieri*, the case remains in
principle the same.   The rigidly " scientific " psychologist—and
this is precisely what creates the special difficulty of his science—
treats the mind of which he discourses exactly as the geologist
might treat a rock, or the biologist a frog.   The mind of which he
speaks is a " typical " human mind not his own, at which he is
looking on, (and at times interfering to see what the result of his
interference will be).   The anthropologist, in like fashion, discourses of the religious cultus, the superstitions, the marriage
customs, the moral codes, of groups of his fellow-creatures as they
look to an outside observer who does not follow the cult, share
the terrors and hopes, or practise the customs of which he treats.
So long as we keep strictly to the methods of the natural sciences,
we never penetrate, so to say, within our own skins.   We deal
with human practice in all its forms and with the convictions it
expresses simply as " objects presented to our notice," as they
might .equally be presented to the notice of a being who shared
none of the convictions and shaped his life by none of them.
It is this attitude of detachment which makes it possible to introduce into our study the quantitative and numerical precision which
is the peculiar glory of science.   But it ought to be clear to us
that our acquaintance with our own inmost self and character,
however come by, is not originally got by observation of an " object
presented to our notice."   Our loves, our hates, our hopes, our
despondencies, our pleasures, our pains are not revealed to us by

inspection of them as presented objects but by living through the experience of loving, hating, hoping, despairing and the like. It is only after we have learned by living through them what these experiences are that we can artificially, if we like, contrive to put ourselves in the position of the observer with a microscope and look on at the expressions of personal mental life in another, or even in ourselves, *as if* it were a presented object. If it were only that, the " experimental psychologist " would be attempting an impossible task, because he would be without any key to the real significance of his observation of the behaviour of himself or of any one else. This, as it seems to me, is the real reason why all that gives human action its significance for the poet, the biographer, the historian, falls, and must fall, wholly outside the purview of the scientific psychologist and the anthropologist. The " trick," if I may call it so, on which these sciences depend for their special success, lies just in treating human doings and thoughts as though they were " events " forming part of the great event which is Nature. But in truth the thoughts and deeds of men are not mere " events " but something more : they are personal acts. Hence, I submit, the information of the psychologist and the anthropologist is true and valuable so far as it goes, but it does not go very far. The knowledge of man which makes the great biographer or historian or dramatic poet, the knowledge of the self, its strength and weakness, won by meditation and prayer go infinitely deeper ; that is knowledge of self from within, and this explains why such knowledge brings wisdom where the knowledge of the other kind amounts at best to science. A life spent in the psychological laboratory, or in anthropological research, may leave a man no more than a learned fool, but a fool will never be a great historian, whatever his learning. In fact, the confusion of knowledge with the sub-species of it which we call natural science would lead directly to the conclusion that there can be no history of a human society, except in the loose sense in which we might talk of the history of an ant-heap or even of a lump of sandstone.[1] If any of my readers are acquainted, as I hope some of them may be, with the writings of St. Bonaventura on practical religion, they will remember that consideration of what is around

---

[1] For a fuller discussion of the difference between scientific and historical knowledge I may perhaps refer to a short essay by myself in MIND, N.S., No. 124, where some rival views on the matter are also expressed by Dr. Schiller.

us, consideration of what is within, consideration of what is above us, are with him three successive well-marked stages of the intellectual ascent to knowledge of God. The restriction of the facts to which we look for the vindication of religion to facts which fall within the purview of the natural sciences and no others would, of course, cut off at one stroke all material for the higher stages of this contemplative ascent.

They are, however, not rightfully excluded from our survey. Even if no one fact or group of facts which can be dealt with by the methods of the museum and the laboratory of itself points Godward, it may well be that when we attempt to take a philosophic, or, as Plato says, a " synoptical " view of physical Nature as a whole, when we ask after the ultimate presuppositions of natural science, we shall find that Nature " as a whole " exhibits unmistakable indications of being after all not a " whole," but something incomplete and dependent, hints at least at the existence of a reality beyond itself which is at once its source and its completion. When we further take into view the aspirations of man as a moral person, we may find that they carry us further. They may be found not only to point to the existence of a reality above and beyond Nature but to indicate, however dimly, something of the character of that reality. And when we further come to consider the specific experiences which are the supports of personal religion, and, so far as we can see, must have been the origin of the different religions known to us from history, we may have reason to think that here we are actually in the presence of a genuine self-disclosure, always imperfect but none the less real, of this " super-nature " itself. If this can be maintained, we shall have a justification for following Bonaventura's line of thought. There will be a witness of Nature to God, a witness of Ethics to God, and a witness of Religion itself to God, none of which can be disregarded without mutilating the rich content of human experience, and the three witnesses will be at one in pointing to the same reality. On each of these three lines of thought I propose to offer a few remarks.

(It may be thought strange that I have so far said nothing about a topic which bulks very large in most philosophical discussions of religious problems, the *metaphysical* way to God. The omission has been made of set purpose. So far as we can draw any distinction between metaphysics and science, the difference seems to be little more than that metaphysics is, as it has been called by someone, " an unusually hard effort to think clearly." Or, to put it in a different way, any attempt to discover the most *ultimate* presuppositions on which any branch of knowledge falls back is the metaphysic of that particular branch of knowledge, and, since we cannot be said to have mastered any subject until we have discovered what its most ultimate presuppositions are, the study of any organised body of knowledge, scientific or historical, must finally culminate in metaphysics. This is, so far as I can see, the meaning of the old definition of metaphysics as " the science of first principles," or " the science of being as such." From this point of view there is no real distinction between a peculiar metaphysical way to God and the ways we have just enumerated. In studying them we are from start to finish within the region of metaphysics and there is no fourth special " way of metaphysics " to follow. It will be the object of the remainder of this essay to urge that, no matter which of the three " ways " we may choose to follow, we are conducted from similar starting-points along similar lines to the same goal, the difference being only that the character of the route and the goal is clearer if we follow the second route than if we confine ourselves to the first, and again if we follow the third than if we confine ourselves to the first two. Thus we shall agree with Bonaventura that in truth there are not three different routes, but three distinguishable stages on the same route.[1])

[1] The references to Bonaventura are primarily to the well-known *Itinerarium Mentis in Deum* and the *Soliloquium de quatuor mentalibus exercitiis* (in *S. Bonaventurae opuscula decem*, Edit. Minor, Quaracchi, 1900).

Among modern works I may specially mention, as illustrative largely of the first " way," Professor James Ward's *Naturalism and Agnosticism* and *The Realm of Ends*, and Professor A. S. Pringle-Pattison's *The Idea of God* ; as illustrative of the second, Professor Sorley's *Moral Values and the Idea of God* ; as illustrative of the third, such a work as Otto's now famous *Das Heilige* (English tr., *The Idea of the Holy*, Oxford University Press, 1923).

See further the note appended at the end of the essay. Naturally one or other of these " ways " will appeal to us with special force according to our individual interests and education. But it leads to mental one-sidedness, and religious one-sidedness too, to disregard any of them. Thomism suffers from exclusive devotion to the first, Kant from his undue concentration on the second. Excessive preoccupation with the third leads to a blind Fideism and leaves us at the mercy of our own personal uncriticised fancies and feelings.

I. From Nature to God

(1) The argument " from Nature up to Nature's God " can be presented in very different forms and with very different degrees of persuasiveness, corresponding with the more or less definite and accurate knowledge of different ages about the detailed facts of Nature and the greater or less degree of articulation attained by Logic. But the main thought underlying these very different variations is throughout the same, that the incomplete points to the complete, the dependent to the independent, the temporal to the eternal. Nature, in the sense of the complex of " objects presented to our notice," the bodies animate and inanimate around us, and our own bodies which interact with them and each other, is, in the first place, always something incomplete ; it has no limits or bounds ; the horizon in space and time endlessly recedes as we carry our adventure of exploration further ; " still beyond the sea, there is more sea." What is more, Nature is always dependent ; no part of it contains its complete explanation in itself ; to explain why any part is what it is, we have always to take into account the relations of that part with some other, which in turn requires for explanation its relation to a third, and so on without end. And the fuller and richer our knowledge of the content of Nature becomes, the more, not the less, imperative do we find the necessity of explaining everything by reference to other things which, in their turn, call for explanation in the same way. Again, mutability is stamped on the face of every part of Nature. " All things pass and nothing abides." What was here in the past is now here no more, and what is here now will some day no longer be here. " There stood the rock where rolls the sea." Even what looks at first like permanence turns out on closer examination to be only slower birth and decay. Even the Christian Middle Ages thought of the " heavens " as persisting unchanged from the day of their creation to that of their coming dissolution in fiery heat and new creation ; modern astronomy tells us of the gradual production and dissolution of whole " stellar systems." Thoughts like these suggested to the Greek mind from the very infancy of science the conclusion that Nature is no self-contained system which is its own *raison d'être*. Behind all temporality and change there must be something unchanging and eternal which is the source of all things mutable and the explanation why they are as they

are. In the first instance this sense of mutability gave rise only to a desire to know what is the permanent stuff of which what we call " things " are only passing phases ; is it water, or vapour, or fire, or perhaps something different from them all ? The one question which was primary for the earliest men of science was just this question about the stuff of which everything is made. To us it seems a very different thing to say " all things are water," or to say " I believe in God," but at bottom the quest after the stuff of which things are made is a first uncertain and half-blind step in the same direction as Aristotle's famous argument, adopted by St. Thomas, for the existence of an " unmoved Mover " (who, remaining *immotus in se*, is the source of all the movement and life of this lower world), and as all the since familiar *a posteriori* proofs of the existence of God.

(2) It is but a further step in the same direction, which was soon taken by the early founders of science, when it is perceived that the persistence of an unchanged " stuff " is no complete explanation of the apparent facts of Nature, and that we have further to ask where the " motion " which is the life of all natural processes comes from. This is the form in which the problem presented itself to Aristotle and his great follower St. Thomas. They believed that " Nature is uniform " in the sense that all the apparently irregular and lawless movements and changes with which life makes us familiar in the world around us issue from, and are the effects of, other movements (those of the " heavens "), which are absolutely regular and uniform. On this view, the supreme dominant uniform movement in Nature is naturally identified with the apparently absolutely regular diurnal revolution of the whole stellar heavens round the earth. But Aristotle could not be content to accept the mere fact of this supposed revolution as an ultimate fact needing no further explanation. No motion explains itself, and we have therefore to ask the " cause " or reason why the heavens should display this uniform continuous movement. That reason Aristotle and his followers could only explain in the language of imaginative myth. Since nothing can set itself going, the movement which pervades the whole universe of Nature must be set going by something which is not itself set going by anything else ; not mutable and changeable therefore, but eternally selfsame and perfect, because it already is all that it can be, and so neither needs nor permits of development

of any kind. "From such a principle depends the whole heaven." [1] And it follows from certain other presuppositions of Aristotle's philosophy that this "principle" must be thought of as a perfect and living intelligence. Thus in Aristotle's formulation of the principles of natural science we reach the explicit result that Nature is in its inmost structure only explicable as something which depends on a perfect and eternal source of life, and this source is not itself Nature nor any part of Nature ; the "transcendence of God" has at last been explicitly affirmed as a truth suggested (Aristotle and St. Thomas would say demonstrated) by the rational analysis of Nature herself. In principle their argument is that of every later form of the "cosmological proof."

Meanwhile with the transference of interest from the question about the stuff of which things are made to the question of the source of their movement and life, another line of thought had become prominent. The connection between organ and function is one which naturally struck the far-away founders of the science of biology. For living things show adaptation to their environment, and the various organs of living beings show adaptation to the discharge of specific functions conducing to the maintenance of the individual or the kind. And again, the living creature is not equally adapted at all stages of its existence for the full discharge of these functions. We can see it adapting itself to one of the most important of these as we watch the series of changes it undergoes from infancy to puberty, and we see the same process more elaborately if we widen our horizon and study the pre-natal history of the embryo. From such considerations derives the further suggestion which ultimately becomes the "argument from design." Aristotle is convinced that the biological analogy may be applied to all processes of the organic or inorganic world. Every process has a final stage or "end" in which it culminates, as the whole process of conception, birth, post-natal growth culminates in the existence of the physically adult animal ; and it is always the "end" to which a process is relative that determines the character of the earlier stages of the process. One seed grows into an apple-tree, another into a pear-tree, not because the two have been differently pulled or pushed, heated or cooled, wetted or dried, but because from the first the one was the sort of thing which was going, if not interfered with, to become an apple, the other the sort

[1] Aristotle, *Metaphysics*, 1072b, 14.

of thing which was going to become a pear. In the same way, there is definite order or plan everywhere in the structure of Nature, though Aristotle, unlike his master Plato, will not account for this orderliness by appeal to the conscious will and beneficent intention of his supreme Intelligence, but regards it rather, in the fashion of many modern biologists, as due to an unconscious and instinctive " quasi-purposiveness " in Nature herself.[1]

Let us look back at this line of thought, out of which the familiar " proofs of the existence of God " brought forward in popular works on Natural Theology have been developed, and ask ourselves what permanent value it retains for us to-day and how far it goes towards suggesting the real existence of a God whom a religious man can worship " in spirit and in truth." We must not suppose that the thought itself is necessarily anti-quated because the language in which it is clothed strikes us as old-fashioned, or because those who gave it its first expression held certain views about the details of Nature's structure (notably the geocentric conception in astronomy) which are now obsolete. It may very well be that the substitution of contemporary for antiquated views about the structure of the " stellar universe " or the fixity of animal species will leave the force of the argument, whatever that force may be, unaffected. There are two criticisms in particular which it is as well to dispose of at once, since both sound plausible, and both, unless I am badly mistaken, go wide of the mark.

(*a*) The point of the argument about the necessity of an " unmoving source of motion " must not be missed. We shall grasp it better if we remember that " motion " in the vocabulary of Aristotle means change of every kind, so that what is being asserted is that there must be an unchanging cause or source of change. Also, we must not fancy that we have disposed of the argument by saying that there is no scientific presumption that the series of changes which make up the life of Nature may not have been without a beginning and destined to have no end. St. Thomas, whose famous five proofs of the existence of God are all of them variations on the argument from " motion,"

---

[1] For an excellent summary account of the early Greek science referred to above see Burnet, *Greek Philosophy : Thales to Plato*, pp. 1–101 ; and for what has been said of Aristotle, W. D. Ross, *Aristotle*, chap. iii. pp. 62–111, chap. iv. pp. 112–128, and chap. vi. pp. 179–186 ; or, for a briefer summary, A. E. Taylor, *Aristotle* (Nelson & Sons, 1919), chaps. iii.–iv. pp. 49–98.

or, as we might say, the appeal to the principle of causality, was also the philosopher who created a sensation among the Christian thinkers of his day by insisting stiffly that, apart from the revelation given in Scripture, no reasons can be produced for holding that the world had a beginning or need have an end, as indeed Aristotle maintained that it has neither. The dependence meant in the argument has nothing to do with succession in time. What is really meant is that our knowledge of any event in Nature is not complete until we know the full reason for the event. So long as you only know that A is so because B is so, but cannot tell why B is so, your knowledge is incomplete. It only becomes complete when you are in a position to say that ultimately A is so because Z is so, Z being something which is its own *raison d'être*, and therefore such that it would be senseless to ask *why* Z is so. This at once leads to the conclusion that since we always have the right to ask about any event in Nature why that event is so, what are its conditions, the Z which is its own *raison d'être* cannot itself belong to Nature. The point of the reasoning is precisely that it is an argument from the fact that there is a " Nature " to the reality of a " Supernature," and this point is unaffected by the question whether there ever was a beginning of time, or a time when there were no " events."

Again, we must not be led off the track by the plausible but shallow remark that the whole problem about the " cause of motion " arose from the unnecessary assumption that things were once at rest and afterwards began to move, so that you have only to start, as the modern physicist does, with a plurality of moving particles, or atoms, or electrons to get rid of the whole question. Nor would it be relevant to remark that modern physics knows of no such absolutely uniform motions as those which Aristotle ascribes to " the heavens," but only of more or less stable motions. If you start, for example, with a system of " particles " all in uniform motion, you have still to account for the rise of " differential " motions. If you start, as Epicurus tried to do, with a rain of particles all moving in the same direction and with the same relative velocities, you cannot explain why these particles ever came together to form complexes. If you prefer, with Herbert Spencer, to start with a strictly " homogeneous " nebula, you have to explain, as Spencer does not, how " heterogeneity " ever got in. You must have individual variety, as well as " uniformity," in whatever you choose to take as your postulated original data if you are to get out of the data a world like ours, which, as Mill truly says, is not only uniform but also infinitely various. *Ex nihilo, nihil fit,* and equally out of blank uniformity nothing *fit* but a uniformity equally blank. Even if, *per impossibile,* you could exclude all individual variety from the initial data of a system of natural science, you might properly be asked to account for this singular absence of variety, and a naturalistic account of it could only take the form of deriving it from some more ultimate state of things which was not marked by absolute "uniformity." Neither uniformity nor variety is self-explanatory ; whichever you start with, you are faced by the old dilemma. Either the initial data must simply be taken as brute " fact," for which there is no reason at all, or if there is a reason, it must be found outside Nature, in the " supernatural."

(*b*) Similarly, it does not dispose of the conception of natural processes as tending to an " end " and being at least " quasi-purposive " to say that the thought originated with men who knew nothing of " evolution " and falsely believed in the fixity of natural kinds. In point of fact the notion of the gradual development of existing natural species made its appearance at the very dawn of Greek science and was quite familiar to the great philosophers who gave the Greek tradition its definitive form, though they rejected it because, so far as they knew, the evidence of facts seemed against it. The admission of the reality of the " evolution " of fresh species has, however, no direct bearing on the question of " ends in Nature " : it actually suggests the raising of that very question in a new form. Is there, or is there not, in organic evolution a general trend to the successive emergence of beings of increasing intelligence ? And if so, must the process be supposed to have reached its culmination, so far as our planet is concerned, in man, or must man be regarded as a mere stage in the production of something better, a *Pfeil der Sehnsucht nach dem Uebermenschen* ? These are questions which we are still asking ourselves to-day, and though the strict positivists among our scientific men may insist that they probably cannot be answered and that it is certainly not the business of natural science to answer them, it is at least curious that the scientific man not infrequently unconsciously betrays the fact that he has privately answered them to his own satisfaction by the very fact that he talks of " evolution " as " progress," a phrase which has no meaning except in relation to a goal or an end, or even, on occasion, permits himself to assume that what is " more fully evolved," *i.e.* comes later in the course of a development, must obviously be brighter and better than whatever went before it. Thus the old problem is still with us and we cannot take it for granted that the old answers have lost their meaning or value.

We may, for example, consider how the old-fashioned argument from " motion " to the " unmoving " source of motion, when stated in its most general form, might still be urged even to-day. As we have seen, the argument is simply from the temporal, conditioned and mutable to something eternal, unconditioned and immutable as its source. The nerve of the whole reasoning is that every explanation of given facts or events involves bringing in reference to further unexplained facts ; a complete explanation of anything, if we could obtain one, would therefore require that we should trace the fact explained back to something which contains its own explanation within itself, a something which is and is what it is in its own right ; such a something plainly is not an event or mere fact and therefore not included in " Nature," the complex of all events and facts, but " above " Nature. Any man has a right to say, if he pleases, that he personally does not care to spend his time in exercising this mode of thinking, but would rather occupy himself in discovering fresh facts or fresh and hitherto unsuspected relations between facts. We need not blame him for that ; but we are entitled to ask those who are alive to the meaning of the old problem how they propose to deal with it, if they reject the inference from the unfinished and conditioned to the perfect and unconditioned. For my own part I can see only two alternatives.

(i) One is to say, as Hume [1] did in his " Dialogues on Natural Religion," that, though every " part " of Nature may be dependent on other parts for its explanation, the *whole* system of facts or events which we call Nature may as a whole be self-explanatory ; the " world " itself may be that " necessary being " of which philosophers and divines have spoken. In other words, a complex system in which every member, taken singly, is temporal, may as a complex be eternal ; every member may be incomplete, but

---

[1] Or rather, the sceptical critic in the *Dialogues*. We cannot be sure of Hume's own agreement with the suggestion.

the whole may be complete ; every member mutable, but the whole unchanging. Thus, as many philosophers of yesterday and to-day have said, the " eternal " would just be the temporal fully understood ; there would be no contrast between Nature and " supernature," but only between " Nature apprehended as a whole " and Nature as we have to apprehend her fragmentarily. The thought is a pretty one, but I cannot believe that it will stand criticism. The very first question suggested by the sort of formula I have just quoted is whether it is not actually self-contradictory to call Nature a " whole " at all ; if it is, there can clearly be no apprehending of Nature as something which she is not. And I think it quite clear that Nature, in the sense of the complex of events, is, in virtue of her very structure, something incomplete and not a true whole. I can explain the point best, perhaps, by an absurdly simplified example. Let us suppose that Nature consists of just four constituents, A, B, C, D. We are supposed to " explain " the behaviour of A by the structure of B, C, and D, and the interaction of B, C, and D with A, and similarly with each of the other three constituents. Obviously enough, with a set of " general laws " of some kind we can " explain " why A behaves as it does, if we know all about its structure and the structures of B, C, and D. But it still remains entirely unexplained why A should be there at all, or why, if it is there, it should have B, C, and D as its neighbours rather than others with a totally different structure of their own. That this is so has to be accepted as a " brute " fact which is not explained nor yet self-explanatory. Thus no amount of knowledge of " natural laws " will explain the present actual state of Nature unless we also assume it as a brute fact that the distribution of " matter " and " energy " (or whatever else we take as the ultimates of our system of physics) a hundred millions of years ago was such and such. With the same " laws " and a different " initial " distribution the actual state of the world to-day would be very different. " Collocations," to use Mill's terminology, as well as " laws of causation " have to enter into all our scientific explanations. And though it is true that as our knowledge grows, we are continually learning to assign causes for particular " collocations " originally accepted as bare facts, we only succeed in doing so by falling back on other anterior " collocations " which we have equally to take as unexplained bare facts. As M. Meyerson puts it, we only get rid of the

" inexplicable " at one point at the price of introducing it again somewhere else. Now any attempt to treat the complex of facts we call Nature as something which will be found to be more nearly self-explanatory the more of them we know, and would become quite self-explanatory if we only knew them all, amounts to an attempt to eliminate " bare fact " altogether, and reduce Nature simply to a complex of " laws." In other words, it is an attempt to manufacture particular existents out of mere universals, and therefore must end in failure. And the actual progress of science bears witness to this. The more we advance to the reduction of the visible face of Nature to " law," the more, not the less, complex and baffling become the mass of characters which we have to attribute as bare unexplained fact to our ultimate constituents. An electron is a much stiffer dose of " brute " fact than one of Newton's hard impenetrable corpuscles.

Thus we may fairly say that to surrender ourselves to the suggestion that Nature, if we only knew enough, would be seen to be a self-explanatory whole is to follow a will-of-the-wisp. The duality of " law " and " fact " cannot be eliminated from natural science, and this means that in the end either Nature is not explicable at all, or, if she is, the explanation has to be sought in something " outside " on which Nature depends.

(ii) Hence it is not surprising that both among men of science and among philosophers there is just now a strong tendency to give up the attempt to " explain " Nature completely and to fall back on an " ultimate pluralism." This means that we resign ourselves to the admission of the duality of " law " and " fact." We assume that there are a plurality of ultimately different constituents of Nature, each with its own specific character and way of behaving, and our business in explanation is simply to show how to account for the world as we find it by the fewest and simplest laws of interaction between these different constituents. In other words we give up altogether the attempt to " explain Nature " ; we are content to " explain " lesser " parts " of Nature in terms of their specific character and their relations to other " parts." This is clearly a completely justified mode of procedure for a man of science who is aiming at the solution of some particular problem such as, *e.g.*, the discovery of the conditions under which a permanent new " species " originates and maintains itself. But it is quite another question whether " ultimate pluralism " can be the last word of a " philosophy of Nature." If you take it so, it really means that in the end you have no reason to assign why there should be just so many ultimate constituents of " Nature " as you say there are, or why they should have the particular characters you say they have, except that " it happens to be the case." You are acquiescing in unexplained brute fact, not because in the present state of knowledge you do not see your way to do better, but on the plea that there is and can be no explanation. You are putting unintelligible mystery at the very heart of reality.

Perhaps it may be rejoined, " And why should we not acknowledge this, seeing that, whether we like it or not, we must come to this in the end ? " Well, at least it may be retorted that to acquiesce in such a " final inexplicability " as final means that you have denied the validity of the very assumption on which all science is built. All through the history of scientific advance it has been taken for granted that we are not to acquiesce in inexplicable brute fact ; whenever we come across what, with our present light, has to be accepted as merely fact, we have a right to ask for further explanation, and should be false to the spirit of science if we did not. Thus we inevitably reach the conclusion that either the very principles which inspire and guide scientific inquiry itself are an illusion, or Nature itself must be dependent on some reality which is self-explanatory, and therefore not Nature nor any part of Nature, but, in the strict sense of the words, " supernatural " or " transcendent "—transcendent, that is, in the sense that in it there is overcome that duality of " law " and " fact " which is characteristic of Nature and every part of Nature. It is not " brute " fact, and yet it is not an abstract universal law or complex of such laws, but a really existing self-luminous Being, such that you could see, if you only apprehended its true character, that to have that character and to be are the same thing. This is the way in which Nature, as it seems to me, inevitably points beyond itself as the temporal and mutable to an " other " which is eternal and immutable.

The " argument from design," rightly stated, seems to me to have a similar force. In our small region of the universe, at any rate, we can see for ourselves that the course of development has taken a very remarkable direction. It has led up, through a line of species which have had to adapt themselves to their " environment," to the emergence of an intelligent and moral creature who adapts his environment to himself and even to his ideals of what he is not yet but ought to be and hopes to be, and the environment of the species he " domesticates " to his own purposes. It is increasingly true as we pass from savagery to civilisation that men make their own environment and are not made by it. On the face of it, it at least looks as though, so far as our own region of Nature is concerned, this emergence of creatures who, being intelligent and moral, freely shape their own environment, is the culminating stage beyond which the development of new species cannot go, and that the whole anterior history of the inorganic and prehuman organic development of our planet has been controlled throughout by the requirements of this " end." I know it will be said that we have no proof that the same thing has happened anywhere else in the " universe " ; our planet may, for all we know, not be a fair " average sample." Again, it may be urged that there are reasons for thinking that the history of our planet will end in its unfitness first to contain intelligent human life, and then to contain any form of life ; consequently man and all his works cannot be the " end of evolution " even on this earth, but must be a mere passing phase in a process which is controlled by no " ends," and is therefore in no true sense of the term a " history." One would not wish to shirk any of these objections, and yet it is, I think, not too much to say that, to anyone but a fanatical atheist, it will always appear preposterous to regard the production of moral and intelligent masters of Nature as a mere by-product or accident of " evolution on this planet," or indeed as anything but the " end " which has all along determined the process. " Nature," we might say, really does show a " trend " or " bias " to the production of intelligence surpassing her own. And further, we must remember that if there is such a " trend," it will be necessary to include under the head of the processes it determines, not only the emergence of the various forms of prehuman life on our earth, but the " geological " preparation of the earth itself to be the scene of the ensuing development and the pre-preparation during the still remoter astronomical period of the formation of our solar system. Thus to recognise so-called " quasi-purposiveness " even in the course development has followed on " one tiny planet " inevitably involves finding the same quasi-purposiveness on a vaster scale, throughout the whole indefinite range of natural events.[1] The more we are alive to this simple consideration that " *de facto* determination by ends," once admitted anywhere in Nature, cannot be confined to any single region or part of Nature but inevitably penetrates everywhere, the more impossible it becomes to be satisfied with such expressions as " quasi-purposive " or " *de facto* " teleology and the like.

The vaster the dominating " plan," the more vividly must it suggest a planning and guiding intelligence.   Nature herself, we may suppose (if we allow ourselves to use the miserably misleading personification at all), may, as has been said, be like a sleep-walker who executes trains of purposive acts without knowing that he does so.   But the plan itself cannot have originated without a wakeful and alert intelligence.   (Even the sleep-walker, as we know, only performs trains of acts adjusted to ends in his sleep because he has first learnt consciously to adjust means to ends in his waking life.) Let " Nature " be as unconscious as you please : the stronger is the suggestion that the marvellous, and often comical, " adapta-tions " of a highly complex character which pervade " Nature " are the " artifices " of one who neither slumbers nor sleeps.   What look like " accidents " may very well be deliberate designs of a master artist, or, as Plato says, contrary to the proverbial expression, it may be Nature which " imitates " Art.   I will not attempt to estimate the amount of probative force which ought to be ascribed to these suggestions.   It is enough for my purpose that they are there, and that their drawing has notoriously been felt with special

---

[1] This is not to say that man is the sole or chief end of Creation, a proposition which, in fact, no orthodox Christian theologian would make ; at least not without very careful explanations and reservations.   But it is worth while to remind ourselves that there is nothing in itself absurd in the view of the Middle Ages that human history is the central interest, the main plot, of the drama of the universe.   For all we *know*, our planet may be the only home of beings " with immortal souls to be saved."   If it is, then the fact that it is "*tiny*" is obviously irrelevant as a reason for denying its central importance. When I reflect on the capacities of a man for good and evil, I see nothing ludicrous in the supposition, which, however, I am not making, that it might have been the chief purpose of a wise Creator in making the solar system that the sun should give us men light and warmth.

All I seriously wish to insist on, however, is that to let in " purpose " *anywhere* into natural fact means letting it in *everywhere*.   Give it an inch and it will rightly take infinite room.   (This as a reply to the arguments based on the allegation that we cannot regard the part of things with which we are acquainted as a " fair average sample."   What we are acquainted with is not a definite isolated " part " or " region," but has ramifications which extend indefinitely far.)

intensity by so many of those who are best acquainted with the facts, even where their metaphysical bias has led them to withhold assent.

The spectacle of movement and change which we call " Nature " thus at least suggests the presence of some " transcendent " source of movement and change which is strictly eternal, being above all mutability and having no succession of phases within itself, and is omnipotent, since it is itself the source of *all* " becoming." The orderliness and apparent purposive " trend towards intelligence " in Nature similarly at least suggest that this omnipotent and eternal " supernatural " is a wholly intelligent Will. The force of the suggestion seems to have been felt by man in every stage of his history so far as that history is accessible to us. It is noteworthy that the more intimate our inquiries become with the " savages " who by our estimate stand nearest to a pre-civilised condition, the clearer it becomes that even those of them who have been set down on first acquaintance as wholly " godless " turn out, on better knowledge, to have their traditions of a " maker of life " and the like. And at the same time we are not dealing with anything which can be set aside as a " relic of primitive savagery." *Our* conception of " One God the Father Almighty, Creator of heaven and earth," has come to us from two immediate sources, Greek science and philosophy and Hebrew prophecy, and both science and prophecy, as cannot be too often repeated, began by a complete break with the " primitive superstition " of the past. Belief in God as the source of Nature is thus a " survival of primitive superstition " only in the same sense in which the same could be said of belief in causality [1] or, if you prefer it, in " laws of uniform sequence."

So far, however, our attention has been confined to what Bonaventura calls the " things around and below us," and they clearly have taken us a very little way indeed in the direction of suggesting the reality of a God who is God in the religious man's sense, a being who can be loved and trusted utterly and without qualification. In the creatures we may have discerned the " footprints " of a Creator, but we have seen no token of his " likeness." Perhaps, if we turn our attention to " what is

---

[1] It is significant that Wittgenstein's penetrating though unbalanced *Tractatus logico-philosophicus* definitely *identifies* " superstition " with the belief in causality. *Op. cit.* 5·1361.

within us," we may find in our own moral being the suggestion
of something further. We may get at any rate a hint that the
creative intelligence we divine behind all things has also the
character which makes adoration, love, and trust, as distinguished
from mere wonder, possible. In man's moral being we may discern not the mere " footprints " but the " image " of God.

II. FROM MAN TO GOD

With the line of thought we have now to consider we can deal
more briefly. If meditation on the creatures in general leads us
by a circuitous route and an obscure light to the thought of their
Maker, meditation on the moral being of man suggests God more
directly and much less obscurely. For we are now starting a
fresh stage of the " ascent " from a higher level, and it is with the
road to God as with Dante's purgatorial mountain : the higher
you have mounted, the easier it is to rise higher still. In Nature
we at best see God under a disguise so heavy that it allows us
to discern little more than that someone is there ; within
our own moral life we see Him with the mask, so to say, half
fallen off.

Once more the general character of the ascent is the same ;
we begin with the temporal, and in a certain sense the natural,
to end in the eternal and supernatural. But the line of thought,
though kindred to the first, is independent, so that Nature and Man
are like two witnesses who have had no opportunity of collusion.
The clearer and more emphatic testimony of the latter to what
was testified less unambiguously by the former affords a further
confirmation of our hope that we have read the suggestions of
Nature, so ambiguous in their purport, aright.

A single sentence will be enough to show both the analogy
of the argument from Man to God with the argument from
Nature and the real independence of the two lines of testimony.
Nature, we have urged, on inspection points to the " supernatural "
beyond itself as its own presupposition ; if we look within ourselves we shall see that in man " Nature " and " supernature "
meet ; he has both within his own heart, and is a denizen
at once of the temporal and of the eternal. He has not, like
the animals, so far as we can judge of their inner life, one
" environment " to which he must adapt himself but two,

a secular and an eternal. Because he is designed ultimately to be at home with God in the eternal, he can never be really at home in this world, but at best is, like Abraham, a pilgrim to a promised but unseen land ; at worst, like Cain, an aimless fugitive and wanderer on the face of the earth. The very " image " of his Maker which has been stamped on him is not only a sign of his rightful domination over the creatures ; it is also " the mark of Cain " from which all creatures shrink. Hence among all the creatures, many of whom are comic enough, man is alone in being tragic. His life, at the very best, is a tragi-comedy ; at the worst, it is stark tragedy. And naturally enough this is so ; for, if man has only the " environment " which is common to him with the beasts of the field, his whole life is no more than a perpetual attempt to find a rational solution of an equation all whose roots are surds. He can only achieve adjustment to one of his two " environments " by sacrifices of adjustment to the other ; he can no more be equally in tune with the eternal and the secular at once than a piano can be exactly in tune for all keys. In practice we know how the difficulty is apparently solved in the best human lives ; it is solved by cultivating our earthly attachments and yet also practising a high detachment, not " setting our hearts " too much on the best of temporal goods, since " the best in this kind are but shadows," " using " the creatures, but always in the remembrance that the time will come when we can use them no more, loving them but loving them *ordinate*, with care not to lose our hearts to any of them. Wise men do not need to be reminded that the deliberate voluntary refusal of real good things is necessary, as a protection against the over-valuation of the secular, in any life they count worth living. And yet wise men know also that the renunciation of real good which they recommend is not recommended for the mere sake of being without " good." Good is always renounced for the sake of some " better good." But the " better good " plainly cannot be any of the good things of this secular existence. For there is none of them whatever which it may not be a duty to renounce for some man and at some time.

I do not mean merely that occasions demand the sacrifice of the sort of thing the " average sensual man " calls good— comfort, wealth, influence, rank and the like. For no serious moralist would dream of regarding any of these as more, at best,

than very inferior goods. I mean that the same thing holds true
of the very things to which men of nobler mould are ready to
sacrifice these obvious and secondary goods. For example, there
are few, if any, earthly goods to compare with our personal
affections. Yet a man must be prepared to sacrifice all his
personal affections in the service of his country, or for what he
honestly believes to be the one Church of God. But there are
things to which the greatest lover of his country or his Church
must be prepared in turn to sacrifice what lies so near his heart.
I may die for my country, I may, as so many a fighting man does,
leave wife and young children to run the extreme hazards of
fortune, but I must not purchase peace and safety for this country
I love so much by procuring the privy murder of a dangerous and
remorseless enemy. I may give my body to be burned for my
faith, I may leave my little ones to beg their bread for its sake,
but I must not help it in its need by a fraud or a forgery. It
may be argued that for the good of the human race I ought to
be prepared to sacrifice the very independence of my native land,
but for no advantage to the whole body of mankind may I insult
justice by knowingly giving sentence or verdict against the
innocent. If these things are not true, the whole foundation of
our morality is dissolved ; if they are true, the greatest good, to
which I must at need be prepared to sacrifice everything else,
must be something which cannot even be appraised in the terms
of a secular arithmetic, something incommensurable with the
" welfare " of Church and State or even of the whole human race.
If it is to be had in fruition at all, it must be had where the secular
environment has finally and for ever fallen away, " yonder " as
the Neo-Platonist would say, " in heaven " as the ordinary
Christian says. If this world of time and passage were really our
home and our only home, I own I should find it impossible to
justify such a complete surrender of all temporal good as that
I have spoken of ; yet it is certain that the sacrifice is no more
than what is demanded, when the need arises, by the most familiar
principles of morality. Whoever says " ought," meaning " ought,"
is in the act bearing witness to the supernatural and supra-temporal
as the destined home of man. No doubt we should all admit that
there are very many rules of our conventional morality which
are not of unconditional and universal obligation ; we " ought "
to conform to them under certain specified and understood

conditions. I ought to be generous only when I have first satisfied the just claims of my creditors, just as I ought to abstain from redressing grievances with the high hand when society supplies me with the machinery for getting them redressed by the law. But whoever says " ought " at all, must mean that at least *when* the requisite conditions are fulfilled the obligation is absolute. There may be occasions when it is not binding on me to speak the truth to a questioner, but if there is one single occasion on which I ought to speak the truth, I ought to speak it then, " though the sky should fall."

Now, if there ever is a single occasion on which we ought to speak the truth, or to do anything else, " at all costs " as we say, what is the good in the name of which this unconditional demand is made of me? It cannot be any secular good that can be named, my own health or prosperity or life, nor even the prosperity and pleasurable existence of mankind. For I can never, since the consequences of my act are endless and unforeseeable, be sure that I may not be endangering these very goods by my act, and yet I am sure that the act is one which I ought to do. No doubt, you may fall back upon probability as the guide of life and say, " I ought to do this act because it seems to me most likely to conduce to the temporal well-being of myself, my family, my nation, or my kind." And in practice these are, no doubt, the sort of considerations by which we are constantly influenced. But it should be clear that they cannot be the ultimate grounds of obligation, unless all morality is to be reduced to the status of a convenient illusion. To say that the ultimate ground of an obligation is the mere fact that a man thinks he would further such a concrete tangible end by his act involves the consequence that no man is bound to do any act unless he thinks it will have these results, and that he may do anything he pleases so long as he thinks it will have them. At heart, I believe, even the writers who go furthest in professing to accept these conclusions do themselves a moral injustice. I am convinced that there is not one of them, whatever he may hold in theory, who would not in practice " draw the line " somewhere and say, " This thing I will not do, whatever the cost may be to myself or to anyone else or to everyone." Now an obligation wholly independent of all temporal " consequences " clearly cannot have its justification in the temporal, nor oblige any creature constructed to find his good wholly in the temporal. Only to a being who has in his structure the adaptatior to the eternal can you significantly say " You ought." [1]

It will be seen that the thought on which we have dwelt in the last paragraph is one of the underlying fundamental themes of Kant's principal ethical treatise, the " Critique of Practical Reason." It is characteristic of Kant that, wrongly as I think, he wholly distrusted the suggestions of the " supernatural " to be derived from the contemplation of Nature itself, and that, from an exaggerated dread of unregulated fanaticism and super-stition, characteristic of his century, he was all but blind to the third source of suggestion of which we have yet to speak. Hence with him it is our knowledge of our own moral being, as creatures who have unconditional obligations, which has to bear the whole weight of the argument. Here, I own, he seems to me to be definitely wrong. The full force of the vindication of religion cannot be felt unless we recognise that its weight is supported not by one strand only but by a cord of three intertwined strands ; we need to integrate Bonaventura and Thomas and Butler with Kant to appreciate the real strength of the believer's position. Yet Kant seems to me unquestionably right as far as this. Even were there nothing else to suggest to us that we are denizens at once of a natural and temporal and of a supernatural and eternal world, the revelation of our own inner division against ourselves afforded by Conscience, duly meditated, is enough to bear the strain. Or, to make my point rather differently, I would urge that of all the philosophical thinkers who have concerned themselves with the life of man as a moral being, the two who stand out, even in the estimation of those who dissent from them, as the great undying moralists of literature, Plato and Kant, are just the two who have insisted most vigorously on what the secularly-minded call, by way of depreciation, the " dualism " of " this world " and the " other world," or, in Kantian language, of " man as (natural) phenomenon " and " man as (supernatural) reality." To deny the reality of this antithesis is to eviscerate morality.

We see this at once if we compare Kant, for example, with Hume, or Plato with Aristotle. It is so obvious that Plato and Kant really " care " about moral practice and Aristotle and Hume do not care, or do not care as much as they ought. In Hume's

---

[1] I owe the expression to a report of a recent utterance of some Roman Catholic divine. I regret that I cannot give the precise reference.

hands moral goodness is put so completely on a level with mere respectability that our approval of virtue and disapproval of vice is said in so many words to be at bottom one in kind with our preference of a well-dressed man to a badly-dressed. Aristotle cares more than this. He reduces moral goodness to the discharge of the duties of a good citizen, family man, and neighbour in this secular life, and is careful to insist that these obligations are not to be shirked. But when he comes to speak of the true happiness of man and the kind of life which he lives " as a being with something divine in him," we find that the life of this " divine " part means nothing more than the promotion of science. To live near to God means to him not justice, mercy, and humility, as it does to Plato and the Hebrew prophets, but to be a metaphysician, a physicist, and an astronomer. Justice, mercy, and humility are to be practised, but only for a secular purpose, in order that the man of science may have an orderly and quiet social " environment " and so be free, as he would not be if he had to contend with disorderly passions in himself or his neighbours, to give the maximum of time and interest to the things which really matter. We cannot say of Hume, nor of Aristotle, nor indeed of any moralist who makes morality merely a matter of right social adjustments in this temporal world, what you can say of Plato or Kant, *beati qui esuriunt et sitiunt justitiam.* " Otherworldliness " is as characteristic of the greatest theoretical moralists as it is of all the noblest livers, whatever their professed theories may be.

The point is again strikingly illustrated by a difficulty raised by a moralist who was also a noble liver in our own times, T. H. Green. He rightly makes it a fatal objection to the current utilitarianism of his day that pleasure or gratified feeling, which according to the utilitarian theorists is the only good, is not a *moral* good—*i.e.* their view is that the end for which the good man acts is the same as that for which the bad man acts. The difference between the good and the bad man is made a mere difference of the method by which each pursues an end which is common to him with the other ; the object sought by both is the same. To escape this reduction of virtue to prudent calculation of means Green goes on to say that true good means " moral good," " what satisfies a moral nature as such." This seems at first sight to leave us with a vicious circle. A moral agent is one who aims at " true " good, but " true " good again can only be defined as

" the sort of thing a moral agent as such aims at." Green's way of escape from this circle is to add that we do not know in its fulness what this true good is, but we can see at any rate that the belief that it really *is* has been the source and impulse of all attempts to obtain it, and we can learn from the history of the past along what lines progress towards its attainment has been made.[1]

Now these observations, so far as they go, are manifestly sound. It is plain that moral progress would be arrested if it were not at every stage inspired by an aspiration towards what has not yet been attained; so Herbert Spencer frankly stated that the very notion of " ought " would vanish from a " fully evolved " society— that is, that such a society would have ceased to be a moral community. It is equally plain that none of us has a " clear and distinct idea " of what it would be like to be a just man made perfect. We all walk by faith, not by sight. The conclusion which Green clearly ought to have drawn from his premises is that, since the goal of the moral life cannot by any possibility be attained under temporal conditions, and yet its reality (which, in the case of an ideal which ought to inspire and regulate all our conduct, must mean its real attainability by *us*) is the necessary condition that the inspiration to progress shall not fail, our final destiny must lie in the non-temporal. But when Green comes to face this issue, his fear of incurring the reproach of " other-worldliness " is so great that he merely equivocates about the " last things," and proves false to what was clearly his own inmost faith.[2]

Of course we could put the thought I am labouring in many other ways. We might, for example, say that it cannot be insignificant that man alone of all creatures of whom we know has a sense of sin. Animals, in a wild state, seem to show nothing of

[1] T. H. Green's *Prolegomena to Ethics*, bk. iii. chap. i. §§. 171–179.

[2] See the shuffling language, *op. cit.*, bk. iii. chap. ii. §§. 187–189, where Green simply runs away under a cloud of words from his own emphatic statement (§ 185) that moral progress can only mean progress *of* personal character *to* personal character. The same terror of being thought " otherworldly " by secularists is much more marked in Green's illustrious disciple, the late Professor Bosanquet. To my own mind it absolutely ruins his philosophy on its ethical side, besides making him a very unsafe guide as an interpreter of Plato. A Christian, or even a Platonist philosopher, should make light of the charge of "otherworldliness"; "Let us therefore go forth unto him without the camp, bearing his reproach. For here we have no continuing city, but we seek one to come." One might have a worse motto as a moralist than ἔξω τῆς παρεμβολῆς.

the kind. Mr. Bradley, it is true, once suggested that you might find the beginnings of moral self-condemnation in the sulky brooding of a tiger which has missed its spring. But I think there is here a confusion which was long ago exposed by Butler in his distinction between the feelings of a man who has been disappointed of an expectation and one who knows he has deservedly suffered for his own misdoing. " In the one case, what our thoughts fix upon is our condition : in the other, our conduct." [1] Dogs which have been well brought up are thought by some observers to be capable of " knowing they are doing wrong " and to feel ashamed of it. I cannot pronounce any opinion on the soundness of this as psychology, but supposing the fact to be so, it is important to remember that these dogs have been brought up by man, and that any approach they make to a sense of wrongdoing, as distinct from a shrinking from expected unpleasant consequences, is presumably an effect of their domestication by a being who is already moral. The alleged fact proves nothing as to the presence of a rudimentary sense of sin in an animal in the " state of nature," any more than the shameless sexual irregularities of our domesticated animals prove that before their domestication they had not their special pairing seasons. In any case the human sense of sin has peculiarities of its own which no sound psychologist can afford to neglect. There is, first of all, its special poignancy and indelibility. As to the poignancy, any one who has felt the sword-point of guilt knows, without my telling him, how it pierces to the very marrow. The indelibility, too, must not be overlooked. The dog which has disgraced itself does, perhaps, for the time being, feel shame, as well as fear of an impending unpleasant consequence. But when the temporary disgrace is once fairly over, there is no indication that the dog which has disgraced itself and been punished is troubled again about its past " misdoings." Its past self is dead and buried. Not so with us. If a man has a high standard and a sensitive conscience, it is not enough for him that he is honestly repentant for his past misdoings and has long honourably striven, perhaps with full success, to " make good," but the remembrance loses little, if anything, of its bitterness. A sincere Christian may be satisfied that he has received the remission of his sins and may trust with assurance that he will be preserved by grace from falling back to them, but he does not forget them ; the remembrance and

[1] *Dissertation upon the Nature of Virtue* (ed. W. R. Matthews, § 6).

the shame remain, like disfiguring and aching scars which testify to ancient wounds. For us, the past may be dead, but it is not yet the dead and buried past it seems to be for the animals. There is the keen sense of " pollution " by our wrongdoing, testified to by the world-wide practice of trying to get rid of the pollution by ablution, sprinkling with the blood of sacrificial victims and similar rites, exactly as we might try to get rid of a bodily defilement or infection. Even where we cannot point to any member of human society who has suffered hurt or infringement of rights by the sinful act, the feeling still persists that a sin is a wrong done to a person of infinite sanctity, a personal affront, an act of *lèse-majesté*. We may no longer be convinced by the old argument that it is just that the least sin should be visited with unending torments, because, as an act of treason against an infinite Deity, it is always an infinite treason. But I believe that we do still feel about what a third human party might call our *peccadilloes* that, trivial as they look, they are infinitely polluting. It is the " saint " not the " notorious evil-doer " to whom it most readily occurs to cry " Woe is me, for I am unclean." Kant expresses the same thought in a different way, which is all the more remarkable from his violent prejudice against " anthropomorphic " conceptions. According to him the one and only specific moral feeling is reverence for the sanctity of the moral law as such. He will not say reverence for a divine Author of the moral law ; that would be " anthropomorphism." Yet when he is trying to make it quite clear what this feeling of reverence for the majesty of the law is, he observes that reverence is, properly speaking, a feeling which is only evoked by moral character, and compares it with the feeling of constraint an ordinary man would have if he were suddenly called on to enter the presence of a " superior," the sort of feeling you or I might have if we were informed that in an hour or two we should have to dine with the King or the Pope. The natural inference, as Professor Clement Webb has remarked, is that the reverence we feel for the moral law really is an attitude towards an unseen being of transcendent purity and holiness of character.[1]

Or the whole argument may be once more put in the form in which we find it in the great scholastic thinkers, a form which goes back in the end to Plato and Augustine. Man, like all living

[1] *Divine Personality and Human Life*, Lecture V, especially pp. 125-126.

creatures, is first and last a conative and striving being.   He has a " good " which he can consciously enjoy and without the fruition of which he is discontented and unhappy.   So too with his animal congeners.   But the good which secures content to them is one for which the conditions of secular existence, when favourable, make adequate provision.   An animal wants food, shelter, warmth, movement, repose, the gratification of its pairing or parental instincts when they are aroused ; it usually also wants to be " let alone," to be left unthwarted in its movements, and when these wants are gratified it is content and as happy as an animal can be. Man has all these wants and many more created by his possession of intelligence.   He wants, for instance, to secure himself against the uncertainties of to-morrow, hence his desire of wealth, power, command of the forces of Nature.   He wants to provide himself with sources of interest and excitement, one chief reason for the attractiveness of the curious game of politics.   He wants to know in order to satisfy his curiosity, to surround himself with things of beauty or to make them for himself, he wants to feel himself beloved and so forth.   Yet the singular thing is that none of these satisfactions, singly or together, really satisfy him.   He is unhappy in deprivation and wearied in fruition by satiety.   And even where there is neither deprivation nor satiety he is discontented with the best things time has to give him, because they will not last.

Most of us would perhaps say that the purest content and happiness earth has to give us is that which comes from the known possession of the life-long personal affection of a friend or a wife or a son.   Yet there is something which forbids us to be really content and at peace even in such possession.   However well we may love and be loved, there is always some barrier between the self and the second self in another.   A man always knows at once too much and too little of the wife of his bosom and she of him.   Again in these dearest intimacies we are never really assured against the changes and estrangements time brings with it.   I may change subtly and imperceptibly or my other self may change, and by and by one awakens with a heartache to the perception that the old confidence and love are a thing of the past.   And finally, if none of these things happen, we all know that when hands have been joined in wedlock or in friendship, they will be unjoined again by death.   " One shall be taken and the other shall be left " is the irrevocable sentence on the dearest of all earthly ties.   There is thus a drop of poison in the chalice of the fullest secular happiness—a poison infused, a Christian would say, by the heavenly Lover of all souls to prevent us from finding abiding and complete happiness outside Himself. Nothing seems plainer than this, that if true peace and content are to be found by man at all, they cannot be found in anything temporal or secular. They must spring from a conscious intimate possession of personal union of heart and will with a being who knows us through and through as no man knows another, or even himself, who contains within Him an inexhaustible wealth of being which excludes all risk of satiety, who is utterly eternal and abiding and therefore can never change or fail. The final peace of man, if it is to be found at all, can only be found in a God who is eternal by nature and imparts by His grace a " participated " eternity of perseverance to the other party to the relation. Our true, final good thus lies not in the world of Nature, but in that "other-world" of the supernatural which everywhere interpenetrates and sustains Nature and yet absolutely transcends her.

" If found at all," we said. But possibly the " final good " is simply not to be found ? It may be an illusion, like the horizon which seems to be the end of the visible world, but recedes as we approach it. But at least the facts about human aspirations of which we have spoken are real facts, as the whole of the great literature of the world testifies. Any philosophy has to give some coherent and rational-seeming explanation of the fact that the " illusion " is there. We cannot say that it is an inevitable consequence of the fact that man is finite and perishable. We have all heard of

> " Infinite passion and the pain
> Of finite hearts that yearn."

But the finitude of the hearts does not explain the infinity of the passion ; it makes it a paradox. The animals, too, are finite, yet their finitude causes them no unrest. But man is not only finite ; he *knows* that he is finite ! There you come to the heart of the mystery. How is a creature who is merely finite to know that he is finite ? Is this any more possible than it would be, for example, that a dog should know that he is " only a dog " ? This is the real crux which a simple "this-world" philosophy persists in ignoring. Or how comes it that a race of beings shaped *by* purely temporal conditions to maintain their existence by adaptation *to* temporal conditions so obstinately insists on demanding something more ?   How obstinate is the insistence is shown by the reluctance of the very thinkers who hold in theory that man is just one of the " products of natural evolution " to advise him to behave himself accordingly.   Of the many who repeat glibly enough that man is just an animal, who would say to a son setting out on life for himself, " Be an animal " ?   Yet if any of us would count it wiser and better advice to his son to say " Live like a creature destined for eternity," is he not virtually confessing that the in-stinct, or whatever we may prefer to call it, for eternity, however questionable the forms in which it sometimes expresses itself, is at bottom a sound one ?

We see that the general character of the argument from Nature and from our moral being to God is the same in both cases.   In both we reason from the temporal to the eternal.   But there is this difference, that the elusive being to which we reason is, in the second case, something richer.   Reflexion on what is below and around us suggested only an eternal intelligent designer and source of Nature.   Reflexion on the moral nature of man suggests a being who is more, the eternal something before whom we must not only bow in amazement, like Job, but kneel in reverence as the source and support of all moral goodness.   This is as it should be, since in the one case we are attempting to see the cause in the effect, in the other to see the features of the father in his child. If Nature shows us only the footsteps of God, in man as a moral being we see His image.

III. From God to God

The apparently paradoxical heading I have given to this section of my essay has been purposely chosen.   We have con-sidered already the suggestiveness of what Bonaventura calls reflexion on what is beneath us and within us, and have now to take into account his " reflexion on what is above us."   Here, if the phrase stands for anything real, we have clearly done with mere suggestions ; we are dealing with the interpretation of a direct manifestation of the divine and super-temporal, within the limits imposed by the finitude and temporality of the human recipient.   To use phraseology which is more familiar to us of to-day, we have to consider the worth of the so-called " religious experience " as testimony to the reality of its own object, and there is no line of argument which lends itself more readily to abuse. Every kind of faddist and fanatic will appeal as readily to " experience " for testimony to his own pet fancies as the credulous appeal to the " evidence of their senses " for proof of the existence of ghosts or the reality of sorcery. We seriously need to remember, as Dr. Temple in *Christus Veritas* has reminded us, that just as the " artist's experience " means the way in which the *whole* natural realm is experienced by the man who is an artist, so " religious experience " means not some isolated group of bizarre experiences but the special way in which the whole of life is experienced by the " religious " man. And yet, true as this is, the very statement implies that there are some experiences which stand out in the life of the religious man as characteristically predominant and determining the colouring of his whole experience of the world. This is equally true of the artist. A man with the artist's eye, we very rightly say, " sees beauty " everywhere, while a man without it goes through life not seeing beauty any-where, or at best seeing it only occasionally, where it is too prominent to be missed. Still no one doubts that even a man highly endowed with the gifts of the artist has to develop his sense for the beautiful. If he comes to find it present where the rest of us would never suspect it at all but for the teaching we may get from his work, this must be because he began by being specially alive to and interested in its presence where it is more visibly displayed. This again means that, however truly beauty may pervade the whole of things, there are special regions where its presence is most manifest and obvious. What is characteristic of the artist is that he makes just these elements of experience a key to unlock the meaning of the rest. So the religious man, no doubt, means the man who sees the whole of reality under the light of a specific illumination, but he has come to see all things in that light by taking certain arresting pieces or phases of his experience as the key to the meaning of the rest. In this sense we may properly speak of specifically religious experiences, as we may speak of a man's experience in the presence of a wonderful picture or musical composition, or at a moment when a weighty decision which will colour the whole tenour of his future conduct has to be made, as specifically æsthetic or moral experiences. The question is whether there really are such specific experiences or whether what have been supposed to be so are only illusions, misinterpretations of experiences which contain nothing unique.

This question is not settled by the admission that some experiences which have been reckoned by those who have had them as religious are illusory. All experience is liable to misinterpretation. We must not argue that sense-perception does not reveal a world of really existing bodies, which are no illusions of our imagination, on the ground that there are such things as dreams and hallucinations, any more than we may argue from the general reality of the things perceived by sense to the reality of dream-figures or ghosts. So again we may neither argue that there is no real beauty in the visible world because the best of us are capable of sometimes finding it where it is not, nor that because there is real beauty, every supposed beauty detected by any man must be real. In a sense, "everything is given." If there were no arresting perception of beauty in the region of colour or tone, we should never come to be on the look out for it where it is less manifest. On the other hand, every man's immediate verdict on beauty is not to be trusted. We have to learn how to interpret our experience in the light of the judgment of the artist who is specially endowed with a fine discrimination of beauty and has cultivated his eye or ear by long and careful attention to the æsthetic aspects of the sensible world before we can trust our own immediate " taste " for colour or line or tone. So, too, in matters of morality, if a man has no direct perception of what " ought " means, it is impossible to convey that meaning to him ; but a man would be led sadly astray in his morality if he assumed that his own first judgments of right and wrong are infallible. He needs to learn " sound judgment in all things " by a training which puts him in possession of the moral tradition of a high-minded society, and by comparing his own judgment in cases of perplexity with that of men of high character, ripe reflexion, and rich knowledge of life. (This is why, though without conscientiousness there can be no true moral goodness, the faddist, who insists on treating his own " private " conscience as infallible, is a mere moral nuisance.)

We may readily admit, then, that much which the experiencer is inclined to take for " religious " experience is illusion. He may mistake the vague stirrings and impulses of sex, or æsthetic sensibility, or even pure illusions of sense or perception, for the self-revelation of the divine, just as any of us may, in favourable conditions, mistake what he has merely dreamed of for an event of waking life. And such confusions may very well lie at the bottom of widespread aberrations ; they may account very largely for the puerility of many of the " religious " beliefs of mankind, and the lewd or bloody practices which defile so many of our ritual cults. And we must insist that if there are specific and unique religious experiences, they must not all be taken " at their face-value " ; like all other alleged experiences they stand in need of " interpretation " in the light of the judgment of the " expert " who is at once keenly sensible of the actual " experience," and has brought a tried and sane judgment to bear upon it.[1] We thus find ourselves face to face with a second question, and we have to ask (a) are there specific *data* which furnish the basis for a " religious " interpretation of life, (b) and if there are, who are the " experts " whose interpretation of the *data* should guide the interpretation ?

(a) As to the first question. It has, as we all know, been denied that there are any specific data to furnish such an interpretation with its starting-point. The supposed *data* have been explained away, now as ordinary physical facts misunderstood by the curious but ignorant savage, now as emotional reactions to dreams, fear of the dark or of lonely places, now as vague emotional reactions attendant on the different sexual modifications characteristic of adolescence, and in other ways. The question is whether *all* the known facts can be disposed of without remainder in this fashion. *A priori* we have no right to assume that this can be done. It may be true, for example, that " conversions " are more common at or shortly after the reaching of puberty than at any other time of life. It is equally true that the same period is often marked by the sudden appearance of other new interests or the sudden intensification of old ones. Thus a boy often suddenly develops a vivid interest in literature, or a new sensitiveness to art, in the years of dawning manhood. Clearly this does

---

[1] This sort of interpretation is needed even for sense-perception. Any one who has, *e.g.*, ever used a microscope must remember how he had at first to learn to " see " with it. At first the beginner does not " see " what his teacher says is there to be seen, or (*experto crede*) he " sees " a great deal that is not there. I can vividly recollect the trouble I had in this matter when first shown sections of the spinal medulla under the microscope. Cp. again the sharp disputes of astronomers about many of the markings which some of them claim to have " seen " on the disc of Mars.

not prove that the qualities we admire in literary style or in painting or music are not really there, but only supposed to be there in
virtue of an illusion of sexuality. *A priori* it is just as likely that
the effect of a crisis which affects our whole bodily and mental life
should be to awaken a heightened perception of a reality previously
veiled from our eyes, as to create the " illusion " of a reality which
is not there.   The experiences of adolescence may be, as a matter
of my private history, the occasion of my first discovery of beauties
in Keats or Chopin which I do not find in the ordinary rhymester
or manufacturer of " music " for the piano.   But how does this
prove that in reality the poetry of Keats does not differ from that of
writers for the provincial newspaper, or the music of Chopin from
the average waltz or polka ?   The problem is not how I came
to make a certain " find," but what the worth of the " find "
may be.

So with the part played by fear of the dark or of desert solitudes
in creating beliefs in gods.   The real question is not whether
emotions of this kind may not have influenced men's religious
emotions and beliefs, but whether the emotions and beliefs, however they may have been developed, *contain* nothing more than
such fears or contain something else which is quite specific, just as
musical perception may be prompted or quickened by adolescence
but certainly, *when once it is there*, contains a quite specific core
or kernel of its own.   However our sensibility to music began,
it is quite certain that what we perceive when we appreciate it is
nothing sexual.   There are, I honestly believe, men who only
respond to the appeal of music so far as, crudely or subtly, it is made
to sexual feeling, but such men are the typically " unmusical."
What they value is not musical beauty itself, but a mass of suggestions which have to be got rid of before one can begin to
appreciate " pure " music at all, exactly as one has to get rid of the
tendency to demand that a picture shall " tell a story " before one
can begin to understand the values of colour, line, disposal of
light and shade.   We have also to be on our guard against the
standing " psychologist's fallacy " which no one has done more to
expose than Dr. Otto in the work to which reference has already
been made.   It is too often assumed that because there is an
analogy between our mental attitude towards an object of our
adoration and our attitude towards something we fear, or something which attracts us sexually, the two attitudes must be the

same. Thus our reverence for the God we worship is in some
ways like our dread of a strange and powerful natural object ;
our love for God is in some ways like the feelings of a devoted
human lover, as the language of religious devotion is enough to
prove. But it does not in the least follow that the likeness is
more than a likeness ; it is still perfectly possible that even the
rudest savage's attitude in the presence of that which he " worships "
has a character of its own quite distinct, *e.g.*, from his mere fear
of a formidable beast or of the dangers of the dark. Since language
has been primarily adapted to express our attitude towards " things
of this world," when we want to speak of our attitude in the
presence of our *numina* we have to make shift, as best we can, with
words which properly designate an analogous but different attitude. The psychologist and anthropologist are only too apt to
take these makeshift expressions *au pied de la lettre* ; because we
have to say that we " fear " or " love " God, they assume that we
mean no more than when we say that we are afraid of an angry
bull or that we love a young lady. Thus the specifically
" religious " character of certain experiences, if it is really there,
eludes them because they have not taken Bacon's warning against
the *idola fori* which arise from excessive belief in the adequacy
of language. They have not understood that the name of GOD
is necessarily the " ineffable " name

That civilised men, in the presence of anything they take as
divine, have this sense of being face to face with the " ineffable "
is quite certain, and we can see by reading the cruder utterances of
the uncivilised in the light of what has grown out of them that they
too must have it. It is the great service of Dr. Otto to the philosophy of religion that he has worked out this line of thought in
full detail in his careful analysis of the meanings of " holy " and
corresponding words, as revealed by the historical study of language
and literature. The main point to be made is that, as far back as
we can trace the beginnings of religion, the " holy," even if it is
no more than an oddly shaped stone, does not simply mean the
strange or the formidable ; it means, at the lowest, the " uncanny,"
and the " uncanny " is precisely that which does not simply belong
to " this " everyday world, but directly impresses us as manifesting
in some special way the presence of " the other " world. As such,
it repels and attracts at once, is at once the awful and the worshipful, but above all in both aspects the absolutely transcendent and

" *other*-worldly." At different levels of spiritual development the object which awakens this special sense of being in the presence of the " absolutely transcendent " may be very different. A low savage may feel it in the presence of what to us is simply a quaintly shaped stone or a queer-looking hill ; the prophet feels it, and is crushed by the sense of its transcendent " otherness," in his vision of the Lord of hosts ; the disciples of Christ feel it in the presence of a living man, who is also their friend and teacher, when we read of Him that " he was going before them on the road and they were *astounded* (ἐθαμβοῦντο), and as they followed they were *terrified* (ἐφοβοῦντο)" (Mark x. 32). It is precisely the same feeling which has prompted, *e.g.*, the utterance of the words of institution in the Eucharist *sotto voce*, and inspired the old Eucharistic hymn σιγησάτω πᾶσα σάρξ βροτεία,[1] as well as the modern saying that if Shakespeare came into the room we should all stand up, but if Jesus Christ came into the room we should all kneel down. It is equally the same sense of being in the presence of the wholly " other-worldly " which finds expression in such an exclamation as the prophet's " Woe is me for I am unclean, for mine eyes have seen the Lord of hosts," or St. Peter's " Depart from me, for I am a sinful man." We should quite misunderstand such language if we read it as a confession of any special wrongdoing on the part of prophet or apostle. It is the universal voice of the mutable and temporal brought face to face with the absolutely eternal ; hence in Scripture even the sinless seraphim are said to " veil their faces " as they stand before their Lord. This, again, is why it has been the belief of all peoples that he who sees a god dies.

As nearly as we can express our attitude towards that which awakens this sense of being immediately in the presence of the " other-worldly " by any one word, we may say that it is the attitude of " worship." But even here we need to remember the inadequacy of language. In our own Marriage Office the bridegroom speaks of " worshipping " the bride ; a mayor or a police magistrate is to this day officially " his worship." The word *worship*, like all other words, is really hopelessly inadequate to express the attitude a man experiences in the presence of what he feels to be the " absolutely other " made directly manifest. (We

---

[1] See the working out of this thought in Otto, *op. cit.* (English tr.), chap. xiv. pp. 159 ff.

do not say anything, we are simply silent when we kneel at the INCARNATUS EST.) Yet it is hard to believe that the most sceptical among us does not know the experience. There are those to whom it is present as a constant experience during their lives, and those to whom it comes but seldom ; there are those who bestow their " worship " on inadequate objects, like the man who " worships " his money or his mistress. But it is as doubtful whether there is really any man who has never worshipped anything as it is doubtful whether there is any man who has never feared or never loved. The experience moreover seems to be specially characteristic of man ; as the Greeks said, " Man is the only animal who has gods." (Possibly indeed, the attitude of some dogs to their masters may offer a remote analogy, but we must remember that these are dogs who have been brought up by man and become at any rate distantly humanised by the process. There is no reason to think that " Yellow Dog Dingo " could ever have developed in this way.)

And again, there can be little doubt that the men in whom the spirit of true worship has been most constantly present are they who show us human nature at its best. It is the " brutalised " man who is marked by the temper of habitual irreverence. Even if we judge of men solely by what they have effected in the way of " social reform," history seems to show that the men who have achieved most for the service of man in this world are men whose hearts have been set on something which is not of this world ; " the advance of civilisation is in truth a sort of by-product of Christianity, not its chief aim." [1] We may reasonably draw the conclusion that religion is just as much a unique characteristic and interest of humanity as love of truth, love of beauty, love of country, and that the saint's " experience " is no more to be dismissed as an illusion than the thinker's, the artist's, or the patriot's.

(*b*) Of course, like all other immediate experiences, the peculiar experience of the immediate presence of the divine requires interpretation and criticism. A man may be moved to adoration by an unworthy and inadequate object, like the heathen

[1] W. R. Inge, *Personal Religion and the Life of Devotion*, p. 84 ; cf. *ibid.* pp. 59–60. A careful study of the debt of " civilisation " to St. Francis would afford an admirable illustration. No one in the course of many centuries has done more for " civilisation "; no one, probably, ever thought less about it.

who " in his blindness, bows down to wood and stone," or the lover
who lavishes his spiritual treasure on a light woman.   Religion
is not proved to be an illusion by its aberrations, any more than
science by the labour wasted on squaring the circle or seeking the
elixir and the philosopher's stone, or love by the havoc it makes of
life when it is foolishly bestowed.   The sane judgment of reflexion
is required to direct and correct all our human activities.   We are
neither to suppose that there is no way to God because some ways
which have been found promising at first have led astray, nor yet
that because there is a way, any way that mankind have tried must
be as good a road to the goal as any other.   We may freely assert
that even the most puerile and odious " religions " have had their
value ; they have this much at least of worth about them that those
who have practised them have been right in their conviction that
the " other-world " is really there to be sought for.   But to
draw the conclusion that " all religions are equally good," or even,
like the " Theosophists," that at any rate every religion is the best
for those who practise it, and that we are not to carry the Gospel
to the heathen because they are not at a level to appreciate it, is
like arguing that all supposed " science " is equally good, or that
we ought to abstain from teaching the elements of natural science
to a Hindu because his own traditional notions about astronomy
and geography are " the best he is capable of."   Views of this
kind rest in the end on an absurd personal self-conceit, and
a denial of our common humanity.   A true religion, like a true
science, is not the monopoly of a little aristocracy of superior
persons ; it is for everyone.   We may not be able to teach the mass,
even of our own fellow-countrymen, more than the first elements
of any science, but we must see to it that what we do teach them
is as true as we can make it.   And so even more with religion,
because of its direct relation with the whole conduct of life.   A
savage may be capable only of very elementary notions about God
and the unseen world, but at least we can see to it that the ideas
he has are not defiled by cruelty or lewdness.   Not to say that
you never know how far the capacity of *any* mind for receiving
true ideas extends, until you have tried it.   The " Theosophist "
usually claims to show a broad-minded humanity, which he contrasts complacently with the " narrowness " of the Christian who
wishes all mankind to share his faith.   But he belies his own profession the moment he begins his habitual disparagement of the

missionary. To say that in religion, or in any other department of life, the vile or foolish is good enough for your neighbour is the arrogance of the half-educated. The neighbour whom we are to love as ourselves deserves at our hands the best we can possibly bring him.

The point I chiefly want to make, however, is that the specific experience of contact with the divine not only needs interpretation, like all other direct experience, but that, though it is the directest way of access to the "wholly other," it is not the only way. If we are to reach God in this life, so far as it is permitted, we need to integrate the "religious experience" with the suggestions conveyed to us by the knowledge of Nature and of our own being. It seems clear that in its crudest manifestations the experience of this direct contact is not specifically connected with superiority in knowledge or in moral character. At a sufficiently low level of intelligence we find the idiot regarded as God-possessed in virtue of his very idiocy. (He is supposed to be in touch with the transcendent "other" because he is so manifestly out of touch with our "this-world" daily life.) [1] And the "holy men" of barbaric peoples are very seldom men who show anything we should call moral superiority over their neighbours. Even among ourselves it is often the simple and ignorant who make on us the impression of spending their lives most in the sense of God's presence, and again the men who show themselves most keenly sensitive to "religious impressions" are by no means always among the most faultless. Indeed, "moral excellence" itself, without humility, seems only too often to close the soul's eye to the eternal. A self-absorbed prig is in deeper spiritual blindness than many an open sinner. But if we would look at the Lord "all at once," we must of course integrate the glimpses we get in our moments of direct adoring contact with all that Nature and Morality suggest of the abiding source of them both. In particular, we need to have the conception of the "holy," as the object of adoration, transformed in such a way that it is fragrant with moral import before "Be ye holy because I am holy" can become the supreme directing note for the conduct of life. In principle this work of integrating our experience has been already accomplished for us by Christianity, with its double inheritance from the Jewish

[1] *Cf.* Wordsworth's application to idiots of the words "Their life is hid with Christ in God."

prophets and the Greek philosophers who freed their " reasonable worship " from entanglement in the follies and foulnesses of the old " nature-religions." But the root of the old errors is in every one of us ; we cannot enter into the highest religious experience available to us except by a perpetual fresh interpretation of the given for ourselves. We may have Moses and the prophets and Paul and the evangelists, and yet, without personal watching unto prayer, all this will not avail to ensure that we shall think Christianly of the unseen, or that our sense of its reality will of itself lead us to a noble life rich in good works. And this answers for us the question " Who are the experts ? " [*cf. (b)*, p. 73 *supra*]. The true " expert critic " of the constructions and hypotheses of science is the man who has already learned what the men of science have to teach him. The true expert critic of the painter or the musician must first have learned to see with the painter's eye and hear with the musician's ear. Without this qualification, mere acuteness and ingenuity are wasted. In the end, all effectual criticism must be of what a man has first seen and felt for himself. So the verdict on the religious life if it is to count must come from the men who have first made it their own by living it. Only they can tell " how much there is in it."

I have urged that the suggestions of an eternal above and behind the temporal are derived from three independent sources, and that the agreement of the three in their common suggestion gives it a force which ought to be invincible. But I would end by a word of warning against a possible dangerous mistake. The fullest recognition of the reality of the transcendental and eternal " other " world does not mean that eternity and time are simply disconnected or that a man is set the impossible task of living in two *absolutely* disparate environments at once. The two worlds are not in the end isolated from one another, since the one shines, here more, there less, transparently through the other. In man, in particular, they are everywhere interdependent, as Kant held that the real (or moral) and the apparent (or natural) realms are. We are not to spend half our time in the service of the eternal and the other half in the service of the secular. If we try to do this we shall merely incur the usual fate of the man with two masters We are not called to be *pukka* saints half the week and " worldlings " for the other half. Strictly speaking, we cannot divide a man's occupations and duties into the " religious " and the " secular."

The true difference between the religious man and the worldly is that the religious man discharges the same duties as the other, but in a different spirit. He discharges them " to the glory of God," with God as his chief intention, that is, with his eye on an end the attainment of which lies beyond the bounds of the temporal and secular. The truest detachment is not retreat to the desert, but a life lived in the world in this spirit. Thus, for example, a man discharges the duty of a husband and a parent in a secular spirit if he has no aim beyond giving his wife a " happy time of it " and bringing up his children to enjoy a lucrative or honourable or comfortable existence from youth to old age. Marriage and parenthood become charged with a sacramental spirit and the discharge of their obligations a *Christian* duty when the " principal " intention of parents is to set forward a family in the way to know and love God and to be spiritual temples for His indwelling. It may be that the temporal will never cease to be part of our environment ; what is important is that it should become an increasingly subordinate feature in the environment, that we should cease to be at its mercy, because our hearts are set elsewhere. Christianity has always set its face against the false treatment of the eternal and the temporal as though they were simply disconnected " worlds." In the beginning, it tells us, the same God created heaven and earth, and its vision of the end of history has always included the " resurrection of the flesh " to a glorified existence in which it will no longer thwart but answer wholly to the " spirit." If we are told on the one hand that a man who is in Christ is a " new creation," we are also told by the great Christian theologians that " grace " does not destroy " nature " but perfects and transfigures it.

Bibliographical Note.—Besides the books referred to or quoted in the text I would specially recommend to the reader the following. Of course they are only a selection out of a much larger number. Perhaps I may also mention, as further illustrating some points touched on in the first part of this essay, an essay by myself in the volume on *Evolution in the Light of Modern Science* (Blackie. 1925).

HÜGEL, F. VON. *Eternal Life.* T. & T. Clark. 1912.
— — — *Essays and Addresses on the Philosophy of Religion.* Dent & Sons. 1921.
SOLOVIEV, V. *The Justification of the Good.* Eng. Tr. Constable. 1918.
WARD, J. *Naturalism and Agnosticism.* A. & C. Black. First published 1899.
— — — *The Realm of Ends.* Cambridge University Press. 1911.

AUTHORITY

EY ALFRED EDWARD JOHN RAWLINSON

AND

WILFRED L. KNOX

CONTENTS

I

AUTHORITY AS A GROUND OF BELIEF

By A. E. J. RAWLINSON

1. *The Authoritative Character of Christianity*

THE Christianity of history is a definite, historical, and positive religion. It is not (in the phrase of Harnack) " Religion itself," neither is it true to say that " the Gospel is in no wise a positive religion like the rest." [1] On the contrary, the Gospel is in such wise " a positive religion," that it came originally into the world in a particular context, and as the result of a particular historical process. It has ever claimed to be the divinely intended culmination and fulfilment of an even earlier historical and positive religion, that of the Jews. It has been characterised, in the course of its persistence through the centuries, by a specific and definite system of religious beliefs, as well as by what has been, in the main, a specific and definite tradition of spiritual discipline and *cultus*— a system of beliefs and a type of *cultus* and discipline, which have been discovered in experience to have the property of mediating (in proportion as they are taken seriously) a spiritual life of a highly characteristic and definite kind. From all of which it follows that Christianity is not anything which could be discovered or invented for himself by any person, however intellectually or spiritually gifted, in independence of historical tradition. The term " Christian " is not an *epitheton ornans*, applicable in the spheres of religion and ethics to whatever in the way of doctrine, ideal, or aspiration may happen to commend itself to the judgment of this or that individual who is vaguely familiar with the Christian tradition as the result of having been born and brought up in a country ostensibly Christian. It is a term which to the historian possesses a definite content, discoverable from history. And because Christianity is thus an historical and positive religion, it is impossible, in the first instance, for the individual to know any-

---

[1] The statements controverted are quoted from Harnack's *What is Christianity?* (E.T.), p. 63.

thing about it at first hand. He must be content to derive his knowledge of it from authority, whether the authority in question be primarily that of a living teacher, or of past tradition.

It belongs, further, to the essential character of Christianity that (in common with all the great prophetic and historical religions) it claims to be a religion of revelation, and as such to proclaim to mankind an authoritative Gospel in the name of the living God. " The idea of authority," writes Friedrich Heiler, " is rooted in the revelational character of the prophetic type of religion." [1] This certainly has been the characteristic of Christianity from the beginning. It appears to have been characteristic of the historical attitude of Jesus Christ, as may be seen from the story of the scene in the synagogue at Capernaum in St. Mark (Mark i. 21 sqq.). It has been pointed out by the German scholar Reitzenstein that the Greek word ἐξουσία, which we render " authority," was employed in Hellenistic Greek to denote, in a religious context, the idea of a combination of supernatural power with supernatural knowledge of divine things. [2] So in St. Mark's narrative the word is used to suggest the combination in Jesus of supernatural power with supernatural authority to teach. " What is this ? A new teaching ! With authority, moreover, he commandeth the unclean spirits, and they obey him ! " (Mark i. 27). " He taught them as one having authority, and not as the scribes " (Mark i. 22). The Lord, as a matter of actual historical fact, astonished people by teaching independently of scribal tradition, with the unhesitating " authority " of immediate inspiration. In this respect His manner and method of teaching resembled that of the great Old Testament prophets, but with the significant difference that whereas the Old Testament claim to prophetic authority was expressed through the formula " Thus saith Jehovah," our Lord said simply " I say unto you." The authority claimed by the Lord Jesus in matters of religion may thus be described as prophetic and super-prophetic : that is to say, He claims for Himself, without any hesitation, the plenitude of spiritual authority inherent in God's Messiah, *i.e.* in the Person in whom God's spiritual purpose of redemption, in every legitimate sense of the word, is summed up and destined to be realised,

[1] F. Heiler, *Das Gebet*, p. 266.
[2] R. Reitzenstein, *Die hellenistischen Mysterienreligionen* (2nd edn.), pp. 14, 101, 125.

in the first instance for Israel, but ultimately also, through Israel, for mankind.

And this attitude of spiritual authority, characteristic of Jesus, is characteristic also, according to the New Testament, of the Church. To the Church as the redeemed Israel of God is entrusted the word of the Christian salvation as an authoritative Gospel, a message of good news, to be proclaimed as the truth of God " in manifestation of the Spirit and of power." " He that heareth you heareth me : and he that rejecteth you rejecteth me : and he that rejecteth me rejecteth him that sent me " (Luke x. 16). "As the Father hath sent me, even so send I you " (John xx. 21). Fundamental in Christianity is this claim of the Church to have been divinely commissioned, divinely "sent." The Church is not primarily a society for spiritual or intellectual research, but a society of which it belongs to the very essence to put forward the emphatic claim to be the bearer of revelation, to have been put in trust with the Gospel as God's revealed message to mankind, and to have been divinely commissioned with pro-phetic authority to proclaim it as God's truth to all the world, irrespective of whether men prove willing to hear and give heed to the proclamation, or whether they forbear. In this respect the tone of the Church must always be " Thus saith the Lord " : she must proclaim her message in such a fashion that men may receive it (like the Church of the Thessalonians in the New Testament) " not as the word of men, but as it is in truth, the word of God."

It is, moreover, in this sense—that is to say, as an authoritative Gospel—that the message of Christianity comes home, whenso-ever and wheresoever it does come home with effect, to the hearts and consciences of men. " Faith cometh by hearing, and hearing by the word of Christ " ; and the Gospel, thus authoritatively proclaimed, proves itself still to be " the power of God unto salvation unto every one that believeth." The apologetic work of reasoned argument and philosophical discussion, the dissipation of prejudices, the antecedent clearing away of difficulties, the removal of intellectual barriers, may in particular cases be the necessary preliminaries to conversion. But conversion to Chris-tianity, in any sense that matters, is not primarily the result of an intellectual demonstration. It is the work of the Spirit. "No man can say ' Jesus is Lord,' but by the Holy Ghost." Nevertheless, when a man *is* thus enabled by the power of the Spirit to say " Jesus is Lord," he does so for the reason that he has been made aware, in the very depths of his soul, that he has been brought face to face with a truth which he did not discover, but which has been spiritually revealed to him, even the truth of God, " as truth is in Jesus " ; and he knows henceforward that he is no longer his own master : he has given in his allegiance, in free and deliberate self-committal, to the supreme authority of Him who is the truth : he is from henceforth " a man under authority," being " under law to Christ."

2. *The Relation of the Gospel to the Church*

With what has been thus far written, it is probable that the representatives of almost all types and schools of thought in Christianity would find themselves to be, upon the whole, in substantial agreement. It is common ground that " grace and truth came by Jesus Christ," and that the Gospel is God's authoritative message to mankind. The main difference between the Catholic and the Protestant traditions in Christianity lies in the kind and degree of recognition which is given, side by side with the authority of the Gospel, to that of the Church. How is the relation of the Church to the Gospel properly to be conceived ? Is the Church the creation of the Gospel ? Or is the Church, in a more direct sense than such a view would suggest, the supernatural creation of God—a divine institution—the Spirit-filled Body of Christ ?

Now, it can be recognised freely that the Spirit operates to-day, in varying measure, outside the borders of any institutional Church, that " the wind bloweth where it listeth," and that " Jordan overfloweth his banks all the time of harvest." Nevertheless it must be affirmed that according to the New Testament the Church (the idea of which is rooted in that of Israel, the holy people of God) is the covenanted home of the Spirit, and the Church is historically the society which is put in trust with the Gospel for the benefit of the world. The Gospel does not descend from heaven immediately, as by a special revelation. It reaches men through the instrumentality and mediation of the Church. This is true obviously in the case of all those who are born and brought up within the fold of the Church, and who acknowledge themselves to be her spiritual children. It is true equally, though less obviously, in the case of those Christians who would be disposed to deny the idea of any ecclesiastical mediation, and who would conceive themselves to derive their faith directly from the New Testament ; since it is a plain fact of history that the very existence of the New Testament presupposes the prior existence and activity of the Church, of whose authoritative tradition it forms a part.

The Church, therefore, is not the creation of the Gospel. The Gospel is rather the divine message of redemption which is entrusted to the Church.   There is ideally no opposition or antithesis between " Catholic " and " Evangelical."   If Catholicism has ever in any degree failed to be Evangelical, it has to that extent and in that degree failed signally to be true to its vocation. Catholicism stands, according to its true idea, both for the presentation of the Gospel of Jesus Christ in its fulness, and also for a certain wholeness, a certain completeness, in the development, maintenance and building up of Christianity as a system and spiritual " way," or manner of life.   The Catholic Church in idea is not simply the redeemed Israel of God : it is also the missionary of Christ to the world, the society which is put in trust with the Gospel.   It is bound therefore of necessity to regard itself as an authoritative society, in so far as it is entrusted with an authoritative message, and empowered with divine authority to proclaim it.   Beyond this, as the Beloved Community of the saints, the familiar home and sphere of the operations of divine grace, the ideal Fellowship of the Spirit, the Church possesses a legitimate claim upon the allegiance of its members, and exercises over them a teaching and pastoral authority, an authority not of constraint, but of love, in respect of which those who are called to the office of pastorate are enjoined in the New Testament so to fulfil their ministry as to seek to commend themselves to every man's conscience in the sight of God.

There are accordingly different types and kinds of authority in the Church, all of which are important and real, even though admittedly all (because of the frailty of men, and of the earthen vessels to which the divine treasure is committed) are liable to abuse.   There is the fundamental and primary authority of the Gospel, the divine message of revelation.   There are the subordinate and totally different questions of disciplinary authority in the Church, of the administrative authority of Church officers, of the prescriptive authority of custom, of the obligation or otherwise, in varying degree, of different types of Church ordinances and rules. There is further the moral and religious authority of the saints, and of the devotional and ascetic tradition of Christendom, in relation to the proper development of the spiritual life in its most characteristically Christian forms. Any one who is wise will, if he desires to develop such spiritual life, go to school to the saints and pay heed to the devotional traditions of Christendom. The sciences corresponding to this type of authority are those of moral, ascetic and mystical theology. They are essentially practical. They presuppose the desire to make progress in the life of the spirit in its Christian form, and the readiness to learn from the experience of the saints and of former generations of Christians. But the proper concern of this essay is not with any of these forms of authority : it is with authority as a ground of belief—belief, not in that comprehensive sense of faith as the response of the " heart," or of the whole personality, to the primary appeal of the Gospel, but in the sense of the acceptance of beliefs, the acknowledgment of particular doctrines or historical assertions as true.

3. *Authority as a Ground of Belief*

For it is, in point of fact, obvious that the preaching of the Gospel, considered simply as the proclamation of a divine message which is primarily prophetic in type, presupposes as the intellectual ground of its validity a number of truths—philosophical, historical, and theological—which it is the business of Christian apologetics and theology to substantiate, to interpret, and to defend. It is possible to point, even in apostolic times, to the inevitable tendency to draw up short statements of Christian truth, dogmatic summaries of the intellectual content of the faith. The work of the teacher in apostolic times went on side by side with that of the evangelist or preacher. The proclamation of the Gospel as a divine message of Good News presupposed, and required as its supplement, the teaching of doctrine. Unless certain dogmatic assertions are true, the whole Gospel of Christianity falls to the ground. The truths, therefore, which to the Christian mind have appeared to be implicit in the truth of the Gospel, or to be presupposed by the assumption of the validity of Christian Church life and devotional practices, were eventually formulated, more and more explicitly, in the shape of dogmatic propositions ; with the result that a body of *credenda* arose, which in the traditionally Catholic presentation of Christianity are proposed for the acceptance of the faithful on the ground of the teaching authority of the Church.

From the point of view of the effectual handing on of the Christian tradition such a method of teaching was in practice inevitable, and has analogies in all branches of education. The acceptance of alleged truths on the authority of a teacher who is trusted is commonly, in the initial stages of the study of any subject whatever, the dictate of wisdom. Authority, for those who are under instruction, is always, at least psychologically, a ground of belief ; nor is there anything irrational in the acceptance of beliefs on authority, provided always that there is reasonable ground for believing the authority on the strength of whose assurance the beliefs in question are accepted to be trustworthy, and that the degree of " interior assent " is proportioned to what is believed to be the trustworthiness of the particular authority concerned. There is nothing therefore *prima facie* irrational in the attitude of a man who in religious matters elects, even to the end, to submit his judgment to authority, and to accept the guidance of the Church, since it may be argued that in respect of such matters it is *a priori* probable that the wisdom of the community will be superior to that of the individual, and the question may be asked : If the Christian Church does not understand the real meaning of Christianity, who does ? The Church in each successive generation has always included within its membership a considerable proportion of such unspeculative souls, who have been content to accept such teaching as has been given to them " on authority," and to live spiritually on the basis of a faith the intellectual content of which they have not personally thought out, and the purely rational grounds of which they have not personally attempted to verify.

Even in the case, however, of those who could thus give no other intellectual account of their beliefs except to say simply that they had accepted them on authority, it is probable that the real grounds on which the beliefs in question are held are not exhausted by such a statement. A doctrine may have been accepted, in the first instance, on authority, but it remains inoperative (save as a purely abstract and theoretical opinion) unless it is at least to some extent verified in the experience of life.   It is doubtful whether those who have accepted their beliefs on authority could continue to hold them, if the experience of life appeared flatly to contradict them ; and conversely the extreme tenacity with which Christian beliefs (seriously challenged, very often, by contemporary critical thought) are not uncommonly maintained by those who in the first instance accepted them " merely on authority," is to be explained by the fact that the beliefs in question have mediated to those who entertain them a spiritual experience—valuable and precious beyond everything else which life affords—of the genuineness of which they are quite certain, and with the validity of which they believe the truth of the beliefs in question to be bound up.

It was on an argument of this general kind, based on the pragmatic value of the " faith of the millions " (*i.e.* on the capacity of traditional Catholic doctrine and practice, as shown by experience, to mediate spiritual life), that the late Father George Tyrrell was at one time disposed to attempt to build up a " modernist " apologetic for Catholicism.   And the argument is of value as far as it goes.   It suggests that in such religious beliefs or religious practices as are discovered in experience both to exhibit " survival value," and also to be manifestly fruitful in the mediation of spiritual life of an intrinsically valuable kind, there is enshrined, at the least, some element of truth or of spiritual reality, of which any adequate theology or philosophy of religion must take account. It is the function of theology in this sense to interpret religion, to explain it, without explaining it away.   The argument of Tyrrell at least constitutes a salutary warning against any such premature rationalism as, if accepted, would have the latter effect rather than the former.

But the argument of Tyrrell, while suggesting that in every spiritually vital religious tradition there is *some element* of truth, of which account must be taken, does not obviously justify the intellectual acceptance at face value of the *prima facie* claims of any and every tradition, as such.   The plain man may be provisionally justified in accepting religious beliefs and practices upon the authority of the Church—or more immediately, in actual practice, upon the authority of some particular religious teacher whom he trusts—and may discover in his own subsequent experience of the life of the spirit, as lived upon the basis of such acceptance, a rough working test of the substantial validity and truth of the doctrine in question. But what the plain man is thus enabled directly by experience to attest is rather the spiritual validity of Christianity as a way of life, and the fundamental truth of the spiritual reality behind it, than the strictly intellectual adequacy or truth of the intellectual forms under which he has received it as a dogmatic and institutional tradition. Meanwhile, in the world of our time, all Christian teaching whatever is very definitely under challenge, and the issues are further complicated by the existence of variant forms of the Christian tradition, and of a number of more or less conflicting religious authorities. The plain man may indeed simply choose to abide by the tradition in which he has been personally brought up and which he has to a certain extent " proved " in experience, and to ignore the whole issue which the existence of current contradiction and conflict is otherwise calculated to raise. But a large number of plain men are not able to be thus permanently content with the practice of a religion which they have in no sense thought out, and with the acceptance of doctrines the properly intellectual basis of which they have never considered. They ask for a reason of the hope and of the faith that is in them. In some cases they become conscious of a vocation to serve God with their minds. The mere existence in the world of conflicting religious authorities raises problems enough. It is clear that religious authority has been claimed in different quarters for a large number of statements which, because of their manifest conflict, cannot all of them be equally true, and in some cases are definitely false. No claim has ever been made with more emphasis by religious authority than the modern Roman claim that the Bishop of Rome, under certain narrowly defined conditions, is possessed *ex officio* of a supernatural infalli-bility. The writers of this volume are united in the conviction that the claims made in this respect for the Papacy are in point of fact untrue. The question inevitably arises, What is the ulti-mate relation between authority and truth ? What of the in-tellectually conflicting claims put forward by different self-styled authorities in the sphere of religion ? Or again, What is the strictly rational authority of the main intellectual tradition of Christian theology ?

It is obvious that these questions, when once they are raised, can only be solved, in the case of any given individual mind, on the basis of an act, or a succession of acts, of private judgment. This is true even in the case of an individual whose solution of the problem assumes the form of submission to Rome. There is a recurrent type of mind, fundamentally sceptical and distrustful of reason, and yet craving religious certitude and peace, which will gravitate always towards Rome ; and for minds of this type it is probable that only the Roman Communion is in the long run in a position to cater. The demand of such souls is not for any form of strictly rational or verifiable authority. It is for authority in the form of a purely external and oracular guarantee of intellectual truth, an authority of which the effect, when once its claims have by an initial act of private judgment been definitely acknowledged, shall be to exempt them from any further responsibility of a personal kind for the intellectual truth of the religious beliefs which they entertain. There are indeed good reasons for believing that such a solution is an illegitimate simplification of the intellectual problems involved in religious belief, but it is clearly a solution the attractiveness of which to some minds is exceedingly strong. In the earliest days of Christianity the Church does not appear to have made claims of a kind strictly analogous to those of the Papacy. The modern Roman conception of authority is the result of a development in the direction of rigidity and absoluteness of claim, which appears to have been at least partly the result of reaction from, and opposition to, the religious confusions of Protestantism.

Reaction and antithesis are not commonly the pathways to absolute truth. In any case it would appear to be clear that for the allegiance of those who, in despair of existing confusions, demand simply the kind of authority which, in virtue of the sheer absoluteness of its claim, shall appear to be its own guarantee, independently of any further appeal either to reason or to history, no other Christian communion will ever be in a position effectively to compete with the great and venerable communion of Rome.

The rejection of the claim of the Roman Church to be possessed of authority in the form of what I have ventured to describe as an external and oracular guarantee of the intellectual truth of its doctrines carries with it, in the long run, the rejection of the purely oracular conception of religious authority altogether. Neither the oracular conception of the authority of the Bible, nor that of the authority of the ecumenical Councils and Creeds, is in a position to survive the rejection of the oracular conception of the authority of the Pope. This does not of course mean that the authority either of the Bible, or of the Church, or of the ecumenical Documents and Councils, has ceased to be real. It means only that such authority is no longer to be taken in an oracular sense, and that the final authority is not anything which is either mechanical or merely external, but is rather the intrinsic and self-evidencing authority of truth. It means that authority as such can never be ultimately its own guarantee, that the claims of legitimate authority must always be in the last resort verifiable claims. The final appeal is to the spiritual, intellectual and historical content of divine revelation, *as verifiable at the threefold bar of history, reason and spiritual experience.*

This of course does not mean that the individual is capable in all cases, or in any complete degree, of effecting all these forms of verification for himself. It is the wisdom of the individual to pay reasonable deference to the wider wisdom of the community, and to regard as tentative the conclusions of his individual reason, save in so far as they are confirmed and supported by the corporate mind, as well as by the spiritual experience, not only of himself, but of his fellows. It does mean, however, that there exists a very real recognition and conception of religious authority which is capable of being reconciled with inner freedom, a conception of authority which is capable of forming the basis of such an essentially liberal and evangelical version of Catholicism as that for which the Anglican Communion, at its best, appears ideally to stand. It is not at all true to say that the Church, on such a theory of authority, would be precluded from teaching clearly and dogmatically those foundation truths on which Christianity may be reasonably held to rest. On the contrary, the Church will be enabled to teach doctrine with all the greater confidence in so far as she is content to make an essentially rational appeal—in so far, that is, as her authority is conceived to rest, not simply upon unsupported assertions, but upon the broad basis of continuous verification in reason and experience. The true authority is that which is able to flourish and to maintain itself, not simply under a *régime* of intellectual repression, but in an atmosphere of intellectual and religious freedom. I submit that it should be the aim of the Church so to teach her doctrines as by her very manner of teaching to bear witness to her conviction that they are true, and that they will stand ultimately the test of free enquiry and discussion : to teach them, in other words, not simply as the bare assertions of an essentially unverifiable authority, but as the expression of truths which are capable of being verified—spiritually verified, in some sense, in the experience of all her members ; verified intellectually, as well as spiritually, in the reason and experience of her theologians and thinkers and men of learning.

It is involved in such a conception of Church authority that the tradition of Christian orthodoxy will not be in its essence a merely uncritical handing on of the beliefs and conclusions of the past : it will rather assume the form of the stubborn persistence of a continuously criticised, tested and verified tradition.   I have argued elsewhere [1] that the amount of strictly intellectual and rational authority which attaches to the broad theological consensus of orthodox Christianity is in direct proportion to the extent to which it can be said to represent the conclusions of a genuinely free consensus of competent and adequately Christian minds, and in inverse proportion to the extent to which unanimity is secured only by methods of discipline.   There have been periods and countries in which the expression of unorthodox opinions has been attended by danger, not merely of ecclesiastical penalties, but of physical violence and suffering to those who professed them. To that extent what would otherwise be the overwhelming intellectual and rational authority attaching to the virtually unanimous orthodoxy of such countries and periods requires to be discounted. Nevertheless, intellectual sincerity is a virtue which cannot be wholly eliminated by any system of discipline from the minds of Christian men.   It may fairly be argued that the broad doctrinal tradition of orthodox Christianity has both maintained itself through long periods under considerable intellectual challenge, and has also exhibited very considerable powers of recovery after apparent defeat—a good example being the revival of Nicene and Trinitarian orthodoxy within the Church of England, after the widespread prevalence in intellectual circles, during the eighteenth century, of Deism.   The weight of rational authority attaching to the proposition that Trinitarian orthodoxy represents an intellectually true interpretation of the doctrinal implications of

---

[1] In the Bishop Paddock Lectures for 1923, published by Messrs. Longmans, Green & Co., under the title of *Authority and Freedom*, pp. 14 sqq.

Christianity in respect of the being and nature of God is, on any view, very far from being negligible.

To sum up the argument : The fundamental authority which lies behind the teaching of the Church is the authority of revelation, in the form of the (primarily prophetic) message of the Gospel, which the Church is divinely commissioned to proclaim. The purely dogmatic teaching of the Church represents the statement in intellectual terms of such truths as the Church holds to be either implicit in the truth of the Gospel, or else presupposed by the assumption of the validity of her spiritual life. The weight of intellectual authority which, in the purely rational sense, attaches to such statements is in proportion to the extent to which they represent a genuine consensus of competent and adequately Christian minds.

It will be obvious that, from the point of view of an argument which thus regards rational authority as attaching to statements of doctrine in proportion to the extent of their real acceptance, and to the impressiveness of the consensus which they may be said to represent, the weight of actual authority attaching to particular statements of doctrine will be a matter of degree. The weight of rational authority will be at its maximum in the case of such statements of doctrine as are commonly ranked as " ecumenical," and that on the ground both of the extremely wide consensus of genuinely Christian conviction which lies behind them, and also of the large number of Christian thinkers and theologians by whom they have been sincerely and freely endorsed. It will be at its minimum in the case of doctrines or practices which have either failed to gain wide-spread acceptance, or else are apparently only of temporary, local or insular provenance. Nevertheless, it needs to be recognised that *some* degree of rational authority attaches to every doctrine or practice which at any time or in any place has commanded the serious allegiance of Christians, and in the power of which men have been enabled to have life unto God, and to bring forth the fruits of the Spirit. What is merely sectarian or local need not necessarily be taken into account, indeed, at its own valuation. But it needs to be taken into account, and to have such truth and reality as it in fact represents fairly treated and adequately represented, in whatever may eventually prove to be the ultimate and finally satisfying statement of Christian theology.

H

II

The Authority of the Church
By Wilfred L. Knox

1. *The Divine Commission of the Church*

ALL Christians of whatever shade of belief would agree that the Church, in whatever sense the term is to be interpreted, is a body possessing a divine commission to preach the Gospel to the world. This claim proceeds inevitably from the belief that the one God, who revealed Himself partially to the prophets, law-givers and wise men of the old covenant, revealed Himself fully and finally in the person of Jesus, and continues to speak to mankind through the Holy Spirit, who dwells in the whole Church which is the Body of Christ.   In this sense all Christians would agree that the Church has a divine authority, in virtue of which it can claim the absolute assent of the reason and conscience of all mankind. Unfortunately this agreement does not carry us very far towards solving the many controversies which have arisen with regard to the authority of the Church.   These controversies concern the interpretation of the divine revelation committed to the Church by our Lord, the nature of the body to which He committed that revelation, and the means by which that body is able to formulate the true interpretation of His teaching.   It is with these contro-versial matters that this essay is chiefly concerned.

2. *The " Infallibility " of Scripture*

It will be convenient if we begin by clearing up a controversy which time and the progress of knowledge have solved for all but the blindest partisans.   This is the old controversy as to the position of the Bible in Christian teaching.   The Church from the outset accepted the old Jewish Scriptures and regarded them, just as the Jewish Church had done, as the verbally inspired teaching of God.   It avoided the obvious difficulties of harmonising the letter of the Old Testament with the teaching of Jesus by the use of allegorical interpretations often of a rather desperate character ; in the conditions of human knowledge in the early Christian centuries it had no other means of solving the problem, unless it was prepared to abandon the whole claim that Christianity was the true development of the old Jewish faith. This the Gnostic heretics did ; but their attempt to reject the Old Testament, and where necessary parts of the New, was obviously fatal to the whole belief that Christianity is the one true revelation of God.

To the Old Testament the Church added its own Scriptures, the New Testament. With the origin and formation of the New Testament canon we are not here concerned ; it is sufficient to notice that for centuries before the Reformation the Church had possessed a body of sacred literature, which was universally accepted as divinely inspired and absolutely true, though the most important truth of certain portions might lie in an allegorical rather than in the literal meaning. In order to harmonise the Scriptures with the practice of the Church, as it had developed in the course of history, Catholics claimed that the Bible must be interpreted in the light of ecclesiastical tradition. Although the claim may often have been abused, and although the prevalent conception of the nature of ecclesiastical tradition may have been untenable (a point which will be considered later), there can be no doubt that the Catholic claim, that the Bible without some standard of interpretation cannot be applied to the daily life of the Christian individual or community, was in itself true. The Reformers claimed as against this that the Bible as it stands is the only source of authority for the teaching and practice of the Church. The Reformers were in many cases justified in appealing to the New Testament against the errors of much popular teaching and the abuses of their age ; but the claim that the Bible alone is the final and sufficient guide for Christian belief and morality was entirely untenable. In actual fact it involved not the appeal to the Bible, but the appeal to the Bible as interpreted by the system of some particular Reformer, who claimed that his particular system was the only true interpretation of the Scriptures ; the result was to produce a multitude of warring bodies, each holding to a different system of belief and anathematising all others ; the only ground of agreement being their denunciation of the errors of Rome.

The scientific development of the last century has rendered untenable the whole conception of the Bible as a verbally inspired book, to which we can appeal with absolute certainty for infallible guidance in all matters of faith and conduct. On the one hand the exact meaning of its various parts and the authority which they can claim are matters to be discussed by competent scholars ; it is hardly to be supposed that they will ever reach absolute unanimity as to the various problems which the Scriptures present ; and even such unanimity could only be provisional, for it is essential to scientific thought that it should always contemplate the possibility of further progress. On the other hand the Christian body as a whole needs a standard of faith and life which it can accept as being, if not absolutely true in every sense, yet absolutely adequate as a means of salvation. Obviously this distinction is one which will need careful examination later ; for our present purpose it is sufficient to point out that the Church as a whole, and the individual—at least the individual who is not a highly trained theologian—need some means of deciding precisely what the Christian message is. If the Church is to bring men to God through the person of Jesus, or if the individual is to come to God through Jesus, there must be some means of ascertaining Who Jesus is, and how we are to find Him. It is perfectly possible that many people have found Him by merely reading the Bible ; but it is obvious that we cannot merely hand the Bible to the inquirer, with no further guidance, and be certain that he will find Jesus there aright. In practice the Reformed bodies have attempted to solve the difficulty by drawing up their own confessions of faith ; but the drawing up of such confessions was really an admission of the inadequacy of the Bible, since these confessions, while claiming to be the only true interpretation of Scripture, are found to differ widely in important matters of doctrine. Clearly the claim that the Scriptures alone are a sufficient guide in matters of faith could only be maintained if all impartial inquirers arrived at the same conclusions. It may be added that the measure of agreement to be found in these documents is largely due to the fact that on many points of fundamental importance they adhered to the doctrines of the Catholic Church, which Catholics and Protestants alike believed to be clearly stated in the Scriptures ; in reality, however, these doctrines were only made clear by the earlier developments of Catholic theology. At the time they were not disputed by any party, and were therefore accepted by all as the clear teaching of the Scriptures ; it is now clear that they can only be regarded as the clear teaching of Scripture if it is admitted that the orthodox Catholic interpretation of the Scriptures on these matters in the first four centuries was in fact the correct one.

3. *Nature of the Authority of Scripture*

At the same time all Christians would agree that in some sense the Bible possesses a paramount authority in matters of belief and conduct. Although it can no longer be regarded as a collection of infallible oracles from which it is possible at any moment to draw with certainty a complete answer to any question that may arise, it would be generally admitted that any development of Christian teaching must very largely be judged by its compatibility with the teaching of the Scriptures as a whole. Opinions may differ as to what this teaching is, and how it is to be ascertained; in particular, Christian scholars and teachers, and organised Christian bodies may differ as to which elements both of the Old and New Testaments are to be regarded as of final and permanent importance, and which possess only a local and temporary value ; but it is universally recognised that the Scriptures contain a divine revelation, which in its essential elements lays down the lines which all subsequent developments of Christianity must follow. This authority proceeds from the nature of Scripture itself. The Old Testament shows us the process by which the religion of the Jewish nation was developed from a system of mythology and folk-lore similar to that of the other Semitic nations into a severe monotheism, based on the identification of the nature of God with ethical perfection, and safeguarded by an elaborate religious code from contamination with the lower religious systems of the ancient world. The New Testament contains the history of the full and final revelation of God to man in the person of Jesus, as recorded by the men who had lived under the influence of His earthly life, together with their interpretations of His life and teaching in its bearing on the relations of God to man.

It is impossible to believe that the literature which records and interprets this historical process was compiled by the human authors without a special measure of divine assistance. It is of course possible to deny the account of the origin of the Scriptures given above : but obviously to do so is to reject Christianity as in any sense a divine revelation. If it be accepted, it follows for the Christian that God must have chosen the men who were to carry out the task, and given them special gifts of the Holy Spirit for doing so. This need not imply in any way that they wrote with explicit consciousness of anything but ordinary human motives, or that they were divinely delivered from the possibility of human error. It does imply that these writings possess an inspiration different from that which is to be found in the greatest monuments of human literature and that they contain in substance the record of a divine dispensation to which all subsequent developments of Christianity must conform.

4. *The Method of Christian Development*

Anyone who is acquainted with the methods of modern investigation of the Old Testament recognises that the historical development of Israel was very different from that which the narrative describes. Instead of a series of catastrophic divine revelations to the patriarchs and Moses resulting in the permanent codification of the Jewish system of law and worship, we find a very slow evolution which only reached its final form some three centuries before the Incarnation. Although this evolution was largely due to the work of individuals whose writings we possess, it is obvious that their labours would never have led to any result, if they had not been able to appeal with success to the religious and moral ideas of their contemporaries. Any prophet or reformer in any branch of life depends for his success on his power to commend his message to his hearers. Their response may not be immediate ; but he must in some way gain the assent of those whom he addresses, if his work is not to be an absolute failure. Thus although we may truly say that the development of the Jewish religion was the work of the prophets and law-givers of the nation, yet it is equally true to say that it was the work of the hearers, who accepted the progressive stages of that process of modification which transformed the national faith from the worship of the original tribal deity and such other local deities as attached themselves to the nation in the course of its history into the worship of the one God, who is the Creator and Ruler of the universe.

We see the same process in the history of the earthly teaching of Jesus. Although He taught as one having authority, yet He does not appear as a teacher of a dogmatic system. Even in His ethical teaching He continually appeals to the conscience of His hearers to make it clear that the teaching He gives is the logical conclusion to be drawn from the Mosaic Law as accepted by them.

The first incident in His public ministry which has a really dogmatic importance is the question put to the disciples at Caesarea Philippi. " Who do men say that I am ? " and the subsequent question, " But who say ye that I am ? " The disciples are challenged to say whether in the light of their more intimate experience of His work and teaching they can regard the views of the general public as being in any way adequate ; St. Peter's answer is an admission of their inadequacy, and a confession of the supernatural character of the origin and mission of Jesus, which is the germ of Catholic Christology. Its importance for our present purpose lies in the fact that it is only elicited by our Lord in reply to a question which presupposes some months of experience of His life and teaching ; incidentally it may be noticed that it comes from one of the three disciples who had a more intimate experience of that life and ministry than the rest. A similar phenomenon may be observed with regard to the death of our Lord. It is only after the incident at Caesarea that He prepares His disciples for the shock of His crucifixion ; and although at the moment the blow was too much for their faith, yet it did not completely destroy it. For the disciples were still an united body, apparently looking for some further development when our Lord appeared to them after His resurrection. In other words their experience of Him made it impossible for them to suppose that His death was really, as it seemed, a complete and final catastrophe.

If we examine the later history of the apostolic period we find a similar process of development. The first serious issue of controversy which the Church had to face was that which arose over the admission of uncircumcised Gentiles. Even the autocratic personality of St. Paul could only solve the question when the natural leaders of the Jewish party, St. Peter and St. James, had come to realise that the essential elements of Christianity lay in the new powers bestowed by Jesus on His followers, which rendered it unnecessary to insist on the old methods by which Judaism had preserved itself from heathen contamination. In the later books of the New Testament we see a steady process of development. The Fourth Gospel and the later Pauline Epistles show a marked tendency to appreciate more fully the implications of the belief in the supernatural character of the person of Jesus, and to concentrate the attention of the Church on this aspect of Christianity rather than on the supposed imminence of His return. In other words we see the mind of the Church, as reflected by the writers of these works, developing under the influence of Christian experience.

5. *The Meaning of Christian Experience*

Since the terms " religious experience " or " Christian experience " will play a considerable part in the remainder of this essay, it will perhaps be well to explain at this point the exact sense in which they will be used. By Christian experience is meant that apprehension of God through the person of Christ which is vouchsafed to all Christians who in any way attempt to live up to the standard of their profession. It may be no more than an experience of power to overcome temptation and to advance in the direction of Christian holiness in however rudimentary a degree. It includes any sense of communion with God in prayer and worship, whether that sense of union is of the elementary type described by theologians as " sensible devotion " or rises to the higher forms of prayer to which the great mystics have attained. It covers also such indirect forms of communion with God as the sense of deliverance from the burden of sin. To a greater or less extent, according to the religious development of the believer and his power to adjust his religious beliefs to his daily life, it covers the whole of his outlook upon the world in general. It is not in any way confined to any kind of mystical experience of God, nor yet to that " sensible devotion " which a certain type of modern theology seems to regard as the main element of religion. The person who finds no particular consolation in his prayers, but only knows that by using the means of grace he is able to attain to a higher standard of life than he would otherwise achieve, has a Christian experience as genuine as the greatest mystic, though of a much lower degree of intensity. On the other hand the higher forms of experience of God through our Lord are an important part of the whole sum of Christian experience, though not the whole of it.

Clearly from the Christian point of view religious experience cannot be treated as a purely natural phenomenon. It is the knowledge of God vouchsafed to man by the power of divine grace and the illumination of the Holy Spirit. Its method of operation has already been indicated in the foregoing section. The reforms of the religion of Israel by prophets and lawgivers were the result of their own personal experience of God, achieved by prayer and reflection on the nature of the divine Being. In the case of many of them it is obvious that the experience of God was of a peculiarly intense character. In the same way their ability to commend their message to their hearers depended on the fact that the latter had, in however elementary a form, some sort of consciousness of the nature of God, in virtue of which they were able to recognise the truth of the prophetic message. Naturally this recognition was only slowly effected, since the hearers as a rule possessed a far more limited consciousness of God than the prophet ; often no doubt it took several generations to enable the mass of the nation to assimilate even the general outlines of his teaching. But without some religious experience of however elementary a kind in their hearers the prophets would have had nothing to appeal to.

The same phenomenon appears in the New Testament. Our Lord appeals, as has been noticed above, to the religious consciousness of those brought up in the atmosphere of prophetic teaching and ardent Messianic expectation which prevailed in Galilee in His days. On the basis of this religious experience He builds up His own exposition of the true nature of the Kingdom of God, primarily in His disciples, but to a lesser extent in the general body of His hearers. In appealing to the Gentiles, St. Paul appeals to a religious experience already moulded either by familiarity with the Judaism of the synagogues of the Dispersion, or in a few cases by the highest religious teachings of Gentile philosophy. In both cases his main appeal is to a sense of sin as a barrier between man and God, and the impotence of Judaism or of human wisdom to provide a means of escape from it. His teaching is to a peculiar degree modelled on his own religious experience, especially on his conversion ; but it necessarily appeals to the religious experience of his hearers, however slight that experience may have been at the moment when he first addressed them.

6 *Religious Experience and the Development of Christian Doctrine*

In modern controversies on the subject of the nature of Christian authority and the proper organisation for its exercise, the part played by Christian experience has often been overlooked.

It may be doubted whether the sterility of these controversies has not in part at least been due to the omission. In the actual history of the process by which the historical system of Catholic Christianity has been built up the part of the general religious experience of the whole body of Christians has necessarily been of primary importance. The actual formation of the canon of the New Testament was almost entirely due to the general sense of the Christian communities of the first two centuries. Books were indeed often admitted because they were believed to be the work of Apostles, but others were rejected although they bore no less venerable names. But although the reason for their rejection was the belief that they were spurious, yet in an age which had little knowledge of critical methods the main test of authenticity was whether the doctrines laid down in such books were a correct interpretation of the implications of the religious experience of the Christian body as a whole. In certain cases, indeed, we find appeals to a supposed body of unwritten teaching left by the Apostles ; but although much teaching given by the Apostles must have been left unrecorded, there is no evidence whatsoever that there was any coherent body of traditional teaching which has not survived. The appeal is fairly frequently met with in the first three Christian centuries, especially in the controversies of the Church with Docetism and Gnosticism. But while it cannot be justified in this form, yet it represents a quite legitimate appeal to that interpretation of the original deposit of Christian doctrine to be found in the canonical books of the New Testament, which was vouched for by the Christian experience of the Church in all places and in all generations since the Incarnation. The importance attached in these centuries to certain sees which claimed apostolic founders was not justified, in so far as it was claimed that they possessed over and above the written records of the New Testament a further body of apostolic doctrine ; it was justified in so far as the circumstances of their foundation and early history guaranteed that the Christian consciousness of those Churches had from the first rested on a basis of orthodox Christian teaching.

It may indeed be said that in these centuries it was mainly due to the general religious sense of the Christian community that these entirely destructive heresies were eliminated from the Church. Although we possess the names and writings of some of the orthodox theologians of the time, it may well be doubted whether their labours would, from a purely intellectual point of view, have won the victory. On the other hand, their attitude was felt to represent the true development of the original deposit of the Christian faith, while the doctrines of the various heresi-archs were rightly rejected as alien additions or false interpreta-tions which were fatal to that religious experience which the faithful felt themselves to have enjoyed in the Church. This reason for the rejection of these doctrines was perfectly legitimate. The claim of a religion to acceptance lies in its power to awaken religious experience in the believer — naturally the Christian claims that Christianity is unique in respect both of the nature of the experience it conveys and of the manner in which it conveys it. A doctrine which is fatal to the enjoyment of that experience must be rejected, unless we are to admit that the experience was an illusion, and to abandon the religion which appeared to convey it. This, of course, does not mean that the individual's judgment as to a particular doctrine is necessarily correct. On the other hand, the rejection of a false doctrine or the establishment of a true one can never be the work of an individual. Even when it is largely due to the labours of an individual theologian the reason for the success of his labours must in all cases be the fact that he has succeeded in commending his teaching to the general Christian consciousness. Just as the success of the Jewish prophet depended on his ability to commend his view of God to the nation, so the Christian teacher must commend his doctrine to the Christian consciousness as a whole, if his labours are not to perish. For our present purpose the point of primary interest is that in the first three centuries the Church overcame the gravest perils that ever faced her without any organised method of formulating the true developments of doctrine or rejecting the false ones by the instinc-tive action of the corporate consciousness of the Christian body as a whole. The orthodox Church proved the truth of its teaching by its survival : the falsehood of rival forms of teaching was proved by their disappearance.

7. *The Formulation of Christian Doctrine*

It is clear, however, that the general Christian consciousness is by itself a vague and fluctuating mass of individual opinions, approximating in each case to the truth, yet perhaps in no case fully grasping the whole truth with no admixture of error. Even in the most rigidly orthodox body of Christians different individuals will base their religious life more definitely on some elements of the whole Christian system than on others. A Christian who could grasp not only in theory but in the practice of his life the whole system of Christian teaching in all its fulness and with no admixture of error would obviously be a perfect saint and a perfect theologian ; he would indeed see the truth as it is present to the mind of God and correspond with it perfectly: for moral failure inevitably carries with it failure to apprehend the truth. The whole sum of the Christian experience of the Church at any given moment must be an inarticulate mass of opinion comprehending in general the whole body of divine truth as revealed in Jesus ; its only way of articulating itself will be its power to express approval of some particular statement of the faith as put forward by an individual theologian, unless the Church is to have some means for expressing its corporate voice. Hence it was natural that with the ending of the ages of persecution the Church should find some means of articulating her teaching and putting into a coherent form the sense in which she interpreted in the light of Christian experience the original deposit of faith which she had received from her Lord.

We are not here concerned with the history of the Councils which decided the great Christological controversies, nor yet with the process by which the decisive influence in all matters of doctrine passed, at the cost of the Great Schism between the East and West, into the hands of the Papacy. The important matter for our present purpose is to consider the claims which are made on behalf of the various definitions of Christian doctrine by bodies claiming to voice the authority of the Holy Ghost speaking through the Church, and the sense in which those claims can be regarded as justified.

It has in many if not in all cases been claimed that the various doctrinal pronouncements of Councils and Popes are simply the affirmation of what the Church has always believed. In the strict sense the claim cannot be maintained ; for it is easy to find cases in which theologians of the most unquestioned orthodoxy put forward doctrines which were subsequently condemned, or re-jected doctrines which were subsequently affirmed as parts of the Catholic faith. Hence it is now generally admitted that such pronouncements are to be regarded as affirmations in an explicit form of some truth which was from the outset implied in the original deposit of the Christian revelation, though hitherto not explicitly realised. This claim is in itself a perfectly reasonable one. For the Christian revelation begins with the life of Jesus, presenting itself as a challenge first to the Jewish nation and then through His Apostles to the whole world, not with the formulation of a dogmatic system. It was only when Christian thought began to speculate on the whole subject of the relations of God to man and man to God implied in that revelation that the need was felt for some body of authoritative teaching which would serve both to delimit the Christian faith from other religions and to rule out lines of speculation which were seen, or instinctively felt, to be fatal to the presuppositions on which the religious experience of the Christian body rested. It should be borne in mind that the great majority of authoritative statements of doctrine have been of the latter kind, and that they usually aimed rather at excluding some particular doctrinal tendency, which was seen to be fatal to the Christian life, than at promulgating a truth not hitherto generally held.

In this sense it seems impossible to deny that the Church ought to possess some means for formulating her teaching, which will enable her to adjust that teaching to the developments of human thought, while eliminating doctrines which would, if generally accepted, prove fatal to the preservation and propagation of the life of union with God through the person of our Lord, which it is her duty to convey to mankind. It might indeed be argued that even without such means for formulating her teaching the Church did in the first three centuries eliminate several strains of false teaching, which would appear on the surface to be more fatal to the specifically Christian religious experience than any which have threatened her in later ages. It must however be remembered that unless the Church has some means of defining her teaching in the face of error there is always a grave danger that the simple may make shipwreck concerning the faith. This might not be a very serious matter, if we were merely concerned with intellectual error as to some abstruse point of theology ; the danger is that large numbers of the faithful may fall into conceptions of the nature of God which are fatal to the attainment by them of the specifically Christian character and the specifically Christian religious experience. Even though in the long run the truth should, by the action of the Holy Ghost on the whole Christian body, succeed in overcoming error, the Church is bound to exercise the authority given to her by our Lord in order to preserve her children from this danger. If this account of the reasons which underlie the formulation of the teaching of the Church be accepted, certain conclusions will follow. The organ through which the Church pronounces must be in a position to judge correctly what the Christian religious experience really is. This involves not merely intellectual capacity to understand the meaning of any doctrine and its relation to the rest of the Christian system, but also that insight into the Christian character which is only derived from a genuine attempt to live the Christian life. The same applies to all theological thought : Christian theology no less than other sciences has suffered profoundly from the disputes of theologians and authorities who, often unconsciously, confused the attainment of truth with the gratification of the natural human desire to achieve victory in controversy or the natural human reluctance to admit an error.

It is however more important for our present purpose to observe that if the authority of the Church is to decide whether a particular doctrine is compatible with the religious experience of the whole Christian body, it must be able to ascertain what the religious experience of the whole body really is. In other words it must be able to appeal not merely to the religious consciousness of a few individuals, however eminent they may be in respect of sanctity or learning. So far as is possible, it must be able to appeal to the whole body of the faithful in all places and in all generations It must inquire whether any particular form of teaching is compatible with that experience of union with God through our Lord which all generations and nations of Christians believe themselves to have enjoyed ; whether it is implied in it or whether it definitely destroys it. The extent to which any pronouncement can claim to be authoritative will depend on the extent to which it can really appeal to a wide consensus of Christian experience representing the infinite variety of the types of man who have found salvation in Christ. Naturally it will not be content merely with counting numbers ; it is also necessary to consider how far the consensus of the faithful on any given matter represents the free assent of men who were able to judge, or on the other hand merely represents the enforced consent of those who either through ignorance or even through political pressure were more or less compelled to accept the faith as it was given to them.

8. *The Claims of Catholic Authority*

It is from this point of view that the claims of the Catholic tradition are most impressive. For it cannot be denied that the Catholic tradition of faith and devotion manifests continuous development reaching back to the origins of Christianity. In spite of wide divergences in its external presentation of religion, it can show a fundamental unity of religious experience throughout all ages and all nations of the world, reaching back to the times when the Church had to propagate her teaching in the face of the bitter persecution of the State. Although in later times the Catholic Church has lost her visible unity, yet the general system of Catholic life and worship has shown its power to survive and even to revive from apparent death. The exercise of the authority of the Church has indeed been impaired by the divisions of the Church ; but the general unity of the trend of Catholic development in spite of these divisions is an impressive testimony to the foundations laid in the period of her unity.

None the less it is necessary to inquire exactly what measure of assent may be claimed for those definitions of doctrine which have the authority of the undivided Church, and how we may recognise those pronouncements which really have the highest kind of authority. It is usually held that any definition of doctrine promulgated by a Council which can really claim to speak in the name of the whole Church, as a doctrine to be accepted by all Christians, is to be regarded as the voice of the Holy Ghost speaking through the Church, and is therefore infallible. The same claim is made by those who accept the modern Roman position for pronouncements made by the Pope, in his character of supreme Pastor of the whole Church, on matters of faith and morals. The exact extent to which any pronouncement, whatever the weight of authority behind it, can be regarded as infallible will be considered in the following section. It is however convenient to consider first the whole conception of authority as residing in the nature of the organ which claims to speak with final authority. From this point of view it is in the first instance only possible to defend the claim that any organ can claim infallibility by means of the distinction generally drawn between doctrinal definitions which all Christians are bound to believe and disciplinary regulations intended to govern the details of ecclesiastical procedure and the popular exposition of the Christian faith. In itself the distinction is a sound one ; for it is reasonable that the Church should have the right to exercise some control over such matters as the conduct of Christian worship and also the teaching of the Christian faith. For instance, it may be desirable to control the extent to which new teaching, which at first sight seems difficult to reconcile with existing beliefs, should be expounded to entirely ignorant audiences. A further complication arises from the fact that it is by no means always clear whether a particular organ has the right to speak, or is at any given moment speaking in the name of the whole Church. For instance, there are numerous cases in which bodies professing themselves to be general Councils have promulgated decisions which have since been seen to be untenable. It is usually said that these bodies were not in fact general Councils at all. The same difficulty applies under modern Roman theories to papal pronouncements, for it is difficult to say with precision which pronouncements on the part of the Papacy are promulgated with the supreme authority of the Holy See and which are only uttered with the lesser authority of disciplinary pronouncements. Hence it has happened in the past that the decisions of Councils which claimed to be general Councils have been reversed by Popes or later Councils, and that papal decisions have been tacitly abandoned. Thus in fact the mere nature of the authority which utters a decision, whether Pope or Council, is by itself of no value as a test of infallibility.

If in fact we inquire what decisions made by authorities claiming to speak for the whole Church are generally regarded as infallible, we shall find that they are those which have won the general assent of the whole Christian body, or, as in the case of more modern Roman pronouncements, of a part of that body which claims to be the whole. It has been urged above that the function of authority in the Church is to formulate and render explicit, where need arises, truths implied in the spiritual experience of the Christian consciousness, and it is therefore not unnatural to suspect that the measure of truth, which any such pronouncement can claim, is to be tested by the extent to which after its promulgation it commends itself to the authority which it claims to represent. In point of fact it is manifest that this is what has actually taken place. Pronouncements which have in fact commended themselves to the general Christian consciousness have gained universal acceptance and have come to be regarded as expressing the voice of the whole Church. Those which have been found in practice to be inadequate, or have been shown to be untenable by the advance of human knowledge, have been relegated to the rank of temporary and disciplinary pronouncements, or else the body which promulgated them has been held not to have spoken in the name of the whole Church, sometimes at the cost of a considerable straining of the facts of history.

It seems however more reasonable to recognise the facts rather than to strain them in order to suit a preconceived idea of what the authority of the Church should be. From this point of view it would appear that just as the inherent authority of a particular pronouncement depends on the extent to which it really represents a wide consensus of Christian experience, so the proof of that authority will lie in the extent to which it commends itself by its power to survive as a living element in the consciousness of the whole Christian body. Its claim to validity will depend very largely on the extent to which that body is free to accept it or not, and also on the extent to which it is competent to judge of the matter. It will be observed that this does not imply that the truth of a pronouncement is derived from its subsequent acceptance by the faithful. Obviously truth is an inherent quality, due to the fact that the Holy Ghost has enabled the authority which speaks in the name of the Church to interpret aright the truth revealed by our Lord and realised in the devotional experience of the Church, and to formulate that truth correctly. But the test of any individual pronouncement, by which it can be judged whether it possesses the inherent quality of truth or not, will be its power to survive and exercise a living influence on the general consciousness of Christendom over a wide area of space and time.

9. *The Certainty of the Catholic Tradition*

At this point the obvious objection will be raised that on the theory outlined above the Christian will at any given moment be unable to know precisely what he is bound to believe. He will never know whether a particular doctrine, which has for centuries enjoyed a wide veneration, but has in later days come to be assailed, is really as true as it seems to be. This objection is often raised in controversy from the Roman Catholic side and has a specious sound. In reality its apparent force is due to the fact that it rests on a confusion of thought. For it confuses the act of faith by which the individual submits his mind and conscience to the authority of Jesus in the Catholic Church with the quite different act of acceptance of the whole system of truth as the Church teaches it at any given moment. The first of these two acts is necessarily an act of private judgment pure and simple. The individual can only accept the faith on the ground of his own purely personal conviction that it is true, although that conviction may be very largely determined by the fact that the faith is accepted by others, and by the impressive spectacle of the faith of the Catholic Church. The second act is a surrender of the private judgment by which the individual, having decided that the Catholic faith as a whole is true, proceeds to accept from the Church the detailed filling-in of the main outlines which he has already accepted.

Now on the theory put forward in this essay the position of the individual is no worse than it is on the most ultramontane theory of ecclesiastical authority. For the determining factor in his acceptance of the Catholic system will be, as it must always be, the belief that it is the truest, and ultimately the only true, account of the relations of God to man. This act of faith, rendered possible by a gift of divine grace, can never rest on anything but the personal judgment that the Catholic system as a whole is true. As regards the structure of Christian doctrine he will find, precisely as he does at present, a large body of doctrine and ethical teaching which is set before him with very varying degrees of authority. Some elements in the system will present themselves to him with a vast amount of testimony to their proved efficacy as means for enabling the believer to attain to the genuine religious experience of Christianity, in other words to realise communion with God through the Person of Jesus, dating back to the most venerable ages of the history of the Church. Some, on the other hand, will present themselves as no more than minor local regulations, judged desirable by the Church as aids to his private devotion. Between these two extremes there will lie a certain amount of teaching which presents itself to him with varying degrees of authority. This he will accept as true on the authority of the Church ; and unless he be a competent theologian he has no need to trouble himself about it. He will know that it has behind it the guarantee that it has proved fruitful as an aid to the development of the Christian life ; and even if he is unable to find in some parts of it any assistance for his personal devotion, he will be content to recognise their value for others. If, on the other hand, he be a theologian, he will still respect the various elements in the Catholic system as a whole merely on the strength of the fact that they form a part of so venerable a structure. Further, he will recognise that every part, in so far as it has in practice served to foster the spiritual life of the Church, contains an element of truth which all theological inquiry must account for. The greater the extent to which it has served that purpose, the greater will be the respect he will accord it. At the same time he will regard the Catholic faith as an organic whole, the truth of which is guaranteed more by its intrinsic value as proved by past experience than by the oracular infallibility of certain isolated definitions. He will indeed reverence such definitions, and he will reverence them the more in proportion to the extent and the quality of the assent they can claim. But he will recognise that their claim to be regarded as absolutely and finally true is not a matter of absolute certainty or of primary importance. It may be that the progress of human knowledge will lead to a better formulation of the most venerable articles of the faith ; but it will always preserve those elements in them which are the true cause of their power to preserve and promote the devotional life of the Catholic Church. It will be observed that in acting thus he will be acting precisely as the investigator does in any branch of science, who recognises that any new advance he may make must include all the elements of permanent truth discovered by his predecessors in the same field, even though it may show that their discoveries had not the absolute truth originally supposed.

It should further be observed that the theologian will recognise that any formulation of doctrine by the Church has the highest claim on his respect. Even if he cannot hold its absolute truth, he will realise that it contains an element of truth which any new definition must preserve, and he will also respect the right of the Church to restrain him from putting forward his own views, where they differ from the authoritative statements of the Church in such a manner as to disturb the faith of the simple or to lead to unedifying controversy. He will admit that the mere fact that a particular statement has been solemnly put forward by the whole Christian body creates a strong presumption in favour of its embodying a very high degree of truth, and will be careful to avoid the danger of denying the truth which a formula contains, even if the formula seems to him to be defective.

It will certainly be objected that this view leaves the door open to " Modernism." The answer is that Modernism as hitherto expounded has obviously undermined the foundations on which Christian experience rests. If a new type of Modernism were advanced, it would either have the same effect or it would not. If it did not (we need not concern ourselves with the question of the possibility of such an hypothesis), there seems no reason to deny that it would be a valid restatement of the essential truth of the Catholic system, and it would stand simply as a more accurate statement of those truths which it is the function of the Church to teach to her children in order to attain to salvation through Jesus.

It may be added that the fear of " Modernism " seems to suggest a lack of trust in the power of the Church to eliminate false teaching from her system. It may be desirable to restrain the dissemination of teaching of an unsettling kind ; but the Christian should have sufficient confidence in the inherent strength of the Catholic system to view with equanimity the exploration of every possible avenue of inquiry. If a particular line of thought is really, as it seems to him at the moment, fatal to the whole content of Christian devotion, it will certainly come to nought. If his fears are unfounded, it can only lead to a fresh apprehension of the truth and the enrichment of Christian devotion.

NOTES

1. The Holy Roman Church

Anglicans have tended in the past to a rather facile depreciation of the claims of the See of Peter. It must be admitted that the aggrandising policy of certain Popes was largely responsible for the division of Christendom ; but it must also be admitted that the

See of Constantinople was by no means free of blame in the matter. In the same way the papal court was largely responsible for the rejection of the demands of the more moderate Reformers ; but the excesses of the Protestant leaders rendered the preservation of Christian unity impossible. If the general position put forward in this essay be accepted, it will follow that there is some error in the claims usually made on behalf of the Papacy, in view of their proved tendency to destroy the unity of Christendom, but also an element of truth in that devotion to the Holy See which has done so much to preserve the Catholic faith in Western Europe.

As regards scriptural authority the Petrine claims cannot claim to be more than a development of the commission given by our Lord to St. Peter and the position held by him in the primitive Church ; it is only by the results that we can judge whether they are a legitimate development or not. Hence controversies as to their exact meaning are bound to prove futile. In general it may be said that the question at issue is whether the Papacy is to be regarded as the organ through which the Holy Ghost speaks directly to the whole Church, or whether it is the organ for articulating the experience of the Christian body as a whole, that experience being produced by the influence of the Holy Ghost on the corporate consciousness of the Church. It may seem that this is a somewhat subtle distinction ; but it is one of supreme practical importance. From the former conception is derived the tendency to regard the Pope as an autocratic ruler of the Church, responsible to God alone ; he has only to speak and the faithful are bound to obey. From the latter point of view the Pope is the representative of the whole Church, whose function is not to promulgate truth but to regulate the general line of Christian thought in so far as it may be necessary to save the simple from the disturbing effects of false teaching and to preserve that measure of uniformity in matters of faith and conduct which is necessary to the welfare of the Church. In this case he is to be regarded as holding a pastoral office as first among his brothers the Bishops of the Catholic Church. At the present time it is impossible to say which of these conceptions is the true one from the Roman point of view. Either can be made consistent with the definitions of the Vatican Council, and both are held in different quarters within the Roman Communion. It is clear that the former view is entirely incompatible with the position advanced in this essay ; but that does not justify

Anglicans in refusing to recognise the element of truth which may be claimed for the Papacy if it be regarded in the latter light. There can be no doubt that the Holy See has on many occasions preserved Catholicism from the gravest dangers ; but it has always done so by acting as the voice of the Christian community in general as against fashionable errors. It is when the Papacy has claimed to speak with the direct authority of the Holy Ghost and without reference to Christendom as a whole that it has aroused that hostility which has led to or kept alive the disruption of Christendom. In any question of reunion the vital issue is whether the Church can be safeguarded against that natural tendency to self-aggrandisement which is the besetting vice of all human institutions, and which has caused the Papacy to claim prerogatives which large bodies of Christians have felt bound to reject. But such a rejection of autocratic claims need not involve the rejection of the view that the Papacy has a special function to fulfil in the life of the Church. Further, just as the authority of the episcopate is held to be *de jure divino* on the ground that by a process of legitimate development the episcopate has become the repository of the authority given to the Apostles, so it might be held that the Papacy possesses authority *de jure divino* as having become by a similar process the repository of a primacy held by St. Peter. Anglican theologians can and should be prepared to discuss this possibility with an open mind. But while doing so they cannot concede the actual claims made or presupposed by the majority of Roman theologians in regard to the position and authority of the Papacy.

2. The Religious Experience of Protestantism

In this essay for the most part only the religious experience of Catholicism has been considered. Obviously, however, the various schools of Protestantism have in history proved for many a means of access to God through the person of our Lord of a very genuine kind. On the other hand, it is to be observed that the dogmatic systems of historical Protestantism are showing a tendency to disappear, if they have not already been tacitly abandoned. This fact shows that the element of permanent value in them was not the dogmatic systems which the original Reformers regarded as essential. This, however, is not intended to deny or to belittle the importance of the religious experience of historical Protestantism. It must, however, be observed that much of it has been drawn from its insistence on the power of the believer to enter into immediate personal communion with God through Christ, and its strong personal devotion to the humanity of our Lord. But these or similar features of historical Protestantism are simply aspects of the Catholic faith, which the Reformers regarded as having been obscured by the Catholicism of the time. It must be admitted that to a very large extent they were right in thinking so. Yet, in so far as it is these elements of Protestantism which have in the past given it value as a means of providing the Protestant with the experience of Christian devotion, and are still in fact a living force in the Protestant bodies, the strength of Protestantism lies in the fact that it emphasises certain elements of Catholicism. Further, Protestantism, although in its positive dogmatic systems it failed to establish any final truth, may claim to have rendered a genuine service to Christianity by showing the untenable character of much of the old tradition of Catholicism, and by its insistence on the necessity of justifying Christian doctrine by the appeal to the Scriptures and to human reason. In the sweeping away of false conceptions, and establishing a truer conception of the nature of the means by which truth is to be apprehended, Protestantism has played a vital part in the life of the Church and the progress of mankind.

THE CHRISTIAN CONCEPTION
OF GOD
BY LIONEL SPENCER THORNTON

CONTENTS

" THE God of Abraham and the God of Isaac and the God of Jacob. . . . He is not the God of the dead, but of the living ; for all live unto him." These words of our Lord take us to the heart of the Bible and the revelation which it records. The Christian's God is One who has to do with living men because He is Himself the living God. He is the Covenant-God who enters into the course of history and communicates the knowledge of Himself in a special way to a particular people, at first partially and in various stages, then finally and completely in the Person of Jesus Christ. All this is without prejudice to the truth that there is a wider and more general revelation of God given to all men, to which all religions bear witness, whose evidences are written in the book of nature and upon every human heart. If we claim that in the religious history of our race a special revelation occupies the foreground of the picture, nothing is to be gained by overlooking this far-stretching background. Yet from the point of view of historic Christianity the Gospel provides the clue which alone can interpret the riddle of God's world-wide Self-revelation.

The argument of this essay starts from the conclusions reached in a preceding essay on " The Vindication of Religion." Assuming the truth of theism, we are concerned with the content of that conception of God which the Christian Church has received. The subject falls naturally into two main parts : (i) The attributes of God ; (ii) The Holy Trinity. In discussing these subjects certain pressing questions of current thought will be kept in view, such as the idea of revelation, the possibility of reconciling different aspects in the traditional doctrine of God, and the meaning of personality in God.

I

THE ATTRIBUTES OF GOD

1. *The Contrasted Aspects of Deity*

When religion is traced back to its beginnings in the history of man, nothing is more striking than the dominating position which it appears to occupy. Religion is the thread upon which are strung whole systems of cultus, custom and taboo, tribal morality and mythological explanation. Thus from its first appearance religion is concerned with the whole man and with the whole of human life. But again the first stirrings of the religious impulse appear to take the form of definite emotional moods in which man reacts to the mystery in his environment and to the mystery in his own life. Doubtless there were even in man's primitive experience a variety of emotional moods and attitudes of this general character. But all varieties ultimately resolve themselves into two main types of attitude. The object of man's worship is terrible and awe-inspiring and yet in other moods is felt to be protective and friendly. Religion means abasement before divine majesty and yet fascination which draws men to seek communion with the divine. The religious revelation given to Israel emerges out of this dim background and continues in its progress to exhibit these general characteristics. There is the religious fear awakened by local theophanies or manifestations of deity, or again by the infringement of some taboo ; and on the other hand there are homely and joyful festivals at the local shrines. Yahweh is revealed in fire, thunder, and storm-cloud. He marches with the tribes to the destruction of his enemies ; He is a jealous God. But there is also another picture : the God who enters into friendly covenant with patriarchs and kings, who promises protection and blessing to the race. When Hebrew religion rises to the level of theism we still find these contrasted aspects of majesty on the one hand and homely intimacy on the other. But the combination attains a new significance. For in the development of prophetic monotheism the majesty of God is seen ever more and more clearly to transcend the crude imaginations and limited horizons of primitive religious thought until He is known in prophetic faith to be the perfectly holy and righteous God who rules all the nations, the Creator of heaven and earth. Yet this revelation of divine transcendence does not crush out the more homely aspects of religion. Rather those aspects are purified of their grosser elements and reappear in deeper and more penetrating forms.

Meanwhile the religion of Israel, like other religions, concerned itself with a people and all its national and local interests. But, unlike most other religions, it overleapt the boundaries of these restricted interests and preoccupations and provided an interpretation of Israel's history and destiny which gave to that people an unparalleled consciousness of divine mission and religious vocation. All the changing events of national experience are woven into the texture of this historical interpretation by a long succession of prophets and prophetic writers.   Like other Semitic peoples they explained all events in terms of direct causation by the will of the deity.   But the action of the divine will is related to a moral purpose which has nothing capricious or arbitrary about it.   It is this purpose which gives unity and significance to history and to Israel's part in history.   Thus through a prophetic interpretation of history in terms of divine purpose there is a steady enlargement of horizon and an enrichment in the content of religion and of religious ideas.   The horizon is enlarged to include all events, international as well as national, within the scope of divine government.   National interests are thus transcended and moral interests are made supreme.   Once this point is reached, it involves a great deal more.   The Lord of history is the moral Governor of the world, the Creator of the universe, the only true object of worship. Thus religion is enriched by entering into partnership with morality and reason, and a conception of God is reached which can satisfy all the awakening faculties of man.   For in the last resort the higher needs of man cannot be separated.   We cannot rest permanently in a moral revelation however sublime, unless it expresses the character of One who is the ground of our lives and of the universe in which we live.   Nor could we yield the fullest worship of heart and reason to a Being who did not manifest His will in the form of a moral purpose controlling and overruling the course of events by which our destinies are shaped.

Now without going further at this stage into the biblical conception of God, we can see that the broad facts of Hebrew monotheism have already decided some of the conditions of our knowledge of God and the limitations which the subject imposes upon human language.   For the God who is disclosed to us in Old Testament prophecy is already in effect the God of Christian theism.   He is the supreme Reality behind all the phenomena of sense and the source of all intuitions of the human spirit.   The external world-process and the interior world of human experience must both alike be traced to Him.   The religious impulse can find adequate satisfaction only in such a God—One who is the ground of all forms of our experience, emotional, moral and rational.   Consequently, when we try to state the content of our conception of God, such a statement must be in terms which cover all the various fields of our experience.   Now since there is a great diversity in the forms of human experience, our approach to the idea of God must be made along a number of different lines, each of which is an attempt to give rational form to some definite part of experience.   These different lines of approach give us what are called the attributes of God.   We can never attain to a completely synthetic view of what God has revealed Himself to be.   For that would involve a level of unified knowledge which can belong to none but to God Himself.   Such a simple and simultaneous knowledge of what God is must exist in God Himself.   But we on our part must be content to approach the sanctuary from the outside and from a number of different points of view.   But if this is our necessary starting-point it is also true that as we seek to penetrate from the circumference to the centre we find the lines of approach to be convergent.   Contrasted attributes are really interdependent and are mutually necessary to one another.   But here the proportion of truth often suffers from the inadequacy of our minds to grasp the whole.   All words that we can use are inadequate and more or less anthropomorphic in character, relating God either by affirmation or negation to human experience.   We cannot avoid this difficulty.   But it calls for a severe discipline of the mind and not least by criticism of such conventions of thought as happen to be familiar or congenial to ourselves or to the age in which we live.   For example, it has often been too readily assumed that, in dealing with moral qualities or categories which enter deeply into human experience, transference of such ideas from a human to a divine context can be effected with security in proportion to the familiarity of the ideas.   It has sometimes escaped men's observation that they have been defective in their grasp upon those very ideas from which they have argued.   Failure to realise this has been in part due to that very familiarity which has been the ground of confidence.   It is easy to detect this danger in the thought of the past.   It is not so easy to remember that it is still operative. When we look back over Christian thought about God we see, in different ages of history, special prominence given to this or that particular idea.   Thus we have the impassible divine substance or nature of Greek theology, the conceptions of legal justice which have characterised Latin theology through many centuries of its history, or again ideas of the omnipotent sovereign will of God dominating men's minds in the age of the Renaissance and the Reformation. The currents of thought in our own age are running strongly in other directions and largely in reaction from these ideas. In the necessary reconstruction we must needs be on our guard against being content with a mere swing of the theological pendulum, replacing the ideas of Augustine, Anselm, and Calvin by some modern version of Marcion's gospel.

2. *The Development of these Contrasts*

If we return now to our starting-point, the characteristics of Hebrew monotheism as it emerged from its origins in more primitive religion, there is another characteristic which needs further consideration. Reference has been made to two contrasted aspects of deity which are clearly developed in Hebrew prophecy, but which can be traced back to two different kinds of emotional mood everywhere present and operative in the religious experience of mankind. The contrast in question—between the majesty of God on the one hand and His willingness to enter into intimate relations with His creatures on the other—is one which can be traced through the whole course of revelation in the Scriptures. God is holy and righteous, yet also loving and gracious. He is Judge and King, yet also Father and Saviour. He is Creator of the world and Sovereign over the nations, yet He dwells with the humble and lowly in heart and the contrite in spirit. But once more, these ideas are not simply held in contrast. Again and again they are blended in one experience. In the experience portrayed in Psalm cxxxix. the writer's conviction of God's nearness to and knowledge of his own soul is blended with a parallel conviction of God's omnipresence and omniscience with regard to the world as a whole ; and the two ideas appear to reinforce one another in his mind. In the book of Job, which perhaps more than any other part of Scripture emphasises the inscrutable majesty and power of the Creator, it is precisely by a revelation of this aspect of the Godhead that an answer is given to all Job's searching questions about the divine handling of his individual life. Moreover, this experience of Job's is in line with the experiences through which some of the great prophets received their call. Isaiah and Ezekiel witness a theophany of the divine holiness and glory and then a Voice speaks to them and they are given a personal mission.

As the revelation of God to Israel moved forward it became more universal in form and at the same time more effectively concerned with individual worth and destiny, more penetrative of the spirit of man and on the other hand more transcendent of this world-order.   When we pass to the New Testament and the teaching of our Lord, we find that the heavenly Father of whom He spoke stands in a universal relationship to all men without respect of persons.   Yet this relationship reaches to the heart of man more completely than was possible under the Old Covenant.   The souls of sinful men and women are now set in concentrated rays of light and seen to be mysterious treasure, over which the Heart of God yearns and travails.   Moreover, these things are not simply set forth in idea.   They are already in operation.   They are part of the hidden reality of a Kingdom, which is here and now present as the action of God upon the world.   Christ Himself is the truth of the Kingdom which He preaches.   This Kingdom is proclaimed in the language of apocalyptic as something which altogether transcends the course of history and which finally breaks the bonds of mere nationalism.   Its claim is absolute against every earthly counter-claim.   Yet this Kingdom has come down to earth in the human form of Jesus Christ and it is actualised in the fellowship of His little flock.   Thus the Incarnation was the final ratification of the principle that God is revealed to us under contrasted aspects.   In the very inadequate language of theology we say that God is both transcendent and immanent.   But these two ideas are not sheer opposites in an insoluble contradiction. They exemplify that " double polarity " of Christianity with which Baron von Hügel has made us familiar.   The Incarnation not only ratified this principle of a union of opposites.   It embodied the principle in a new form.   Christianity is the universal religion, and at the same time it is the religion which raises individual personality to its highest power.   In the New Testament we see the creation of a wholly new experience of fellowship between God and man reaching down to the roots of the human spirit.   Yet the individual is thus recreated within the compass of a religious movement which breaks through all the old particularist limitations and claims for itself universal scope as the bearer of an absolute and final revelation of God.

The immediate effect, therefore, of God's love " shed abroad in our hearts " was an immense enlargement and enrichment of the whole idea of God.   The idea now called for a new language in which it could be expressed.   The search for such language already appears in some of the great doctrinal passages in the writings of St. Paul and St. John.   As the development of Christian thought proceeded, it was impelled to borrow from philosophy's vocabulary of abstract words and impersonal categories of thought.   Only by the use of such language, it was found, could justice be done to a revelation which was, as given to experience, intensely personal and concrete in form.   Thus in the traditional list of the divine attributes there is a large proportion of such abstract and impersonal terms side by side with others which are drawn more directly from the vivid, personal language of religious experience.   Again, although we are not as yet primarily concerned with the doctrine of the Holy Trinity, the formulation of that doctrine provides a further illustration of what has been said. To sum up, the limitations of the human mind and the facts of revelation alike require that the content of the idea of God should be formulated under a variety of aspects.   No true simplification is effected by attempts to reduce the diversity of our religious experience, or to submerge under the dominance of any one idea the diversity of divine attributes which reflect that experience. Moreover, Christian theism, as the trustee of all religious revelation, bears witness to a fundamental duality running through all our experience of God ; and the contrasts which this experience implies are ultimately irreducible facts, of which theology is bound to take account.   These considerations impress themselves upon the mind in a great variety of ways.   God guides the stars and He also touches the heart.   He embraces all the worlds and He is also the Voice that speaks in Jesus Christ.   He is to be known in His cosmic relations through the severe impersonal studies of science and philosophy.   Yet He can be vividly known to each one of us in the penetrating sway of conscience and in the hidden depths of prayer.   We know Him through very varied schools of discipline and through many channels of revelation.   None of these can be left out of account.   For all contribute to the enrichment of each and every particular field of experience with which as individuals we may be most concerned.

K

3. *Revelation and the Attributes*

Much light is thrown upon these questions by two principles of great importance in the speculative thought of to-day. These are (*a*) the principle that there are different grades in the structure of reality ; and (*b*) the principle that all knowledge is trans-subjective. Both of these principles illuminate the religious concept of revelation and have an important bearing upon the whole subject of the divine attributes.[1]

(*a*) It is the glory of Christianity that God has been revealed to us in terms of a human life ; because humanity is what stands nearest to us. But if we consider man's place in the world-process this must mean a great deal more. For man is a microcosm of nature, and human life is the meeting-point of an inner world of spirit with the external world through all its levels. Further, the revelation of God in Christ is an historical revelation and, on any Christian interpretation, must be regarded as occupying the centre of history. Its universality is exhibited upon the background of the ages, through which its eternal principles are refracted both forwards and backwards for our clearer understanding. Here, then, we have a series—Nature, Man, History, the Incarnation— a series which forms a graded sequence with interconnections. The four factors in the sequence taken together provide all the data we possess for our knowledge of God. Revelation in its widest sense must be spread over the whole of this field and through all its stages and levels. Now it is precisely this fact which is represented in what are called the attributes of God. Moreover, as the different stages and levels of revelation are interconnected, so must it be with the attributes. There is here a real parallelism which is worthy of notice.

If we consider the attributes from this point of view we find, in the first place, that for Christian thought God is above the whole order of nature and the historical process of events which is unfolded upon nature's system. He is infinitely more than can ever be apprehended by man, the microcosm of nature and the subject

---

[1] For the first point cp. the recent Gifford lectures, *Space, Time and Deity* by Prof. Alexander and *Emergent Evolution* by C. Lloyd Morgan ; also W. Temple, *Christus Veritas*, ch. i., and F. W. Butler, *Christianity and History*, cc. i. and ii. For the second point cp. Von Hügel, *Essays and Addresses*, pp. 51–57, and L. A. Reid, *Knowledge and Truth* (a recent criticism of the " new realist," " critical realist " and other modern theories of knowledge).

of history, either through the medium of the external world and its temporal processes or through man's own inner life. God must for ever be contrasted with all the positive content of these things. This is the principle of negation. We do not know what God is in His ultimate Being. Such knowledge of Him as we possess is as a flicker of light upon a background of cloud and mystery. He is infinite, eternal, ineffable, absolute, inscrutable, wholly beyond this world of our experience and not subject to its changes and chances. In form these attributes are negative ; but their meaning for us is not simply negative. They are symbols of God's greatness and of our smallness, through which the attention of the mind is strained towards the Object of all desire. But, secondly, there is another knowledge of God which is mediated to us through the same series of our temporal experience. We may know the Creator through His creation, however inadequately, yet with sufficient clearness and certainty to satisfy the cravings of the human spirit. God is revealed through all levels of creation in the measure which is possible to each level. What He possesses as an undivided treasure is refracted through nature and man in an ascending scale. God possesses in a more eminent sense all the true goods which exist in this world, all fulness of energy, life, mind and personality. He is rational, free, self-determining Spirit. In Him are realised all the values which these words connote. Thirdly, God is in active relations with His creation through all its stages as its ground, cause, and sustainer. All processes and events of the temporal order are within the compass of His knowledge and the control of His will. So, too, with the spiritual life of man and the expression of that life in society and in history. In this sphere also man can recognise what God is, both by contrast with himself and through the best in himself. God stands to man in a series of relations as Creator to creature, Deity to worshipper, Lawgiver to conscience, Sinless to sinful. These relations of contrast are asserted when we speak of God's majesty and glory, of His holiness, righteousness and goodness, of His perfect beatitude. Finally, through the Incarnation in its whole context and issues God is revealed as Love and Mercy, as Father, Saviour and Friend.

In this survey of the attributes we see a sequence which corresponds broadly to the factors or stages through which revelation is mediated. We move from the negative to the positive, from the abstract to the concrete, from transcendence to immanence, from the limitations of our knowledge to the light of positive revelation ; from nature to man as set in the order of nature and then to man on the field of history, from man in the social order of history to man the individual recognising his God through religious and moral intuitions ; finally from man and his aspirations to their fulfilment in the Incarnation.

(*b*) A prevailing characteristic of thought in the nineteenth century was its tendency to seek for an explanation of the world in terms of some one comparatively simple idea either of causation or of development. Such a principle the mechanistic theory seemed at one time to provide, or, again, the idea of evolution conceived as the continuous and inevitable unfolding of what existed in germ or in essence from the first. In all this the spell of Descartes' " clear and distinct idea " was still potent. But as the sciences steadily won their way to autonomy, this method became less and less adequate. Now we are faced with a new conception of reality in the graded series of matter, life, mind and spirit which the hierarchy of sciences discloses. This change of outlook is driving out the old monistic theories of knowledge. Descartes left the awkward legacy of an unresolved dualism between subject and object. Upon this fierce onslaughts have been made ever since and are still being made.[1] Yet even Professor Alexander, who surely sings the swan-song of evolutionary monism, is unable to eliminate this dualism of subject and object.[2] Each grade of reality has its own " system of reference " and lays upon the knower its own categories of thought. The real yields up its secrets only to those who accept it as something given, to which the mind must be receptive. Now here we gain a flood of light upon the whole idea of revelation, which comes forth from its place in theology to claim a wider field. This given-ness of the objects of knowledge persisting over every stage of so vastly varied a range throws a new meaning into the question as to what sort of knowledge we may possess in a revelation of God. At every step in the scale the given reveals itself to mind as something of which we may have real knowledge ; and yet in such a way that our knowledge is never complete. Knowledge is trustworthy as far as it goes ; yet the object always escapes from the knower's net.

[1] *E.g.* by the American " New Realists " and in the philosophy of Croce.
[2] *Space, Time and Deity*, vol. ii. bk. iii. ch. iv. B., pp. 109-115.

There is always attainable a degree of certainty sufficient for a further advance. But there is always an unsolved mystery left over. The higher we go in the scale of revelation the more significance this double principle attaches to itself. Moreover, throughout the whole series, consciousness of mystery remaining in no way conflicts with an assured confidence of knowledge already attained. We may even suggest that of these two characteristics the one is an ingredient in the other. The things which we feel are most worth knowing are known not as solved problems but as fresh vantage-grounds, providing new horizons and fascinating fields for further exploration. The more we are at home in the world which we know, the more strange and mysterious it is to us. How much more, then, is this likely to be true in the knowledge of that Being, who is the ground of all that is and all that knows, the source of all revelation and the all-inclusive object of knowledge. It is this truth which is reflected in the contrast of transcendent mystery and condescending love, which we have found to be a permanent factor in religious experience and in that intellectual formulation of the attributes, which endeavours to do justice to such experience. But this is not the whole truth. It has its complement in the fact that, unlike all finite objects of knowledge, God is Himself the ground of the knower. As the ground of all our experience He is less strange to us than any finite creature can be. He comes as the infinite Creator to the rescue of our finite powers and embraces our aspirations with immense condescension. The paradox of revelation has its reverse side. He who is wholly beyond us is infinitely near. The Creator's love is more native to our spirits than any affinity of His creatures can be.

The conception of revelation outlined above cuts across certain currents of theological thought which have been running strongly since Ritschl's day. These were congenial to that whole type of thought which we have seen to be characteristic of the last century. A variety of causes, into which we need not here inquire, led men to seek, in the break-up of traditional foundations, for some one clear and simple foundation upon which to build anew. They found this in the human figure of our Lord and in the moral revelation of divine love disclosed in His life and teaching. They rightly saw that here if anywhere the light of revelation shone most clearly. But they did not sufficiently consider the fact that what is in itself most luminous will not remain luminous if it is taken out

of its context.   The context of Jesus Christ is all that we can know
of nature, man and history.   The context of divine love is all
that we can know of God at all levels of reality and through all
channels of knowledge.   The Gospel is too tremendous to be
apprehended on any narrower stage, and that just because the
revelation of God's love in Christ transcends all other stages of
revelation and is the culminating point of the whole series.   Again,
underlying all these considerations is the fact that religion makes
its ultimate appeal to the whole of human nature.   Religion,
indeed, has its roots in emotional types of experience.   But it was,
as we have seen, the special province of Hebrew prophecy to bring
religion and morality into permanent alliance in such a way that
religion itself might ultimately claim the whole of human nature
and so be able to justify itself in satisfying the claims of both
morality and reason.   In the Old Testament revelation the
emphasis remains upon the moral response to God, that is to say
upon religion moralized in the form of obedience to the Law.
In the Gospel revelation of divine love religion becomes completely transcendent of morality, whilst taking morality up into
itself and transfiguring its character.   Thus the eternal fascination
of religion, which consists in man's deepest levels of desire being
met and satisfied by the self-communication of the divine—this is
now charged with moral quality and meaning ; and morality itself
in turn is fused with mystical and emotional power.   This is the
peculiar ethos of the New Testament.   It is summed up in the
word ἀγάπη, the most pregnant word of apostolic Christianity.
We therefore feel rightly that love is the most significant of all
the aspects under which God is revealed to us.   But it is so, not
as an idea which excludes other ideas, but as a ray of light which
illuminates everything which it touches.

II

The Holy Trinity

The Catholic doctrine of the Holy Trinity is believed by the
individual Christian in the first instance on authority.   It is the
tradition to which he has been delivered at his baptism.   He has
accepted it in accepting the general trustworthiness of the Church's
mental outlook and the body of experience which that outlook
represents.   He continues in this faith because his own religious
experience corroborates the value of what he has received.   But in

the third place, in so far as he reflects upon the contents of his religious beliefs, he must necessarily seek to understand the Church's doctrine with the help of such light as can be obtained from human knowledge as a whole. It is with this third stage that we are here mainly concerned.[1]

1. The Word and the Spirit

It is a familiar thought that revelation and inspiration are complementary ideas ; that the Word of God *aptat Deum homini* and that the Spirit of God *aptat hominem Deo*.[2] In other words, all revelation may be regarded from the side of the object revealed and also from the side of the recipient of the revelation. Thus we think of God's self-revelation as an objective manifestation mediated through nature, history, and the life of man. But this idea requires for its counterpart an interior unfolding of man's powers of spiritual apprehension. These two conceptions provide a background for the Christian belief that Jesus Christ is the revealing Word of God and that the revelation thus given has been committed to a community of persons whose inner life is quickened and illuminated by the Holy Spirit.

(*a*) In theology the doctrine that Christ is the Logos or Word of God has from the first had two contexts, both of which are to be found in the Prologue of St. John's Gospel. There the Word is the author of creation and the light which enlightens mankind through a revelation given in the order of nature. But the Word is also, in the same passage, said to have been manifested in history to His own people, in a process whose climax was the Incarnation. Following part of St. John's thought we may therefore regard the revelation in Jesus Christ as the goal towards which all earlier and lower stages of revelation were tending. The conception of Christ as the goal of the world-process conceived as a single divine plan unfolding through the ages is also one of the leading ideas in the Epistle to the Ephesians.[3] The word there used indicates, not that our Lord is the last term in a series, but that He is the summation of the whole series. He includes in Himself all the

---

[1] The writer is not here concerned to raise, still less to prejudge, questions concerning the respective functions of authority, faith and reason in religion. The remarks in the text are confined to a general statement of facts.

[2] The phrases are taken from Du Bose, *The Gospel in the Gospels*, Part I, c. iii.

[3] Eph. i. 10 ; cp. also *ib.* iv. 13.

content of revelation as exhibited through all its stages. He is the final expression of the purpose of God as disclosed in nature, man and history. He is the "perfect Man." But we cannot rest satisfied with such an idea. There is a correlative truth stated emphatically by St. Paul and St. John. Creation is not only " unto Him " ; it is also " through Him " and " in Him." He is not only the substance of all revelation given to man and its ultimate meaning. He is also the ground of the whole created order through which revelation comes.[1] The Christ of the New Testament is not evolutionary precisely because He is the Word, the absolute revelation. This antithesis becomes clear if we follow up the conception of revelation already outlined in this essay. In all revelation there is a disclosure to man of some aspect of reality which yet transcends our power of knowing. As we ascend the scale that which is given to knowledge increasingly transcends and escapes from the dissecting analysis of intellect ; and yet at the same time comes ever closer to what lies within and at the root of man's most significant experiences. Thus at the top of the scale truth, beauty and goodness have infinitely larger meanings than we can ever find in them. Yet they correspond to our deepest intuitions, and are not only the ends which we seek but the grounds of our seeking. They are always beyond us and yet always with us. They are wholly native to our minds and yet altogether transcend every sequence in our mental and moral life. But they are only rays of that " light which lighteth every man," who is the Way, the Truth and the Life.

It follows that if Christ is the summation of that series in which such values appear and the goal towards which they point us, then the double principle of revelation must reach in Him its final and absolute expression. He sums the series of revelation because He transcends it entirely. He spans all avenues of revelation because He is the supreme Revealer, the personal Word, who is the source of all partial utterances of revelation and of all particular parts and sequences of that temporal order through which they are mediated to us. The Christ of history stands in an historical succession ; yet He cannot be explained from within it. He enters it *ab extra* ; and, to say the least, such an idea appears both national and intelligible on the view that all revelation exhibits characteristics of transcendence. A previous essay has urged that

[1] Col. I. 15–17 ; John i. 1–4.

Nature and man are not self-explanatory, that both point to a supernatural world which is the ground of this world, and again that man himself belongs to both of these worlds.[1] It is in virtue of such considerations that man appears pre-eminently fitted to be the recipient of a revelation from that supernatural order. Now the Johannine doctrine that Christ is the Word made flesh declares that the whole revelation of God to man, the final summation of all that man can know of God, was projected into human life at a point in the historical sequence in the Person of Christ.[2] The possibility of such an event St. John finds in the fact that He who enters thus into human nature is Himself the author and sustainer of the cosmic process, of that humanity which He took and of that historical succession into which He entered. " In the beginning was the word and the word was with God and the word was God." From this cycle of Johannine ideas springs that theological tradition which connects together Creation and Incarnation as two stages in one divine action, and which finds the ground of both in the deity of the Word or Son of God. St. Paul reached the same result, but along a different line of approach. Here the experience of redemption from sin was the principle governing the process of interpretation. Christ not only reveals God to man ; He also redeems man to God. He brings down the supernatural to man and also raises man to that supernatural order. Where these two lines of thought meet, as they did conspicuously in St. Athanasius, there theology most truly reflects the balance of the New Testament. But both lead to the same conclusion. For it is through the experience of Christ's redeeming action that God's character is revealed to us ; and the substance of the revelation is that God is redeeming Love. The conclusion in both cases is that God is revealed to man and man is redeemed to God by One who is Himself within the life and being of God.

(*b*) The idea of revelation requires for its counterpart the corresponding idea of inspiration. Man is indeed fitted to be the recipient of a revelation by the fact that he is made in the image of the Word ; since the Word is alike the author of man's being and the ground and substance of that revelation which is made to him.

---

[1] Essay II.

[2] This in no way precludes us from recognising the limitations of Christ's earthly life ; cp. what was said above on the " context" of the revelation in Christ, pp. 133, 134.

Nevertheless, since what is given in revelation is from a super-natural source, man stands in need of divine assistance or grace from the same supernatural source, that he may be able to appre-hend what is revealed.   This process of inspiration entering into the spirit and life of man goes forward *pari passu* with all stages of revelation.   It is as wide in scope and as diverse in form as we have found revelation to be.   But in particular, as the Old Testament revelation developed, Jewish thought distinguished the Spirit from the Word and looked forward to a full outpouring of the Spirit as a special mark of the Messianic Kingdom.   This hope was fulfilled in the Pentecostal experience of the apostolic Church.   The recipients of this experience traced the gift of the Spirit to their incarnate Lord, and found in the fellowship of the Spirit a new life whereby they were enabled to appropriate the meaning of that revelation which had been given in Christ.   In the place of that objective historical manifestation of divine love in terms of human life which they had seen in Christ they now possessed an interior presence of indwelling love in the fellowship of the Christian community   This presence was personal in its action, creating a new social fellowship and renewing the life of individuals within that fellowship.   The Spirit experienced as the source of such rich personal values was understood to be Himself personal [1] and yet distinguished from the incarnate Lord, whose revealing life He illuminated and whose historical redeeming action He transmuted into the form of an abiding interior principle of sanctification.   There were, therefore, in this new cycle of experience two distinct features.   God has revealed Himself through the redeeming action of Christ ; and God so revealed is present in the Christian community and in its individual members through the gift of the Spirit.   The love of the Father is revealed in the grace of the Son ; and the grace of the Son is possessed and enjoyed in the communion of the Spirit.[2]

It does not fall within the scope of this essay to trace in full the development of the doctrine of the Trinity in the early Church until it reached its final expression in the fourth century.   In the New Testament we find no formulated doctrine ; but rather the materials for such a doctrine taking shape in the form of a developing

---

[1] *E.g.* such phrases as ἐνεργεῖ . . . καθὼς βούλεται in 1 Cor. xii. 11 suggest an active subject rather than an impersonal influence. Still more definite is the use of the pronoun ἐκεῖνος in John xiv.–xvi.

[2] 2 Cor. xiii. 14.

experience which is already feeling its way vigorously towards adequate intellectual expression. This stage is already manifest in the Pauline epistles. It reaches its maturest expression in St. John's Gospel. Here Father, Son and Holy Spirit are Three " Subjects " or " Persons " ; and on the other hand the distinctions drawn between the Three are balanced by emphatic statements of divine unity and mutual relationship. The development of patristic thought consisted in a series of attempts to do justice to such language and still more to the apostolic experience which lay behind it. Not all of such attempts were successful ; each advance was made at the price of many abortive experiments. But the controlling principles of the process are sufficiently clear. The twofold experience of redemption through Christ and of new life in the fellowship of the Spirit is the continuous link between the apostolic Church and the Church of Tertullian and Origen, and again of Athanasius, Basil and Augustine.

2. *Personality in God*

It has often been pointed out that to the influence of Christianity must be assigned a large part in the development of modern conceptions of personality. The case is somewhat parallel to that of another comparatively modern conception, that of history. In both cases the development of the Christian idea of God in the Bible and in theology has had much to do with the emergence of these conceptions. Of history something has already been said in this essay. The question of personality confronts us in any discussion of the doctrine of the Trinity. In its modern connotation personality probably includes two main aspects. On the one hand there is the idea of mental life organised in relation to a conscious centre. What is distinctive of man as an individual, on this view, is self-consciousness. But on the other hand consciousness of self as a centre of mental life already involves the further idea of other such centres of consciousness. Personality has a sociological as well as a psychological significance. It involves the idea of relationship with other-than-self. It has a social as well as an individual aspect. It is awareness of self and of not-self. It means self-regarding reflection and activity on the one hand, and capacity for passing out of self into social relationships on the other.

There can be no reasonable doubt that religion has played an important part in the long process of thought which lies behind these developed ideas.   But the connection between the two ideas of God and of personality in human life becomes strikingly manifest if we concentrate attention upon the New Testament and the early Church.   Here we see blossoming forth new conceptions of God, of society and of individual life.   These are three aspects of one creative experience, three strands intertwined.   We see the Christian community emerge as a new sociological factor, a new experience of fellowship.   We see also the Christian individual with a new consciousness of his individual worth and ends and of their possibility of attainment.   A deeper meaning for personality in both its individual and social aspects has begun.   Thirdly, within the same movement there emerges a new conception of God, in which the living, personal God of earlier revelation becomes known as a fellowship of Persons.   We must now follow up this clue of a connection between personality in God and in man.

Any attempt to translate the formula of Three Persons in One Substance into modern language is beset with acute difficulties. For example, Descartes has given to the idea of " consciousness " a new meaning and emphasis for us which differentiates our habits of thought from those of the Nicene Fathers.   Such a phrase as " Three Centres of One Consciousness " represents a bold attempt to grapple with this difficulty.[1]   But do we know enough of consciousness to be quite sure of our ground ?   No formula can be adequate.   But, in view of the fluid state of modern psychology, it would perhaps be better to avoid the word " consciousness " altogether and to speak of *Three Centres of One Activity*.[2]   In the case of human personality relationship can exist only between separate individuals.   The Nicene formula, and any modern equivalent, must mean that such relationship exists in God, but *not* as between three individuals.   The three centres of relationship are here comprehended within the unity of One Absolute Activity.   Such a statement presupposes that personality exists in God after a manner to which human personality offers some analogy, but in a more eminent sense as is the case with all positive statements about God.[3]   The main difference would seem to be

---

[1] Dr. Temple in *Christus Veritas*.

[2] The word " Activity " was suggested to me by Professor A. E. Taylor, to whose kind criticism this essay owes much.   See Additional Note B (p. 451).

[3] As Professor C. C. J. Webb well says, we speak of " Personality in God " rather than " the Personality of God."   See his *God and Personality*.

that characteristics and functions, which at the human level of personality appear in tension and conflict as antithetical tendencies, exist in God within a unity and harmony which transcend all analogies from human experience. In man the individual and social aspects of personality are in tension and conflict. In God the self-regarding and other-regarding aspects of personality are integrated within the unity of one mental life. Within this unity there may indeed be tension, deeper tension than we can know. But if so it is tension within harmony. We can dimly perceive that this means a higher kind of personality than ours. Moreover, although the mystery of the Blessed Trinity far transcends our powers of understanding, yet there are features of human experience which point directly towards the truth of the mystery.

We turn naturally to the special forms of experience within which the Christian conception of God as a Trinity first appears and to which reference has already been made.[1] Christianity came into the world as a way of life with a specific doctrine of life.[2] Man attains his true self through the principle of sacrifice or dying to self. By this means he may transcend the purely self-regarding aspect of personality and find a larger life of fellowship. The New Testament shows this transcendence of the self-regarding ego as the Way of the Cross which our Lord inculcated and which He Himself followed out, fulfilling that Way to the uttermost in His death. The same principle of self-transcendence is also set forth as something actually and vividly realised in experience by the early Christian community. It was realised in the fellowship of the Spirit and was recognised to be an operation of the Spirit. But what the Spirit wrought in the Christian life was a mystical union with Christ, whereby the self-transcending power of Christ's life passed into the soul and, bursting through its natural bonds of selfishness, carried it up to a supernatural level of love, where the dualism of self and other was in principle already solved. It was not, however, solved by the annihilation of self, nor by the merging of the individual's personality in the community, nor again by the absorption of that personality into the life of God in any pantheistic sense. What is characteristic, for example, of St. Paul's doctrine of mystical union is exactly the reverse of such absorption. The transcendence of self which is

[1] See above, pp. 139 f.
[2] Cp. Royce, *The Problem of Christianity*, vol. i.

there described leads to the transfiguration of self. " I live, yet no longer I but Christ liveth in me ; and that life which I now live in the flesh I live by faith which is in the Son of God. . . ." " I can do all things in Him that strengtheneth me." Where life is all grace, all Christ, all death to self, there also it means enlargement and enrichment of self. Now this supernatural experience, as we must call it, carries us both in promise and in fulfilment to a level beyond the range of natural human capacity. The development of culture and civilisation in itself shews no tendency to overcome the tensions existing between the individual and society and again between society as a whole and smaller groups within it. On the contrary the development of human society leads of itself to increasing stress and complexity.[1] The evolutionary process as a whole appears to be characterised on the one hand by increase of complexity and on the other hand by the emergence, at various stages, of new factors which take control of this growing complexity.[2] On this view the Christian experience of grace, union with Christ and the fellowship of the Spirit, might be regarded as the emergence in, or rather entrance into, the series of a yet higher factor, which takes control of the complexities of self-conscious human personality.

This Christian doctrine of life sets the movement of human life in train towards a goal already achieved in Christ, who in this way, as Pauline Christology declares, sums up in Himself the cosmic process. As has already been said, however, Christ is not only the goal but also the ground of this process in the developed teaching of St. Paul and St. John.[3] The truth of this now appears from another point of view. What Christian experience and the New Testament alike declare to be the true direction of human life, the higher possibility of self-conscious personality under the action of divine grace, *this* Christian theology from St. Paul onwards declares to be, not simply achieved within the historical order in the life of Christ and in process of attainment in the fellowship of the Spirit, but already existing in the life of God and in the eternal activities which belong to that life. The harmony of reciprocal personal relationships, which when carried to its highest

[1] This point has been worked out at length by Royce. See *op. cit.*
[2] On this point cp. J. Y. Simpson, *Man and the Attainment of Immortality*, cc. ix.–xi.
[3] Cp. pp. 135–137 above.

level is called ἀγάπη in the New Testament, this is the true end of man because it is the eternal mode of God's life. The inner reality of this mystery of Triune Love is something utterly beyond us. All thought and speech are helpless and impotent before it. Yet this same mystery is utterly near to us. For all avenues of Christian experience lead up to it and lead back to it. Because the truth of this doctrine is rooted in experience, its formulation was inevitable. No formulation indeed can be adequate. But we can at least endeavour to see what sort of difficulties must, from the very nature of the case, accompany all thought upon the subject.

3. *Two Primary Difficulties*

There are really two primary difficulties which beset human thought upon this matter. One is the difficulty of conceiving rightly the unity in the Godhead. The other is the difficulty of conceiving rightly the distinction of Persons. It does not matter which of these questions we consider first. For each leads eventually into the other. Our mental life is of such a kind that it is always bringing unity into the manifold of sense impressions through the medium of abstract concepts and ideas. Abstraction is the unifying principle of all intellectual activity. Consequently, the mind inevitably tends to think of unity itself as having the characteristics of an abstract principle or idea. It is a fact well-known in the history of thought that the philosophic and scientific mind finds personality difficult and intractable to system. From this point of view, if the idea of God is introduced, it is valued chiefly as providing a rational ground for the unity and order of the world-process. Modalism is the interpretation of the Trinity which is most congenial to this type of thought. The Persons become aspects, modes or phases of a single principle rather than centres of consciousness in relationship. This conception of unity is however very inadequate to reality as we know it to-day. The unities which the sciences reveal to us consist in the correlation of different kinds of energy and in the harmony and balance set up by the reciprocal interactions of these energies. As we move up the scale of reality the characteristics of unity necessarily change as the higher factors of life and mind emerge and take control. But the changes which occur move steadily in the direction of self-conscious personality and personal relationships. This series, as we know it, is unfinished.   Personality, as known to the psychologist, is an imperfectly realised unity, in which conflicting tendencies have not yet attained to such a harmony as it is necessary to presuppose as the goal of personality.   Moreover, this incompleteness in the unity of the individual is reflected in his corresponding inadequacy as the unit in a system of social relationships. Yet this unfinished series is a clue as to the direction in which we ought to look for our ideas about unity and personality in God.

A different line of approach is that of religious experience which starts, not from the idea of unity, but from the experience of personal relations.   For that is in essence what religion means, even in the earliest stage of religious history, when the object of worship is not clearly recognised in terms of such relationship.   The peculiar difficulty with which religion is beset is not abstraction but anthropomorphism.   Consequently, religious thought, in attributing personality to God, finds it difficult to strip off from the idea of personality the associations of human imperfection and limitation which cling to it.   Now the essential Christian experience of God is, in its completeness, what the New Testament records, namely personal communion with Father, Son and Holy Spirit, a threefold experience of personal relationship.   This involves the idea of a fellowship of Persons in God ; and this fellowship is partially and imperfectly but truly reflected in the fellowship of the Christian community.   On the whole, therefore, it seems true to say that, as reason is primarily interested in the unity of God, so religious experience is primarily concerned with the distinction of Persons.   Owing to the difficulty referred to above, this distinction may easily be conceived in a form which approaches to Tri-theism.   The human mind tends to think of the essence of personality as consisting in what sets one individual apart from another.   The whole *nisus* of human personality towards self-realisation seems to confirm this idea ; because in our natural experience there is a deep fissure between the individual and social aspects of personality which it is hard to bridge over. But the Christian reading of this natural experience is that it is in large part to be explained in terms of sinful pride and selfishness. It points away from the true meaning of personality, not towards it. Philosophy also teaches a very different lesson.   The higher values or goods of life are of such a kind that they can and must be shared. For they can be fully realised or enjoyed by each only in community with others. If then we strip off our present limitations from the idea of personality, that idea in its most perfect form would mean something not less but more truly social than anything of which we have experience. It would mean precisely what is indicated in the mysterious doctrine that there is a complete mutual indwelling and interpenetration of the Three Persons in the Godhead.

III

CREATION, MIRACLE AND PROVIDENCE

In conclusion, something must be said as to the view of God's relation to the world and to human life which follows upon this conception of God. For Christians, creation has always meant that God made the universe " out of nothing." No other view is compatible with the absolute and transcendent character of the Deity as understood by Christian theism. It follows that God is the necessary ground of creation. Can we in any sense speak of creation being necessary to God? Here there is need of careful distinction. Some philosophers seem to think that a perpetual process of creation is a necessary counterpart to the idea of a living personal God. Whether there is such perpetuity of creation is surely an irrelevant question, which we have no means of answering. The vital point is that God does not create under any necessity *external to Himself*, but by the perfectly free action of benevolent will. Since, however, there is nothing arbitrary in the divine will, this is the same thing as to say that He creates in accordance with the laws of His own nature. He does not create because He stands in need of creatures, but through the overflowing fullness of His love which must manifest itself in condescension. It is unfortunate that the English language possesses no convenient way of distinguishing between these two kinds of necessity. But whatever language we use the distinction must be maintained. Upon this difficult subject the doctrine of the Trinity throws a flood of light. In a Unitarian conception of God, where there is no subject-object relation within the Godhead, the idea of creation inevitably comes to mean that the world is the necessary object of divine activity. The world thus takes the place of the eternal Son, and God is subjected to external necessity. If, however, there are hypostatic distinctions within the Godhead, we can find in God an eternal ground and possibility of creative action without introducing such necessity. The creative capacity which we know in human personality attains its ends through growth and succession ; and such attainment is but a mode of self-realisation within the created order of which we are parts.   But a transcendent Creator cannot be thought of as finding His adequate object in a created order, which is and must always remain less than Himself.   Such an adequate object the Father possesses in the Son, who is the eternal reproduction of Himself.   The doctrine of the Trinity indicates in God eternal activities of personal relationship such as provide a rational ground for creative activity.   Eternity is no mere negation of succession. For the most significant forms of human experience transcend successiveness and yet they are immanent in a succession.   We may therefore believe that in the eternal activities within the Godhead there exists in a more eminent way all that is abidingly significant in the temporal process.[1]

Closely connected with the subject of creation are important questions concerning miracles and providence.   Upon these matters nothing more can be attempted here than the indication of a point of view.   We have seen that the graded series of reality known to us through the sciences is actually an unfinished series.[2] Moreover, as new factors emerge in the series, horizons proper to the lower stages are transcended.   Again, the whole series is transcended by God its Creator.   It follows then that God's action upon the world as a whole must transcend our experience of what falls within the series.   The series itself contains the principle of transcendence and points beyond itself to horizons outside our experience of the system which we call Nature.   In other words, it points to a supernatural order.   It is, to say the least, hazardous, therefore, from our partial standpoint to prejudge the question as to what kinds of special action might or might not be appropriate to the fulfilment of God's redeeming purpose for His creatures.   The Christian conception of God and of His relation to the world involves at least the possibility of miracles.   Miracles may be defined as unusual events in which we catch a glimpse of a divine purpose which is actually embodied in all events.   Further, they are unusual to such a degree that in that respect they fall outside the horizon of our normal experience altogether.   The

---

[1] This is what I understand Dr. Temple to mean in *Christus Veritas*, ch. xv.
[2] See pp. 143, 144.

term " miracle," as thus defined, has a more restricted meaning than the term " supernatural," which covers operations of grace as well as abnormal events. The distinction seems to be mainly relative to our experience (we have continuous experience of grace, but not of miracle). If, however, miracles are *contra quam est nota natura*, the same is really true of the whole action of grace upon the soul. For the power of grace overcomes the sway of natural propensities and enables freewill to assert itself. Thus psychological laws are transcended by grace as physical laws are transcended by miracle. The idea of miracle belongs to a group of ideas which includes freewill, providence, prayer and grace. These in turn run back to creative will and a revelation of personality in God. We cannot properly dissociate any of these ideas from one another. There are as substantial arguments available against human freewill and against the validity of prayer as against any physical miracle. If it is appropriate for human freewill to break through psychological laws by the aid of divine grace, then we cannot rule out the possibility that it is appropriate for the Creator Himself, for sufficient reasons, to supersede the normal sequences of the physical universe. The universe exists, not primarily for the purpose of exhibiting unvarying sequences of law, but that it may be sacramental of God's glory and goodness and may be the medium through which God fulfils His providential purposes for man. The providence of God is directed towards personal ends and is concerned with the priceless treasure of human souls. In the last resort the universe is best understood as the unfolding expression of God's love. Its deepest secrets are disclosed in such sayings of our Lord as " Come unto me and I will give you rest " and " There is joy in heaven over one sinner that repenteth " ; or again in the words of St. Paul, " All things work together for good to them that love God." [1]

---

[1] In these brief remarks the writer has intentionally confined himself to one point only in the modern controversy about miracles, namely its metaphysical aspect, this being the only point which seemed relevant to the subject of this essay. The writer is well aware that other aspects are raised by the bearing of modern anthropological and psychological inquiries upon the evidence for particular miracles. An admirable discussion of the metaphysical aspect will be found in Dr. F. R. Tennant's recent work, *Miracle and its philosophica presuppositions.*

ADDITIONAL NOTE
By E. J. BICKNELL

The Trinitarian Doctrine of Augustine and Aquinas

The aim of this note is to examine the statement that in Augustine and Aquinas the personal distinctions of Father, Son and Holy Spirit are reduced to mere functions or activities within one single divine mind or consciousness.

The terms " Una Substantia," " Tres Personae," are first found in Tertullian. While the precise meaning of " substantia " is disputed, there is a general agreement that " personae " is in origin a grammatical term, taken from texts used to prove the distinctions of the Persons, as where the Father addresses the Son, or the Spirit speaks of the Father and the Son, *i.e.* the Three are regarded as holding intercourse with one another. Hence, as in ordinary speech, " persona " means a party to a social relationship.

Augustine, unlike earlier Latin writers, approaches the Trinity from the side of the divine unity. " The Trinity is the one and true God " (*De Trinitate*, i. 4). " The Father and the Son and the Holy Spirit intimate a divine unity of one and the same substance in an indivisible equality" (i. 7). Whatever is spoken of God according to substance or, as he prefers to call it, essence (vii. 10), is spoken of each Person severally and together of the Trinity (v. 8). All that God is He is essentially. In Him are no accidents. For what is accidental can be lost or changed. His substance is at once both simple and manifold (v. 5, vi. 8). Each Person is as great as the other two or as the entire Trinity. It is hard to say either " the Father alone " or " the Son alone," since they are inseparable and are always in relation to one another (vi. 9). The divine substance is in no way a fourth term. We do not say three Persons out of the same essence in the same way as three statues out of the same gold, for it is one thing to be gold, another to be statues. Nor, are they like three men of the same nature, since out of the same nature can also be other three men. " In that essence of the Trinity in no way can any other person exist out of the same essence " (vii. 11). The truth that each is equal to the three is difficult because the imagination uses spatial images. In all their operations *ad extra* the Three have one will and activity (ii. 9). Their unity is by nature and not by consent. Hence the Son takes an active part in His own sending (ii. 9), and the Angel of the Lord in the Old Testament is the appearance not of the Son, but of God, that is the Trinity (ii. end).

Yet, though inseparable, they are a Trinity. As their names cannot be pronounced simultaneously, so in Scripture they are presented to us through certain created things in distinction from, and mutual relation to, one another, *e.g.* at the Baptism (iv. 30, cp. Ep. 169). The reality of essential distinctions within the Trinity is maintained by the theory of relations. The Persons cannot be accidents. But " every thing that is said about God is not said according to substance. For it is said in relation to something, as the Father in relation to the Son and the Son in relation to the Father, which is not accident." The terms are used reciprocally. " Though to be the Father and to be the Son is different, yet their substance is not different ; because they are so called not according to substance, but according to relation, which relation however is not accident, because it is not changeable " (v. 6).

Such teaching is only a development of the doctrine of coinherence as found in the Cappadocian Fathers. It is unfortunate that in vii. 7–12, through his ignorance of Greek, Augustine's treatment of their terminology is so confused that it is not worth discussion. They indisputably did not reduce the Persons to three aspects of a single self. Augustine goes further in this direction. The analogies of ix.-xiv. are all taken from the activities of a single mind. He begins by asserting that it is through love that we can best attain to the knowledge of the Trinity, and finds in the threefold nature of love a trace of the Trinity. " Love is of someone that loves, and with love something (or in one place someone) is loved. Behold then there are three things : he that loves and that which is loved and love " (viii. 14). Elsewhere he identifies the Spirit with the love of the Father for the Son (vii. 3–8), or with the will of God which is a will of love.

On the other hand, he did not wish to be a modalist. Though he disliked the word " Personae " as unscriptural, yet he recognized that something had to be said to deny the teaching of Sabellius (v. 10, cp. vii. 9). In his " Retractations " (I. iv. 3), composed at the end of his life, he corrects " He who begets and He who is begotten, is one," by changing " is " into " are," in conformity with John x. 30. Further, in a famous passage of the *De Trinitate* he expressly affirms that each Person has a knowledge and memory and love of His own. There emerges at length a view inconsistent with the idea of God as a single self (xv. 12). It cannot be set on one side as a mere slip. It is anticipated in xv. 7, and occurs independently in Ep. clxix. 6. It is so elaborately worked out that it represents an essential element in his theology. Lastly, though his psychological illustrations are borrowed from the functioning of a single self, he ends a prolonged apology for their inadequacy. " But three things belonging to one person cannot suit those three persons, as man's purpose demands, and this we have demonstrated in this fifteenth book " (xv. 45).

Two other considerations deserve notice. First, he gets more modalistic, the further that he gets away from Scripture into the region of logic. Secondly, the influence of Neoplatonism has at times led him to force the Christian idea of God into moulds of thought borrowed from pagan philosophy, so as to endanger its Christianity.

In Aquinas, the dominant analogy is that of distinct functions within a single human mind. The relation of Father to Son is that of a thinker or speaker to his thought. The Spirit is love. The Son proceeds by way of intellect as the Word, the Spirit by way of will as love. Is then the Son only the divine thought, and the Spirit the love which God has for the object of His thought ? This simple explanation is hard to reconcile with other passages. " Persona " is defined, in the words of Boethius, as " rationalis naturae individua substantia " or " subsistentia " or " hypostasis." " Persona " is not used in the case of God in the same sense as in the case of creatures, but " excellentiori modo." It denotes a relation existing in the divine nature " per modum substantiae seu hypostasis," not as a mere accident. "Cum nomen ' alius' masculine acceptum non nisi distinctionem in natura significet, Filius alius a Patre convenienter dicitur." We say " unicum Filium," but not " unicum Deum," because deity is common to more than one. A neuter signifies a common essence, but a masculine a subject (suppositum). "Quia in divinis distinctio est secundum personas non autem secundum essentiam, dicimus quod Pater est alius a Filio sed non aliud : et e converso quod sunt unum non unus" (*Summa Theol.* I. xxxi. 2). Again, "Apud nos relatio non est subsistens persona. Non autem est ita in divinis. . . . Nam relatio est subsistens persona" (xxxiii. 2). In xxxvii. the name love is only applied to the Spirit as " personaliter acceptus." In his discussion of the Incarnation he decides that though it was fitting that the Son should become incarnate, it was equally possible for either of the other Persons to have been incarnate (III. iii. 5 and 8). Further words predicated of God and creatures, are predicated not univocally, but either analogically or equivocally (I. xiii. 5). In xxxix. 4, he shows that persona is not used equivocally. Therefore it must be used analogically. This analogous use implies some likeness between the divine and human persons.

In short, even in Augustine and Aquinas there is evidence of the inadequacy of the single human mind with its functions to furnish a complete illustration of the threefold process of the divine life. It suggests that it needs to be supplemented by something like the analogy from a perfectly unified society.

THE CHRIST OF THE SYNOPTIC GOSPELS

BY SIR EDWYN CLEMENT HOSKYNS, Bт.

CONTENTS

" There is an absence of all reason in electing humanity to Divinity."
                                    TERTULLIAN, *Apology*.

" Beloved, outward things apparel God, and since God was content to take
a body, let us not leave Him naked and ragged."—JOHN DONNE.

" Doe this, O Lord, for His sake who was not less the *King of Heaven* for
Thy suffering Him to be *crowned with thornes* in this world."—JOHN DONNE.

> " Wherein lies happiness ? In that which becks
> Our ready minds to fellowship divine,
> A fellowship with essence ; till we shine
> Full alchemiz'd, and free of space.   Behold
> The clear religion of heaven."
>   KEATS, *Endymion*.

> " ' What think you of Christ,' friend ? when all's done and said,
> Like you this Christianity, or not ? "
>   ROBERT BROWNING, *Bishop Blougram's Apology*.

I

THE PROBLEM

FOR the Catholic Christian " *Quid vobis videtur de Ecclesia,
What think ye of the Church ?* " is not merely as pertinent a
question as " *Quid vobis videtur de Christo, What think ye of the
Christ ?* " : it is but the same question differently formulated.
This unity between Christ and the Church, vital though it is for
Catholic religion, raises a historical problem as delicate as it is
important : delicate, because of its extreme complexity ; important, because the study of the history and development of primitive Christianity has a subtle though direct bearing upon Christian
belief and practice.

The problem is this : What is the relation between the life
and teaching of Jesus of Nazareth and the Christ of St. Paul, of
St. John, and of Catholic piety ?   And further, what is the relation between the little group of disciples called by Jesus from
among the Galilean fishermen and the *Corpus Christi* of St. Paul
or the *Civitas Dei* of St. Augustine ?   This problem was first
clearly recognised, when, in the latter half of the eighteenth
century, the exegesis of the books of the New Testament was taken
out of the hands of the dogmatic theologians and entrusted to the

historians. Since that time many theories have been advanced in order to explain the development of Christianity in the apostolic age, and many attempts have been made to analyse and describe its essential character. These, however, show such radical disagreement, and are so mutually exclusive, that it can occasion little surprise if the intelligent observer grows sceptical of the ability of the historian to reach conclusions in any way satisfactory ; " facts being set forth in a different light, every reader believes as he pleases ; and indeed the more judicious and suspicious very justly esteem the whole as no other than a romance, in which the writer hath indulged a happy and subtle invention." [1]

The chaos is not, however, so great as would at first sight appear. There is at the present time a fairly widespread agreement among a large number of scholars as to the main outline of the development within primitive Christianity. The conclusions arrived at accord so well with modern demands that they have strayed into quite popular literature, and are found to be exercising considerable influence outside strictly academic circles.

II

The Liberal Protestant Solution

The reconstruction is roughly as follows [2] :

Jesus was a Jewish prophet, inspired by the Spirit of God at his baptism by John, and called to reform the religion of

[1] Henry Fielding, *Joseph Andrews*, Book III, chapter i.

[2] The more popular exposition of this view may be found in the following books : E. F. Scott, *The New Testament To-day* ; J. Estlin Carpenter, *The First Three Gospels* ; W. Wrede, *Paul*, English translation by E. Lummis, preface by J. Estlin Carpenter ; C. Piepenbring, *La Christologie Biblique* ; B. W. Bacon, *The Beginnings of the Gospel Story*, esp. pp. 38–40 ; A. Harnack, *What is Christianity?* ; T. R. Glover, *The Jesus of History*, *Jesus in the Experience of Men*, esp. chap. ix ; G. Frenssen, *Dorfpredigten*.

Such expositions are largely based upon elaborate literary and historical critical studies, and upon the more important critical commentaries on the books of the New Testament. The following have been of especial importance : H. J. Holtzmann, *Hand-commentar zum Neuen Testament, Lehrbuch der Neu-Testamentlichen Theologie* ; A. Harnack, *Beiträge zur Einleitung in das Neue Testament, Lehrbuch der Dogmengeschichte* ; E. Klostermann, Commentary on the Synoptic Gospels in the *Handbuch zum Neuen Testament*, edited by H. Lietzmann ; J. Wellhausen, *Das Evangelium Marci, Das Evangelium Lucae, Das Evangelium Matthaei* ; R. Jülicher, *Die Gleichnisreden Jesu* ; A. Loisy, *Les Évangiles Synoptiques* ; W. Bousset, *Kyrios Christos* ; R. Reitzenstein, *Die Hellenistischen Mysterienreligionen* ; Claude Montefiore, *The Synoptic Gospels* ; F. J. Foakes-Jackson and Kirsopp Lake, *The Beginnings of Christianity*, (esp. I. pp. 265–418).

the Jews, which in the hands of the scribes and Pharisees had been overlaid with burdens which the common people were unable to bear, and in the hands of the Sadducees had been bereft of all spiritual content.   After the death of John, he continued the Baptist's work, discarding, however, his crude and inhuman asceticism.   Jesus came to interpret the Mosaic Law and to awaken in men the love of God and the love of one another.   A true Jew, he felt himself one of the great line of prophets and proclaimed that union with God and the brotherhood of men depend upon righteousness and purity of heart.   In the Sermon on the Mount, with unerring insight, he emphasised the essential characteristics of that righteousness which is pleasing to God, and his teaching was embodied in his life.   The authority of his teaching and the power of his life rested upon his own intense faith that God was his Father ; a belief which, owing to his regular practice of silent and lonely prayer, led to an actual experience of union with God.   In the parables his simple teaching was presented to the crowds in language which they could understand, and his miracles of healing were the natural expression of the power of the spiritual over the material.   It is true that at times he chose the exaggerated and poetic language of Jewish eschatology as a vehicle for his teaching, but such language was natural at the period in which he lived, and causes little surprise.   His essential Gospel is not to be found in the eschatological speeches, but in the Sermon on the Mount, and in the parables of the Sower, the Prodigal Son and the Good Samaritan.[1] Whether or no he claimed to be the Messiah, and in what sense he used the title, if he did use it of himself, we cannot now know.   Nor can the modern historian recapture the exact significance of the phrase the ' Son of man ' ; perhaps it was but the expression of his consciousness of the dignity of his essential humanity.   These are problems which need further consideration, and which may perhaps be insoluble.

---

[1] Recently, however, since the publication of Johannes Weiss' monograph, *Die Predigt Jesu vom Reiche Gottes*, and of the works of Albert Schweitzer, *Skizze des Leben Jesu, Das Abendmahls Problem*, and *von Reimarus zu Wrede*, most New Testament scholars have been compelled to treat the eschatological element in the teaching of Jesus far more seriously.   The consequent readjustment in the reconstruction of the development of primitive Christianity is best studied in Kirsopp Lake's *Landmarks of Early Christianity*.

But one negative conclusion may be regarded as certain.   He did not claim to possess a divine nature.   The possibility, however, must always be allowed that his sense of union with his Father in heaven may have led him at times to claim to be the Messiah and even the Son of God ; if so, these titles were the expression of his sense of divine vocation and of the complete surrender of his human will to that of his Father.

The crucifixion was the greatest of all human tragedies. True to their traditions the Jews killed the greatest of their prophets.   But history has reversed the judgment of Caiaphas. He is only remembered as the man who chose to hand over Jesus to Pilate as a leader of insurrection against the emperor, rather than to accept his teaching and himself undertake the reform of the Jewish religion.

The divinely inspired ethical humanitarianism of Jesus, originally evolved within the narrow sphere of an attempt to reform Judaism, could not be thus permanently confined. At times Jesus seemed to feel that his religion was capable of infinite expansion, for if every human soul were of infinite worth in the eyes of the Father of all, there could be no peculiar people and Jewish particularism was therefore undermined at its foundations.   But he foresaw no formal mission ; he founded no Church to propagate his ideals ; he left them to grow and expand in the hearts of those who had heard him, conversed with him, and lived under the influence of his personality.

The influence of Jesus over his disciples was immensely increased by their belief that he was still alive after the crucifixion.   The importance of the resurrection experiences for the later development of primitive Christian faith cannot be exaggerated.   The disciples were convinced that Jesus was the Messiah, and that he would shortly return in glory to destroy the power of evil and inaugurate the final rule of God. By a process of enthusiastic reflection upon the death and resurrection of Jesus, and upon vague memories of certain obscure sayings of his, they advanced the first step toward Catholicism.   Whereas Jesus had preached a Gospel, his disciples preached him.   And yet they still remained Jews, loyal to the traditions of their fathers, and distinguished from other Jews only by their claim to know the Messiah, and by the intensity of their expectation of his coming. They waited for Jesus, the Christ.

This Messianic enthusiasm spread, as such beliefs are known to spread in the East; but its progress can with difficulty be traced, for it moved underground, just as the piety of the Balymous (Plymouth) brothers spread up the Nile valley during the nineteenth century. Groups of disciples appeared at Damascus and at Antioch and even some Greeks were converted to the new faith. With the mission of St. Paul the number of believers grew, and, since his converts were drawn chiefly from the Greeks and not from the Jews, popular Greek ideas penetrated Christianity, and his epistles were largely influenced by this new element. Paulinism both in form and content is popular Greek paganism Christianised. Jesus Christ became the Lord and Saviour, the centre of a sacramental cult based upon the interpretation of his death as a sacrifice, and Christian phraseology was so turned as to suggest that the Oriental-Greek cult deities had been superseded by Jesus, the Son of God. What was historically the gradual apotheosis of a Jewish prophet under the influence of Greek-Christian belief and worship was then thrown back upon the Jesus of history and the story of his life and death was related as the Epiphany of the divine Son of God. This stage of Christian development was completed when the author of the Fourth Gospel completely re-wrote the narrative of the life of Jesus, and borrowed the language of Greek philosophy in order to interpret his significance for the world. He was the Logos incarnate.

Thus Christianity became a mystery religion which tended increasingly to express its doctrines in terms of Greek philosophy. In other words, by the beginning of the second century the main features of Catholic Christianity had been evolved. In one respect, however, Christianity was infinitely superior to all other mystery religions. Christian immortality was morally conditioned to an extent which is not found elsewhere. Initiation involved moral conversion, and the Eucharist involved a moral conformity to the footprints of the Son of God, the *vestigia Christi*. In this way the teaching of the Jesus of history was preserved within the growing Catholic Church; it was not altogether submerged under the mythical interpretation of his person.   This moral sincerity ultimately saved Christianity from the fate of other mystery religions.   They perished, but it endured.   The gradual disappearance of the Jesus of history, however, constituted a grave danger to the persistence within Catholicism even of this moral earnestness.

The rediscovery of the Jesus of history in our own days by the application of the historical method to the study of the earliest Christian documents, and the consequent reconstruction of the development which issued in the Catholic Church of the second century, is far more than a monument to the skill and honesty of the historian.   A basis is now provided for a new reformation of the Christian religion, capable of ensuring its survival in the modern world.   In the Gospel of Jesus is to be found the pure religion of civilised and united humanity. Thus the assured results of liberal historical criticism form as necessary a prelude to the Christianity of the future as the preaching of John the Baptist did to the original proclamation of the Gospel.

III

Its Reflection in Catholic Modernism

This reconstruction of the origin and development of primitive Christianity is undeniably attractive, not so much on account of the sanction which it gives to modern idealistic humanitarianism, but because for the first time Christian historians have presented a rational account of the relation between the Gospel of Jesus and the Catholic Religion, on the basis of a critical analysis of the documents contained in the New Testament.   The method is historical and the conclusions are supported by evidence drawn from the documents themselves.   These conclusions have not left even Catholic scholars unmoved, and Catholic Modernism is, in one of its aspects, an attempt to explain and defend Catholicism on the basis of this historical reconstruction.   It is maintained that Catholicism is the result of a development in which the Gospel of Jesus formed but one element.   The dogmas of the Church and its sacrificial sacramentalism are pagan in origin, and for this reason can be shown to correspond to demands essentially human.   Catholicism is a synthesis between the Gospel of Jesus and popular pagan religion ;   and, because it is a synthesis, Catholicism can claim to be the universal religion.[1] Thus, while Liberal Protestantism tends to find the religion of the future safeguarded by the discovery of the Jesus of history, and by the consequent liberation from the accretions of Catholicism, so foreign to the modern mind,[2] Catholic Modernism welcomes the broadening of the basis of Christianity, due to the recognition of its having preserved and purified the mythology and worship of countless ages of men, and feels no regret that a way of escape from the tyranny of a Jewish prophet has been so solidly secured by the historical and critical approach to the study of the New Testament.

The conclusions, which give this newly discovered liberty the sanction of unprejudiced and scientific historical research, have, however, been shown to be open to very severe criticism, which is by no means confined to those who may be suspected of a desire to defend orthodoxy. These critics do not only question the details of the reconstruction ; they judge the whole to have sprung less from a nice historical sense, than from an impatient anxiety to interpret primitive Christianity " in terms of modern thought." [3]

Those who regard the writing of history as a gentlemanly accomplishment which requires little more than sufficient leisure to ascertain the relevant facts, and a certain facility for embodying them in adequate literary form, not unnaturally discover in the

---

[1] Loisy ably defended Catholicism along these lines in his *L'Évangile et l'Église* (esp. chap. iv). The book was a criticism of Harnack's *What is Christianity?* and of A. Sabatier's *Esquisse d'une Philosophie de la Religion.* Loisy's point of view was developed by G. Tyrrell in *Through Scylla and Charybdis* and in *Christianity at the Cross-Roads* ; it appears in more modern form in Friedrich Heiler's recent book, *Der Katholizismus* (esp. pp. 17–78, 595–660).

[2] "Above all, the figure of Jesus stands out all the more grandly as the mists of theological speculation are blown away from him, and we come to discern him as he really sojourned on earth. It is not too much to say that by recovering for us the historical life of Jesus criticism has brought Christianity back to the true source of its power. The creeds, whatever may have been their value formerly, have broken down, but Jesus as we know him in his life, and all the more as his life is freed from accretions of legend, still commands the world's reverence and devotion. The theology of the future, it is not rash to prophesy, will start from the interpretation of Jesus as a man in history."—E. F. Scott, *The New Testament To-day*, pp. 89 ff.

[3] G. A. van der Bergh van Eysinga, *Radical Views about the New Testament* ; Arthur Drews, *The Christ Myth* ; P. L. Couchoud, *The Enigma of Jesus*, preface by Sir J. G. Frazer ; V. H. Stanton, *The Gospels as Historical Documents* ; Pierre Batiffol, *The Credibility of the Gospels.* To these must be added the learned and voluminous writings of Theodor Zahn. These authors agree in recognising that the Gospels stand within the sphere of Christian orthodoxy ; they disagree, however, completely as to their historical value.

disagreements of the critics nothing more than a fresh instance of that persistent and irrational hatred which theologians are commonly supposed to feel for one another. Those who assume that the Gospel of Jesus was a simple gospel are equally irritated by the inability of the critics to reach agreed conclusions, and attribute this disagreement to the innate tendency of the academic mind first to complicate what is obvious, and then to perform mental gymnastics as prodigious as they are unnecessary. Books written under the influence of such prejudices are, however, calculated rather to inflame the imagination than to sharpen the intellect, and fail to lead to an accurate appreciation of the canons of historical criticism or of the peculiar problems which confront the historian of the beginnings of Christianity.

English theologians, trained in the study of the Classics, and accustomed to an exacting standard of scholarly accuracy, have looked with suspicion on such popular accounts of Christian origins, and have shown far less confidence in the "assured results of modern criticism" than their colleagues in Germany, Holland,[1] and France. The effect of this tradition of learned conservatism has been that, whilst English theologians have made important contributions to the study of the history of the text of the New Testament, to the literary analysis of the first three Gospels, technically known as the Synoptic Problem, and to the exegesis of the various books of the New Testament, they have generally refrained from attempting any comprehensive reconstruction of the development of primitive Christianity on the basis of these exhaustive preliminary studies, and have been content mainly with a criticism of the critics.

IV

NEED OF A SYNTHETIC SOLUTION

It can hardly be denied that English theology stands at the cross-roads. The preliminary studies with which it has been chiefly concerned are now on the whole so well-worn that the results have passed into the textbooks ; and the attempt to force the energy of all the younger men into these channels threatens to involve them in work which must be largely unproductive. On

---

[1] Eldred C. Vanderlaan, *Protestant Modernism in Holland*, provides a useful survey of recent Dutch literature; cf. K. H. Roessingh, *De moderne Theologie in Nederland*, and *Het Modernisme in Nederland*.

the other hand, the analysis of the religious experience within primitive Christianity, and of the beliefs by which it was stimulated, offers a new line of approach to the history of Christian origins, and provides a field of investigation almost untouched, except by those who have little or no first-hand knowledge of the necessary prolegomena. If this be a correct statement of the present situation, there can be little doubt that the time has come for English theology to make its contribution to the study of Christian beginnings, a contribution which may be all the more valuable for this long preparatory discipline. An examination of the reconstruction outlined above provides a convenient point of departure. Should it survive the examination, it only remains to perfect the whole by a greater attention to detail ; if it be found unsatisfactory, an alternative reconstruction must be attempted and submitted to the judgment of scholars. The main purpose of this essay is to state the problem afresh, and to indicate the lines along which a solution may perhaps be found.

1. *Literary Structure of the Gospels*

The literary analysis of the four Gospels has shown that the first three Gospels are closely related documents. Both St. Luke and the editor of St. Matthew's Gospel made use of St. Mark's Gospel in approximately its present form, and also of an early Christian collection of the sayings of Jesus. Since both writers, apparently independently, made constant use of the same documents, it may not unreasonably be deduced that they regarded them as of especial importance. In addition to the material common to the First and Third Gospels each editor has incorporated into his narrative special material not found elsewhere. Therefore, if St. Mark's Gospel be called M, St. Matthew's Gospel T, St. Luke's Gospel L, the collection of sayings Q, the special material in St. Matthew's Gospel $S1$, and the special material in St. Luke's Gospel $S2$, T is composed from $M + Q + S1$ and L from $M + Q + S2$. But it must not be assumed that the editors incorporated their sources unchanged. They show considerable freedom in the use of their sources, a freedom which is however considerably curtailed when they record actual sayings of Jesus. The literary construction of the First and Third Gospels may therefore be expressed by the formulae $T (M + Q + S1)$ and

$L(M+Q+S2)$.   The first three Gospels depend ultimately upon tradition, which was preserved not in the interest of accurate history, but for the guidance and encouragement of the Christians.   It is therefore always possible that the tradition may have been transformed before it was committed to writing.   It must be borne in mind, however, that the belief that the same Jesus who had been taken from them into heaven would return in like manner may well have been more powerful in preserving an accurate tradition of His words than any theory of unprejudiced historical investigation.

The Fourth Gospel occupies a peculiar position in the New Testament.   In form it is a narrative of the actions and sayings of Jesus ; that is, it is a Gospel.   In substance it is primarily an interpretation of Christianity in the light of Christian experience.   The author has no doubt made use of oral tradition, or of a part or the whole of the Synoptic Gospels, or of apostolic reminiscences, or of all of these, but they have been transformed in such a way that it is almost impossible to disengage the tradition from the interpretation.   Therefore, whereas the historian is free to make full use of the Fourth Gospel in describing the Christian religion at the close of the first century, it is dangerous for him to use it as an authority for the earliest form of the Christian tradition.

Since none of the Gospels can have been written down in their present form before the second half of the first century, the Pauline Epistles are the earliest written Christian documents which survive.   The Epistles, therefore, offer important evidence of the primitive Christian tradition in those passages where St. Paul refers to the teaching he had " received," and where, when writing to those who had not been converted through his preaching, he assumes certain beliefs to be held by all Christians alike.

If this literary analysis be accepted as sound, it follows that though the documents do not provide sufficient material for a detailed " life of Jesus," they ought not to be dismissed as entirely untrustworthy.   There is no reason to assume that the characteristic features of His teaching could not have been accurately preserved, or even that incidents recorded as giving rise to sayings of especial importance were entirely due to the creative imagination of the Christians.   This, however, needs careful testing.

The investigation of the origins of Christianity must begin with the exegesis of St. Mark's Gospel (M) and of the sayings common to Matthew and Luke (*Q*), and then proceed to an examination of the Matthean-Lucan corrections of *M* and of the variant forms in which the *Q* source has been preserved. The treatment of the special material (*S*1, *S*2) is best reserved until this has been completed, since the valuable check afforded by a comparison of Matthew and Luke is no longer available.

Assuming the exegesis of *M*, *Q*, *S*1, *S*2 and of the Matthean-Lucan corrections of *M* and *Q* to have been completed, two important questions arise. Do these surviving extracts from primitive Christian tradition agree or disagree in their description of the Gospel proclaimed by Jesus ? and Do they agree or disagree with the tradition received by St. Paul ?

The Synoptic Tradition consists of sayings, miracles, parables, and a careful record of the events which immediately preceded the crucifixion. A Gospel as a literary form emerges when, not merely the events immediately preceding the crucifixion, but the whole tradition is arranged and narrated as the Way of the Cross crowned by the resurrection. This arrangement gives unity to the whole, and the reader is hardly conscious of the fragmentary nature of the parts. Whence came this order? Was it a literary device of the Evangelists? Was it the result of the faith of the Christians?[1] or did it go back to the Lord Himself? No reconstruction of the Gospel of Jesus is possible unless it is possible to answer these questions.

The unity which is achieved by ordering the material so as to secure movement towards a fixed point is also achieved by the central position given to the Kingdom of God, or of Heaven, as a concrete reality ; the whole tradition, including the narrative of the crucifixion, being brought into the closest relationship with it. The recognition of this unity of direction and standpoint leads, however, to a simplification more apparent than real. The Kingdom eludes definition. It is both present and future. The full significance of the phrase " the Kingdom of God " is presumed to be intelligible only to those who believe in Jesus as the Christ, and yet when Peter declares his belief, the obscure title Son of Man is

[1] The literary structure of the Gospels has been minutely examined by three German scholars since the war. The conclusion arrived at is that the Gospel framework is a literary creation, which emerged from the Hellenistic Christian community ; *cf.* K. L. Schmidt, *Der Rahmen der Geschichte Jesu*, 1919 ; M. Dibelius, *Formgeschichte des Evangeliums*, 1919 ; R. Bultmann, *Die Geschichte der synoptischen Tradition*, 1921.

substituted for that of the Christ (Mark iv. 11, viii. 29–32). Thus the Christology underlies the idea of the Kingdom, and the title Son of Man underlies the Christology, and the eschatology underlies the whole. The problem which has to be solved can be clearly formulated. Is this complexity due to the existence within the Synoptic Tradition of various strata of Christian piety with which the original tradition has been successively overlaid, or is the origin of this obscurity to be sought in the life and teaching of Jesus ? If it be maintained that the latter is demanded by the evidence of the documents, then a synthesis of the apparently divergent elements in His teaching must be found.

2. *Canons of Historical Criticism*

No solution of these intricate problems is possible without strict adherence to carefully defined canons of historical criticism. Some of these need stating by way of illustration. (1) Passages which do not occur in the earliest documentary sources, but which are found in later sources, should not be dismissed as necessarily originating at the date of the document in which they are found. Therefore *S*1 and *S*2 may be as valuable as *M* and *Q*. They may be even more primitive. (2) Editorial corrections of an older document need not necessarily be bad corrections. If a document be open to misinterpretation, an editorial correction, however clumsy, may nevertheless correctly elucidate its meaning. Therefore the Matthean-Lucan alterations of *M* and *Q* require careful and sympathetic attention. For example, " Blessed are the poor *in spirit*" (Matt. v. 3) may well be an admirable gloss on the saying recorded by St. Luke, " Blessed are ye poor " (Luke vi. 20). (3) If a word occurs only in a comparatively late document, it does not follow that what is expressed by the word is secondary. Therefore, for example, from the fact that the word " Church " is not found in the Synoptic Gospels except in *S*1, and then only twice (Matt. xvi. 18, xviii. 17), it cannot be assumed that the existence of a corporate body of believers, into which men and women could enter and from which they could be excluded, did not form an integral part of primitive Christian tradition.[1] (4) If the analysis of a document disentangles distinct strata of subject-matter, it must not

[1] Commenting on Matt. xvi. 18, Montefiore writes : " This passage could only have been written after the death of Jesus, for the Christian community was hardly founded by Jesus, but only after his death on the basis of his supposed

be presumed that the dates of their origin can be arranged in definite chronological order.[1]   Therefore, if the analysis of the Gospels reveals Jesus as a prophet, as the Messiah, and as the Saviour of the world, and His teaching as consisting of moral exhortations, of eschatological predictions, and of the promise of supernatural re-generation and immortality, it does not follow that this represents merely successive stages in the development of Christian faith and experience.   And as a rider to this it also follows that, in dealing with religious texts which chiefly record supernatural events, and yet contain much that is normal and human, it must not be assumed that what can easily be paralleled from human experience is historical, and that what is supernatural has been superimposed by the irrational credulity of later enthusiastic believers.   It must, nevertheless, be allowed that an experience felt to be supernatural tends to be expressed symbolically, and the symbolical language or actions are capable of misinterpretation as literal fact, without, however, the symbolism being thereby necessarily obscured. Alterations in religious texts, which appear at first sight to be caused merely by a " love of heightening the miraculous," are more often due to an instinctive desire to perfect the symbolism in such a way that the reality may thereby be given more vivid and adequate expression.   Therefore, for example, when it is found that $S2$ contains a parable, the subject of which is the destruction

resurrection."   With this may be compared the interpretation of Matt. xviii. 15–18 given by Estlin Carpenter: " The church whose authority may be invoked is very different from the Master's ' Kingdom of God ' ; and the rejection of the evil doer on to the level of the heathen or the publican hardly savours of the tireless love which came to seek and to save the lost.   Here, likewise, may we not say, the practice of the later community seeks shelter under the Founder's sanction" (*The First Three Gospels*, chap. i. 4).   Compare the conclusion most solemnly stated by H. Holtzmann : " Therefore it is generally recognised that Mt. (in xviii. 17) has substituted the Church for the Kingdom of God just as he has done in xvi. 18, 19.   To-day, the impossibility of finding in Jesus a founder of a church is accepted by all theologians who can be taken seriously " (*N. T. Theologie*, 2nd Ed., vol. ii, p. 268, n. 3).

[1] Upon this assumption Bousset built the theory which he elaborately developed in *Kyrios Christos :* " There will emerge from the presentation (i.e. of the history of the Christology) a clear distinction between the original community in Palestine and in Jerusalem, and between Jerusalem and Antioch. At the same time it will, I hope, become clear how far Paul belongs pre-eminently to the Hellenistic primitive communities, thus making a contribution to the solution of the great problem of the relation between Paul and Jesus.   The first two chapters of my book, which treat of the primitive community in Jerusalem, form also no more than the introduction, the starting-point, for the presentation which follows " (*Kyrios Christos*, p. vi.).

of a fig-tree (Luke xiii. 6–9), and that *M* includes an incident in which a fig-tree is cursed and destroyed (Mark xi. 12–21) it is possible that the latter is a later form of the former.   But in both cases the fig-tree symbolises Judaism, which failed to produce the fruit (righteousness) demanded by the Messiah, and the transformation of the parable into a miracle emphasises rather than obscures the symbolism.   Considerable portions of the Synoptic Tradition may perhaps have been influenced by similar transformations.

Finally, (5) In cases where a word or a phrase in an ancient document can be translated or paraphrased by a word or phrase in common use at a later period, it does not follow that the meaning of the original is best reproduced by such a translation or paraphrase : it may be even completely obscured.   For instance, " Thou art my beloved Son " seems an obvious rendering of the original Greek in the narrative of the Baptism (Mark i. 11, Luke iii. 22), but the suggestion of uniqueness, which belongs to the Greek word ἀγαπητός [1] is in no way reproduced by the English word " beloved."   Hence the use of such phrases as " the call of Jesus," or " the supreme intuition of his divine mission," [2] tends to obscure the meaning of the passage, by employing easily understood language to paraphrase language which is strange and allusive.

3. *Fallacies in the Liberal Protestant Reconstruction*

Tested by such canons as these, the popular reconstruction of the various stages in the development of primitive Christianity is found to rest upon a series of brilliant and attractive intuitive judgments rather than upon a critical and historical examination of the data supplied by the documents.   *S*1 and *S*2 are used just in so far as they are convenient.   The parable of the Prodigal Son (Luke xv. 11–32, *S*2) is held to be original because forgiveness of sin is not complicated by any reference to the atoning death of the Christ, whilst the speech at Nazareth (Luke iv. 16–30, *S*2), which concludes with the prophecy of the rejection of Jesus by the Jews and of His acceptance by the Gentiles, is treated as a Lucan

---

[1] Cf. *The Journal of Theological Studies*, July 1919, pp. 339 ff., Jan. 1926, pp. 113 ff., and the detached note on " The Beloved " as a Messianic title in Armitage Robinson, *St. Paul's Epistle to the Ephesians*, pp. 229 f.

[2] Loisy, *Évangiles Synoptiques*, i. 408, quoted by Montefiore, *The Synoptic Gospels*, i. 47.

composition [1]; and the important sayings, "But I have a baptism to be baptised with ; and how am I straitened till it be accomplished !" (Luke xii. 50, *S*2), and "Fear not, little flock; for it is your Father's good pleasure to give you the kingdom" (Luke xii 32, *S*2) are hardly mentioned. The subject-matter of the Sermon on the Mount is accepted as authentic throughout (Matt. v.–vii., *Q* + *S*1), but no reference is made to the parable of the Drag-net (Matt. xiii. 47–50, *S*1), or to the saying addressed to St. Peter, embedded in the episode of the Stater in the Fish's Mouth, "Therefore the sons are free" (Matt. xvii 26, *S*1).

St. Mark's Gospel is regarded as a primary source, but the narratives of the Stilling of the Storm, the Walking on the Sea, and the Transfiguration are dismissed as altogether untrustworthy, even though they record the awe experienced by the disciples in the presence of Jesus and their halting, stammering questions, "They feared exceedingly, and said one to another, Who then is this?" (Mark iv. 41), "They were sore amazed in themselves" (Mark vi. 51), "They became sore afraid . . . questioning among themselves what the rising again from the dead should mean" (Mark ix. 6, 10). Nor is any serious attempt made to explain the significant fact that this attitude is accepted and even encouraged by Jesus, which suggests that He regarded a true interpretation of His Person as only possible on the basis of some such experience Sayings firmly rooted in the tradition, such as

---

[1] Montefiore comments on Luke iv. 14–30 : "Luke now makes a great change from the order of Mark. B. Weiss supposes that in doing this he followed his extra special authority (L) ; it is more probable that the transportation of the rejection in Nazareth to this place, and the variants in, and additions to, the story are entirely the work of the Evangelist. His aim is to symbolise the rejection of the Gospel and the Christ by the Jews, and their acceptance by the Gentiles. The miracles which Jesus is said to work outside Nazareth represent the diffusion of the Gospel beyond Israel. The widow of Sarepta and Naaman are types of Christians who were once heathen" (*Syn. Gosp.*, ii. 872). Commenting, however, on Luke xv. 11–32, he describes the parable of the Prodigal Son as "the purest Judaism," and quotes with approval the remarks of J. Weiss: "The gospel of the grace of God is announced without any reference to the cross or the redemptive work of Christ. There is no hint that the love of God must first be set free, so to speak, or that a redeemer is needed. Jesus trusts in His heavenly Father that without more ado He will give His love to every sinner who comes to God in penitence and humble confidence. Thus our parable is in fact a 'gospel' in miniature, but not a gospel of Christ or of the cross, but the glad tidings of the love of the heavenly Father for His children" (*Syn. Gosp.* ii. 991 ; cf. Jülicher, *Die Gleichnisreden Jesu*, ii. 365).

" The Son of man is delivered up into the hands of men, and they shall kill him ; and when he is killed, after three days he shall rise again" (Mark ix. 31), or "The Son of man came not to be ministered unto, but to minister, and to give his life a ransom for many " (Mark x. 45), are held to be secondary and to owe their present form either to the influence of Paulinism or to the first efforts of the Christians to create formulas which were developed later into creeds entirely foreign to the teaching of Jesus.

The use in the New Testament of language which can be paralleled from the surviving records of popular Greek and Eastern religious cults is presumed to imply an assimilation of primitive Christian piety to Greek-Oriental models. The possibility that such language may have expressed and effectually reproduced a relationship to Jesus which existed from the beginning, and which it had been the main purpose of His life and death to evoke, is hardly ever seriously discussed.

The assumption that the original preaching of the Gospel was simple and at once intelligible to ordinary people, and was only misunderstood by the Jewish authorities, whose sympathy had been perverted by hard and unbending ecclesiasticism, underlies the reconstruction outlined above, and conditions the manipulation of the analysis of the subject-matter of the Synoptic Gospels. What is supernatural is transferred to the period of growth, what is human and merely moral and philanthropic and anti-ecclesiastical is assumed to be primitive and original. The miracles and the Christological passages are, therefore, treated primarily as presenting literary and historical rather than religious problems. Consequently their value as evidence for the existence of a unique experience dependent upon a unique faith is entirely overlooked. The possibility has, however, to be reckoned with that the experience of salvation through Christ, or as St. Paul calls it, Justification by Faith, rather than an ethical humanitarianism was from the beginning the essence of the Christian religion, and that the conviction of salvation was from the beginning the peculiar possession of the body of the disciples who surrounded Jesus, and that the peculiarly Christian love of God and of men followed, but did not precede, the experience of salvation by faith in Christ, and the incorporation into the body of His disciples. In other words, not only may the supernatural element have been primitive and original, but also that exclusiveness, which is so obviously a characteristic of Catholic Christianity, may have its origin in the teaching of Jesus rather than in the theology of St. Paul.

These criticisms are not, however, wholly to the point unless the exegesis of the Marcan narrative of the Baptism, upon which the whole reconstruction ultimately rests, can be shown to be unsatisfactory and misleading. It is claimed that the natural meaning of the narrative is that Jesus, conscious of the need of repentance, and therefore possessing a sense of sin, came to be baptised by John. At the moment of His baptism He passed through a religious experience, of which He alone was conscious, and that He then felt Himself called to associate Himself with the work of the Baptist. Thus, in spite of all the later Christological accretions, there is preserved in St. Mark's Gospel a genuine reminiscence of the consecration of Jesus to the work of a prophet, in the light of which the claim to the Messiahship, if He did make the claim, must be interpreted. The Matthean version of the Baptism shows the early church in the process of obliterating all traces of this human experience by the insertion of the preliminary conversation between Jesus and John, and by the substitution of " This is my beloved Son " for " Thou art my beloved Son," which has the effect of transforming an intimate personal experience into a public proclamation of Jesus as the Messiah (Mt. iii. 13–17, $M + S$1).

But is the Marcan narrative really capable of such psychological treatment ? And is it necessary to convict Matthew of such wilful and unprincipled editing ? The Second Gospel opens with the description of John the Baptist as the forerunner of the Christ, preparing " the way of the Lord," and proclaiming the advent of the Messiah to baptise with the Holy Spirit. Jesus is then immediately introduced, coming unknown and unrecognised among the crowd, and His baptism is narrated as the fulfilment of the great Messianic passages in Isaiah xi. 1–9, xlii. 1–4, lxi. 1–3, and in Psalm ii. 7. Most significantly the latter half of the citation from the Psalm (ii. 7), " This day have I begotten thee," is omitted, and an echo of Isaiah xlii. 1, " In whom I am well pleased," substituted for it.[1] No less significant is the inser-

---

[1] The citation from Ps. ii. 7 is completed in some manuscripts of the Lucan version of the Baptism (D a b c ff²). Canon Streeter considers this to be the original reading of Luke iii. 22 (*The Four Gospels*, pp. 143, 276). It is more easily explained as an assimilation to the Psalm. Even if it were original in Luke, its Christological significance cannot be unduly pressed, since in Acts xiii. 33 the citation is applied to the resurrection.

tion of the word "beloved," which at least suggests uniqueness, and may be a synonym for "only begotten."[1] Thus the intelligent reader, who is expected to feel the allusions, is from the outset initiated into the secret of the Messiahship of Jesus. The question as to whether there was or was not a moment when He became the Son of God is neither raised nor answered by the Evangelist. Having made it perfectly plain that Jesus is the Christ, the Son of God, he proceeds to record the steps by which the disciples were led to accept Him as the Messiah. The introduction to the Gospel which consists of the preaching of John the Baptist, and the account of the Baptism of Jesus, must therefore be interpreted by the whole narrative which follows, and especially by the Transfiguration, the Crucifixion, and the Resurrection.

If the Marcan narrative be open to this interpretation, the Matthean corrections admit of a comparatively simple explanation. They do not involve the transformation of a human prophet into a supernatural Messiah, since the Marcan source itself implies a supernatural Christology. They do, however, gloss over the reiterated emphasis laid by St. Mark on the fact that the Messiahship of Jesus was recognised by none except by the evil spirits until the confession of Peter, and that it was not proclaimed in public until the trial before Caiaphas. The use of the baptismal narratives for an analysis of the religious experience of Jesus is at best a very hazardous procedure, and almost inevitably results in confining His experience within a framework supplied by an incomplete knowledge of the psychology of vocation.

The conclusion to which these arguments have been leading is that, so far as the subject-matter of the Gospel is concerned, no one of the Synoptic Gospels can be contrasted with the others, nor can portions of the Gospels be set over against the remainder, nor is there any evidence of the existence of older lost Christian documents which contradict those which survive. The main problem of the origin of Christianity can, therefore, be stated with considerable precision. Was this unity of subject-matter achieved in the period between the crucifixion and the date when the Christian tradition was first committed to writing ? Or did

---

[1] In the LXX the Hebrew word יָחִיד is translated indiscriminately by μονογενής or ἀγαπητός (Judg. xi. 34, Tob. iii. 15, vi. 14, Ps. xxxv. 17; Gen. xxii. 2, 12, 16, Am. viii. 10, Jer. vi. 26 ; cf. Mk. xii. 6, Lk. xx. 13, vii. 12, viii. 42, ix. 38). See references, p. 166, note 1.

it originate with the teaching of Jesus ? In solving this problem the personal judgment of the historian can never be wholly eliminated. For example, even if it be granted that the Marcan narrative of the Baptism implies a supernatural Christology, it is still possible for the critic to claim that Mark was himself influenced by a developing Christology, and that he has allowed his narrative to be controlled by it. This must, however, remain no more than a supposition so long as it is supported by no documentary evidence ; and the necessity for some such supposition is considerably reduced if it can be shown that the elements which together form the subject-matter of the Gospels are capable of a synthesis.

V

GOVERNING IDEAS OF THE GOSPELS

1. *The Kingdom of God*

The petitions of the Lord's Prayer, " Thy Kingdom come. Thy will be done, in earth as it is in heaven," indicate that the phrase " the Kingdom of God," or " of Heaven," is more than a poetical representation of an ideal. It presumes that the Kingdom of God exists in heaven. In the immediate presence of God His sovereignty is complete and absolute, and heaven is the sphere in which that sovereignty operates perfectly and eternally. The genitives which qualify the word " Kingdom " are primarily genitives of origin. If the Kingdom is to be established on earth, it must come from God or from Heaven. Thus the salvation of men, that is their incorporation into the sphere in which the sovereignty of God operates, is only possible either by their ascension into the heavens, or by the descent and extension of the supernatural order from heaven to earth. Salvation is therefore conceived of as necessarily dependent upon an act of God. The conception that the human order can be transformed into the Kingdom of Heaven by a process of gradual evolution is completely foreign to the New Testament.

The Synoptic Gospels assume throughout that the supernatural order has descended to earth. The Kingdom has come. The Beelzebul speech (Mark iii. 20–30, Matt. xii. 22–30, Luke xi. 14–23), in which our Lord's interpretation of His miracles, of the call of the disciples, and of their acceptance of His call is recorded, gives this classical expression.   Beelzebul, the Prince of the evil spirits, has usurped authority over men, and has become, as his name indicates, the master of the house (*cf.* Matt. x. 25).[1]   The miracles of Jesus are effectual signs that a stronger than Beelzebul has come.   The Mighty One is robbing the Prince of evil of his authority, and spoiling his goods.   When the twelve accepted the call of Jesus, they passed from the sovereignty of Beelzebul under the authority of the Christ ; and the family of Jesus who do the will of God is thus sharply distinguished from the house of Beelzebul (Mark iii 33–35, *cf.* Matt. xii. 30, Luke xi. 23).   But the underlying distinction is between the Kingdom of God and of His Christ, and the Kingdom of Satan.   The Matthean-Lucan addition to the Marcan narrative, " Then the kingdom of God is come upon you " (Matt. xii. 28, Luke xi. 20), is admirably appropriate.   The authority of Satan is undermined by the advent of the Christ, and by the descent of the Kingdom of God (*cf.* Luke x. 18).   The new supernatural order has descended upon earth, and is realised in Jesus and His disciples.   Because He is the Christ from heaven, they have become the sons of the Kingdom and the Messianic people of God, to whom the mystery of the Kingdom has been given.   The true love of God and of men is thus embodied in a living organism.

Judaism is, therefore, superseded and fulfilled.   The authority exercised by the chief priests and scribes and Pharisees passes to the disciples of the Christ, and especially to the twelve apostles, who as the twelve patriarchs of the new people of God are to lead the Messianic mission to the world, to cast out devils and fish for men.   Finally, they will sit on twelve thrones judging the twelve tribes of Israel : " Fear not, little flock ; for it is your Father's good pleasure to give you the kingdom " (Luke xii. 32, xxii. 28-30, Matt. xix. 28, *cf.* Mark i. 17, xii. 9).   This radical attitude to Judaism, which gives point to the parable of the Wicked Husbandmen and to the Cursing of the Fig-Tree, underlies the whole of our Lord's teaching.   Judaism is superseded, not because a new

---

[1] The name *Beelzebul* may mean either *Lord of dung* or *Lord of the habitation*.   Mt. x. 25, and the whole sense of the Beelzebul speech, seem to demand a play upon words.   Jesus is the true, Beelzebul the false, *Lord of the house*. The variant reading *Beelezebub*, which occurs in no Greek manuscript, is best explained by assimilation to 2 Kings, i. 2, 6, when the significance of the name *Beelzebul* was not understood (*cf.* Swete, *St. Mark* ad Mk. iii. 22).

prophet has arisen, but because the Messiah has come and effected the purification of the heart and brought into being the new People of God. The Messianic Kingdom has arrived and Judaism is fulfilled by the advent of the Messiah and by the actual righteousness which belief in Jesus carried with it. Of this Messianic purification and illumination the miracles are signs and symbols. The blind who see, the dumb who speak, the lepers who are cleansed, the hungry who are fed, and the dead who are raised have their more important counterparts in the apostolic vision of the Christ at the Transfiguration, in St. Peter's convinced declaration after a long period of inarticulate stammering that Jesus is the Christ, in the cleansing of Mary Magdalene, Levi, and Zacchaeus, in the Eucharistic bread and wine, and in the eternal life which is promised to those who leave all and follow Jesus. The apostles, having heard the call of the Christ and having been incorporated into the supernatural order of the Kingdom, are the true believers in God and the true lovers of men, and as such are given especial authority. They are the salt of the earth, and to them is entrusted the Messianic purification of the world.

2. *The Humiliation of the Christ*

During the earthly ministry of the Christ all this is veiled in obscurity, not because the Kingdom will only come with the end of the world, but because He must first complete His work. The humiliation of the Christ of divine necessity (Mark viii. 31) precedes the apostolic mission to the world, because this mission, to be effective, depends upon His death and glorification. Until this is accomplished His disciples are ignorant both of the meaning of His life and teaching and of their own significance for the world. The humiliation of the Christ underlies the Synoptic Tradition throughout, and is carefully emphasised, as a comparison with the Apocalypse clearly shows. He was subject to temptation, His power was dependent upon faith and prayer, the sphere of His work was limited to Jews resident in Palestine, He was compelled to face the united opposition of the Jewish authorities. He spoke in parables and His actions were symbolic, because the Gospel could not be nakedly expressed. Of this humiliation the crucifixion was both the climax and the completion, for by it the Christ was both freed and glorified.

" I have a baptism to be baptised with ; and how am I straitened till it be accomplished ! " (Luke xii. 50).

" The Son of man must suffer many things, and be rejected by the elders, and the chief priests, and the scribes, and be killed, and after three days rise again " (Mark viii. 31).

The death of the Christ was, however, far more than a necessary stage in His personal glorification; it inaugurated a new order, as the sacrifice on Mount Sinai inaugurated the Old Covenant. Our Lord's words at the Last Supper must be taken primarily as assigning to His death redemptive significance.

3. The Via Crucis

It is not, however, suggested that this liberty of the Christ, accomplished through His death and glorification, will carry with it at once the liberty of His disciples.   They must remain in the world and succeed to His former position.   If He was the humiliated Son of God, they are to be the humiliated sons of God. The persecuted and humiliated Christ is to be succeeded by the persecuted and humiliated disciples ; but whereas His work was limited to Jews, the sphere of their work will not be thus bounded (Mark xiii. 9–13, 27).   In other respects they must follow in His footsteps.   Possessing supernatural power, they will be tempted from within and from without to misuse it ; their power will be dependent, as His was, upon faith and prayer ; they must take up their cross, for they also will be brought before governors and kings for His sake [1] ; they must be willing to die.   For some, as for Judas, these demands will prove too severe and they will return whence they had been rescued—that is, they will pass from the Kingdom of God to the Kingdom of Beelzebul.   Into this life of Christian humiliation the disciples were initiated by the words

---

[1] Professor Burkitt (*Christian Beginnings*, p. 147) holds that "governors and kings" (Mark xiii. 9) are Roman officials and Herods in Palestine, and that "the mental horizon is still Palestine, not a formal worldwide evangelization." In the context, however, in which the saying stands, the horizon is not Palestine merely (xiii. 8, 13, 27).   The eschatological mission of salvation before the End can, it is true, hardly be described as a *formal* evangelization.   Mark xiii. contains no suggestion of *formality*.   If it be granted that the chapter refers to an eschatological mission which, after the death of the Lord, the disciples are to lead beyond the boundaries of Palestine, there seems every reason to regard Mark xiii. as, at least, reminiscent of words spoken by Jesus.

spoken at the Last Supper. The Last Supper, therefore, both gave formally to the death of the Christ its redemptive value and also formally initiated the disciples into the mystical and actual participation in His sacrifice and of its benefits. The disciples must share in His *broken* Body and His *outpoured* Blood. Only thus could they be enabled to continue His work, to share in His victory over sin and death, to take up their cross confidently and follow Him, and to endure the hostility of the world until the End.

4. *The New Righteousness and Eternal Life*

The Synoptic Tradition presumes eternal life to be dependent on moral conversion effected by belief in the Christ and by incorporation into the body of the disciples of Jesus. The apostolic Gospel, therefore, is both a gospel of supernatural moral purification and a gospel of immortality. Possessing the supernatural righteousness of the heart, the disciples possess also eternal life, and those who have received and maintained this righteousness need not fear the Judgment which is to come. The Christian gospel of immortality has its roots in Jewish eschatology as transformed by our Lord, rather than in the cycle of ideas and experiences characteristic of Greek-Oriental mystery cults.

The character of the new Messianic righteousness, upon which the Christian hope of ultimate immortality is based, is illustrated in our Lord's teaching on marriage and divorce. Moses, He allowed, wisely permitted divorce, because of the hardness of men's hearts, and Judaism rightly followed his teaching. But with the coming of the Christ and the consequent entrance of those who believe on Him into the sovereignty of God, this hardness of heart has been removed, and His disciples can not only, therefore, fulfil the law of God promulgated in the second chapter of Genesis, " Therefore shall a man leave his father and his mother, and shall cleave unto his wife : and they shall be one flesh " (Gen. ii. 24, quoted Mark x. 7, 8, Matt. xix. 5), but they can even, for the sake of the Kingdom, remain celibate without falling into sin (Matt. xix. 12). Hence adultery and fornication among Christians are not to be regarded as lapses from a moral law, but as apostasy from the Kingdom. Similarly, the purpose of the Sermon on the Mount is to describe the new Messianic righteousness by which the old is authoritatively superseded and fulfilled, rather than to construct a new moral law on the basis of the old.   Still less is the Sermon on the Mount a loosely constructed list of ideal moral virtues.   The advent of the Christ and the existence of the Messianic community which He has brought into being are presumed throughout.   The most serious humiliation of the Christians is that this righteousness which they have received has to be maintained in the face of manifold temptations, and may be lost.   It is possible for the salt to lose its savour, and of this Judas becomes the terrible symbol.

The emphasis on the humiliation of the Christ and on the subsequent humiliation of His disciples is crossed by the eschatology which alone renders the whole position tolerable and intelligible. Though the humiliation of the Christ ends with His death and resurrection, the humiliation of His Ecclesia must last until He returns, not this time unknown and unrecognised, but in glory, on the clouds, and visible to all.   Then the righteous will be separated from the unrighteous, and the Kingdom will be established in glory and for ever.   The final reunion of the Christ and His disciples is also foreshadowed in the words spoken at the Last Supper. The Eucharist looks forward beyond the humiliation of the Christ, beyond the humiliation of His disciples, to the time when it will be no longer possible for them to share in the sacrifice of His body and blood, for He will drink the wine new in the Kingdom of God (Mark xiv. 25, Luke xxii. 18 ; the Matthean addition *with you*—Matt. xxvi. 29—that is, *with the Apostles*, giving correctly the sense of the Marcan saying; *cf.* p. 164).[1]   The Eucharist is, therefore, as St. Paul says, the commemoration of the Lord's death " *till he come* " (1 Cor. xi. 26).   But when the Kingdom will come in glory, or when the Christ will return, no one can know ; of this even the Christ Himself was ignorant.   Only this is certain : the Gospel must first be preached to all nations, and, what is a far more difficult task, it must be preached in all the cities of Israel.   But the impression given by the Synoptic Gospels is that the End will not be long delayed.

---

[1] Dr. Gore, however, informs me in a letter that he considers that " there can be little doubt that St. Mark gives the original and true tradition, and that it referred to the experience of the Christ, as it was to be, without reference to the Apostles." (Letter dated Sept. 9, 1926.)

VI

CONCLUSION

From this reconstruction it will be seen at once that a whole series of contrasts underlies the Synoptic Tradition. These contrasts, however, do not break the unity of the whole, since they are capable of synthesis. The failure of most modern scholars to formulate the contrasts correctly has led to their failure to recognise the possibility of a synthesis. The contrast is not between the Jesus of history and the Christ of faith, but between the Christ humiliated, and the Christ returning in glory ; the two being held together by the title Son of Man which suggests both (Ezek. ii. 1, Psalm viii. 4–6, Dan. vii. 13, 14, interpreted by Enoch xlvi. 2, 2 Esdras xiii.) : " The Son of man must suffer " (Mark viii. 31) ; " The Son of man hath not where to lay his head " (Luke ix. 58) ; " Ye shall see the Son of man sitting at the right hand of power, and coming with the clouds of heaven " (Mark xiv. 62) ; " And he said unto his disciples, The days will come when ye shall desire to see one of the days of the Son of man, and ye shall not see it. And they shall say to you, Lo, there ! Lo, here ! go not away, nor follow after them : for as the lightning, when it lighteneth out of the one part under the heaven, shineth unto the other part under heaven ; so shall the Son of man be in his day. But first must he suffer many things and be rejected of this generation " (Luke xvii. 22–25). The double significance of the title Son of Man may have caused our Lord to use it for the interpretation of His Person, in preference to the easily misunderstood title " the Christ." The contrast is not between a reformed and an unreformed Judaism, but between Judaism and the new supernatural order by which it is at once destroyed and fulfilled : not between the disciples of a Jewish prophet and the members of an ecclesiastically ordered sacramental cultus, but between the disciples of Jesus, who, though translated into the sovereignty of God, are as yet ignorant both of His claims and of the significance of their own conversion, and the same disciples, initiated into the mystery of His Person and of His life and death, leading the mission to the world, the patriarchs of the new Israel of God. The contrast is not between an ethical teaching and a dreamy eschatology, or between a generous humanitarianism and an emotional religious experience stimulated by mythological beliefs, but between a supernatural order characterised

N

by a radical moral purification involving persistent moral conflict and the endurance of persecution, and a supernatural order in which there is no place either for moral conflict or for persecution. Thus stated the contrasts are capable of synthesis by a fairly simple view of history. Judaism is fulfilled by the advent of the Christ, who inaugurates the new order, which is the Kingdom of God on earth. The existence, however, of the Kingdom of God and of the kingdoms of the world together involves conflict and opposition, which is to last till the return of the Christ and the final destruction of evil, when the Kingdom will come in earth as it is in heaven, or, to use St. Paul's phrase, when God shall be all in all.

A synthesis of the contradictory elements within the Synoptic Tradition having been thus achieved, the last step in the historical reconstruction of the origin of the Christian religion is almost inevitable. This was the Gospel proclaimed by Jesus, and these were the claims made by the Jesus of history for Himself and for His disciples. Ultimately this conclusion is, and must be, a subjective judgment, but it is a conclusion from which it is exceedingly difficult to escape.

It remains only to point out what is gained by this alternative reconstruction. The historian is freed from the necessity of being compelled to assume that a foreign influence was exerted upon primitive Christianity between the crucifixion and the appearance of the earliest Pauline Epistles, and he is therefore enabled to treat the development represented by the Pauline Epistles, the Johannine writings, and the literature of the Catholic Church of the second century primarily as a spontaneous Christian development. The commentator will find that the New Testament is one book, not merely because certain documents have been collected together by ecclesiastical authority or by common Christian usage, but because it presumes an underlying unity of faith and experience.

In conclusion it may be suggested that the results of a purely historical investigation of the origins of Christianity have a more than purely historical importance. There seems no reason to doubt that the characteristic features of Catholic piety have their origin in our Lord's interpretation of His own Person and of the significance of His disciples for the world. The religion of the New Testament provides, therefore, a standard by which the Catholicism of succeeding generations must be tested, and which it must endeavour to maintain.

THE INCARNATION
BY JOHN KENNETH MOZLEY

CONTENTS

THE doctrine of the Person of Christ, in its historic form, gives the fullest illumination to the doctrine of God and the fullest expression of the doctrine of grace. That is because the *theologia Christi* is essentially, as Kaftan, the theologian of the Ritschlian right wing, says, the doctrine of Christ's Godhead. "Christ is spoken of as God": so, in opposition to assailants of the Lord's real divinity, writes an anonymous author quoted by Eusebius, with an appeal to the Fathers of the second century. If Christ is perfect in His Godhead, then in Him God's self-revelation reaches its highest point, nor is there any peak beyond this peak which man will, under the conditions of his earthly life, ever need to ascend in order to gain the light of a fuller knowledge of God. The Catholic doctrine of the Incarnation rules out every thought of a repetition of that supreme act in which God became man. It is concerned with one who is truly God incarnate, not a temporary *avatar* of deity. And the wealth of God's favour to man is pledged and given in the gift of the Son. "How shall He not with Him freely give us all things?" The great problems of theism, as they affect both speculative inquiry and practical religion, come to the fullest rest which man can enjoy, in that faith which has been the foundation of the victories of Christianity in the world and the power in which those victories have been won. Browning only puts in an absolute form the confidence which the doctrine of Christ's Godhead inspires:

> I say, the acknowledgment of God in Christ
> Accepted by thy reason solves for thee
> All questions in the earth and out of it.

It is natural enough that round this doctrine the most dramatic controversy in the history of the Christian Church was fought out; it is equally natural that in the religious world of to-day, with all its cross-currents and hesitations, it is in relation to this same doctrine that the most real divisions, productive of the most far-reaching consequences, appear. The religious discussions and confessions of faith, to which so large a space has recently been given in popular journalism, all come to their critical turning-point, whether the writers have perceived the fact or not, when the choice has to be made between a Jesus as divine as the Father and a Jesus whose divinity, if the term is used, is the immanental divinity of the race at the highest point which it has yet reached. And it is the crisis within all that calls itself Christian as well as between Christianity and the world that lies without.

I

The Doctrine and the Gospels

In the previous essay the question has been approached from the side of the study of the Gospels and of the picture which they give of Jesus Christ. Such a treatment is indispensable. In the Christian religion historical facts and theological doctrine cannot be detached from one another and put into separate compartments. That issue was effectively settled in principle when the Gospels came to be written. But the relation between the Gospels as documents which certainly intend (let us for the moment put it no higher than that) to record facts of history and the doctrine of the Incarnation calls for much accurate discrimination. In the first place, the Gospels are products of the doctrine in the form which that doctrine possessed about the middle of the first century or a few years later, and witnesses to it ; they were not written to establish it ; that is no more true of St. John's Gospel than of St. Mark's. And, secondly, it is not necessary to hold that one, and only one, evaluation of the historical matter in the Gospels is essential to the doctrine. Among the various attempted re-constructions of the Gospel history and delineations of the central Figure, some, of course, make the interpretation which the Church regards as the one true interpretation at least difficult. But even radical criticism may compel the recognition of a mystery *sui generis* about the Person of Jesus, and not compel but allow of the belief that nothing less than the Catholic doctrine is an adequate explanation of the facts. That the " reduced Christology," to use Dr. Sanday's phrase, of the liberal theologians of Germany did cohere more or less closely with views as to the unreliability of the Gospel narratives, especially of the Fourth Gospel, in the report of sayings and doings of Jesus in which the element of transcendence comes notably to the front, is undeniable. But it makes a great difference whether this element is judged to have been intruded into the history, because an examination and comparison of strata and traditions can be brought to show or suggest the unauthentic character of the Gospels at the points in question, or whether the Gospels are pronounced to be unreliable in the relevant passages because of the intrusion of this element. It is not necessary, nor would it be right, to present these alternatives as though, in practice, they could be quite clearly and sharply differentiated from one another. But in so far as a place has to be found for the second alternative, we are thrown back on to distinctively theological issues. For the determining of those issues other considerations must be present than the data of the Gospels can by themselves, if taken in isolation, supply.

II

The Reaction against the Doctrine

We turn then to the doctrine itself, to the belief that in the Person of Jesus Christ we have the incarnation of the eternal, divine Son of God ; and, first of all, to the reaction against that doctrine, or, at least, the deflection from it, characteristic of the many Christologies which can be studied from rather different angles in Schweitzer's " Quest of the Historical Jesus," and in Sanday's " Christologies Ancient and Modern." It is noteworthy that the very idea of a Christology, of a doctrine of Christ's Person, implies that in that Person there is present something, some overplus, as compared with what is true of other persons. It is possible to adopt what may be called a wholly humanitarian view of Jesus. Some world-views necessitate such a conclusion. In such cases the break with the Christian tradition is absolute. But whenever, against a theistic background, it is recognised that there is something in respect of the relation of Jesus to God which can be associated with none other than Him, a step has been taken within the borders of Christology. Though they may not be aware of the fact, modern writers often raise just the same problem as underlies the doctrine of the Church. But in their thought there is less thoroughness and less care than is manifested in the theologians of the Church. It is a curious fact that the accuracy with which the theologian feels that it is necessary for him to try to approach the expression of a coherent world-view seems, at times, almost to be imputed to him as a fault, whereas the metaphysician is not subject to this charge.

What are the objections to a Christology which, while admitting an overplus in the Person of Jesus, surrenders the Catholic doctrine of Christ's Godhead, thus opposing itself to the Creed of Nicaea not less than to the Definition of Chalcedon? In the first place the break, at this point, is made with tradition precisely where tradition is strongest. For the strength of tradition consists not merely in consistency of belief but in the sense of what is indispensable to life and health. If the Christian conception of the meaning of existence is untrue, then the doctrine of the Incarnation falls ; but if that conception is maintained and defended as giving the true religious interpretation of the world ; if that interpretation is found to be consistent only with a doctrine of a personal God whose relations with the world are expressed by such terms as creation, providence and redemption ; if, further, Jesus is regarded as, in a special way, illuminating and even mediating some of those relations, as possessing (a point on which Ritschl laid great stress) a unique historical vocation ; and if, finally, a distinct place is kept for the truth and importance of the resurrection of Jesus, with whatever dissent from the form of the Gospel narratives—then, in such case, the rejection of the doctrine which has, in the history of Christian thought, been associated not formally and externally, but by the most intimate of internal connections, with the affirmations of Christian faith and the struggles, heroisms and achievements of Christian practice, needs to be justified by weightier arguments than are usually forthcoming. The pages of criticism in Loofs' small book "What is the Truth about Jesus Christ?" may be referred to as a careful and temperate, while definite, attempt to show that the Catholic doctrine is untenable. But apart from the fact that the Incarnation, as a possibility for God, cannot be disproved by the exhibition of resulting paradoxes which are then pleaded in support of the view that the doctrine is irrational, it is, I think, fair to say that the weakness of Lutheranism, and of German liberal theology in general, in its grasp of the idea and importance of the Church, makes it difficult for Loofs to appreciate the force of a question which might be written across his book taken as a whole—If, in such large respects as this work reveals, what the Church has believed about Christ is true, is not the Church likely to be right in that further belief about Him which makes of the Church's faith a coherent unity? Obviously it is impossible to reach more than a measure of probability along the lines of such a question, and the argument involved possesses in this context the characteristics and the limitations of an *argumentum ad rem* : nevertheless, it ought to be faced by those who agree that the Church is right in ascribing to Christ a unique place in relation both to God and to man and in striving to bring the world to an acknowledgment of this His position, but is wrong in the interpretation it offers—an interpretation which, in the fourth century crisis, was essential to the survival of Christianity as vital religion. Anyone who reads the fascinating account of the beginnings of the Arian controversy, and especially of the contrasted doctrines of Arius and Athanasius in Harnack's "History of Dogma," may well feel that he is preparing for himself a position of unstable equilibrium if he tries to make his own what is, in effect, Harnack's conclusion, that Athanasius was religiously at the centre, dogmatically absurd.[1]

Then, secondly, Christian experience decidedly favours the Nicene doctrine of Christ's true Deity. Warily though it is necessary to walk in the attempt to apprehend the character and to determine the tests of the argument from experience, it is possible for any careful observer to arrive at certain results after a broad survey of the course of Christian history. And whether attention be directed to the Church as a whole or to the great Christian souls who have revealed themselves to us, or, so far as that can be known, to the piety of the individual Christian who has achieved no supereminent degree of saintliness and progressed not far along the mystic way, the strength and the inspiration of life have been that devotion and self-committal to Him, that trust in Him as Saviour and loyalty to Him as Lord, which finds its completion in the adoration of Him as God. But that is not all : not only are Christian piety and the Christian life historically bound up with the confession of the Godhead of Christ, so that each is intellectually coherent with the other, but the highest ascents and the most far-going adventures of Christian saints who have made of life a continual means of sacramental or mystical communion with God have been, at the same time, the attempt to win a fuller

---

[1] I have adapted a phrase quoted by Mr. H. G. Wood as used of W. Herrmann, "religiously at the centre, dogmatically worthless." Like all such epigrams it is too sweeping. But Herrmann's view of the relation of Christian religion and faith to dogma makes it intelligible in his case, whereas in the case of Athanasius the disjunction is far less tolerable.

knowledge of Christ, and to discover more of the meaning of what has been already confessed. If Christians had not believed in the Godhead of Christ, both the most distinctive and the most wonderful things in Christian experience would never have come into existence. That to which they witness is that from which they have sprung. It is not simply a case of the creed being an intellectual explication of the experience. If that were all, there would be comparatively little difficulty in allowing that a change in the creed would, after the necessary readjustments in thought, make no difference to the future history of the experience. But what has happened, when belief in Christ's Godhead has been given up and some other form of doctrine has taken its place, gives no ground for any such idea. If the richest and the most penetrating kind of Christian experience is to continue, its conditions will remain what they have always been.

And, thirdly, whereas the Catholic doctrine gives a rational interpretation of the Person of Jesus in relation to God, and, in connection with Him, of God in relation to the world, the Christologies which stand on the other side find it hard to rise above description to explanation. After accounts with historical criticism have been settled the individual scholar or theologian must, if he wishes to go as far as possible into the depths of his subject-matter, put to himself such questions as " How is it that Jesus was the kind of person that the sources, after cross-examination, show Him to have been ? " and " Why did the primitive communities think of Him after the fashion revealed throughout the New Testament ? " It is not easy to answer the first question along the lines of a non-Catholic Christology, while keeping a firm hold on the uniqueness of Christ. Arianism, in its historic, dogmatic form, is as dead as an opinion can be, but the root-difficulty of Arianism remains in Christologies which are quite differently expressed and seem free enough from everything of a mythological character. Historic Arianism made of Christ an intermediate being whose physical characteristics isolated Him both from God and from man. The Christologies of modern times do not isolate Christ so far as His nature is concerned ; as to that He is man, simply and exclusively, with whatever affinities to God man possesses in virtue of his Creator's will, or, if the background of thought is pantheistic rather than theistic, of the terms of the cosmic and evolutionary process. But the grand solitariness of Christ, His moral and spiritual difference, has been constantly emphasised, and much made of those features in His life and teaching which belong to Him as they do not belong to others, and which we do not associate with mankind in general. As to how and why this should be so, a Christology which rejects the doctrine of the Incarnation cannot readily explain. As the medium of the conceptions of the world and of God's dealings with men which appear in the teaching of Jesus, Messianic and apocalyptic notions may rightly be exhibited. But these do not account for Him, and that is the heart of the problem. The belief that in Jesus the Spirit of God was present in the highest degree is the nearest approach which liberal Christologies make to the Catholic doctrine : but this doctrine does not so much solve one problem as raise another, namely how we may understand the action of God in the choice of a particular person at a particular time for this superlative endowment ; or, if the stress is laid rather on the achievement of Jesus than on the work of God, how we may understand the supremacy of Jesus in the moral and spiritual sphere. Christologies of an immanental or inspirational character involve in this case an ethical development *per saltum* to which no parallel can be offered. This perplexity, at least, does not confront the believer in the Incarnation, since in that case what we have is not a sudden break in the normal moral history of the race, but a new beginning. St. Paul's contrast drawn between the first Adam and the second is one way of expressing the difference which Christ makes for mankind. But to find the material for such a difference in the history of one individual member of the race involves an assertion of spiritual relevance in this one person such as challenges us to go further into the meaning of a truth of which the phenomenon of His life affords the one and only example.

But the belief that the historic doctrine of the Church has advantages of a purely rational character over its rivals ought not to prevent those who hold it from feeling a very real sympathy with others who have been able neither to make the Church's doctrine their own nor to evacuate the Gospels of personal mystery. A logic which may seem insuperable to others should not lead to the attempt to force hard and fast alternatives on those who can more easily be impaled upon a dilemma than saved by one. The Liberal reconstructions in Christology were not built to be

immortal; yet amid all the confusion of an era which inevitably
set its sons searching for guiding-posts to take the place of their
fathers' landmarks, which were for the time at least, and some
thought for ever, being submerged beneath the incoming flood
of discovery and criticism, they did service to their own generation
and even beyond. They aimed at showing the religious view
of the world to be concentrated in and mediated through the
Person of Jesus; they refused to admit that Christianity was
merely a department of religion, and religion of philosophy.
When all the reservations on which they insisted had been made,
it was still clearly the case that the history of Jesus Christ and
of Christianity was much more than one chapter in the comparative history of the religious experiences of mankind.

III

LIBERALISM AND ESCHATOLOGY

A word may be said on the greatest difference in scientific
outlook between the Liberals on the one hand and their critics
from the side of eschatology on the other. For the former it
was natural to try to present the Person of Jesus as rationally
intelligible and interpretable in terms of the standards and ideas
of an age far later than His own. That age, their own, was
being immensely affected in its world-view by the science and
criticism which were so striking a feature in the development
of its intellectual life. It would almost seem as though the
unconscious notion prevailed that He could be of use to the nineteenth century only by being shown to lack the characteristics
of a Jew of the first. So rationalisation entered not only into
explanations of narratives in the Gospels but also into the
delineations of the figure of Jesus. Against this the eschatologists
set their faces, and with much right. They had strong arguments
to bring forward both in criticism and in theology. And when
those who have stood on this side have been penetrating enough,
as was the case with von Hügel, they have deepened the impression
of mystery, to which the Liberals were not insensitive, in connection with Jesus. They have called attention to the strain
and tension which the Gospels reveal, by what they report of
some of His words and of His actions, to have beset Him. And
so, especially in connection with the life of the Church and its
dependence upon Him, they have heightened the sense of some-

thing extraordinary attaching to His Person by the very fact that they have viewed it in its historical context. The eschatological side of the Gospels, even if we admit the truth contained in von Dobschütz' valuable phrase " transmuted eschatology," involves perplexities which neither the critic nor the theologian can hope wholly to straighten out. But perplexity is not the only word. The eschatological sayings of the Lord give us, as perhaps no other part of the Gospels does, the power of appreciating something of the results in consciousness that might be expected to follow upon that bringing together of God and man which the doctrine of the Incarnation presupposes. Von Hügel speaks of the " junction between Simultaneity and Successiveness " ; and unless the human were to be simply lost in the divine, it would seem inevitable that conflict, or at least strain, should follow upon junction. The narrative of the Temptation suggests its presence in one way, the eschatological sayings in another. In both cases it is in connection with Christ's Kingdom that the signs of tension appear, and, even more fundamentally, in connection with Jesus as King. In comparison with this side of the Gospels the language of Nicaea and still more of Chalcedon seems to present us with a static impassive union of two elements human and divine. But the comparison is not apposite, and ought not to be raised to the level of a contrast. In a formulary the content of a historical situation does not need to be mentioned, except in the briefest way and with reference to some fact that has a special dogmatic significance, as when in the Nicene Creed, it is said that Christ " was crucified also for us under Pontius Pilate." The abstractions of a formulary are not to be taken and applied as they stand to the concrete experiences of which historical narratives tell. The four words of the Chalcedonian Definition which we translate " without change, without confusion, without division, without separation," do no more than say that in Christ what is divine remains divine and what is human remains human, while they are not isolated from one another as they would be if there were one Person who was divine and another Person who was human. How the divine and the human acted in relation to and upon each other in Christ they do not try to declare. Such statements were, indeed, not lacking ; but, whatever be thought of them, they are not essential deductions from the language of approved dogmatic decisions.

IV

THE DOCTRINE OF THE TWO NATURES

If criticism has at times its conventions which are obstacles to a clear understanding of the way in which progress may best be made, that is also true of theology. In the doctrine of Christ's Person the disparagement of the formula of the Two Natures has become in some circles almost a convention. It is one from which we have gained very little. Chalcedon can be criticised as offering to us a psychological puzzle which we can never hope to solve by any help which it gives us ; but if the doctrine of the Incarnation is true, we cannot escape from a psychological puzzle. If either the divine or the human element could be abandoned or explained away we could avoid such puzzles. But if the elements are allowed to be there, in the life, then, whether we do or do not use the phrase Two Natures, we recognise what the formula recognises and puts on record.

But, it is said, the doctrine of the Two Natures is incompatible with the unity of Christ's Person. Dr. Mackintosh, in his well-known and highly (and rightly) valued book, "The Person of Jesus Christ," lays great stress on this :—" The doctrine of the two natures, in its traditional form, imports into the life of Christ an incredible and thoroughgoing dualism. In place of that perfect unity which is felt in every impression of Him, the whole is bisected sharply by the fissure of distinction. No longer one, He is divided against Himself. . . . The simplicity and coherence of all that Christ was and did vanishes, for God is not after all living a human life. On the contrary, He is still holding Himself at a distance from its experiences and conditions. There has been no saving descent. Christ executed this as God, it is said, and suffered that as man." [1]

Now it is quite true that inferences can be drawn from the traditional statement of the doctrine which are very prejudicial to real unity, and that a mode of expression, "He did this as God, that as man," became habitual, which seems to suggest that the danger was not avoided. But that is not to say that the Chalcedonian phraseology is no longer possible for us, still less that we cannot make the meaning of Chalcedon our own. Certainly Christ was, and is revealed in the Gospels as, really one. His personal unity is as unquestionable as Dr. Mackintosh affirms,

[1] P. 294.

and as the theologians, who spoke in ways which suggest the bisection of which he complains, would most sincerely have confessed. And following out the line of thought of which Dr. Moberly made so much we shall say that all the experiences of Christ were the experiences of God in manhood. But unless we are prepared to say that the divine is human and the human is divine, we must admit a distinction between the two in the Person of Christ and discover a relationship between them which is dependent upon the fact that each of the terms " divinity," " humanity," expresses a real truth about the one, whole Person. Let us take three descriptive phrases from documents of the fifth century and see how the truth expressed by the Two Natures' formula can be expressed in language which lacks the disputed phrase, while at the same time exactly the same distinction is made as that which is inherent in the theology and terminology of the Two Natures. In *Quicunque vult* the writer points out, as against views which were supposed to follow from the principles of Apollinarius, that in the oneness of Christ we are to see not a conversion of the Godhead into flesh, but a taking of the manhood into God. That does not mean a change of the substance of manhood, but a new relationship of manhood to Deity under the new conditions which have come into existence with the Incarnation. Again, Leo in his " Tome " speaks of Christ as " complete in that which is His, complete in that which is ours " ; the distinction is clear enough, but so also is the intimacy of the relationship, since everything falls within the circle of the unity of the one Person. Lastly, the Chalcedonian Definition itself says that the one Lord Jesus Christ is " complete in Godhead, complete also the selfsame in manhood."

If what the Church means by the word " incarnation " is a true belief, it is impossible not to speak in such ways as the above references illustrate. If the words φύσις and *natura* had been scrupulously avoided, the problem, except for a greater exactness in definition, would have remained just the same.

The famous passage in Ignatius concerning the one physician who is " spiritual and fleshly, of Mary and of God," [1] contains the whole theological meaning and truth of the doctrine of the Two Natures. And when we say, as believers in the Incarnation are bound to say, that Christ is truly God and truly man, while

[1] *Ad Ephes.* vii, 2.

at the same time we do not and cannot allow that He is the one in virtue of being the other, we affirm what the traditional statement affirms and mean the same thing.

In the passage which I have quoted, Dr. Mackintosh exaggerates the dualistic impression which methods of employing the doctrine of the Two Natures can convey, through not allowing for the orthodox emphasis on the unity of the Person which is the correlative of the emphasis on the duality of the natures. And further, when he charges the doctrine with leaving no place for a human life as lived by God, one may ask what the truth is which this phrase implies and which Chalcedon omits and by implication denies. For it is the one orthodox doctrine—and all orthodox theologians, whatever differences appear among them, agree in this—that all the experiences that fall within the circle of the incarnate life are experiences of the one divine Person. If the objection is that in the traditional theology a number of experiences are selected as essentially human, and Christ is said to have had them in respect of the flesh or of His humanity, one may agree that, in so far as this suggests an alternation or action by turns on the part of Christ, now as God, now as man, an artificial oscillation as between the human and the divine is introduced into the picture of a life which is at unity with itself. And further, it may be allowed that we can get very little way along the lines of such distinctions within the sphere of the Incarnation. But unless we are to be greatly embarrassed by a drift in the direction of pantheism we must bring in the idea of human nature as intermediate between God and human experience. The Alexandrine Christology, with all its stress upon the divine aspect of the Incarnation, was compelled to do this when, in its best representations, it stopped short of monophysitism. So Cyril of Alexandria in his " Epistola dogmatica " explains the ascription to the Logos of birth and death.

The doctrine of the Two Natures does not endanger the unity of the Person when it is associated with that other doctrine to which so much exception has been taken, that Christ's human nature is impersonal. This difficulty arises from the failure to distinguish between the abstract and the concrete. Catholic theology never meant that, in the concrete, the human nature of Christ lacked its *persona*. Leontius of Byzantium brought in no new idea by his employment of the term *enhypostasia*. All that went on within the incarnate life, all that was static and all that was dynamic, was covered, if the word is permissible, by the Person of the Son. But regarded in abstraction the human nature of Christ is rightly spoken of as impersonal, since in this case and this alone discrimination can be made between human experiences and a human subject of the experiences.

The Chalcedonian Christology holds its ground as the only one which has a right to be regarded as fully Catholic. But, for the very reason that its implications undoubtedly present difficulties, and that the attempt to follow out the meaning of the doctrine to its further conclusions in respect of the incarnate Christ can be made only with the utmost care—while yet, if it is to be made at all, it must be made with the boldness that comes from a grasp upon first principles—honourable reference is due at this point to the chapter entitled " Towards Solution " in the late Bishop Weston's " The One Christ."[1] No one but a real theologian could have written it. Its peculiar strength lies in the consistency with which Bishop Weston conceives of the manhood of the self-limited Logos as the one medium of all that took place within the state of the Incarnation. When the Logos " took human flesh which, with its own proper and complete soul, He constituted in Himself so that He became truly man, living as the subject or ego of real manhood,"[2] He imposed upon Himself such a " law of self-restraint " that " He has, as Incarnate, no existence and no activity outside the conditions that manhood imposes upon Him."[3] This law, as we may call it, determined the character of all the relationships involved in the state of in-carnation. With this Bishop Weston combined the thought of " the essential inseparableness of the universal relations of the Logos from His relations as Incarnate, seeing that all are based in one and the selfsame Person."[4] The same idea appears in " Christus Veritas," where the Bishop of Manchester speaks of the value of thinking of God the Son as most truly living the life recorded in the Gospels, but adding this to the other work of God.[5] And to such a conclusion the logic of the Christian doctrine of God may point, but even the best of analogies (and Bishop Weston's were more than ordinarily good) can do very little to enable us to form a conception of the reality involved.

---

[1] Second edition, 1914.   [2] Pp. 150 ff.   [3] P. 153.
[4] P. 181.   [5] P. 143.

V

FURTHER CONSIDERATIONS IN RESPECT OF THE CHALCEDONIAN CHRISTOLOGY

On the strictly theological side the objections to the Chalcedonian Christology as a statement of the doctrine of the Incarnation are less formidable than the propounders of them suppose. And the failure to replace the old terminology by something equivalent in value and equally effective as a bulwark against restatements which involve an alteration not only in the form but also in the substance of the doctrine is important ; for it is an argument against the view that it is no serious loss if we regard the Definition put out by the Council as possessing only the interest which attaches to an historical landmark, and of no inherent validity for the guidance and regulation of our conceptions. On the philosophical side the difficulties are greater. A doctrine of Christ's Person that approached adequacy and completeness would go along with a satisfactory doctrine of personality. Such a doctrine did not exist in the fourth and fifth centuries, and though the problem of personality has come to the front in philosophy as one that demands serious attention, the stage of an agreed solution has not yet been reached. If what Dr. Cave, the writer of the latest monograph in English on the subject of Christology, calls " the beginnings of a philosophy of personality " [1] in the works of modern philosophers is further developed, theologians may find avenues of insight into the Christological problem opening out before them from the side of metaphysics. Du Bose, had he been able to handle the question simply as a philosopher, and been gifted with greater lucidity of expression, might have contributed much in this connection.

As it is, while the Chalcedonian doctrine neither answers nor professes to answer all the inquiries which naturally arise out of the faith in Christ as one who is both God and man, it remains the bulwark of that faith, and does not, as is the danger with some modern restatements and speculations, render the faith itself precarious. It has not barred the way to the study of the conditions of our Lord's life on earth, and it has left ample room for different types of devotion, resting on the clearer apprehension of His Godhead or of His manhood. And it decisively prevents the conversion of a doctrine of incarnation into the highest form

[1] *The Doctrine of the Person of Christ*, p. 240.

of a doctrine of divine immanence.   This latter mode of thought gives us a Christ who is as we are, except that He has in richest measure what we have in small portions.   Grace is poured into Christ, as into us, but in His case without stint.[1]   But, that being so, there is no place for the thought of an absolute dependence upon Christ as Redeemer.   He does not have for us the value of God. Something in Him does, since the value of that which indwells Christ is divine.   But so it is with ourselves.   And if Christ is, by virtue of God's indwelling within Him, the most highly privileged member of the human race, then the faith, the mysticism and the ideas of sacramental union which we find in the New Testament, directed towards Him and placing Him in a position where He Himself and not something in Him becomes everything to man, cannot be justified.   It is not as though immanence and incarnation were two theological ways of expressing the same thing.   They are the beginnings of different religions, though along the divergent lines there may be points of resemblance. We do not know all that it means to say that God is immanent in a man ; and we do not know all that it means to say that God is incarnate ; but we know enough, and the religious history of mankind helps us, to see that a real difference is involved.

The faith of the Church and its doctrinal expression set before us Christ as one who is man, but also God.   That is its account of the facts, but what kind of a thing, viewed apart from the facts, the incarnation of God would be it does not try to say.   But if we take the idea of the Two Natures as one which asserts the diverse realities of divinity and humanity, and then try to conceive of the consequences of those two realities being united, neither fused nor lost, in a Person who does not result from the union but is precedent to it and enters into new conditions because of it, we shall come under the unescapable difficulties which attach to the attempt to determine in the abstract the character of what is, *ex hypothesi*, a new kind of fact and the single instance of it.

[1] Cf. S. J. Davenport, *Immanence and Incarnation*, p. 229: "Does the immanental theory imply that . . . given a perfect man *ipso facto* we are presented with an Incarnate God ? If such is a necessary implication of immanentism, then, as we have argued above, this is not the Christian conception of Christ.   He is Absolute.   Even a perfect man a priori would derive his perfection through the Logos, from whom he derives his constitution, his existence.   Perfection is by no means synonymous with hypostatic union, for the former is possible, abstractly, for all men, but the latter belongs to the Second Person of the Trinity alone, that is, to Jesus Christ."

If the word "incarnation" is rightly used, then the fact of the Incarnation is the one instance of the particular being its own universal. We should have to say the same thing in another way if we possessed no heritage from Aristotle and the Scholastics. But as to speculations in Christology, the data afford us little opportunity for supposing that we can lay down rules for the testing of the validity of our conclusions. There have been such speculations, but they fall right outside the faith and the dogma of the Church, which is concerned to make decisions only with reference to the concrete historical fact. So it is with regard to kenotic theories, and, in partial opposition to them, to speculation as to the work of the Logos outside the circle, but during the period, of the incarnate life. Such a tentative idea as Dr. Temple has put forward in " Christus Veritas," [1] that supposing from the life of Christ the presence of God incarnate were withdrawn we should not be left with nothing, but with the life of a man, belongs to the same order of untestable suggestions. All that the Church asserts as positive truth is what must be asserted if we are to think of a real incarnation. For that, Christ must be both God and man, not successively and by division but wholly and simultaneously.

VI

FINAL DIFFICULTIES AS TO THE DOCTRINE OF THE INCARNATION EXAMINED

When all necessary explanations have been given, two obstacles to faith may still remain. The first is that the notion of incarnation involves an incredible relationship between God and the finite order ; that God, the Eternal, cannot be thought of as entering into time after the manner expressed in this doctrine. In popular form the objection takes exception to the discovery of a final

---

[1] Dr. Temple writes (p. 150) : " If we imagine the divine Word withdrawn from Jesus of Nazareth, as the Gnostics believed to have occurred before the Passion, I think that there would be left, not nothing at all, but a man." If the Bishop had stopped there, one might feel that an incursion had been made into the region of the most unverifiable speculation, and that behind it lay a really inadequate view of the meaning of the Incarnation. But he continues, in words which (especially with the note calling attention to the avoidance of the phrase " human person ") make all the difference in substance, whatever be thought of their form, " yet this human personality is actually the self-expression of the Eternal Son, so that as we watch the human life we become aware that it is the vehicle of a divine life, and that the human personality of Jesus Christ is subsumed in the Divine Person of the Creative Word."

revelation in something which happened a long time ago in an obscure corner of the world. A full consideration of this objection and of the answer to it would necessitate an examination of the significance of the pre-Christian history to which the title *preparatio evangelica* is given, and a discussion of the doctrine of God as the background against which the idea of incarnation becomes intelligible. Here it must suffice to point out that while Christian theology has repudiated all explanations of the Incarnation which imply that God immerses Himself in such a manner in the finite order that He becomes for a time no more than part of it, it has presented the doctrine as the one in which alone the gap between God and the world is effectively overcome. The world-order is raised potentially to the level of the divine life which has been manifested within it. That is the truth of the idea of deification. But this idea is not construed as though the Incarnation worked like leaven to the production, by a quality of permeation, of a human super-nature. The Christian tradition, if account is taken of its chief emphases and of its total character, has viewed the Incarnation in relation to God's redemptive and ethical purposes, which man must receive and make his own if he is to know the joy of communion with God. The ethical confusion to-day is the result of uncertainty as to the existence of an ethical interpretation of life, which is the real meaning of life and not superimposed upon life, while a grasp of the ethical character of life becomes less firm in the absence of knowledge of where to look for the true ideals, standards and laws of moral well-being. The Incarnation brings light at the point where lack of light must work out in lack of power. It gives the assurance of the reality of moral values in God and in the world-order. It reveals God as making Himself one with man, and entering into the world's moral life and undergoing the passion which is born of the travail of good in its struggle with evil. It is only as we view the Christian Church and the Christian life, both of which derive from the Incarnation, that its moral fruitfulness begins to be manifested both extensively and intensively. But immediately following upon conviction of the truth of the Incarnation comes the realisation of a new unity accomplished, which gives the best of all answers to those most poignant of all doubts, in which the drama of the world and of the soul seems to have nothing moral at its heart and to move towards no moral end.

The other principal difficulty arises out of the study of the Gospels. The picture which they bring before us is held to be incompatible with the faith in Jesus as God incarnate. Something that bears on this has been said earlier. The extent of the difficulty will depend upon the judgment formed as to the miraculous sections of the Gospel.[1] But it is largely the consequence of *a priori* assumptions, which may be held with no full consciousness of their nature, as to the form which an incarnation of God will take. The sense of injurious speculation concerning the Person of Christ which kenotic doctrines often produce must be ascribed to preliminary judgments of what is both possible and fitting in the case of one who is God incarnate. But the doctrine of the Incarnation, as the one that best satisfies all the facts which are bound up with the beginnings and history of Christianity as religion and way of life, is not to be rejected on the ground that the life of Jesus contains features of a surprising and unexpected character. Like the Apostles we have to learn that apparent stumbling-blocks may be the way in which God effects His will. If the Cross has not prevented the confession of the Godhead of Jesus, but has revealed the full glory of the self-impoverishment of the Eternal Son, the recognition of limitations in His knowledge and His power while on earth need not do so.

The question of the finality of Christianity as the "absolute religion" has come into some prominence of late. It is a question which depends altogether for any valid answer upon the view taken of Christ. Christianity is not primarily the most satisfactory philosophy of religion, embodying in the most perfect form certain universally valid religious principles, but faith in a Person, to believe in whom is to believe in God. If that is not true, then all that is most distinctive in Christianity falls, and even though a sentiment about Him and an attachment to Him remain, Jesus Christ will no longer be the Way, the Truth and the Life. The Church at least knows what is at stake. Her life is not centred in herself but in Him. Her tradition, derived in the first instance from the faith of the apostolic age, is the rational account which she has given of her experience. And believing herself to be the trustee, not only of the Christianity which deserves the name, but of vital religion and of its continuance within human life, she sees no future for her office and no security for

[1] See the appendix to this essay.

her efforts except in the acknowledgment and adoration of Jesus Christ as Lord and God.

APPENDIX ON MIRACLE

The stage which the question of the miraculous element in the Gospels has reached seems to be describable as follows : The opposition to miracle from the side of those sciences which reveal the orderly flow of sequences in nature, and are thereby responsible for the phrase " natural law," is no longer formidable. It is clear that no decision can be reached without taking into account the prior questions which arise around the problem of theism. With regard to literary criticism of the Gospels, no discovery has been made which suggests the existence of any primitive nonmiraculous documentary deposit which has been overlaid by later strata.

On the other hand, there is no sign of a return to the old kind of argument which built upon miracle (and upon prophecy) for evidential and theological purposes. The miracles are not taken just as they stand, as though no problem were raised by their appearance. Though they may be regarded as " in place " in the life of Christ, they are so regarded in consequence of an interpretation of His Person ; they are not usually appealed to directly for establishing the truth of that interpretation. It is inevitably impossible to reach a settlement which could be put forward as representing objective truth, since the approach to a decision can be reached only along the lines of this or that *praejudicium*. The non-Christian, and more definitely the nontheist, may admit that the historical evidence has its strong points, that the narratives are not far removed in time from the facts, that they are not worked up into a form which suggests mere legend-mongering, and that they are embedded in a context which there is no reason to distrust. But even so he will reject them because it is impossible for him to find a place for them in a non-theistic world-view. His non-theistic successor ages hence may be able to accept them on the basis of knowledge which is at present hidden. But that is mere hypothesis ; at the present time a non-theist will not and cannot accept the truth of the Gospel miracles. He may or may not be able to explain the accounts in a way satisfactory to himself and to others. But even if he cannot do that, even if his conjectures seem as absurd as some of the methods taken to find a way round the Gospel-narratives of the morning of Easter Day and of the resurrection, he will be guilty of no irrational behaviour when he denies that these wonderful things happened. His fault lies further back. Where he is wrong is in not believing in God, and in Christ as the Son of God. In other words it is, broadly speaking, only from within the Christian tradition that he is capable of a true verdict upon the miracles of the Gospel.[1]

But because the Christian is free from a *praejudicium* which is anti-miraculous because it is anti-theistic, he will not necessarily go on to the assertions which the other has denied. He still may feel difficulties. Unless he believes in the verbal inerrancy of Scripture he is not able to affirm that a miracle which appears in one of the Gospels must have happened as a miracle. He knows that stories of miraculous events appear all over the world in connection with different religions, and he is probably not prepared to accept those which have their place in religions which are rivals to Christianity. What is it, he may ask, which gives the New Testament miracle-narratives a special claim to be accepted as true statements of wonderful occurrences in the natural order ?

I can do no more than suggest the lines along which an answer may be found. In the first place I would say that the problem of miracle concerns not God's will to produce certain results through acts attributable immediately to Him without the appearance of any mediate agencies, but God's will to produce those results under certain conditions which involve a particular relationship between Him and the human soul. There is a mediate agency, namely man in fellowship with God. In a theistic world-view, which finds the greatest of all powers under God to be those of spiritual beings in fellowship with God, and cannot regard the material side of existence to be at any point simply intractable and unmalleable, it is impossible to set limits to the results which might be produced, given favourable conditions in respect of communion with God.

Then, secondly, whatever be the case with other conditions under which miracles have been said to have occurred, the context of the Gospel miracles raises no difficulty. That Jesus Christ lived in the most intimate communion with the Father, that His power was the natural fruit of that communion, and was manifested in a moral holiness which, apart from questions of " Christology," gives evidence of His pre-eminence among men, is the picture of His life which we can derive from the Gospels. That in His case, in response to the faith in which He drew upon God for help, certain things happened in God's world of nature, which revealed in a way that we call miraculous the supremacy of spirit over matter, is not surprising. And the miracle-narratives do not appear in their context oddly and awkwardly as might be expected if they were really

---

[1] That seems to me true with this reservation. The evidence for the resurrection possesses a specially impressive character, and makes a more general appeal than any other miraculous section in the Gospels. Why this should be so is not difficult to understand. The truth of Christianity and the truth that Christ is risen are inseparable, and part of the evidence for the resurrection is the account of the tomb that was found empty.

out of place. If the element of miracle in them is untrue, they are, if not conscious inventions—a most improbable supposition—, the product of pious imagination misinterpreting certain natural phenomena. Such a view does not, at least as a rule, arise spontaneously out of the study of the Gospels without the presupposition of a theory adverse to miracle.

And, thirdly, if Christianity is the true religion because Jesus Christ is the Son of God incarnate, the record of the Gospel-miracles possesses this essential difference from the record of other miracles, that the personal Subject differs from all other persons. His divine-human sovereignty in the sphere of the spirit, in virtue of which He is Lord, Judge, Saviour and King, has as its other side a divine-human sovereignty in the sphere of nature. The Son of Man has power in both. Incarnation and miracle do not, perhaps, cohere so closely together as to enable us to say that where the one is the other must be found ; but, on the other hand, if the Incarnation is in any real way apprehended as the greatest event in human history, miracle cannot be ruled out as possessing no fitting occasion for the manifestation of such a mode of divine operation.

These considerations may be particularised in reference to the miracle which, through its relationship to the beginnings of our Lord's earthly life, Christian theology has viewed in specially close connection with the doctrine of the Incarnation. Here, I think, we may legitimately contrast with great clearness and sharpness two propositions. On the one hand, if we did not believe that Christ was truly the Son of God, we should not believe that He was born of a Virgin. Some of the Ebionites could do so, but that does not matter : no lengthy argument is needed to convince us that their position is untenable. On the other hand, if we do believe that Christ is truly the Son of God, the Virgin-Birth appears as a truth in respect of His advent into this world congruous with the truth of His eternal being and essential Deity. Chary as we may be of pressing arguments which cannot be conclusive because they contain an element of unverifiable speculation, the difficulty, to which defenders of the orthodox tradition, most recently the learned American Baptist scholar Dr. A. T. Robertson,[1] have called attention, of combining the notion of incarnation with the belief that Jesus was the Son of Joseph and Mary, is not an unreal one. And the fact that disbelief in the Virgin-Birth, and belief in other doctrines of the Person of Christ than that He was the Son of God incarnate, do very largely go together suggests that the Incarnation and the mode thereof are neither easily nor truly dissociated from one another. The possibility of theoretical abstraction of the one from the other does not prove that they are not, in fact, a living unity.

There is one point to which attention may be drawn. May we not lay stress on the part actively taken by the Blessed Virgin in co-operation with God, coming along the avenues of mystical experience ? The

[1] In his book, *The Mother of Jesus*, p. 28 f.

importance of this idea, which is not inconsonant with the story of the Annunciation in St. Luke's Gospel, lies in the fact that it recognises in connection with the physical miracle the relevance of the human, spiritual, mediate agency. Mary did all that she could do, by making her will one with the will of God, to make it, from her side, possible for the Son of God to be born of her. It is, therefore, quite wrong to treat the Virgin-Birth as though no spiritual significance were to be discovered in connection with it. A narrative in which the woman's part was of no essential worth, and nothing emerged except a divine decision that a particular birth should be brought about in a miraculous way, might fairly be regarded as of no spiritual consequence, except for the exhibition of the power of God. But that is not St. Luke's narrative. In his account the faith and willingness of Mary show that, even in such an event as this, all the factors are not exhausted in the one idea of divine omnipotence. There is spiritual response and spiritual preparation from the human side. We cannot define the exact character of the Annunciation. We may quite properly hold to its objective reality without thinking of the angel coming to the Blessed Virgin in any way parallel to a person coming into a room through its door. The word " vision " may help, and so may the word " experience." In any case St. Luke has given us what he did not make up, a most appropriate spiritual context for the physical wonder of the Virgin-Birth. And both the context and the wonder are appropriate to Him who came, in the fulness of time, true God made man.

ASPECTS OF MAN'S CONDITION
BY EDWARD JOHN BICKNELL
AND
JOHN KENNETH MOZLEY

CONTENTS

I

SIN AND THE FALL

BY E. J. BICKNELL.

1. *Basis in Experience of the Theological Doctrines of the Fall and Original Sin*

(*a*) THE doctrines of " original sin " and " the Fall " are pieces of theology. Theology is the science of religion. It springs from the effort of man to understand his own life. Always religion comes first, and theology second. Experience precedes reflection on experience, and the two must not be confused. Man lives first and thinks afterwards. Accordingly we shall not be surprised to find that these two doctrines, so closely connected, were not revealed ready made, but have behind them a long history of development in time. Our first duty therefore will be to consider what are the facts of experience which they attempt to express and to correlate. What is their relation to practical religion ?

Let us start from common ground on which all Christians are agreed. We all have no difficulty in understanding what is meant by " actual " sin. It is a concept that can be denied by no one who believes in a personal and righteous God and in some measure of free-will in man. Actual sin denotes an act of disobedience to God or the state of mind and heart that results from such acts of disobedience. Christ depicts sin as the alienation of the will and heart of a child from an all-righteous and all-loving Father. It is important to remember for our present discussion that sin is always against God. The term belongs to the vocabulary of religion, not to that of moral or political philosophy. To an atheist sin can only appear to be an illusion. " Against thee and thee only have I sinned " is always the cry of the awakened sinner. No doubt historically the content of the term sin has varied enormously in accordance with the conception of the character of God attained by the community. Even within the Bible we find a development in the idea of sin *pari passu* with a development in the understanding of the character of God. In primitive times sin is simply that which displeases God. Exclusive attention is paid to external acts, not to motives. Individual responsibility is hardly recognised. Ritual irregularities are not distinguished from moral offences. Unintentional breaches of custom are put on a level with wilful disobedience. But gradually personality comes to its own and distinctions are made. The root of sin is seen to lie in the will. Merely ceremonial defilement is felt to be of small account beside moral evil. The development reaches its culmination in the teaching of Christ that nothing from outside a man can defile him but only that which comes from within. Still always and everywhere sin is that which offends God. We do not wish to discuss here the difficult question of the relative degrees of guilt or accountability which sin involves. We only assert summarily that in the last resort only God who knows the heart can estimate the exact measure of guilt in any case. Nor can we discuss the relation between sin and the sense of sin. We deliberately put these problems on one side.[1] All that we are concerned to maintain is that the one constant element in the concept of sin is that which puts man out of fellowship with God.

(*b*) So far our path is clear. When, however, we look into ourselves we discover the fact, so mysterious to all who believe in a good God, that we find there evil tendencies and desires, similar to those which result from indulgence in actual sin, but which are prior in time to, and independent of, any such actual sin. For these bad tendencies and impulses we do not recognise any personal responsibility. They are not the consequences of our own acts of choice. They seem to come to us ready made. Yet, quite as fully as those bad habits which are the result of actual sin, they incapacitate us from full fellowship with God. They hamper and thwart our better purposes They are not simply imperfections : they are positively evil. They are loyalties that conflict with and weaken our loyalty to God. Nor do we show any signs of outgrowing them. They do not disappear as we get older. In other words our nature, as we receive it, appears to be not merely undeveloped but to possess a bias towards evil, a disunion within itself, an inability to rise to higher levels. We find ourselves out of sympathy with God from the start.

This analysis of human nature is confirmed when we look

[1] For a discussion of them see Bicknell, *The Christian Idea of Sin and Original Sin*, pp. 43–49.

outwards and study human life as disclosed in history and politics. The history of the race is that of the individual writ large. There is no doubt marvellous progress in many directions. It is the recognition of this that prompts the objection that man has not fallen, he has risen. But the rise is only in certain limited directions. He has gained an increased mastery over the material world. He has accumulated a vast amount of experience and turned it to good account in ministering to the needs and comforts of the body. He has also advanced in intellectual knowledge. He has before him more material from which to draw conclusions and better methods of sifting and arranging that material. He has also developed more complex and refined moral ideals. There is among civilised men less open brutality and cruelty, less violence and unabashed lawlessness. But there is no evidence that his moral and spiritual powers have proportionately developed. The wonderful inventions of science are in themselves morally neutral. They may be used in the interests of the common good or for selfish ends. Science provides impartially a hospital or the latest poison bomb. It may well prove that man's moral powers are so inadequate to stand the strain of all this increasing mastery of the material world that he will use it to destroy himself. So, too, though the outward forms of human selfishness have changed, there is no ground for believing that men are at the bottom less selfish than they were. The highwayman has been superseded by the profiteer, but the only gain is a loss of picturesqueness. Nor do improved conditions of life necessarily go hand in hand with an improved condition of soul. Men can be as selfish and godless in a palace as in a slum. Vice does not cease to be vice because it is gilded. The polite and polished self-indulgence of the smart set hides the glory of God even more effectually than the brutality and coarseness of the savage. Nor does mere learning carry with it an increase in holiness and righteousness. A professor can be further from the kingdom of God than a coal-heaver. Nor is it enough to have higher and more elaborate ideals. The real question is how far we live up to them.

In short when we study the causes that underlie the decay of nations and the degradation of public life, or the misuse of new powers and knowledge, we always come back to man himself. There is nothing outside him that hinders a triumphant upward movement turning all fresh discoveries into means for promoting the highest welfare of each and all. The hindrance lies in man himself, in his inability to love the highest when he sees it and to subdue his antisocial impulses. History lends no support to the idea that these are being outgrown. At bottom the problem is one of moral and spiritual weakness.

(c) This impression is deepened when we turn to the human life and example of Jesus Christ. There we see man as he was intended in the divine purpose to become. We realise anew his imperfection and degradation by placing ourselves beside the concrete picture of the ideal. Christ shows up not only the weakness but the fallenness of human nature. His life throughout is based on unbroken communion with God. He exhibits a perfect harmony between all the faculties and impulses of His human nature. His growth is uniform and unbroken. He is in full sympathy with the mind and purpose of God. Taken by itself, the life of Christ might well only provoke us to despair. We see in it what we acknowledge that we ought to be, but what we are wholly unable in our own strength to attain. It makes us all the more conscious of the evil impulses within us. It shows up our " fallen " condition. Thus introspection, a study of human history, and the example and teaching of Christ all unite in witnessing to our present state as unnatural. By what name are we to designate it ?

(d) Since it is indistinguishable in all except the consciousness of personal responsibility from that condition of heart and will which results from actual sin, in theology it has long received the name of " original sin." Indeed the two are so closely intertwined in actual experience that it is often hard to distinguish them. The alienation from God that they produce is almost identical. We cannot wonder at the choice of the term. To-day, however, the term " original sin " is widely criticised, and with good reason. Many writers argue that the word sin should be restricted to actual sin—that is, to states of character or conduct for which the individual is personally responsible by acts of moral choice. The wider use of the term, they say, only leads to confusion of thought and endangers morality. It is a relic of the days when the concept of sin had not yet been moralised. Its retention to-day only tends to blur the sense of the heinousness of sin or to lead to morbid scruples. If we were starting theological terminology, there would be much to be said for a clearer distinction. But the use of the term sin to include other states of character than those for which the individual is personally responsible, not only has a long history behind it, but witnesses to certain truths of great importance. What are we to substitute for the phrase " original sin " ? Various suggestions have been made, but none of them is entirely satisfactory. " Inherited infirmity " expresses the important truth that our unhappy condition does not carry with it guilt in the sense of accountability or expose us personally to the wrath of God, but is hardly adequate to the seriousness of the situation. " Moral disease " has the advantage that it brings out the positive danger to spiritual health. But neither phrase sufficiently emphasises the important truth that by this state of heart and will we are disqualified for that full communion with God which is the indispensable condition of all sound human life. Religion is not mere morality, but is a walking with God ; and " two cannot walk together unless they be agreed." Further, the old term has this additional advantage that it leaves room for the idea of corporate sin. In his moral and spiritual life the individual is interpenetrated by the community. The will of the community is not simply the sum-total of the wills of the individual members who compose it, though indeed it has no actual existence outside of or apart from them. There is such a thing as a group mind, though probably not a group consciousness. And though an act of moral choice can only be made by an individual, he makes it not as an individual, but as shaped and moulded by the community. Thus we find corporate action which can only be described as sinful since it is objectively opposed to the will of God, though it is certain that not every member of the body is personally responsible for it. Our Lord judged not only individuals, but cities, as Capernaum or Jerusalem. If we attempt to limit sin to states of character or acts for which the individual is personally in the sight of God responsible, we shall find ourselves in difficulties about those corporate sins which are both recognised in the teaching of Christ and implied by modern psychology.

2. *Various Forms of these Doctrines in History*

If, then, we decide to retain the term in spite of its manifest disadvantages, that does not mean that we accept all doctrines of original sin. It is most important to study the various forms which this doctrine has assumed.

P

(*a*) If we begin with the Old Testament, we find there a full recognition of the badness of human nature, but hardly any theory of original sin or any attempt to account for it.   In the third chapter of Genesis there is a vivid picture of temptation and of actual sin by an act of disobedience to a command of God recognised as binding, but though the act of disobedience is followed by punishment, it is not suggested that this included a bias towards evil in Adam's descendants.   Further, when the conspicuous wickedness of a later generation is recorded, the explanation of it is found not in Adam's transgression, but in the strange tale about the " sons of God " and the " daughters of men."   Nor is there any certain reference to the story of Adam to be found in the whole of the canonical books.   When we pass on to the post-canonical literature, we find more than one apparent attempt to account for the empirically universal wickedness of man.   There is the Rabbinic doctrine, based on Genesis viii. 21, of the evil impulse already existing potentially in the heart of man and only waiting for the right stimulus to emerge in a sinful act.   There are the more popular theories which connect man's present condition with the disobedience of Adam or with the unions of evil angels and women.   Thus it may be said that a doctrine of original sin in some form was held by many in the Jewish Church in the time of Christ, but hardly as an official doctrine of the Church.   Nor was there any agreed doctrine of the fall of man.   The word " fall " does not occur in this connection in the canonical writings. It is first found in a quite untechnical sense in Wisdom x. 3.

(*b*) In the teaching of Christ Himself as recorded in the Gospels there is no formal theology of original sin.   Indeed we should not expect such.   What we do find is the full recognition of the facts of human nature and history which the theological doctrine was formulated to express.   It is not too much to say that in His teaching and ministry He assumes that all men are in a condition of " fallenness."   They are sick and need a physician.   They cannot cure themselves.   They need not only enlightenment, but redemption.   They are in bondage to a strong and cruel tyrant.   They are no longer free and cannot deliver themselves. They are not only undeveloped, but misdeveloped, and therefore must undergo not simply growth and education, but new birth. The existing world order is largely under the domination of evil powers.   It resembles a field in which an enemy has sown tares

among the wheat. The wheat and tares are hopelessly inter-
mixed both in the hearts of man and in all human life. Nothing
is more startling than the way in which He assumes the presence
of evil in all human hearts. " If ye then, being evil, know how
to . . . ," He says. The Lord's Prayer includes a petition for forgiveness. The only class of people of whom He seems to despair
are those who are unaware of any need for repentance or change of
mind. We cannot develop this subject at length, but it is plain
that in all His teaching He implied that mankind as a whole had
strayed from the right path and swerved away from God's purpose.
This judgment on all men is in the sharpest contrast to His own
claims to an unbroken communion with the Father and undimmed
insight into and sympathy with His purposes. While He sum-
moned all men without exception to repent He displayed no need
of repentance Himself. No prayer for pardon or amendment for
His own life passed His lips. His own sinlessness, if we use
what is too negative a term to express the positive and harmonious
energy of His life towards the Father, shows up the failure and
disharmony of all other human lives.

(c) In St. Paul we find the beginnings of a Christian doctrine
of original sin, starting from the Jewish speculation which connected
man's present condition with the disobedience of Adam. In the
famous sentence " as through one man sin entered into the world,
and death through sin ; and so death passed unto all men, for that
all sinned : for until the law sin was in the world : but sin is not
imputed where there is no law," we find a foundation on which
many large and imposing structures have been built. Unfortunately St. Paul's meaning is most obscure. His primary interest
in the whole chapter is in the universality and completeness of the
redemption brought by Christ. Man's sinful condition is only
brought in as a foil to this. Indeed the actual sentence which
speaks of all men sinning is never finished. It may simply make
the statement that as a matter of fact all men after Adam did for
some reason or other commit sin, without connecting this with
Adam's sin. That is exegetically possible, and it may be argued
that if " in Adam " was to be added, the addition is so important
that it must have been expressed. But the context is against this
interpretation. The whole passage is based on the parallelism
between Adam and Christ, and there is little doubt that the words
" in Adam " are to be supplied in thought, though the fact that

St. Paul did not actually insert them proves that the dominant purpose in his writing here was not to give a theory of the origin of sin. Further, what is the connection between the sin of Adam and the universal sinfulness of his descendants? Is the tendency to sin transmitted by heredity? The passage gives no answer to such questions. They clearly were not in St. Paul's mind at this moment. Perhaps all that we can say with certainty is that Jewish tradition connected man's present sinfulness with Adam's transgression, and St. Paul assumes a general familiarity with this idea. If we press for a closer examination of St. Paul's meaning, we may perhaps find a clue in the parallelism between " in Adam " and " in Christ " which pervades the whole context. Christians are " in Christ," and a study of his general line of thought shows that this means more than that they individually adhere to Christ by personal faith, though it includes this. It also conveys the idea of membership in His Body the Church. For St. Paul the Christian life was always mediated by fellowship in the divine society, the people of God. So "in Adam" may well convey the idea of membership in an unregenerate humanity. This would suggest that Adam's sin affected his descendants not merely by way of bad example, but by the subtle influences of social tradition in all its forms.

It is also important to remember, though the point is often overlooked, that when at the opening of the Epistle, St. Paul develops the picture of mankind as wholly given over to sin and needing a new power for righteousness, he never mentions Adam. He never suggests that Jew and Gentile have fallen away from God because they inherited a weakened or depraved nature. He blames them for wilfully turning away from the light given to them. His language is consistent with a recognition of the social nature of sin but hardly with a strict theory of heredity.

(*d*) When we turn to the early Church, it is long before we meet any formulated doctrine of original sin. Before the time of St. Augustine there is neither in East nor West a single and consistent theory of original sin. The early Christian writers were more concerned with deliverance from demons from without than with deliverance from an inherited bias towards evil within. In the main, the Greek Fathers represent a " once-born " type of religion. Under the influence of St. Paul's language, they often allow that Adam's sin has affected his descendants, but it is very difficult to be certain of the way in which they regard this effect. The general tendency is to lay stress on the inheriting, through the solidarity of the race and its unity with its first parent, of the punishment of Adam's sin rather than of the moral corruption of the sin itself. Where emphasis is laid on the effects of the Fall on human nature, they are regarded rather as a *privatio* than as a *depravatio*, a loss of supernatural light and gifts. There is always a strong insistence on the reality of free will and responsibility. Even though in Origen and in Gregory of Nyssa we find the germs of a doctrine of original sin similar to that of St. Augustine, there is no doctrine of original guilt and the consequences of such a doctrine are not thought out.

In the West, Tertullian's traducianism led him to formulate a theory of a hereditary sinful taint—" vitium originis." Adam's qualities were transmitted to his descendants. Yet, as his arguments for the delay of baptism show, he was far from regarding human nature as wholly corrupt. Nor did he deny free will. But he established a tradition in the West which was continued by Cyprian and Hilary and developed by Ambrose until it attained a systematic form at the hands of St. Augustine.

(*e*) In St. Augustine we reach for the first time a systematic theology of original sin. In considering it we must take into account all the factors that have gone to its construction. We place first among these the profound spiritual experience which he had undergone in his sudden and violent conversion, similar to that of St. Paul. His religion was essentially that of the twice-born type and gave him an insight into the meaning of St. Paul's Epistles possessed by few of that age. As he reflected on his experience, it seemed to him that his former life had been one of entire badness from which he had been rescued by an act of divine love. God had done all ; he had done nothing, except to offer a vain opposition to God's irresistible grace. Secondly, in the face of this conviction, the teaching of Pelagius that every man at any time, whatever his past conduct, was able to choose equally and freely either right or wrong, seemed unmitigated folly. No less inadequate was the Pelagian view of grace as primarily the nature bestowed on man in virtue of which he enjoyed this free will, or a merely external assistance such as the example of Christ, or at most an inward inspiration useful indeed as seconding man's efforts but in no way indispensable for salvation. Accordingly in revolt against Pelagius, who taught that all men at birth receive a sound and uncorrupted human nature, he emphasised to the utmost the corruption of human nature.   Mankind was a " massa perditionis." [1]   We do indeed possess free will by nature in the sense that the sins which we commit are our own choice, but we do not possess a truly free will in the sense that we have the power to choose right.   Apart from the grace of God we can only choose sin.   In support of this teaching he appealed to the authority of St. Paul.   The Pelagians argued that practically universal sin was due to the following of Adam's bad example and to the influence of bad surroundings, regarded in a purely external way.   Against this, relying on the mistranslation of Romans v. 12, " In whom *(in quo)* all sinned," he taught that Adam's sin involved the sin of all his descendants and that they in some sense sinned when he did.   Thus, going beyond the teaching of St. Paul, he insisted not only on original sin, but on original guilt, a conception which it is impossible to reconcile with either reason or morality. When driven to offer a defence for this indefensible position, his replies were by no means either clear or consistent.   At times he put forward the theory of our seminal existence in Adam, as Levi existed in the loins of Abraham.   At other times he fell back on a mystical realism in which he held that not only Adam's nature, but his personality was shared by his descendants.   Elsewhere he appealed to the mystery of divine justice.   In close connection with this view of inherited guilt involving the further assertion that unbaptised infants were condemned to hell, was the theory familiar to Gnostics and Manicheans, but strange in the writings of a Christian teacher, that inherited sinfulness consisted mainly in that concupiscence through which the race was propagated, since under the present conditions of a fallen world marriage, in itself right and sinless, was inevitably accompanied by passions which are sinful.   Few theories have had more disastrous results in later Christian thought.   Such teaching as this would seem logically to carry with it some form of traducianism, but, though he inclined towards it, he never actually adopted it.

In this short summary of St. Augustine's teaching it is clear that he has gone very far beyond the teaching of St. Paul.   Not only does he omit the other side of St. Paul's teaching where he insists on the need of human effort, but the novel conception of

[1] e.g. *De correptione et gratia*, 12.

original guilt gives a new colour to the concept of original sin. To St. Paul, original sin is of the nature of a deadly spiritual disease disabling man from full fellowship with God, objectively contrary to the will of God and in that sense sinful, but not blameworthy. Men stricken with it are unable to help themselves, but their plight appeals to God's pity rather than to God's wrath. This teaching does full justice to man's need of redemption, and is in full accord with the facts of life. St. Augustine on the other hand ignores a large field of facts, and though his interpretation of religion goes far deeper than that of Pelagius, his theology is one-sided. His doctrine of man as inheriting a totally corrupt nature by physical transmission from a historical Adam and involving guilt in the sense of accountability is often taken to be the Catholic doctrine of original sin, but this is by no means the case. We must not confuse the doctrines of the Fall and of original sin with the Augustinian presentation of them.

A short survey of Church history is sufficient to show that the complete Augustinian system has no claim to be considered Catholic in the true sense of the term. As we saw, the teaching of the Fathers before him, even in the West, gives no certain voice on the subject. The Church agreed with him in his rejection of Pelagianism, but was by no means ready to accept the system that he offered in its stead. The Eastern Church has never received Augustinianism as a whole. Its teaching on original sin does not at most go beyond that of Gregory of Nyssa. In the West his views aroused at once considerable opposition, especially in South Gaul. The so-called Semi-Pelagian School protested with effect against his doctrine of grace and election as a novelty, and maintained that even man as fallen had some power of free choice, though weakened, so as to be able to co-operate with grace. The celebrated " Commonitorium " of Vincent of Lerins, in which " semper, ubique, ab omnibus," is laid down as the test of Catholicism, was probably aimed at the teaching of Augustine. The Synod of Orange in 529 maintained a considerably modified Augustinianism. While emphasising the need of grace, including prevenient grace, it expressly condemned the idea of predestination to evil which was implied in the doctrine of irresistible grace. As regards the Fall it asserted that Adam's sin affected not only himself but his descendants, and that it has impaired not only the body but the soul. Nothing however is said about entire corruption.

In the Middle Ages the general movement was away from the stricter teaching of St. Augustine, in spite of the veneration for his name.   Aquinas taught that on the positive side original sin was a wounding of nature, a disordered condition, the result of a loss of superadded graces which Adam had enjoyed in his state of original righteousness.   In contradiction to Augustine he denied that natural goodness was forfeited by the Fall or free will destroyed, and held that concupiscence is not properly sin.   Duns Scotus represented an even greater departure from the standpoint of Augustine.   He insisted more strongly on man's freedom and taught that the first sin, whose gravity he tended to minimise, had affected not man's nature, but only his supernatural gifts.   The Council of Trent with an ingenuity worthy of our own Thirty-Nine Articles contrived, while using the language of St. Augustine, to produce a formula which could be interpreted in accordance with the much milder Scholastic teaching.   The Fall is said to have involved the loss of original righteousness, the tainting of body and soul, slavery to the devil, and liability to the wrath of God. Original sin is propagated by generation.

It is to the Reformers that we must principally look for a revival of Augustinianism.   Calvin and Luther agree in describing the depravity of human nature in the strongest terms, in insisting on the guilt of original sin, and in maintaining the doctrine of irresistible grace.   They both did what Augustine shrank from doing, namely, taught explicitly that some men are predestined to evil.   Here again, if we study the history of Protestantism, we find an increasing reaction against such teaching.   It is hardly too much to say that modern Protestantism, so far as it has any doctrine of the Fall and original sin, has repudiated the stern but logical teaching of Calvin and Luther.

3. *The Need for Restatement*

Within the last century new knowledge has accumulated which compels a reconsideration and restatement of the whole question. New data unknown to the theologians of the early Church and of the Middle Ages may well cause us to revise their teaching in the interest of truth.   All that reverence for Catholic tradition demands is that the new theology of original sin should be no less adequate to the facts of the Christian life and should possess the old spiritual values.

We may especially consider three sources from which fresh light has been thrown on the subject.

First, literary and historical criticism has shown beyond any reasonable doubt that the opening chapters of Genesis do not give us literal record of fact. They are, to use a phrase of Bishop Gore, "inspired mythology." This does not diminish their value for religion, however. The picture of the temptation to disobedience followed by the act of sin is of abiding value as an analysis of the spiritual drama that is constantly being re-enacted in our own souls. No words could bring out more clearly the subtlety of temptation, the nature of actual sin, and the alienation from God that it brings. On the other hand the value of these chapters as literal history has been for ever shattered. There is a strange reluctance in many quarters to face the consequences of this discovery. Historical facts can only be proved by historical evidence. We have therefore no right to draw from the stories in Genesis deductions about the condition of Adam before his disobedience and make them a basis for theories about the condition of unfallen man. How much theology has centred round the purely hypothetical supernatural graces of an Adam for whose existence we have no historical evidence ! The chapters of Genesis do indeed bear witness to man's conviction that his present condition is unnatural and not in accordance with God's will. They attest a sense of fallenness, but give us no information whatever about a historical Fall.

Secondly, we have come to realise that man has been evolved from a non-human ancestry, and that he has inherited impulses and instincts which he shares with the lower animals. Recent psychology has emphasised the fact that not only the human body, but the human mind has been thus evolved.

Thirdly, psychology has given us the concepts of the " unconscious mind and purpose." Whatever be the ultimate verdict about the theories connected with the names of Freud and Jung, there can be very little doubt that they have thrown light on the structure and mechanism of the human mind, and that this will have to be taken into account in all attempts to understand and deal with our spiritual life.

How, then, can we apply these considerations to the doctrine of original sin ?

(*a*) We owe to Dr. Tennant the first attempt, at least in England, to reinterpret the doctrine in the light of biology. It is quite unfair to regard his treatment as merely naturalistic. He limits the term sin to actual sin, claiming that this limitation brings out all the more clearly the seriousness of sin. So-called original sin he regards as the survival in man of animal tendencies, useful and necessary at an earlier stage, but now felt to be an anachronism. Our consciousness of divided self is due to the fact that these animal impulses are only in process of being moralised. As man has evolved he has exchanged a life of merely animal contentment and harmony for one of moral struggle and effort. He has become dissatisfied with his brute life and contrasts his animal passions and habits with what he would fain become. So his sense of dissatisfaction is really a sign of moral advance and is the inevitable outcome of man's development.

Though we are unable to accept this as an adequate explanation of all the facts, we owe much to Dr. Tennant for his treatment of the problem. But we feel that he has underestimated the gravity of the situation. He has explained admirably the origin of the raw material of our evil impulses and tendencies, but the real problem is not the possession of these animal tendencies but the universal failure to control them. We believe that the human life and character of Christ were based upon just such elements of instinct, but in Him they were directed and harmonised into a perfect whole. There is in this material of instinct and impulse nothing that is intrinsically evil. It is all capable of right direction. The problem is that men universally fail to control and direct it. The mere possession of these impulses could not be called sinful in any sense of the term. It is in full accord with the will of God. But it certainly results in very much that cannot be in accordance with the will of a good God. We may also criticise Dr. Tennant on the ground that he regards sin as a purely moral problem. He passes over lightly the religious aspect. He has replied indeed that there was no need to emphasise the fact that sin is against God, because no one had ever disputed it.[1] But there is always a danger of allowing too little weight to considerations which are taken for granted. Sin is a religious term and religion is more than mere morality. The seriousness of original sin is that it cuts man off from God and from that fellowship with Him for which man was made.

[1] *Journal of Theological Studies*, Jan. 1923, p. 196.

(*b*) Let us then look at the facts again. Science and psychology unite in teaching us that we must regard human nature not statically but dynamically. It does not come to us ready made. It is a process. When we are born, we are so to speak candidates for humanity. We inherit a number of quite general instincts out of which we build up our life through experience. We also inherit certain mental dispositions and capacities, though there is a wide difference of opinion as to their number and nature. Our powers are undeveloped. What if this mental structure has been already misformed before the conscious life begins ? May we not find on these lines an explanation of those phenomena which are comprised in the term "original sin" ? Older theology regarded men as inheriting a tendency to evil by generation much in the same way as physical peculiarities. This is still the official doctrine of the Roman Church, following St. Augustine. It comes very near to reducing moral evil to a physical taint. Further the transmission of any such bias to evil would be a case of what is called the transmission of an acquired characteristic. The possibility of this is strongly denied by the dominant school of biologists. They hold that modifications acquired during the lifetime of an organism cannot be passed on to its descendants by heredity. It is true that many scientists are of an opposite opinion, but until science has made up its mind on the question—and it is for science to decide—it is rash to explain original sin by heredity. Further, it is hard to see in what way any element in our nature can have become intrinsically bad, since God created nothing evil in itself. Rather it is the balance of our nature that is upset, and desires and impulses good in themselves and necessary for the completeness of our human life have become attached to wrong objects or got out of control.

We suggest therefore that more weight should be attached to what is often called, not quite accurately, " social heredity." We have already called attention to the fact that there is no such thing as a mere individual. The individual only comes to himself as a member of a community. This truth long familiar has received a new application through modern psychology. We have come to see that from his earliest moments, even perhaps in the period before birth, the infant is having his tastes and tendencies moulded by the influence of those around him. And all through life we are being shaped by social tradition in all its many and subtle forms.

In all his moral and spiritual life the individual is being inter-penetrated by the moral and spiritual life of others. There is a real solidarity of mankind. Herd instinct prompts our conduct far more than we like to assume and, let us remember, herd instinct is in itself at best morally neutral. When we have attained a certain stage of development, mere herd instinct tends to lower the moral level of the individual. We must distinguish between mere herd or mass suggestion and the group mind or mind of an organised society, which is able to raise the minds of the members of a group to higher levels of moral and intellectual life. This innate capacity for social life is then itself morally neutral. As it may be the condition of progress, so it may be equally the condition of movement away from the purpose of God. We may see in original sin the result of misdirected social influence. Some such concept is an intellectual necessity. Social sin is as much a fact as social righteousness. Every society has in a real sense a corporate mind, the product not only of its present members but of its past members also, and all who belong to and share its mind come consciously or unconsciously under its sway. We suggest that original sin is to be found not simply in the possession of animal impulses and passions imperfectly disciplined and in the failure to discipline them by the individual, but rather in the positive mis-directing of such instinctive tendencies by bad social influences at every stage. Psychologists have invented a new term " moral disease " to describe a mental condition in which instinctive tendencies which conflict with moral standards have been repressed into the unconscious and from there exercise a pernicious influence on the conscious life. Without committing ourselves to the position that original sin consists merely in repressed complexes, we may see here one way in which the moral life may be disordered through no fault of the individual but simply through social environment.

In a review of Dr. Tennant's book in the " Journal of Theological Studies " [1] Mr. C. S. Gayford wrote : " Granted that the propensities which constitute the *fomes peccati* come to us from our animal ancestry, and are in themselves non-moral, the last step in the evidence should tell us what attitude the will itself at its first appearance is seen to adopt towards these propensities. Is it neutral ? Does it incline towards that higher law which is just

[1] April 1903, p. 472.

beginning to dawn upon the consciousness ? Or is it found from the first in sympathy and alliance with the impulses which it ought to curb ? " Modern psychologists would complain that this language treats the will as a separate faculty, whereas they regard it rather as the whole man moving in response to some stimulus. But if we modify this view of the will, the quotation corresponds to our suggestion. When man becomes responsible for his actions, his power of choice is limited and perverted by " sentiments " and " complexes " formed under the influence of his social environment during the time when his power of moral choice was still undeveloped. While these do not destroy his power of free choice, they curtail the range within which such choice is now possible.

(c) Dr. Tennant's view has also been attacked from another direction. It has been argued in several quarters lately that we cannot isolate the evil tendencies in man from the evil in nature : that the process of evolution was vitiated long before man ever appeared on the scene. It is impossible to suppose that a perfectly good and wise God would have created, say, the cobra or the cholera germ. It is not enough to say that the world is imperfect. The existence of "dysteleology" in nature, the ruthless competition and cruelty all go to show that it does not perfectly express the will of God. So the nature which man inherited from his animal ancestry was fallen before ever he inherited it. He appeared on the scene burdened by an inherently self-centred nature dominated by instinctive structures of animalism whose overpowering bias towards evil he could not be expected to control. Those who maintain such views as these make out a strong case. They argue for a " Fall," but a Fall which is " pre-organic "—that is, prior in time to the whole evolutionary process. Certainly this idea clearly emphasises the reality and seriousness of original sin.[1]

4. The State of Fallenness

The doctrine of a Fall of some kind is an inevitable deduction from the recognition of original sin. If we hold that our present condition is not in accordance with the will of God we must believe that the race as a whole has fallen away from the divine purpose. As we have seen, we can no longer use the story in Genesis as historical evidence. Nor have we any other source of

[1] See e.g. Formby, *The Unveiling of the Fall.*

light on the moral and spiritual condition of primitive man.   We do
not even know for certain whether all mankind are descended from
a single pair or not.   Nor does the study of the scanty remains of
primitive races throw light on our problem.   It seems as if man
had made one or two false starts, and that races who had attained to
a certain degree of development died out.   It can also be inferred
from the possessions buried with the dead that they believed in some
kind of future life, and therefore had some kind of religion.   More
than this we cannot say, nor does it seem as if we shall ever get any
clear evidence on this point.   It is quite conceivable that there once
was a time when the human race was developing on right lines,
a period of what we might call, to use the old term, " original
righteousness."   Science is more ready than it was to admit of
leaps forward in evolution.   We can picture one such when man
became aware, however dimly, of a spiritual environment and of
his capacity to correspond to it.   It may have been that for a
time long or short he did respond and began to develop on right
lines and then failed to respond.   He refused to make the moral
effort to live up to his calling and so forfeited that full fellowship
with God which could alone give him the power to control his
animal impulses.   Science cannot say anything against such a
hypothesis.   Indeed, Sir Oliver Lodge in his last book puts forth
a similar view.   Man experienced " a rise in the scale of existence,"
but fell " below the standard at which he had now consciously
arrived.   The upward step was unmistakable ; mankind tripped
over it and fell, but not irremediably." [1]

Another possible view is that there never existed in actual
history any period when man fulfilled God's purpose for him,
but that before ever he emerged, the evolutionary process was
marred by some rebellious spiritual influence.   Some have
attempted to revive Origen's teaching of a Fall of individual souls
in a pre-existent state.   This is open to all the arguments against
pre-existence and is hard to reconcile with the justice of God.
If our present lot is the rightful consequence of disobedience in
some previous existence, then it is morally useless to punish us
for it unless we are able to remember it.   Others again have put
forward a theory of a world-soul which by some pre-cosmic act
was shattered and defiled so that the life-force is in itself tainted.
This is a piece of pure mythology, and corresponds to nothing in

[1] *The Making of Man*, pp. 84, 151.

human experience. It is difficult to criticise it because it eludes both the understanding and the imagination. It is more reasonable to conjecture that the world-process has been distorted by rebellious wills other than human. There is nothing irrational in supposing that there are other conscious beings than man in the universe. We know in our own experience the possibility of disobedience to the will of God. If sin can arise in our own lives in this way, it is not unreasonable to hold that it arose in like manner in other beings who, however unlike ourselves, resemble us in this, that they enjoy some measure of free will. This certainly can claim the support of Scripture, which assumes the activity of rebellious spirits other than human behind the world-order. St. Paul includes in the redemption won by Christ not only mankind, but angels above man and nature below man.

To sum up : Christian tradition and experience unite in bearing witness to a belief that mankind as a whole and not merely individual man has fallen away from the purpose of God. What is important is to recognise the fact of fallenness. The practical value of this belief is great. To believe in original sin is to face the facts, but not to take a depressing view of human life. It is to make an act of faith that we ourselves and human society are not what God intended us to be, and that our present condition is a libel on human nature as He purposed it. The human race as a whole and every member of it needs not only education and development, but redemption. It cannot save itself, but must be as it were remade or born again. And we believe that in Christ God has provided exactly what we need. In Him the human race made a new start.

Further, just as we saw that original sin was propagated by membership in a fallen humanity, so in the Church, the Body of Christ, we see the new people of God, the new humanity. The Church is in literal truth the home of grace. By baptism[1] the

---

[1] The question may be asked whether the rejection of much of the traditional theology connected with the Fall of man does not necessitate a revision of our doctrine of baptism. We must first insist that much of the language employed in connection with baptism, which is taken from Scripture, was used in its original context to refer to adult baptism. It dates from a time when, as in the Mission field to-day, infant baptism was the exception and not the rule. Accordingly when it is transferred to apply to infant baptism we cannot wonder that its meaning needs to be modified. Thus an adult coming to be baptised needs forgiveness of his past actual sins. He needs not only to be cleansed but to be pardoned. But an infant is not in the least responsible for

Christian is born again, because he is brought within the sphere of the new life achieved by Christ and imparted normally by membership in His Body. "For as in Adam all die, so also in Christ shall all be made alive." Over against original sin we set the redemptive power realised through fellowship with God and with one another in Christ.

II

GRACE AND FREEDOM

BY J. K. MOZLEY

1. *The Idea of Grace*

THE differences which inhere in any two individual lives are, in part, the result of the differences of the two persons concerned. But they are also, in part, the result of the differences of the two particular environments. For no two persons, at any stage, is environment precisely the same, and the secret of a life, which may be revealed though very incompletely at some moment in its course, and is more fully disclosed when that course has reached its earthly end, is the secret of the interaction between the self and its environment. Yet this is not the whole truth. The Christian sees the deeper truth of the self and its earthly environment in the

his share in a fallen humanity. He needs indeed the grace of God to counteract the perverting influences which have already begun to work upon his life, but God cannot be said in any sense to blame him for his present condition. Nor can we believe that infants are personally exposed to the wrath of God. All that we can assert is that God hates and condemns that condition of humanity which shuts men out from fellowship with Himself. Only in this quite abstract sense can sin that is only "original" be said to deserve God's wrath. The unhappy use of St. Paul's phrase "children of wrath" in the Church Catechism has been responsible for many misunderstandings. In its context, as all New Testament scholars agree, it only means "objects of wrath." There is no reference whatever to infancy. St. Paul insists that men by "nature," that is apart from the assistance of God's grace, cannot overcome their evil tendencies and be pleasing to Him. Even so God's wrath is directed, as we have seen, against their condition, not against themselves. God cannot condemn men for a state for which they are not accountable. Rather, as suffering from a disease of the soul which disqualifies them for the highest life, they are the objects of His pity and redeeming purpose. So, again, when infants are said to be born "in sin," the term is being used in its widest sense, to include all tendencies of life that are contrary to the divine purpose. The phrase means "born into an environment that will mis-shape them."

light of the relation of each to a higher order of reality which supplies the only adequate account both of what is and of what is intended to be. There is a unity underlying variation. A two-fold relationship, constituting a twofold environment, forms the permanent setting of the life of every individual. We are one through our membership of a fallen and sinful humanity ; we are one through our membership of a redeemed humanity which offers us the hope of such a final liberation from all sin and every form of evil as will mean the fulfilment of a glorious destiny.[1]

Both these are real environments. They give the spiritual conditions of our lives. There are certain moral facts connected with humanity, out of which no individual can contract. This is clear enough of the evil. It has penetrated too deeply for any sort of Pelagianism to hold its ground, when the appeal goes to the facts. It is on the moral side that pessimism has its strength. There is a real facing of a mass of evidence in the belief that though humanity is conscious of a call to moral idealism and achievement it neither has nor ever will have the power to attain. The other condition is not equally clear. Indeed, to some it may seem too great a paradox to speak of humanity both as though in it a kingdom of evil held sway, and also as in fact redeemed. Some who reject pessimistic conclusions, while seeking to face bravely and honestly the widespread signs of evil strongly entrenched, would probably prefer to describe humanity and the world as to be redeemed rather than redeemed. But the Christian Church will never allow its songs of triumph to be set in the minor key. The work of Christ means something more than a specially powerful movement in the long warfare between good and evil. The two great epistles *Colossians* and *Ephesians* bear testimony to that. We have but dim conceptions and inadequate words for expressing what is known as the cosmic work of Christ. A veil hides from us the mysteries both of creation and of redemption. But the Church with all the richness of its life is not to be understood as the means to the attainment only of moral ends, nor is the Kingdom to be reckoned as no more than that " far-off divine event " which will some day close the book of world-history. The Church is here, and the Kingdom comes because of the eternal present value of Christ's work of salvation. We have our place in a new world-order as truly as in that which binds us with the chains of its ancient evil.

[1] *Cf.* Romans viii. 18–25.

But though the belief in a new order is characteristic of Christianity, the relationship of the individual to this order in which the old things have become new is not " given " in the same sense as his relationship to that sinful humanity which represents the continuance of the old order. For the efficacy of his member-ship in it depends upon his personal response to it and use of it. He himself, for this to be possible, must become a new creation. No utterance of the New Testament better expresses the nature of the environment in which the believer has his dwelling and of the change which the reaction between it and himself involves than 2 Corinthians v. 17 : " In Christ . . . a new creation " ; that description briefly comprehends the reality of the new life as possessing and possessed by the individual. And the word which gives the best and fullest description of this new life, expressing both its nature and also the individual's proper reaction to it, is the word Grace.

This word is one of the classic words of Christian theology, as an exposition of its frequency and importance as χάρις in the New Testament, and of its standing in the great dogmatic *schemata* of Catholicism and of Protestantism, would show. Yet the framing of a wholly satisfactory conception of it has not been unattended by special difficulties, and both in popular religious thought and in theological interpretations, it has occasioned mis-understandings and perplexities which have not been chiefly on the surface or at the circumference of Christian faith. We must allow first of all for impressions, which can hardly be called intellectual conceptions, of grace as an impersonal force, a " thing " which can be brought into touch with persons by some process of permeation. That is the danger of the phrase " infused grace." We cannot abandon it. It has both too honourable a history and too essentially religious a meaning. But we must not let it convey to our minds the idea that grace is a kind of invisible fluid which passes into persons and produces effects through contact. The materialism of attenuated and etherialised substances is still materialism ; and though matter and spirit are not contrary the one to the other, seeing that each is dependent upon God and serves God's purposes ; though, further, matter can be used in the highest interests of spirit, else the Incarnation would be impossible and the sacraments possess no inward part ; it is always true that spirit remains spirit, and matter matter. Grace stands for the personal dealings of God with man in various ways and through various media. He does not start a process which ends in the pouring of grace into man; but grace means God in action, regenerating, blessing, forgiving, strengthening. It is the suggestion of impersonal operation which has found an entrance into the terminology of grace that needs to be eradicated. Then, secondly, difficulties arise in connection with the place given to grace and with the effects ascribed to its activity. It is both intellectually justifiable, and also of great spiritual value, to believe that man is not the victim of illusion when he claims to possess a measure of freedom, and that that freedom is never overwhelmed or destroyed. Man's free self-expression is variously limited, and in no two persons is it of exactly the same quality, but the moral aim of life is towards an expansion not a contraction of it, and in all moral attainment free action of personality is involved. Now the workings of grace have been so expounded as to leave no place for freedom. The Augustinian tradition so emphasised the necessity of acts of will being in accordance with the state of human nature which lay behind the will, that grace was in danger of being regarded as an invasive and irresistible force which so changed man's nature that man was then "free" to do what had formerly been impossible for him. For Augustine the true freedom was the *beata necessitas boni*,[1] and the goal of the spiritual life. To this description of the ideal no exception is to be taken : but there is grave objection to the idea that the human will, or, better, the willing person, never makes any contribution in connection with salvation except that of willing what he has to will because his whole being is in the control of a force which turns it like a ship's rudder.

There is no hope of escape from this annulment of freedom by the delimitation of the moral and the religious life as two different spheres, with freedom the characteristic description of the one, and grace of the other. This is an unsatisfactory and unreal compromise. Even if grace could ever be regarded as operating in man in such a way as to leave his freedom alone and not to invade that region of his life in which moral decisions have to be made and moral values achieved, that could be applied only to quite low levels of experience. Only on such levels is any divorcement between ethic and religion conceivable. Ethic is not religion, and religion is not ethic, but

---

[1] Cf. *De Civ. Dei*, xxii. 30. The phrase itself I take from Harnack's *History of Dogma*, v. p. 113.

only as they meet and interpenetrate in experience are the highest levels of either attainable.[1]   If grace is to be allowed for at all, that is progressively the case as the moral life grows to higher stature and becomes richer and more comprehensive.   And the consciousness of dependence upon grace is the best way to moral attractiveness.   It is the lack of this consciousness which is the most serious and suggestive defect in the pagan moral ideal.   How little Aristotle conceives of a way out of the moral struggle whereby the individual may reach a higher state of goodness and abide therein is clear from his comparison in the seventh book of the " Ethics " of the ignorance of the incontinent man, and its cessation, with the phenomena of sleep and awakening.   There is simply an alternation of contrary experiences.   As for the Stoic sage, we may admire him, without impulse or desire to imitate him.   Whatever theory be held of the matter, it is the union of religious dependence with moral independence in the Christian saint which gives him his pre-eminence religiously and morally.   It appeals as a unity, not as two admirable but isolated facts lying side by side within one personality.

2. *The Idea of Grace in the Bible and Christian Theology*

Before we go further into the question of the presence and scope of grace in the Christian life, and of the character of its relation to freedom, a sketch of the idea of grace as we find it in the Bible, and of the place it occupies in the historical development of Christian thought, will be useful, and may point us in the right direction for a solution of the difficulties which have gathered round the subject.

We may note at the start that the general notion involved in the word "grace" is, when viewed in relation to God or the gods, that of divine favour flowing outwards to man, and, when viewed from the side of man as the recipient of that favour, enhanced powers which may reveal themselves in physical or spiritual growth and capacity.   According to the character and development of religion, so will be the conception of grace.   If we take two definitions of grace when it is conceived in accordance with the whole Christian outlook—that of Dr. Gore that it is " God's love

---

[1] Otto's insistence on this point has been strangely overlooked by many of his critics.

to us in actual operation," [1] and that of Dr. W. N. Clarke who describes it as " the suitable expression, in such a world as this, of the fact that God's gracious purpose is to bless sinners " [2]—we see how far such phraseology goes beyond the primitive ideas of grace which we find in ethnic religions. [3] But wherever there is the conception of a mysterious power or virtue attaching to particular things, or, more personally, of beauty and strength bestowed on men by a divine being, there we may recognise the rudiments of what was to become the Christian belief in grace. A passage in the " Odyssey " shows how χάρις can be construed as a physical gift from the gods. Before his meeting with Nausicaa Odysseus is beautified by Athene ; she makes him " greater and more mighty to behold, and from his head caused deep curling thick locks to flow like the hyacinth flowers . . . and shed grace about his head and shoulders. Then to the shore of the sea went Odysseus apart, and sat down, glowing in beauty and grace." [4] Yet, though materialistic or quasi-physical conceptions of the gods involve similar conceptions of grace, we must not exclude a primitive moral interpretation. The favour of the gods possesses this moral connotation, in that the opposite of the divine favour, namely the divine anger issuing in punishment, is the result of offences which draw down upon individual or tribe supernatural wrath. And though, at early stages of religion, no sharp division between the ceremonial and the ethical is possible, allowance must be made for the presence of an element truly, though in quite primitive fashion, ethical. [5]

The Old Testament is permeated with the conviction of God's gracious dealings with man. But we must recognise different levels of insight into the character of these dealings. There is the primitive conception of grace as it comes before us in the story of Noah's sacrifice [6] ; there is the highly developed teaching of the Prophets whose doctrine, on its side of hope and promise, is one of grace specially directed towards the Community. [7] There is

---

[1] *The Epistle to the Romans*, i. p. 49.

[2] *The Christian Doctrine of God*, p. 89.

[3] For primitive notions of grace and the concept of " mana " see R. R. Marett, *The Threshold of Religion*, pp. 101 ff.

[4] *Odyssey*, vi. 229–237 (tr. Butcher and Lang).

[5] See the chapter entitled " Morality " in Dr. F. B. Jevons' *Introduction to the Study of Comparative Religion*.

[6] Genesis viii. 21.

[7] *Cf.* Amos v. 15 ; Hosea xiv. 2 ; Is. xxx. 18.

nothing akin to pagan conceptions of grace as won from supernatural powers through magical processes.   In the sacrifices of
the Law, it is God who through the cultus gives man the means of
approaching Him and being accepted by Him.[1]   Where the Old
Testament, as a whole, is incomplete is in placing so predominant
an emphasis on the national covenant-relationship with God that
the individual is in danger of being overlooked, and in the confinement of God's gracious purposes and blessings to Israel.   But the
manifestation of grace as the antithesis of sin and the source of
mercy and forgiveness is constantly found in the Old Testament,
beginning with the Protevangelium.   It would take us too far
away from the subject to pursue this thought further, but it may
be said that modern misconceptions of the religion of the Old
Testament and its doctrine of God are largely due to a failure to
pay attention to the place and importance given in the Old Testament to God's manifestation of His grace.

In the New Testament, though the word " grace " is unevenly
distributed through the various portions of its literature, the reality
for which the word stands is of the essence of the revelation of
God's attitude towards man.   The Gospel is always one of grace.
It is so in our Lord's preaching of the fatherhood and the love
of God, nowhere more prominently than in the parables which
St. Luke has preserved for us.[2]   And when we pass to St. Paul's
epistles, grace appears as " that regnant word of the Pauline theology " [3] in which is contained the answer to the fact and problem
of sin, bound up with the Incarnation and cross of the Son of God,
and linked on, as the Dean of Wells shows, with the extension of
the Gospel to the Gentiles.[4]   Any adequate discussion of St. Paul's
understanding of grace would have to take account of problems
which can only be mentioned.   These concern the universality of

---

[1] *Cf.* Lev. xvii. 11.

[2] *Cf.* Dr. Townsend's *The Doctrine of Grace in the Synoptic Gospels.*   On
p. 106, writing of the first two parables in St. Luke xv. he says : " In the Christian
religion the emphasis is on the divine quest of God for man.   God is the seeker,
and these parables affirm the restlessness of His grace in Christ, until that which
was lost is found."   *Cf.* what St. Paul says of " being known of God " in 1 Cor.
viii. 3 and Gal. iv. 9.

[3] Miss E. Underhill's expression in *The Mystic Way*, p. 178.

[4] See, in his edition of *Ephesians*, the exposition on ii. 10, pp. 52–3 : " It
was the glory of grace to bring the Two once more together as One in Christ.
A new start was thus made in the world's history.   St. Paul called it a New
Creation."

grace, the relationship in which it stands to the divine righteousness, its doctrinal connections with the Apostle's theology of the indwelling Christ and of the Holy Spirit, and its bearing upon his conception of the sacraments.   It is sufficient for our purposes to point out that the problems or even dilemmas of which he was conscious, at least in part—and we still more when we try to systematise the controlling features in St. Paul's religion—must not be solved or evaded by any compromising formula which is always in danger of missing the point of the Apostle's meaning.   For him the true interpretation of religion depends on the recognition of the priority of grace to all human endeavours.   This grace he found at its richest and most illuminating in Jesus Christ, the Son of God, crucified and risen, and when he thought of the working out of God's purposes in the ages to come, he saw it as an increasing manifestation of " the exceeding riches of his grace in kindness towards us in Christ Jesus." [1]

As in the New Testament, so in Christian theology, grace is one of the dominant words.   Yet in the first centuries it gained no special attention.   The sacramental associations of grace are, as early as Ignatius, deriving from the Incarnation and pointing forward to a climax in " deification." [2]   No one was concerned to go deeply into the question of the effect of grace upon human freedom.   Origen has something to say on the matter, and ends his discussion with the declaration that both the divine and the human element must be maintained. [3]   But for the full significance of grace to be expounded, both a man of quite uncommon religious history and genius and the occasion of a great controversy were necessary. The need was supplied by Augustine and the issues which rose round the sharp reactions from one another of himself and Pelagius. We must leave on one side the story of that first great clash of rival efforts to state a Christian anthropology.   Suffice it to say that Augustine's whole doctrine of grace rests on two pillars which rise from the ground of one of the profoundest of religious experiences.   One of them stands for the absolute necessity of grace, as the source of all real goodness, the other for the character of grace as real power infused into the human heart.   A determinist in the modern philosophical sense Augustine was

---

[1] Eph. ii. 7.
[2] *Ad Ephes.* xx. *Cf.* also Irenaeus, *Haer.* v. 2, 3.
[3] *De Principiis*, iii. 1, 22.

not.[1] But the only freedom which interested him was freedom to do right, and that freedom was obtainable through grace alone. His opponents, on the other hand, conceived of grace as no more than a help, interpreted it, partly at least, as a description of such external assistance to well-doing as law and doctrine,[2] and displayed great zeal for the emphasising of man's natural freedom to choose the good, and of the obligation resting upon him precisely in virtue of that freedom. Augustine triumphed, but within the Catholic Church Augustinianism as a fully articulated system has, practically from the first, been subject to reservations. When in A.D. 529 the Council of Arausio or Orange, while maintaining against Pelagianism or Pelagianising tendencies that grace was necessary and prevenient and not based on antecedent merits, declared that sufficient grace was given to all the baptised,[3] a place was left for the action of the will which involved by implication a kind of differentiation between grace and freedom that Augustine could not have admitted.[4] For Augustine identified salvation with the gift of final perseverance, which was not bestowed on all the baptised ; and as that gift was both in itself indispensable for salvation, and the culmination of the economy of grace, sufficient grace, in the sense of being sufficient for salvation, was not, in Augustine's view, a gift of which every member of the visible Church had the advantage.

Large contributions to the theology of grace were made by the Schoolmen, and the conception of actual grace as the motive

---

[1] " The *libertas arbitrii* in the psychological sense he never denied ; within the region of his ability man possesses a *liberum arbitrium* (that is freedom of choice): Augustine was no determinist." Loofs' *Leitfaden zum Studium der Dogmengeschichte*[4], p. 411.

[2] In the *De gestis Pelagii*, 30, Augustine refers to Pelagius' repudiation of an opinion ascribed to Coelestius that " the grace and help of God is not given for individual acts, but exists in free-will or in law and teaching." Thus interpreted, grace becomes the revelation of what we ought to do, and the formal possibility of doing it, not a re-enforcement of man's will by divine power. Harnack, while allowing that just at this point it is hardest to reproduce Pelagian views, concludes that the Pelagian doctrine " in its deepest roots . . . is godless " (*Hist. of Dogma*, v. p. 203).

[3] Towards the end of *Capit. XXV* it is said : " This also we believe according to the Catholic faith, that through the grace received in baptism all the baptised, Christ helping them and working with them, can and ought, if they are willing to strive faithfully, to accomplish those things which concern the soul's salvation."

[4] For Augustine the way in which freedom and grace are related to one another is all-important. He says (*De corrept. et grat.* 17) " the human will does not attain grace by freedom, but rather attains freedom by grace."

power whereby habitual grace, consisting in the natural or theological virtues, is exercised, is in line with the Augustinian tradition,[1] though the scheme is much more elaborate. When at the Council of Trent neither the Dominicans, carrying on the Augustinian doctrine, as it had come down through St. Thomas Aquinas, nor the Jesuits, with their much more definite semi-Pelagianism and affinities with Scotist thought, were able to secure full dogmatic expression for their views, the result was an Augustinian assertion of the necessity of grace, which, at the same time, refused to treat the will as other than a real co-operant, with its own part to play by assent and by preparing itself for the grace of justification.[2] It is a synergistic doctrine, and, in view of it, Jansen's later attempt to revert to the severest conclusions of the logic of the great African Father was sure to fail. With regard to the sacraments, the Council in its seventh Session taught that these contained and conferred the grace which they signified.

The rigour of Augustine's doctrine reappeared in the Continental Reformers. Both Luther and Calvin by insisting on the bondage of the will of the natural man under sin left no room for any factor in salvation except that of grace, while Calvin's emphasis upon a double Predestinarianism, in the absoluteness of which he went beyond Augustine, closed the circle so completely that man appeared as a wholly passive instrument controlled by forces which he could do nothing to help or resist. The Continental Confessions of Faith give formal statements in accordance with these estimates of grace and the will. An instance may be given from the Canons of Dort. In them it is taught that as a result of their corrupt nature, " all men are thus children of wrath, incapable of any saving good ; without regenerating grace neither able nor willing to return to God, to reform the depravity of their nature, nor to dispose themselves to reformation." The knowledge of God which belongs to man through the faint light of

[1] "Besides the supernatural superadded 'organism' (habitual grace, virtues, and gifts), the human soul, in order to produce supernatural actions meritorious of life everlasting, requires, each time, the impulse from God, which enables it to perform now a supernatural action " ("Grace, Doctrine of (Roman Catholic)," in Hastings' *Encyc. Rel. Eth.*, vol. vi, p. 368).

[2] Session VI, chapter V, of the decree on Justification. The beginning of justification springs from the prevenient grace of God, who calls sinners in such a way that " through His awakening and assisting grace they may be disposed to convert themselves with a view to their own justification, by freely consenting to and co-operating with that same grace."

nature has no saving value. Salvation results from God's un-feigned calling, and as to the unsaved " the fault lies in men them-selves, who refuse to come and be converted. But that others obey and are converted is not to be ascribed to the proper exercise of free will whereby one distinguishes himself above others equally furnished with grace sufficient for faith, but it must be wholly ascribed to God who calls effectually in time the elect from eternity, confers upon them faith and repentance . . . that they may glory not in themselves but in the Lord." [1]   It is the paradox which goes back to Augustine : the wicked are rightly condemned because they will evil, yet apart from grace it is impossible for them to will anything else.

Where the Reformation theologians broke with Augustine was in substituting the doctrine of justification by faith only for that of infused grace. Yet at this point there was not perfect consist-ency. Luther, who in connection with the baptism of infants had invented the idea of infused faith, taught an Eucharistic doctrine which involved the thought of the infusion of the power of Christ's body and blood. The notion of the sacraments as *efficacia signa gratiae* belongs to him as much as to the twenty-fifth article of the Church of England. Earlier articles reveal, on the problem of grace and freedom, an Augustinianism which avoids the full rigour of that system by not pushing its positive statements beyond a certain point and by the indeterminate character of its exposition of predestination.

With a brief account of the bearing of certain aspects of modern religious thought upon the subject with which we are concerned, this section may close. It is a natural deduction from all the evidence we possess that, to understand the place which grace holds in Christianity, we must view it against the background of belief in revealed religion as involving in a very definite way the incursion of the supernatural. It was precisely that belief which the growth of sceptical and deistic philosophies in the seventeenth and eight-eenth centuries assaulted ; and that meant a depreciation of the need for grace, for if Christianity was " as old as creation," the whole notion of supernatural grace, however interpreted, directed manwards through, and as a result of, the Incarnation, was jeopardised. Stages in the progress of this tendency may be ob-served in Socinianism with its " school-Christianity " and its

[1] See W. A. Curtis, *History of Creeds and Confessions of Faith*, p. 245.

Pelagian outlook, in the pantheistic philosophy of Spinoza, in the Arianism and Deism which so suddenly threatened the dogmatic well-being of the Church of England and of English Dissent, in the anti-miraculous thought of Hume, in the philosophy of the "Enlightenment" on the Continent, and even in Kant. For Kant's profound moral reaction against the "Enlightenment" left no place for the idea of grace, inasmuch as he held it necessary to exclude something which seemed to him prejudicial to human freedom and so to a real morality. Kant here stands in almost formal opposition to Augustine, since for him " the only true means of grace is a morally good life." [1] At the same time Kant came nearer to the orthodox standpoint and refused to range himself with a merely facile liberalism in that he both left a place for original sin and did not deny man's reception of supernatural help as a supplement to his own endeavours. In the nineteenth century the " liberalising of theology," which was on the whole anti-sacramental as against Catholicism and anti-evangelical as against the Reformation *doctrine*, was inimical to any emphasis upon grace, though the greatest of nineteenth-century liberal theologians, Albrecht Ritschl, refused to interpret Christianity either as the climax of natural religion or as the supreme ethic. But one must allow that his exact position as to grace is not at all easy to grasp. In England, while liberalism in theology had its influence, that could hardly be described as a positive and reconstructive one in the fields either of dogmatics or of the Christian philosophy of religion. On the other hand, the Oxford Movement laid the fullest stress on the supernatural, and brought once more into prominence the sacramental system as a principal means for the bestowal of grace; while, in a very different quarter, the Keswick School, with its special devotion to the theme of the work of the Holy Spirit in sanctification, proclaimed the inspiration of grace in the Christian life.

3. *The Supernatural Order, Grace and Freedom*

The question, What is grace and wherein may we recognise it? is wrapt up in that larger and most crucial question, What is the supernatural and where may we look for its manifestation? Exception is sometimes taken to the word " supernatural," but it is on any adequately Christian view impossible to dispense with the

[1] C. C. J. Webb, *Problems in the Relations of God and Man*, p. 95.

idea for which it stands. And whether the word be favoured or not, this idea of the essentially transcendent which establishes itself by a special kind of immanence within the natural order, and gives to that order a new centre, control and destiny, could hardly be denied by any believer in the Incarnation. But the Christian understanding of the relation of the supernatural to the natural is not content to see it concentrated in one supreme manifestation. The new unity in Christ's Person overflows into the whole of life with the power of unifying all life on a new and higher level. There is no denial of natural goodness or the value of natural and this-worldly ends. But when that goodness and those ends are isolated from their true destiny—which is to be integrated into an excellence and to serve purposes which transcend their own nature—then the Apostle's vision of a redemption of the natural order is retarded not only by the positive evil which has found a place within it, but also by the short circuit of its own virtues. So, as a recent writer has pointed out,[1] the New Testament conception of a moral life is that of one " deriving from, and determined by, fellowship with God," a life to which, minting a phrase of more than common value, from a passage in the Epistle to the Hebrews, he has given the title the " worshipful life." And I believe that he is entirely right and gives intelligible application within the sphere of morals to the distinction between the natural and the supernatural, when he writes : " that there is a fundamental difference not merely between good and evil, but between good and good, in the spiritual condition of men ; that the second includes but transcends the first ; and that it is the second which is of primary significance for religion, because it is concerned with men's relationship to the eternal Good Himself—these are propositions which appear to have overwhelming testimony in the mind of the Christian Church." And the secret of the power of the higher good lies in the revelation of the supernatural in the light of that Eternal Light which came into the world in the Person of Jesus Christ full of grace and truth. With this belief in a supernatural order belief in grace will be found congruous, since grace stands for the outflow into the existing given natural order of the powers of the world to come, the world which *a parte temporis* is conceived of as subsequent to our world and yet in present relationship to it. But that

[1] E. G. Selwyn in *The Approach to Christianity*, pp. 138–145.

is not the only result. One of the problems which has followed in the wake of modern science and has engaged the attention of those who have sought to vindicate the reality of the mental and spiritual side of human life and to refute that account of it which involves the conception " that all mental states are *epi-phenomena*, superfluous accessories, which arise in the course of the connected series of bodily changes," [1] is the problem of freedom. A one-ordered interpretation of reality makes it, at least, exceedingly difficult to find any place for freedom. Stoicism is prophetic in the consequences of its monism. Its teaching was that the only freedom possible was freedom to follow obediently the leading of the world-order, of Zeus or Destiny. In any case " follow still I must," is the testimony of Cleanthes.[2] Modern determinism has no other message. Entirely different is the witness of the New Testament. Unconcerned as it is, except by way of implication, with speculative problems that belong to the territory where science, philosophy and theology all try to make themselves at home and stake out their claims, it leaves us in no doubt where it stands on this issue. Its Gospel is a Gospel of freedom in the moral life from the bonds of a world-order which, so far as it had organised itself apart from God, meant slavery for all who were caught in its net.[3] With the will as the subject of philosophical discussions neither the Old Testament nor the New is at pains to deal. With man as the servant either of God or of his own lusts and the powers of evil the Bible is occupied from beginning to end. And had our modern expressions been at the disposal of the Biblical writers,

---

[1] A. E. Taylor, *Elements of Metaphysics*, p. 318.

[2] The four lines run thus : " Lead me, O Zeus, and thou, O Destiny, whithersoever I am appointed by you to go. I will follow without shrinking ; but if I turn evil and refuse, none the less shall I follow."

[3] At this point I insert the following note by Professor A. E. Taylor : " *Cf.* the allusions of St. Paul to bondage under the στοιχεῖα, which seem to mean the planets. Is not this aimed directly against the current astrology which, as is now known, was, in its Hellenic form, definitely Stoic ? The thought is that true freedom consists in getting loose from the evil world-order which is subject to the planetary revolutions. You get this thought equally in the Hermetic writings, where the main point is that the divine part in the soul came from God who is above the planetary system, or from the super-planetary " aether " where God dwells. But *how* this direct contact with God is to be established is just what the Hermetists cannot tell us and St. Paul does tell us. It is the thought of the starting of the process *from God's side* which is lacking to Stoics, Hermetists and Neo-Platonists alike."

they would not have said that the character of man's service was wholly determined by the circumstances of his human nature and its environment—that is, by the world-order expressing itself through him and controlling him through his physical and psychical con-stitution.   We must not generalise too widely ; but it is a fact that the ruling out of the supernatural order and of grace does not tend to strengthen belief in human freedom.   If we think of the Christian view of the world as one which holds to the reality of freedom as the condition for there being any life truly deserving the title of " moral " at all, we see the significance of the fact that a threat to one is often a threat to both.   It suggests that grace and freedom alike are living forces only when we view reality as a whole as something richer and deeper than it is in the power of the natural sciences by themselves to reveal to us.   And it also suggests that, as this enlarged world-view is able to provide satisfaction for those who wish to maintain the truth of human freedom, and also for those who assert that religious experience and its theological interpretation are not astray as to the actions upon and within human life of that divine energy which is called grace, it is a reasonable supposition that grace and freedom are not antitheses, and that the notion of discord between them errs by conceiving of them as though they were objects occupying space, and the one were excluded by the fact that the other was already in possession.

To consider the question more closely.   When we think of the meaning of grace, not simply as the energy of the divine favour and good will, but as that energy operative within the con-ditions of human life, bringing man into such contact with God that life is progressively raised to a higher than the natural level of this-worldly experiences, we see that grace involves a dependence of man upon God, a set of relationships between man and God over and above the fact that man is God's creature.   And because man's one true end is God, it is clear that the fuller his dependence upon God the truer will the direction of his life be and the richer will be its content, since it will neither consciously limit itself to the goods of the natural order nor fail to interpret and use those goods for purposes whose realisation lies beyond that order.   So for St. Paul the body, while belonging to the natural order, is also a temple of God, to be redeemed and raised in glory.

Now when we seek to understand the meaning of freedom

we find it impossible to give any rational account of it which does not take into consideration the sphere or order within which it is or may be a real fact, and the ends for which it exists. Freedom, in isolation, means nothing, and when, being expounded as a "freedom of indetermination," it is held to imply that "our choice between motives is not determined by anything at all," [1] it has neither philosophical sense nor religious value. Freedom is not given once for all. Rather do we begin to give it its true place only when we remember that life is the opportunity for man's progressive growth in independent moral personality, so that his personality represents something truly individual and distinctive. Of course if the moral world—what Professor Ward has called the Realm of Ends—is itself an illusion, then, so far as freedom is concerned, *cadit quaestio*. But if it is reality, and a higher reality than the physical world, then each person can enter into that realm only by making moral ends his own. He cannot do so by being wound up like a clock to a state of exact correspondence with the objectively good. Nothing but a purely external relationship would thereby be brought about. The objectively good must become goodness in him, the very stuff of his life. And this goodness is of his own choice. He is good because he chooses to be good. If we deny this, we not only destroy freedom but endanger personality as well ; for how shall we preserve the distinction between person and thing, unless we say that a person recognises certain purposes as purposes for him, and makes active contribution towards the bringing of those purposes within the circle of his own life ? This is what no thing can do, and animals other than man can do, if at all, only to a very limited extent.

When we think of the religious relationship to God and the life of grace, the moral relationship to goodness and the life of freedom, dependence and independence, we seem to postulate two circles, never intersecting, yet each enclosing human life,

---

[1] The late Dr. McTaggart's view of freedom as understood by its defenders, on which he based his attack. In the article, "Libertarianism and Necessitarianism," in *Encyc. Rel. and Eth.*, vol. vii, Dr. Pringle-Pattison's quotation of and repudiation of Dr. McTaggart's interpretation is given. Professor Taylor finds the true place of freedom to lie in the comparative judgment of the goodness of two objects of pursuit, A and B. When the judgment is made the will is determined by the judgment, but the judgment is not decided in advance by character up to date plus circumstances. William James, it may be remembered, insisted on the freedom of attention.

each indispensable. But in point of fact these relationships, blessings and ideals are held together within the unity of the personal life, and the moment we begin to think of the matter concretely, on the basis of what we can experience or observe, the whole idea of the delimitation of spheres, of so much being given to freedom and so much to grace, fades away.[1] It is not that we can be satisfied simply with an interpretation of freedom as " ideal " freedom, freedom to do right, as contrasted with the faculty of self-determination ; but the unconstrained activity of personality directed towards the attainment of ends which will involve in the case of the personality itself a self-realisation or self-fulfilment lies within that system of relationships which represents God's continual re-creative energy upon and within the world-order with a view to its establishment in a true religious and moral attitude to Him. This is not a work of divine omnipotence. A kingdom of good cannot be established by force ; there would be no value in man being constrained from without to become what he was not becoming from within.[2] At the same time, to suppose that anything good which he becomes from within he becomes in detachment from divine grace, or, differently expressed, from the inspiration of the Holy Spirit, is an atheistic delusion, since it means a discrimination at some point between goodness and God. If we treat the problem as one that concerns the relations of two abstractions known as " grace " and " freedom " to one another, we pose it in a *milieu* which forbids the hope of the discovery of a way out. For it implies an isolation of man from God just at the point where religion, and especially Christianity, affirms that isolation is exactly the wrong

---

[1] *Cf.* the quotation in von Hügel, *The Mystical Element of Religion*, vol. i. pp. 69 f., from St. Bernard, *Tractatus de Gratia et Libero Arbitrio*, cap. xiv. § 47 : " That which was begun by Grace gets accomplished alike by both Grace and Free Will, so that they operate mixedly not separately, simultaneously not successively, in each and all of their processes. The acts are not in part Grace, in part Free Will ; but the whole of each act is effected by both in an undivided operation."

[2] Two sayings of early Christian writers may be quoted in this connection. The author of the *Epistle to Diognetus* argues that in the sending of His Son God was saving men by persuasion, not compulsion, " for compulsion (βία) is not an attribute of God " (vii. 4). And Irenaeus, in a very interesting passage (iv. 62, in Harvey's edition), suggests that the education of the human race towards perfection is due to the fact that, whereas " God was indeed able to give man perfection from the beginning, man was unable to receive it for he was a child."

word and conception. No religion has contributed as much as Christianity to faith in the value of man, to appreciation of his dignity, and to hope of his destiny. It has done so by viewing him as the redeemed child of God, enabled by grace to enter upon his inheritance.

When we speak of the grace of God we mean that the divine favour goes forth towards man and rests upon him to bless and strengthen him. Spirit communicates with spirit ; the personal God is active towards the sanctification of the persons He has created and redeemed. He has ways at His disposal beyond our power to search out or define. Yet the phrase "means of grace" certainly stands for a method of His activity on which we can count, for instruments or channels which He uses, through and in which we can be sure that what He wishes to give us is to be found. Like more than one other famous expression of Christian theology it is capable of being misconstrued. It could be taken to allow of the idea that grace was a quasi-physical substance poured into men, which would mean a passing out of the region of moral relationships into the region of impersonal forces. But avoidance of such an error will enable us to make free and natural use of such words as "means" and "channels," which stand for truths congruous with the character of Christianity as the religion which, above all others, asserts the harmony and not the discord of matter and spirit. And while grace is present and operative in the historical process, in the formation of institutions and in the material order, so that we shall not seek to exclude it from anything but sin, with which it has a different kind of relationship, there are points within the historical, the institutional and the material at which grace is revealed as of special potency and relevance. We do no injustice to the universal operation of grace when we point to the cross as the place where God has manifested the full measure of His graciousness, or to the Church as the body in which that graciousness is the consciously realised background and meaning of all its distinctive actions,[1] or to the sacraments as objects which God selects, that through them as *efficacia signa* He may bring Himself into contacts of particular kinds with men and enable them to realise what He does. In them the divine life, everywhere

---

[1] *Cf.* Dr. Bicknell's remark on p. 223: "The Church is in literal truth the home of grace."

R

present, imparts itself in ways which answer to man's need, not only of a general environment of God's graciousness, but also of acts and ordinances which mediate to him the blessings which the gracious God gives in answer to his various necessities.   And the life of man, enriched by these blessings, and making a response which is itself possible only because man himself is never simply a natural phenomenon, becomes different.   It is in that difference as it is expressed in moral and spiritual progress that we recognise the grace which sanctifies.   There is nothing automatic, nothing magical, nothing unethical intruded at this point.   Sacramental grace does not involve any such incredible supposition as that God, in this province of His loving energy on our behalf, ceases to deal with us as persons and treats us as though we were things. It would indeed be an astonishing paradox if the richness of the sacramental life, rooted in and bearing its flowers in the ground of the conviction of the reality of sacramental grace, flourished alongside of so profound a misunderstanding of its own nature. It is possible, of course, to think of the sacraments sub-personally and sub-ethically, but so it is possible to do of God's grace and love, quite apart from the sacraments.   When we think truly, as the Gospel inspires us to think, of God's grace and love as realities which express the being of One in whom is the perfection of moral and personal life, we shall think of no other grace and love as given to us in the sacraments, that we may grow up into the ever fuller self-identification with the ideal of the καινὴ κτίσις.   Nor is there any obliteration of freedom.   The life strengthened by the sacraments is one in which man, by making his own the one true objective and personal ideal which exists for him, the ideal of the perfect humanity of Jesus Christ, is on the way towards that highest personal achievement which we understand by the word character.   And the more character is unified in its tendency and moves towards unity in expression, the freer, because the more completely himself, does man become in the correspondence that exists between himself and the spiritual order.   More and more is he raised above the natural order, to which he is indeed linked as an element within it, but which is neither the explanation of him nor his home.   It is only in his true home, and as he begins to be a native of it, that he learns the salvation which is God's purpose for him, for which God's grace is given.   And as he learns that, depending at all times upon the grace to which he owes the redemption won for him by Christ, he becomes what he already is, his Father's son, and gains his own self.

Christianity is the religion of redemption. And, not in addition to that, but in and through that, it is the way of the highest moral life and the completest personal attainment, a life of service wherein is perfect freedom. All this it is, and as a unity, and no one word so well explains this many-sidedness and this unity as the word Grace.

ADDITIONAL NOTE

To those who are acquainted with that very remarkable book, " Grace and Personality," by Dr. John Oman, Principal of West-minster College, Cambridge, it may well seem strange that I have not hitherto referred to it. I desire neither to overlook the book, which, in fact, I reviewed in *The Journal of Theological Studies* (July 1920 : xxi. 84), nor to fail to acknowledge the debt which I owe to its author. But I should have overburdened my pages had I referred at the various relevant points to Dr. Oman's positions, or dwelt on controversial matters where I should feel it necessary to diverge from his conclusions. " Grace and Person-ality " is written round the conviction that the distinguishing characteristic of a moral person is autonomy, and that grace must be a personal relationship between God and man, involving fellow-ship between God and man, and not suppressing freedom. The problem as he sees it is that of combining the dependence upon God which is an essential quality of a religious person and the independence which is an essential quality of a moral person. And the way to unity is neither by a compromise between religion and morality nor by the isolation of one from the other, but by such a relationship that " our absolute religious dependence and our absolute moral independence are perfectly realised and made perfectly one " (p. 82). I am sure that he is right in holding that the problem of grace can be handled properly only when all vestiges of sub-personal relationships are excluded from our thought of what can be true as between God and man. And neither the Augustinian emphasis upon the irresistible might of the grace which saves those who are called according to God's purpose, nor the Pelagian appeal to the obligation of obedience to the moral law as indicating that man has the power to keep the commandments, necessarily involves that thorough personalising of relationships. On the other hand, Dr. Oman is pressing his point too far when he attributes a kinship to the " extremest Catholicism and the extremest Evangelicalism . . . just because both depend on the same conception of grace as arbitrary acts of omnipotence." Not only would most of the theologians implicated in this indictment have vehemently rejected the word " arbitrary " : they would also have been justified in doing so because they did not find the source of right in God's particular appointment, but in the unchangeable moral perfection of God's nature. Even as to Duns Scotus important reservations have to be made,[1] while it is certainly no part of St. Thomas's doctrine that " God's appointment makes things reasonable and right," though Dr. Oman associates the two doctors in this belief (pp. 163-4). Dr. Oman insists on the need to recognise that " in all things God is gracious," and that we should not treat " the rest of experience as mere scenery for operations of grace which are canalised in special channels " (p. 174). Certainly ; but Catholic theology knows quite well that it must seek to do justice to the world and experience as a whole, and that it must exclude the possibility of contact with God and of doing God's will from nothing whatsoever except the morally evil. At the same time, whatever language be used, the Incarnation is a special channel of God's graciousness, and the religion sprung from belief in it reflects that fact in ways which do not at all impair the truth that all experience is usable for the knowledge of God and for fellowship with Him. Dr. Oman seems to me to be too much outside the particular and characteristic field of sacramental praxis and theology which we

---

[1] See the article " Scholasticism " in *Encyc. Rel. and Eth.* vol. xi. " Assuming that the content of duty depends on the constitution of human nature, it follows that, if human beings were constituted differently in certain fundamental ways, then the content of morality would be fundamentally altered. There is, however, no evidence that Duns Scotus intended to teach that morality could be determined differently by the will of God, human nature being constituted as it is." Professor Taylor draws my attention to Bonaventura, *Breviloq.* vi. 1, 5 (ed. minor, Quaracchi, p. 205) : " Huiusmodi sacramenta dicantur gratiae *vasa* et *causae* nec quia gratia in eis substantialiter contineatur nec causaliter efficiatur, cum in sola anima habeat collocari et a solo Deo habeat infundi ; sed quia in illis et per illa gratiam curationis a summo medico Christo ex divino decreto oporteat hauriri, licet Deus non alligaverit suam potentiam sacramentis."

associate with Catholicism to be first a satisfactory interpreter and then an adequate critic. There is not enough sympathetic penetration, at least at this point; and mental, and even spiritual, power, richly as his book is endowed with both, do not make up for that lack. He sees negatives in the positions of others which they would deny, or of which they would give a different description. The positive in his own position which he knows at first-hand is of very high religious value.

THE ATONEMENT
BY KENNETH E. KIRK

CONTENTS

I

The Problem of the Death of Christ

Ex ore infantium . . . The Catholic theory of the Atonement, with all its affirmations, its reticences, its possibilities of diverse interpretation, its consequent or collateral problems, is stated more clearly perhaps in three verses of the children's hymn than in any other document. Taking them as a starting-point, we shall have an opportunity of gathering, first, the affirmations in which all Christians are agreed; then those to which Catholic theology is more firmly wedded than other modes of Christian thought; finally the problems which are raised by the contrast between Catholic affirmation and non-Catholic doubt or silence.

> He died that we might be forgiven,
>   He died to make us good,
> That we might go at length to heaven,
>   Saved by His precious blood.
>
> There was no other good enough
>   To pay the price of sin,
> He only could unlock the gate
>   Of heaven, and let us in.
>
> Oh dearly, dearly has He loved,
>   And we must love Him too,
> And trust in His redeeming blood,
>   And try His work to do.

"He died that . . . " Christ's death is *central* in Christian thought. Christ's submission to death was *purposive.* On these two points there is substantial agreement between all types of Christian thought. *Why* it is central, or with *what* purpose He submitted to it, is the question which it is the object of this essay to consider. It suffices at the moment to say that those who would hush reason to silence at this point, and let loving faith dwell on the mystery without seeking to pierce its truth or meaning, ignore the God-given desire to know and understand which is the inheritance of every thoughtful man. Thought must go on till it is checked by the failure of its own powers : it admits no other or more artificial barriers.

The problem, therefore, of the purpose of the Lord's acceptance of death, or (in other words) of the manner of the Atonement, cannot be evaded. We must notice, however, a tendency among Christians, particularly of the present day, to take " death " as a mere paraphase or metaphor for " life." To them it would be the same or almost the same if our hymn ran—

> He *lived* that we might be forgiven,
> He *lived* to make us good,
> That we might go at length to heaven,
> Saved by His precious *love*.

The death of Christ, appealing, arresting though it is, is in their view no more than the focus of His life—" it only added a crowning illustration of the ethical principle which ran through all His teaching." [1] There was no absolute need for the cross and passion, nor anything new contributed by them ; they have no " exclusive efficacy " [2] ; they are simply accessories introduced by the cruelty of circumstance. They point the moral, no doubt ; but in strict thought they do no more than adorn the tale. If (as some of Athanasius's opponents urged) Christ had lived the same life of purity, self-denial and love, but passed away in a quiet and honourable old age, the dramatic appeal would have been less (for " no other way of ending the earthly life could so fully embody or symbolize the fundamental thought of Christianity that God is love "),[3] but the atoning effect the same. To such a conception our hymn, as it stands, offers no obstacles ; yet the divergence from traditional Christianity and from the New Testament writers is really extreme. We must, at some stage of our argument, face the question : If the death or " blood " of Christ saves, does it do so merely as summarising in itself the message and purpose of His life which is the true medium of salvation ; or does it contribute some-

[1] H. Rashdall, *Idea of Atonement* p. 46.
[2] Rashdall, *op. cit.* p. 149.
[3] Rashdall, *op. cit.* p. 361.

thing to our salvation which His earthly Incarnation, had it ended in any other way, would not have secured to us ?   Is His death, and that the death on the cross, a *sine quâ non* of salvation ; or no more than an appropriate but not strictly necessary conclusion of His life ?

II

Its Necessity for Salvation

" There was no other good enough . . . "   " He only could unlock . . . "   Here there can be little explicit [1] disagreement. Even though some writers use language which suggests that (given Christ's *life* on earth) His *death* was a mercy strictly speaking superfluous, vouchsafed to men by the abundant love of God to point the moral of His life, few would go so far as openly to allege that the life itself was, in the same strict sense, superfluous.   This would involve a belief that man can save himself (whatever is meant by salvation) if he only bestirs himself sufficiently ; and that the Incarnation was a divine gift which no doubt makes it easier for us to bestir ourselves, but with which the most saintly and noble souls can dispense.   Such a theory we can unhesitatingly reject. No coherent body of Christian thought has ever consciously regarded the incarnate life of Christ as a mere luxury, easing the moral man's path to perfection indeed, but in no way making that path practicable for the first time.   If man had not sinned, perhaps, it might have been so ; but since sin entered in, we have " no power of ourselves to help ourselves " ; our sufficiency—if ever we attain to sufficiency—is " of God," and of God " through Christ alone."

As to this necessity of an atonement, however, different minds will be impressed by different arguments.   The point is one to which we must recur [2] ; at the moment we need do no more than establish its inherent probability.   That probability depends upon a doctrine which clearly dominates St. Paul, that sin and circumstance are inextricably allied as forces from which man longs for

[1] The words "explicit," "openly," "consciously," are used in this paragraph because, in the writer's opinion, the theory he has ventured to call "exemplarist" involves an implicit though probably unconscious denial of the position here stated.   See further, Note A, fin. p. 276.

[2] *Infra*, pp. 267–270.

deliverance. " Sin," to the apostle, is a force hostile to God and goodness permeating all life and nature, and manifesting its power at every point. To adopt the words of another New Testament writer, here is an enemy or a combination of enemies, in fear of which every man goes " all the days of his life." [1] He may have little sense of moral sterility within himself—and it is in this respect, no doubt, that the " sense of sin " most fully manifests itself ; but he is conscious of an environment full of menaces, dangers, and hidden possibilities, all of them potent enough to destroy in a moment the work of his hands, and to reduce his efforts and aspirations to a cipher. Against such an environment he sees himself to be in fact powerless ; though it tolerate and even further his activities for the time, he cannot tell at what moment it may turn against him and overwhelm his work in disaster. From all such dread of circumstance he needs—and indeed, if he be a man of any sensibilities at all, he desires—" salvation," and he feels himself to be incapable of finding it spontaneously. He may not see in Christ his Saviour ; but at least he says, " There is *none other* good enough."

This deep-rooted disorganisation of the universe, investing all man's efforts with pain and threatening them with annihilation, of which every serious-minded man is conscious and from which he must naturally seek deliverance, is presented in the early chapters of Genesis as the consequence or punishment o₄ sin. If the invariable imminence of death be taken as its most obvious symbol, then St. Paul is found to be in complete agreement ; death is the wages of sin.[2] Such a representation of the dependence of physical upon moral disorganisation is not without its difficulties —death and disaster appear to have been laws of nature at epochs before conscious morality or immorality were possible. Yet there is a connection between the physical and the moral in this matter so intimate and unbreakable that to apply the name " sin " to both, and to recognise both together as that from which man needs to be saved, is wholly warranted. That connection shows itself in two respects at least. (i) As we have said, sin and circumstance combine to frustrate, or threaten with frustration, all man's hopes and efforts ; they form thus an unholy alliance, or conspiracy, against him, so intimate that one name fitly covers both. (ii) Without a change of moral attitude (a " salvation " from " sin "

---

[1] Heb. ii. 15.   [2] Rom. vi. 23.

in the narrower sense) no change in man's environment could make him happier, or better, or more confident of the future, *i.e.* could " save " him from " sin " in the wider sense. He might be assured that Nature would further his every effort and crown him with length of days, but reflection would still convince him that his own moral deficiencies might bring disasters more bitter than Nature's worst ; health, prosperity, rank, reputation avail nothing to lighten the burden of sin upon a guilty soul. Escape from circumstance would be valueless except to those who could also escape from sin. To equate the idea of " salvation " with any-thing less than " full personal righteousness " is not merely—as Dr. Moberly so fairly pointed out [1]—" a pagan rather than a Christian " thought ; it is also a thought in itself futile and doomed to disillusionment.

Scripture has good grounds, therefore, for regarding sin and circumstance together as an alliance of enemies from which man needs deliverance. And it is just this fact of the alliance between physical and spiritual menace which makes it so natural for us to assert that man cannot " save " himself. Were our enemies spiritual only, we might not be able to prove that man is so debased in moral capacity as to be unable, unaided, victoriously to meet them. But they are physical, or cosmical, as well. This, on the one hand, enhances the demand for moral effort, for a new moral outlook to make man master of his fate and captain of his soul ; on the other it threatens all such effort with futility. Of what avail will be self-sacrifice, devotion to the cause of others, patience, courage, endurance when all but hope is gone, if there is only one event to the good and the wicked, if man is no more than dust, and to dust must return ? " Salvation "—at the very least—demands not merely that new moral outlook of which we have spoken, but also the assurance that Christian fortitude must in the end triumph over all the powers of cosmic evil ; that the gates of hell cannot prevail against it. And such an assurance the experience of human life does not seem to give. The grave is still the inevitable termination of all our hopes. There is a further aspect of this corporate or cosmical character of sin, to which we shall come. But even the aspect just suggested is enough for our present purpose. We are forced to the conclusion that man cannot save himself ;—that, apart from Christ, there can be " none

[1] R. C. Moberly, *Atonement and Personality*, p. 72.

other good enough " to overcome that combination of spiritual and physical enemies which St. Paul personifies as Sin.

III

Its Function as an Example

" Oh dearly, dearly has He loved, and we must love Him too." Here again all are, almost without exception, agreed.   The life and death of Christ (whether the death stands by itself in purpose, or is simply the appropriate consummation of the life) constitute an example which calls for human imitation within the measure and limits of human capacity ; whose call, moreover, is of infinite power in inspiring men to a new and devoted service of God and their fellows.   Whatever other benefits may have been secured for us by this mystery which we call the Atonement, one benefit was not secured, offered, or intended—that man should be saved without any contributory effort of his own will towards good.   Phrases have been used by Christian thinkers which sometimes can be distorted into this latter meaning, as of the sacraments, so of the death of Christ.   But no responsible theologian would ever have accepted the implication.   Some indeed might be so full of the thought of " grace " or " communion " as the means of holiness (whether mediated by the sacraments, or given apart from visible channels in response to the appeal of naked faith ; and whether, again, thought of primarily as a moralising force, or as a force lifting man into a realm far transcending all moral distinctions) as to suggest that man's efforts should primarily be directed, not to the imitation of Christ, but to the pursuit of " grace "—" grace " itself, on some theories, being thought of as attainable on conditions other than those of a constant striving after moral excellence.[1]   But even so, it would be admitted by all except the most extreme, that *if* in the " state " or " life " of grace moral problems arose demanding a " yes or no " answer—problems of the form, " Must I do this ? " or, " May I do that ? "—the life and death of Christ must form a final test or standard by which to measure the rightness or wrongness of the action contemplated. As an example, that life and death can be neither surpassed nor

---

[1] For the exaggerated teaching of Luther in these directions see H. Rashdall, *Idea of Atonement*, pp. 401–409.

ignored.   At the very least they mark out a path from which we deviate at our peril.   At the most they constitute a challenge which, in the last event, no human will, unless far advanced on the road to perdition, can disregard.   And to all the world they present, as realised in actual history, the picture of an ideal which few would not be glad to have constantly before their eyes, to keep their efforts from flagging and their hope from extinction.

IV

CRITICISM OF EXEMPLARIST THEORIES

So far all ways have lain together.   Theologians of every shade of thought travel in company.   The landmarks they have passed are these :   (*a*) No man can save himself ;   (*b*) the life of Christ incarnate was therefore *essential* to man's salvation, though its significance hitherto has mainly been found to lie in the fact that it makes the one appeal without which humanity could never have raised itself far out of the slough of sin ;   (*c*) the death of Christ, even though no more than the appropriate consummation of the life, was *so* appropriate that it may, symbolically at all events, be regarded as itself necessary also.   But at this point many theologians halt.   No more (according to them) is required by man, no more has been given by God ;   the example of Christ's suffering and obedience is all-sufficient.

Theories which go so far and no further have been designated by two names, equally question-begging ;   their upholders call them " ethical," their opponents " subjective." [1]   " Ethical," of course, they are, and " subjective " also, in the best senses of those much-abused words—that is to say, they demand of the human subject an ethical or moral effort towards righteousness.   But, in this respect, all genuinely Christian theories are ethical and subjective.   Nor can it even be said that the type of theory we have under consideration is *necessarily* more ethical or subjective than any other ;   that depends entirely upon the degree of effectiveness with which the interpreter endows the example of Christ, which (as we have seen) is the only lever of salvation recognised by the theory.   If he says (as for the theory's sake alone he might be

[1] Though Dr. Rashdall constantly uses the word " subjective " of his own theory with approval.

induced to say) that the moral appeal of the death of Christ is so overwhelming that no reasonable man can resist it, his theory partakes to an almost unlimited extent of the " unethical " or " objective " character which he deprecates in, or which his opponents claim for, the fuller theories to which we are to come. He is saying in effect: "The lion hath roared, who will not tremble; the Lord God hath spoken, who will not prophesy ? "—" Christ's death makes such an appeal to all that is best in human nature that only the insensate can remain unmoved ; all others *must* rise up from sin in the desire to imitate." The analogies on which the theory rests [1] are just those instances in which the example of one human personality removes out of another's path stumbling-blocks which hitherto have remained insuperable. A single hero may, by the stimulus of example, turn a craven rabble into a band of heroes like-hearted with himself ; and under that stimulus they can and do perform—with ease and without reflection upon the cost—acts of valour which at an earlier stage appeared entirely impossible. Their efforts, no doubt, are still voluntary and conscious (and therefore " ethical " and " subjective "), but so inspired by the example and magnetism of a great personality that they have ceased to be " efforts " in any ordinary sense of the word. The leader has lent his followers his own strength and daring. They are themselves and yet other than themselves ; or—we may say—they are their real selves at last, and no longer the cowards they appeared to be.

Here is a theory of the Atonement at once comprehensible, admirable and inspiring—one, moreover, without doubt true to life; but the more the influence of Christ's example is emphasised, the more He is thought of as lending His followers His strength, the less can it be called " subjective," or " ethical " either, in any sense in which emphasis is laid upon the efforts of the Christian to imitate. If we must have a name for theories of this type, let us choose a non-committal term and call them " exemplarist "— because their emphasis is upon the moral value of Christ's example. Terms such as " ethical " or " subjective " simply confuse the issue ; they suggest either that partisans of the theory claim too

---

[1] *E.g.* the " leader of men," Rashdall, *op. cit.* p. 43 ; *cf.* p. 51—our Lord thought of His death " as a kind of service which His disciples ought to imitate." As a matter of fact, and naturally enough, few exemplarist writers emphasise this " objective " aspect of their doctrine. *Cf.* p. 257, note.

much for it, or that opponents attack it at points where it is not necessarily assailable.

The "exemplarist" theory is not therefore, at first sight, either unworthy or unchristian. It is indeed a part, and a vital part, of every theory that can be called Christian. It might even be urged that it exhausts the data of Scripture, and is wholly adequate to the needs of man. But brief consideration will show that, whether it be the only truth derivable from reflection upon the death of Christ or no, its adequacy is a very different question. The example of Christ, we are told, appeals to love and will ; and so it does. But it does so, except in the case of His historical contemporaries, indirectly and at not one but many removes. It appeals to love and will only by way of imagination ; the mind which cannot visualise the life and death of Christ, as an example of self-sacrificing devotion, must go untouched. And imagination is a weak, fickle and erratic servant ; if we are to depend upon *this* for our salvation our chances are tenuous at best. In the long run, therefore, exemplarism holds out little hope to the ordinary man. The will, as we know, we can to some degree command, even in our state enfeebled by sin. But imagination and emotions are our servants only to a far slighter degree ; if the dedication of the will is to depend upon a prior captivity of emotion and imagination, our state is precarious indeed.

This criticism might perhaps be met by the addition to the theory of a doctrine of objective grace, to be won on such conditions that not even the most unimaginative soul would stand at a disadvantage as regards salvation [1]—and such indeed is the character assigned to grace in traditional Christian thought. But few exemplarist theologians seem disposed to make this addition. The cause of their reluctance does not concern us here ; it is connected with a shrinking from the objectively supernatural in general, characteristic of much modern thought. But the absence of any such doctrine of grace in exemplarism marks the theory out not only as inadequate to human needs, but also as profoundly inequitable. On the exemplarist theory, those will benefit most

---

[1] Such a theory, on strictly exemplarist lines, is involved in that " objective " aspect of exemplarism to which we alluded on the preceding page. But to adopt it would be to introduce an element of objectivity as aggressive as any contained in the traditional doctrines of grace. It is for this reason that exemplarists as a whole ignore the interpretations we have suggested.

by the example of Christ, *ceteris paribus*, who are most highly endowed with the capacity for emotional or imaginative quickening. Less moral effort will be required of them than of others of more stolid natures. In some cases, indeed, the force of example playing upon imagination and emotions will be so potent that a minimum of conscious moral effort will serve, when aided by this influence, to achieve results which in other natures, less richly endowed, even heroic struggles may fail to reach. The traditional theories, whatever form they take, all assume as a fundamental proposition something which common sense and Christian sentiment alike endorse—that (in the measure in which man is called upon to co-operate with God and grace in his salvation) the greater the moral effort the greater the certainty, if not the degree, of achievement. This plain and obvious piece of natural justice exemplarism sets aside ; it makes attainment depend primarily not upon moral efforts for which the man is consciously responsible, but upon accidents of heredity for which he can claim no merit. The theory is not merely *less* ethical than traditional Catholicism ; it is even more unethical and arbitrary than any but the most absolute Predestinarianism.[1]

Finally, the insufficiency of mere exemplarism is shown once more by the fact that it does not, in itself, provide any hope against that complete disorganisation of the universe which we have seen to be comprehended under the title of " sin." The moral appeal of the character of Christ is infinite and compelling ; but what guarantee does it give of a successful issue to the struggle ? The universe conspired to drive Him to the cross and to a forgotten grave ; was not this total failure ? There is still one event to the good as to the evil ; "vanity of vanities, all is vanity." The Christian is forced to proclaim the victory of his Master's earthly life by appealing to the truth of the resurrection ; and once that appeal is made, exemplarism, whilst never losing its elements of truth and final value, is forced into a secondary position. New factors come into view which wholly change the balance of doctrine : factors which traditional Christianity has always placed in the forefront of the scheme, though the exemplarist, by the very urgency with which he advocates the essentials of his own theory,

---

[1] For a possible reply to this argument, and further discussion, see Note **A**, " Exemplarist Theories of the Atonement," at end of this essay.

is compelled to give them little attention, if not wholly to ignore them.[1]   What these are we must briefly consider before passing to the central affirmation of Catholic doctrine.

V

The Resurrection the Guarantee of the Atonement

" He only could unlock the gate of heaven, and let us in." We must add then to the inspiration of the example of Christ the guarantee of ultimate victory over all the powers of evil, of disorganisation, of the malignancy of circumstance, given by the resurrection of Christ.   Our primary emphasis will no longer be upon the heroism with which He struggled against the powers of evil, but upon the manifest victory with which the struggle was crowned.   St. Paul in various passages arrays the army of forces against which the Christian has to fight, or from which he desires deliverance ;   in other passages he is meticulously careful to show that each of these forces has been severally and individually conquered by Christ—robbed of its sting ;   stripped of its power ; nailed to the cross ;   made a mockery.[2]   Similarly he never tires of speaking of the " redemption " won for us, as though we were prisoners emancipated from captivity or slaves bought back into freedom in the market-place.[3]   The meaning of all this is transcendently clear.   The resurrection and ascension of Christ, above all if taken in connection with the doctrine of the Holy Spirit as the agent through whom man accepts and makes his own the obedience which was in Christ, guarantee as a certainty what the world had always groped after as a pious aspiration.   The ills of this life, against which a moral revelation of character would indeed strengthen us to endure (though only transcendent faith would enable us to believe the endurance to be more than a noble but quixotic vanity), will come one day to an end for the moral man.

---

[1] This point is noticed in regard to Abailard by Canon Storr, *Problem of the Cross*, p. 132.

[2] So of " sin," Rom. viii. 3 ; " death," 1 Cor. xv. 54 ; the " law," Rom. x. 4, Gal. iii. 25, Eph. ii. 15 ; *cp.* Col. ii. 14 ; the " curse," Gal. iii. 13 ; the " present evil world," Gal. i. 4 ; the " powers of darkness," Col. ii. 15 ; etc.

[3] λυτροῦσθαι and compounds, Rom. iii. 24, viii. 23 ; 1 Cor. i. 30 ; Eph. i. 7, iv. 30 ; Col. i. 14 ; 1 Tim. ii. 6 ; Tit. ii. 14 ; ἀγοράζεσθαι and compounds, 1 Cor. vi. 20, vii. 23 ; Gal. iii. 13, iv. 5.

His struggles shall usher him into a glorious immortality of body as well as soul, where there shall be no more crying nor any pain, and God shall wipe away all tears from his eyes. Redemption, won by the cross, is guaranteed by the resurrection ; and for the righteous, at least, it shall be redemption not merely from temptation and the sinfulness of the flesh, but also from all the disorganisation and hostility of the universe. For him at least there shall be a new heaven and a new earth, for the old heaven and the old earth are passed away. St. Paul goes further, and in a mystic passage suggests that the whole universe, inanimate as well as animate, shall be relieved from a condition so terrible that it can be described only as a " universal moaning in pain." [1]

Is such a consummation guaranteed by the resurrection of Christ ? The question, properly, belongs to other chapters of this book, but two points may be noticed here. (i) The advantage of a doctrinal position which emphasises *not merely* the example of Christ's life and death *but also* the guarantee of His resurrection, over any theory which concentrates solely upon the example, is independent of any theory of grace, sacramental or otherwise, which may be taken into account. Its superiority stands assured even though no doctrine of the agency of the Holy Spirit be added to it. We are for the moment considering questions merely of example and guarantee—questions, that is, of purely " natural " influences, into which " supernatural " considerations do not enter at all. If " grace " and " the Spirit " be thought of as no more than summary terms to describe natural operations such as these—and in this manner, it may be conjectured, do most exemplarists conceive of them—we shall indeed have little enough comfort to offer to the sick soul ; but even so it remains true that a guarantee of victory as well as an example of heroism is a greater gift, or act of " grace," than the example taken solely by itself could be. Our contention that no doctrine of the atonement is complete apart from explicit emphasis upon the Lord's resurrection is independent therefore of any controversy as to, let us say, the personality of the Spirit, or the character or means of grace ; it can be considered (as the preceding paragraphs have considered it) on its own merits alone.

(ii) It gives to the death of Christ, and in particular to the special circumstance of tragedy with which it was surrounded,

[1] Rom. viii. 22.

exactly that unique significance which we have seen that Catholic theology has always attributed to it. A tiny example may inspire, in others, efforts altogether out of proportion to itself in magnitude ; but the adequacy of a guarantee always depends upon an *a fortiori* argument. The example of the spider inspired, no doubt, in Robert Bruce heroism far greater than that which the spider itself manifested ; but it could give him no guarantee of victory, because the obstacles which the insect overcame were not demonstrably more serious than those which confronted the patriot. He might reasonably have argued : " The example of this persevering animal is no doubt highly laudable, but what evidence does it give me that a renewal of *my* efforts will not be crowned with disasters even greater than the present one ? " The example was adequate ; the guarantee insufficient.

But the resurrection of Christ does give a guarantee ; and where it is combined with a doctrine of grace which puts the assistance of the Spirit of God within the reach even of the most unimaginative man, we may fairly urge that the guarantee is one of triumph over every conceivable obstacle. The guarantee is sufficient, precisely because the death of Christ was attended by every circumstance which could conceivably add completeness to the apparent defeat sustained in it. The treachery of a familiar friend ; the cowardice and flight of all who were most bound to stand their ground ; the *volte-face* of a multitude demanding to-day the crucifixion of Him whom yesterday they claimed as King ; the uprising of the leaders of religion against one whose only concern is with religious integrity and ideals ; the failure of a justice which, by its very indifference to purely national and sectarian interests, might reasonably be supposed impartial ; even the deliberate refusal of the Sufferer Himself to call upon the legions of angels who only waited His summons to intervene ;—these, far more than any physical pangs, constitute the real tragedy of the crucifixion. These too, to every sensitive mind, exhibit in their highest degree the cruel refinements of that adverse circumstance which it is the aspiration of Christian virtue to conquer and transcend. The death of Socrates is often quoted as a parallel to the crucifixion of our Lord ; in effect it provides, not a parallel, but a glaring contrast, which only enhances the offence of the cross. Beyond a combination of events such as those which culminated in Calvary, the mind can scarcely picture anything more terrible ; and therefore the resurrection of the Lord is a guarantee that the tyranny of circumstance is not eternal and unconquerable, just because it is a resurrection following upon *such* a death and not upon one less unnatural or cruel. It is for this reason that He is able to help *to the uttermost* them that call upon Him.

We have reached a second halting-place. Here again many theologians are content to rest in their exposition of what is called the doctrine of the Atonement. The death and resurrection of Christ are not merely an example of righteousness, but a guarantee that the righteous man who sets himself in the way of salvation (at least if this be thought of as a life ennobled and strengthened by grace) may triumph over every temptation, hindrance, or power that sin and circumstance can array against him. But our hymn carries us further still ; it proclaims that there is yet another factor in man's degradation and weakness of which we have taken no account ; but that the Lord took account of it, and provided by His death a remedy.

VI

CHRIST'S DEATH THE PRICE OF SIN

" He died that we might be forgiven . . . to pay the price of sin." It is of phrases such as these that Catholic thought finds itself most called upon to offer an explanation. We may dismiss at once any explanation which leans to the suggestion that a ransom had to be paid to the devil to rescue man from his clutches ; or that God demanded a victim—*any* victim, but still a victim—on whom to wreak vengeance for man's sin—" as if God did, according to the manner of corrupt judges, take so much money" (it matters not from *whom*) " to abate so much in the punishment of malefactors." [1] It need scarcely be pointed out that theories of this kind find no support in the New Testament. They have at times no doubt been popular in Christian thought, and their popularity has left marks upon Catholic language which may sometimes prove misleading ; but we must distinguish between such mere phrase-survivals and the deeper and truer thought to which, by a not unnatural transition, they have become attached.

Put in its simplest form, that thought is something as follows. The benefits of the death of Christ to which we have so far alluded

---

[1] R. Hooker, *Eccles. Polity*, vi. 5.

are all directed towards enabling man, as we may say, to " turn over a new leaf," to adopt a new and nobler attitude for the future towards both temptation within and adverse circumstance without. Yet if a sinner were so to lay hold upon grace and turn from sin without any allusion to, or apparent recognition of, his past offences, we should all rejoice, no doubt, at the result ; but equally we should all feel that something demanded by the circumstances of the case remained unsatisfied. " An improved attitude on the part of men to the law, a moral re-identification with it, is not sufficient ; for the temporal future cannot meet the demands of the temporal past." [1] " Afterward he repented and went" is without doubt a better conclusion to the story of the elder brother in the parable than " he went not " to the story of the younger, and the word " repented " may cover a multitude of acts of reparation. But if we take the story at its face value we cannot resist the conviction that the elder brother was something of a boor. He had refused his father's request, and that abruptly and insolently ; and though his subsequent repentance cancelled, in a sense, the original refusal, the abruptness and insolence must have created an atmosphere of mutual tension which it would take more than the formal obedience of the mood of penitence to dispel. Some kind of apology, acknowledgment or recognition of the intentional and uncalled-for offence offered to the father would have gone far to restore the family relationship which the son's perversity had subjected to so severe a strain. " Afterward he went " is no doubt a technical expiation of " I go not " ; but a sullen " going," without apology, could hardly restore the original harmonious relationship to which the father appealed with his courteous " Son, go labour to-day in my vineyard." The offence was a slight one, and no more than a mere apology was needed ; yet, as the story stands, the elder brother's repentance seems less adequate to the circumstance than that of another son, of whom we are told that he said, " Father, I have sinned against heaven, and before thee . . . ."

Where offence has been offered, therefore, a mere cessation of the offence does not restore the original relationship which existed before the offence. Even a complete reversal of behaviour can scarcely be thought to suffice, though it comes

---

[1] J. K. Mozley, *Doctrine of the Atonement*, p. 210 ; *cf.* Augustine, *Serm.* 351 ed. Ben). ; Anselm, *Cur Deus Homo*, i. 11.

nearer to sufficiency. Something more is demanded—something in which the offender explicitly acknowledges his fault and asks for forgiveness and restoration, even though he knows that forgiveness and restoration are his without the asking. But when we come to say *what* it is which demands this reparation for the past, our limited knowledge of eternal truth makes it difficult to give an answer. Phrases have been multiplied to express the source of the demand. "God's offended majesty," "God's holiness," "natural justice," the "craving of the soul for expiation," "the constitution of the universe as a moral order," all suggest the truth, yet we hesitate to say that any one of them expresses it fully. Perhaps we can do no more than borrow a theological term popular in many other connections ; it is πρέπον, *conveniens*, "fit" that the past be explicitly acknowledged in this way, before we turn to the future with its hoped-for newness of life. Such reparation is a part of the "natural fitness" of things.

It may indeed be alleged that in employing the phrase "the demand of natural fitness" rather than, let us say, the "demand of God's holiness," we have availed ourselves of a facile euphemism to evade a real difficulty.[1] Such an objection would be true enough if the substitution involved any suggestion that the ideal demands of nature did not coincide with the demands of God ; to contrast God and nature in this way would reduce theology to confusion. In common fairness it must be admitted that "natural fitness" and "divine decree" do mean the same thing ; and that the necessity for what we have called explicit recognition of past sin is to our mind of divine institution. Nevertheless, something is gained, in this connection, by using the name of "nature" rather than that of "God." For to say that God "demands" such and such things involves, in much modern anthropomorphic and unphilosophical thought about God, the

[1] A similar criticism could with some plausibility be urged against Canon Storr's theory that while the "consequences of sin" (degeneration of character, etc.) may fitly be called "the divine reactions against our sinning, expressed in the laws of the universe" (*Problem of the Cross*, p. 86), they can *not* be described as "the direct, personal acts of God" (*ib.* p. 84). It is difficult to see what is gained by this delicate distinction—or indeed whether it is a real distinction at all. At best it marks a difference between two modes of divine action—on the one hand, antecedent legislation ; on the other, *ad hoc* intervention. But this difference does not affect in any way the real question, which is simply, "Are the 'consequences' of sin of divine ordinance or not ? "

attribution to Him of characteristics at once tyrannical and pedantic :—tyrannical, because it suggests that He selects, of his own unfettered choice, conditions which He then imposes upon man as necessary preliminaries to salvation ; pedantic, because it might be inferred that, once He had laid down the law, He suffered not the slightest deviation from it to go unpunished whatever extenuation could be pleaded. Until Christian thought has wholly emancipated itself from the possibility of interpreting God's " demands," " decrees," or " laws " in an unnatural and unethical sense, it is wiser perhaps, and certainly safer, if we wish to argue the essential morality of a principle such as that of acknowledgment of sin, to base the argument upon phrases whose appropriateness and cogency all will recognise, rather than upon others which, though just in themselves, are at the moment liable to misinterpretation. When Christendom regains its appreciation of exact theology it will be possible to say plainly : " God, in no arbitrary or vindictive spirit, calls for acknowledgment of past sin as a piece of natural justice " : and the conscience of man will recognise the essential truth of the statement without falling into the errors so common in modern thought.[1]

At all events it is easy to show that some such idea as that which has been indicated underlay the whole Jewish system of sacrifice, crowned as it was by the final aspirations of the Day of Atonement. Other ideas were present no doubt—ideas which have an integral place in the scheme and which, like this one, have their own counterpart in Christian doctrine—ideas of communion with God, of sharing in His nature. But the " covering " of sin by sacrifice, the offering of atonement, is a primary thought of the system. With a humility as deep as their sense of sin itself, the Jews believed that only unwitting offences could be atoned for in this way ; for the "sin with a high hand " there was no known form of atonement. And with a like humility the greatest of their prophets invariably reminded them that the whole system of sacrifice could never be

---

[1] M. Rivière puts the argument of the above paragraph with inimitable precision and effect : " Nous ne prêtons pas à Dieu, comme on nous en accuse, je ne sais quelle susceptibilité mesquine de grand seigneur piqué ; et la raison en est que l'honneur de Dieu n'est pas, à vrai dire, un droit personnel et comme une affirmation hautaine de sa supériorité : il se confond avec la loi de subordination nécessaire des êtres, avec ce qu'on appelle parfois—d'un mot vague, mais juste— l'ordre des choses."—J. Rivière, *Dogme de la Rédemption*, p. 4.

regarded as *adequate* atonement for the past. Sacrifices were
a symbol of penitence no doubt—an explicit recognition of sin
before God—but in no way a substitute for that newness of life
which He desired to see. And this introduces a consideration
of primary importance. The function of sacrifice is wholly
different from the function of newness of life ; the latter is the
end after which man, by God's grace, should strive ; the former
a necessary preliminary as restoring, by the admission of wrong
done, the condition of harmony making future sanctification
possible. Sacrifice and conversion, therefore, are two separate
acts in the restoration of man ; each has its distinct part to
play. Only a debased mind will infer, from the necessity of
sacrifice, that it can take the place of conversion ; only a
shallow mind, that conversion is adequate without sacrificial
reparation.

The fact that sacrifice to the prophetic mind appeared valueless unless accompanied by a genuine effort of contrition brings
out a further truth of real importance—that the intrinsic cost
of the sacrifice to the offerer is not in itself a condition of its
reality or worth. It must not indeed be so valueless as to make
it only another insult to the offended person ; but because it is
the explicit symbol of an implicit sense of sin rather than an act
of legal restitution, appropriateness to the occasion rather than
cost to the offerer should be its dominant characteristic. If we
revert to the Parable of the Two Sons, we see that all that was
required to restore the ruptured relationship was the utterance
of a single sentence of regret. "Restitution" such as the circumstances demanded was made by the work in the vineyard,
it was the apology that was lacking. Without the restitution,
indeed, the apology would have been an added insult ; without
the apology the restitution was at best ungracious and inconsiderate.
But to one genuinely intent on the restitution the apology could
scarcely, in the case in question, have involved a great additional
effort ; it is not so much the actual as the symbolic value of the
sacrifice that makes it acceptable. From this it may further be
inferred—and the inference is one of crucial importance—that, if
A has no appropriate sacrifice of his own that he can bring to the
altar, he can avail himself of, associate himself with, B's offering ;
if he is, for any reason, tongue-tied, another can speak the necessary
words for him, provided only that he signifies his assent. Another's

gift can still be offered validly, if the desire to offer sacrifice is there, and no other means avail.

The importance of this conclusion for Christian theology becomes at once apparent. To all who fail to find within themselves adequate means for that expression of real contrition of which we have spoken, the Church offers her doctrine that the death of Christ is the divinely appointed means of help in this respect, as in those other respects which have been considered above. " On the cross," she says, " we see One wholly akin to ourselves offering a sinless life to the Father as representative for man. There is no confession of sin on His lips, for He did no sin ; otherwise His sacrifice would have been, in its measure, imperfect as ours have always been. And if we attribute to the Father the intent to give His only-begotten Son for the world's salvation, we can scarcely be wrong in seeing in His death this purpose also, that man should be provided with an adequate sacrifice and symbol of penitence—a symbol sufficient to satisfy the demand of ' natural justice ' or the ' fitness of things.' "

That one who has no other means of adequate sacrifice at his disposal may associate himself with another's offering we have already seen. That the sacrifice of Christ is *appropriate* for this purpose need hardly be argued ; that it is *adequate* will scarcely be doubted by anyone who sees in Jesus the Son of God, of the essence of the Godhead, incarnate for the salvation of the world The only question that arises is whether we can in all strictness call the death of Christ *necessary* in this respect, as in those others in which its necessity has already been argued ; or rather, whether this aspect of the matter *demonstrates* that necessity for the death which our earlier arguments only led us—though with a high degree of cogency—to assume.[1] Is man unable adequately to make an appropriate acknowledgment of his sin ? Some will have no doubt on this point. " Christianity," they will say, " gives us a doctrine of human depravity which renders it antecedently unlikely that any-one not far advanced in spiritual grace could appreciate the depths of sin into which he had fallen, and give his appreciation adequate expression. Experience, again, teaches us that no acknowledgment of sin before God of which we are capable is wholly free from selfish sentiments and motives. It is mingled with wounded self-respect

[1] *Supra*, pp. 251-253.

and remorse for folly unbefitting the sinner's fancied dignity ; it is not without unworthy hopes of a response of divine favour showing itself even in temporal benefits ; it is hypocritical, as promising in the moment of emotion a dedicated life which it knows it cannot guarantee." Confession of sin may be a higher thing than sacrifice ; but arguments such as these suggest that it can never on human lips be pure enough to satisfy that natural fitness of which we have spoken.

Those who are convinced by these and similar lines of argument will not hesitate to agree that " some better sacrifice " than the blood of sheep and goats—better even than contrition of the heart and confession with the lips—was universally necessary ; and they will the more unhesitatingly and willingly accept the claims made by the Church for the death of Christ in this regard.   Others, not so convinced, may believe themselves—theoretically at least—*capable* of such contrition and confession as is needed by the circumstances of their sin.   Yet, even so, it is unthinkable that they should actually be *content* with any contrition they had exhibited or confession they had voiced.   Contentment of such a kind would be of the very essence of self-righteousness ; it would indicate not sorrow for sin, but complete analgesia towards the real character of sin in the soul.   If, then, there should be a genuinely spiritual man who said "I see the need for confession, but not the need for sacrifice as well," he would never reject without examination any offer of help that *might* conceivably enable him to make his confession more adequate ; rather he would *only* reject such offered help if it proved either idle or immoral.   He might indeed be less inclined to emphasise the necessity of Christ's death in this respect.   But, on the arguments hitherto advanced, he would not hesitate to attribute to it sacrificial character in the fullest measure.   He would recognise the unspeakable gift of God which enabled him to say : "Whether my own life, renewed as it is by the Spirit of God, is an adequate expression of sorrow for my past sins, I cannot say.   But I know that some such expression was a necessary condition of my reconciliation with my Father in Heaven ; and my own attempts at expression, be they sufficient or otherwise, are infinitely enhanced when I contemplate the cross and say 'There, O Father is the sacrifice I would have made if only I could.   There is the sinless life of obedience unto death which—if I could offer it—

would be a fitting reparation for the past. Accept, I pray, this sacrifice on my behalf. It is not mine ; yet by every grace given to me I associate myself with it, promising to mould my life upon that pattern not only for righteous service in the future, but also, and equally, as my open acknowledgment of grievous sin in the past.' "

Yet even this consideration moves within too limited a circle of argument. " Sin," as we have seen, involves a deep-rooted disorganisation of the universe, mysteriously bound up with human sin, yet infinitely more terrible than even the complete sum of all the sins that ever have been or can be committed. " Sin " is a corporate matter involving both animate and inanimate creation, and to the reflective mind even an endless offering of individual reparations would not suffice to repair the breach thus made between the creation and the Creator. Natural fitness, we may say, demands that human nature—if not universal nature too—shall in one symbolic corporate act express the conviction, shared by God and man alike, that sin is foreign to its ideal constitution. If the boorish son of the parable had been not one but fifty in number, individually and collectively offending against the father's love, separate and private acts of reparation, however complete, would not have effected the necessary reconciliation. A conspiracy can only be expiated by the corporate submission of the conspirators ; ideal justice remains unsatisfied if they merely pass over, severally and one by one, to the side of the aggrieved. And whatever be the truth of the disorganisation of nature, it is clear that human sin partakes of this character of conspiracy. Men make an implicit compact not with Death and Hell alone, but with one another, to hold down the truth in unrighteousness, to connive at an outraged social order, to tolerate the inertia of selfishness, to prostitute the divine standard of purity to the debased usage of the world. Once we revert to the Pauline conception of the corporate character of sin, the absolute necessity for some such act as the death of Christ becomes transcendently clear. We are in a position to endorse the familiar statements that in Him humanity paid the price as a whole, and that He died as the Representative Man ; for it is only a soul preoccupied with the thought of " my sin " to the exclusion of that of " sin " as a whole which can hesitate any more to confess that, without such an offering, the sacrifice demanded by natural fitness is still unoffered,

and salvation, which must at least involve full and final reconciliation with the loving Father of all mankind, remains not merely
difficult or doubtful of attainment, but completely and finally
impossible.[1]

VII

THE VOCABULARY OF THE ATONEMENT

There is no " Catholic " doctrine of the Atonement in the
sense in which, for example, there is a " Catholic " doctrine of
the Incarnation.   Conciliar definition has never asserted any one
theory of the manner in which Christ's death avails for the salvation of men.   But the main stream of Christian thought has
carried along with it certain definite phrases as applicable to the
Atonement, and it is by reference to these that we may test what
has been written above.   That, on the theory thus outlined,
the death of Christ may with peculiar appropriateness be called a
sacrifice is self-evident, and in this respect the test is wholly satisfied.
That it provides *expiation*, or due acknowledgment, for the past
sin of mankind, and so removes the obstacle on man's side which
impedes the resumption of harmonious relationship between man
and God, we have already argued ;   that it *propitiates*, or *satisfies*[2]—
not, indeed, an arbitrary, angry, or tyrannical deity, but that natural
fitness which is none the less a divine ordinance for being also an
admitted demand of human reason, has been our main contention.
Similarly, there can be no doubt as to the description *vicarious* ;
the death was offered by the divine Victim on man's behalf,
and, as we have argued, is available for man to identify himself
therewith.   That it can fitly be called *substitutionary* is not, on
the theory we have stated, very apparent ;   but we have frankly
to recognise that, whilst the New Testament constantly speaks
of Christ suffering " on our behalf," it very rarely indeed uses
language suggesting that he suffered "in our stead "[3]; and it may
reasonably be supposed that such language crept into Christianity
through an interpretation of Isaiah liii. which neither the author

[1] See further, *infra*, p. 276, Note B, " Dr. Moberly's Theory of the Atonement."
[2] See further, *infra*, p. 277, Note C, " The Term ' Satisfaction ' as applied
to the Death of Christ."
[3] *Cf.* Rashdall, *op. cit.* p. 93.

nor, for example, his Septuagint translators would for a moment have endorsed, or from a similar vulgarisation of the ritual of the Day of Atonement.

We may pass on to a much more important problem, and that our last one : have we done sufficient justice to the undisputed fact that the death of Christ on the basis of New Testament evidence is constantly spoken of as winning for us *justification* and *forgiveness* of sins ?

This is scarcely the place for a detailed discussion of the meaning of St. Paul's *justification by faith.* Two facts, however, are sufficiently clear : (i) that he discards the gospel phrase of *forgiveness* whilst introducing and emphasising that of " justification " ; (ii) that no amount of argument can rob the latter word of its primary forensic sense ; it is redolent of the Law.[1] These facts are surprising and disturbing enough in all conscience. It would seem that the apostle of the Gentiles showed himself, at the central point of his gospel, more Jewish than the Jew, a Pharisee of the Pharisees in the worst sense ; that he abandoned the free air of the new law for the bonds of Rabbinic legalism just at the point where such a lapse would prove most disastrous. The motive may, indeed, have been mainly controversial—to prove to his opponents *not* that " forgiveness " must be taken in the sense of " justification," but rather that " justification " could have no religious meaning unless set in a context of " forgiveness." Yet even so it can hardly be denied that St. Paul perpetuated, in Christianity, a Jewish idea singularly difficult for the Gospel to assimilate with other elements as fully, or more fully, integral to itself—the idea of the " wrath of God " from which man has to find " justification " ; and that he added to it a conception which to many appears equally infelicitous—the conception, namely, that this wrath could be evaded, by the unrighteous, on the basis not so much of a conversion to righteousness as on that of the appropriation of justification—a righteousness not of obvious fact but of apparent legal fiction—from another source.

Yet we have to notice that he is not happy in his adoption of the phrase " the wrath of God "—he tends throughout to

---

[1] *I.e.* " to deem righteous." Modern commentators are practically agreed on this point : W. L. Knox, *St. Paul and the Church of Jerusalem*, p. 117, and A. C. McGiffert, *Christianity in the Apostolic Age*, pp. 143, 144, are the principal dissentients.

avoid it and substitute an impersonal "wrath." [1] This tendency eliminates—partially, if not entirely—one of our difficulties. We can interpret this " wrath " in the sense of that " fitness of things " or "natural justice" which demands of a sinner some overt recognition and abhorrence of his past sin. Such a recognition, as we have seen, is independent of "newness of life," fulfilling as it does a different function ; it can therefore avail itself, for its explicit self-expression, of the actions of another. So, too, St. Paul's "justification" is independent of "newness of life." Ideally, sanctification follows it ; but St. Paul is clear that Christians, already "justified," will still have to answer "in the body" for their life after justification, and that an unsanctified life will not be able to evade condemnation by any appeal to precedent "justification." That being so, the element of " evasion by fiction " goes. Justification is far from being salvation ; it is just that acknowledgment of past offences without which salvation is impossible, but which does not in itself guarantee salvation. The Jew, St. Paul suggests, had made his mistake in identifying justification with salvation, and the identification was a false one. It is necessary to "justify" oneself for the past, or to associate oneself with another's act sufficient to secure "justification"; but this is only the beginning of the righteous life, not (as the Jew supposed) the beginning and the end as well.

We come, then, to the other question, In what sense does the death of Christ win " forgiveness of sin " ? Forgiveness obviously means resumption, by the injured party, of the same *attitude* towards the offender (*e.g.* an attitude of friendliness) as was exhibited by him before the offence. Forgiveness, therefore, is (in strict thought) different from the resumption between the two parties of the same *relations* as before the offence. It is the act of one party—the injured—and not of both. But the *goal* of forgiveness is obviously the resumption of the relations of which the resumption of the attitude (of friendliness or the like) is a part but no more than a part. There is therefore a sense in which forgiveness may be called incomplete until these relations are resumed ;—it is not incomplete in character indeed, but it is incomplete in its effects. No one has put this paradox more finely

---

[1] ὀργή with Θεός, Rom. i. 18, iii. 5, ix. 22 ; Eph. v. 6 ; Col. iii. 6 ; without Θεός, Rom. ii. 5, 8, iv. 15, v. 9, ix. 22, xii. 19, xiii. 5 ; Eph. ii. 3 ; 1 Thess. i. 10, ii. 16, v. 9.

than Dr. Moberly. " Love wears the form and carries the name of ' forgiveness,' " he writes,[1] " in its anticipatory and provisional relation to the penitent. We *call* love ' forgiveness ' just when and just because the penitent, whose very life it is, yet makes and can make no claim to deserving it. But the *full forgiveness* to which I aspire is the righteous love which, *seeing in me at last the very righteousness of Christ*, embraces in me the righteousness *which is really there.*" Although, therefore, the death of Christ does not alter God's attitude to man—that attitude of unswerving love could never and needed never to alter ; indeed, it showed itself in its highest degree in the self-oblation of Christ—it *does* alter the relations subsisting between man and God, and in such a way that God's forgiveness of man, formerly incomplete, is put on the road to consummation. There may be other and deeper ways in which Christ made atonement for man ; but even the way suggested above makes it possible to say with a meaning in every respect conformable to the tests of Christian tradition and of unbiassed reason, and passing beyond everything contained in our previous affirmations, that " He died that we might be forgiven," that " He paid the price of sin," and that we are " saved by His precious blood."

That being so, we may with confidence revert for the last time to the New Testament and to Catholic thought, and draw from them one more universal phrase to express our meaning. It is true that St. Paul eschewed the words " forgiveness of sins " ; but it is profoundly untrue that he did so to substitute for them the idea of justification ; the new idea—his great contribution to Christian soteriology—was the word " *reconciliation*," " atonement." Furthermore, his consistent use of the word implies that the fulfilment of God's purposes depends even more upon man being reconciled to God than upon God being reconciled to man.[2] But it is in reconciliation that forgiveness first comes to rest and finds its goal ; without reconciliation forgiveness remains an offer to which no answer is vouchsafed. And reconciliation sums up in itself every aspect of that restoration of relations between the offender and the offended which we have seen to be the crucial need in man's salvation. Where sin is not thought of as an offence

---

[1] Moberly, *Atonement and Personality*, pp. 62–72, condensed ; the italics have been added.

[2] Sanday and Headlam, *Romans*, pp. 129, 130 ; Rashdall, *op. cit.* p. 100.

against the living God, it is true this need cannot be felt ; but where sin is not so thought of, the soul has far to go before it begins to realise the fulness of its needs. Even so, Christ's death has a message and a promise for it—the message of example to inspire present effort, the promise of victory in the end. Is it not true to say that meditation upon the goodness of God revealed in this promise and message must lead to a sense, by contrast, of human unworthiness of God—unworthiness whose most piercing sting lies just in the fact that it is the result of human sin ; and that this sense must sooner or later bring with it the knowledge that frank penitence and open confession are the first steps towards reconciliation ? Once this knowledge is attained, the need for a sacrifice is felt ; and where the need is felt, in whatever degree, great or small, to recognise that in the death of Christ God has Himself provided a Lamb for the sacrifice is to lay aside remorse, despondency and despair, and to be reconciled to God.

NOTE A.—EXEMPLARIST THEORIES OF THE ATONEMENT (see p. 258)

It is perhaps in a subconscious effort to avoid the criticism here adduced that Exemplarist writers lay more stress upon *gratitude* than upon *respect for example* as the motive to which the death of Christ appeals (*cp.* Rashdall, *op. cit.* p. 101 *et pass.*) ; for " gratitude "—" the last spark of the divine image to disappear from the soul of man " (Rashdall, *op. cit.* p. 361)—may be thought of as a more widespread emotion than "respect for example," and so less dependent upon the intermediary offices of imagination. If this, however, is the real object of the insistence upon gratitude, it depends on a fallacy. A man can only be grateful in response to some objective service, and on the Exemplarist theory the *only* objective service contributed by the death of Christ to man's salvation is its appeal as an example of unswerving obedience to the will of God. That this is an objective service we need not deny, indeed (as we have attempted to show above, p. 256) it has more objectivity about it than Exemplarist writers would care to admit ; but the *realisation* of its objective value depends wholly upon its appeal to the imagination ; and therefore the question as to whether it will or will not in any given case elicit responsive gratitude depends in equal measure upon that appeal. The shifting of emphasis from the motive of *respect for example* to that of *gratitude* is a specious obscuring of the issue, which leaves the real gist of our criticism untouched.

It might however be held that *any* theory of the atonement depends for its efficacy in eliciting a response from the individual upon an appeal to the imagination, and that this is evidenced by the facts that all theories of justification alike are theories of justification *by faith* ;—for faith in the atoning work of Christ for us is only possible when imagination has been stirred to embrace its atoning value. On such grounds it would appear that the assertion in the text above, that in the traditional doctrines of grace the unimaginative man stood at no disadvantage as compared with his imaginative brother, was wholly illusory. This objection, however, depends upon a dangerous confusion between imagination and common sense. The older theories of atonement, however inadequate or misleading they may have been—the Ransom theory, the *Wergeld*-satisfaction theory, and the like—all depended upon an appeal to common sense which would be universally recognised. Man is Satan's prisoner,—*of course*, therefore, someone must ransom him ; man owes a debt to God which justice cannot remit,—*of course*, therefore, someone must pay it for him. As Canon Storr has pointed out (*Problem of the Cross*, pp. 10–13), these traditional theories were erected upon the universally accepted axioms of contemporary thought. Common sense would therefore at once see their relevance and necessity ; no effort of imagination was necessary ; faith—and consequently grace—was in reach of the most pedestrian and prosaic mind. But the Exemplarist theory is not so. Here common sense is satisfied with some such dictum as " Man must live the moral life ; conscience, Scripture, the Church tell him in what that moral life consists " ; it does not rise to the affirmation, " *of course* he must have an example." Whether a given example—even the highest—will help a sinner or not depends, therefore, wholly upon the exercise of his imagination.

No doubt the verdict of common sense changes with the ages ; and what to patristic or mediæval thought seemed obvious may appear to us fantastic or untrue. But modern " objective " theories are all of them attempts to find a basis in common sense—in some proposition whose cogency will be universally admitted—and not in imagination. Thus the theory outlined in the later paragraphs of this essay (pp. 262–270), however imperfect and inadequate it may be, must stand or fall entirely in accordance as the reader's common sense accepts or rejects the postulate on which it depends—namely, that where offence has been committed, " natural fitness " demands not merely reformation of character but also some form of overt acknowledgment as an appropriate and adequate means of restoring ruptured relations.

Dr. Denney (*Death of Christ*, p. 177) launched a somewhat confused criticism of the appeal to gratitude in Exemplarist theories, based on the fact that *some* Exemplarists had forgotten to emphasise the objective value of an example of loyalty to the service of God and man. By restoring the emphasis, Dr. Rashdall had little difficulty in rebutting this criticism at its face value (*op. cit.* pp. 440 ff. —note that the references to the pages in *The Death of Christ* appear to be incorrect). But the real point of Dr. Denney's criticism remains unaltered. The " rational connection " between the death of Christ and the " responsibilities which sin involves and from which that death delivers "—the " intelligible relation " between the two—is scarcely apparent to the ordinary mind, unless the " natural fitness" of the explicit acknowledgment of guilt be admitted. Without that admission a relationship may indeed be established, as we have admitted, between the example of Christ and the needs of man, even on the Exemplarist basis ; and in his implicit denial of this Dr. Denney would seem to have overstepped the limits of his argument. But it is certainly not a *rational* relationship ; for, as the argument in the text is designed to show, it makes grace proportionate not so much to the moral earnestness as to the imaginative capacity of the recipient.

One final criticism of exemplarism may be mentioned. The theory fails to show any grounds for belief in the *necessity* of the death of Christ. The ultimate arguments for that necessity must be drawn, as we have seen, even more from the *corporate* character of human sin (demanding as it does corporate or representative acknowledgment—see above, p. 269) than from its *cosmic* character (above, pp. 251–253). It is just this need for a corporate acknowledgment which the Exemplarist denies ; his theory loses all distinctiveness unless he insists that the example and teaching of Christ were the *only* benefits conferred on man by His life and death. Were he to allow that possible interpretation of his theory which emphasises (p. 256 above) a psychological compulsion to Christian heroism objectively resulting from the example of Christ, we might still be in a position to assert the necessity of that example with some appearance of plausibility ; the more the compelling character of the example were emphasised, the more it would appear unlikely that without it (and consequently without the death of Christ) man could work out his own salvation. But few Exemplarist writers care to emphasise this aspect of their theory, for the reason that they wish to avoid *any* suggestion (not merely that involved in so-called " transactional " theories) that a change in man's spiritual condition can be brought about by any agency external to his own conscious moral efforts. They are therefore compelled to postulate that the example of Christ can only be effective in the lives of those who *consciously meditate* upon His life and death. We should be the last to deny the ᴗupreme value and importance of such conscious meditation ; but if this be the *only way* in which the life and death of Christ can alter man's spiritual condition, it must be conceded that it can hardly be a *necessary* way. For it to be necessary it would have to be asserted that *no other possible subject* of meditation could be depended upon to rouse the Christian to a moral effort sufficient to win salvation ; and such an assertion would at once be too unsubstantiated, and too suggestive of a " magical formula," unfailingly efficacious in the case of all who had recourse to it, to commend itself to Exemplarist thought.

It follows, therefore, that on the strict logic of the Exemplarist theory, its supporters would be unable to subscribe to the belief that man cannot be saved apart from the death of Christ, without sacrificing all the distinctive positions for which they are really contending. Where writers of this school of thought commit themselves to language which appears to assert the universal necessity of Christ's death for men, the fact can only be attributed to a failure to grasp the full implications of their system ;—or better, and probably more truly, to the victory of a genuinely Christian sentiment over a faulty human logic.

It remains only to notice Canon Storr's version of exemplarism. To him the death of Christ is principally not an example of obedience to the will of God, but a revelation of God's sympathy with sinful man and His consequent suffering on account of man's sin (*Problem of the Cross*, pp. 133, 136, 152, etc.— with quotations from Canon Wilson and Dr. White). It is noteworthy that although this position (which of course contains in itself a profound and wholly Christian truth) might establish a better case for the necessity of Christ's death than other versions of exemplarism, Canon Storr himself evades the test (" The burden lies on the shoulders of those who criticise," p. 139), which elsewhere he regards as " very important " (p. 108) and applies rigorously to theories which he rejects (pp. 93, 108, 111). However this may be it remains true that the other criticisms we have urged against exemplarism hold with equal force in this case.

Note B.—Dr. Moberly's Theory of the Atonement

The debt which this essay owes to Dr. Moberly's *Atonement and Personality*, and especially to the sixth chapter of that great book, is so obvious that any comment on its position might seen unnecessary. But those who, with the present writer, find themselves continually recurring to Dr. Moberly's pages for fresh light upon the mystery of the Atonement, will notice in this essay the omission of two of his most important phrases—" Christ the Perfect Penitent " and " Christ inclusively man." Canon Storr (*Problem of the Cross*, ch. ix.) has published a very fair and friendly appreciation of the merits and defects of these two phrases to which little need be added. The first (" Christ the Perfect Penitent ") is a beautiful and arresting paradox, whose meaning cannot be obscure to any but the most pedantic and literal mind ; it has not been avoided here of strict purpose, and its meaning has as far as possible been expressed in analogous ways. The second (" Christ inclusively man ") is perhaps more open to question, as witness Dr. Rashdall's criticisms (*Idea of Atonement*, pp. 424, 425 ; *J.T.S.* iii. 178–211—Dr. Rashdall censures similar phrases used by Dr. Ottley and Mr. Mozley ; Canon Storr also quotes a kindred passage from Dr. Du Bose). The phrase covers three (if not four) distinct ideas which it is well to keep apart, as confusion between them may produce an erroneous impression that their implications have not been fully thought out, if not that the phrase itself is virtually meaningless : (*a*) that atonement by a Representative is the *natural* or even the *necessary* way in which corporate guilt can be acknowledged ; (*b*) that such representative acknowledgment, if fitly expressed, will be adequate in the case of each individual offender who chooses to associate himself therewith ; (*c*) that " incorporation in Christ," of which the sacraments are at once a symbol and a means, is for Catholic thought the most obvious way in which man can (i) associate himself with Christ's acknowledgment of sin on his behalf, and (ii) derive from God those other benefits of the death and resurrection of Christ (victory over sin and circumstance and the like) to which allusion has been made. It has been the purpose of this essay to keep these separate implications of the phrase as distinct from one another as possible (for (*a*) see p. 269 ; for (*b*), pp. 266 f.; (*c*) (i) has not been dealt with here, but is fully treated in the concluding essay of this book ; for (*c*) (ii) see p. 261) ; and to this end the phrase itself has not been used. But analysis is not necessarily the best way of expressing Christian truth ; and though the writer has thought himself bound, in the present case, to use the analytic method, he would take this opportunity of wholly and gladly associating himself with what he takes to be the rich complex of meanings underlying Dr. Moberly's synthetic phrase.

Note C.—The Term " Satisfaction " as applied to the Death of Christ

A note on the traditional (but not Scriptural) term *satisfaction*, as applied to the death of Christ, will not be inapposite, especially as it is the term to which critics of the doctrine of Atonement most commonly take exception. The application is first made by Radulphus Ardens in the eleventh century (Rivière, p. 289), but it was really popularised by Anselm. It is often thought to be derived from the Teutonic concept of the *Wergeld*, or compensation paid by (*e.g.*) a homicide to his victim's clan (see reff. Rivière, pp. 308–309 ; *cp.* Rashdall, p. 352, note 1) ; and the necessary corollary that Christ (on the theory of satisfaction) paid a penalty due from man which exempted man from any further responsibility is rightly stigmatised as clearly immoral. But there seems to be no doubt that the phrase was in fact borrowed by soteriology from the penitential system of the Church, where it had been used since Tertullian's time to designate the penitential acts (or, as they are now called, *penances*) which should accompany contrition (Rivière, Rashdall, *ut sup.*). At first sight this does not appear to affect the inherent immorality of the theory, until the full implications of *satisfactio* are seen. In legal Latin the word meant not so much " compensation " as " surety," " guarantee "—not that which satisfies a creditor in full, but that which satisfies him of the good faith of the debtor. " Non idem sunt *satisfacere* et *solvere*; nam *solvit* qui creditori pecuniam omnem numerat; *satisfacit* qui quocumque modo creditorem placat—v.g. cautione, satisfactione, pignore, partis debiti solutione " (Forcellini, *Lexicon*, s.v.). Hence in classical

Latin, when applied to offences, it may mean no more than " making suitable apology"—"purgare se de injuria illata, verbis excusare, deprecari, veniam petere culpam fatendo " (*ib.*) ; cp. *Digest*, 46, 3, 52.

No doubt the idea of "payment in full" attached itself in popular thought to the term in its penitential usage (*e.g.* to avoid the *poena temporalis* of sin) ; but the other conception was never lost. Thus Ambrose, *de poenit.* ii. 9 (80), points out that penitential works could never *merit* forgiveness ; though called " satisfaction " the idea of " full compensation" was wholly absent. So too Hooker, commenting upon Tertullian, points out that " repentance and the works thereof are termed *satisfactory*, not for that so much is thereby done as the justice of God can exact, but because . . . they draw the pity of God towards us (*illices divinae misericordiae*—Tert. *de poenit.* 9)." "Satisfaction as a part [*i.e.* as distinct from contrition] comprehendeth only that which the Baptist meant by works worthy of repentance " [καρποὺς ἀξίους τῆς μετανοίας Lk. iii. 8] (Hooker, *Eccles. Pol.* vi. 5). Furthermore, " satisfaction" was not a *sine quâ non* of absolution ; the latter could be given before penance was performed (as in the present discipline—which Hooker (*ut sup.*) indeed calls a " strange preposterous course," though what he is really inveighing against is the distinction between eternal and temporal punishment on which many of its defenders based it) ; or could be waived by the Bishop (*Conc. Anc.* can. 5 ; *Conc. Nic.* can. 12)—though there was always some doubt as to the validity of this (Bingham, *Origines*, xviii. iv. § 6).

From this it would appear that we are not going beyond the strict limits of patristic thought if we say of satisfaction (in the sense of "penitential works") that though (*a*) generally necessary, it is (*b*) quite different from repentance, (*c*) inoperative without repentance (this is universally agreed), (*d*) not an "adequate compensation" to God for the offence committed, but rather a " suitable acknowledgment" thereof, and a pledge of newness of life. This gives to " satisfaction" in Christian theology a meaning identical with that assigned in the text above to "reparation" (pp. 263 ff.), and allows us to use the term of the death of Christ (as in the case of the Anglican Prayer of Consecration) not with any implication of the idea of an "angry God" who has to be placated, but as suggesting that Christ, by His death, provided a suitable symbol of human guilt with which man, to make that due acknowledgment of his sin which otherwise could not be made, can associate himself.

Space forbids any discussion of the meaning of the word " propitiation." In the text above it has been used as the equivalent of " satisfaction " ; but note should be taken of Westcott's contention that " the scriptural conception of the verb is not of appeasing one who is angry . . . but of altering the character of that which, from without, occasions a necessary alienation and interposes an inevitable obstacle to fellowship." " The ἱλασμός, when it is applied to the sinner, so to speak, neutralizes the sin." (Additional note on 1 John ii. 2, *Epistles of St. John*, pp. 83 ff.) If Westcott's view be adopted, *propitiation* would correspond with the meaning we have given to *expiation*. Considerations suggesting caution in the acceptance of this view will be found in Sanday and Headlam, *Romans*, p. 130 ; and Moulton and Milligan, *Vocabulary of Greek Testament*, s.v. 2 ; Deissmann, *Bible Studies* (E.T.), pp. 124 ff. Driver, Art. " Propitiation " in Hastings' *Dictionary of the Bible*, should also be consulted.

THE RESURRECTION

BY EDWARD GORDON SELWYN

CONTENTS

I

INTRODUCTORY

THE resurrection and ascension of Jesus Christ have from the earliest days formed a cardinal element in the *credenda* of the Christian Church. They focus with peculiar intensity that faith in the Gospel as at once historical and supernatural, which enabled Christianity to conquer the pagan religions of the Græco-Roman world ; and by the same token they focus also those doubts and problems which are characteristic of modern criticism and enquiry. If it be true that the religion of Christ belongs at once to this world and to the other ; if it claims to provide a synthesis between the agelong antinomies of Time and Eternity, of Nature and Supernature, of Successiveness and Simultaneity, of Fact and Value ; and if it asserts that the secret of this synthesis lies in the mediation of a Person ;—then clearly supreme importance attaches to those happenings in history in which the Mediator is alleged to have decisively and finally vindicated His character. In an earlier essay it has been shown that the Christ of the Synoptic Gospels must remain " a stranger and an enigma " to us unless we recognise the reconciliation of the two principles of suffering and of glory in the unity of His single experience as giving the clue to His life and teaching ; and others have drawn out the dogmatic implicates of this fact, and its reactions upon human sin, freedom and forgiveness. It remains to be shown that the revelation thus made to the reason and the redemption thus offered to the will are not illusory, but were sealed as genuine by a divine action credibly attested in history and in character with the momentous issues at stake.

Various causes combine to make the task one of great complexity. The resurrection, and still more the ascension, in so far as they are facts, are facts on the borderland of history and symbol. In the case of the ascension the symbolical element greatly outweighs the historical ; one might almost say that the faith of the Church would not be other than it is, if by some mischance the few verses in the Acts which St. Luke devotes to the ascension had not survived. The primary evidence, that is to say, is the Church's experience of Christ's sovereign power from St. Stephen's day to our own. The resurrection presents a far closer balance between the two elements. Who would not feel, for example, if we were without the last chapter of each Synoptic Gospel or the last two of the Fourth, that the whole significance of the story had been changed ? The precise determination of the fact behind these records is perhaps impossible ; but that some historical fact of an unusual order occurred at that point is required not only by the existence of the documentary evidence, but by the evidence of Christianity ever since. Yet here two important cautions must be borne in mind. In the first place, while the Christian creed asserts an unequivocal belief in the fact of the Lord's resurrection, it lays down nothing as *de fide* in regard to the manner of it ; and on the latter point many different interpretations have been given by theologians of unquestioned orthodoxy at different times. This does not mean that any such teaching, particularly if it seems to endanger the faith-values of the fact, should be exempt from criticism. But it does mean that the Christian scholar may claim here a large latitude of enquiry and thought, and that such criticism as he either makes or receives should be frankly *in foro theologiae*. In the second place, it must be observed that the risen Lord appeared only to believers. The fact was not of a kind, that is to say, to convert men by its stark and palpable marvellousness against their will. We may assume, then, that much will depend for our understanding of the resurrection on the atmosphere or " spirit " of our minds. It belongs to that order of " spiritual things," of which St. Paul says that they must be " spiritually discerned." Apologetics must beware, therefore, of trying to do too much—of trying to demonstrate to the natural reason a fact which in its historical happening was witnessed only by those whose minds had been trained by Jesus. If we reach a point where we have to admit that the historical evidence can only give probabilities, we may well remember that *a priori* in a matter of this kind historical evidence cannot be expected to do more.

The method which I propose to adopt in this essay is the familiar one of arguing from the better known to the less known ; or, in other words, from the doctrine to the fact. We do know with singular precision what was authoritatively taught and believed in the Church within a generation of Pentecost ; and we can determine the significance, and observe the centrality, of Christ's resurrection in relation both to doctrine and ethics for those first writers and believers.   The next section will therefore be devoted to considering the resurrection as part of the apostolic teaching.   But we cannot stop there.   The Apostles are convinced that what they preach as the resurrection was a fact of history for which unimpeachable testimony existed.   Examination of this testimony will show that it is concerned partly with "appearances" of the Lord, and partly with circumstances of a different kind pointing to the fact that He had risen from the dead. In the third section of this essay, therefore, I propose to discuss the evidence for the "appearances" as evidence relating to the experience of the disciples, to appraise their meaning, and to consider how far they provide an adequate explanation for the Catholic dogma ; while the last section will be devoted to an estimate of the probabilities in regard to the remainder of the evidence.

II

The Resurrection in the Apostolic Teaching

Christianity went out into the world as a gospel of emancipation.   To the Jew it brought emancipation from the cramping fetters of the Law ; to the Gentile from the doubt and despair which haunted the pages of his greatest teachers ; and to both a new freedom from the power of sin.   It did this by opening up afresh, on the strength of a new and authoritative revelation, the true nature of God.   It proclaimed Him to be transcendent both above the Law, which had once been the embodiment of His will, and above those circumstances of sin and death which seemed to set such inexorable limits to the possible worth of human life. Moreover, this opening up of truths and riches as yet unguessed in men's conception of the Being of God carried with it the uncovering of new worlds for the spirit of man to move in.   Access was now given to that heavenly and supernatural order of fellowship with God, whose doors had seemed fast closed hitherto : the citizenship of Christians was in heaven, and they were heirs of eternal life.   This call involved new powers and new hopes— new powers of conquering sin in this life here, new hopes of immortality hereafter. And the fact which more than any other was asserted as the ground of this whole revelation, opportunity and call was the resurrection of Jesus Christ.

In this first preaching of the Gospel the resurrection is set forth as primarily a mighty act of God in relation to His only-begotten Son. It is a revealing act which at once designates the Son and declares the nature of the Father. It designates Jesus as the head of the corner, the only Saviour of men,[1] the Fulfiller of Messianic prophecy,[2] the Lord and Judge of men,[3] the Son of God.[4] At the same time it declares the nature of the Father as "a living and true God"[5]; it was through His power that Jesus was raised and now lives[6]; Christ's resurrection and ascension are demonstrative proofs of God intended to lead men to repose in Him their faith and hope.[7] And this new understanding of God through Christ and His resurrection bears the hall-mark of a true revelation in spiritual experience. It is, that is to say, fundamentally vocational. This sense of call or mission, of a new and divine direction given to life, is one of the means by which men are made aware of that element in the transcendent Deity called by Otto "energy" or "urgency." The resurrection of Jesus was felt by the first Christians to be a signal example of this divine urgency, laying upon them generally the duties of their vocation and upon their leaders in particular their apostolic commission. The power and purpose of God stand out now with a new definiteness and a richer content. In it St. Paul finds rooted his own title to be an Apostle[8]; by it the disciples are emboldened to claim to obey God rather than men[9]; through it believers are made certain of the limitless spiritual resources now put at their disposal.[10] Faith in the resurrection has thus mediated a new experience and vision of God—a vision and an experience which are attested in the positive fruits of new vocation.

This revelation of the purpose of God and of His power to

---

[1] Acts iv. 11, 12. The identity of teaching as to the resurrection in the speeches in Acts and in the Epistles is one of the important points of internal evidence in favour of the genuineness of the former, as at least a reliable reflexion of the Christian ideas of the time : though a modern historian such as Eduard Meyer regards the external evidence as in itself sufficient.

[2] Acts ii. 25 ff.
[3] Rom. xiv. 9; Phil. ii. 9 ff.
[4] Rom. i. 4.
[5] 1 Thess. i. 9.
[6] 2 Cor. xiii. 4.
[7] 1 Pet. i. 21.
[8] Gal. i. 1; 1 Cor. i. 1; 2 Cor. i. 1; *cf.* 1 Cor. ix. 1.
[9] Acts v. 29.
[10] Eph. i. 19.

achieve it has its counterpart in a great expansion of men's ideas as to the meaning and worth of human life. In the age which witnessed the dawn of Christianity no conviction was more widespread than that of the vanity and corruption of the world and all that pertained to it. What the Gospel did was not to deny this, but to change its significance by showing that the world was only a part of that whole structure of reality with which men had to do. It was true that the creation was "subjected to vanity"; but it was of God's set purpose and for a time only. For the natural order—so St. Paul says in a famous passage—is but the vestibule of the supernatural; its bondage is but the presage of liberty; its corruption preparatory to a glorious redemption; the world as we know it is no more than a kind of enclave, soon to be removed, within the reality of eternal life.[1] And the assurance of this reality derives from the resurrection of Jesus.[2] It is the risen Lord who has "abolished death and brought life and incorruption to light through the gospel."[3] Once before in history God's people had known what it was to enter upon a new inheritance. It was when Israel saw the fulfilment of long-cherished hopes at the entrance into Canaan. But there the analogy ends. For the new inheritance opened up to Christians is infinitely more satisfying than their storied land ever was to the Jews. Its wealth is incorruptible, its boundaries inviolable, its resources permanent, its nature not of earth but of heaven. And its possession is secured to believers by Christ's resurrection.[4] New ends are thus proposed to human life; its destiny is given a fresh scope; man's spirit breathes in a new air.

One effect of this changed outlook and proportion is a transvaluation of those very experiences in which man enters most sensitively into the sorrow and vanity of the world. In a passage of poignant intimacy [5] St. Paul tells how the Christian life, and particularly the life of an Apostle, is a perpetual reproduction of the Lord's death and resurrection. In his weariness, perplexity, persecution he feels himself to be "always bearing about in his body the dying of Jesus." But it is compensated for and balanced by a parallel manifestation of the life of Jesus, both in the Apostle himself and yet more signally in the life of the Church he serves.

[1] Rom. viii. 18 ff.   [2] Rom. viii. 11, which governs the context.
[3] 2 Tim. i. 10.   [4] 1 Pet. i. 3 ff.
[5] 2 Cor. iv. 7–15.

Here we have that principle of life through death and glory through humiliation, which is the clue to the synoptic portrait of the Christ, transferred from the Master to the disciple, from the field of history to that of spiritual experience. The gospel of the resurrection is a gospel of salvation, because it offers fellowship with God in a new quality of life, and this is the ground of rejoicing. But this rejoicing does not mean that the Christian is exempt from trials ; it means that he finds in them a new significance as a test and proof of his faith.[1]

But it is the moral element involved in the new relation to God which the Apostles press most urgently upon their converts. St. Peter at Cæsarea and St. Paul at Antioch in Pisidia alike insist that the message of the resurrection is a message of " the remission of sins." [2] He who was "delivered up for our trespasses " was likewise "raised for our justification." [3] The resurrection makes a new start in the moral life of men, which every believer is called to reproduce and manifest in his own case. New ethical motives, new powers of conquering sin, new standards of right living are now proclaimed and accepted. Christ risen from the dead now " lives unto God," and creates in the hearts of believers a life motived by a like fellowship with God [4] ; the purpose of His death and resurrection was that men might abandon their selfish interests and make Him the centre of their affections and the end of their activities.[5] And the moral resolutions so originated are capable of achievement. The power of God manifested in the raising of Christ from the dead is what has raised Christians from paganism to the moral freedom of the converted life [6] ; and it is for ever available to them as a potent instrument for the conquest of sin. The purpose of the resurrection was that believers should be joined with the living Christ,[7] and find grace through that union. And this privilege carried with it obligations of a most definite kind. It involved renunciation of sin and of the "lusts of the flesh." In writing to the Corinthians St. Paul lays particular emphasis on the incompatibility of any breach of the law of purity with the Christian profession.[8] But it would probably be an

---

[1] 1 Pet. i. 6–8 ; *cf.* 2 Tim. ii. 8–10.   [2] Acts x. 43, xiii. 38, 39.
[3] Rom. iv. 25.   [4] Rom. vi. 4.
[5] 2 Cor. v. 15.
[6] Eph. ii. 5 ; Col. ii. 13 ; Rom. viii. 2.   [7] Rom. vii. 4.
[8] 1 Cor. vi. 14, 15.

error to restrict his allusions to the mortification of the flesh to impurity alone.[1] Rather we should interpret them as coterminous with the whole range of purely selfish impulses and desires which in St. Paul's philosophy are characteristic of the natural man. In reference to all of them the faith of the resurrection meant for the Christian the deliberate pursuit of the " purgative way." But it involved likewise new standards of positive conduct—a walking in " newness of life." [2] A fresh worth-whileness has been given to the spiritual life as such. " If then ye are raised together with Christ," says the Apostle, " seek the things that are above, where Christ is, seated on the right hand of God. Set your mind on the things that are above, not on the things that are upon the earth." [3] Thus the claims of the unseen order upon men's thoughts and interests are laid upon them by virtue of their relation to the risen Lord.

So decisive is the ethical teaching of the resurrection that St. Paul can write definitely, " If Christ hath not been raised, your faith is vain ; ye are yet in your sins." [4] It is part of one of the arguments he uses against sceptical opponents at Corinth who mocked at the notion of immortality. He would not have done this, and the argument would not have served its purpose, had not Christian morality been regularly and closely linked with Christ's resurrection in his own and the Church's teaching. He seems indeed to be prepared to admit the strength of the Epicurean—or rather the Cyrenaic—argument for pleasure as the highest good, if the resurrection is a myth. For the resurrection is the one sure pledge and guarantee men have of the reality and claim of that other order of ends and values whose existence proves the fallacy of hedonism. Christ's resurrection, the Christian's experience of moral redemption, and his hope of immortality are three facts so closely locked together that none of them can be disowned without the repudiation of the others. It is significant of the whole outlook of the first age of Christianity that this great chapter on the Christian hope should close with the note of practical exhortation. " Wherefore, my beloved brethren, be ye steadfast, unmovable, always abounding in the work of the Lord, forasmuch as ye know that your labour is not in vain in the Lord." [5]

---

[1] Rom. vi. 12-19, viii. 12.   [2] Rom. vi. 4.
[3] Col. iii. 1 (The Epistle for Easter Day).
[4] 1 Cor. xv. 17 ; cf. 1 Cor. xv. 32.   [5] 1 Cor. xv. 58.

But we are already trenching upon that further issue which for large numbers of Christian believers throughout the ages has given to the resurrection of Jesus its most significant appeal. It is true to say that thousands to whom the doctrinal or the moral bearing of the Easter message means little or nothing yet pin their faith to it as the main assurance we have of the life beyond the grave. And in this the popular sentiment of Christendom undoubtedly reflects the mind of the New Testament. It is by that act of raising Jesus from the dead, and by that in unique measure, that God has certified believers of their immortality.

A full discussion of the New Testament doctrine of immortality would fall outside the scope of this essay ; and we must confine ourselves to those aspects of it which have a direct and detailed bearing upon the problem of the resurrection of Christ. The two passages of particular importance are both to be found in the letters which St. Paul addressed to the Church of Corinth.[1] It is not an accident that that cosmopolitan city should have elicited a peculiarly full treatment of the subject. The Church there contained both Jews and Greeks, and it was in close contact with a world where every phase of speculation passed rapidly from mouth to mouth. Thus the Jewish element found little difficulty in believing in a resurrection ; but they were no less exercised than the Jewish Christians of Thessalonica as to what the belief portended for those who died before the " coming " of the Lord. To the Greek element, on the other hand, the whole idea of resurrection was perplexing. If they had avoided the current scepticism of the philosophical schools, it was usually through recourse to some Orphic or Platonic conception which asserted only the immortality of the soul and despaired altogether of the body. St. Paul, who was at once Jew and Greek, was well equipped for handling such a situation ; and we can, in fact, see him in 1 Corinthians xv. addressing himself now to the Jewish and now to the Greek section among his readers.[2]

The Apostle's teaching in this chapter, so familiar to us from the Burial Service, may be summarised as follows. Christian immortality is conceived after the analogy of a grain of corn, which is sown in the earth dead and renews itself in the grains of the ensuing harvest. It involves, that is to say, a continuity of indivi-

[1] 1 Cor. xv. ; 2 Cor. v.
[2] *Cf.* Lake, *Earlier Epistles of St. Paul*, p. 218.

dual life, but a transformation of the form or " body " in which that life finds expression. There is a connection between the earthy body and the heavenly body, in that each in its time is appropriate to the individual life which it embodies ; though the point is emphasised that the heavenly embodiment is the gift or act of God. In the case of Christians already dead, or dying before the Lord's " coming," the transformation from the earthy to the heavenly body entails the dissolution of the former in death, followed by a period of waiting ; whereas for those who survive to that day the transformation is immediate and sudden. But in point of fact death is really irrelevant for Christians. For them the only thing in connection with death which matters is sin. They share the physical mortality of all the sons of Adam ; but, if they have laid sin aside, this mortality is overwhelmed in and swallowed up by that other life which Christians also now share, the immortal life of Christ.

The irrelevancy of death as a barrier to immortality, and the certainty of the spiritual body, are proved by Christ's resurrection. In one sense the Greeks are right ; " flesh and blood," the material particles of the body, cannot as such inherit eternal life. But they are wrong in not seeing that there must be a body in that life. At the same time there are differences between the resurrection of Christ and that of those who are His, corresponding to the difference of rank which belongs to Him in the hierarchy of spiritual beings.[1] So He experienced " on the third day " that completeness of transformation for which Christians who are dead have to wait until His " coming." He is distinguished from Christians already dead in that His body knew no decay ; from Christians now living in that the spiritual body is already His. His bodily transformation, though it involved death, did not involve corruption ; and, though it involved resurrection, did not involve an interval of waiting.[2]

[1] 1 Cor. xv. 23. Canon Streeter's whole treatment of the resurrection in *Foundations* is governed, as he admits, by the assumption that the parallelism between the resurrection of Christ and that of Christians is complete. But this is surely too facile. What is true, as Professor Lake points out, is that certain important features in St. Paul's view of the resurrection of Christians are based on his knowledge of the resurrection of Christ.

[2] The argument is not affected if we adopt Dr. McNeile's thesis (*The Problem of the Future Life*, p. 107) that " in some sense the formation of the spiritual body has already begun [*sc.* in this life here], and is being progressively formed with our spiritual progress." The idea is attractive, and, as he points out, is consistent with much N.T. teaching. But it would still remain true that for

That is the gist of St. Paul's teaching in the two great passages under review. It is sometimes said that the later passage (2 Cor. v.) is inconsistent with the earlier. But careful examination does not endorse this. There is a change of phraseology through the use of the metaphors of a heavenly " house " and of heavenly " clothing " to describe the spiritual body. There is a change in the practical point of the argument, which in the earlier passage turns on popular doubts and questionings, in the later on the contrast between the sufferings of the present and the glory of the future. And there is, further, the addition of a new idea—the idea that Christians already dead are if anything more privileged than those still living, because they are in closer proximity to their Lord. But so far as the main principles of the teaching are concerned, there is no alteration. It still remains true that, for St. Paul, immortality means a body of different texture from that of earth ; that this body is an endowment given to each believer by God ; that Christians already dead pass by resurrection, after a period of waiting, to the manifestation of this transformed or spiritual body, while those who survive to the "coming" enter upon it suddenly and without delay ; and that of both these hopes the resurrection of Christ is the great security and pledge.

It has been necessary to describe St. Paul's teaching in these chapters with some fulness, because it is sometimes stated that his doctrine would not be stated as it is, if he had accepted the traditional ideas connected with the empty tomb. That, however, is to overstate the case. Not only is there a very wide agreement among critical scholars, including even Schmiedel, that one who like St. Paul had been brought up in Pharisaical circles must be assumed to have accepted these traditional ideas, unless he definitely states the contrary ; but it also ignores some important considerations. It ignores, for example, the care with which St. Paul sets Christ in a " rank " of His own distinct from those of other Christians ; and still more it fails to recognise that details of the manner of Christ's resurrection would be foreign to the argument which the Apostle is here developing. On the other hand, it can fairly be urged that the very fact that St. Paul keeps these details in the background, even though he assumed them as part of the

St. Paul Christ's resurrection is differentiated from that of Christians in that the process of transformation was in His case completed without corruption and within a very brief period of time.

regular belief of the Corinthian Church, is not without its significance ; while the emphasis he lays upon the difference between the earthy and the spiritual body in the case of Christians does require us to suppose that he conceived of Christ's risen body as spiritual too, transcending the ordinary properties of matter, in conformity with that heavenly order into which at the resurrection He had passed. It will be important to bear this in mind, when we come to deal with that subject more closely.[1]

II

THE APPEARANCES OF THE RISEN LORD

1. *The Nature of the Evidence*

We have considered at some length the evidence for the reaction of the resurrection-faith on the first generation of Christians ; and we have seen that it postulates the occurrence in the historical order of some fact of transcendent significance touching Jesus Christ. It is now time to examine the more direct historical evidence. In part, we have already touched it ; for St. Paul's teaching in 1 Cor. xv. is prefaced by a brief historical summary, which is in fact the earliest documentary testimony we have as to the resurrection. Its date is somewhere in the middle fifties of the first century ; and it points back to still earlier dates—one the period of St. Paul's first preaching in Corinth, which may be placed in A.D. 49 or 50 ; the other that of his conversion, probably in 35 A.D., when he received authoritative instruction in the truths of the Gospel. The facts, that is to say, of which he reminds the Corinthians, are facts which he had received and believed for several years past ; and they were the common property of the Church in Jerusalem within at most six years of the crucifixion. The summary itself, moreover, falls into two parts. The first has all the marks of a primitive *credo*. It not only contains the death, burial, resurrection, and appearances of Jesus, but notes that

---

[1] It may be pointed out, further, that both the passages we have been considering may be dependent on the Book of Wisdom. *Cf.* W. L. Knox, *St. Paul and the Church in Jerusalem*, pp. 128 f.

the death was " for our sins," that the resurrection was " on the third day," and invests both events with the dignity of religious dogma by adding that they were fulfilments of Scripture. The second part contains further allusions to appearances of Jesus, closing with that which had been experienced by the Apostle himself ; the purpose of this second section being to reinforce the evidence for the resurrection, to expand its significance, and to account for St. Paul's own title to be an Apostle.[1]

The evidence of the Gospels is naturally of a different kind from that of St. Paul ; for here we are dealing with narratives definitely purporting to be historical. Nowhere does the criticism of the Gospels present more complicated literary and historical problems than in regard to the resurrection.

The earliest narrative, St. Mark's, unfortunately breaks off after recording the discovery of the empty tomb and before coming to speak of any appearances of Jesus ; and the concluding twelve verses are usually recognised as a précis, compiled by a much later hand, of other accounts then current in the Church, some of which are more fully given in our other Gospels. St. Luke appears to have material of his own for this part of his story no less than for that of the Passion, derived perhaps from some member of the Herodian household [2] ; and it is possible that his concluding chapter may have belonged to the first edition of his work,[3] if such were indeed prepared, and so have been written no later than St. Mark. The internal evidence of this Gospel cuts both ways : for while the naturalness of the narrative, especially of that of the walk to Emmaus, tends to bear out the high opinion of St. Luke's trustworthiness as a historian which his own preface and the study of his works as a whole have led scholars to form, yet there are features in it which many will regard as secondary and as presuppos-

---

[1] A division of this kind seems to me necessitated by the phrasing. To the end of verse 5 (" then to the twelve ") each clause is introduced by the conjunction ὅτι, while from verse 6 onwards the direct statement is used (ἔπειτα ὤφθη). Moreover it is impossible that the record of the appearance to St. Paul himself (v. 8) could have been part of the primitive *credo* ; so that a division somewhere in the list of appearances is inevitable. This is also Meyer's view. At the same time it is quite possible that the whole list represents an agreed statement arranged between St. Paul and the other Apostles on one of his visits to Jerusalem, with a view to making clear his title to the Apostolate.

[2] *Cf.* Sanday, *Outlines*, p. 172.

[3] *Cf.* Canon Streeter's hypothesis of a Proto-Luke, which has secured influential support.

ing problems and questionings of a later day than the resurrection itself.[1] Nevertheless it is important to remember that St. Luke was brought into close touch with St. Paul and the other Apostles, and no doubt had access to several streams of oral testimony. St. Matthew's account is from the historian's point of view perhaps the most baffling. It has commonly been supposed to incorporate part at least of the " lost ending " of St. Mark ; but this is impossible to prove, and internal evidence points to certain features of the record as having been amplified in transmission. The verdict of the historian on the Synoptic evidence for the resurrection would recognise that in St. Mark and St. Luke we have two independent lines of testimony of whose general worth we can form a clear estimate ; while the first Gospel, if in some respects it follows St. Mark, also incorporates elements of floating tradition the value of which cannot to-day be determined.

There remain the Fourth Gospel and the Acts. Our estimate of the Johannine evidence must clearly be very largely affected by the view we take of the historical value of the Gospel as a whole ; though it must be recognised that no part of it falls in so well with the belief that the writer was, or was in immediate touch with, an eye-witness and disciple of Jesus as the last two chapters. The narratives are detailed, and yet marked by the greatest reserve ; they are marked by inward consistency, and yet this consistency does not appear artificial ; and they imply such a conception of the resurrection as we may well suppose St. Paul to have held. Canon Streeter has recently gone so far as to conjecture that St. John xxi. rather than St. Matthew xxviii. is our best guide as to the " lost ending " of St. Mark. Be that as it may, it is difficult to believe that the historian who approaches these chapters without *parti pris* can fail to be arrested by their intrinsic claims to his serious consideration.

Before we pass to a study of what the records tell us, a word should be said with regard to the importance of the Acts of the Apostles. What the Acts does is to attest beyond all question a fact which must govern our whole estimate of the historical evidence for the resurrection. It is the fact of the changed lives and characters of the Apostles. Whatever else we may say of the resurrection, we are compelled by the narrative in the Acts to see in it a historical happening adequate to account for the vast psycho-

---

[1] *Cf.* Loisy's view that it is influenced by reaction against Docetism.

logical and spiritual change thus attested.[1]   What Paley said of
" the Christian miracles " in general is true of the resurrection,
that " many professing to be original witnesses . . . passed their
lives in labours, dangers, and sufferings, voluntarily undergone in
attestation of the account which they delivered, and solely in consequence of their belief of these accounts ; and that they also
submitted, from the same motives, to new rules of conduct."
That is a fact which may not take us very far in the determination
of historical detail ; but it will at least absolve us from giving
serious attention to the views of those who attribute the rise of
belief in Christ's resurrection either to some skilful fraud or to
some trivial mistake.[2]

Further, a very striking symbol of this change in the lives of
the disciples may be seen in the religious observance of the first
day of the week, of which Acts records the beginnings.[3]   It is
clear that the primitive Church in Jerusalem maintained, even
with some ostentation, the customs of the Jewish Church and not
least that of the Sabbath ; but they added to this the regular
observance of the first day of the week as their especial day of
worship, and this gradually came to supersede entirely the observance of the Sabbath.   When one reflects on the tenacity with
which devout people cling to religious customs of long standing,
it is obvious that some unusually strong cause must have operated
to produce so startling an innovation as that involved in the institution of the Christian Sunday.   Such a cause can be found in the
association of the first day of the week with the Lord's resurrection, but in nothing else.   There is no suggestion in antiquity that
this observance had any other root but the commemoration of that
fact [4] ; nor is there any trace of evidence for any kind of apostolic

---

[1] It does not seem to me necessary here to discuss the narratives in the
apocryphal *Gospel according to the Hebrews* and the *Gospel of Peter*.   These
are clearly *Tendenzschriften* belonging to the second century, and cannot be
regarded as independent sources.   The former is interesting, however, as stating
that the appearance to St. James was accompanied by an eucharistic action—
" He took bread and blessed and brake "—analogous to that at Emmaus.

[2] As, for instance, that the women went to the wrong grave, or that the
Lord was not really dead when taken down from the cross.

[3] Acts xx. 7 ; *cf.* 1 Cor. xvi. 2.

[4] There appears to be no suggestion that the occurrences of Pentecost
recorded in Acts ii. were responsible for the observance of Sunday.   Pentecost
remained for Christians, as it had been for Jews, an annual festival (Acts xx. 16),
and no connection with the weekly Sunday can be traced.

decree initiating the usage. It grew up, that is to say, as the natural and spontaneous expression of the faith that on the first day of the week Jesus rose from the dead ; and it thus affords strong indirect support to that note of time in regard to the resurrection in which all the documents agree.

It has often been observed that the Gospel narratives of the resurrection present a number of discrepancies,[1] which it is exceedingly difficult and indeed probably impossible to harmonise. Some of them are insignificant ; but others, such as the place of the appearances, whether Jerusalem or Galilee or both, and the length of time over which they were spread, are more substantial ; and we need not shrink from admitting that the evidence forbids our giving upon them a decisive verdict. But this is by no means, as is sometimes supposed, to discredit the evidence as a whole. On the contrary, it is rather a testimony to its honesty. When we remember that the facts it handles were *ex hypothesi* such as baffled a complete explanation, and that the first witnesses confessed themselves incredulous and bewildered in face of them, then the existence of discrepancies in the accounts argues a close contiguity with the experiences related ; whereas a compact and coherent narrative would have given us cause to suspect the deliberate artifice of later hands. Precisely similar discrepancies, moreover, meet us in the evidence available for many of the most striking events in history ; and yet we do not for that reason reject them. What we do is to weigh the documents by reference to the position and character of their writers ; to weigh the different statements of each by reference to the access which the author may be supposed to have had in each case to means of observation ; to prefer eyewitnesses or those who have had access to the testimony, whether written or not, of eyewitnesses ; and not to reject evidence simply because it is of later date or lays more emphasis on the supernatural.[2] Our duty towards the evidence is not to harmonise it, but to weigh it, and so doing to form as true an estimate as we can of the happenings to which it relates.

[1] These are fully set forth by Schmiedel, in *E.B.*, art. Resurrection.

[2] *Cf.* Sir Edwyn Hoskyns' essay above, pp. 164 ff. Also Dr. E. A. Abbott's *St. Thomas of Canterbury*, i. pp. 348, 388. Note, for instance, Dr. Abbott's observation that the account of Herbert of Bosham, though biassed against "miracle," is often wrong where others are right.

2. *Theories of Visions*

One of the main characteristics of modern attempts to account for the evidence thus briefly surveyed is the emphasis laid on the records of the appearances of Jesus and the interpretation of these by some theory of visions. The kernel of truth, it is urged, which underlies the resurrection narratives, is the fact that the disciples saw visions of their Master soon after the crucifixion, and passed to the inference that He had risen from the dead ; and out of this belief and the experiences behind it grew up the legends of the "miraculous" resurrection. The theories of visions fall broadly into two classes, according as the visions are regarded as "subjective" or "objective." Supporters of the former view, which is well represented by Schmiedel in the *Encyclopædia Biblica*,[1] insist that the disciples' visions were "subjective" in the sense of being simply a product of their mental condition at the time. This theory, however, encounters acute difficulties from the standpoint both of psychology and history. On the psychological side it requires us to ascribe to the disciples morbid and pathological dispositions which their whole subsequent conduct appears to belie ; while historically it involves us in the almost grotesque belief that a world-wide religion of some nineteen centuries' vitality was founded on a series of delusions. It is not surprising that more sober critics, such as Harnack and Meyer in Germany and the English school generally, should have sought for a version of the theory which would not be open to such palpable objections. So arose the theory of "objective" visions, which, ever since Keim propounded his notion of the "telegram from heaven," has had weighty supporters. According to this view the belief in the resurrection sprang from the disciples' visions ; but these visions were caused by the invisible Christ Himself, really present with them. The disciples were inspired by God to see what they saw : Jesus was really alive, and the eye of faith could behold Him.

An initial criticism of this theory of visions, in whichever of these two forms it be presented, is that it involves the use of a distinction between "subjective" and "objective" which has no warrant either from psychology or from philosophy ; and the facts which the theory is advanced to explain are left as much hanging

[1] Art. " Resurrection."

in the air as ever. It is arguable that the distinction corresponds closely with that which psychology makes between hallucinations and illusions ; but it has been used, at least by supporters of the "objective" version, to support a conclusion which involves the philosophical judgment of "true" or "false." The truth is that all visions are objective as well as subjective, in that what is seen in them, be they dream or hallucination or mystical insight, is as much an object as in the case of normal perception : the question is whether or not the object which the mind images is real or unreal. In the former case, the vision may be called " true " or " veridical "; in the latter case it may be called " false " ; and in the case of our Lord's resurrection that is the issue which is of primary importance

It is necessary, therefore, to discard the distinction which has dogged the theory of visions in the literature of Higher Criticism on the resurrection. Yet various considerations should make us pause before we discard the theory itself. We have to remember certain facts which make it difficult to believe that, in the narratives of the Lord's appearances, we are dealing with cases of normal perception by the disciples. These facts are partly of a historical, partly of a doctrinal order. On the historical side we have the fact already alluded to, that none but believers (so far as the Scriptural evidence goes) saw the risen Lord ; the Fourth Gospel makes it clear that His entrances and exits were mysterious ; and the presumption is not unnatural that, if a Herod or a Caiaphas had been present in the upper room, he would not have seen Jesus. This presumption is strengthened by considerations of doctrine. We have St. Paul's clear statement that " flesh and blood cannot inherit the kingdom of God "—a statement which, as Professor Lake points out,[1] appears to rest on his knowledge of Christ's resurrection and to be inconsistent with the belief that His risen body was "material." We have, finally, our Lord's own teaching about the resurrection state, in which " they neither marry nor are given in marriage, but are as the angels in heaven." There is, therefore, very strong ground for saying that the Lord's risen body was not physical in the sense that it possessed metrical properties, and therefore not perceptible to any normal percipient.[2] In such circumstances we are

[1] *The Resurrection of Jesus Christ*, ch. i.
[2] It would, I suppose, be possible to argue that the risen Lord, though normally " spiritual," could and did " externalise " Himself for the duration of each appearance, and invest Himself with " mass " for that period. This seems to rest on the belief that the appearances of our Lord afford stronger

justified in saying that the theory of visions deserves on its merits a more sympathetic consideration than it is apt to receive from orthodox theologians. It has a value, that is to say, which is largely independent of the question of its adequacy to account for the Church's belief in the resurrection. The appearances of Jesus,

evidence for His resurrection if they involved normal sense-perception on the part of the disciples than if they were " spiritually discerned." The following passage from an article by a modern philosopher, Dr. C. D. Broad (*Hibbert Journal*, Oct. 1925, pp. 42, 43), will serve as a reminder of how complicated the matter in fact is :

" Perception may roughly be defined as being in direct cognitive contact with an existent something which manifests certain qualities to the percipient, and is instinctively regarded by him as a part or an appearance of a more extended and more enduring object which has certain other qualities that are not manifested to the percipient at the moment. *E.g.* when I say that I see a penny, I am in direct cognitive contact with something which manifests the qualities of brownness and approximately circular shape ; and I instinctively regard this as a part or an appearance of something which is permanent, which has an inside as well as an outside, and which has qualities like hardness and coldness that are not at present being manifested to me. If this belief be mistaken, I am not perceiving what would commonly be called a ' penny.' Now it is notorious that in ordinary sense-perception we are often deluded, and sometimes wildly deluded. A simple example is mistaking a mere mirror-image for a physical object, and a still more striking example is perceiving snakes or pink rats when one is suffering from *delirium tremens*. It is quite certain, then, that there are delusive sense-perceptions. Now, in the case of sense-perception there are several tests which we can use to tell whether a perception is delusive or not. We can check one sense by another, *e.g.* sight by touch. We can appeal to the testimony of others and find out whether they see anything that corresponds to what we see. Finally, we can make inferences from what we think we perceive, and find whether they are verified. We can say : ' If there are really rats running about my bed my dog will be excited, bread and cheese will disappear, and so on.' And then we can see whether anything of the kind happens. Now it does not seem to be possible to test the alleged supersensible perception which some people claim to have of God by any of these means. Very few people have had the experience at all ; they are very difficult to describe, and therefore to compare ; and it is very hard to point to any verifiable consequences which would follow if, and only if, these perceptions were not delusive."

On this we may observe that, on the theory here advocated, precisely the same three tests are applicable to the disciples' perception of our Lord. (*a*) Sight is checked by hearing, and *vice versa*. St. Luke implies—though he does not state—that touch also was used. But, as Professor Goudge has pointed out, this sense no less than sight or hearing has its counterpart in mystical experience. (*b*) The testimony of others. So the Emmaus story is checked by the Eleven ; that of the Eleven by St. Thomas ; that of the women by the two disciples from Emmaus, etc. And the collective character of some of the appearances is here in point. (*c*) The verification of inferences in practice corresponds to what the masters of the mystical life speak of as the vocational effect of a true mystical experience.

in short, require, and will be found to repay, a careful study simply as mystical or vocational experiences of the disciples.

3. *Tests and Types of Mystical Experience*

When we place the " appearances " of Jesus in that category, we render them comparable at once with a series of religious phenomena with which Catholic theology has a long familiarity It is theology, moreover, of a type fully as critical of its subject-matter as that which we are accustomed to associate with modern Protestantism. Mystical writers, for instance, such as St. Theresa or St. John of the Cross, insist constantly that the extraordinary phenomena of the religious life—ecstasies, visions, locutions and the like—are subject to countless dangers, imitations and delusions. This is no occasional concession to scepticism, but is a fundamental principle of their whole treatment of the subject. Their phraseology differs in many respects from that of our psychologists to-day; but they are no whit less alive to the distinction between the false and the true, the pathological and the spiritual, and to the frequent occurrence of morbid states of mind which closely simulate those of healthy life. They set themselves, therefore, to diagnose the symptoms of each condition ; to formulate canons applicable to them ; and to prescribe remedies, such as more exercise and fresh air, in cases where there is reason to suspect delusion. In all cases, moreover, subjects of abnormal experiences are advised to submit them to the criticism, and their lives to the guidance, of some competent director. The writings of the great mystics are thus characterised by precisely those qualities of vigilance, candour, and love of truth which we find in any scientific tradition of thought to-day ; and in applying their criteria to the records of the risen Lord's appearances, we are not removing these " into the clouds," but are submitting them to tests of a very concrete and searching kind.

Among the many criteria by which the mystical writers are wont to test the truth of visions and locutions, two stand out pre-eminently. One is that expressed in the saying of Richard of St. Victor : " I will not believe that I see Christ transfigured, unless Moses and Elias are with Him." [1] He means that no mystical

---

[1] Cited by Miss Evelyn Underhill in *Theology*, x. 10—an article to which I am much indebted.

experiences can be trusted as true, unless they are in concord with the moral law and with divine revelation. They must be in relation, that is to say, with the authoritative tradition which forms the background to the subject's spiritual life. This does not mean that they are not individual and original ; St. Theresa insists that divine communications made in this way are commonly sudden in their occurrence and unexpected in their content. But they are not fantastic. They have their context. The form, whether visual or auditory, in which they are clothed, must have palpable links with the corporate and institutional life to which the subject belongs, however much abstraction from it or re-association of its elements there be.[1] We cannot, of course, always trace these connections in the records of their experiences which prophets and seers have left to us ; but salient illustrations of the principle come readily to mind. Thus, Isaiah's vision is plainly coloured by his knowledge of the mysterious figures which brooded over the mercy-seat. The "showings" of the Seer of Patmos are steeped in the imagery of the Book of Ezekiel and of the Jewish apocalypses. St. Augustine's hearing of the words, *tolle, lege,* was the experience of one who knew that the Christian faith was contained in Scriptures. The heavenly beings seen by Joan of Arc were modelled on the statues familiar to her in her parish church at Domrémy. Comparison of the Lucan narrative of the Nativity with some of the stories in Judges will suggest that the visions of Mary were deeply influenced by her familiarity with the records of her nation's saints.

The importance of this principle is that it provides a point of contact between the saints and modern psychology. The " traditional " element in the mystical experience on which the saints set such store is nothing else than what psychologists denote to-day as the product of the unconscious or subconscious mind. They assert that visions, trances, dreams and the like are the precipitate, so to speak, of activities in which the mind has been engaged below the surface of consciousness. The phenomenon, moreover, is

[1] My friend, the Rev. H. K. Skipton, points out to me what is probably an interesting example of this in the life of Bunyan. According to *Pilgrim's Progress,* what eases Christian of his burden is the sight of a crucifix: and various facts make it likely that this was a crucifix thrown to the ground some years before Bunyan's day within the precincts of an old monastic house (now called The Chantreys) beside the Pilgrim's Way, which is the "road" of Bunyan's book.

by no means restricted to religion. The well-known French mathematician, Henri Poincaré,[1] gives a remarkable example of its occurrence in the development of his own researches ; and similar first-hand evidence is available for Lord Kelvin. In recognising, as the mystical writers do, that the thoughts and images round which the mind was working before the vision or audition is experienced determine in large part the form of the experience, they exhibit a close agreement with the scientific thought of to-day as to the psychological mechanism underlying it. Where they differ is in refusing to regard this admittedly subjective element as the whole story ; the ultimate truth or value of the experience as a whole depends on its harmony with the truest and most valued convictions and experiences of their conscious life ; and by use of this criterion they drew a distinction (which was not a psychological distinction) between veridical and non-veridical visions—the former coming from God, the latter, either by the suggestion of hallucination, or by direct experience, from the devil. And those who believe that truth was really reached in analogous ways by a Poincaré or a Kelvin will not hesitate to say that on that point the saints were right.

A second and more certain test of the validity of such visions and locutions is to be found in their effect. The first fear and confusion are tranquillised into peace and joy ; the soul is humbled, not elated ; the words heard are rich in meaning and implication and are never forgotten ; their truth is whole-heartedly believed, and they are charged with a life-giving authority and power.[2] They are, that is to say, fundamentally vocational.[3] The test provided by the traditional imagery in which such experiences are clothed is by itself inconclusive ; its absence renders them suspicious, but its presence is not a sufficient guarantee of validity. It is when this criterion is reinforced by the further and more telling criterion of the effect of the experience on character and life that its veridical

---

[1] Cited by Canon Streeter in the *Hibbert Journal* for January 1925. It is curious that Canon Streeter does not notice the inconsistency between this citation and his own unproven assertion that this method of arriving at truth is characteristic only of " primitive " ages or peoples.

[2] *Cf.* especially *The Interior Castle*, Mans. vi.

[3] This is so in the case of religious experience. In the case of scientific knowledge a better word would be *illuminative*. It is significant that H. Poincaré mentions " conciseness, suddenness, and immediate certainty " as leading characteristics of this experience.

nature becomes evident. The demonstration that the visions of an Isaiah or an Ezekiel were no product of delusion lies in the activities to which they were called and through which they left an abiding mark upon history ; and the same is true of St. Peter's vision at Joppa, and of St. Paul's on the way to Damascus. The experiences bore precisely those fruits of penitence and peace, of certainty, and above all of clear vocation which the " higher critics " of the mystical life assert with unanimity to be the hall-mark of divine revelation.

Once more, the critics of the mystical life discriminate not only between true and false in the experiences we are considering, but also recognise differences of type among those which are veridical, and classify them accordingly. Three kinds of visions and locutions especially are distinguished, and are called respectively exterior, imaginal,[1] and intellectual : a classification which is probably psychological, corresponding to the degree of visualisation in each case. Exterior visions and locutions are those in which the subject believes himself to see the object with his bodily eyes and to hear the words with his bodily ears. These are regarded as very rare ; and they are marked by an element of error, in that the object seen is not entirely such as in the vision it seems to be. The resurrection appearances are commonly assigned to this category, in that the Lord's body, though real, was glorified and no longer subject to ordinary physical laws.[2] Imaginal visions, on the contrary, are those in which the subject is aware that his physical senses are not employed : he sees with the eye, and hears with the ear, of the soul ; the bodily eyes and ears may be closed. Such experiences are often accompanied by ecstasy, and sometimes by anæsthesia ; the image seen is often an infused light ; and it is gone in a flash, though it leaves a permanent impression. The visions of Isaiah, of St. Stephen, and of " St. John the Divine " are commonly classed here ; a more modern example would be St. Francis's vision at the time when he received the *stigmata*. It is significant that a modern mystic like the Sadhu Sundar Singh, who appears to have been unacquainted with this classification of visions

---

[1] Dr. Thouless has coined this word as a substitute for the word " imaginary " (used by the mystics themselves) as less open to misunderstanding. *Introduction to the Psychology of Religion*, p. 73.

[2] *Cf.* St. Thomas, *Summa Theol.*, III. qu. 54, art. 1–3, where the nature of angelic beings is discussed.

and locutions when describing his own, made precisely the same distinction between the exterior and the imaginal experiences in his own life on purely empirical grounds. The third type of phenomena are those which are called " intellectual," when the subject is aware of a divine presence and communication, but without either sense or imagination appearing to be impressed. These may often be of long duration ; and the mystical writers agree in regarding them as the most valuable, because the least liable to error, of all the three types of experience. It is to this class, in all probability, that we should assign the vision described in the closing pages of Dante's *Paradiso* or that which Pascal records in his " Memoriale," or that again which is recorded by Sir David Shackleton in *South*.[1] Finally, we find records of experiences which, like some of the " showings " vouchsafed to Julian of Norwich, cannot be assigned to any one of these classes simply, but can only be styled " mixed," in that they present characteristics belonging to more than one class.

In dealing, however, with the resurrection-appearances of our Lord, there is an important discrimination to be made. Several of the recorded appearances were to a number of people at the same time ; whereas the mystical experiences we have been considering are normally those of individuals alone. This point is important, not for its bearing on the truth or falsehood of the visions and auditions (for any argument that might be based on the psychological theory of collective hallucinations is open to correction at once from the historical fact of collective vocation), but for its bearing upon our estimate of the evidence. The effect is greatly to broaden our basis of judgment. We have no reason to assume that, in the case of these collective appearances, the experiences of all the witnesses were of the same type : indeed it is probable that they differed considerably in the degree of their visualisation, and consequently in the details which they recorded. A cause of this

---

[1] " I know," he writes, after describing the march across South Georgia (chapter x), " that during that long and racking march of thirty-six hours over the unnamed mountains of South Georgia it seemed to me often that we were four, not three. I said nothing to my companions on the point, but afterwards Worsley said to me, ' Boss, I had a curious feeling on the march that there was another person with us.' Crean confessed to the same idea. One feels ' the dearth of human words, the roughness of mortal speech ' in trying to describe things intangible, but a record of our journeys would be incomplete without a reference to a subject very near to our hearts."

kind may explain, for example, the discrepancy between the Lucan and the Johannine accounts of the appearance to the Eleven on the first Easter evening. To some who were present it may really have appeared that the Lord " did eat before them," and St. Luke may have preferred this testimony as a safeguard against Docetism [1] ; while St. John preferred evidence in which the " exterior " elements in the experience were less prominent. We can be certain that these collective experiences gave rise to various streams of oral tradition, and that St. Luke—and probably also the author of the Fourth Gospel—was conversant with these. Each Evangelist selected the version which best fitted his general purpose and his whole conception of the resurrection. But it is a mistake to suppose that the versions are mutually exclusive for the historian. On the contrary, the differences are what we should expect, if the experiences were of the mystical type.

4. *Application to the Records of the Appearances*

The application of these principles to the narratives of the resurrection produces results of importance in more ways than one ; and we may summarise them as follows :

1. The conclusion, which seems dictated by general considerations of psychology and history, that the visions of Jesus which the disciples saw and the locutions which they heard were veridical is filled in and confirmed. A new factor is introduced into our estimate of the internal evidence for the Lord's appearances ; and features in the records which historical criticism has tended to fasten upon as pointing to the " subjectiveness " of the experiences are found in no way to prove them valueless or untrue, but rather to point the other way. Thus, it has been urged that the allusions to the breaking of bread at the conclusion of the walk to Emmaus and to the exposition of Scripture in connection with that vision and with others provide the real clues as to what happened ; and that the repetition by the disciples of that solemn rite and of the searchings of prophecy to which Jesus had accustomed them produced an atmosphere of tense devotion, and led to their supposing that they saw and heard Him. But, if the rigid canons of criticism proper to experiences of this kind be applied, the contention loses

---

[1] Though I think that a simpler reason may be found in the fact that St. Luke was a doctor.

much of its force. The breaking of bread and the exposition of the Scriptures provide precisely those links with the context of the disciples' previous life which in parallel cases are regarded as a mark of genuineness.[1] The feedings on the hill-side, the Eucharist at the Last Supper, the many occasions when they had listened to Jesus interpreting the Old Testament in public or in private—these experiences had sunk deep into their minds and been the food of their constant thoughts, until the shock of the cross had seemed to dismiss them as only an idle memory. And so they must have remained, had not the events of " the third day " stimulated them afresh into consciousness, not now as a medley of bewildering and unrelated ideas, but as a coherent and convincing revelation of truth, the answer to a thousand questions. A sound psychology will demand a cause for such a mental revolution [2] ; but, when the cause is forthcoming, it will see in the features of the narrative—the breaking of bread and the exposition of Scripture—symptoms of the mind's working which it knows to be wholly natural.[3]

2. Still more significant is the way in which the resurrection appearances answer to tests of vocational effect. The twice-repeated " Peace be unto you " prefacing the investiture of the disciples with their priestly calling in St. John, the apostolic commission to preach the gospel recorded in St. Matthew or St. Luke, the threefold charge addressed to St. Peter, the words addressed to St. Paul at his conversion—all these represent the impression made on the minds of the Apostles by these experiences. They belong to every strand available in the documentary evidence ; and their testimony is unanimous that the visions and locutions which the disciples received at this time were vocational. And they provide, as nothing else can, an adequate explanation for the fact that

---

[1] Thus, H. Poincaré says that experiences of the type he describes in his own life are not fruitful unless they come as the crown of " days of voluntary effort " on the subject in hand.

[2] It is not perhaps inconceivable that such a revulsion of mind might have occurred spontaneously, *given sufficient time*. But it is asking too much to believe that it could have occurred spontaneously within forty-eight hours of the crucifixion. And no fact is better attested historically than that the change occurred on " the third day."

[3] St. Theresa seems to have come very near to the conception of the subconscious mind. Speaking of imaginal locutions, she says that " whether from the lower or the higher soul, or from outside, these originate from God." She recognises, that is to say, that in these experiences God frequently speaks to the soul along the lines of the mind's natural pre-occupations and ideas.

the men of broken faith who forsook their Master in the **hour** of danger went out into the world a few weeks later fearless and certain, proclaiming Christ as the Saviour and Judge of mankind.

3. This emphasis on the vocational character of the appearances which is so marked a feature of the narratives in the Gospels has a direct bearing on the interpretation of the earliest testimony to the resurrection, that of St. Paul. The fact that in his first letter to the Corinthians St. Paul places the appearance to himself on the way to Damascus in the same category as the other appearances which he records has long been felt by theologians to present a difficult problem ; and criticism has not been slow to suggest that St. Paul regarded his own experiences as the norm of the others and as having equal evidential value with them for the resurrection of Christ. The inference, however, is premature. St. Paul's language undoubtedly requires us to understand that *on some plane, and in some important respects*, his vision and those of the other Apostles were strictly parallel and of equal value. But to assume, as is commonly done, that he regarded them as of equal value on the evidential plane is to jump to unwarrantable conclusions. Careful study of the records of the appearances in the Gospels suggests, on the other hand, that for the Evangelists the vocational elements in these experiences were fully as important as the evidential : in some they are manifestly predominant. The appearances of Jesus are recorded, that is to say, to account not only for the resurrection, but also and equally for the mission of the Apostolate and the Christian Church. They are as much the first chapter of Church history as the last of the story of the Incarnation. What if this be their primary meaning and interest for St. Paul ? Various considerations make it probable that this was, in fact, the case. His title to the Apostolate was, as we know, hotly challenged at Corinth ; and from the beginning circumstances must have made it essential that his position in the Church should be defined according to some recognised principle. The principle chosen was the fact that he had seen the Lord. His vision, that is to say, was accepted by the leaders of the Church as having the same vocational character as that experienced by themselves. And, finally, if we turn again to St. Paul's words, we find them entirely consistent with such a view. Not only does he close the chronicle of the appearances with a discussion of

his own title ; but the chronicle itself is introduced as though it constituted a distinct article of belief[1] in the Gospel which he had received—as distinct from the resurrection as that was from the burial, or as the burial was again from the redemptive death. Linguistic considerations, that is to say, confirm what we have already seen to be probable on other grounds, viz., that the appearances, owing to their vocational character, were regarded by the early Church as having a credal value independent of their testimony to the resurrection. They represent the divine commission of the Apostolate and the Church ; and in that context St. Paul needs to make no discrimination between the various appearances which he records.

4. At the same time, it does not follow that in other respects discrimination should not be made ; and the testimony of the mystical writers suggests that in fact the appearances were not all of the same type, even though all were equally veridical. Thus, St Paul's conversion-experience bears all the marks of an imaginal vision. We are told that a bright light shone round him ; but in none of the accounts is it said that he saw the figure of Jesus[2] ; while, on the other hand, the locutions were clear and it was Jesus who spoke them. It would, of course, be hazardous to attempt to classify the recorded appearances of Jesus with any precision; but it is at least possible that some of them were of the same kind as St. Paul's. The story of the walk to Emmaus, again, presents some of the characteristics of an intellectual vision ; the emphasis throughout is on what the disciples " knew " rather than on what they saw or heard, and the experience is of long duration. This difference of character, moreover, might perhaps account for the fact that this appearance is ignored by St. Paul. At the same time the evidence points clearly in certain cases to the visions and locutions being exterior. That to Mary Magdalene was evidently of this type, and St. Luke's narrative implies that the appearance to the Twelve on the evening of the first Easter Day was likewise ; for in both

---

[1] Each article is introduced by the conjunction ὅτι, which is well represented by inverted commas in English. Thus St. Paul says his teaching was: " Christ died," " He was buried," " He rose again," " He appeared." The argument is independent of whether or not the " primitive *credo* " ends with verse 5 ; *cf. supra*, p. 292.

[2] His question, " Have not I seen the Lord ? " is none the less fully justified but as an interpretation rather than as a description of his experience. So, too, Acts ix. 27, xxii. 14.

cases we find the element of mistake which is a characteristic of exterior visions.   It is probable, also, that the ascension is best explained in this way.   But the evidence in fact does not admit of our speaking with confidence.[1]   There is good reason to suppose that the Church at Jerusalem did everything possible to discover and to record what took place on each occasion, and this tendency must always be set off against any tendency to "materialise" experiences which were essentially part of a mystery.   But in any circumstances such experiences are difficult to describe with accuracy ; and the Apostles had not at hand those principles of classification which theology was later to develop.

Peculiar significance attaches to the appearance to St. Peter. Not only does St. Paul place it at the head of his list ; but St. Luke alludes to it in a way that conveys the strongest impression of veracity.   At the same time, it is nowhere described.   Various reasons might be conjectured for this, but none is more probable than that the experience was in fact indescribable in its clarity and power.   One is tempted to conjecture that we may have here the clue to the abrupt ending of St. Mark's Gospel.   The Pauline and Lucan evidence points to the fact that this incident would normally have followed next in his narrative.   St. Mark may have written some account of it, and on further reflection have torn it up ; or he may have come to feel, when he reached this point, that he could indeed go no further.   In either case he might feel loth to record any of the other experiences, if he could not record this, the chief and most striking of all.   The conjecture is, of course, no more than a guess ; but it at least absolves us from postulating a "lost ending" for which no evidence exists, and gives a reason for the abruptness of the ending that we have.[2]

5. The study of the appearances of the risen Lord as mystical or vocational experiences of the disciples goes far to mitigate the difficulty presented by the discrepancies in the evidence for the

---

[1] Allowance must also be made for the possibility that the experiences were of a " mixed " character ; *cf.* Thouless, *The Lady Julian*, p. 44.

[2] Canon Streeter thinks that the appearance to Peter of which St. Luke and St. Paul speak is identical with that described in St. John xxi.   This seems impossible to reconcile with the time assigned to it by St. Luke and (by implication) by St. Paul.   Nor is there any difficulty in supposing that there was more than one appearance to St. Peter.   The Johannine statement that the appearance by the Lake was the third appearance *to the disciples* seems to call for no such elaborate explanation as Canon Streeter gives it.

ascension. In the Acts St. Luke dates the ascension forty days after the resurrection [1] ; but from his Gospel we should gather that the story of Christ was complete on the evening of the first Easter Day itself ; while St. John gives no account of the ascension but suggests that it was closely coincident with the resurrection, and that His appearances were manifestations of One whose journey to the Father was already advanced beyond the borders of time and space.[2] The discrepancy becomes less formidable, however, in the light of the foregoing discussion. The experience known as the ascension will then be regarded as an " exterior vision " from which the disciples learnt that their Lord had ascended into heaven.[3] There is no real inconsistency in St. Luke. In his Gospel he records those visions and locutions which were especially evidential for the resurrection. In the Acts he singles out for particular mention that experience which more than any other brought home to the disciples the reality and scope of their new vocation. In both cases he is serving the purposes he had set himself as the historian first of Christ and then of Christ's Apostles. St. John, on the other hand, writing as a theologian with his whole attention concentrated upon the Person of the incarnate Son, sees nothing in the incident called the ascension which adds or can add to men's knowledge of Him and of His glory. Whatever be the process of interior personal change through which the Lord passed in His relations with the Father after the resurrection, it was not such as could be measured in time. All that could be measured in time was the education of the disciples, and he records moments in this education and brings out their vocational significance. But the Lord whom they see has already resumed the heavenly life which He had with the Father before the creation, and it is from that mysterious other world that He appears to His Church on earth

---

[1] It is significant that the Epistle of Barnabas implies that the ascension took place on a Sunday.

[2] *Cf.* especially St. John xx. 17 (" Touch me not," etc.). Few utterances of our Lord are more difficult to interpret. But, if the text be right, I should paraphrase as follows : " The old reserve and detachment which have marked our intercourse still hold good : for I am still with you, but not yet in you, and my journey is not yet finished. But go and tell my brethren that it is ending and I am already ascending, etc." The present tense ἀναβαίνω, rather than ἀναβήσομαι, is significant.

[3] The " element of error " which characterises exterior visions was in this case the belief that our Lord was lifted physically from the earth.

6. Finally, it may be claimed that consideration of the appearances as veridical visions goes some way towards solving the problem of where they took place. The problem does not lie merely in the fact that St. Matthew and the Johannine appendix describe appearances in Galilee, whereas St. Luke restricts them severely to Jerusalem and its environs. That the disciples should have journeyed to Galilee and back again to Jerusalem within the forty days before the ascension is by no means impossible. The real difficulty, however, lies further back, in the meaning of the Lord's promise, " I will go before you into Galilee." It has been observed [1] that these words occur at a crucial point in the Marcan narrative ; and that, if they were literally meant, they represent an anticlimax hard to reconcile with the known principles of our Lord's discourse. It can be shown, moreover, that both to St. Mark and to St. Luke they presented a puzzle, which each unravelled in his own way. The true clue, however, is provided by St. Matthew who, when recording the appearance in Galilee, lays the whole emphasis upon the fact that the disciples received from Jesus the revelation of His plenary authority and their own world-wide commission to the Gentiles. What the Lord had meant by Galilee, in short, was contained in the prophet Isaiah's phrase, " Galilee of the Gentiles " ; it was the symbol of the world waiting to be evangelised. The Lord's allusion, in fact, was precisely to that vocation of the Apostles which, as we have seen, was the main meaning of the appearances and caused them to constitute for St. Paul almost a distinct article of his creed.

This does not of itself go very far towards settling the historical question as to whether there were appearances in Galilee. But it illuminates other evidence which does. We need not suppose that the Johannine appendix represents the " lost ending " of St. Mark in order to justify ourselves in giving credence to the tradition of a Galilean appearance there embodied ; and the Matthæan record of the appearance on the mountain in Galilee has usually been regarded as providing the occasion for the appearance, to which St. Paul refers, " to five hundred brethren at once." I do not

---

[1] By Sir Edwyn Hoskyns, in *Theology*, vii. 14 ff. I can do no more than summarise the arguments and conclusions of that article. The difficulty is also faced by Spitta in his *Streitfragen der Geschichte Jesu* ; *cf*. Montefiore, *The Synoptic Gospels*, p. 1089. *Cf*. also Dr. Wade, *New Testament History*, p. 480

think that we can get rid of the evidence for the occurrence of appearances in Galilee. But, if the ascension be interpreted as we have interpreted it above, and as apparently St. John interpreted it, the discrepancy with the Lucan tradition ceases to be grave. The broad difference of character between the Jerusalem and the Galilean appearances—the former evidential, the latter vocational —is seen to go back to the mind and purpose of our Lord Himself. St. Luke is concerned with those appearances whose primary meaning lay in their testimony to the Lord's resurrection. St. Matthew, in the majestic conclusion of his Gospel, lays the emphasis rather on the world-wide vocation to which the risen Lord now called His disciples. The Fourth Gospel, as its manner is, combines the two, and brings out in unmistakable fashion the dominant significance of each series. Nor is it difficult to see why the second lesson needed different surroundings from the first. The vast truth of their vocation which the disciples had to realise as implicit in the resurrection was not one that would easily come home to them amid the bustling multitudes of the Jewish capital. For that, as for the realisation of the fact itself, other influences would be needed as well as the words of the risen Lord Himself ; and foremost among these would be all the associations of Galilee— its memories of earlier missions and commissions, and all that the Lord's teaching and ministry there had made it to mean. Only after this lesson had been learnt were the minds of the disciples ripe for understanding the truth declared in the ascension, that the Lord had indeed entered into His glory.[1]

To sum up. The study of the appearances of the risen Lord as mystical experiences of the disciples is justified by the fact that the resurrection was itself a " mystery," and that the manifestations accompanying it were confined to those whose faith Jesus had Himself trained. The details of the evidence, moreover, confirm the view, which on broad psychological and historical grounds is seen to be most probable, that the visions and locutions experienced

---

[1] The view here advocated suggests a change in the traditional interpretation of 1 Cor. xv. 7 (τοῖς ἀποστόλοις πᾶσιν), which is usually referred to the ascension. But there appears to be no reason whatever for this identification, except the desire to " harmonise " the accounts. The E.V. translation of τῷ ἐκτρώματι (1 Cor. xv. 8), " to one born out of due time," probably suggested the idea that St. Paul has in mind the fact that his vision was in the period after the ascension. But the word has no note of time about it, and refers simply to the suddenness and violence of his conversion.

by the disciples—even though in the strict sense " subjective "—
were veridical : for it shows them to be traditional in form and
vocational in character ; and this vocational character is the
common element in virtue of which St. Paul speaks of all the
appearances as of the same validity for faith. At the same time
there are signs that the experiences in question were not all of the
same type, though all alike were veridical; and the differences revealed in the narratives, though they may not be pressed, correspond
in many ways with those clearly distinguished types which are
familiar to the saints. And, finally, all the appearances, to whichever type they belong, admit readily of the Johannine interpretation
of the Lord's risen life, in the sense that they are appearances of
the heavenly and glorified Christ. What St. Luke records in the
Acts was that particular vision which taught the disciples what
they could not have apprehended immediately, that their Lord had
indeed departed to the Father. The Galilean appearances were
concerned to impart a fuller revelation of the resurrection and of
all that it involved for the universal mission of the Church.

Before passing on to consider the adequacy of this theory to
compass the whole faith and fact of the resurrection, it is worth
while to pause and note how much it involves. Whatever
philosophy we profess—whether we call the resurrection mystery
or miracle—we have to recognise that in such a matter as this a
point must be reached sooner or later where the mind's progress is
arrested in a reverent agnosticism. For believers generally that
point is reached at a stage further than we have so far travelled ;
it is reached, that is to say, when we stand by the empty tomb.
But there are many thoughtful believers to-day who cannot go so
far, and who halt at the point which our enquiry has now reached.
They do not regard the evidence as certifying us of more than the
fact that the Lord appeared to His disciples and gave them a clear
call to work in His behalf. It is desirable, however, that both
orthodox and modernist should realise how much this belief signifies.
It signifies accepting as true a number of occurrences or experiences
which the saints do not hesitate to describe as " miracles." It
involves also accepting them as acts in which God has definitely
intervened in human experience to reveal and to teach. These
acts are interpreted, moreover, in a way which gives to the
occurrences a profoundly spiritual meaning, and which renders
irrelevant alike the liberal's question as to how the risen Lord was

clothed [1] and the traditionalist's assertion that the earth was lighter by so many pounds when the Lord ascended into heaven.[2]   Finally, they are of that transcendent and supra-normal character which claims and receives the homage of a man's whole surrender and obedience ; so that those who accept in practical faith this theory of veridical visions cannot but commit themselves to that Spirit who prompted them and who built upon them the Church of the Apostles.

5. *Limitations of this Analogy*

Nevertheless, while all this is true, we must face at the same time the limitations of this faith.   In the first place, in so far as it is a doctrine of Christ, it is a doctrine of His foundation of the Church and of His giving commission to the Apostolate rather than of His resurrection from the dead.   No one who seriously believed this faith could belittle the Church's supernatural calling or doubt its vocation to holiness or question its title to be the Body of Christ. In that sense it exacts a Churchmanship which is unquestionably Catholic.   But it does not reach by itself to the Catholic belief in Christ's resurrection.   It is not in essence the Easter message. For that message is first and foremost a message of the Person rather than of the doings of the Son of God.   It declares something that happened to Him as the climax of His human life and death. Its primary reference is to His experience, not to the experience which others had of Him.   Behind the mystery of His new relation to the disciples lies a prior mystery concerning only Himself and the Father and embodying in one signal event the mighty power of God.   And it is this which is the kernel of the Easter faith.

Secondly, the act of God involved in the theory of visions is an act which determines the future rather than interprets the past. But the gospel with which the primitive Church went out into the world, though it claimed to represent the authoritative word of God and vision of Christ, was first and foremost a gospel of divine redress.   It was the gospel of the cross, because it was at the same time the gospel of the cross's reversal and transvaluation.   It is

---

[1] Cf. *Liberalism in Religion,* by the Dean of St. Paul's.   Dr. Wade, in his admirable (even if unduly modernist) *New Testament History,* says, I think, all that we need say : " The details of the Appearances (dress, speech, wounds, etc.) were mediated through the memory."

[2] Cf. *Some Loose Stones,* by the Rev. R. A. Knox.

possible that the appearances alone might have led the disciples to infer that their Master had survived death ; but what they said was far more than this—they said that He had conquered death. This is a belief which quite outranges any doctrine of immortality. The first Christians believed, as we have seen, that those who died before the Lord's coming were immortal in the sense that they survived death ; but they did not say of them that they conquered death. They reaped indeed the benefits of the conquest ; but the conquest itself was Christ's. And the certainty of their faith on this point calls for some more substantial ground than was provided by the appearances alone. It calls for an act of God in the life of Christ which matched at every point the apparent defeat which He suffered on the cross. Christ's conquest of death must be as complete, as convincing, as all-embracing as death's apparent conquest of Him had been. It must extend to every relation of His Person which death had touched, and show that at no single point was the power of sin and death left in possession of the field.[1]

And assurance of that kind is not sufficiently accounted for by any theory of visions. There is nothing in the theory which conflicts with it, except the claim that it is inadequate. But its inadequacy requires us to review the evidence again ; to restore the appearances, which we have isolated for a particular purpose, to their place in the whole narrative ; and to pick up along with them those other strands of testimony which the documents offer to our investigation.

IV

THE RESURRECTION OF CHRIST

1. *Convergent Testimony*

Few facts are more strongly attested by the documentary records of the resurrection than that the disciples' belief in it rested in the first instance upon a number of converging lines

---

[1] Professor Taylor draws my attention to the striking passage on resurrection where Soloviev urges that, *unless* the physical dissolution of life is reversed by resurrection, evil is *obviously* more potent than good. (*Three Dialogues on War, Progress, and the End of History*, English translation, pp. 162 f.)

of evidence, none of which by itself was convincing. This is a feature of the narratives which is not easy to account for, unless it be authentic. It is perhaps intelligible that, if the disciples had reached the conviction that Christ was risen simply on the strength of the appearances, their belief should have come to embody itself in a legend of the grave being empty ; but it is not at all easy to believe that a legend of this kind should have presented us with a picture of the formation of the conviction so natural, inwardly consistent, and free from artifice as that which we have. Such evidence is of a high degree of credibility. It is discordant and uncertain precisely on those details of time and place which men easily forget ; it is harmonious, on the other hand, and coherent on that which they most easily remember—namely, the impact of great experience on the development of their own minds. And when we find this impact varying with different individuals and at different moments in the story, and varying in ways which our own experience of life shows us to be intrinsically probable, we have a right to conclude that our evidence is in close contact with the truth.

Little more need be said here with regard to the appearances. The view which regards them as analogous to the mystical experiences of the saints will seem to some inadequate ; and they will prefer to think of the risen Lord " as one who no longer felt physical obstacles, but who could still submit, if His purpose so demanded, to physical conditions." [1] The present writer does not feel that this doctrine of what one may call occasional externalisation contains any truth which is absent from the theory of veridical visions, while it entails, in his judgment, difficulties of its own, and particularly in regard to the ascension. But the conditions of our Lord's risen life are confessedly outside our experience, and our interpretation of them cannot be other than partial. In either case the question is not so much whether an analogy with mystical visions exists, but how far it can be pressed ; and on that issue there may well be difference of opinion.

Mention has already been made of two other factors besides the

---

[1] Gore, *Belief in God*, p. 269. *Cf.* also Dr. Sparrow Simpson, *The Resurrection and Modern Thought*, p. 418 : " In that glorified body the penetration of matter by spirit was so complete that He could at will re-enter into terrestrial conditions and become perceptible to the senses of human beings upon earth." Yet I am not sure that this fully represents Dr. Sparrow Simpson's view on the whole.

appearances which contributed to the disciples' conviction of the resurrection — the exposition of Scripture and the breaking of bread. Both these occur in St. Luke's narrative of the walk to Emmaus ; but it is significant that he does not say that they led the two disciples to the inference that Jesus was risen. The effect was to cheer and encourage them with the belief that He was not far from them. Other narratives in the Gospels illustrate the occurrence further. Thus, St. Luke records that on one occasion Jesus ate before them, in proof that He was not a ghost. The silence of St. John on this incident, though otherwise he records the appearance, suggests that St. Luke is recording a version of an act which was in reality of a piece with that at Emmaus [1] ; and the narrative in the Johannine appendix points to a similar experience. What would appear probable is that the solemn distribution of food, recalling the mysterious feedings on the hill-sides and still more the rite at the Last Supper, was used by the risen Lord as a means of recognition.

Not less striking is the part played by the exposition of Scripture. " Did not our heart burn within us, while he talked with us by the way, and opened to us the scriptures ? "—there we seem to have a glimpse of a real experience often repeated since in the story of the Church. Both St. Luke and St. John in different ways point to the fact that the understanding of Scripture played an essential part in the formation of the resurrection faith. St. John records as exceptional the fact that the beloved disciple believed in the resurrection on the strength of the empty tomb alone, seeing that he and St. Peter " as yet . . . knew not the scripture, that He must rise again from the dead." St. Luke narrates in connection with the appearance to the Eleven and their commission on the first Easter evening a repetition of the exposition of prophecy which was so signal a feature of the walk to Emmaus. And both Evangelists are recording a feature of the disciples' experience at this time which the severest critic must submit to be intrinsically probable. For it is not the kind of fact which the weavers of legend, eager for miracle, would have any interest in recording. On the contrary, it supplies a link in the evidence which shows the

---

[1] St. John xx. 20 contains an allusion to Jesus showing His hands and His side—language which the writer of the Fourth Gospel might well use, if he had in mind the Eucharistic rite. The incident belongs to the appearance recorded in Luke xxiv. 36–43 and John xx. 19–25.

disciples to have been reasonable men. The fact of the resurrection, that is to say, despite its external attestation, was not faith for them, until it had been integrated with the rest of their religious life. For this life the Scriptures had a peculiar authority, second only to the words of the Lord Himself. Only when they saw that the cross and the resurrection were the fulfilment of prophecy could they fully believe that Christ had risen from the dead.

Once more, this emphasis on the understanding of Scripture has a close bearing on the adequacy of the theory of visions. For, if the visions of Jesus rather than the empty tomb were the decisive factor in the formation of the disciples' faith, we should suspect that the parts of Scripture now unveiled would have reference to them. We should expect St. Paul to say that Jesus " appeared " " according to the Scriptures," as he said this of the death and the resurrection ; and there were many passages in the Psalms and the Prophets which he and the Evangelists could have cited. But neither in St. Paul nor in the Gospels is the exposition of Scripture given any bearing whatever upon the appearances. They lie side by side as collateral evidences to a great fact other than themselves, for which the main evidence was of a different character.

2. *The Empty Tomb*

We come, therefore, finally to that evidence which was regarded by the primitive Church and has been regarded ever since, as the principal guarantee for Christ's resurrection—I mean, the empty tomb. It is no exaggeration to say that, so far as the documentary evidence is concerned, no fact recorded in the New Testament is better attested than this. Not only is St. Mark's narrative available here to confirm those of St. Paul and of the later Evangelists ; but the discovery is told with a directness and simplicity which seem to be the echo of the eyewitnesses themselves. It is reasonable that those who reject the entire Gospels as historically valueless should reject this testimony too ; but to accept them generally as good sources of historical information and yet to refuse to follow them on this point argues an *apriorism* and an arbitrariness in dealing with evidence which is an affront to scientific method.

It is not surprising, therefore, that contemporary criticism should concentrate rather on accounting for the grave being empty than on questioning whether or not it was so.   Various theories have been advanced on this score.   The earliest, viz., that the disciples secured the Lord's body by stealth, is no more credible to-day than it was when the first Evangelist wrote his Gospel.   Nor can we attach credence to the view that the Jews themselves removed the body ; for, had they done so, they could have nipped Christianity in the bud by avowing the fact when the resurrection was first preached.   Insurmountable difficulties, in fact, attend any theory which attributes the removal of the body either to the devotion of friends or to the malice of enemies.   And the same difficulties really attach, though at a stage further on, to the view that " the Romans, fearing a public disturbance, took advantage of the Sabbath quiet to remove the body." [1]   For it is incredible that the Lord's disciples and friends should have been the only persons interested in the grave and likely to visit it.   Even if we reject the intrinsically probable statement of Matthew that the Jewish leaders asked for and obtained a guard, we may be perfectly certain that they would not leave the grave entirely unvisited and unwatched, at least by day ; and it could not have been long before they too were asking the question as to why it was empty.   Had Roman soldiers removed the body, or had such a statement had the slightest foundation in fact, the Jews must have given it currency, and the Romans would have had good cause to encourage the notion.   The saying, still current when the first Gospel was written, that the disciples removed the body by stealth represents in fact the bankruptcy of all attempts on the part of the Jews to suggest any other explanation.

The truth is that the empty tomb presents the mind with one of those issues where the decision is made at a deeper level of personality than that which is concerned simply with the weighing of historical evidence.   If a man follows the evidence so far as to envisage the empty tomb but then deserts it for pure hypothesis, it is because he is drawn aside by other than historical considerations.   It is because he has been overcome by that arrested wonder which underlies all serious agnosticism.   And the effect of the empty tomb is either to arrest wonder or to expand it.   The case with us who study the evidence is the reverse of what it was with the first witnesses.   We first satisfy ourselves as to the appearances of the Lord, and find our wonder expanding as we do so, until it

[1] Canon Streeter, in *Foundations*, p. 134.

comes either to arrest or to yet further expansion at the empty tomb. The first disciples begin to wonder when they hear of the empty tomb. Mary's first impulse is one of dismay : "They have taken away the Lord out of the sepulchre and we know not where they have laid him." Peter and John run to verify the tidings ; and, though for the beloved disciple wonder at the state of the grave ripens swiftly then and there into faith, Peter departs "wondering in himself at that which was come to pass." The two disciples walking to Emmaus have heard that the grave is empty, but can only find in it matter for astonishment. Only when the Lord has appeared decisively and when Scripture has been added to interpret their experience—only then does the first wonder expand into faith and adoration. Nevertheless, for us as for them the full truth of the resurrection requires each strand of the three-fold cord of evidence for its apprehension. It requires the appearances as the basis of a transcendent vocation deriving from the risen Lord ; it requires Scripture as the bond which links the resurrection with the cross in one redemptive Gospel ; it requires the empty tomb as the great pledge that death has indeed been conquered.

The reality to which the evidence thus points is of an order beyond our comprehension. Reason can estimate the evidence ; but when that is done, it must make way for other functions of the mind—for constructive imagination, for wonder, and for faith. What is involved is such a change in the body of Jesus as takes it out of the category of things to which the laws of natural science apply, and sets it in a relation to experience, both His and ours, to which we know no parallel. Various terms have been coined to describe it, such as sublimation or etherealisation ; but these are no more than symbols of our ignorance and wonder. We do not know what are the potentialities of matter when indwelt by the soul of the Son of God, though we can well believe that in such a case it is exempt from the sentence of corruption. What faith claims is that, in embodying the manhood of God Incarnate, the whole course of physical evolution reached its highest destiny, and through the conquest of death passed over into forms of energy as yet unguessed. Into the mystery of that mode of being only the heart of the worshipper can penetrate ; and its only language when it does so is that of St. Thomas, MY LORD AND MY GOD.

THE SPIRIT AND THE CHURCH
IN HISTORY
BY ERIC MILNER-WHITE

Y

CONTENTS

The Distinctiveness of the Church in History due to its Possession of Spirit

THE Church is a nation without race, without boundaries, with no common language or courts of law, without army or fleet. Yet it is never treated as of no account. States and men may love or hate, they cannot ignore it. Its bonds of unity, even in outward disunion, constantly prove to be tougher than ties of tongue and kindred ; its boundaries are never at any moment settled, and claim indeed to extend beyond the visible world. Though without arms, it is always at war ; though without codes, courts and police, its moral ideal is in all quarters of the world heroic ; and in practice the heights of moral beauty are its common fruit. For it has a *spirit*.

The spirit, whatever it be, which thus binds and inspires this supernational body calls for serious consideration merely on account of its obvious achievements. First, because it has brought so large and lasting a people into existence. Since that baptismal Day of Pentecost the world has seen many empires of colossal strength shiver and sink, many changes of catastrophic importance to the development of man, much increase of know-ledge with consequences subtle, profound, bewildering. Yet this peculiar people has not only survived, but has driven its founda-tions deeper with every change : it has not merely kept together a remnant living on the tradition of ancient faith and fame, but has increased with every century, gathering in recruits by the brilliant newness of an old appeal. The peoples enter it because it gives life. The empires, armed and coherent, fall ; the Church, by human standards incoherent and weaponless, stands. The mystery of its survival is at least a title to respect ; it is the body which first claims investigation if we would investigate the eternal in human affairs.

Not less mysterious is the influence of this spiritual nation upon the individuals of its obedience. Here almost all analogy to the secular state ceases. And if we turn to other faiths and philosophies, comparison again is difficult, simply because these too have proved mortal. Faiths have perished in their hundreds and philosophies in their thousands. They were influential, but only for a day and days. But the Church lives and grows, commanding a devotion which is both passionate and steady. Its liveliest rival is Mohammedanism ; yet here Christianity has nothing to fear in depth or quality of influence, or in appeal to the higher intellect, or in moral achievement. Its " spirit " is a superior one, or a loftier, fuller, manifestation of the same.

Observe the intensity, steadiness, and range of this influence. Unlike the impulses of patriotism which awake suddenly at crisis, and, when it is over, doze again, the inspiration of the Church presses more or less evenly upon its members throughout all the days of their conversion. It is not evoked from without at any special danger, but works from within, in the daily aspiration of heart and mind, and the efforts of an abiding devotion. Temper is tuned, selfishness purged, suffering transfigured, diverse purpose unified, all the variations of daily experience made to contribute to wealth of character, and the peace of active charity. There appears to be no kind of temperament, no rank of life, no difference of circumstance or intellect or ability or race or civilisation, which this influence cannot grip and bless. And it is true to say that to the individual its onset comes always as a surprise, an ever new thing to man despite its frequency amongst men, a welcome thing despite its disturbing nature—a witness at least to the general sense that it comes from without.

Over and beyond the force with which it wakes the individual and changes his life, it has extended its moral and ethical ideals over the peoples most conspicuous for progress, civilisation, and power ; and all attempts to break from these seem to end in weariness and failure, sometimes, as in the German following of Nietzsche, in world-disaster. The noble pagan of to-day cannot but live, up to a point, by the ethical teaching of Christ's Church, lest he fall below the highest standard he meets. Christian character is an argument impossible to ignore; to be answered, as it is propounded, only in terms of living. The search for a superior ethic has conspicuously failed. The best and most thoughtful non-believers, therefore, submit to Christian influence in the sphere of living where they do not in the sphere of thought. The history of Western civilisation is inextricably bound up with the steady establishment of a less imperfectly Christian ethic, and the East begins to move uneasily to the same stimulus. Apart then from any question of the truth of Christianity, the Christian ideal of actual living has a living influence, and is to some exten⁺ effective outside the converted, beyond the Church's nominal adherents. That is to say, the spirit which is the bond and inspiration of the Church itself, does a work through it which is indisputably important to the whole world.

Nobody wishes to pretend that even the best lives of Christians, much less their actual average standard, approach the ideal of the Church Catholic. But the ideal, which is to be "like Christ," "to be conformed to His image," "to abide in Him and He in us," "to be perfect as our Father in heaven is perfect," has never for one instant ceased to be presented to its members ; and the pattern of the Head has produced in every generation not a handful but hundreds of acts and lives of a heroic virtue. The great merciful activities which the sympathy of the Church first found to do, the abolition of slavery, the institution of hospitals,[1] the raising of the status of women, the zeal for education when none other cared, have now passed into the very fabric of Western civilisation. But it is seldom noted that even now the hardest works of mercy are still left to those whose devotion to Christ provides them both with the perseverance for the task and with the readiness to remain unknown and obscure in the doing of it. The worst wreckage of indulgence and sin can still be dealt with only by the Church's Homes of Mercy. The educational and medical care of backward races is left to the Christian missionary. The bulk of such social work as is unpaid and voluntary is done demonstrably by people who "go to church." And though in sentiment most people desire social reform, it is still only the minister of Christ and his little band of helpers who live in the midst of the conditions which others lament.

Then what is the *claim* of the Church ? Does it match these facts ? From so potent and deathless an empire, we should expect high claims ; and find them. This, we are told, is the

---

[1] The Church was not the inventor of the hospital any more than our Lord was the inventor of the name "Father" for God. But Christianity at once transformed human thought and practice by raising the care of the sick to the plane of essential religious and civic duty.

people of the Eternal God, the fellowship of His incarnate Son, inspired and guided by His very Spirit, a holy priesthood, steward of the mysteries and dispenser of the gifts of God's love, of the forgiveness of sins, of a new life in grace and of a communion with God which will develop and deepen world without end.

It is to the examination and explanation of this claim that the rest of this essay must be devoted. The sins of the Church must of course be thrown in against the achievements ; the achievements be regarded more carefully to see if they correspond, and how they correspond, to the claim ; and whether they justify it. We must start with the premise (surely indisputable) that there is a spirit within the Church—a unique and remarkable spirit—which gives it aim, character, force, indestructibility, and essential unity ; but is it *holy* spirit, the Spirit of God ?

II

The Development of the Church in History progressively reveals its Spirit as Holy Spirit

The Church of God on any showing existed before the coming of Christ. He indeed was born into it. The Jewish race had long been conscious of itself as what we should now call a Church. This sense was denied to other peoples, whose development, if under the guidance of God, was so unconsciously. The Hebrew people may have been mistaken, but their literature puts their conviction of special privilege beyond all possible doubt. And their history corresponds impressively to the conviction. Never did a folk so feeble, with a history so chequered, and situation and politics so impossibly difficult, give such gifts to the world. They were gifts to the spiritual development of mankind, and to nothing else at all. We cannot even date the Church's birth ; like the mysterious Melchizedec, it is without descent, having neither beginning of days, nor end of life. Whether the call of Abraham be history or legend, it bears undeniable witness to a sense of special vocation and divine guidance, implanted at an early date in this obscure Semitic tribe. No one can mistake that it was this sense, pressing invisibly and perpetually over long spaces of time, which gave the race its peculiar tenacity, and explains its strange line of development. The story of Abraham is a parable of the early stages of a profound religious growth. With the awakening of vocation in man and race it embodies also the discovery of monotheism, the conception of a moral God who demanded faith, the sacrifice of mind and heart, rather than the cruel sacrifices of fear ; who punished the guilty, but whose righteousness the righteous man could approach for lavishness of mercy. In that undated dawn, and in silent ways, a new spirit entered earth and was comprehended ; without doubt, a higher spirit than prevailed elsewhere, a spirit of higher truth.

Thenceforward the Hebrew people had *a sacramental value to the world.* It neither posed nor presumed ; it did not try to teach other peoples, but itself was taught. Like any naughty schoolboy, it hated rather than liked its lessons, and rebelled against its teachers, yet consistently it learned. It thought that it learned for itself, a learning real and long and hard enough ; but time has shown that its learning was a deeper thing, for the whole world, a learning sacramental, almost vicarious, still of fundamental value. Under Moses and Joshua, the sense of divine guidance grew unescapable. Jehovah was their own, as other gods belonged to other races ; but how different He ! At the same time, the acceptance of the primitive law marked a further inflow of spirit, and involved both a clearer definition of God and a new conscience towards Him : His moral demand became the first obligation both of state and individual. The code has never gone wholly out of date in so far as the duty towards God and neighbour has become the foundation of almost universal morality. Again then, a spirit of truth entered, worked within and issued forth from an insignificant race, which claimed a particular character for God, and a particular vocation from Him ; which in the face of constant distress it held fast and finally delivered to mankind.

The vocation was deepened and fostered by the line of Hebrew prophets. There has never been in history a phenomenon more remarkable, nor one which bears so easily the appearance of an irruption of spirit. About the prophets' own interpretation of themselves there is no doubt at all. " Thus saith the Lord," they cry. They stand between Yahwe and His people, convey His reproofs and encouragements, expound His character and demands, discern His will and intentions. They do not address themselves to the individual, but to the nation. It is to a national conscience, to the Church, that they appeal. And the God whom they represent is a moral personality, "inexorable in His requirement of a righteousness corresponding to His own." From this standpoint, unparalleled in that age, they could develop their doctrines of sin, of suffering, of responsibility national and individual, of a Messiah to come, of the triumph of the Kingdom of God, carrying them to new spiritual heights, and driving them into the consciousness of the nation-church, so that they became an abiding possession on the earth.

So remarkable a phenomenon indeed is this, both in content and persistence, that questioning minds of the capacity of Bishop Gore's have seen here a foundation powerful enough on which to base their faith in God. Such glory and power belong to the pre-Christian Church of God even in these most modern days. It is therefore fair to say that the Old Testament Church, the elect race, has been to the world sacramental, not only of a monotheistic creed, but also of the development of man on his spiritual side, in his spiritual character. Salvation came indeed of the Jews ; and every step of their spiritual progress has been sacramental of that world-salvation. Through them, what we may now call Holy Spirit has entered the world in ever greater degree, as a living and abiding force, its own evidence and its own gospel.

—Entered the world and secured permanence *through an organisation, an institution* bounded and disciplined, not primarily by law or doctrine, but by *race*. Holy Spirit came by a people. This is not to say, that the Spirit of God worked only in Israel. He worked and works throughout His own poem of creation. But in Israel His life was concentrated, confined, guarded, fostered in an institution dominated by that vocation only. To Israel He came expressly as Captain of the Lord's host, and pre-eminently through His own host He revealed Himself to the nations of men. If the host had failed . . . but it did not. It ought to have failed by all human chances ; except for this single pertinacity, its history was ignominious ; but the call of God was without repentance ; the most feeble folk persisted by the Spirit that was with it and in it.

John, the last prophet, was followed immediately by the Christ, and a new revelation, too large to be confined any longer to one race, overturned the old barriers and spread north, south, east, and west. It overleapt the barriers not only of race, but even of death, by the rising of Jesus from the dead. The new covenant did not destroy, but fulfilled the old : and what had been racial became universal. It was part of Christ's declared gospel that it should. It was not part of Christ's gospel that His adherents should lose their cohesion. On the contrary, He conceived their new unity as more august and absolute than anything earth had seen or prophets dreamed—akin to and partaking of the very unity of the Godhead. Both in their writings and actions His immediate followers stressed this character of the new ecclesia. St. Paul spent his active life in tearing down the middle wall of partition, and building the new fellowship that should know no distinction of race or class. To his writings the Church is a most glowing inspiration, no mere organisation or propagandist machine, but a new race, a new kingdom, the very Body of Christ. St. Peter's description is not dissimilar nor less lyrical : " Ye are an elect race, a royal priesthood, a holy nation, a people for God's own possession." The sense of the vocation of the holy nation was not less because it now ceased to be identified with Israel after the flesh, but infinitely greater. The stress upon its unity, now that it was changed from a unity of blood to one of spirit, was infinitely exalted. With the new revelation, the task of the elect race was more clearly seen and understood, and the new power which had come into the world for its fulfilment was recognised, palpably felt, personified and named the Holy Ghost. These things only enhanced the distinctiveness of God's people. They peculiarly possessed His Spirit, and were peculiarly knit by it. They felt a divine responsibility, a vocation, as a body. So much is a mere matter of history. It is matter of history also that the consciousness of fellowship and vocation drove them by successive steps into a definite, though loose, outward organisation : it is indeed hard to see what else could have happened, considering the extraordinary nature of the ministries which Christians felt bound to share amongst themselves and to give to the world. The process began with the Founder Himself, who made deliberate choice of twelve apostles. The apostles took their duty of ordering the new society outwardly as seriously as any other of their responsibilities : there is no more sacerdotal writing in existence than the very first chapter of the Acts. The rest of the book continues the tale of the establishment of the new race. The worst difficulty was faced at once and marvellously overcome—the breaking down of the barrier between Jew and Gentile.   No power on earth could hold up a Spirit capable of that.   Nobody imagines that the original leaders, Peter, James, or Paul, wholly understood what they were doing, or laid the conscious plans of politicians which always prove so vain.   But they felt the inspiration of a mighty cause of God, which demanded unremitting propaganda, and which not only required unity in the inspired fellowship, but *made it*.   The unity of Christ's fellowship was indeed to be, as He intended, utter ;   to be expressed not only by outward organisation and not only by inward love, but in both and all ways.   It should have no boundaries which could cramp expansion, such as race, or which could limit the free flow of Christ's spirit, such as a law ; and yet it must draw bold the lines which should define and pro-claim its revelation, simple boundaries of belief and discipline and outward order, alike the guarantees of its reality as a fellow-ship or kingdom, and the visible, audible expression of its sacra-mental vocation to a non-Christian world.

Since then, nineteen hundred years have rolled by ;   time sufficient, surely, to judge how this fellowship, the Church, has performed its function ;   and whether we can with any certainty detect the divine guidance and relationship which it claims, and with any reasonableness yield it allegiance.

III

The Witness of Historical Achievement to the Claim of the Church

In the first place, the New Race has shown, on a more am-bitious field, that remarkable characteristic of the old, indestructi-bility.   It has had a no less stormy passage through time.   The armed tribes and empires over the little Hebrew boundaries gave place to the criticism of the whole world, and every known weapon, fair and unfair, of thought and word and deed.   No institution on earth has sustained such constant attacks from without and betrayals within—and the Judas works always more havoc than the Caiaphas.   Yet so far from showing signs of disappearing with its day, unexpected resources have again and again turned the worst moments of apparent failure into a new era of growth. Indestructibility may not be an argument for faith, but it is for reverence, and for serious study of the principle which secures a life so unique. For this survival has not been that of a fortress standing foursquare and uncaptured ; but that of an army with banners, moving, advancing, ubiquitous ; increasing ever, not in mere numbers—though, without the witness of missionary pertinacity, the case for the Church would be weaker—but in the width and depth of its spiritual message and in the purity of its moral ideal. Just as the Jewish race developed in largeness of faith and hope, so the Christian ; often enough, too, like the Jewish, through its sorrows and failures. The truths on which, historically, it was founded, have proved themselves to be ceaselessly and vigorously dynamic, and capable of boundless expansion and applicability without any loss of either simplicity or definiteness. They do not grow out-of-date. The noblest livers need them. Mohammedanism as a faith is static ; Buddhism and Hinduism as certainly retrograde, despite spasmodic efforts of moral and theological reform in places where they are face to face with Christianity : the situation in India, indeed, vividly resembles the conflict of religions in the later Roman Empire. The Christian explosive shatters every civilisation which it enters, making way for one based on higher sanctions. Before the war of 1914 it had become a popular article of faith that civilisation in itself was progressive. If men are wiser now, they have not yet grasped the truth which gave rise to that easy philosophy, that in a Christian civilisation the Christian motive present is, regarded broadly, always progressive. Its own swift motion, indeed, creates more difficulties for Christianity than the attacks of all its foes. The army is frequently terrified at the far-marching of its pioneers, and would cling to ancient bivouacs. Yet onward it goes, not by virtue of the courage or generalship of its earthly chiefs, nor yet by the often ill-directed ardour of its warriors ; but by something implicit in its nature, some irresistible yearning towards more perfect achievement and more profound interpretation, some persevering disgust with things that are ; in fact, by the drive of Holy Spirit.

The impressiveness of this impulse gains in force when we turn from its general movement in time to its particular influence on individuals. Inspiration is a common experience beyond any conceivable bound of the Catholic Church or of conscious religion. The poet, the musician, the artist, the thinker know it well. That does not alter the facts that the Church is the very home of spiritual experience ; that its life consists primarily in such purely spiritual energies as prayer ; that it, alone of institutions on earth, proposes to guide, heal, and perfect the soul. However Christians may live in practice, they never cease to be urged to unselfishness, humility, and love as their first glory. The love, labours, and lowliness of the Crucified stand ever before their eyes ; union and communion with Him is their single goal. And in millions, some greatly, some slowly and partially, they respond. The true history of the Church has never been written in human book, and never will be ; for it has taken place not in courts, curias, and councils where power is great and decisions are registered, but in cottages, streets, and places where men work and pray. Its spiritual fervour issues in the preaching and practising of good morals, blazes forth in conversions, mounts to God by a ceaseless series of heroisms, which are often more than martyrdoms, just because they are secret and humble and new every morning.

The Church has no monopoly of such high and holy spirit ; but it exists for it and illustrates it, not at intervals or by chance, but constantly ; and thereby is a sacrament of Holy Spirit, perpetually reserved, daily reconsecrated, in a selfish and material world. Because of the Church, the standards of mankind are doomed ever to be faced by the standards of the saints, and are forced to some measure of imitation, lest inferiority of fruits reveal too clearly inferiority of truth.

The inspiration of the Church has proved strong enough to alter the course of history, more profoundly than is often appreciated, by its production of the Christian character. And that brings us to the phenomenon of Christian missions. There are three sides of this strange and constant energy to emphasise. The first is the obvious one of " foreign " missions. Christianity is not, of course, the only missionary religion, but it is the most missionary, and the only one which seems to appeal to all peoples— white, yellow, brown, and black. Nineteen hundred years have not exhausted the impulse ; on the contrary, it has never been more eager than it is now : the last century has seen more devotion and wealth put into missionary effort than any period in history :

and the success rivals the sacrifice. But, again, not only is Christianity the most missionary of faiths, but it has the most enduring results to its credit. It began with the conversion of Southern Europe, passing on to the North and West. The consequence in every case has been the establishment and rapid growth of what we call civilisation. Civilisation[1] is primarily a growth in love and goodness, in wisdom and truth of outlook : the increase of mercy and opportunities for education alike are inevitable, when the love of Christ, and of the neighbour for whom He died, becomes the most solemn duty of men. In the missionary work which often seems so inexplicable and ill-judged to the modern Englishman, the Church seeks to do for African, Polynesian, and Asiatic what once it did for Saxon and Frank. And the task has an urgency now which is new in history. For the less advanced races suffer bitterly from the impact of the developed civilisation of the West : they are wholly at its mercy even when it wants to be disinterested and benevolent (which is, again, only the case where Christian sanctions are strong): they cannot appropriate its virtues without a long training in morality, and an education, practical and spiritual, in wholly new categories. But its vices are easy to adopt : there is no doubt that without the faith of the West many races would perish by its sins. And as it is only the Christian ethic, however im-perfect, of their rulers which saves them from the worst forms of exploitation, so it is only the Christian missionaries, those un-modern moderns who, for love of Christ, marry poverty, loneliness,

---

[1] The writer can give no meaning to the word civilisation which is barren of moral and spiritual content. Of course civilisations may degenerate and fall ; for the very gains and graces of living originally inspired by moral advance, and inevitably attendant upon it, may grow rank and abuse the soil from which they sprang. That moral decay time and again sets back civilisa-tion is only proof of the necessity of moral vigour and ideal to advance it. Herein lies the world-importance of the Church's power of revival, mentioned later in the essay. It is the best, perhaps the only, *guarantee of progress* which mankind possesses. Recent events have only shown the incapacity of intellectual advance as a guarantee, apart from moral. But the " divine discontent " and the unflagging hope of the Church must for ever climb ; the Body which exists to realise the perfection of Christ cannot be content with the moral conscience of any moment of its past, even the fairest. It looks back to no golden age. It does gaze continually on Jesus Christ, and does take courage from the achievement of individual saints,—but only that it may reach forward. This spirit is now *within* civilisation, and its surest hope : there is no precedent for its final failure yet !—what it has done in less than 2000 years is marvellous enough in our eyes.

and exile, who can and do give them the long, patient teaching, and the moral discipline, which is the hope of their future.

The third side of this missionary ardour of the Church has been less noticed, but is not less valuable as witness of the impulse of Holy Spirit. The only weapon of propaganda is *persuasion*. It has taken the Church, indeed, a long time to understand its only allowable method, the Spirit of a God who is Love, and the example of the Christ who never used force. There is no love in haste, and only a curse in force. Men find it hard ever to forgive the use of force by the Church, and their instinct is right. The regimentation of the Church of Rome even now governs disastrously the popular conception of the Catholic Church, since it suggests the atmosphere of compulsion, the use of force, or the loss of freedom in that which claims and means to be the very Body and organ of love and spiritual liberty. But in reality force has played a very small part, less perhaps than no part at all, in the expansion of Christianity. Even the words and teachings of missionaries have accomplished little enough, apart from the lives behind them. Alike the spread, the maintenance and the growth within Christian countries of Christianity has been due to the persuasion of Christ-like lives. The witness therefore of missions to the presence of Spirit within the Church does not rest merely upon the pertinacity of a peculiar and unworldly vocation amongst men, or upon the results to converted nations, or upon the constant expansion of the Body of Christ ; it rests still more upon the amazing phenomenon of lives that are *different*, of men who never teach and preach, it may be, by word of mouth, but who convert, simply by means of the beauty and power of the Spirit that is in them.

IV

MODERN PERIODS OF DECADENCE AND REVIVAL ; AND
OF INTELLECTUAL STRESS AND PROGRESS

The drive of the Spirit within the Body has in the fields of character and propaganda been constant. But there are other fields in which to the modern mind it does not seem so true. In the first place, some of the Christian centuries or generations in Europe have been not only stagnant but decadent ; and secondly, when new truth, especially scientific truth, has emerged, the fiercest resistance to it seems to have proceeded from the citadels of organised religion. These objections to " institutional religion" weigh heavily to-day ; the modern man has come to confound orthodoxy with obscurantism ; and to regard the Catholic Church, the admitted centre and strength of the Christian world, as a foe to intellectual freedom and to the discovery of truth.

It is not enough to urge that the primary duty of the Church is to conserve its revelation in its completeness and purity for the benefit of all, and to sift and test the spirits carefully and long before they are admitted to the rank of divinity. Admittedly there have been periods when general Christian standards have been low, and the authorities of the Church a byword of reproach. We need do no more than point to the fourteenth and fifteenth centuries before, and the eighteenth century after the Reformation. In the former period, the corruption at the headquarters of the Western Church can hardly be exaggerated, and it infected the whole with malign disease. Yet, paint we never so darkly the papal leadership and morals, the Catholic community never stayed quiet under the scandal. The voice of protest and appeal rose loud. Sometimes it was the voice of states, seeking to safeguard themselves against this bewildering, degenerate power, in claim so supernatural, in practice so mercenary and unholy ; and the methods of reform by general councils, and by emphasis upon the indepen- dence of the National Church, declared themselves, as at Basle and in Gallicanism. Sometimes it was the voice of a single prophet of reform, a Wycliffe, a Hus, a Wessel, a Savonarola, an Erasmus. At no time did the humbler and more persuasive speech of saint and mystic falter, of Catherine and Bernardino, both of Siena, of the German mystics and the Dutch schoolmasters, of Thomas à Kempis. Fresh springs of devotion were many, piety deep, in the century before the Reformation ; it was the liveliness of Christian devotion, not only its deadness, which made the revolt. Similarly in the eighteenth century, Christianity was not dead because its officials were cold and worldly, and because it was suffering through its new disunity the devastating experience of provincialism. The peoples waited for their Wesleys and followed them.

To say that the action of the Spirit is constant, is not the same as saying that the professing Christian world receives it equably, levelly, consistently. What is not true of any other movement of human thought is not to be thought true of religious. The facts of history only correspond to the laws of the individual mind, which moves in seasons germinal, creative, and absorptive. Far more important to any just criticism of the Church than its times of stagnation is its power of revival. This indeed has proved constant. The seasons of sloth and sin (real or apparent) have been but the prelude to some amazing outburst of spiritual energy, unpredictable, defying human probabilities, working enormous transformations, vitally changing the prevailing categories of thought. More and more it appears that in these revivals the intellectual and the spiritual combine, unwitting allies ; that is to say, the paths of the Spirit do not move merely in the province of what we call so narrowly the " religious " or still less the " ecclesiastical " ; but, for advance here, instigate and require movement in the whole higher powers of man. Thus the Renaissance and Reformation are not truly two movements, two awakenings, this intellectual and that spiritual, but two sides of one. The godliest deed of those unpleasing fifteenth-century popes was their welcoming of pagan thought. Man's failure is often enough God's opportunity ; so too the failure of His Church the Spirit of God can turn to His praise. Renaissance and Reformation act and counteract, influence and counter-influence, hurt and counter-hurt, mingle, achieve, transform, and yet leave huge tasks for the centuries of rest to work out after the centuries of tumult pass. Similarly, the age through which we are still passing shows the Spirit at work liberating spirit at once through scientific criticism and discovery, and through the emulation (at first hostile, but eventually friendly, and certainly inevitable) of the deeper moral and spiritual forces, which make available the conquests of mind to character and life.

Here indeed we stumble upon a general truth, hitherto too little recognised, we believe, both by believers and by others : that there never is, nor can be, a great spiritual movement apart from the company of an intellectual advance ; nor a great movement of mind without a corresponding burst of spiritual progress. Usually, but not always, the new knowledge or ideas function first ; and intellectual renascence passes into spiritual, as the new comes into contact or conflict with the old in the fields of faith and conduct. The Church, as the guardian, interpreter, and inspirer of the highest faith of man, is bound by its very being to sift and to test ; and it cannot do this quickly, for it tests not only by the processes of thought, but by those also of prayer and of living. The mind fares forth, the prophets cry in the desert, of the people some are inspired but most perplexed, the Church examines with a care involving experience as well as thought ; and so the Spirit's new impulse of spirit gains a home which will hold the new, now reconciled, added, mingled with the old, in trust for all men and all time. To recognise the inevitability of some such cycle is to lessen the chances of conflict and disaster, both by softening the impatience of pioneer and prophet, and also by modifying their unpopularity and terror to those whose outlook is bounded by what has been and what is. Prophet and priest have always feared and hated one another, each blind to the fact that both are ministers of the same Spirit. At the moment it seems to be the peculiar mission of the Church of England to reconcile the antagonism of the intellectual and the churchman, by saying and showing, first, that the Church has no fear of the thinker, but rather welcomes and thanks him ; that his meaning to it ultimately (however one-sided and singly-concentrated on his novelty he may be for the present) is that of a revivalist, the seer of new truth being the minister of new Spirit : and secondly, that, on the other hand, the Church of the Holy Spirit is the final critic of all new ways of thought, the final test of truth, and its trustee for the future ; in that its one interest and ministry is to add to the one treasury of truth the things new to the things old, guarding them fast and distributing them freely, not merely to the mind (which the schoolmaster can do) but to the inmost spirit and whole character of man.

This "sacramental conception" of the Church's place and work in the world is growing conscious and apparent, we believe, by that which is its best illustration, the history of the last seventy years. A crisis of mind and spirit, comparable to any in history, only less great than that consequent upon the coming of Christ Himself, declared itself in the second half of the last century. It had been gathering force for several decades, but, in this country at least, came into the open with the publication of "The Origin of Species" and of "Essays and Reviews." The one was a great and permanent book, the other a little and transient. But they served to announce to every man the two lines of new

z

thought, the one the result of the scientific investigation of the natural world, the other consequent upon the scientific historical criticism of the Scriptures. Both affected and upset the received beliefs of the Western world. The inevitable conflict of old and new took place in the religious field : it must always do so, because that is the dearest and most vital place of man's possession ; there he houses the innermost sanctities and sanctions of his being, and loss elsewhere counts nothing in comparison with loss here. Man, being of little faith, fears the diminution of his treasure more than he believes in its increase. That should not be put down to the fault of religion which is the fault of man's nature. For awhile in the seventies and eighties the world grew dark even to those of most faith ; many left the Christian fold, and among the prophets were false ones who proclaimed the death of Christ. The Church as trustee of truth seemed to small visions to be failing just when, as a matter of fact, it was performing its proper function in the most signal manner. Just as the impact of the new thought had been gradual, so too was the Church's examination and appropriation of the new gifts of the Spirit to spirits. Each was a matter of three or four decades, less than a man's lifetime, a short space for so vast a revolution and reconciliation. It would not be true yet to say that the stress is over, because, by the mercy of God, the scientists are still researching, and the critics still upon their documents. Nevertheless, not only have the main principles of reconciliation and appropriation been perceived, but the religious revival which was in progress before the crisis asserted itself has received from it that enrichment which makes the Catholic revival in the Church of England, with all its consequences within and without, one of the loveliest and strongest reformations in Christian history. Christ did not die, nor the Church of Christ fail. So far from that, to compare the Church of 1826 with that of 1926 is almost a comparison of death with life. Not one grain of spiritual treasure which the people of Jesus possessed at the earlier date has been lost ; and the gains, who shall count ? And the witness of one more revival, assured and fearless, in circumstances which it is hard to imagine can ever seem so desperate, has been added to the positive gains of truth and of spirit.

The sacrament of the Church therefore has not only survived, but has strengthened both its claims and function.

If it has done this in England, it has done so throughout Christendom ; for what is true of the triumph of Holy Spirit in one part of the field holds good for all. We do not pretend anything so absurd as that the English Church has—if the military metaphor be allowed—fought and won this battle alone ; the old guard of Rome and the East lay behind ; sharpshooters, pioneers, and allies, protestant, modernist, and independent, played essential, if unorganised and sometimes embarrassing, parts in the forefront ; but the brunt fell upon that Communion which, under the standard of the Catholic creeds and the discipline of Apostolic order, had the necessary freedom and mobility to march to the guns and make contact with the armies of science. The work of the Church of England through the scientific and critical revolution has been at least of an importance sufficient to justify at the bar of history her position in temporary separation from the fellow-communions of East and West. She has done for the Catholic Church that which Rome was not free to do, and which the East was too far from the centres of modern thinking to comprehend. It is not merely that Catholicism has not suffered by the new categories ; new knowledge of the world has meant in every direction new understanding of God ; criticism of the two Testaments—the fiercest effort of mind in history—has not only revealed the rocks on which they stand, but has given a re-interpretation of their place and meaning in religion which is well-nigh a new revelation ; the concentration of study upon the figure of Christ has but lit up the unique majesty of His perfection and love. That such is now bound to be the result of the nineteenth-century renaissance in the religious sphere can scarcely be denied. A revolution of mind, in itself glorious and wonderful, has led to glorious revelation of God. The Church has lost nothing but what is good to lose ; it has gained rich reality and outpouring of Holy Spirit.

V

The Catholic Church a Sacrament of Holy Spirit to the World

And by the Church we mean deliberately and primarily the Catholic Church. Of course all Christianity everywhere has gained by the passing of error or inadequacy of understanding ;

but these inadequacies were more vital to the Protestant position of seventy years ago than to the Catholic; the Catholic verities at the base of Protestantism have stood the test, and have been more and more liberated from outworn dressings. But far more important is the sight, ever growing in clearness, of the function of Catholicism as the trustee for all Christendom of the religion of Christ; and therefore of the sacramental value of the historic Church for the truths deepest and clearest to the world, those which reveal God to man, and man to himself. Protestantism is greatly valuable not only to the world of men, but to Catholicism itself; yet all the time, in the last resort, it depends upon the Church of which it is a criticism. The Catholic Church of early days is its acknowledged inspiration, the Catholic Church of these days its unacknowledged buttress. It is not with any wish to decry the Protestant bodies that we suggest that, in their general meaning, they stand to the Church which is the formal sacrament of Holy Spirit to mankind as, in the sphere of Christian devotion, the sermon stands to the Eucharist or momentary prayer to age-long liturgy.

The Ecclesia, which is to fulfil so sacramental a function, will necessarily show outward and visible signs of its inward grace. Inevitably that will be displayed outwardly amongst other things by some ordering or articulation representative of its perpetual witness. Order and Succession are not ecclesiastical inventions, burdens grievous to be borne, but the unavoidable clothing of the Church's sacramental meaning. You cannot break up and re-start divine sacraments, or they cease to carry their own evidence of validity. The continuity befitting a sacramental race the Catholic Church shows impressively. Its continuity even with that previous election of the Hebrews is unchallengeable, because at the critical point of process the two eras are perfectly united by the Person of Christ, and the expansion is the command of Him who elects. Continuity, however, is a possession of no great independent value in itself; as a guarantee and servant of the sacramental vocation of the Church it is vital. It carries with it also the requirement that we should read the lengthening tale of the historic Church as modern theologians and historians agree to read that of its pre-Christian beginnings. No one has seriously attempted that; perhaps, for the very reason that the essential meaning of the Church to the world has been too vast and far-reaching for isolation and description. It was not the mistakes and backslidings of the Jewish people which made their meaning to mankind, except in so far as these prepared the way to plainer knowledge of God. Nor is it the mistakes and sins of the Catholic Church which matter first, however much they have hindered the coming of its own proposed kingdom of goodwill amongst men. Its meaning and worth to the world have been just this constancy of ideal and of the high beliefs which inspire it. The histories of doctrine, which have been thoroughly written up to and including the Reformation, show that these " high beliefs " are not static, but ever developing in depth and fruitfulness. Other chapters of history confirm the swift development of mind and spirit in the countries ruled or influenced by Christianity, and in none other ; for even Japan's copy of the Christian West forms no exception. The peculiar phenomenon of Christian missions testifies both to the confidence and unselfish energy of the disciples of Holy Spirit, and also to the power of persuasiveness wielded by lives so inspired through all the ages. Not that we assert for one moment that the Christian countries are Christian, or that the Catholic Church at its best moments has been worthy of the Spirit which it knows, loves, and teaches. But it lives and grows, seeming only to be purified and enriched by the successive attacks of states and thinkers and savants ; inspiring millions to seek virtue and love ; and to find both in weal and woe the knowledge and peace of God. So the main fact and true meaning of this Church, apostolically articulated, unbrokenly continuous, become clear. It is the one sacramental institution of all time, sacramental of the gift of Holy Spirit, instituted by God, trustee of the birth, death, resurrection, and eternal love of Jesus Christ the Lord.

The phrase " institutional religion " is to-day unpopular, because men see the blemishes of the institution, and wish it holier, freer, still. So much the better. For the enemy of the Church, and that which cramps it most, is not new knowledge or any criticism, but, always and only, sin. The very request, from within or without, for greater holiness and fulness of the Church will bring its own fulfilment, and makes straight the path of Holy Spirit. Priests and preachers may now cease to demand allegiance to the Catholic Church merely as an obligation, and can call men into loyal fellowship with it as a vocation. There can be nothing higher, holier, and truer than to be part of this sacrament of ageless and unaging celebration, consecrating gifts to the world which grow ever richer and purer. The Catholic Church can cease to fear the splendid labours of mind in particular fields, which by dispelling ignorance and making godly use of the intellectual gifts of God, reveal not only scientific but religious truth. Science will cease to lose so heavily by its departmentalism, and good thought will have freer course to the ends of the earth, when thinkers and scientists refuse any longer to weaken the Church by a distrust and aloofness caused by conflicts, fears, misunderstandings which are now too old. For this sacrament to the world will only be complete when it becomes the world, and the Royal Priesthood is universal.

THE REFORMATION

BY A. HAMILTON THOMPSON

CONTENTS

I

Character and Effects of the English Reformation

In one of his poems George Herbert, that most loyal and devout son of the Church of England, writes with enthusiasm of the perfect lineaments of his spiritual mother, and contrasts her studied moderation of aspect and attire with the allurements of the wanton of the hills upon the one hand, and upon the other with the dishevelled array of the wayward inhabitant of the valleys. Between Rome and Protestant Nonconformity with its warring sects, the British Church, double-moated by the grace of God, pursues a middle path and finds in the mean her praise and glory.[1]

Such congratulation, if it came from a source less sincere and pure, might be accused of insular self-complacency. But from the doctrine and rites of the Church of England, as organised under the Elizabethan settlement, Herbert derived the spiritual nourishment which satisfied his soul and quickened his pious imagination. Born in 1593, when Whitgift was prosecuting the struggle between episcopacy and puritanism, he died in 1632, the year before the translation of Laud from London to Canterbury. Amid the strife of rival parties, he preserved that ideal of the historic position of the Church of England as a true branch of the Catholic Church, claiming its right to hold the essentials of Catholic doctrine, and exercising the ministry of the Word and Sacraments through a properly ordained priesthood, which, through all the vicissitudes which that Church has undergone, has never been lost. The example and teaching of Herbert and of those who shared his convictions, within a century from the breach with Rome, remind us that the Reformation, in spite of the efforts of extremists and the uncertainty of individual aims, did not effect a complete severance with the past. So far as England was concerned, it was a work of reconstruction. It had its full share of the errors of judgment which beset the restoration of all ancient fabrics : it suffered from the competition of rival

[1] George Herbert, *The British Church.*

architects, some of whom preferred demolition to repair : the compromises which were the result of their disputes led to diversities of opinion which have lasted to our own day and are still hotly in debate. But the historic basis of the fabric was preserved. The renovated structure stood firm upon its old foundations, and the fact was apparent, not only to those whose faith was rooted in tradition, but to those also who had vainly endeavoured to bring it under the domination of novel schemes and systems of reform.

In considering the Reformation and its effects upon the Church of the present day, we must face it as a fact of critical importance in our national history. It brought changes with it which cannot be overlooked or disregarded at will. Contemptuous references to "the so-called Reformation," implying that it was a mere illusion, are out of date. They have never carried weight with serious historians, nor have they improved the credit of those who have indulged in them. It is equally impossible to be satisfied with the view that the Reformation was primarily a political movement to which religious considerations were entirely subordinate. Politicians, it is true, used the movement freely to serve secular ends : its history is so closely connected with politics that it is constantly difficult to distinguish between its religious and secular aspects. But in this respect the Reformation is not peculiar : the arguments founded upon the influence of Tudor monarchs and their ministers on its progress might be applied, *mutatis mutandis*, to the age of Constantine, Justinian, or the Saxon emperors. Or again, the adverse verdict which has been passed upon the Reformation in the light of social and economic changes which accompanied and followed it depends upon a romantic and sentimental conception of the Middle Ages which is at variance with fact. In the breaking-up of the medieval polity the Reformation took a prominent part, but as a consequence, not as a cause of a tendency which was present in every department or life and thought.

II

The Break-up of the Medieval Polity

When all is said and done, the religious force which was behind the Reformation remains. Although its energies were frequently diverted into alien channels and to unworthy ends, its motive power was the necessity of ecclesiastical reform. The demand for the reform of the Church in head and members had arisen within the medieval Church itself, during the period which had succeeded the disastrous end of the strife between the papacy and the empire. The theory of a dual control of Christendom by a spiritual and a temporal monarch, each exercising within his own sphere an authority derived from God, and working in harmony towards the same end, the establishment of the kingdom of God on earth, had come into existence as the result of the need of temporal support by the spiritual power. It had failed in practice : the continual attempt of one power to overrule the other contradicted its possibility.

1. *Failure of the Conciliar Movement*

The field of strife was narrowed into a contest between a German king, with a shadowy claim upon the imperial crown, and a papacy in complete subservience to a foreign monarch, its ally and captor. When the Schism succeeded the captivity of Avignon, the problem of the rivalry between spiritual and temporal rulers receded into the background. The new problem was the preservation of the unity and spiritual sovereignty of the Church beneath an undivided rule. To the would-be reformers during the conciliar period, their immediate task was the settlement of internal polity and discipline. Re-statement of dogma did not occupy their minds : their business was to prevent the recurrence of schism by restoring the papacy upon a sound basis. Their efforts at reconstruction failed, however, in face of the obduracy of the popes to reform by conciliar methods. Their divided interests and jarring schemes were confronted by the august tradition of the papal monarchy, able to hold its own against an unwieldy opposition with no concerted plan. National ambitions and jealousies crossed the path which led to Catholic unity ; and the dispute between pope and council gradually took the form of a new alternative between an united Church governed by papal mandates and a group of Churches, federated by a nominal recognition of the spiritual authority of the Roman pontiff, but ruled by local law and custom and, as a logical consequence, closely allied with the policy of national governments.

2. *Lollardy and Orthodoxy*

England, during this period of dispute, adopted no independent policy of her own. Throughout the great schism she had been faithful to the Roman pope : at this juncture she remained within the Roman obedience. Apart from the natural divergency of her attitude towards the papacy from that of France, the accession of the house of Lancaster to the throne had ensured a *régime* of strict orthodoxy. During the troubled reign of Richard II, Lollardy, with its popular interpretation of Wycliffe's theological and political doctrines, had gained some ground, in spite of the efforts of bishops to repress it. But, even then, it had not attained the proportions of an organised movement. Opponents of clerical government coquetted with it, as long as it seemed to promise an attack upon the temporal endowments of churchmen as the main feature of its programme ; but they were not prepared to connive at heresy, and the development of heretical doctrine forfeited it their support.[1] Archbishop Courtenay dealt promptly with its academic defenders at Oxford and forced them to recantation or flight : its adherents in country districts were persons of little influence and, with some exceptions, of low social standing, who were isolated by the vigilant policy of the bishops. Although cases of heresy are frequent in the ecclesiastical records of the fifteenth century, they represent individual opinions which have a common likeness but no common ground of action. The attempted rebellion of Sir John Oldcastle, the most prominent Lollard of the Lancastrian period, was a complete failure ; and popular disturbances, from the Peasants' revolt in 1381 onwards, though they doubtless found encouragement from sympathisers with Lollardy, were symptoms of social unrest and discontent with which theological opinion had no fundamental connection. If unusual intellectual activity, in an age of mediocrity, led Reginald Pecok, a bishop of the Church, into heresy, his heterodoxy had nothing in common with popular Lollardy. The clergy of his day found in him its most powerful and eloquent defender against detractors, and his subsequent deprivation and imprisonment were due as much to his political sympathies as to his theological vagaries.

[1] For the attitude of John of Gaunt to Wycliffe and his followers, see *Fasciculi Zizaniorum* (Rolls Ser.), pp. 114, 300, 318.

3. *England and the Papacy*

In this orthodox atmosphere, however, the spirit of nationalism, though not aggressively active, was not absent from ecclesiastical affairs.　It is impossible to attempt to trace in this context
the successive steps by which the conception of the medieval
Church in Europe had become indissoluble from that of the
supremacy of Rome.　The first assertions of that supremacy lie
far back in history : the authority of the pope, alike as bishop of
the old capital of the world, as exercising a patriarchate founded
upon the apostolic origin of his see, and as the successor of the
prince of the Apostles, had developed into a spiritual monarchy
wielded by a prelate who claimed the title of vicar of Christ and
commanded the obedience of kings and princes.　It could hardly
be said that England was backward in recognising this supreme
power.　The Norman conquest had been sanctioned by a papal
bull ; and, if the Conqueror had decreed that he himself was the
sole judge within his realm of the apostolic pretensions of any
pope and of the validity of his mandates, what pronouncement
could be more reasonable as coming from the faithful supporter
of Gregory VII, whose throne was menaced by schism ?
William, it is true, made a careful distinction between the civil
and ecclesiastical spheres of law, so as to prevent mutual encroach-
ment ; but it would be a mistake to interpret this action as wholly
in the interests of the control of the Church by the Crown.　On
the contrary, disobedience to the Church incurred coercion by
the secular arm, while unauthorised civil intervention with the
Church's affairs was prohibited.[1]　The freedom thus granted to
the ecclesiastical courts was greatly curtailed by the legislation of
Henry II.　By the constitutions of Clarendon, the judicial power
of the Church over the laity was limited by safeguards, appeals to
Rome were carefully restricted by the necessity of reference to
the king's approval, the question of the possession of disputed
benefices was brought within the final cognisance of the king's
court, and the Crown claimed the right of nominating bishops
and of controlling the subsequent elections.

The spirit of the constitutions of Clarendon, however, was
Caesarism, not nationalism.　The papacy, indeed, during the
century in which it rose to its highest eminence, was the champion

---

[1] See the ordinance printed in Stubbs, *Select Charters,* ed. Davis, pp. 99, 100.

of local freedom against secular tyranny. The pope who supported Becket encouraged the nascent independence of the Lombard republics and humbled Barbarossa. During the conflict between John and his barons, the influence of Innocent III and of the Church generally was on the side of the rebels ; and the refusal of John to accept the papal nominee to the see of Canterbury added fresh ground to the quarrel. The submission of John to the pope, with all its humiliating circumstances, was a temporary relief from the struggle, and its immediate consequence was the absolution of England from the interdict. Not until the position was changed, and the pope appeared on the side of John, was the action openly condemned as a national disgrace.[1] It was at any rate with the aid of the archbishop appointed by the pope that the barons eventually forced from the king those concessions which, subjected to a wider application than was actually contemplated by their framers, came to be regarded as the chief guarantee of national liberty ; and, in the forefront of the charter in which they were embodied, the freedom of the *ecclesia Anglicana* was formulated. In so far as this famous clause defines the position of the Church within the realm of England, it may be said to countenance the theory of a national Church. But the tyranny against which the English Church protested was not papal, but regal, the tyranny of a national king. The charter in which the protest occurs was witnessed by a primate who was also a cardinal of the holy Roman Church and by the papal subdeacon who had received John's resignation of his crown to the pope : at the head of the names of those who counselled its re-issue in 1216 and 1217 was that of the apostolic legate Gualo. It would be useless to argue that the Church of the English nation was an Anglican body which claimed to be independent of the Holy See. It was an integral part of a Church which is described in the official language of English bishops as Catholic, Apostolic and Roman.

As time went on, circumstances changed. Even Innocent III was willing to absolve John from his oath to observe the Great Charter. The popes of the thirteenth century interfered freely

---

[1] In 1216 the barons, according to Matthew Paris, spoke bitterly of the relations between John and the Pope : " Haec facit charissimus in Christo filius papae, qui suum vassallum tam liberum et nobile regnum inaudita novitate subiugantem tuetur." The same author credits them with strong expressions against the pope : " Ut quid ad nos extendit Romanorum insatiata cupiditas ? . . . Ecce successores Constantini, et non Petri."

in national politics, siding with kings against their subjects and fostering the growing power of France in the interest of their own domination in Italy, until Boniface VIII, asserting his sovereignty with a boldness which exceeded that of his greatest predecessors,[1] overreached himself and destroyed the autocracy which he sought to vindicate. During this period, and still more during the century which followed, a strong current of anti-papal feeling set in throughout England. Popes who were subjects of a hostile power made intolerable demands upon the compliance of the nation. The system of reservation and provision of bishoprics and rich benefices traversed the rights of cathedral chapters and patrons of churches, and challenged the competence of royal courts of justice. Appeals to the papal Curia, provocative of long and expensive litigation, overrode the jurisdiction of prelates and their delegates. Bishops found their appointments to vacant dignities and prebends forestalled by the appearance of proctors of foreign cardinals and papal officials to prosecute the claims of their principals to fill such vacancies. The payment of first-fruits to the pope and of periodical fees in lieu of personal visits to Rome or Avignon landed bishops in debt and involved them in financial complications with Italian bankers.[2] The papal court was a market in which spiritual privileges were bought and sold, and the pope's collectors in England kept a watchful eye upon all possible sources of revenue. Parliament took advantage of the most successful period of Edward III's war with France to pass the statutes of 1351 and 1353, in which provisors and appellants outside the king's courts were subjected to legal penalties ; and these statutes were more stringently enacted forty years later. Praemunire, however, long remained a dead letter [3] ; and the statutes of Provisors merely had the effect of establishing a *modus vivendi* between pope and king, without benefit to the freedom of the Church as postulated in the Great Charter.

---

[1] See the declaration in the bull *Unam sanctam* (Extrav. Comm. I. viii. 1) : " Porro subesse Romano Pontifici omni humanae creaturae declaramus . . . omnino esse de necessitate salutis." This may be a logical inference from the claims put forward by earlier popes, but it goes far beyond their actual statements in the unconditional inclusiveness of its terms.

[2] Valuable evidence upon this subject may be gathered from the wealth of financial detail contained in the unpublished register of Archbishop Melton (1317–40) at York, under the heading *Intrinseca de camera.*

[3] For recent commentary upon the statute of 1393 and its working, see W. T. Waugh, *The Great Statute of Praemunire* (*Eng. Hist. Rev.*, xxxvii. 173–205).

No temporal legislation, as a matter of fact, could affect the spiritual supremacy of the pope. Anti-papal statutes were passed in parliament without the concurrence of the spiritual lords, who shrank from compromising the allegiance which they owed to the visible head of the Church. So far as the Crown was concerned, a deliberate rejection of the Roman see as the source of ecclesiastical preferment would have been impolitic.

The pope might be restrained from impinging upon the rights of English patrons; but, if English incumbents were to enjoy the advantages of plurality and non-residence, the sanction of the Holy See was necessary. The parliaments of Edward III and Richard II, in safeguarding the temporal power of the Crown, insisted on the theory that ecclesiastical endowments were the gift of royal and noble benefactors, and that the descendants of such donors inherited claims which could not be set aside by papal interference[1]; but they asserted no principle which vindicated independence of the spiritual supremacy of Rome for the Church in England.

The fact that, upon so important a point as the patronage and disposal of benefices, the common law of the realm held its own is by no means to be overlooked or minimised. At the same time, in matters within the competence of ecclesiastical courts, the judges resorted to no national code of law. The canon law of England was the canon law of the Western Church, and the canon law of the Western Church was papal law, in whose authoritative texts the canons of early councils and the opinions of individual fathers of the Church were reinforced by an enormous mass of papal pronouncements upon every conceivable subject. Many of these, as a very casual study of the first five books of the Decretals will show, had been delivered with relation to English cases : under Alexander III and Innocent III, England had taken its full share in augmenting the law of the Church as decreed by the popes. It is true that successive archbishops of Canterbury had issued constitutions in their provincial synods, and that these had their due weight in Church courts. It might also be possible, as in the case of Pecham's constitution concerning pluralities, that a primate, by inadvertence or excessive zeal, might

---

[1] This theory was expressed in the statute of Carlisle (1307), and repeated in the preambles of the statutes of 1351 and 1390. See *Statutes of the Realm*, i. 150, 316 ; ii. 90.

contradict the purport of an apostolic decree. The final interpretation, however, depended upon the Roman solution of the problem. Further, even had provincial constitutions possessed a local superiority to the law of the Church as a whole, they formed in themselves no complete body of law. Their volume is relatively insignificant, and, comprehensive as they are, they provide no full or satisfactory answer to the questions which came before ecclesiastical lawyers in their ordinary practice. All that they contributed was a general summary of the law of the Church upon subjects which constantly came within the scope of that practice ; and in this respect their authority was conditioned, like those of the legatine constitutions of Otho and Ottobon, for which English lawyers had at least equal respect, by the terms of documents included in the vast body of canon law. In the fifteenth century Lyndwood, with a masterly command of his sources, provided the authoritative commentary upon the provincial constitutions, and, in so doing, deserved the gratitude of English practitioners. But Lyndwood's book is not a *Corpus juris*. It is merely a guide to the interpretation and amplification of the *dicta* of English primates by reference to canon law and to the Roman civil law on which the foundations of canon law were laid. The appearance of Lyndwood's *Provinciale* did not mean that the English lawyer abandoned Gratian and the Decretals : all that happened was that he was enabled to find his way about them with much less trouble than before, and this is the advantage which Lyndwood still offers to the reader who would derive profit from his pages.[1]

Lyndwood's exposition of the provincial constitutions is almost contemporary with the victory of the papacy over its conciliar opponents. It is unequivocally the work of a lawyer who recognises the papacy as the fountain-head of ecclesiastical law. It belongs to a period at which the idea of an English national Church was as yet unformulated. But, even so, the principle of nationalism was gaining ground. There was a current theory that Henry V, in his joy at the termination of the great schism and his devout gratitude for his successes in France, had promised

---

[1] See the essay on Lyndwood in Maitland, *Roman Canon Law in the Church of England*, 1–50. Maitland's conclusions on these points are inevitable in the light of ecclesiastical documents: see, *e.g.* the elaborate arguments upon points of law in *Hereford Reg. Trefnant (Cant. and York Soc)*, pp. 73–90, 103–114. In these documents the appeal is entirely to Roman law, civil and canon.

to allow Martin V an unprecedented control over English benefices at the disposal of the Holy See.[1] This was not the policy of the regency which, at Henry's early death, entered upon the administration of the *damnosa haereditas* which he bequeathed to his infant son. The story of the translation of Kempe to the see of York in 1425 illustrates the principle that, where the temporal power chose to press its will upon the pope, his policy was to comply with its demands. An examination of the appointments to English sees from the middle of the fourteenth century onwards indicates that, even where the papal right of translation was exercised to avoid the difficulties which might arise in consequence of the Statutes of Provisors, the will of the Crown was not ignored.

The normal method was for the pope to confirm the nomination made in the name of the Crown. The chapter of the cathedral church received the *congé d'élire* : on the transmission of the election to the pope, the letters of provision were made out which were necessary to the spiritual validity of the appointment. It is possible that, in unimportant sees, cathedral chapters were allowed a free hand. But the fact remains that the Crown, as founder and patron, treated appointments which were nominally elective as presentations to benefices in its gift, with a growing disregard of constitutional formalities. Its nominees were given custody of the temporalities of vacant sees to which they were elected and provided as a matter of course. At his election the nominee of the Crown was already virtually in possession. Moreover, a comparison of such documents as the official headings prefixed to episcopal registers will show that, while bishops reckoned their pontifical years from the date of their consecration or translation, the act by which their temporalities were restored to them was regarded with increasing importance as putting them in full control of their diocesan jurisdiction.[2]

This was the position upon the eve of the Reformation. The supreme authority of the pope in matters spiritual was respected

[1] See *Cal. Papal Letters*, viii. 216–18. The whole series of documents of which the letter of Eugenius IV, containing the statement that Henry V had this intention, is one, is very instructive as illustrating the relations between the Crown and papacy in the case of a disputed appointment to a see.

[2] This may be remarked in the rubrics at the beginning of the registers of the 15th and early 16th century bishops of Hereford. These omit all mention of election. In 1504 Bishop Mayew is stated to have been called to the see by apostolic authority and the nomination of the Crown : in the case of Bishop Bothe (1516), only nomination by the Crown is mentioned.

implicitly. Whether he was the true source of episcopal jurisdiction is still a moot point on which canonists disagree : large as
are the assumptions which can be and have been made on behalf
of the vicar of Christ, there are obvious limits to the powers of a
vicar. But, as vicar of Christ, he possessed a jurisdiction which
transcended that of any diocesan bishop and was superior to the
patriarchal authority of the successor of Peter. He was the " universal ordinary," wielding powers which superseded the mandates
of bishops and the decisions of their judges in the ecclesiastical
courts. If a bishop was slow in executing a commission entrusted
to him in his own diocese by the Holy See, and in a matter which
he might reasonably consider to belong to his own province as
local ordinary, the pope could transfer execution to a commissioner
who could take the business in hand without reference to the diocesan. An offender who was unwilling to stand to the judgment
of his bishop could evade it by procuring absolution from the
collector who acted as the pope's agent in England.[1] At the
same time, where the temporal power was concerned, the pope
was obliged to walk warily and submit to compromise. As the
papacy, from the temporal point of view, fell into the position of
an Italian principality, it became involved in the intricacies of
national politics which it could no longer direct, and its power of
enforcing its will upon kings and their ministers was seriously
curtailed. Thus, at the period of the English Reformation, the
English Church, although subject to the jurisdiction of Rome,
had become definitely national in composition. If, in the early
part of the sixteenth century, Italians were promoted to English
sees, this was merely a logical result of the understanding between
the papacy and the government. Where their mutual interests
were concerned, pope and king were ready to accommodate each
other ; but, where those interests collided, the advantage lay with
the Crown. The Church, in fact, was in service to two masters ;
and, in a trial of strength between the two, the allegiance of the
Church was necessarily influenced by the temporal sovereign
who could bring the most direct pressure to bear upon her.

[1] Instances of both types of case mentioned here may be found in the history
of the small chantry college of Irthlingborough (*Assoc. Archit. Soc. Reports*
xxxv, 267 *sqq.*). The authority of the " universal ordinary " is stated explicitly
in the bull *Sancta* (Extrav. Comm. I. iii. 1) : " Sancta Romana ecclesia quae
disponente Domino super omnes alias ordinariae potestatis obtinet principatum a
Deo, utpote mater universorum Christi fidelium et magistra."

III

THE REFORMATION ON THE CONTINENT

The truth of the matter is that, at the beginning of the sixteenth century, the preservation of the papal jurisdiction depended upon the compliance of the pope with the will of temporal monarchs. At no time was the spiritual influence of the papacy lower. The power which, three centuries earlier, had stood for righteousness against the kings of the earth was reduced to defending its precarious position upon Italian soil by fostering political combinations against the foreign powers which threatened its security in turn. Its hope lay in its ability to maintain the balance between national jealousies. Meanwhile, however, there were ominous signs that, in the pursuit of its Italian policy, its hold upon Christendom was relaxed. In countries whose orthodoxy was beyond question, that orthodoxy was a matter of national conservatism. Spain, of all nations, repressed heresy most sternly and effectively ; yet the attitude of the Spanish kings to the Holy See during the century which followed the union of the crowns of Castile and Aragon was by no means that of submissive children. Their filial obedience, constantly tried, was tempered by the consciousness that their spiritual parent needed to be kept in order by admonitions and even by open threats. In the north of Europe, heresy developed openly. The climax of tendencies which could no longer be kept in abeyance was reached in 1527, when the forces of the Most Catholic king who was also ruler of Germany, a mixed multitude of divided creeds and diverse national sympathies under the leadership of a French renegade, attacked and plundered Rome. The pope lay at the mercy of Charles V. Two centuries and a quarter earlier, Dante, with all his hatred for Boniface VIII and the corruption of the papal monarchy, had seen with horror the lilies enter Anagni and Christ bound and reviled once more in the person of His vicar.[1] In 1527 pious minds might still feel compunction for the captivity of the pope ; but the catastrophe was the result, not of such an effort to re-assert a spiritual dominion over princes as gave the fall of Boniface VIII a certain nobility, but of a long course of diplomacy in which that dominion had been well-nigh forfeited. Henceforward the

[1] *Purg.* xx. 86 *sqq.*

business of the papacy was to regain its spiritual authority, with the help of the nations which were still ready to admit it ; and the problem of the internal reform of the Church became once again a pressing question.

IV

THE ANGLICAN SOLUTION

Nevertheless, the disaster had come, and must in any case have come, too late for the revival of a spiritual monarchy, uniting all national Churches into a compact body under one head. On the one hand, revolt against that headship was spreading, and involved rebellion against the whole doctrinal system of which the pope was the chief representative. The attack upon traditional dogma, with its appeal to the freedom of private judgment in matters of faith, assailed the entire mechanism which guarded the faith of the medieval Church. New systems of spiritual polity were invented to suit new theories : a large portion of the Christian world was split into sects, united only in their rejection of the doctrine of the transmission of divine grace through the ministry of a hierarchy which culminated in the person of the vicar of Christ. On the other hand, this manifold division and lack of settled purpose were confronted by the hope that unity still could be maintained under a spiritualised and reformed papacy. To hold the political aspirations of the papacy in check was not to hinder its exercise of legitimate authority, but to promote its influence in its own proper sphere and to justify its claim to dominion over the souls of men considered as members of the Christian commonwealth, apart from their position as members of distinct nationalities.

Thus the Reformation upon the continent became a conflict between two ideals of reform. In face of destructive schemes which did away with the old ecclesiastical system and all that it represented, the conception of the reform of the Church from within, long dallied with and postponed, became a practical object. The choice lay between the abandonment of outward unity for a sectarianism guided by individual caprice and the maintenance of the compact symmetry of ecclesiastical order under the quickening influence of a renewed spiritual fervour. To both parties the idea of a hierarchy without the papacy was inconceivable. The necessity of a vicar of Christ as head of the visible Church, as supreme legislator and tribunal of appeal, was the question at the root of their differences. Impugners of the papal jurisdiction attacked the whole system which it had overshadowed and included beneath its working. The defenders of that system set themselves to strengthen and assert the papal authority as the permanent safeguard of its active existence. Between a spiritual autocracy on the one hand and the will-worship of the individual on the other there could be no intermediate path. At best, the alternative to unquestioning surrender of the will and judgment was the adoption of a loose congregationalism, which might assume temporary form under the control of some commanding personality, but had no guarantee of permanence or consistency.

This alternative has long survived the circumstances in which it arose. To the continental protestant of to-day it is as present as ever : it finds expression in the *obiter dicta* of members of our own Church who are more closely in touch with novel readings of theology than with the teaching of history. We are invited to see, in the English Church as the Reformation settlement left it, one of many protestant sects, allied in general sympathy with the reformed systems of the continent, and differing from them only in its retention of the semblance of an antiquated and obsolete machinery. No candid student of the English Reformation will overlook or endeavour to explain away certain features in its development. It began in a formal renunciation of spiritual allegiance to Rome, and in the transference of that allegiance to the Crown as supreme head of a national Church. The political circumstances in which this came about severed England from its connection with the great Catholic powers and made it seek alliances with the princes who had embraced the protestant cause abroad. As a natural consequence, close relations arose between the continental reformers and that party in the Church which regarded the breach with Rome as an opportunity for welcoming novel experiments in doctrine and ecclesiastical government. During the reign of Edward VI this party was in the ascendant : the English liturgy of 1549, which preserved a close continuity with historical models, was superseded three years later by a form of common prayer and worship in which the influence of foreign refugees was allowed to have a disproportionate part. Had that *régime* continued longer, it is not improbable that the Church of England would have been led irrecoverably into a position of mere sectarianism. As it was, this revolutionary progress was checked by the accession of Mary, followed by the temporary return to communion with Rome. But, if conservative sentiment was strongly in favour of strict orthodoxy on the old pattern, it also had a strongly nationalistic bias. Reconciliation with the Holy See was closely associated with an unpopular foreign alliance, and was accompanied by a policy of religious persecution, which, although from one point of view it was no new thing and had the sanction of English law, was nevertheless a tactical error of the gravest kind. In no respect was Mary more to blame than Henry VIII : her motives indeed were purer than his. Persecution, however, of loyal subjects for the sake of religion was a very different thing from persecution exercised, with whatever ruthlessness, against the supporters of a foreign jurisdiction in opposition to the national monarchy ; and the fact remains that, rightly or wrongly, the Marian suppression of heresy affected the minds of Englishmen with a greater and more permanent feeling of repulsion than was caused by the tragedies of the Pilgrimage of Grace and, at a later date, the Rising of the North.

It would be fruitless to speculate what might have happened, had Elizabeth chosen to accept the Roman obedience. However tortuous the policy which she followed at the opening of her reign, there can be no question that in the course which she took she tested national sentiment and gauged it accurately. The Elizabethan settlement was not a glorious thing. It was a compromise which included parties and persons of very diverse views in one religious establishment. Its motive was political : the Church was regarded by the framers of parliamentary legislation as a department of state in which uniformity of practice was an essential condition of stability.[1] The formulae of doctrine which emerged from the settlement were couched in studiously ambiguous terms. Only a special pleader will argue that the Thirty-Nine Articles say one thing and mean another ; but their compilers, where points were in dispute, succeeded in saying two things in one breath

---

[1] The relations between Church and State under Elizabeth have lately been re-examined by Dr. W. P. M. Kennedy, *Elizabethan Episcopal Administration* (Alcuin Club), and his conclusions fully stated in his introduction (vol. i.) to a series of episcopal injunctions and other documents.

with remarkable adroitness. There was no question of concili-
ating a definitely Romanising party in the Church. What was
needed was to provide a *modus vivendi* between the party attached
to episcopal government and the innovators who came back from
exile in centres of foreign protestantism in love with alien methods
of Church polity, a common ground upon which both might
work together as agents of the state, irrespective of mutual
differences.

The idea of the Church as an instrument of national policy
was not new. It was a corollary of the theory of national
monarchies which had superseded the medieval ideal of a world-
wide empire, and during the later Middle Ages, as we have seen,
the civil government had exercised a prepotent influence over the
appointment of bishops. It was a new thing, on the other hand,
to see a temporal ruler controlling a Church within which rival
factions, divided upon fundamental points of doctrine and practice,
strove for the mastery. It is easy, of course, for a certain type of
critic, who regards the Elizabethan settlement merely as a clever
stroke of statecraft, to speak disparagingly of the religious issues
which it involved : such a view neglects the genuine conviction
which lay beneath the controversies of the period, and looks upon
their superficial aspect with hardly concealed scorn. We may
sympathise more entirely with the attitude of the faithful Romanist, who, in that day as now, could not conceive of the Church
without its visible head and postulated that catholicity implied
obedience to the Apostolic Roman see. His Church was busy
with the work of reforming itself. New influences had arisen
in its borders, bent on kindling religious fervour and on strengthening the papal position as the first necessity in their programme.
The faith of the medieval Church was being defined and restated
at Trent ; old heresies were being condemned ; dogma was
assuming a settled rigidity. To such a spectator England had
fallen into heresy ; her monarch had incurred excommunication ;
the subjects of the pope were prescribed and hunted down, fined
and imprisoned. The Elizabethan Romanist was ready to risk his
life on behalf of the Holy See, and in so doing he found no foes
more dangerous than the bishops of the Church of England, policing
their dioceses and keeping as strict a watch upon the disaffected
as their predecessors had kept upon the Lollards. He himself
was naturally incapable of discerning in the religious body which

prosecuted him a member of the true Church : it was an apostate communion to which the dignities of the historic Church of the country had been transferred, and its endowments, or such of them as had survived the rapacity of the Crown and the court, had been appropriated. His view survives to-day, not as a mere suspicion or as a weapon of controversy, but as a genuine conviction. The Church of England might congratulate itself on putting an end to the papal usurpation ; but all the while it was usurping the titles, goods and foundations which it had wrested from their ancient holders and had misapplied.

Such a point of view has its logical basis, and outward appearances did much to strengthen it. The traditional liturgy of the Church, round which the fabric of medieval faith had been built and compacted, had gone with all its venerable associations, and was banned as popish and superstitious. In its place there was a form of worship which, if it had not entirely obliterated, at any rate partially obscured its most familiar aspects, and was celebrated with a bareness of ritual in strange contrast with the solemnity of the ancient rite. The process of denuding churches of all ornaments which recalled the past went on under the direction of prelates whose learning and love of antiquity were somewhat inconsistent with their destructive zeal. Yet, amid all these changes, the old machinery of ecclesiastical government remained unimpaired and in perfect working order. Within less than a quarter of a century, four reigns had produced startling fluctuations. Henry VIII had transferred the papal authority over an orthodox Church to the Crown. Under Edward VI the Church had been protestantised. Mary had brought it back into submission to Rome. Elizabeth had deromanised it and subjected it to interests of state. But, through all this, the processes of ecclesiastical law had gone forward in the old way. Apart from the changes of constitution in certain cathedral churches consequent upon the suppression of the monasteries, and from the creation of a few new dioceses, there are few alterations to be traced. The ordinary jurisdiction of bishops remained as in the past. Officials and vicars-general still exercised their delegated authority. In the official records of English dioceses for this period traces of contemporary change are few and far between. Bishops were deprived of their sees and burned for heresy, but the business of diocesan administration, founded upon centuries of long practice, was not interrupted for a single day.[1] The machine whose efficiency in the past had been so largely controlled by papal law could work without the help of the pope.

More than this, in spite of the changes of *personnel* among the bishops themselves, the episcopal succession was not visibly broken. It was preserved throughout the reign of Edward VI at a time when foreign non-episcopal bodies were gaining ground in the country and novel systems had their best chance of success. Without the maintenance of the episcopate, uniformity of religious practice was impossible: the Church, split up into sects, would fall into anarchy and become the prey of civil strife. Episcopacy formed the essential link with the past which ensured order and discipline. It is possible that this, which is not the highest view of the institution, was the most powerful motive which influenced the filling up in 1559 and 1560 of sees vacant by the death or deprivation of Marian bishops. Even so, the consecration of new bishops was not undertaken without the careful provision of valid means to secure the historic continuity of the office. The controversy which has raged round the consecration of Parker has wasted much energy on both sides ; but it has at any rate had the effect of displaying the uneasiness and uncertainty of opinion prevalent among those who have sought to impugn the act.[2] The ground of attack has constantly shifted from one objection to another, until it is reduced to the mere presumption that the act was invalidated by the intention of the consecrators. To this *petitio principii* common sense has only one answer, that, so far as human judgment is capable of defining private intention, the end which the consecrators had in view was the transmission without breach of the apostolic gifts derived in the beginning from the Founder of the Church. Otherwise, their action would have been pointless.

The preservation of episcopal order and jurisdiction, with the far-reaching consequences which it involved, is the distinguishing feature of the English Reformation. It had the inevitable effect of restoring confidence, as time went on, to a Church distressed by internal conflicts of opinion. The hold which foreign pro-

[1] Episcopal registers for this period were not always well or fully kept ; but this was due, not to interruption of business, but to negligence in keeping official records posted up to date.

[2] See the searching review of the whole controversy in Dixon, *Hist. Ch. England*, ed. Gee, v. 205 *sqq.*

testantism had obtained upon the English Church weakened
throughout the Elizabethan period. Puritan zealots found their
cherished doctrines incompatible with episcopacy. In a primate
like Whitgift, waging war on behalf of law and order, they saw
an authority as dangerous to their ideals as any pope, and an
authority backed by all the resources of the civil government.
For the stringent measures which the prelates of the sixteenth
and seventeenth centuries employed against papists and puritans
alike we can have little sympathy in an age of easy toleration.
But it is impossible not to recognise that, with all the drawbacks
to spirituality involved in the conditions of the Elizabethan settlement, the historic conception of the mission of the Church as
the accredited guardian of the appointed means of divine grace
held its own and steadily grew in strength. The position of a
national Church, free from external interference, which Parker
and Whitgift had used their power to uphold, was defined un-
mistakably by Laud and his supporters. In such men as Lancelot
Andrewes, Jeremy Taylor, and George Herbert the power of
that Church to attract and to nurture, through its ministry of the
Word and Sacraments, the highest type of religious devotion was
manifest. Loyal to the Reformation and recognising the protestant attitude of their Church to Rome, they yet proved that
such loyalty was consistent with a theology and with forms of
worship hallowed by antiquity, and justified the *via media* taken
by the English Church as scriptural, primitive and truly Catholic.

It is true that their work was temporarily checked by the
puritan revolution. But the religious disorders of the Commonwealth proved the impossibility of the maintenance of civil order
without the principle of cohesion provided by the national Church :
sectarianism meant confusion and anarchy. The conflict between
royalist and republican, between High Churchman and precisian
left its permanent mark upon English thought. It perpetuated
within the Church itself that opposition of parties which had been
inherited from Elizabethan times. On the one hand, orthodox
divines upheld episcopacy and its divine origin : on the other, the
formalism of episcopal government and the mechanical theories
which it seemed to encourage were undervalued by the defenders
of less confined views of the operation of divine grace. It must
be conceded that the political events of the close of the seventeenth
century left behind them an orthodoxy which laid more stress

upon bare forms than upon the spiritual meaning of ordinances, and that the Church of the eighteenth century, as a whole, was spiritually at a low ebb. It is a mistake, however, to suppose that the revival of spiritual life which showed itself openly during the second half of the century was wholly promoted by disaffected enthusiasts. It was accompanied, as for example in the Wesleys, by a devout desire to give warmth and reality to the services and doctrines of the Church ; and it was only the distrustfulness and reluctance of ecclesiastical authorities which alienated the would-be reformers and laid the foundations of modern nonconformity. The unreadiness of a privileged institution to set its house in order was still as manifest as it had been three hundred years before.

V

The English Church of the Future

Yet the vicissitudes which the Church of England has undergone since the Reformation have failed to weaken the conviction of her children to-day that she, as a true and living member of the Church of Christ, is in full possession of the means of grace and of the authority for their dispensation. Those means may at times have been underprized, their nature may have been disputed, that authority may have been minimised ; but no careful student of her history can overlook its witness to the constant working of the Spirit of God within her borders. From the days of the Evangelical revival onwards, she has made continual progress as a spiritual force. Under the influence of the Tractarian movement, she recovered a lively sense of her mission and its opportunities which, in spite of opposition and internal controversies, has permeated her whole organisation at home and abroad, so that even those who still raise the cry of warning against a betrayal of the principles of the Reformation argue almost unconsciously from a point of view complacently familiar with much that an earlier generation denounced. The marked growth of mutual forbearance between ecclesiastical parties, though not wholly without its dangers, is due to a heightening of spiritual ideals visible in every department of the Church's activities. The truth has come home to all Churchmen that the life of the individual soul needs for its quickening and sustainment a full sense of loyalty to its corporate responsibilities, that such life finds its true refreshment in that sacramental union with the Head of the Church which binds all faithful souls together in unity and supplies the Church with never-failing strength. And, while this closer cohesion is being effected among members of the Church of England, the need of it is felt as strongly in the religious bodies which stand outside its pale. Contemporary movements in nonconformist communions in England and among protestant bodies abroad are signalised by the desire to abandon a policy of isolation and dissidence, and to seek a common ground of reunion with those who, through all changes and chances, have held to the historic conception of the Church and its ministry.

At the present time, it is possible to look back too apprehensively to the perils which beset the English Church at the Reformation and to the risks which she has subsequently encountered. By identifying ourselves too closely with her past anxieties and controversies, we may lose our sense of perspective. These things cannot be overlooked by the historian, but a sound judgment will regard them as dangers incident to the growth of a living organism which has survived them and gathered from them strength to meet and overcome the trials of the present and the future. Throughout her post-Reformation history, the Church of England has given proof of a steadfastness of purpose and a power of recovery amid such perils which we may well review with thankfulness and confidence. The path on which she entered in the sixteenth century was new and untried, and its beginnings were dark and uncertain ; but no one who watches her progress along it can doubt that she was guided by the Spirit of God, acquiring stores of spiritual energy which have revived her in periods of faintness and have quickened her to fresh and accumulated effort. Under this guidance, she has achieved successes which were beyond the dreams of the medieval Church. She has prosecuted her apostolic mission and planted apostolic faith and order in regions outside the hope and imagination of the most sanguine of Crusaders. Without novel or sensational experiments, adhering closely to traditional lines of doctrine and practice, she has made her influence felt as a permanent element in the life of the Christian Church, fostering in her sons a devotion and a temper of mind which have added no small strength and supplied new impetus to the spiritual activities of the modern world. From the protestantism of her early reformers she has found her way to a positive assertion of her claim to an abiding place in the Catholic community from which she has never separated herself by any action or declaration. The Reformation severed old ties and disunited bodies of professing Christians who owed obedience to the same Lord : it put an abrupt end to an old order of things which had long threatened disruption. The restoration of that visible unity of the Church in its medieval form is hardly possible to-day. But, to those in whose minds the hope of reunion is strong and is not dominated by conceptions, however venerable, belonging to one particular age of human history, the English Church has its part, and perhaps a deciding part, to play in the work of restoring Catholic unity to the Church at large, so that its Lord, at His coming, may present it to Himself a glorious Church, not having spot or wrinkle, or any such thing.

THE ORIGINS OF THE
SACRAMENTS

BY NORMAN POWELL WILLIAMS

CONTENTS

I

INTRODUCTORY

It has been said that the radical difference between the Catholic and the Protestant presentations of Christianity consists in the fact that the former is built upon the idea of justification by grace imparted through the sacraments, and the latter upon the idea of justification by faith only. Like most theological epigrams, this sentence purchases its concise and arresting form at the cost of exact veracity. Yet it contains at least a kernel of truth ; for it is a matter of common knowledge that the sacraments occupy a central and dominating position in the spiritual life of the Catholic Christian which the specifically Protestant type of devotion does not concede to them. A recent writer has described the part now played by the sacraments in Protestant Christianity as being, on the whole, that of " optional appendages " to religion [1] ; and the theory of their nature which this part presupposes may not unfairly be stated in the following terms :—

1. The sacraments are not primarily " means of grace," but rather means whereby the believer publicly declares that he has already received grace. Considered in themselves, they are not *signa efficacia* but *signa mera*.

2. They may, however, become, relatively to given individuals, and in a secondary and improper sense, " means of grace," or " efficacious signs," in so far as their impressive dramatic symbolism works upon the subjective emotions of the worshipper, and serves as an aid to devotional auto-suggestion. This subjective efficacy may be heightened by the reciprocal hetero-suggestion which the members of a devout congregation naturally exercise upon each other when assembled for common participation in a solemn rite. When the collective imagination of the worshipping community is keyed up to a given pitch of exaltation, Christ may be said to be " present "—in the sense that His universal presence is then realised with special vividness—and to fulfil the promise " Where two or three are gathered together

[1] A. E. J. Rawlinson, *Authority and Freedom* (1924), p. 97.

2 B

in my name, there am I in the midst of them " ; though this promise has no special reference to the sacraments, and may come to fruition in meetings for Bible study, praise, or prayer of any kind.

It follows that there can be no such thing as an absolute duty to assist at sacramental ceremonies (except, presumably, for the officials who are commissioned to organise them).   An individual citizen, who does not care for military pageantry, clearly requires no justi-fication for habitually absenting himself from the " trooping of the colour " ; and in like manner a Christian, who finds that the symbolic actions known as " sacraments " leave him cold, must be at liberty to discard them from his personal religious practice in favour of other modes of approach to God more congenial to his temperament, without forfeiting the title of " a good Christian." It cannot on this showing be affirmed that the sacraments are " generally necessary," but only that they are *ceteris paribus* helpful, " for salvation."

In clear and unmistakable contrast with this " declaratory," " subjective," and " optional " theory stands that which is characteristic of Catholic Christianity.   We may, for the sake of convenience, and without begging any question, describe the former as the " minimising," and the latter as the " maximising " view of the nature of sacraments.   For the " maximiser," the sacraments are the most precious things in life, the breath of his nostrils and the staff of his pilgrimage.   In his description of them the epithets " declaratory," " subjective," and " optional," as explained above, are replaced by " unitive," " objective," and " generally necessary."   He will, indeed, join with the " mini-miser " in affirming the universal presence of Christ and of the Holy Spirit in every place and at every time ; but he will add to this the conviction that They are specially present in the sacra-mental actions, not merely in the sense that the divine power is then imaginatively realised more than at other times, but in the sense that it is objectively accessible and operative in a quite unique degree and after a manner to which Bible-reading and the like offer no analogy, for the purpose of creating, maintaining, or restoring that secret union with God which is the basis of the supernatural life of the soul.   And, whilst not eliminating *in toto* the idea of a certain subjective efficacy which may be deemed to flow from the visible, audible, or tangible symbolism, he will maintain that this is always accidental and relatively unimportant, and may on occasion (as in the cases of the baptism of infants and the absolution of unconscious persons *in extremis*) be dispensed with altogether. If it be appropriate to translate the Catholic theory, like its rival, into terms of " suggestion," it may be said that the thoughtful and instructed " maximiser " would not by any means deny that part of the efficacy of the sacraments (except in the two cases just mentioned) may flow from auto-suggestion or from congregational hetero-suggestion, though he would, in the light of his belief in the Communion of Saints, enlarge the conception of the " congregation " so that it would always include both the whole Church militant here in earth and also " angels, archangels, and all the company of heaven." But he would also assert that, in addition to these influences, which represent the working of his own mind and of other finite minds, there is present an element of divine invasion and hetero-suggestion—a power which comes entirely from without and which transforms and quickens the emotional forces evoked by the mere symbolism of the rite from within, as in an estuary the brimming salt flood-tide of the ocean penetrates, suffuses and overwhelms the fresh waters of the river gliding to meet it—a mighty Energy which cannot be rationalised or explained away as the resultant of merely " endopsychic " factors, but proclaims itself, to those who have experienced it, as simply " given," objective, catastrophic, numinous.

This conception contains an implicit challenge, which has been replied to by the counter-cry of " Magic ! " In so far as this counter-cry involves the allegation that sacramental grace is believed by Catholic Christians to operate irrespectively of the moral dispositions and will of the recipient, or to be based upon some supposed power of men to constrain the divine rather than upon the voluntary condescension of the divine to meet human need, its refutation may be found in any text-book of Catholic theology. But in so far as the term " magical " is merely a disparaging synonym for " including an element of objective efficaciousness," it may be candidly admitted that the Catholic Christian must make up his mind to endure this reproach with equanimity. For it belongs to the essence of the Catholic position that the sacraments are in some sense *causal* ; they are *verae causae*, and not merely symptoms, of the reception of grace. It would be a task of considerable complexity and difficulty, and it is in any case unnecessary for the purposes of this essay, to find a more precise definition of the mode of this causality which would be equally applicable to each of the specific operations of the several rites commonly known as "sacraments." The task has indeed been attempted by Latin theology, and six centuries of speculation have not proved sufficient for its solution. Nor need English Churchmen feel themselves necessarily bound to defend any one of the hypotheses which have from time to time been produced by outstanding theologians of the West.[1] Though Article XXVII employs the Thomist conception of "instrumental causality" in connection with baptism,[2] it would be unreasonable to assert that we are on that account debarred from holding, if we think fit, the Scotist theory of "occasional causality," which represents the sacraments not so much as *causae per quas*, but rather as *causae sine quibus non*, and conceives the relation between the reception of the outward sign and the bestowal of the inward grace as one of "pre-established harmony," resting upon the appointment of God. Even St. Thomas relapses into vagueness with regard to this subject, when he tells us that "the sacraments of the Church have their virtue specially from the Passion of Christ, the virtue whereof is in a certain manner joined to us (*quodam modo nobis copulatur*) by the receiving of the sacraments."[3] The theologians and official documents of the Eastern Church confine themselves to a general affirmation of a causal relation between the reception of the sacraments and the reception of grace, and do not attempt any narrower determination of this subtle and mysterious question.

Such, in rough outline, are the two main theories of the place of the sacraments in our religion which at present divide the allegiance of Christians ; and though we do not forget the existence of mediating positions and points of view, in practice the choice presents itself as one between two clearly contrasted alternatives

---

[1] For an account of these (frequently over-subtle) speculations, see *The Catholic Encyclopaedia*, xiii. p. 302.

[2] "Baptism is not only a sign of profession, and mark of difference, whereby Christian men are discerned from others that be not christened : but it is also a sign of Regeneration or new Birth, whereby as by an instrument (*per quod tanquam per instrumentum*) they that receive Baptism rightly are grafted into the Church . . . etc."

[3] *Summa Theol.*, III. lxii. 5.

The individual Christian must necessarily order his devotional life either on the assumption that the sacraments are "generally necessary" means of objective grace, or on the assumption that they are no more than optional pieces of declaratory symbolism. It is self-evident that such a choice must be determined by the mind and the purpose of the Founder of Christianity, if they can be discovered. But the question of our Lord's intentions relatively to the place and the importance of the sacraments turns upon the further question, whether He can be truly said to have " instituted " sacraments or not ? It is universally agreed that our Lord's teaching, explicit and implicit, was confined to the broadest and most fundamental principles of Christian faith and conduct. He never concerned Himself with otiose or non-essential details. He did not act in the spirit of a Rabbinical casuist, nor lay down minute ceremonial ordinances for the purpose of making a " hedge around the Law " ; He is not likely (if we may so say without irreverence) to have devised fresh modes of tithing mint, anise and cummin, or to have invented an improved type of phylactery. If, then, the true view of the sacraments is that they are "optional appendages to the Christian religion," it is not likely that they can be traced to His direct institution ; and, conversely, if they can be traced to His institution, it is certain that they must be a great deal more than " optional appendages." I venture to draw especial attention to this argument, inasmuch as the remainder of this essay presupposes its validity. If our Lord, with all His indifference to mere ceremonial, did actually " institute " the rites known as "sacraments," then those rites must be of the very highest and most central importance in the Christian life ; and it is difficult to see how such an importance can be ascribed to them, unless it is the case that through them God does something for man which man cannot do for himself, that is, unless they are the means or vehicles of supernatural grace. In other words, there would seem to be in logic, as there always has been in Catholic belief, a tenacious mutual connection and cohesion between the ideas of " Dominical institution," " general necessity for salvation," and " objectivity of operation." And if " Dominical institution " can be proved, then the further question which has sometimes been mooted—namely, whether it might be possible to regard the sacraments as Spirit-inspired ecclesiastical developments, which, though not commanded or even contemplated by the historical Jesus, have nevertheless acquired an obligatory character through the witness of the Church's corporate experience to their actual efficacy—manifestly does not arise.

II

THE NUMBER OF THE SACRAMENTS

Before, however, proceeding to investigate the strictly historical question of the " Dominical institution" of the sacraments, it is necessary to fix with greater precision the exact denotation of the term " sacraments," as it will be used in this essay. The term " sacrament" has borne different significations in the history of the Church, varying from the indefinite meaning sanctioned by the usage of patristic times, when it could be applied to almost any solemn rite or part of a rite, to the clear-cut denotation enforced by the sevenfold enumeration of the Schoolmen, or the even more restricted enumeration familiar to us from our own formularies. Article XXV appears to confine the term " sacrament," in the sense of a rite for which divine institution can be claimed, to Baptism and the Lord's Supper, describing the rest of the mediaeval seven (" those five commonly called sacraments "), in somewhat loose and sweeping phraseology as " such as have grown partly of the corrupt following of the Apostles, partly are states of life allowed in the Scriptures "—neither of which descriptions applies to Confirmation. From the standpoint of Catholic Christianity as interpreted by the " Vincentian Canon," it would seem that the general distinction drawn by the compilers of the Thirty-Nine Articles between " sacraments of the Gospel," that is, sacraments which belong to the very heart of the Catholic redemptive system—and " those that are commonly called sacraments," that is, other rites or institutions which have been given the name of " sacraments " in order to make up the mystical number of seven—is amply justified. But it may be questioned whether Article XXV, the language of which, as we have pointed out, has been somewhat carelessly framed, draws the line at precisely the right point, when it places Baptism and the Lord's Supper alone in the former category, and assigns all the rest of the mediaeval seven indiscriminately to the latter. It is certainly true that Matrimony is not specifically a "sacrament of the

Gospel " ; for our Lord expressly declared, when He repealed the Mosaic permission of divorce, that He was founding nothing new, but merely republishing a natural law which had existed " from the beginning." [1] Nor is it possible, in the light of the historical evidence collected by Father Puller,[2] to describe Unction as a sacrament instituted by Christ ; it is rather a sacrament gradually shaped by the Church, during the first three centuries of our era, out of an indefinite and floating custom of anointing sick people as a means for the " spiritual healing " of physical disease—a custom which would seem to have been employed by the Twelve during our Lord's ministry, presumably with His approval, and is commended by St. James, but concerning which it cannot be shown that our Lord gave any direct command for its continuance. It is doubtless the case that Ordination would be generally held by traditionalist Christians to be a " Dominical sacrament " in the sense of resting upon our Lord's own declared will ; but it can hardly be counted as a *sacramentum evangelicum*, inasmuch as its bearing upon the salvation of its recipients would not be claimed by any Catholic writer to be of the same direct and immediate character as that of Baptism, Confirmation, Penitence, and the Eucharist. These four, in fact, would seem to be sharply distinguished from the other three, either in respect of the origin or of the operation claimed for them or of both ; and it may be said that Article XXV would have represented the underlying mind of historical Christendom more accurately if it had divided the conventional "seven sacraments" into four of the first category and three of the second, rather than into two and five.

The conclusion which follows from the foregoing considerations is, that the " sacraments," with which we are concerned in this essay, and which constitute the core and foundation of Catholic sacramentalism (construed in accordance with the Vincentian Canon, and in independence of scholastic and Tridentine definitions), are *four* in number, namely, Baptism, Confirmation, Penitence, and the Eucharist or Lord's Supper. This enumeration is not very far different from the earliest list produced by ecclesiastical authority during the English Reformation, that

---

[1] Mark x. 5 ff. The statement above remains true, even if the "Matthaean exception " (Mt. v. 32, xix. 9) be regarded as having proceeded from the lips of our Lord.
[2] *The Anointing of the Sick in Scripture and Tradition* (2nd edn. 1910).

contained in the " Institution of a Christian Man," or " Bishops' Book," of 1537 ; but we may claim that our numbering appears to do more justice to Confirmation than the work just mentioned, which relegates the completion of Baptism to the same category as Orders and Extreme Unction.[1]

It is, however, possible to simplify the subject-matter of our inquiry still further ; for Penitence, Baptism, and Confirmation were in primitive Catholicism not three distinct sacraments, but rather parts of, or moments in, one great cleansing, regenerating, and Spirit-imparting rite, which was conceived as both symbolising and effecting the complete transition of the soul from sin and heathenism to full Christian life ; which in the earliest days had no one authoritative name, but seems to have been vaguely and popularly designated as " making the act of faith " (πιστεῦσαι) or " being illuminated " (φωτίζεσθαι) or even as " baptism " *tout court*, but understood as including both the preliminary Penitence and the subsequent Laying on of Hands. This single original rite of entrance to Christianity we will designate by the word " Initiation." It is worth while observing, in order to elucidate certain issues which will appear at a later point in this essay, that the main historical factor which has split this single initiatory rite into three is the rise and universal diffusion of the custom of " infant baptism," an ecclesiastical development of which the New Testament writings contain no mention. What is now known in the West as " Confirmation " is the conclusion of the initiatory rite, cut off and made into a separate sacrament, which is postponed until the arrival of the neophyte at " years of discretion," in order that at least a part of the process by which admission is gained to full membership in the Church of Christ may be experienced by him under conditions of full consciousness and intelligent responsibility.[2] And what is known in both West and East as " Penitence " or " Penance " (*poenitentia*, μετάνοια), which normally, though not invariably,[3] involves an oral con-

---

[1] C. Lloyd, *Formularies of Faith put forth by Authority during the Reign of Henry VIII* (1856 edn.), pp. 12S, 129.

[2] This separation of Confirmation from Baptism did not become universal in the West until the sixteenth century ; and it is still unknown in the East, where the Chrism which is believed to be " the seal of the gift of Holy Spirit " is administered immediately after Baptism, even to infants.

[3] For an account of the circumstances under which, according to present Latin discipline, Penance may be administered without any oral confession, see Schieler-Heuser, *Theory and Practice of the Confessional* (1906), p. 645 ff.

fession of sin by the penitent, is the beginning of Initiation, detached from its original context and formed into a substantive rite to serve as a remedy for *post*-baptismal sin, a " second plank after shipwreck " ; and post-baptismal sin is a phenomenon which in the nature of things is more frequent when Baptism is habitually administered to unconscious infancy than when it is received only by adults as the crown and seal of a conscious conversion of the will to God.[1] But Initiation is still very generally performed, in its primitive shape, as a single unitary process including Confession, Washing, and Laying on of Hands, in the mission field, where most catechumens are still persons of adult age, and occasionally in Christian countries, also in the case of adults.

The two fundamental sacraments, therefore, which form the irreducible core or nucleus of the conventional septenary scheme, are Initiation and the Supper of the Lord. It is the historical connection of these with the Founder of Christianity which we now propose to investigate.

III

The Evidence of the New Testament

Such an investigation would, two centuries ago, have been a comparatively simple task, as it still would be if the New Testament documents were universally and unquestioningly accepted at their face value. If we leave out of account the inconsiderable " Sacramentarian " and Socinian sects on the Continent, and the Quakers in England, it will be true to say that all theologians of the precritical epoch—Roman, Anglican, Reformed, Lutheran—were united in affirming that the Dominical institution of Baptism, at least, is proved—not merely by the regular administration of this rite to converts from the Day of Pentecost onwards, and by the exalted language in which New Testament writers describe its spiritual import, as a mystical participation in the death, burial, and resurrection of the Redeemer,[2] and as the " laver of regeneration " [3]—but by indubitable words of the Lord Himself ; firstly, those in which He foretold to Nicodemus the necessity of the

---

[1] This is not necessarily an argument against the custom of infant baptism ; see below, p. 412, n. 1.

[2] Rom. vi. 3–9.   [3] λουτρὸν παλιγγενεσίας, Tit. iii. 5.

new birth " of water and the Spirit " for all who would enter
the Kingdom of God [1] ; secondly, the solemn charge addressed to
the Twelve by the risen Christ, in which He formally instituted
the sacrament, enjoining His hearers to " make disciples of all
nations, baptizing them in the name of the Father and of the
Son and of the Holy Ghost." [2]   Doubtless there was not the
same unanimity in regard to Confirmation and Penitence ; but
the Dominical institution of the Eucharist, once more, would
have seemed self-evident to all, or nearly all, Christian thinkers,
despite their diversity of opinion as to the right doctrinal interpretation of this supremely sacred rite.   The command " This
do in remembrance of me," embodied once in the *Textus Receptus*
of St. Luke's Gospel [3] and twice in St. Paul's account of the Last
Supper,[4] combined with the declaration " Except ye eat the flesh
of the Son of man and drink his blood, ye have no life in
you . . .," [5] would have appeared so overwhelmingly conclusive
in regard to our Lord's intentions of founding a permanent means
of communion with and commemoration of Himself, that they
would hardly have felt it in need of support from the practice of
the Apostolic Church or the teaching of others of the canonical
books.   And when it is remembered that, for theologians of the
epoch which we have mentioned, these testimonies were set, as
it were, in the adamantine framework of a verbally inspired
volume, thus sharing in its supernatural inerrancy, it will be
seen that for many centuries the question of the Dominical
institution of the greater sacraments was not so much settled as
incapable *a priori* of being discussed.

Those who are acquainted with the present position of the
minute critical and historical investigations, which have been for
the last century and still are being carried out with reference to
the origins of Catholic Christianity, will not need to be reminded
that such a general agreement amongst theological scholars is
now a thing of the past, and that the connection of the sacraments
with the historical Jesus is precisely one of the matters which are
most hotly disputed.   It will be convenient at this point to
sketch briefly the change which has come over the attitude of
Christian scholars towards the Scriptural testimonies just quoted

---

[1] John iii. 5.   [2] Matt. xxviii. 19.
[3] Luke xxii. 19.   [4] 1 Cor. xi. 24, 25.
[5] John vi. 53.

Not only has the belief in the divinely guaranteed literal inerrancy of the sacred volume vanished, so far as we can see for ever, but the historical reliability of the principal proof-texts, considered merely as human evidence, is called in question. This is specially true of those which, like the Nicodemus passage, occur in the Fourth Gospel. It is no longer possible to assume that the sayings attributed to Christ by the great mystical writer whom we know as " St. John " represent *verbatim* reports of His *ipsissima verba*, reproduced with phonographic accuracy. Even the most conservative estimate of the value of the Fourth Gospel must admit that the discourse-matter embodied in it is to be regarded rather as a unique blend of Dominical teaching and of the Evangelist's own meditations, a blend in which it is now all but impossible to distinguish the two ingredients, than as a bare transcript, without commentary, of some of Christ's actual sayings. Hence we are not at present in a position to rule out the suggestion that the saying about " water and the Spirit " in John iii. may represent not so much what our Lord actually said on any given occasion as what the Evangelist, after a lifetime spent in the fellowship of baptized and spirit-endowed people, was convinced that He meant ; and so long as this possibility remains open, the scientific inquirer will be debarred from using these words (for all the depths of spiritual truth and splendour which he may discern in them) as assured historical evidence for the conscious prevision by our Lord, during His earthly lifetime, of the saving effects which Christian Initiation would have during the long centuries which were to succeed His death.

Similar considerations apply to the cardinal proof-text traditionally adduced on behalf of the Dominical institution of Baptism, Matt. xxviii. 19. It is now generally agreed, amongst Biblical scholars other than those of the Roman Catholic Church, that the Gospel which stands first in our New Testament can only be described as that " according to Matthew " in the sense that it may include sections of a work by him, perhaps the " Logia " stated by Papias to have been compiled in Aramaic by the Apostle Matthew.[1] The same consensus of critical opinion affirms that the final editor of this Gospel, whoever he was, cannot have been an eyewitness of the events which he records (his dependence upon the Marcan narrative is enough to prove this) ; and that

[1] Eus. *H.E.* iii. 39.

his editorial principles and methods permitted him a degree of freedom in the way of edifying and haggadic modification or amplification of his sources which is hardly in accordance with the more exacting standards of modern biography, and which (in one or two passages [1]) is utilised in a manner reminiscent of the unrestrained thaumaturgy of the extra-canonical Gospels. If this be so, it is difficult to discover any consideration which decisively excludes the suggestion that " Matthew's " attribution of the baptismal charge to the risen Christ may be dogma couched in a quasi-historical form, rather than history proper : that it represents not so much what Christ actually said as what the Christians of *c.* 80 A.D. were convinced that He ought to, and must, have said.[2] Such a suggestion draws a certain amount of force from the fact that the text Matt. xxviii. 19 contains the Threefold Name in its most clear-cut and technical form, " Father, Son, and Holy Ghost "—a form which occurs nowhere else in the New Testament, and of which the next recorded instance is to be found in the *Didache* [3] (which can hardly be dated earlier than A.D. 100). It is urged that a literal acceptation of " Matthew's " statement, that the use of the Threefold Name was prescribed at the very beginning of Christian history by the supreme authority of the risen Lord, is incompatible with a candid interpretation of the Acts and Epistles, which show that Baptism was for long administered " in the Name of Jesus " only, and that the doctrine of the Trinity itself, as summed up in the scholastically precise formula, " Father, Son, and Holy Ghost," was the comparatively late product of a slow and gradual development, which even in St. Paul's lifetime had not advanced further than the embryonic stage reflected in the primitive benediction " The grace of our Lord Jesus Messiah, and the love of God, and the fellowship of the Holy Ghost, be with you all." [4] But if it is a possible supposition that the final editor of the first Gospel has

---

[1] *E.g.* xvii. 27 (the stater in the fish's mouth) ; xxvii. 52, 53 (the resurrection of the " saints ").

[2] The suggestion, first made by F. C. Conybeare, in the *Zeitschr. f. N.T. Wissensch.*, 1901, p. 275 ff., and afterwards adopted by Prof. Kirsopp Lake in his inaugural lecture before the University of Leyden, that the words " baptizing them in the name of the Father and of the Son and of the Holy Ghost " are a late dogmatic interpolation into the text of St. Matthew, has been effectively dealt with by the late Dr. F. H. Chase, *Journal of Theological Studies*, vi. 483 ff., " The Lord's Command to Baptize," and need not be considered here.

[3] c. 7.   [4] 2 Cor. xiii. 14.

(doubtless with the best intentions) read back the developed Trinitarian theology of his own day into the baptismal command, the suspicion is inevitably aroused that the baptismal command itself may be no more than a dogmatic projection upon the background of the past. Such reflections do not, indeed, constitute a decisive disproof of the Matthaean affirmation of the formal institution of Baptism by Christ ; but they are thought by many to remove it from the category of reliable evidence into that of uncertain statements, on which it would be precarious to build a historical case. But if both of the sayings on which the Dominical institution of Baptism is based recede into the limbo of the historically dubious, the institution itself recedes with them : and the field is left open for the hypothesis now widely accepted by the Protestant scholars of the Continent, that the origins of Christian Baptism are to be found, not in any word or declared intention of Jesus, but rather in the Jewish custom of the baptism of proselytes, or in the baptism of John—one or other of which is assumed to have been continued, on their own authority, by the earliest disciples as a natural but purely non-mystical method of symbolising admission to the Christian group, to have been gradually invested, by tradition and usage and other factors which will claim attention presently, with a supernatural awe, and to have been finally ascribed, by a process of *ex post facto* reasoning familiar to all students of ancient religion, to the command of the Saviour Himself.

The evidence for Christ's institution of the Eucharist, as a permanent rite designed to be celebrated after His death and in memory of it, has undergone a similar process of attrition. It is not denied that our Lord at the Last Supper blessed a loaf and a cup, and gave them to His disciples, declaring them to be, in some sense, His body and His blood ; but the question which is debated is that of the intention with which He did so. Was the solemn action, which He then performed, of a purely *ad hoc* nature, consummated once and for all with the view of impressing upon the circle of His intimate friends, and upon them only, the significance of the terrible events which lay before Him ? or did He consciously mean to found a definite liturgical or sacramental ceremony, to be continued by His followers after His visible presence should have been removed from the earth ? If we could be certain that His lips actually uttered the command

"This do in remembrance of me" (τοῦτο ποιεῖτε εἰς τὴν ἐμὴν ἀνάμνησιν), the question would be settled. But this crucial saying, which has hitherto been taken to constitute the main, if not the only Scriptural ground for believing that our Lord intended His action to be repeated, is preserved only in the Gospel of St. Luke (according to the generally received text) and in St. Paul's First Epistle to the Corinthians. And its occurrence in the text of the third Gospel is now held to be highly questionable, inasmuch as it is omitted, at this point, by the great fifth-century Graeco-Latin Codex D, by four Old Latin MSS.,[1] by Tatian, and the Jerusalemitic Old Syriac—facts which have caused such careful and conservative scholars as Westcott and Hort to excise it from the Lucan account of the Last Supper, as a "Western non-interpolation" which has crept into the text of St. Luke through scribal assimilation to I Cor. xi. 24, 25.[2] The statement, therefore, that Jesus commanded His disciples to repeat in memory of Him the symbolic actions which He performed at the Last Supper must, in the present state of our knowledge, be taken as coming to us on the authority of St. Paul, and of St. Paul only. But the authority of St. Paul, in regard to a matter of historical fact of which he cannot, in the nature of the case, have been an eyewitness, is very far from being unchallenged. It is not, indeed, disputed that the Apostle of the Gentiles was in all good faith reproducing what he had learnt from the nucleus of original disciples, who had known the Lord in the flesh. But, as in the case of the Matthaean command to baptize, the possibility that the injunction "This do in remembrance of me" may be due to unconscious aetiological invention spontaneously recurs to the mind. A comparison of the four versions (given by the three Synoptists and St. Paul) of the words spoken by Christ at the delivery of the Bread and of the Cup reveals the fact that no one version agrees precisely with any other, and textual criticism suggests that St. Luke's autograph may have placed the distribution of the Cup (*without* the words "This is my blood") before that of the Bread.[3] It is a reasonable inference from the somewhat confused state of the evidence that the Apostolic Church

---

[1] a l ff[2] i.

[2] *The New Testament in Greek* (1881), Appendix, pp. 63, 64.

[3] D a l ff[2] i omit Luke xxii. 19[b]–20, thus making the cup of v. 17 to be the Eucharistic Cup.

was not in possession of a single, uniform, and rigidly stereotyped account of our Lord's sayings and doings at the Last Supper. But if such oral tradition as existed continued to be fluid for some decades after the event to which it refers, it is not by any means impossible that the words "This do" may have imperceptibly crept into that stream of it which was destined to reach St. Paul, as an *ex post facto* legitimation of a custom, originally perhaps based on mere sentiment, of repeating at the common meal of the Christian community, in remembrance of the Master, the significant acts which He had performed at "the last sad supper with His own." If this suspicion is justifiable, the Eucharistic command "Do this . ." joins the baptismal command "Make disciples of all the nations, baptizing them . . ." in the twilit realm of historical uncertainties. The solitary link connecting the sacramental practice of the Church with the intentions of the Master has been, if not irretrievably snapped, at least attenuated to a degree of fragility at which it can no longer bear the strain which the traditional theory of the Eucharist demands.

It might be objected that, even if the cogency of the foregoing considerations be admitted, they do not prove that our Lord did not institute the sacraments, but only that the existing documentary evidence is insufficient to show that He did. And it might further be suggested that there is at least a possibility of basing the belief in the Dominical institution, not so much upon a couple of proof-texts as upon the universal and immemorial custom of Christendom, which would seem to imply a source not less authoritative than the will of the Saviour Himself. But at this point the non-Catholic critic produces his final, apparently irresistible and overwhelming argument, which (if its validity be admitted) becomes in his hands a logical flail or bludgeon whereby all the attempts of the Catholic apologist to find a basis for traditional sacramentalism in the words and actions of Jesus are mercilessly smitten to the ground. This argument is founded upon the assumption of *the eschatologically limited outlook* of Jesus. During His lifetime (it is contended) Jesus believed that the existing world-order was on the point of dissolution, that the lightnings and terrors of the End might at any moment burst upon mankind, that within a space of time to be measured by months He Himself would be caught up and transfigured in celestial glóry, and would return on the clouds of heaven to inaugurate the Messianic millennium upon a supernaturally rejuvenated earth. Hence He can neither have foreseen nor provided for the long history which the movement kindled by His words was in fact destined to have upon this planet : He can have " founded," or " instituted," nothing—neither Church, nor hierarchy, nor sacraments. If this position, which Friedrich Heiler describes as " the Copernican achievement of modern theology," [1] really represents the facts, then *cadit quaestio* : it becomes unnecessary even to examine the evidence for " Dominical institution," and the hypothesis of a fortuitous origin of the present Christian sacraments assumes the character of inevitability.   Just as Christian Baptism is (on this showing) to be regarded as the accidental survival of the Jewish proselyte-baptism, utilised by the common sense of the new movement as a symbolic means of admitting new adherents, so the Lord's Supper is the relic of the Jewish *Kiddûsh*, or sanctification of the Sabbath or of a great feast by the blessing of bread and wine on its eve,[2] a ceremony which Jesus had in the circle of His friends and hearers occasionally invested with the additional significance of a ritual rehearsal of the " Messianic banquet," which on the last evening of His life He had employed as an acted parable of His imminent death, and which His followers continued to observe at their club-meal or *Agape*, from habit or feeling rather than from any reasoned theory, as a commemoration or reminder to themselves both of His death and of His future return.   For the first few years of Christianity, therefore, these observances were no more than harmless pieces of sentimental symbolism, with no specifically " sacramental " significance, created or adopted by the Christian community to express its collective emotions on certain solemn occasions.   Many non-Catholic critics would add, that it would have been well if they had remained on this level.

---

[1] *Der Katholizismus* (1923), p. 3 : " Die Erkenntnis des eschatologischen Charakters seines Evangeliums ist die kopernikanische Tat der modernen Theologie ; mit einem Schlage stürzt sie das katholische Dogmensystem um."

[2] *Cf.* A. Loisy, *Les Évangiles Synoptiques*, ii. p. 542, n. 4.   The *Kiddûsh* may in any case well have been the foundation of the Christian Eucharist ; see G. H. Box, " The Jewish Antecedents of the Eucharist," *Journal of Theological Studies*, iii. 357.

IV

THE "MYSTERY RELIGIONS"

The theory just sketched requires as its natural complement an explanation of the manner in which the innocuous customs presupposed by it became transformed into the Catholic sacraments of Initiation and Communion, as known to St. Paul, St. John, St. Ignatius, and St. Justin Martyr, and all or practically all subsequent Christian thinkers and writers down to the sixteenth century of our era. This explanation is found by a consensus of non-Catholic scholarship in the well-known "Mystery-religion" hypothesis, which, though familiar to classical and theological students, may be briefly summarised here, in order that the logical bearings of the complete anti-traditionalist case may be fully exposed.

If we leave out of account the bizarre phenomenon of Caesar-worship, it is true to say that official "paganism," that is, the established religious system or systems with which Christianity found itself confronted when for the first time it spread beyond the borders of Palestine into Northern Syria, Asia Minor, and Europe, consisted of an immense multitude of localised and mutually independent cults, closely associated for the most part with the life of the State and of its provinces and municipalities.[1] Where they did not represent mere survivals of primitive magic and fetichism, these "established" cults were based on a strictly commercial view of the relation between the gods and their worshippers, the god being bound to protect the State or the municipality in return for a given *quantum* of sacrifices, but otherwise being under no obligation to interest himself in the community or its members. It will be clear that so purely contractual a system did not even pretend to satisfy the deeper spiritual needs or aspirations of the individual soul, nor were its ministers conceived to be invested with what we know as "pastoral" functions. A Roman who was oppressed by the enigma of the universe, by the weight of unmerited misfortune, or by the sense of personal guilt, would no more have thought of

[1] It is not necessary for the purposes of this brief sketch to take account of private or semi-private worships, such as the cults of the Attic phratries or the *sacra gentilicia* at Rome.

2 C

applying to the *flamen Dialis* or to the *quindecemviri sacris faciundis* for ghostly aid and comfort than of confiding in the Prefect of the Praetorian Guards. Moreover, such reality as the official cults had once possessed had long since been drained out of them, so far as the educated classes were concerned, by the widespread scepticism, which had made it impossible to believe in the substantive and personal reality of the members of the conventional Pantheon. Even those who, under the influence of the most remarkable Hellenic-Oriental religious teacher of the last two centuries B.C., Posidonius of Apamea,[1] had won their way to a philosophic monotheism, seem to have made no effort to relate their creed to the traditional State religion : Cicero's quotation of Cato's cynical apophthegm, about the difficulty which two *haruspices* must have felt in keeping straight faces when they met in the street, illustrates vividly the utter deadness of the old ceremonies, even for a man whose patriotism, no less than his religious feelings, would naturally have disposed him to make the best of them.[2]

It is not surprising that, during the centuries which immediately preceded and followed the birth of Christ, men who felt the need of a vital and personal religion should have turned away from the desiccated State ceremonies to the warm emotional " Mystery Religions " ; which, in virtue of their private character and their interest in the destiny of the individual soul, may without undue anachronism be styled the "evangelical nonconformity" of the pagan world, and which, in the eyes of the prosaic populations of the West, were endued with a unique glamour by the fact that they came from the wonder-world of the East, the immemorial home of religion. Of those mystery-cults, some, like those of the Eleusinian Demeter and the "Great Gods" or Kabeiroi of Samothrace, were strictly localised, being capable of celebration only by a priesthood resident at some particular spot, as in the case of the Eumolpidae at Eleusis, though the votaries who had once been initiated might be, and doubtless were, scattered all over the civilised world ; others were of a more avowedly " catholic " or " œcumenical " character in respect of their organisation, which was not tied down to a

---

[1] The latest study of this enigmatic personage appears to be K. Reinhardt, *Poseidonios* (Munich, 1921).

[2] Cic. *De Div.* II. xxiv.

single centre, but covered the whole Empire with a network of shrines and priestly colleges. The most important of these were the four great faiths which respectively clustered around the divine persons of Dionysus the Hunter (Zagreus), Isis the Egyptian queen of heaven, Cybele the sorrowful Mother of Asia Minor, and Mithra the hero-god of Persia, patron of soldiers, whose altars have been found in Roman military stations from the Euphrates to the Solway. To these must be added a host of lesser cults such as those of Atargatis, Adonis, Hermes Trismegistos,[1] and the like. These various faiths were propagated by the *Diasporai* of the nations in which they had originated, much as Judaism was propagated by the *Diaspora* or " dispersion " of Israel : and the syncretistic tendencies of the age enabled them to borrow from each other, and to fuse their usages and even the personalities of their gods, in every kind of proportion. If the *Metamorphoses* of Apuleius may be trusted, the ethical levels of their professional exponents ranged from the most austere virtue to the vilest charlatanism.

The roots from which the Mystery Religions sprang are not difficult to discern. Some, such as the Eleusinian and Egyptian mysteries, were developments of the vegetation-myth common to many primitive peoples, which personifies the vital force of nature, apparently dying in the winter and blossoming into fresh life in the spring, as a god who dies and rises again : others, such as the Orphic mysteries, appear to be built upon survivals of totemic ceremonial. But our knowledge of their fully developed contents, theological and ritual, is exceedingly fragmentary, a fact which is due partly to the faithfulness with which the initiates observed their pledge of secrecy, and partly to the crusade conducted by the victorious Christian Church, after its establishment by Constantine, against the shrines and sacred books of its rivals. Enough, however, remains, both of literary and of archaeological evidence, to furnish us with some conception of their broad underlying ideas.

The basal human need which all alike claimed to satisfy was the craving of the sick soul for " salvation " (*soteria*). The " failure of nerve," [2] which afflicted great masses of the popu-

---

[1] But see below, p. 392, n. 3.

[2] The phrase is borrowed from the heading of c. iv., in *Five Stages of Greek Religion* (Prof. Gilbert Murray, 1925). The whole chapter is an incomparable sketch of the popular emotional background which was common both to Christianity and to the Mystery Religions.

lation during the first century of our era, the widespread pessimism and world-weariness which supervened upon the close of the Roman civil wars, appeared in the consciousness of the individual as a nameless and oppressive fear—a fear of the universe, of the ruthless power of Fate, of the malefic influences of the stars, of annihilation at death, or of the torments of Tartarus. It was from this fear that the " Mystery Religions " promised deliverance, bestowed by a philanthropic " Lord " (*Kyrios*) or " Saviour " (*Soter*), who himself had known the anguish of death, or at least of poignant sorrow or laborious toil, and who, as it is alleged, promised to transfuse the virtue of his own divine life into the soul of his votary, assuring the latter thereby of pardon, inward peace, and a blessed immortality, through rites of a sacramental character. As the chief needs of the religious soul are purity and inward strength, it was natural, indeed inevitable, that these rites should have taken the forms of a cleansing bath and of a sacred meal.

We are here upon very uncertain ground, and it is impossible to say whether sacramentalism was strictly universal in these cults or not. In the rites of Eleusis we hear of a preliminary bath in the sea prescribed for the *mystae*,[1] and the cistern or *lacus* discovered by Sir William Ramsay in the sanctuary at Pisidian Antioch appears to have been used for baptismal purposes.[2] Demosthenes scoffs at the baptism of the Phrygian Cybele, as carried out by Aeschines in his youth, acting as the acolyte of his mother, a strolling priestess[3] ; and, in the romance of Apuleius which gives us the most exhaustive account now surviving of Isiac initiation, the candidate Lucius undergoes a bath and a ceremonial lustration to prepare him for his enlistment in the service of the goddess.[4] But the most striking parallel (in respect of the spiritual effects claimed for it) to Christian Initiation is to be found in the *taurobolium* or *criobolium*, that is, the bath in the blood of a slain beast, bull or ram, which admitted men to the mysteries of Cybele and Attis, and may have been borrowed from them by the cult of Mithras[5] ; some sepulchral inscriptions

---

[1] ἅλαδε μύσται; see L. R. Farnell, *Cults of the Greek States*, iii. p. 168.

[2] W. M. Ramsay, *The Teaching of Paul in Terms of the Present Day* (1913), p. 287 ff.

[3] Dem. *de Coron.* 313.   [4] Apuleius, *Metamorph.* xi. 23.

[5] Cumont, however, thinks that the *taurobolium* was never strictly a part of the Mithraic liturgy (*Textes et monuments figurés relatifs aux mystères de Mithra*, i. p. 334). For the *criobolium*, see Pauly-Wissowa, *Real-Encycl.*, iv. p. 1718, *s.v.*

testify to the faith of those who had received this horrible rite that they had thereby become "eternally regenerate," *renati in aeternum.*[1] Evidence for sacred meals is tantalisingly sporadic and fragmentary. The most certain instance is to be found in the *omophagia* of the Orphic mysteries, in which the delirious worshippers tore to pieces the sacred ox, believed anciently— though whether in historic times or not, we cannot say—to be the incarnation of Dionysus, and devoured its flesh raw.[2] Sacred meals, including both food and drink, appear to have occurred in the mysteries of Attis,[3] and of the Kabeiroi [4] ; and the rites of Eleusis included the drinking of a mixed cup (the so-called κυκεών) which may or may not have had a sacramental significance.[5] Probably the Mithraic sacred meal of bread and water mixed with *haoma*-juice should be added to the list,[6] though it is possible that this ceremony was a deliberate imitation of, and therefore not a true pagan parallel to, the Christian Eucharist.

This list embodies the principal instances of (apparent) sacramentalism in the pagan mystery-cults. We cannot, however, tell that there may not have been more ; and it is a reasonable presumption that those which we have enumerated would have familiarised the inhabitants of Syria, Asia Minor, and Greece, amongst whom the first expansion of Christianity outside the borders of Palestine took place, with the ideas of cathartic lustrations and sacramental, perhaps even of "theophagic," meals. It is suggested that the specifically Catholic conceptions of Initiation and the Eucharist are the product of a gradual infiltration of such ideas into Christianity from the mystery-faiths described above. a process for the inception of which, it is contended, St. Paul must bear the chief responsibility.[7] The Apostle is not, indeed, accused

---

[1] Other inscriptions, however, imply that the effect of this blood-baptism was only supposed to last for twenty years.

[2] See J. E. Harrison, *Prolegomena to the Study of Greek Religion*, pp. 482–92 ; A. Loisy, *Les mystères païens et le mystère chrétien* (1914), p. 32 ff.

[3] Farnell, *op. cit.* iii. 187.   [4] *Ibid.* iii. 195.   [5] *Ibid.* iii. 186, 195.

[6] F. Cumont, *Les mystères de Mithra* (1913), p. 163.

[7] It should be said that Harnack (*Mission and Expansion of Christianity*, E. tr., 1908, i. p. 230), and two distinguished British scholars, Prof. H. A. A. Kennedy (*St. Paul and the Mystery Religions*, 1913), and Dr. T. R. Glover (*Paul of Tarsus*, 1925, p. 161 ff.), favour or seem to favour a modified form of the "Mystery" theory, which finds the influence of the pagan Mysteries clearly manifested in later Catholicism, but not in the writings of St. Paul, who is thus exempted from the responsibility alluded to above. This position, however, appears ultimately to rest upon the assumption that there is an essential

of having, consciously and with his eyes open, embarked upon a policy of paganising Christianity in order to commend it to the Phrygian and Anatolian populations. The theory is rather that his first converts,[1] on being admitted to the Christian fellowship, and finding that it revered a human Messiah as, in some undefined sense, the "son of God," that it admitted new adherents by means of a ceremonial washing, and that it celebrated a common meal with special and sentimental reference to the death of its hero and prophet, naturally thought of all these matters in terms of the mystery cults with which they were familiar : in other words, that they envisaged Jesus, the Jewish-Christian Messiah, as a *Kyrios*,[2] a mystery-god analogous to Attis, Serapis, Mithras, and the other pagan *Kyrioi* or Redeemers[3] ; that they interpreted the harmless symbol of Baptism as a mysterious and awful sacrament of regeneration, and the "eschatologised *Kiddûsh*," which concluded the club-feast, as a realistic participation in the body and blood of the *Kyrios*. But, instead of striving with might and main to exclude the infiltration of these alien ideas (the theory goes on) St. Paul weakly acquiesced in them. The Apostle, or his immediate coadjutors and *epigoni*, found that the work of evangelisation was immensely simplified and accelerated if the pagan inquirer could be addressed in the terminology already familiar to him, and if the Gospel could be represented as "the last," and the only true, "word" in Mystery Religions. Stated in this way, Christianity spread with a surprising rapidity ; and St. Paul not merely accepted this transformation as expedient, but actually came to believe in it as true. By a kind of un-

---

incompatibility between the "ethical" and the "objectively sacramentalist" conceptions of Christianity ; and as (for the reasons explained in our introductory section) we repudiate this assumption, we may be permitted for the purpose of this essay to confine ourselves to the more thoroughgoing form of the "Mystery" hypothesis, as set forth by its leading Continental expositors.

[1] W. Bousset, *Kyrios Christos* (1921), p. 99, suggests that the beginnings of the transformation described above should be placed in the primitive Christian community of Antioch, the first Gentile-Christian Church to come into existence, before St. Paul's missionary journeys.

[2] See W. Bousset, *Kyrios Christos* (1921), c. iii. pp. 75–104.

[3] The words of St. Paul in 1 Cor. viii. 5 f. "For even if there are so-called gods, whether in heaven or on earth (as there are many 'gods' and many 'Kyrioi'), yet for us there is one God, the Father . . . and one *Kyrios*, Jesus Messiah . . ." show that the idea of a parallelism between Christ and the Pagan Redeemers existed in St. Paul's mind ; but it will be argued later that parallel conceptions need not be related as cause and effect.

conscious auto-suggestion, he persuaded himself that Baptism and the " Lord's Supper " really were and could do what the Mithraic *taurobolium* and the Dionysiac *omophagia* only pretended to be and to do, and that the Eucharist, at least, had been explicitly instituted by Jesus as a mystery of sacramental might. Christianity thus became Catholicism, and its triumph in the Graeco-Roman world was purchased at the cost of a surrender to the pagan sacramentalism which it should have resisted to the death.

Though considerations of space forbid us to dilate upon the matter now, it is worth while to emphasise the fact that the " Mystery-Religion " theory of the origins of the sacraments (or rather of the origins of the belief in their objective efficacy) does not stand by itself ; it is part and parcel of a wider thesis, namely, what may be called the " Mystery-Religion " theory of the origins of Catholicism in general, including the idea of Christ as a pre-existent Divine being and that conception of God which is ultimately necessitated by a " pre-existence " Christology, namely, the idea of the Trinity. The solidarity of the whole *religionsgeschichtliche* explanation of Catholicism is understood well enough in Germany, though in England there seems to be a tendency to speak and write as though its purview were confined to the sole question of the significance of the sacraments. But such an impartial witness as Heiler will tell us that neither in history nor in logic is it possible to dissociate the idea of Jesus as " Kyrios " from the ideas of Initiation and the Supper as " Mysteries." [1] The educated Catholic, from his own point of view, may be grateful for the implied admission that Catholic Christology and Catholic sacramentalism are interdependent. But, from the point of view of the " Mystery " hypothesis, the Christ of traditional dogma is a generalised blend of Attis, Osiris, and Mithras, wearing as a not too-well-fitting mask the features of Jesus of Nazareth ; and the Christocentric mysticism which is the heart of Catholic devotion is derived from Hellenistic-Oriental paganism, not from anything believed by Israel or taught by Jesus Himself. The silent recollection, with which the Catholic believer, kneeling in some still and empty church, fixes his eyes upon the Rood, becomes but the after-glow of the emotions with which the Mithraic initiate, in some crypt or chapel of the warrior-god, contemplated the Tauroctony, or

[1] Cf. *Der Katholizismus*, pp. 48, 49.

carven *retablo* depicting the slaying of the mystic bull. The lights and the Alleluyas of the Christian Easter are in great measure but the mirage-like reflection of the joy which filled the devotees of Attis, when on the *Hilaria*, the crowning day of the vernal commemoration of his passion, the chief priest whispered to them, as he administered the sacramental balm, " The God has been saved ! " [1]

V

CRITIQUE OF THE " MYSTERY " HYPOTHESIS

Such in outline is the great, modern, skilfully articulated and impressively coherent, *alternative* explanation of the genesis of Catholicism which now confronts the traditional belief in the Deity of Christ and in His direct institution of the sacraments.[2] If this alternative explanation can establish itself as the truth, there is an end of historic Christianity as we know it. On the other hand, if it can be shown to rest on arbitrary assumptions and to involve historical or psychological impossibilities, the traditional theory will remain in possession of the field. The scope of this essay is necessarily limited to the question of the sacraments only ; and a few words regarding the method which we propose to follow in examining the " Mystery " theory will conduce to clearness. It will have been observed that the theory, as sketched above, assumes a detailed picture of the state of the " Mystery Religions " during the first generation of Christian history which is by no means universally recognised as an accurate representation of the facts.[3] Most of our evidence for the character of these cults dates

[1] See J. G. Frazer, *Adonis, Attis, Osiris* (1914), i. p. 272.

[2] Signs are, however, not wanting that the " Mystery " theory has reached the zenith of its popularity, and may shortly enter upon a period of decline, even in Germany ; see an article by Robert Eisler, " Das letzte Abendmahl," in *Zeitschr. f. N.T. Wissensch.*, Nov. 1925, in which the author explains that he was once an adherent of the " Mystery " theory, but now considers it " one of the most erroneous conclusions that has ever arisen in the whole history of New Testament study."

[3] A striking instance of the precariousness of the evidence for the " Mystery " theory is provided by the " Hermetic " writings. R. Reitzenstein, perhaps the best-known Continental student of the subject, regards them as " scriptures " venerated by " Hermetic congregations," so that he is able to use them, in conjunction with magical papyri which mention the name of Hermes, for the purpose of reconstructing a scheme of ideas supposed to have been common to all Mystery Religions in the first century A.D., and to have included the conceptions

from the second and third centuries A.D., and there is no proof that we are entitled to employ it as evidence for the first century. The use of Mithraism in this connection is peculiarly unjustifiable, inasmuch as during St. Paul's lifetime it was all but unknown in Europe, and never took root in lands of Greek speech and culture.[1] It has not been proved that all the apparent analogues of Baptism and the Eucharist to be found in paganism were conceived as sacramental, nor yet that all mystery-cults possessed all of the three cardinal points of the generalised " mystery-scheme " presupposed by the theory, that is (1) a *Kyrios*, (2) a ceremonial washing, and (3) a sacred meal.   But an attempt to reconstruct the stages of development to which the various Mystery Religions had severally attained during the period A.D. 29–70 would require far more space than is at our disposal.   In spite, therefore, of the uncertainties just indicated, we will, for the sake of argument, assume that the advocates of the " Mystery " hypothesis have construed the available evidence correctly, and that their picture of the Mystery Religions in the first century A.D. is free from anachronisms. We can afford to concede them this considerable logical advantage, because, if the strongest form of the " Mystery " theory can be overthrown, it will carry with it in its fall any weaker forms which a searching historical analysis might reveal.

Our criticisms of the " Mystery " hypothesis will, therefore, not be concerned with details ; they will refer solely to its fundamental positions, which may be formulated as follows :

(*a*) That there is no reliable evidence that Christ *did* institute the sacraments.

(*b*) That His " eschatologically limited outlook " proves that He *could* not have instituted them.

(*c*) That the parallelism between Pauline and pagan sacramentalism is only explicable on the supposition that the former is directly derived from the latter.

of the " Spirit," " new birth," and the efficacy of the Redeemer's Name. (See especially *Poimandres*, 1904, pp. 1–36, 219, 226 ff., 366, 368 ; *Die Hellenistischen Mysterienreligionen*, 1910, pp. 33 ff., 112 ff.) The latest editor of these documents, on the other hand, Mr. Walter Scott (*Hermetica*, vols. i, ii., 1925), dismisses the idea of a Hermetic " cult " and " congregations " as a pure invention, and pronounces the *Corpus Hermeticum* to be no more than a fortuitous collection of late Greek-Egyptian philosophical and religious writings, only bound together by the fact that their authors happened to use the figures of Hermes and Tat as conventional *dramatis personae*.

[1] F. Cumont, *Les mystères de Mithra* (1913), p. 31 f.

It will be convenient to consider these points in an order somewhat different from that in which we have stated them.

1. "*Parallelism*" and "*derivation*"—*the question of* a priori *probability*

The contamination of a higher religion by surviving elements of a lower which it has conquered or is in process of conquering is a phenomenon familiar to the student of the history of religions : the fusion of Yahwism with Canaanitish *ba'al*-worship denounced by the Hebrew prophets, and the transformation of Buddhism into Lamaism, are instances in point. No one who is intimately acquainted with Catholicism as it exists to-day in Mediterranean countries and amongst peoples of Iberian stock can deny that it contains many details of external observance and of popular piety which are directly borrowed from Graeco-Roman paganism ; a comparison of the model legs, arms, and hands suspended as *ex-votos* before continental shrines of our Lady with the precisely similar objects employed for the same purpose in temples of Isis will bring this fact vividly before the reader's eyes. *Graecia capta ferum victorem cepit*[1]—the well-known Horatian line applies as much to the struggle of her folk-religion with the victorious faith of Judaea as to the contest of her culture with the barbarian rusticity of Rome. From the same source are descended the stories of holy wells and trees, winking pictures, sweating statues, flying houses, and other fetichistic and animistic beliefs which flourish rankly in the underworld of the Mediterranean religious consciousness. It was, perhaps, hardly to be expected that the ark of the Church could traverse the Sargasso Sea of the ancient religions without acquiring some adventitious incrustations of this kind ; and it is not necessary here to distinguish between those which are harmless or even picturesque, and those which definitely retard the speed of the ship. And it may be observed, in parenthesis, that whatever less desirable effects the Reformation may have had, it conferred at least one permanent benefit upon religion in Northern countries by decisively plucking up the roots of all such heathen survivals, so as to make possible, at any rate in England, a fresh start, and the working out of a presentation of Catholicism which should contain no vital element of which

[1] Hor. *Ep.* II. i, 156.

at least the germs were not to be found in the New Testament. But these toys of the uneducated, "miraculous" stocks and stones, *ex-votos*, and the like, stand on an entirely different footing from the sacraments, which are the subject-matter of our inquiry : partly because such things as thaumaturgical images are in principle no more than separable accidents of any version of Catholicism, and could be relegated *en masse* to the dust-heap without any disturbance of its logical structure, and partly because the beginnings of their infiltration into Christianity can be historically controlled and linked with the vast influx of semi-converted heathen into the Church during the fourth and succeeding centuries ; whereas the sacraments, in substantially their Catholic shape, and the conception of Jesus as *Kyrios* which they presuppose, appear in the pages of the New Testament itself. The fact that direct, if unconscious, borrowing can be proved in the later and less important case of parallelism between Christian and pagan custom does not in itself compel us to assume a similar explanation of the earlier and more important.[1]

Considered in itself, the statement that parallelism proves dependence would seem to be entirely arbitrary. As applied to the relations between Christian and ethnic sacramentalism, it is by no means new : it was asserted as strongly by the early Christian Apologists as by the modern non-Catholic critics, the only difference between these two bodies of writers being that, whereas the critics assume the Christian sacraments to be the reflection of the pagan Mysteries, the Apologists held that the Mysteries were Satanic parodies of the sacraments. But both alike appear to have overlooked a third *prima facie* possibility, which would surely occur to a cultivated Martian or other completely unbiassed investigator, namely, that the connection between the Christian and the pagan rites might be *collateral* (in the sense that both might be independent products of the same psychological factors) and not one of direct dependence or causality. The researches

---

[1] The same consideration applies to the facts (1) that in the fourth and succeeding centuries much " mystery " terminology was applied to the sacraments—*cf.* the title of St. Cyril of Jerusalem's instructions on the sacraments, *Catecheses Mystagogicae*—and (2) that certain details of liturgical observance (*e.g.* the use of milk and honey in connection with Christian initiation—see H. Usener, *Rhein. Mus. für Philol.* lvii. 177) seem to have been borrowed from or at least influenced by the procedure of the pagan mysteries. We are here only concerned with the fundamental essence of Christian sacramentalism as it appears in the New Testament.

of anthropologists seem to show that man everywhere tends to satisfy the same instincts in the same way : the works of Frazer, Crawley, van Gennep, Durkheim, Hubert and Mauss, contain thousands of instances of similar myths, rites, customs, and *tabus* which have sprung up, to all appearance independently, in diverse lands in response to the same social or individual needs, and there is no necessity to postulate a " monophyletic " origin even for so elaborate a system as totemism.   In no other department of scientific thought is it assumed as axiomatic that similar phenomena must be directly related as cause and effect ; and there seems no reason for making such an assumption within the sphere of the history of religions.[1]   From the most severely impartial point of view, therefore, it must be at least an *a priori* possibility that the Christian lustration and sacred meal came to be interpreted in the same way as their pagan analogues, simply because it was found by experience that they did (for whatever reason) provide a full satisfaction for the same spiritual needs, that is, for those cravings for purity and ghostly strength, which in the pagan world had created the Mystery Religions as a means to their own partial gratification or sublimation.

But a detached Christian investigator—by which phrase I mean an inquirer who had come to admit, in a general sense, the uniqueness and supremacy of the Christian revelation, without having decided which of the existing forms of our religion appeared to be the truest—would, I submit, be prepared somewhat to enlarge the field of this possibility.   He would at least concede that Almighty God, in accordance with the principle of continuity which can be discerned running through His providential govern-ance of history, *may* have willed to do for man, through His final self-revelation, what man had attempted to do for himself through crude and imperfect means of his own devising ; and that Christianity, as it claims in other respects to sum up and gather into one the various lines of man's secular search for God, may also claim—with pride, and not with apology—to be by divine appointment the supreme and ideal Mystery Religion.   He would see no reason why the " creed of creeds " should not include,

---

[1] We do not forget that some anthropologists, like the late Dr. W. H. R. Rivers, do explicitly assume that all similarities of custom, religious and social, in different nations must be due to the spread of civilisation from a single centre ; but they are far from having converted all their fellow-students to this view.

side by side with an ethic loftier than that of Socrates, and a theology richer and grander than that of Aristotle, " Mysteries " more pure and ennobling than those of which Sophocles wrote :

ὡς τρισόλβιοι
κεῖνοι βροτῶν, οἳ ταῦτα δερχθέντες τέλη
μόλωσ' ἐς "Αιδου.[1]

And, assuming him to believe both in human free will and in God's all-pervasive providence, he would admit that the Mystery Religions may have been an integral element in the vast *praeparatio evangelica* which began with the emergence of man from the ape ; that, viewed from the standpoint of human initiative, they may have been models and symbols, first fashioned by man for himself, which God, condescending to man's limitations, vouchsafed to reproduce within the framework of the final religion ; and that, viewed from the standpoint of divine providence, they may have been, like the Levitical ordinances, types and foreshadowings of " good things to come."

The supposed axiom that " parallelism implies dependence " is, therefore, neither self-evident nor inductively proven, and cannot be used to invest the hypothesis of " pagan infiltration " with a degree of *a priori* likelihood superior to that of " Dominical institution." So far as our argument has gone, both hypotheses would seem to stand on the same level of probability. We may now carry our analysis a little deeper, with the object of showing that the " Mystery theory," so far from being more probable than the traditional view, is actually less so, inasmuch as it involves a gross psychological impossibility. To make this point clear, let me remind the reader of the part which, according to this theory, was played by St. Paul in the genesis of Catholic sacramentalism. As Augustus found Rome brick and left it marble, so St. Paul is said to have found Christianity a vague movement of apocalyptic enthusiasm and to have left it a sacramental *Kyrios*-cult, a more or less organised Mystery Religion—not as the result of any deliberate action on his part, but through his too complaisant acquiescence in the tendency of his converts to construe the Gospel in terms of the Mysteries with which they were familiar. Now we have seen that, on the admission of the most typical champions of the Mystery

---

[1] " How thrice-blest among mortals are they, who having beheld these rites go to the house of Hades " (Soph. *Fr.* 719, ed. Dindorf).

theory, the Catholic ideas regarding Initiation and the Lord's Supper are already present in the First Epistle to the Corinthians, a document which can hardly be dated later than A.D. 55.   But the first conversions of pure Gentiles, that is of persons who were neither Samaritans nor Jewish proselytes—and the theory requires a large influx of pure Gentiles to account for the first beginnings of the "infiltration"-process—cannot have happened earlier than A.D. 30–35, between which dates practically all systems of New Testament chronology would place the persecution which arose upon the death of Stephen, scattering the members of the primitive Jerusalemite community through Palestine and Syria, and thereby bringing to pass the momentous circumstance that certain "men of Cyprus and Cyrene" "spake unto the Greeks also the preaching of the Lord Jesus." [1]   The radical transformation of the whole idea of Christianity which the Mystery theory assumes must, therefore, have taken not more, and probably rather less, than twenty years for its accomplishment.

Consider for a moment the implications of this supposition. It compels us to suppose that, within a comparatively short space of time, St. Paul's Asian and Hellenic converts unconsciously infected their master and father in Christ with what was, on the hypothesis which we are considering, a profoundly un-Christian point of view; and that this mental infection was so thoroughgoing that the Apostle, whilst still at the zenith of his intellectual and spiritual powers, and still enjoying an unimpaired memory of his past life, came to believe—in diametrical opposition to the truth—that he had "received from the Lord," through the Mother Church of Jerusalem,[2] and had always taught to his disciples, traditions and ideas which in fact he had unwittingly imbibed from them.   It necessitates the ascription to him of an incredible degree either of simplicity or of carelessness, in order to account for the alleged fact that—whilst engaged in a campaign against those pagan cults which, in his bitterest moments, he regards, like Justin Martyr, as the work of daemons,[3] and which, in a more tolerant mood, he dismisses contemptuously as the worships of "many (so-called) *Kyrioi*" [4]—he should have unsuspectingly

---

[1] Acts xi. 20.

[2] I here assume the accepted interpretation of $\dot{\epsilon}\gamma\grave{\omega}$ . . . $\pi\alpha\rho\dot{\epsilon}\lambda\alpha\beta\text{ον}$ $\dot{\alpha}\pi\grave{o}$ $\tau\text{o}\tilde{υ}$ $\kappa\nu\rho\text{ί}\text{ου}$ in 1 Cor. xi. 23 ; see below, p. 400.

[3] Compare 1 Cor. x. 20 f. and Justin, 1 *Apol.* 66.

[4] 1 Cor. viii. 5.

allowed the texture of his devotion and his thought to become saturated by conceptions borrowed from those very " Mysteries " which it was the object of his mission to destroy. If this be incredible, and yet the " Mystery " hypothesis be retained, it can only be on the supposition that St. Paul was dominated by the desire to attract converts at any price, even the price of truth. Only if one or other of these suppositions be accepted—only if we assume that the most heroic of evangelists may pervert his message for the sake of a cheap success, or that the most vigorous of thinkers may so befog himself by self-hypnosis as to lose grip on the realities of his own past life—shall we think it a probable explanation of the genesis of Catholic sacramentalism that " St. Paul, though ready to fight to the death against the Judaising of Christianity, was willing to take the first step, and a long one, towards the Paganising of it."

And only if we attribute a hardly believable blindness to the primitive nucleus of Jewish-Christians, can we suppose—as the " Mystery " theory would compel us to suppose—that, whilst attacking St. Paul with unmeasured ferocity for his liberalism in regard to the imposition of the Law upon Gentile converts, the Judaising faction should nevertheless have acquiesced, with inexplicable placidity, in his far-reaching contamination of the faith of Israel with Gentile ideas of a *Kyrios* and of " sacraments." [1]

2. *The evidence for " Dominical Institution " re-examined :* (a) *The Eucharist*

If the foregoing conclusions as to the *a priori* probability of the traditional and the " Mystery " hypotheses are cogent—and I cannot see any way of escape from them—we may now proceed to a re-examination of the *a posteriori* evidence for the " Dominical institution," with the general disposition to trust such evidence, if it can be found. It will be convenient to discuss in the first instance the evidence for Christ's institution of the Eucharist *as a permanent rite.* We may concede at once that the main weight of this hypothesis must rest upon the command which He is believed to have given, "This do in remembrance of me," and

[1] If the Judaisers had raised any serious protests against St. Paul's Christ-ology and sacramentalism, some traces of the fact would surely be found in the Acts and Epistles.

that, in the present uncertainty as to the genuine text of Luke xxii. 17–20,[1] the words of St. Paul in 1 Cor. xi. 24, 25 constitute our sole authority for this command. But, given the conclusions of our last paragraph—and leaving out of account for the moment the " Mystery " critic's trump card, namely, his contention as to the impossibility of our Lord's having made any provision for the future, owing to His " eschatologically limited outlook "— it is reasonable to suggest that St. Paul's authority is *prima facie* good enough. The Apostle's affirmation is so solemn and significant that it may be quoted at length :

" For I received of the Lord that which I also delivered unto you, how that the Lord Jesus, in the night in which he was betrayed, took bread ; and when he had given thanks, he broke it, and said, This is my body, which is for you : this do in remembrance of me. In like manner also the cup, after supper, saying, This cup is the new covenant in my blood : this do, as oft as ye drink it, in remembrance of me."

The opening words of this passage, " I received of the Lord that which I also delivered unto you," are almost identical with those which introduce the list of the resurrection appearances in ch. xv. 3 of the same Epistle, " I delivered unto you that which I also received," and presumably bear the same meaning, namely, that the teaching which St. Paul transmitted to the Church of Corinth he had himself received from the Mother Church of Jerusalem. Such, indeed, is the accepted interpretation of the phrase : Professor Percy Gardner's suggestion,[2] that the Apostle thereby implies some vision or supernormal " revelation " as the medium whereby he " received " this information " of the Lord," has won very little acceptance. St. Paul, then, asserts quite definitely and bluntly, not only that Christ instituted the Lord's Supper as a permanent rite, but that he himself had been informed of the fact by the immediate disciples of Christ. There can be no reason why these latter should have wished to deceive their

---

[1] See above, p. 382. This admission does not invalidate the phrase in our present Prayer of Consecration, " Who . . . did institute, and in his holy Gospel command us to continue . . .," as some recent proposals for Prayer Book Revision seem rather pedantically to assume ; the words " in his holy Gospel " need not mean " in one of the four canonical Gospels," but may more appropriately be taken as signifying " in his general message of salvation to the world."

[2] *The Religious Experience of St. Paul* (1911), p. 110 ff.

great recruit and future colleague ; and we have already shown reasons for rejecting the supposition that St. Paul deluded himself into the belief that he had received the Eucharistic tradition from the original Apostles, in much the same way as George IV deluded himself into believing that he had been present at the Battle of Waterloo. The Pauline testimony, then, holds the field so far. It is not temerarious to add that, if it had been only the acts and intentions of Alexander the Great or of Julius Caesar that were in question, testimony from an analogous source would never have been challenged.

The question may be very reasonably raised at this point : "If the words, ' This do in remembrance of me,' are a genuine *logion* of the Lord, how is it that they are absent from the Synoptic Gospels, and presumably from the ultimate sources used by the Synoptists, that is, the Petrine tradition underlying Mark, and what is usually termed LQ, the early and reliable tradition from which Luke drew his Passion-narrative ? " This question deserves a careful reply, all the more so because an adequate treatment of it will involve coming to close grips with the ultimate contention on which the " Mystery " theory rests and apart from which, as we have seen, it does not possess any measure of probability—the contention, namely, that Christ *could* not have instituted any sacraments or made any provision for a future Church, inasmuch as He believed that this present world was on the point of coming to an end. It will conduce to clearness if we formulate our answer first, and state the grounds on which we base it afterwards.

Our answer is in substance as follows. " The silence of the Synoptists, and possibly of the traditions which they employed, as to the command ' This do ' is amply accounted for—and any argument which might be founded on this silence, of a nature hostile to the hypothesis of ' Dominical institution,' is cancelled— by the fact that both Mark (followed by Matthew) and Luke contain another, more enigmatically expressed *logion*, which, though difficult of comprehension at the time of its utterance, was later recognised as being fraught with the same meaning as ' This do,' namely, the expression of the Lord's purpose that His actions should be repeated by His future Church. This *logion* is the verse, ' Verily I say unto you, I will no more drink of the [this, *Mt.*] fruit of the vine, until that day when I drink it new [with you, *Mt.*] in the kingdom of God' (Mk. xiv. 25 = Mt. xxvi. 29 [1] = Lk. xxii. 18, with apparently a doublet in v. 16). As the Synoptists record this saying, they might well have thought it unnecessary to record the command 'This do,' even if they had known of it.[2]   There is, however, no reason why both sayings should not have been uttered by our Lord at the Last Supper, the Synoptic traditions preserving one and the Pauline tradition the other.[3] "   We must now proceed to justify the meaning which we have attributed to the Synoptic saying, " Verily I say unto you, etc."

We can best develop our exegesis of this passage by sketching the interpretation of it which would be given by thoroughgoing upholders of the view opposed to our own.   The key to its meaning lies in the phrase " the Kingdom of God."   For our Lord's contemporaries, the Kingdom of God meant a new world-order, conceived as a somewhat materialistic millennium, which would immediately succeed the Day of Jehovah with its accompanying cataclysms, in which the present world-order would have been dissolved.   In this Kingdom the sovereignty of God would be exercised by the Messiah, reigning over a rejuvenated earth, which would be possessed by the Saints, that is by pious Israelites, in boundless peace, wealth and happiness.   We have already sketched the theory that these expectations were shared by our Lord, and that His mental horizon was limited, so far as the existing world-order was concerned, by the belief in the imminence of the End ;   from which it would follow that He can have had no idea of providing for the future of His group of disciples under the conditions of this present life by instituting sacraments.   This theory, however, provides what is (given its assumptions) a not unreasonable explanation of His action at the Last Supper and of the *logion* now under discussion.   It was apparently a common device of the apocalyptists [4] to represent the bliss of the millennial

---

[1] We assume that the Marcan version of this saying is more likely to be original, as being more fresh and vivid in phraseology, than the Lucan.   The question as to whether it was spoken *before* the sacred action (Lk.) or *after* it (Mk., Mt.) is irrelevant to the argument.

[2] The presumption is that St. Luke at least *did* know of it, owing to his association with St. Paul.

[3] *Cf.* the two sayings said to have been addressed by our Lord to Judas at the moment of the betrayal—" Comrade, [do] that for which thou art here " (Mt. xxvi. 50), and " Judas, with a kiss dost thou deliver up the Son of man ? " (Lk. xxii. 48)—both of which may well be historical.

[4] *Cf.* 1 Enoch xxv., lxii. 14 ; *Test. Levi,* xviii. 11.

" Kingdom " under the figure of the " Messianic banquet "—
an image ultimately derived from the words of Isaiah xxv. 6,
" In this mountain shall the Lord of hosts make unto all peoples
a feast of fat things, a feast of wines on the lees, of fat things full
of marrow, of wines on the lees well refined."   Now it has been
noticed that the acts of blessing and breaking bread in a specially
solemn manner are recorded as having been performed by our Lord
on at least one other occasion during His earthly lifetime, in
connection with the miraculous feeding of a great crowd (or on
two other occasions, if the stories of the Five and Four Thousand
be regarded as based on two separate incidents).   Dr. A. Schweitzer
has made the brilliant suggestion [1] that, in order to heighten the
vividness of His teaching about the joys of the coming Kingdom,
Jesus was accustomed from time to time to hold what may be
described as a dramatic or symbolic rehearsal of the " Messianic
banquet," distributing to each of those present a tiny portion of
some common food, bread and fish, or bread and wine ; that the
stories of the " miraculous feedings " represent accounts of such
rehearsals, touched up (when their original significance had been
forgotten) by the addition of the assertion that the participants had
previously been fainting with hunger, but were supernaturally
satisfied by the multiplication of the food ; and that the actions
performed by Him at the Last Supper were meant to be the last
and most solemn of these ceremonial rehearsals, carried out within
the privacy of His own circle of intimate friends, under the
shadow of the impending Passion, by which He believed that He
could force the hand of God and compel the Kingdom to appear.
On this hypothesis, the meaning of the declaration " I will no
more drink of the fruit of the vine " is clear.   Roughly paraphrased
it means " This is the last of our ceremonial rehearsals of the
' Messianic banquet,' the last of our symbolic foreshadowings :
the next meal at which we shall meet will be the reality, *the
' Messianic banquet ' itself*, celebrated in the new world-order, in
the unearthly Kingdom of God to be brought down from heaven
by the suffering which lies before Me.   *Now* I drink, and invite
you to share, the old wine of this present world, which is ripe to
rottenness and on the point of passing away ; but *then* we shall
drink the new wine of the world to come."

[1] *Von Reimarus zu Wrede*, E. T., *The Quest of the Historical Jesus* (1910),
p. 374 ff.

It is impossible within the limits of this essay to examine the "eschatological" theory of the life of Christ in detail ; but it is not too much to say that on the whole such writers as Johannes Weiss and Schweitzer seem to have established, as against the older " Liberal Protestant " view, their main contention, namely, the centrality of the conception of the future " Kingdom " in our Lord's message, and the relatively subordinate position of His ethical teaching, as being merely a "propaedeutic" or preparatory discipline designed to qualify men for entrance into the Kingdom. The acceptance of this general position, however, does not by any means carry with it an acceptance of the more particular assumption which has coloured and determined these writers' whole presentation of the life of Christ, that is, the assumption that our Lord meant by " the Kingdom of God " *no more than what His Jewish contemporaries meant by that phrase.* This latter is the fundamental postulate which lies at the bottom of the hypothesis of His " eschatologically limited outlook," and, consequently, at the bottom of the whole " Mystery " theory. But, I submit, it is a postulate which, though not susceptible of mathematical disproof, is contrary to the inherent rationality of things and renders the general course of human history unintelligible ; for it assumes that the greatest Man of all time possessed little or no originality in the intellectual sphere, that He was the slave and not the master of popular phraseology, and that He did not possess even so much power of foreseeing and providing for the future as is attributed by Mommsen to Julius Caesar.[1]

It is not necessary to invoke the Christology of Nicaea and Chalcedon (which consistent advocates of the " Mystery " theory naturally do not accept), or to dogmatise about the very difficult problem of the limitations of the knowledge exercised by our Lord as man, in order to rebut this assumption ; it is sufficient to appeal to the general probability that the supreme Messenger of God to the world (and we cannot, within the limits of this essay, argue with any one who denies the historical Jesus this position) was not a deluded fanatic, whose prophecies were conspicuously

[1] Mommsen (*History of Rome,* E. tr., 1894, V. xi.) credits Caesar with the conscious intention of bringing into existence that unified and homogeneous Italo-Hellenic empire which actually did realise itself under his successors ; why should not a greater than Caesar be credited with the conscious intention of creating that Church and faith which actually did spring from His life and death ?

refuted by the facts, less than a generation after His death. Those who accept this general probability will be prepared to believe that our Lord was perfectly capable of pouring a new and refined content into current popular phrases, and that His prediction (in its Marcan form) " There be some here of them that stand by, which shall in no wise taste of death, till they see the kingdom of God come with power " [1] was fulfilled in very truth at Pentecost, when the Kingdom of God came with power as the Catholic Church and faith, which went forth from the Upper Room, conquering and to conquer. On this hypothesis, the " Kingdom," which is both present and future, both an interior inspiration and an external power, both the product of gradual growth and a catastrophic irruption into the time-series from the eternal world, is nothing other than the new dispensation of faith and grace which actually did spring from Calvary ; it is the " new covenant " consecrated by the blood of the Messiah, the new universal *Ecclesia* or Israel of God. With such an interpretation of the meaning of the " Kingdom " the facts of our Lord's life and teaching, as re-grouped by the " eschatological theory," come into perfect line ; and a new and deeper significance is given to the conception of the " Messianic banquet," as implied in the passages mentioned above.

In the light of this interpretation we may well accept the suggestion that our Lord's action at the Last Supper was not the first action of the kind. It is very probable that the feeding or feedings of great crowds, whether accompanied by miraculous circumstances or not, were meant in the first instance to be symbolic portrayals of the future banquet, which would gladden the hearts of the members of the Messianic Kingdom ; and that the same thought was present to our Lord's mind when He spoke of the Gentiles as " reclining at meat " with the patriarchs, at the mystic feast that was to be.[2] But, if the "Kingdom of God " is the Christian Church and faith, what else can the " Messianic banquet " be than the Eucharist, the *sacrum convivium* which s the centre of its life, and in which the Messiah Himself is believed to be both the Breaker of the bread and the Bread which is broken ?

---

[1] Mark ix. 1 ; the Matthaean version (xvi. 28) misunderstands the point of the saying, and turns it into a prediction of the end of the world and the Parousia of the Son of Man.

[2] Matt. viii. 11 = Luke xiii. 29.

If this is so, the Fourth Evangelist has, at the least, shown a true instinct, and may well be conforming to the historical course of events, when he appends his great Eucharistic discourse at Capernaum to the account of the "miraculous feeding." Whatever the exact purport of the words "This is my body" and "This is my blood"—and I should be trenching on the ground of another writer if I were to discuss this question in detail—it is clear that, on any showing, the communion administered by our Lord at the Last Supper must be regarded as having been *sui generis* and exceptional, because, at the moment when He pronounced these words, His body had not yet been broken, nor His blood shed ; and we may, therefore, without irreverence, conclude that there must have been something, as it were of imperfection, or of a provisional nature, in a communion administered before the accomplishment of that which every Communion is meant to proclaim, namely, the Lord's death.[1] If this is so, then the mysterious *logion*, from which this section of our discussion has started, may be interpreted as meaning : "This is the last of those prophetic actions, whereby I have endeavoured to impress upon you, through type and shadow, the glories of that future ' Messianic banquet,' which will be shared by the elect in the ' Kingdom of God.'   The next time that we meet together on such an occasion as this, I shall still be the Host, though present invisibly, and not in tangible form.   But the next celebration of this Feast will not be, as this is, a provisional and anticipated transaction of the sacramental mystery ; it will be *the mystery itself*, consummated in the Kingdom of God, that is, in My Church, which in its universalised or Catholic form will be constituted by virtue of the great events which lie before us, My death and resurrection, and the coming of the Holy Ghost."

Interpreted in this way, the saying is not indeed a command to continue the observance of the solemn " drinking of the fruit of the vine " : but it is an affirmation that the observance *would in point of fact be continued* in the future Kingdom : and such an affirmation, made by one who believed Himself to be the King-designate, is the equivalent of a command, in so far as it is an explicit declaration of His purpose and intention.   It may therefore be concluded without extravagance that the Synoptic and the

[1] See the Note appended to this essay, " On Mark xiv. 25."

Pauline traditions, taken together, constitute evidence for the " Dominical institution " of the Eucharist (that is, for the performance by Christ of certain actions with the intention that they should be repeated), such as would be considered reasonably adequate for any alleged event belonging to the secular history of the same period and country.

3. *The evidence for " Dominical Institution " re-examined :* (b) *Initiation*

The question whether Christian Baptism can be said to have been " instituted " by Christ or not is in some ways a more difficult one. It is clear that in this connection the term cannot be taken as synonymous with " devised " or " invented " ; for the custom had already been practised by Christ's forerunner, John. It will be used, therefore, during the following discussion in the sense of " adopted," " sanctioned," or " enjoined." At this point the earliest Christian documents which we possess, namely the extant letters of St. Paul, fail us ; for though the Apostle of the Gentiles, as we shall see, attributes the highest value to the rite, he does not make any statement, in that part of his correspondence which has survived, as to its exact origin. The only direct statement on the subject contained in the New Testament is the famous verse, Matt. xxviii. 19, in which the risen Christ is represented, not merely as commanding the universal administration of Baptism, but also as prescribing the Trinitarian formula for recitation in connection with the sacramental act. It is impossible, for the reasons mentioned above in Section III,[1] to deny the force of the suggestion that this passage may be a piece of compendious symbolic narrative, that is, of dogmatic theology cast into a quasi-historical form, rather than of history strictly so called ; and we are therefore debarred from using the Matthaean command, " Go ye therefore . . ." as a means of settling the question without further discussion.

On the other hand, there is a reasonable probability that even " Matthew," with all his lack of the minute scrupulousness demanded by the modern scientific historian, would not in regard to a matter of such crucial importance have made so plain and

[1] p. 380 f.

direct an assertion without any sort of *a posteriori* justification.
Even though his statement as to the exact occasion on which,
and the precise terms in which, the precept was given may not
command the fullest confidence, it is possible to hold that it
embodies a kernel of truth, and that, on some occasion not known
to us, Christ did with His human lips actually enjoin the practice
of the custom upon His disciples.   In other words, whilst we
cannot attribute overwhelming weight to St. Matthew's testimony,
it cannot be reasonably denied any weight at all.   It is at least
good evidence for the belief of the Christian Church some fifty
years after the resurrection.   The most logical view, therefore,
of the function which it may play in our inquiry into the origins
of Christian Baptism, will be to regard it as the feather which may
decisively weigh down that scale of the historical balance which
represents " Dominical institution," if sufficient indirect evidence
can be gathered from the rest of the New Testament to invest
this hypothesis with considerable likelihood.   This text, taken
together with the words attributed to our Lord by St. John,
about the new birth through water and the Spirit,[1] will be just
enough to turn a high degree of probability into reasonable certainty, assuming that such a probability can be established by
other means.   But if the weight of probability turns out to be in
favour of the alternative hypothesis—namely, that which assumes
that the disciples spontaneously copied the baptism of John, or
the Jewish baptism of proselytes, without any explicit instructions
from our Lord so to do—then the Matthaean text, not being more
than a feather, will not avail to weigh down the opposite scale.

We will, accordingly, leave the Matthaean evidence for the
moment on one side, and examine the *data* furnished by the
remainder of the New Testament, in the hope of finding some
independent indications as to the origin of Christian Initiation.
Such a review must necessarily start from the baptism of John
and its Jewish antecedents, but need not go further back into
history : the idea of symbolising purification from uncleanness
by the act of washing in water is so obvious and natural, and has
occurred independently to so many peoples,[2] that it is neither
necessary nor indeed possible to determine its ultimate beginnings.

---

[1] John iii. 5.

[2] For detailed information see Hastings, *E.R.E.*, vol. ii., art. " Baptism
(Ethnic)."

In the Levitical law, ablutions with water are prescribed as a means of removing ceremonial pollution contracted by the touch of a corpse, or in other ways.[1]   These precepts doubtless represent the survival of a primitive stage of religious thought, in which evil is conceived quasi-materialistically as "bad *mana*." From these Levitical lustrations were derived both the baptism of the Essenes,[2] and that by which proselytes after circumcision were made full members of the Jewish Church.[3]   In the latter instance the idea was rather that of cleansing the Gentile from the ceremonial defilement with which he was assumed to be infected through a life spent in idolatry, than that of abolishing " original sin," in anything like the Augustinian sense of the term. John the Baptist adopted the custom, but gave it a distinctly ethical and spiritual, as contrasted with its previous quasi-material, significance. This is shown by the fact that John's baptism is described as a " baptism of repentance," [4] and that it was preceded by, or at any rate closely associated with, a confession of sins.[5]   Here we discern for the first time two of the essential elements of the great Christian rite of Initiation, namely (*a*) Confession, and (*b*) Baptism.   The purpose of John's baptism is said to have been the " forgiveness of sins," [6] and we need not doubt that he and his disciples believed that this was really effected by the act ; the distinction between a declaratory symbol and an efficacious sacrament is too subtle to be grasped by unreflective enthusiasts such as were those who thronged to hear the Baptist's preaching, and is, in any case, alien to ancient modes of thought.   This " remission of sins," it would seem, had an eschatological orientation and purpose.   Those who received it believed that they had been thereby invested with an invisible spiritual " character," which would be their passport through the terrors of the End, and would ensure their entrance into the calm haven of the Messianic millennium.   We are not told that any verbal formula was associated with John's baptism.   Despite his eclipse by his mightier Successor, and his early death, his movement seems to have possessed sufficient vitality to persist in the form of a " Johannite " sect, which survived as a kind of parasite on

---

[1] *Cf.* Lev. xv. *passim*, xvii. 15, 16 ; Num. xix.

[2] Jos. *B.J.*, II. viii. 7.

[3] *Jewish Encyclopaedia*, arts. " Baptism " and " Proselyte."

[4] Luke iii. 3 ; Acts xix. 4.   [5] Matt. iii. 6 = Mark i. 5.

[6] Luke iii. 3.

Christianity, administering the "baptism of John," at least down to A.D. 55. It will be remembered that one of its most illustrious members was Apollos, who was eventually led by Aquila and Priscilla into the larger life of the Christian Church.[1]

It is in contrast with this baptism of John that we perceive most clearly the *differentia* of Christian Baptism, or baptism "into the name of the Lord Jesus." We are told that at Ephesus St. Paul found certain members of the Johannite sect, who are given the title of "disciples,"[2] and must therefore be presumed to have been indistinguishable in most respects from full Christians, but who appear to have manifested none of those supernormal phenomena generally attributed to the action of the "Spirit," and who upon examination confessed that they had not even heard of His existence. St. Paul thereupon rebaptizes them "in the name of the Lord Jesus"; and we are told that when this rebaptism had been completed by the imposition of the Apostle's hands, the Holy Spirit came upon them, with the result that they at once manifested the characteristic signs of His presence, namely, "glossolaly" and prophecy.[3] This incident is instructive. It shows, first of all, that the baptism of John and Christian Baptism at this date were regarded as entirely different things, not as imperfect and perfect forms of the same thing. Secondly, we gather that, on the external side, the *differentia* of Christian Baptism is found in the employment of the "name of Jesus" as part of a spoken formula ; and, thirdly, that on the spiritual side its characteristic effect is, not merely the "remission of sins," which the Johannine baptism also claimed to bestow, but the impartation of "holy spirit." We need not here investigate the psychological *rationale* of the extraordinary phenomena which the early Christians attributed to "holy spirit," or the validity of the conception itself. We are only concerned to draw attention to the fact that, whereas Johannine initiation consisted only of (*a*) repentance, and (*b*) baptism effecting only the "remission of sins," Christian Initiation consisted of (*a*) repentance, (*b*) baptism, and (*c*) laying on of hands, which produced *both* the "remission of sins" *and also* possession of the Holy Spirit.

This ascription to Christian Initiation of a *double* effect, negative and positive, sin-annulling and Spirit-bestowing, appears

---

[1] Acts xviii. 26.   [2] Acts xix. 1.

[3] Acts xix. 1–7.

to run back into the very earliest days of the infant Church. On the Day of Pentecost St. Peter instructs his Jewish hearers as follows : " *Repent* ye, and *be baptized* every one of you *in the name of Jesus Christ,* unto the remission of your sins ; *and ye shall receive the gift of the Holy Ghost.*" [1] In other words, whereas the Johannine practice was a water-baptism only, the Christian rite was both a water-baptism and a Spirit-baptism. At first, it would seem, the illapse of the Spirit was mediated by the baptism alone.[2] Later, when the Apostles began to be confronted by baptisms which did not at once produce the supernormal *charismata* which testified to the Spirit's presence, it was found, as at Samaria,[3] that the imposition of the Apostles' hands was accompanied by the bestowal of what was lacking in the way of spiritual gifts ; and thus, apparently, the impartation of the Spirit became specifically associated with the " laying on of hands " as a distinct, though not as yet a separate, part of the rite. In this way what we now call " Confirmation " came into existence as embodying the positive effects of Initiation, the negative effects being specifically associated with the actual washing ; and in the Epistle to the Hebrews we find the " doctrine of baptisms " and of " the laying on of hands " bracketed together as part of the " foundation," in which it is assumed that adult Christians do not need instruction.[4] The complete continuity between this Apostolic practice and the combined rite of Penance, Baptism, and Confirmation, as we find it in the early patristic period,[5] does not need to be emphasised.

It is clear from the language of the New Testament that the subjects of this initiatory rite were normally adults, who alone were capable of the repentance and confession which formed its initial stage ; though it would be rash to assert that children were never baptized, and the well-known saying of Polycarp, " eighty and six years have I served Christ," [6] seems to show that at least one instance of infant baptism must have taken place before the fall of Jerusalem in A.D. 70. Consonantly with this fact, it appears that " the sins " which are conceived as being washed

---

[1] Acts ii. 38.

[2] Exceptionally, as in the case of Cornelius and his household, the illapse of the Spirit might actually precede the baptism (Acts x. 44 ff.).

[3] Acts viii. 14.   [4] Heb. vi. 2.

[5] *E.g.* Tertullian, *De Baptismo,* 7, 8, 20.

[6] *Martyrium Polycarpi,* 9.

away by Baptism are what we should call *actual* sins.[1]   Yet, in
the exuberant enthusiasm of the Church's youth, it was natural
to assume that interior conversion of the soul and exterior
initiation into the Christian society were, not merely in theory
but in fact, different aspects of the same process, like the concave
and convex aspects of a curve.   At first, Baptism seemed to have
the effect of transforming its recipient into a " new creation," [2]
so effectually that all his sinful impulses and appetites were
destroyed, and sin became both a moral and a psychological
impossibility for him.   We need not now review the steps of the
process whereby it was found, through bitter experience, that
this ultra-optimistic estimate of the transforming effects of Initiation was exaggerated, and whereby, in the teeth of embittered
opposition, " Penitence " was detached from its place at the
beginning of the initiatory rite, and shaped into a subsidiary
sacrament for the purpose of imparting a second remission of sins
to post-baptismal offenders.   We are only concerned with the
ideas which prevailed on these subjects during the lifetime of
St. Paul ; and it is sufficient to refer the reader for an extensive
treatment of the effects of Christian Initiation to cc. v–viii. of
the Epistle to the Romans, in which the Apostle elaborates the
primitive ideas of the " remission of sins " and the bestowal of
" Holy Spirit " into a magnificent sequence of pictorial conceptions, representing the effects of " faith " and Baptism, that
is of the whole change from non-Christianity to Christianity,
under the figures of incorporation into the Messiah,[3] the crucifixion of the " old man," [4] the " annihilation of the body of sin," [5]
a mystical participation in the death, burial and resurrection
of the Redeemer-God, and the reception of the " Spirit of
adoption," [6] which entitles the neophytes to repeat the words of
the Lord's own prayer, " *Abba*, Father," [7] and which will one
day transform them into the " splendour of the freedom of the
children of God." [8]   A more prosaic, but no less characteristic,

---

[1] It is impossible here to examine the *rationale* of Paedo-baptism and its
connection with the doctrine of " original sin " ; a full discussion of the matter
will be found in my forthcoming Bampton Lectures, *The Ideas of the Fall and
of Original Sin.*

[2] 2 Cor. v. 17.   [3] Rom. vi. 3 ; *cf.* Gal. iii. 27.

[4] Rom. vi. 6.   [5] vi. 6.   [6] viii. 15.

[7] viii. 15 : for the interpretation of " Abba, Father " as the opening words
of the Lord's Prayer, see Th. Zahn, *Römerbrief* (1910), p. 395.

[8] viii. 18 ff.

summary of the various elements in Christian Initiation, both inner and outer, is found in 1 Cor. vi. 11, in which passage the Apostle, after having detailed various abominable types of human sin, adds, with considerable frankness—" And such were some of you [in your pre-Christian lives] ; but ye were *washed*, but ye were *sanctified*, but ye were *justified* [i.e. *absolved*] in the *name of the Lord Jesus* Messiah and in the *Spirit* of our God."

It has been said above that this Pauline conception is clearly continuous, indeed identical, with the doctrine of the earliest Christian writers outside the New Testament, that is, for all practical purposes, with the Catholic doctrine. Can it show a similar continuity with the ideas held in regard to Baptism during the earliest days of Christianity ? *Prima facie* the continuity between St. Peter's teaching as reported in Acts ii. 38 and St. Paul's teaching as expressed in the passages just mentioned appears to be without a break ; the threefold scheme, Penitence, Baptism with water in the Name of the Lord Jesus, Reception of " Holy Spirit," runs all through the New Testament allusions to the subject. We have already adduced considerations to show that St. Paul was not likely to have " paganised," or to have acquiesced in the " paganisation " by his converts of, an originally non-sacramental custom ; and these considerations apply just as much to Initiation as to the Eucharist. It is true that his theology of Initiation represents in one respect an advance upon the primitive ideas embodied in the early chapters of the Acts, in so far as the spiritual effect of Baptism is said to include not merely the impartation of "Holy Spirit" but a transcendental or mystical union with Jesus, the *Kyrios* : this, however, is not so much an addition to the primitive teaching as a clarification of it, which necessarily followed from the ever-growing realisation of the personal distinction between " the Lord " and " the Spirit." The suggestion that the Pauline or deutero-Pauline phrase " having cleansed it " (the Church) " by washing of water with a word " [1] implies a magical conception of Baptism (the " word " being the Name of Jesus used as a spell) and therefore the beginnings of " pagan infiltration," seems purely arbitrary.

We are, then, entitled to conclude, on the basis of this survey of the relevant New Testament passages, that one single conception of " Initiation " runs through the thought and the

[1] Eph. v. 26.

surviving literature of the Christian Church between the Day of Pentecost (? A.D. 29 or 30) and the destruction of Jerusalem (A.D. 70). This Christian Initiation, with its *three* members, Penitence, Washing, Reception of " Spirit," is clearly based upon the Baptist's initiation, which included *two* members only, Penitence and Washing.   In fact, the Christian rite may be described as being identical with John's baptism, save for the addition of two all-important features, one external and the other internal, namely, the use of a formula containing the name of Jesus,[1] and the consequent or concomitant impartation of " Holy Spirit " to the baptized person.   By what authority or by whose will were these additions made ?   Three considerations may be adduced, the cumulative effect of which (I would suggest) is to establish a very great probability that the historic cause which transformed the baptism of John into Christian Baptism was the expressed will of Christ Himself.

(1) The language of 1 Cor. x. 1–4, with its reference to the Old Testament types of the two great sacraments, shows that St. Paul bracketed together Baptism and the Eucharist, very much as a modern Christian might, as rites of equal or all but equal dignity and awe.   (" Our fathers . . . were all baptized unto Moses in the cloud and in the sea, and did all eat the same spiritual meat, and did all drink the same spiritual drink." [2])   But there cannot be any doubt that he bases the whole wonder and mystery of the Eucharist on the fact of its Dominical institution, and it is extremely unlikely that he would have coupled with it, as a rite on the same level, a mere Church-custom which could not claim a similar august origin.   It is, further, inconceivable that he can have based his exalted conception of Baptism on nothing at all, or that he naïvely took this rite for granted without raising

[1] The early and universal substitution of the Name of the Father, Son, and Holy Ghost for the " Name of the Lord Jesus " was presumably due to the influence of Matt. xxviii. 19.   In view of the eighteen centuries of prescription which the use of the Three-fold Name can now claim, the modern Church is doubtless justified in making its employment an absolute condition of the technical " validity " of the rite as administered at the present day ; but the Roman Catholic scholar, W. Koch (*Die Taufe im N.T.*, 1921, p. 7) quotes Pope Nicholas I (*Respons. ad consult. Bulgar.*, *ap.* Denzinger-Bannwart, *Encheiridion Symb. et Def.*, 335), Cajetan, and Hadrian of Utrecht (later Pope Hadrian VI) as asserting the standing validity of baptism " in the name of Jesus " or " of Christ."

[2] See Kirsopp Lake, *Earlier Epistles of St. Paul*, pp. 178, 213.

the question of its *provenance*. It is equally improbable that, like Tertullian,[1] he connected the saving effects of Baptism with the intrinsic properties of water, or that he relied on the authority of John the Baptist, whose baptism he expressly declares at Ephesus to have been imperfect and provisional. And it would be anachronistic in the extreme to suppose that his theology of Baptism, as a mystical identification with the death and resurrection of the Messiah, was founded merely on an " induction " from the " observed effects " of a custom which owed its origin and universal diffusion to mere chance. The earliest Christians were not self-conscious enough to analyse their " experience " in the manner of the modern introspective psychologist, or to base scientific " inductions " upon it. The fact that St. Paul's extant correspondence does not contain any explicit attribution of the institution of Baptism to Christ does not prove that other letters of his now lost may not have contained such an attribution ; and an argument *a silentio* hostile to " Dominical institution " cannot legitimately be based upon this fact.[2] We are therefore entitled to claim, on the ground of the great solemnity with which St. Paul speaks of Baptism, implicitly co-ordinating it in respect of majesty and efficaciousness with the Lord's Supper, a very high degree of probability for the supposition that he believed its celebration to be founded on the declared will of Christ. And if such was St. Paul's conviction, it must also have been the current teaching of the Mother Church of Jerusalem. He can hardly have claimed for his teaching with regard to Baptism any other authority than that on which he bases his Eucharistic doctrine— " I received of the Lord " (through the mediation of those who had known Him in the flesh) " that which also I delivered unto you . . ."

(2) The narrative of the Day of Pentecost contained in

---

[1] *De Baptismo*, 3–5.

[2] The much-quoted sentence, 1 Cor. i. 17, " Christ sent me not to baptize, but to preach the gospel," if interpreted in the light of its context, merely means that St. Paul's characteristic function, as Apostle of the Gentiles, was preaching, rather than (what we should call) liturgical ministration ; he usually employed others to baptize for him, in order to avoid the possibility of his converts developing an excessive attachment to his own person. Under circumstances similar to those which prevailed at Corinth, these words would have risen quite naturally to the lips of many Catholic mission preachers, from Savonarola down to Father Dolling ; and it seems purely arbitrary to construe them as a disparagement of Baptism or a denial of its Dominical institution.

Acts ii. represents St. Peter as stating, without a moment's hesitation or reflection, the fully developed theory of Christian
Initiation in its three elements, Penitence, Baptism, and the
reception of Holy Spirit.[1]   If this narrative can be taken as
historically exact, Dominical institution is proved, because there
had been obviously no time in which St. Peter could have considered the results of Christian Baptism and formed an inductive
conclusion to the effect that it really did impart the Holy Spirit.
We do not, however, leave out of sight the fact that the reminiscences of those earliest days transmitted to St. Luke by the
Christians of the first generation, may have been unconsciously
modified and remoulded in the light of subsequent experience ;
and we will not therefore claim this passage as testifying to more
than the conviction of the Palestinian Church, some twenty-five
years after the resurrection, that Peter did on the Day of Pentecost
behave and speak as though he knew beforehand what spiritual
effects Christian Baptism would produce, a knowledge which in
the nature of the case could only have been derived from the
Lord Himself.   This passage therefore indirectly testifies to the
belief in Dominical institution, as held by the Mother Church
of Christendom less than a generation after the end of Christ's
earthly life.

(3) The two foregoing considerations have reference ultimately to the beliefs of the Church of Jerusalem, the fountain-
head of all Christian tradition, shortly after the middle of the
first century of our era.   But to this may be added a consideration
based upon probabilities arising out of admitted facts.   If Christian
Baptism does not rest upon the declared will of Jesus Himself it
must be regarded as the continuation within Christianity, either
of John's eschatological baptism, or of Jewish proselyte-baptism.
(There is not the slightest reason for supposing that the first
Christians were influenced by the practice of the Essenes.)   Now
it is not likely that the disciples of Jesus would, in the absence of
express instructions from Him, have continued the custom peculiar
to John.   From the point of view of our Lord's followers, John
had no importance save as the forerunner of the Messiah (" he
that is but little in the kingdom of God is greater than he " [2]) ;
and there is no reason why a custom of his should have been
supposed to be invested with an authority which did not belong

[1] Acts ii. 38.   [2] Matt. xi. 11—Luke vii. 28.

to its author. This view, moreover, leaves unexplained the immense importance attributed to the use of " the name of the Lord Jesus " by the earliest Christians : it is not likely that the baptism of John was ever administered in the name of John, either by the Baptist himself or by his later disciples. The second hypothesis, that Christian Baptism represents the mere survival of Jewish proselyte-baptism, appears equally unsatisfactory Proselyte-baptism could *ex hypothesi* only be administered to " sinners of the Gentiles," who were assumed to be polluted with idolatry and stained with all the vices of the Graeco-Roman world ; and to invite orthodox Jews, members of the holy nation, such as were the three thousand baptized on the Day of Pentecost, to submit to this rite would have been to offer them a gratuitous insult, if such an invitation had no better authority behind it than St. Peter's own sense of the fitness of things.

Both these hypotheses, therefore, are quite inadequate to explain the deeply impressive phenomenon of the universal prevalence of Christian Baptism from the earliest days of the movement onwards : and the use of the " Method of Residues " suggests that the true explanation is to be found in some command, or expression of purpose, given by the Lord Himself.

We claim, then, that for the unbiassed explorer of the origins of Christian Initiation these three considerations constitute a group of direction-signs, converging upon the supposition that our Lord, during His earthly life or through one of the resurrection-visions, conveyed to His followers some clear indication of His will in the matter ; and that by themselves they would render " Dominical institution " at least much more probable than any other hypothesis, even if no record of any facts which could be interpreted as such an " institution " had survived. Another finger-post, pointing the same way, is to be seen in the prediction of the Baptist that the Messiah would inaugurate a " Spirit-baptism," which (in St. Mark's version) is explicitly contrasted with the speaker's own " water-baptism." [1] Deeply significant, too, is the fact that Jesus Himself, having submitted to John's " baptism of repentance " in Jordan, experiences forthwith the illapse of the Spirit, which mediates to Him the full realisation of His divine Sonship and therewith some unimaginable consciousness of new birth, as expressed in the mystic locution

[1] Mark i. 8 ; Matt. iii. 11—Luke iii. 16.

2 K

"Thou art my Son, to-day have I begotten thee." [1] It does not appear an exaggeration to suggest that by undergoing this momentous experience, in which the interior influx of the Spirit was super-added to the exterior affusion of water, our Lord Himself, in His own Person, transformed the water-baptism of John into Christian Spirit-baptism.

We are now in a position to effect our final evaluation of the evidence. If we place in that scale of the balance which represents "Dominical institution" the cumulative probabilities set out above, adding thereto the feather-weight of the Matthaean testimony ; and if we throw into the opposite scale what is in the last resort the only positive argument for "accidental origin," namely, the assumption of our Lord's "eschatologically limited outlook," an assumption which we have already seen to be of a highly arbitrary nature and devoid of any real weight, the reader will be able to judge for himself which scale must be taken to sink and which to "kick the beam." If, in Butler's words, "probability is the very guide of life," [2] and if, in dealing with events which lie on the further side of a gulf of nearly nineteen centuries, a very high degree of probability may be taken as the practical equivalent of certainty, in sacred as in profane history, the "Dominical institution," in some form, of Christian Initiation may be regarded as reasonably assured.

If a more precise determination of the mode of this "institution" be demanded, the following theory may be tentatively put forward. The Fourth Gospel tells us that, towards the beginning of His ministry, Jesus "came into the land of Judaea, and there . . . baptized," at a time when John was still engaged in administering *his* baptism, at Aenon near to Salim (iii. 22, 23). This statement is amplified in iv. 1 by the note that the baptism o₁ Jesus soon outstripped that of John in popularity, and slightly modified in the following verse by the observation that Jesus (like St. Paul at a later date [3]) did not Himself act as the ministrant of baptism, but delegated this function to His disciples. If these statements are historical (and there seems to be no reason why they should not be [4]) a probable outline of events suggests itself ;

---

[1] Luke iii. 22 (according to the "Western," and apparently more probable, reading).

[2] *Analogy of Religion*, Introduction.   [3] See above, p. 415, n. 2.

[4] It is coming to be universally admitted that the Fourth Gospel contains at least a large infusion of good and reliable tradition, and the details noted above may well belong to such tradition.

namely, (1) our Lord receives baptism from John, and through it the influx of " Spirit " ; (2) He consequently (if we may, without irreverence, employ human language in this regard) conceives the idea of a Messianic baptism, superior to the Forerunner's baptism, which will admit to the " Kingdom " (that is, to the New Dispensation) and impart " Holy Spirit " ; (3) He Himself administers, or provides for the administration of, this baptism during His earthly lifetime, as the means of initiating men into the little group of His adherents, which was the nucleus of the future *Ecclesia* ; (4) this pre-Passional administration of Baptism was, however, necessarily imperfect, just as the one pre-Passional celebration of the Eucharist was imperfect [1] ; though Jesus received the Spirit *for Himself*, at His own baptism, He could not as yet impart Spirit to others, " for Spirit was not yet " [so far as our Lord's adherents were concerned] " because Jesus was not yet glorified," [2] in other words, because He had still to *win* the gift of the Spirit for His new Israel by His suffering and death. Consequently (5) through one or more of the resurrection-appearances He intimates to His followers that the preliminary water-baptism which they have received, whether from John or Himself, will be supplemented and validated by the gift of the Spirit (" ye shall be baptized with the Holy Ghost not many days hence " [3]), and that the complete rite of Initiation is henceforth to be the means of admission into the new People of God.[4]

VI

CONCLUSION

If the foregoing considerations are well founded, we are entitled to conclude that the " institution," in the sense previously defined, of the two original and fundamental sacraments, Initiation and Communion, by the Founder of Christianity Himself, may be taken as proved, in the sense that the historical evidence for this hypothesis would be regarded as sufficient by an unbiassed inquirer. The outlines of the traditional theory stand fast, though a certain amount of reconstruction and restatement has

---

[1] See the Note at the end of this essay. [2] John vii. 39.
[3] Acts i. 5. [4] Matt. xxviii. 19.

been necessary in regard to detail. It may be reasonably asserted that the affirmation of the Dominical origin of the sacraments rests upon a much wider and more nearly contemporaneous consensus of testimony than do the affirmations of the birth of Herodotus at Halicarnassus or of the martyrdom of St. Peter at Rome ; and yet, of these two latter affirmations the first is not challenged at all, and the second is only disputed by those who on other grounds are strongly opposed to the claims which are made in the name of St. Peter by the present Church of Rome. If, then, the reader is still prepared to admit the cogency of the contention developed in the second section of this essay—namely, (1) that *if* the sacraments were really instituted by Christ they must be of quite overwhelming importance in the Christian life, and (2) that if they are of such overwhelming importance, it can only be because the grounds of their efficacy contain an element which is simply " given " or objective—a task of no small significance will have been accomplished.

But though the argument set forth above would, we believe, be good enough for a student who approached the question without *parti pris*, we do not claim for it mathematical irresistibility.   As it will always be possible (*si parva licet componere magnis*) for those who are subconsciously dominated by anti-papal sentiment to deny any sort of connection between St. Peter and Rome, so doubtless it will always be open to those who feel an unconquerable aversion from the idea of objectively efficacious sacraments to reject the case for Dominical institution on one ground or another.   To affirm this is not to fall into the vulgarity of imputing a lack of intellectual honesty to those who, like Eduard Meyer, are convinced *a priori* that " The thought, that the congregation . . . enters into a mystical or magical communion with its Lord through the reception of bread and wine . . . can never have been uttered by Jesus Himself " [1] ; it is merely to draw attention to the well-known fact that, in the concrete processes of psychic life, thought and feeling mutually suffuse and interpenetrate one another, and that men's judgments as to what is true, especially in regard to historical questions on which vital practical issues depend, are apt to be insensibly deflected by the unconscious wish that some particular solution may turn out to be true.   Whether the influence of such disturbing factors has

[1] E. Meyer, *Ursprung u. Anfänge des Christentums* (1921), i. 179.

been successfully eliminated from our own exposition or not must be left to the reader's decision.

It does not in any case fall within the scope of this essay to deal in detail with the ancient and indurated anti-sacramental *praeiudicium*, which is the real, though hidden, source of the inhibition which restrains many religious persons from so much as considering the possibility that historic Christianity may actually be in possession of the marvellous treasure which it claims. The unexpressed conviction, which to those who hold it appears axiomatic, that a religion of priests, sacraments, liturgies, and ecclesiastical institutions—a religion, that is, which avowedly expresses itself through a phenomenal body or time-garment— must in the nature of things be a lower and inferior kind of religion in comparison with one consisting solely of intellectual concepts or ethical values, eludes dialectical attack by virtue of its emotional origin and its unprovable character. It is not, indeed, difficult to formulate the arguments on which it is nominally founded, as (*a*) that it is degrading to our conception of God to suppose that He can or will produce spiritual effects through the direct instrumentality of material things or external and sensible ceremonies ; (*b*) that sacraments understood in any other than a purely symbolic sense involve a sacerdotalism which is inevitably hostile to individual and civic freedom ; (*c*) that the belief in their objective efficacy is refuted by the sins of many who habitually receive them and the lofty Christian virtues of many who, like the Quakers, reject them. Nor is it harder to set against each of these arguments a group of considerations which would seem in logic to cancel it. To the first, it might be replied that God has never told us that He cannot or will not work spiritual effects through matter or the phenomenal world ; that unless we are prepared to accept a Deistic or Manichaean dualism, He is doing so every day through His immanent Real Presence in the vast multiform sacrament of the visible universe ; that (as Bishop Gore has pointed out) no spiritual operation ascribed to the sacraments of the Church is more sharply super-naturalistic, or bears a more frankly *ex opere operato* character, than the miracle whereby the creation of a new, unique, and individual human personality supervenes upon the consummation of what, considered in itself, is a purely material process. To the second the obvious rejoinder is, that whilst any institution existing amongst men is doubtless capable of perversion, Catholic sacerdotalism, involving as it does that impersonal conception of the part played by the human officiant which is expressed in the doctrine that " the unworthiness of the minister hindereth not the effect of the sacraments," is in principle much less liable to abuse by private ambition than theories of the ministerial function which by placing its essence in preaching and exhortation make its efficaciousness to depend entirely upon the talents, virtues and personal qualities of the individual minister ; and that the history of Calvinistic Geneva and Puritan Massachusetts is sufficient to show that ecclesiastical tyranny has no necessary connection with any one type of sacramental theory. The third is sufficiently countered by two principles which are inherent in the Catholic theology of sacramental grace, namely, *Deus non alligatur mediis,* and *Homo potest sacramentorum gratiae obicem ponere.* But the real vitality of the anti-sacramental *praeiudicium* resides in the emotional energy with which it is charged, and which flows from various underground sources—fear of the Papacy, the xenophobia which makes beliefs held by members of other nations than one's own appear for that reason alone as intrinsically repulsive, the unconscious survival of dualistic modes of thought which sunder God from all contact with matter, hereditary influence, and social suggestion. Those who are subject to this prepossession must always argue back from it to a negation of " Dominical institution " ; it will always appear self-evident to them that Jesus, as the highest spiritual teacher known to our race, cannot have intended to found what they believe to be a religion of the lower grade, and that therefore any evidence that He did so intend must be unreliable.

Historical argument alone can no more dissolve so tough and closely knit a psychic structure than it can create the corresponding, but opposite, conviction, the deep, calm, infinitely satisfying intuition which can only be experienced by those who know the Catholic system from within, and which reveals to them the ineffable harmony and homogeneity of the sacramental principle with the kindred truths of God's immanence in the whole world of created being and of His unique self-expression in the Incarnation. But faith can move mountains, and love wear down seemingly adamantine barriers ; and the believer in the traditional interpretation of the Christian sacraments will rely upon their inherent power and mysterious compelling attractiveness to be in the long run their most effective missionary. He will confidently accept the implied challenge of Dr. Kirsopp Lake's words, " If the Catholic theory of sacraments prove in the end to cover all the facts, and to be the only theory which does cover them, it will in the end be universally accepted " [1] ; and he will look for the ultimate fulfilment in a re-united Catholic Christendom of the promise made to the Church of the elder dispensation : " In those days it shall come to pass, that ten men shall take hold out of all languages of the nations, even shall take hold of the skirt of him that is a Jew, saying, We will go with you, for we have heard that GOD is with you." [2]

ADDITIONAL NOTE ON MARK XIV. 25

A point connected with this *logion* may be here further explained, in order to elucidate the view taken in the text as to the significance of our Lord's actions at the Last Supper :

The implied contrast between the " old wine " which our Lord had just drunk Himself (this is clearly indicated by the words " I will not *again* drink . . ."—οὐκέτι οὐ μὴ πίω) and given to His disciples, and the " fruit of the vine " which He would drink " new " in the Kingdom of God, suggests that the *imperfect* and *provisional* character, which in the text of the essay has been attributed to the only pre-Passional " celebration of the Eucharist," may have been so thoroughgoing as to make it true to describe our Lord's actions on that occasion as constituting, not a " Eucharist " as we know it now, but a " shadow " Eucharist— a typical object-lesson, not the mystic and glorious reality which could only be consummated in the " Kingdom of God " (*i.e.* the new Christian dispensation) which His death was to inaugurate. If this is a permissible view, the Apostles at the Last Supper did not feed upon Christ, as we do now, in reality, but only in figure ; their first real and sacramental Communion in the body and blood of Christ can only have been made after that body and blood had been glorified and freed from spatial limitations by the resurrection. This view completely avoids the almost insoluble difficulty inherent in the traditional interpretation—" How could our Lord with His own hands give His body and blood to His disciples (*se dat suis manibus*) whilst evidently standing there before them in His intact, unbroken body ? " It must be admitted that there is no ancient authority for this view : but it appears to be that favoured by Dr. H. L. Goudge, " 1 Corinthians," p. 105.

[1] *Earlier Epistles of St. Paul*, 1911, p. 434. [2] Zech. viii. 22.

THE EUCHARIST

BY WILL SPENS

CONTENTS

I

INTRODUCTORY

IT has often been said that one of the greatest needs of our time is a satisfactory glossary of religious terms. As things stand, the Christian apologist finds himself confronted with a dilemma. On the one hand, it is possible for him to try to discard much of the traditional phraseology in which Christian ideas are clothed, and to use only such language as may be supposed to be intelligible to any educated person. The obvious danger of such a policy is that he will, in fact, fail to convey many of the deeper and more difficult ideas for the expression and transmission of which the technical language was developed. His attempt would be like that of a man of science, who should try to give some account of the physical universe without employing any of those terms which scientists have invented. The other alternative is for the apologist to accept frankly the terminology with which the piety and thought of the Church have provided him, and to draw out its significance for the faith of intelligent men to-day. In pursuing this task he may find that some of the old terms are, in fact, no longer useful ; or, again, he may find that they are only useful if they are given a somewhat different meaning from that which they originally connoted. None the less, this policy has certain advantages. It goes far to ensure, for example, that no elements of proved value in the thought of the past are lost by misadventure ; while, since the terms which he is discussing are not merely intellectual but also emotional symbols, his thought is kept at every point in close contact with the concrete experience of the worshipping Church. These conditions apply with peculiar force in dealing with a subject like the Eucharist, which is the acknowledged centre of the Church's devotional life, and yet has, for many centuries, given rise to acute theological controversy. Here, if anywhere, it is obviously important that discussion should be synthetic, as well as clear ; and for this purpose it is essential that the second of the two possible policies should be adopted.

In the present case, moreover, this course is clearly more convenient, inasmuch as many of the terms which belong to the current coin of Eucharistic theology have been the subject of careful discussion in the preceding essays and the result of those discussions will be assumed here. Thus the seventh essay will have made clear the sense in which the word " grace " is used when we speak of the sacrament as a " means of grace." Again, much has already been said in the essay on the Atonement about the cross as a sacrifice for sin, expressive at once of sin's awfulness and of its forgiveness. Still more germane, of course, to the present essay, is that which has immediately preceded it, in which it was urged that the sacraments are not merely dramatic but effectual symbols, and that they derive their significance from the fact of our Lord's appointment. All these words—grace, sacrifice, sacraments, symbol—will occur again in a rather different setting in our consideration of the Eucharist, together with other terms to which reference has not yet been made ; but the discussion will assume, throughout, the general theological and historical background provided by the rest of this volume.

II

SYMBOL AND SACRAMENT

It would probably not be denied that symbolism of some kind is a necessity of religion as soon as it receives a social and institutional expression. That this is so would seem to be proved not least by the practice of those Christian bodies which have, in fact, set themselves, so far as possible, to do without it. Nowhere is this more clear to us than in the case of the Society of Friends, whose emphasis upon the sovereignty of the inward aspect of religion has not prevented them from adopting a symbolism in dress and speech which was, at one time, a picturesque and well-known feature of English life. Symbols are, in fact, a kind of language which men use when words fail them. One aspect of this use was expressed by Pope Gregory the Great, when he spoke of images as the " books of the unlettered," [1] implying that words would be beyond their wit to read ; another aspect is expressed in civic, no less than in religious, ceremonies, as when the unfurling of a flag or the beating of a drum expresses something for which words would be too weak. Symbolism of this kind occurs frequently in the historical and prophetic books of the Old Testament ;

[1] Gregory, Lib. ix, Ep. cv, *ad Serenum.*

and our Lord's entry into Jerusalem provides a significant example of it in the New. In all such cases, however, the symbolism is dramatic or didactic.

There is, however, another kind of symbolism to which the word effectual may be given, and which is no less a feature of human society ; and it is to this type rather than to the other that the Christian sacraments belong. The distinctive mark of an effectual symbol is that it not merely conveys a message, but effects a result. The accolade is a case in point. More familiar, if less obvious, examples are supplied by token coinage to which an authoritative decision of the State gives certain purchasing value, defined in terms of the sovereign, but quite independent of the coin's intrinsic worth. A little reflection will suggest, in ever-growing number, other illustrations. The essence of such symbolism lies in the association of certain results or opportunities with certain visible signs by a will which is competent to bring about those results or give those opportunities. To the properties which the action or object has in itself are added other properties which may be civic, social, or economic, and it is this second series of properties which is taken for all practical purposes as determining the nature of the symbolic action or object. Those who recognise the authority which appoints the token do not, in fact, use or think of their florins as though they were counters.

From all merely human symbolism, even of this type, the sacraments are, of course, differentiated by the character of the results and opportunities connected with them, and by the fact that these are determined by the will of God Himself ; but none the less the analogy is valuable and real. When we say that the sacraments are effectual signs we mean that certain actions or objects are invested by divine authority with certain spiritual or supernatural properties. The action of washing, for example, in Baptism admits the baptized not merely into the visible fellowship of the Church but into the regenerate order, the Kingdom of God, of which the Church on earth is the expression. In the case of the Eucharist, the bread and the wine are given by Christ's ordinance new properties, which, while they do not annihilate the natural properties of giving sustenance and refreshment, yet so supersede these that we can rightly speak of the objects themselves as wholly changed and transfigured. As Theodoret says, " They remain in their former substance and shape and form, and are still visible and as they were before ; but they are apprehended as what they have become, and are believed and adored as being what they are believed to be." [1]

These considerations, moreover, will enable us to make clear what was involved when Christian theology found itself unable to rest contented with the close parallelism between Baptism and the Eucharist on which the earlier Fathers, notably St. Augustine, used to insist. The form which the development took was the claim that the Eucharist contained not only the two elements which were recognised in Baptism—namely, *sacramentum* and *virtus sacramenti*—but a third element also, which was distinguished as *res sacramenti*. In other words, it was claimed that in the Eucharist there was not only a symbolism of action, but a symbolism of objects as well. And this threefold distinction is a development which is reflected in Anglican formularies, where our Catechism speaks, in the case of the Eucharist, of " sign," " thing signified," and " benefits." If we ask, moreover, the reason which prompted this development we shall be compelled to find it in the words which our Lord is represented as using at the institution of the Eucharist —words which have no parallel in the case of Baptism. To the narratives of that institution we must now turn with a view to discovering what our Lord meant by the effectual symbolism of objects which He then established.

III

The Eucharistic Sacrifice

If a student of comparative religion, not otherwise acquainted with Christianity, were to enter a church where the Holy Mysteries were being celebrated, and were afterwards asked what kind of service he had been attending, he would undoubtedly say that it was some sacrificial rite ; and he would find his answer endorsed if he were to turn from the service which he had witnessed to the earliest narratives of its institution. It is not only that the descriptions of the rite in the New Testament are marked by certain expressions which have all the appearance of liturgical fixity, nor again that the words used by our Lord, such as the reference to the new covenant, are strongly suggestive of sacrifice. Even more significant is the fact that the records are agreed in placing the rite in a context which is replete with sacrificial associations. On the

---

[1] Dialogue II, P.G. lxxxiii. 165–168.

one hand, that is to say, it is made clear, particularly by St. Luke, that the Last Supper, and the Eucharist which was its climax, took place under the shadow of the Passover ; and the force of this fact is not diminished, if we adopt the Johannine view as to the date of the crucifixion. On the other hand, all our evidence makes it clear that the rite at the Last Supper was connected by the closest ties with that sacrifice of Christ upon the cross which was so soon to be consummated.

In the light of these facts the natural meaning of our Lord's phrase, " Take, eat, this is my body," and of the corresponding and even more startling phrase as to His blood is surely not difficult to determine : they must have meant that in receiving the bread which He had broken and the cup which He had blessed the apostles were made partakers in a sacrifice, and thereby in the blessings of a sacrifice, in which He was to be the victim. We need not suppose, nor does the evidence suggest, that ritual participation in sacrifices was always regarded as securing and conditioning spiritual consequences. We cannot assign, for example, to the Paschal meal a clear sacramental significance. But this is bound up with the fact that the Jews had apparently ceased to assign to the killing of the Paschal victims any supernatural consequences. In the case, however, of a sacrifice which was regarded as truly propitiatory (and therefore in the case of our Lord's death) it is impossible to believe that devout ritual participation in an appointed manner would not have been supposed both to secure and normally to condition participation in the blessings which flowed from it.

Or, again, if we turn to passages of the New Testament other than the records of the institution, the same conclusion holds good. St. Paul's language, for instance, seems definitely to require this view ; for he was writing for persons familiar in a greater or less degree with Mystery Religions, and it is incredible that he should not have guarded his language far more carefully, had he not regarded the Eucharist as a sacrifice, and believed that devout ritual participation in this sacrifice secured and conditioned participation in spiritual blessings. There is no evidence, moreover, that St. Paul was subject to any criticism on the score of his Eucharistic teaching, and it must therefore be taken as representing what the apostles understood our Lord to have meant. Once more, even the sixth chapter of the Fourth Gospel gives little real support to any different conception of the Eucharist. If by eating His flesh our Lord is taken to have meant merely the reception of His teaching, then His language as recorded could only be pronounced unaccountably misleading and provocative. A real difficulty is removed if the issue was intended to lie not between the Jews' literal interpretation of His words and a final explanation that eating our Lord's flesh meant receiving His teaching, but between that literal interpretation and the sacramental explanation which the Eucharist afforded. On such a view the phrase " the words that I have spoken unto you are spirit and are life " referred to His whole foregoing teaching, including that on the Eucharist. Whatever view be held as to this or as to the historical character of the discourse—and on that question no view is here expressed—it is safe to say that its language could not be what it is unless the Evangelist either himself understood the discourse as having a sacramental and sacrificial reference or was at least endeavouring to account for a current tradition of Dominical teaching in this sense which he could not ignore. Neither the Fourth Gospel nor any other evidence [1] affords any real ground for setting aside that conception. As we have seen, it is implied by the other Evangelists and by St. Paul ; and it may be summed up by saying that the Eucharistic Host and Chalice not only represent our Lord as appropriable in a visible rite as our sacrifice, but also render Him thus appropriable ; an idea which carries with it participation in His life.

Enough has already been said to justify the earlier statement that a stranger present at the Eucharist would naturally describe it as a sacrificial rite. It is necessary, however, in view of current misunderstandings and controversies, to carry the analysis further, and it is the more profitable to do so at this moment in view of recent developments of Eucharistic theology associated with the

---

[1] *Cf.* the Rev. W. L. Knox's Second Appendix entitled "The Primitive Eucharist " at the end of his *St. Paul and the Church of Jerusalem.* It is not easy to take seriously the attempts which have been made to use the *Didache* as an argument against a sacramental view of the Eucharist. We need only point to the standard of exegesis in the book, which is not merely trivial but on occasion manifestly superficial and untrue. For example, shortly before the often quoted passage on the Eucharist occurs the sentence : " Let not your fasts be with the hypocrites ; for they fast on Mondays and Thursdays, but do you fast on Wednesdays and Fridays " ; while shortly after it occurs the sentence : " Do not test or examine any prophet who is speaking in a spirit ; for every sin shall be forgiven, but this sin shall not be forgiven."

name of Père de la Taille.[1] The definition of sacrifice from which we shall best approach this task is that which describes it as consisting in two main and necessary elements, one the death of the victim, and the other certain ritual acts, very often concerned with the blood, which invested the death with a supernatural significance or effect. The word " death " is used rather than " destruction " because, although it is true that not all sacrificial gifts are animate and therefore cannot be said to die when sacrificed, yet the word " death " is in fact more applicable in cases where a living victim is offered. It does not, that is to say, beg the question of the purpose of the killing of the victim, but leaves the way open for the explanation that at least one purpose of the victim's death is the release and the appropriation of its life.[2] In the case of the sacrifice of the death of Christ the importance of this point is obvious. The technical term generally used for this element in a sacrifice is immolation or mactation. The principal objection which has been urged and rightly urged by Anglican theologians against what has been until recently the dominant tradition of Roman Catholic teaching, is that their doctrine of the Eucharistic sacrifice appeared to suggest a further immolation of Christ in every Mass. This idea is obviously inconsistent with the New Testament, and with its clear belief in the all-sufficing efficacy of the death of Christ. At the same time the alternative to such a view appeared to be that the Mass could only be called a sacrifice in a sense so subordinate and secondary, and so different from that entertained by Roman or Orthodox theology, as to make the description at best misleading. The importance of a definition of sacrifice on the lines suggested above is that it makes it possible to describe the Eucharist as a sacrifice in a primary sense, without involving or suggesting any repetition of the cross.

[1] In view of a considerable similarity between his doctrine of the Eucharistic Sacrifice and my own, it should be said that the position adopted in this essay was worked out independently of Père de la Taille's work, and in fact before I had become acquainted with it. It can be most fully studied in his *Mysterium Fidei de augustissimo Corporis et Sanguinis Christi Sacrificio atque Sacramento*.

[2] This fact has led Père de la Taille to say that "conversion" would be a better term than " destruction " to use of the sacrificial gift. In O.T. sacrifices (and in many others) ritual acts concerned with the blood would often appear to involve this conception, the blood representing the life to the worshippers.

For, in the first place, it is asserted on this view that the act of destruction, in virtue of which the Eucharist is a sacrifice, is the one historical death of our Lord on the cross, not some further act of destruction or other corresponding change. But, in the second place, it goes on to discover in sacrifice a second element which is no less characteristic or essential than the victim's death. We can best see the character and the necessity of this element by an illustration. Suppose that Abraham had slain Isaac without ceremony, instead of preparing to slay him on an altar or in accordance with some other convention which clearly expressed his purpose of sacrifice. Would one regard that as fulfilment of a command to sacrifice his son? Think of any other sacrifice, actual or legendary, and imagine all ritual acts omitted, leaving simply an act of destruction, not performed in a ritual manner. Whatever the purpose of the act, would it fully correspond to what we mean by a sacrifice, save as we have come to apply the term in a metaphorical sense? In short, is not some ritual act which expressly invests the death with its sacred purpose or significance at least as characteristic an element in sacrifice as is the death itself?

If, as appears to be the case, this last question must be answered in the affirmative, the explanation is not far to seek. Consider first honorific sacrifices. It is not possible to regard these simply as gifts to the deity worshipped; the gift is so made as to constitute an act of homage, a formal recognition and acknowledgment of his sovereign claims. There lies the explanation, for example, of the fact that the inherent value of that which is surrendered is, on the whole, less important than that it should have been expressly appointed or that it should possess a natural symbolism; and there also lies the explanation of the need for such act or acts as will expressly invest the rite with its significance. In consequence, if a formal definition of a sacrifice is to be attempted it would appear necessary so to frame it as to treat this aspect as an essential element, by asserting, for example, that a sacrifice is a series of related actions dictated by belief in some Higher Power and involving (*a*) the giving or giving up of something, in and through a death, to a supernatural Being—or to secure a supernatural end or to secure supernatural aid; and (*b*) an act or acts dependent on or closely related to the death, and of such a character as formally to invest this with supernatural significance, and thus to render the rite an express acknowledgment of a relation to some Higher Power.

The need for some such definition appears to be no less real in the case of propitiatory sacrifices than in the case of honorific sacrifices. We would hesitate to describe as a propitiatory sacrifice an act of destruction, even if this was conceived as effecting a propitiation, unless the act of destruction was performed in such a manner or accompanied by such further acts as served to express its purpose and significance. If a god was believed to have required the death, say, of the king's son in consequence of tribal sin, and if the king's son was promptly slain without ceremony, we should say that the purpose of his death was the propitiation of the god, but we should not describe what took place as a propitiatory sacrifice. We should so describe it if the manner of his death, or other closely related ritual acts, gave expression to the purpose and significance of the death ; and an explanation of the apparent necessity for such ritual acts may again be found in the fact that they render the rite an express acknowledgment of a relation to God, in this case a relation which has gone wrong. It is precisely in virtue of the presence and significance of such acts that there is not only a purpose of propitiation, but an avowal of that purpose. The rite thus becomes an express acknowledgment of the need for propitiation and, in so far as this propitiation is held to be necessitated by sin, an acknowledgment of the nature of sin and its significance. Nor is acknowledgment before God the whole story. Propitiatory sacrifices are conceived not only as an acknowledgment by man before God, but, in so far as they are thought of as divinely appointed, as an authoritative declaration to man of the significance and effect of sin. In short, such sacrifices have a manward as well as a Godward reference, and the declaration to man as well as the acknowledgment before God implies ritual acts which expressly assign its significance to the act of destruction.

If, then, we are justified in regarding as an essential and important element in sacrifice, no less essential or important than immolation, acts which expressly invest the immolation with its significance, the first condition is secured for a solution of our problem. It may be noted at once that as shown, for example, by the case of the Passover, it is such acts, rather than the killing of the victim, which are necessarily performed by the priest.

On this ground, and for the sake of brevity, in what follows such acts will be referred to as "sacerdotal acts."

It will by now be obvious that the view to which we are approaching is that the Last Supper and the Eucharist are not separate sacrifices from that of Calvary, but supply a necessary element in the sacrifice of Calvary, by expressly investing our Lord's death before God and man with its sacrificial significance. There is nothing, moreover, in sacrificial conceptions to preclude the multiplication of the sacerdotal acts. In the case of our Lord's sacrifice such multiplication was necessary if that sacrifice was to be truly proclaimed, and its benefits duly appropriated, by successive generations. And this necessity is not less but greater in view of the absolute significance we ascribe to our Lord's death in contrast with the "types and shadows" of the older dispensation. For, as has already been pointed out elsewhere in this volume, the essence of Christ's sacrifice on the cross consists in the fact that it is an acknowledgment before God and man of the nature and consequences of sin. It is sin's "covering" or propitiation, which is a necessary antecedent to man's reconciliation with God. What is asserted here is that the Eucharist is that part of the sacrifice of Calvary which, by our Lord's appointment, expressly invests His death with its significance and thus renders it such an acknowledgment. By it He ensured that Christian worship should be centred in the confession of God's infinite holiness and of the awfulness of sin, and that His worshippers of all times and places should only on the basis of that wholly evangelical confession stand secure in His fellowship and grace. It is not an accident that in every ancient liturgy the prayer of Consecration issues from the solemn accents, at once uplifting and humbling, of the *Sanctus*. In other words, while our Lord's death supplies in itself an adequate expression of the nature and consequences of sin, our profiting from the satisfaction thus effected must surely involve our acknowledgment and recognition of this. Such recognition requires expression no less than any other element in religion ; while, if a particular manner of acknowledgment has been appointed, then it is for us to give our recognition this expression rather than to urge, like Naaman, the equal or greater efficacy of possible alternatives.

On the other hand, we cannot regard the Eucharist simply as an acknowledgment by man that our Lord's death exhibits the

nature and results of sin, an acknowledgment which is effected by
our expressly assigning to that death the significance of an expiatory
sacrifice.[1] At the Eucharist, our Lord's death is invested with
this significance in and through a rite which, since it affords participation in the blessings of our Lord's sacrifice, must be held to be
performed with divine authority. Because it is in and through
such a rite, and therefore with such authority, that the Church's
ministers solemnly invest our Lord's death with an expiatory
significance, and thus acknowledge before God and declare to man
the nature of sin, they may properly be termed priests. On the
other hand, such a statement of the position is something less than
the truth. This Divine authority is possessed, as we believe,
because the Eucharist is celebrated by our Lord's command,
whether given at the Last Supper or through the Holy Spirit to
the early Church. In accordance with our conception of Christians not as external to our Lord, but as members of His body,
Christian acts performed by His command must be thought of less
as performed by His authority, than as performed by Him through
the members of His mystical body. As a result, He is to be conceived as Himself the Priest in the Eucharist, no less than at the
Last Supper ; but because His ministers are also our representatives
we participate in His sacerdotal act.

On such a view the Eucharist is a sacrifice, not only or primarily
because we offer thanksgiving or give money or hallow bread and
wine, or even because Christ is there given to be our food, but
because by word and act, by the words of institution and in the
double consecration and through the act of Communion, His
death is proclaimed, before God and man, as an expiatory sacrifice,
and because this express investing of a sacrificial death with its
significance is no mere declaration, adding nothing beyond declara-

---

[1] The phrase "expiatory sacrifice" is used as best describing a sacrifice
which is regarded as propitiatory alike in intention and effect, and as necessitated
by sin. That this significance is assigned to our Lord's death by the Eucharist,
and that the early Church regarded the institution as assigning to it this significance, is made clear by the words of institution, as given in the various records
and as taken up into the Eucharistic liturgies. Our Lord's body is described
as given for us, His blood as poured out for us, as inaugurating a new covenant,
and as poured out unto the remission of sins. Even apart from the presence of
the last of these phrases we should be justified in reading its meaning into any
description of our Lord's sacrifice which represents this as propitiatory, since
the propitiation thus effected was, from the first and as a matter of course, held
to be necessitated through sin.

tion, but is itself an essential element in such a sacrifice, required, not by some trick of definition, but in order to supply an overt acknowledgment and declaration of the nature and consequences of sin. Whether we think of the cross as the one sacrifice or of each Eucharist as a sacrifice, whether we speak of Christ as having been once offered upon the cross or as being offered in every Mass, depends simply on whether we are thinking in terms of one or other of two essential aspects of sacrifice. If we think of sacrifice in terms of the act of destruction, Christ was once offered upon the cross. If we think of sacrifice in terms of the sacerdotal acts which expressly invest an act of destruction with its significance, then Christ is offered in every Mass. Either view is correct from its own angle : and for either view the death is fundamental. Nor does a choice appear possible or desirable between one or other mode of expression. Both must be used in their proper context if we are not to minimise unduly either the cross or the Eucharist.

There is one subordinate point in regard to sacrifice which appears to be of sufficient value and relevance to deserve emphasis Details in the symbolism of the sacerdotal acts are often highly significant and of real devotional value. It is in this connection that it appears possible to retain and use the truth embodied in conceptions of the Eucharistic sacrifice which emphasise the offering of bread and wine. The fundamental fact in the consecration is that Christ is given to be appropriated as our sacrifice, and that His death is thus expressly invested with a sacrificial significance. But, in subordination to this, we may well dwell on the symbolism of the means by which it is secured : on the consecration of typical gifts of God ; on how much is thereby made of gifts so common or so capable of abuse ; and, by that identification of the worshipper with the thing consecrated, which is so frequent an idea in sacrifice, on the purpose of hallowing ourselves, not to become as many separate and inadequate sacrifices as there are individuals, but to become one with and in Him who is the only perfect sacrifice. If another conception of the Eucharistic sacrifice seems to have been omitted which is too deep-rooted to be thus ignored, it must be replied that the solemn assertion, before God as well as before man, of the expiatory character of our Lord's death is in itself in the strongest possible manner a pleading of that death. Further pleading of that death in the Eucharistic liturgies is valuable as bringing out what is thus involved. It can add nothing to what is involved.

To sum up. The writers of the New Testament, when they speak of the Eucharist, are unanimous in bringing it into the closest connection at once with the Passover and with the cross. They represent our Lord as celebrating this rite, if not for the first time, at least with a new (sacrificial) significance, on the eve of His passion and death. They imply a clear purpose on His part that He should be done to death at the hands of wicked men ; and they show Him forestalling the certainty that His death would appear to His disciples as no more than the judicial murder of a martyr by giving to it, in advance, a significance which, in the light of the resurrection and ascension, would supersede that other interpretation altogether. By what He said and did at the Last Supper, and in our repetition of what He then did, our Lord invested and invests His death with its significance as a sacrifice for sin ; and it was because of this that St. Paul could write, " As often as ye eat this bread and drink this cup ye show forth the Lord's death till he come," and that the writer to the Hebrews could describe the cross as an altar (Heb. xiii. 10). Both alike, the cross and the Eucharist, are integral to the sacrifice of our redemption. The fundamental element—fundamental because of the nature of Him whose life was offered on the cross—is the death of Christ ; and that immolation once made can never be repeated. But equally necessary in its bearing upon the salvation of the world is the rite by which down the long succession of ages our Lord makes His death to be our sacrifice and enables us to appropriate the blessings thus secured.

IV

THE REAL PRESENCE

The doctrine of the Real Presence, more perhaps than any other element in Eucharistic teaching, is charged with all the warmth of Christian devotion. The idea of a special presence of God would seem to be in itself one with which religion cannot dispense. It is what gives to many moments of spiritual experience, described in both the Old Testament and the New, their peculiar vividness and freshness of appeal. When Jacob says " Surely the Lord is in this place, and I knew it not " ; or when Moses, at the burning

bush, " hid his face, for he was afraid to look upon God " ; or wher
the psalmist cries " Whither shall I go from thy spirit ? o1
whither shall I flee from thy presence ? " or, again, " The Lord
is in his holy temple, the Lord's throne is in heaven "—in all
these cases we are confronted with utterances and actions which
belong to the very heart of religion.　Jewish faith in particular
distinguished three modes of this presence—in Nature, in the
Chosen People, and in that central shrine where the invisible glory
of the Shekinah brooded over the Mercy-seat ; yet there is nothing
to show that their emphasis upon any one of these displaced or
weakened their hold upon the others.　In all cases, moreover,
the context of the term presence suggests that its primary
reference is to the experience of grace, and that that reference
provides the best key to its definition.　In the New Testament we
find this element of Jewish faith, as we should expect, transfigured
by the fact of the Incarnation and the dispensation of the Spirit.
Christ is Himself the personal embodiment of the divine glory
and tabernacled amongst men.　He promised that when His visible
presence was withdrawn He would still be present in the midst of
believers gathered in His name ; and the Epistles bear abundant
witness to the way in which the earliest Christian communities
found this promise fulfilled in their experience of the Holy Spirit
and their incorporation into Christ in the Church.　The doctrine
of the Real Presence asserts that in addition to (but as a consequence
of) the more general presence in the Church, the Eucharist
affords a presence of our Lord as our sacrifice, and that this
presence is of such a character as to give opportunity for full and
concrete expression of our worship of the Lamb.

No more than in the case of the Jewish Shekinah are other
modes of our Lord's presence depreciated or excluded ; and,
indeed, all true Eucharistic theology insists that in the Eucharist
our Lord is present as priest as well as victim.　The sacramental
presence, that is to say, depends upon and derives from Christ's
priestly presence in the Church　But that is not to say that the
Eucharistic presence has not its own characteristics and claims.
In the Eucharist, Christ is present as the Lamb slain from before
the foundation of the world ; and the space devoted in each of the
Gospels to the narratives of the Passion and crucifixion imply that
this is an aspect of our Lord's Being and work which it would be
impossible to emphasise too much.

So much will probably be generally admitted ; difficulty arises rather when we come to interpret these ideas in relation to the Eucharistic Gifts. Various terms have been used in Catholic theology to describe this relation. If what has been said in the preceding sections of this essay holds good, we are bound to say that the bread and wine are changed by consecration. They acquire a new property, namely, that their devout reception secures and normally conditions participation in the blessings of Christ's sacrifice, and therefore in His life. Regard being had to their sacrificial context, this is the natural meaning of the description of the consecrated elements, in relation to their consumption, as our Lord's body and blood—His body given for us and His blood shed for us. Outwardly, we have bread and wine ; the inward part and meaning of the sacrament is that these become in this sense the body and blood of our Lord, and as such are received by His people. The act of reception requires appropriation by faith, if reception is to have its proper consequence and complete meaning ; but the opportunity for reception and appropriation is afforded by the sacramental Gifts. The body and blood of our Lord are given after a spiritual and heavenly manner, not by any process separate from, and merely concomitant with, visible administration, but because the bread and wine become in the above sense (without any connotation of materialism) His body and His blood. It is true that this occurs simply in and through their becoming effectual symbols, but wherever the significance of an effectual symbol is certain and considerable we naturally think of it in terms of that significance, as well as in terms of its natural properties. We do not carefully separate in thought the natural properties of a florin and its purchasing value ; rather, we combine the two, and we think of the florin, quite simply, as an object [1] which has certain natural properties and certain purchasing value. We tend to think of the latter as to all intents and purposes a property of the object ; yet it depends simply and solely on the fact that the object is an effectual symbol. The case for a similar view of the Eucharistic symbols is, of course, infinitely stronger. In the first place, the Eucharistic character of the elements turns more directly on the

[1] Here, and throughout the essay, the word object is used to connote a complex of persisting opportunities of experience which have a common situation in space. The properties of an object are the component opportunities. Further analysis of "objects" is of course necessary from various points of view ; the above definition appears adequate for the present purpose.

connection between a certain act—to wit, devout reception—and certain results, and the basis of this connection is identical with the basis of those potential sequences between action and effect which constitute the natural properties of a visible thing. The Eucharistic sequences and the natural sequences are both determined by the divine will. In and through consecration those complexes of opportunities of experience which we call bread and wine are changed, not by any change in the original opportunities of experience, but by the addition of new opportunities of experience which are equally ultimate and have far greater significance.

Such considerations justify the tendency to speak of the consecrated elements as Host and Chalice, or as the Blessed Sacrament, or, using our Lord's words, to describe them as His body and blood, not as asserting any material or quasi-material identity with His natural or glorified body and blood, but as asserting that they render Him appropriable as our sacrifice. Any Eucharistic theology which does not begin by treating the words of institution as an immediate assertion of an identity tends also to use such phrases as the sacramental body and blood or the Eucharistic body and blood. Such phrases have a real value. They avoid much misunderstanding, and at the present day and in present circumstances they probably avoid more and more important misunderstandings than they create. On the other hand, they are in turn open to misunderstanding and to criticism which may be summed up in the incongruous phrase employed in this connection, that they teach a multi-corporal Christ. In the only sense in which we can still think of our Lord's glorified body as identical with His natural body, we must, however, think of His sacramental body as identical with that body. The identity between our Lord's glorified body and his natural body must be held to consist in the facts that opportunities of experience which each includes, and normally conditions, are directly determined by that nature which our Lord assumed at His Incarnation ; and that in each case the whole complex of opportunities of experience exists as such in immediate dependence on that nature and affords immediately an expression of it. All this is, however, also the case in regard to the Eucharistic body or blood. And the doctrine thus resulting admits of more than one philosophical expression. In the terms of a value-philosophy, the word " Convaluation "[1] meets the

---

[1] *Cf.* W. Temple, *Christus Veritas*, pp. 247 ff.

case ; though it may be questioned whether " Transvaluation " would not do so even better. If the doctrine were translated into scholastic terms it would involve the assertion that the substance of the Eucharistic body and blood is the substance of that body and that blood which our Lord assumed at His Incarnation ; and it is in this sense a doctrine of transubstantiation. But it is not such a doctrine of transubstantiation as is condemned in Anglican formularies, and is neither open to the objections nor presents the difficulties to which those testify. It does not overthrow the nature of a sacrament but is directly based on assigning to a sacrament that nature which Anglican formularies assign, and is deduced from the traditional Anglican view simply by insistence on the significance and implications of the facts that in the Eucharist we have primarily a symbolism of objects, and that the effectual symbolism of a sacrament is based on, and determined by, the divine will.[1]

It will be obvious that the views which have been advanced have an immediate bearing on the question of Eucharistic adoration. The danger of idolatry (in its narrower sense) lies in the identification of a material object with a divine person. The position with regard to images is exactly parallel to that with regard to pictures. They may legitimately afford a means for expressing as well as

[1] This is perhaps the most convenient point to notice an important criticism of the line of argument which is being employed. It is urged that this proves too much : that all that is claimed in regard to the Host or Chalice might be claimed in regard to unconsecrated bread or wine on the ground that these have the " property " that they can be consecrated to become the Eucharistic body and blood, and that this " property," and either complex as including this " property," also depend on our Lord's being and nature. When, however, an opportunity of experience depends on a special capacity to utilise an object, which capacity is possessed only by certain persons, the opportunity of experience thus presented cannot be regarded as a property of the object, and is rightly referred to the capacity, not to the object. The possibility of the " Venus of Milo " or of Leonardo's " Last Supper " was not a property of some piece of marble or of certain pigments, although dependent on these. So with the bread and wine. The opportunity which the unconsecrated bread and wine afford is not general, so that the same act by any person in the same (regenerate) order would normally have the same effect. It depends on a special power inherent in the priesthood, even although this power of the priest is, of course, merely the power of an ambassador, and what is involved in his making bread and wine effectual symbols depends not on his will but on the divine will. A further reply can also be made, in the judgment of the writer, by regard to immediacy of dependence and the nature of the " property " in question, but the above consideration appears adequate for the purpose, and is considerably simpler.

stimulating feelings. Unless it is improper for a man to kiss the picture of one he loves, or place flowers before a picture of a dead wife, or for ardent politicians to decorate the statue of Lord Beaconsfield, it cannot be improper for the Catholic to place flowers or lights before the image of a Saint. Nor is this situation different when the image is an image of our Lord, and, in consequence, of a Person to whom adoration may be paid. But there must be no identification of the object with the person : these must consciously be held apart or idolatry results. In the case of the Sacrament the matter is different. On the view advanced we have objects which are a direct expression of our Lord's being and nature ; which exist in direct dependence on that being and nature as such an expression, and which enable us not only to participate in the blessings of His sacrifice but to be strengthened with His life, thus affording a relation to Him even more intimate than that which His natural body made possible. It is, of course, obvious that even such an object may not be worshipped in itself with that worship which may only be properly paid to a person. Even if our Lord were present in His glorified body, when we knelt before it in our worship of Him, we should not be giving to the Body in itself that worship which may be properly paid only to a divine person, but we should be so far identifying the object with the person that our worship of the person found expression in relation to the object. If the Eucharistic body and blood are no less directly related to Him in that they are no less directly dependent on His being and nature, and if they mediate an even more intimate relation than did His natural body, a similar attitude is justified, and our Eucharistic adoration finds natural and proper expression in acts related to the Sacrament.

It may be worth while, finally, to point out the bearing of these considerations on the devotional use of the Reserved Sacrament. It is desirable to emphasise that from the point of view here advanced the question whether our Lord is present and may be worshipped in the Reserved Sacrament, and the question whether Communion may be given by means of the Reserved Sacrament, are not two questions but one question. When it is asserted that our Lord is present in the Reserved Sacrament, it is not a question of asserting something additional to the fact that Communion may be given by the Reserved Sacrament. If the Reserved Sacrament is in fact capable of giving Communion precisely the arguments as to Eucharistic adoration which have already been advanced apply in the case of the Reserved Sacrament. Further, when this finds expression in devotional practices, what is involved is simply the transposition—in time, though not in thought, and for convenience though not in principle—of elements which are intrinsic parts of the Eucharistic rite. Thus, the devotional use of the Reserved Sacrament is not something independent of Communion and deriving from some separate conception. It is precisely because devout reception unites us to our Lord that the Reserved Sacrament is His body, that He is present in a special manner, and that He can be thus adored.[1]

V

CONCLUSION

The foregoing argument will have suggested that the Eucharist is only very imperfectly described in the phrase, so often repeated, that it was given only for the purpose of Communion ; but it will also have been clear that the whole doctrine here advanced is at every point rooted in, and dependent on, the idea of Communion as an integral and culminating part of the rite. If we were to define the purpose of the sacrament, we probably could not do better than use the language of the Catechism, and say that it was instituted " for the continual remembrance of the sacrifice of the death of Christ, and of the benefits which we receive thereby." This essay has been an attempt to draw out the meaning of that pregnant definition. It is, however, by no means the only statement in our formularies which appears to presuppose a Catholic doctrine of the Eucharist. The rubric with regard to reconsecration, for instance, would be unnecessary, if not superstitious, if, instead of the symbolism of the rite being one primarily of objects rather than of action, the acts of individual administration were held to be directly sacramental. The same view is

---

[1] The desirability of the devotional use of the Reserved Sacrament, and the forms which it should take, involve considerations outside the scope of this essay, since practical questions arise as to the risk of inadequate teaching with consequent superstition, and as to such an excess of these devotions as would destroy the proportion of the faith. It may, however, be fairly claimed that objections of these types hold against many other forms of devotion, and that experience in the case of these would appear to show that a remedy is better sought in regulation than in prohibition.

suggested by the rubric as to the consumption of what remains of the consecrated elements ; while more broadly still, the whole structure of the English Communion Office—its requirement of priesthood in the celebrant, its detailed directions as to vesture and ceremony, its preparation of the worshipper by confession and absolution, and not least its truncated Consecration prayer with its abrupt emphasis on the words of institution—points to the symbolism of the rite being conceived as at once sacrificial and effectual.

At the same time, the truth that the Eucharistic sacrifice finds its consummation in Communion is one which cannot be too strongly emphasised. The principle is implicit in the universal fact that no Eucharist is ever celebrated without the priest at least communicating ; and it is an axiom of Catholic teaching that only by devout reception of the Sacrament can the individual worshipper appropriate its benefits. There have been periods in the Church's history, no doubt, when this side of the truth was forgotten ; and it may be admitted that one cause of this has sometimes been an undue stringency of penitential or ceremonial discipline. More serious, however, is a difficulty of an opposite kind, which must be faced before we close. It cannot be denied that to many minds the notion that the partaking of a sacrament should be " generally necessary to salvation " is a great stumbling-block. To such minds the sacramental principle appears to involve a reaction from that pure and spiritual religion which Jesus Christ came to establish. The issue is too large for adequate treatment here, and we must be content with no more than an outline. It will generally be found on examination that this difficulty involves an important underlying assumption—the assumption, namely, that our spiritual experience is, and should be, independent of and separable from our natural experience. But is that true ? Is it not rather the case that spiritual experience, though of course it is more than natural experience, is yet so commonly intertwined with it as to stand to natural experience in the relation of whole to part ? Certainly this is the case in our social relationships. An outstretched hand, for example, may be the expression of an offer of renewed friendship ; and in such a case the offer and its acceptance alike involve this expression as part of the whole experience. In certain circumstances a salute to the national flag is not something separable from our loyalty, but is an integral part of such loyalty and of the experience which this involves. At every turn in our social life acts or opportunities of personal intercourse are ordinarily associated with some outward expression, suitable for its purpose but otherwise arbitrary ; and the facts would appear to suggest that a healthy emotional life requires such an expression in a substantial measure. Within the special field of religious experience the same would appear to be the case. It is easy to say that an excess of sacramentalism is harmful : it is difficult to deny the value of sacramentalism as an element in religion. And sacramentalism found at once a fuller opportunity and a more adequate basis when God became incarnate. By His own acts on earth and through the Church as His mystical body it became possible in a new degree for the Word of God to give expression to opportunities and gifts of grace, and thus to utilise a method of intercourse which men had always employed in their personal relations with each other, and after which they had sought so earnestly, if often so mistakenly, in their relations with God.

There will, of course, always be those whose thought and devotion will tend to lay especial stress upon the " exemplarist " aspects both of the Incarnation and of the cross, and to whom spiritual and moral progress will consist chiefly in the development of the understanding ; and it will usually be found in such cases that the appeal of the Eucharist is not strong. Yet even such people will probably admit that Christ's example, in His life and in His death, is not the whole Christian Gospel, but that this involves an activity of God towards man and in man deriving from the historic and glorified Christ and continuous in the Church ever since. That activity is what we mean by the word " grace." And what the Catholic belief in the Eucharist asserts is that this grace is normally given by means of the Sacrament, which when received in faith—and even for natural nourishment active assimilation is necessary—does in fact renew the believer's union with God. It cannot be too often asserted that it is on the actuality and fruits of that union, and not any conscious feeling of it, that the emphasis is laid in Catholic teaching and practice. It would probably be true to say that " sensible devotion " at the time of Communion is the exception rather than the rule in the case of those who most regularly receive. But " we know whom we have believed," and find in experience that God performs all that

He promises in this rite, so far as our frail faith and feeble penitence allow. More than that we cannot ask ; but less we dare not claim.

NOTE

The above Essay is based on an article on the Eucharistic Sacrifice in *Theology* (October, 1923); on a pamphlet by the late Mr. Arthur Boutwood (Hakluyt Egerton) and myself, *A Cross Bench View of the Reservation Controversy*, published by the Faith Press ; on the Second Appendix to the *Irenicum* of John Forbes by the editor of this volume ; and on other material lavishly supplied by him. I am indebted to the publisher of the above article and pamphlet for permission to incorporate certain passages.

For fuller treatment of the terms used in this essay, and especially of the term " oblation," I venture to refer to page 3 of my review of Canon Quick's *The Christian Sacraments*, published as a "Theology" Reprint (No. 3) under the same title.

ADDITIONAL NOTES

A. Essay 2. The Vindication of Religion

I trust I have done my best to profit by those criticisms of my essay which have come to my knowledge. I should have counted it good fortune to meet with a piece of thorough and dispassionate hostile criticism of the whole argument. Unfortunately the one emphatically unfavourable review which I have seen, that in *The Freethinker*, though couched in heated and rhetorical language, contains much vehement assertion but no reasoning, and appears, indeed, to be the work of a writer who knew no more of the essay he was denouncing than he had learned from a review in *The Church Times*. The author clearly did not know what my argument was, but was singularly anxious to prevent it from getting an unprejudiced hearing. Among friendly critics, I note that one says, apparently with regret, that the argument is " on conventional lines," and a second complains that I have not dealt with the " problem of evil." To the former friend I would reply that I should think it a grave fault if the reasoning of my essay did not proceed on "conventional lines." I do not presume to claim any private and peculiar reasons for belief in God ; if I have any, I apprehend that, just because they are private and personal, they cannot be used as the basis of an argument addressed to my fellow-men at large. As to the " problem of evil," it is purposely excluded from the scope of my essay. Belief in God, in my judgement, neither creates the problem nor removes it, and a complete " solution " of it is impossible alike to reason and to faith, so long as we are still *in via*. Anything I have to say in the matter, and it is little enough, will now be found in a small pamphlet *The Problem of Evil* (Ernest Benn, Ltd., 1929). For a much better treatment I would refer my reviewer to the essay on " Preliminaries to Religious Belief" in von Hügel's *Essays and Addresses on the Philosophy of Religion*.

I pass on to some remarks on a few particular expressions used in the course of the essay.

P. 32, l. 29.—Mgr. Batiffol points out that I have fallen into a slight error, which he readily grants does not affect the substance of the paragraph, about the Vatican Council. The doctrine anathematised in the third session of the Council was that the existence of God " cannot be certainly known (certo cognosci) by natural reason " ; nothing was said about demonstration. I confess that I had been misled into thinking that the expression used was *probari*, and unpardonably forgot to " verify my reference." In point of fact, since express reference was made to Romans i. 20, I take it that the Council, in speaking of " certain knowledge," was thinking of inferential knowledge, valid *proof*, and that I should have been substantially correct if I had not used the word *demonstrated*, with its mathematical associations. It is interesting to see that, in the discussions which preceded the formulation of the anathema, the point was actually raised whether the word *certo* ought not to be omitted. It was retained, apparently, on the grounds that to delete it would amount to divergence from the position of St. Paul in the passage referred to, and that St. Thomas and others often speak of demonstration in the matter.

Pp. 36, 37.—Compare with what is said here about the " principle of Carnot," the pithy remark of Eddington (*The Nature of the Physical World*, p. 74) that a reversal of it would be " something much worse than a violation of an ordinary law of Nature, namely, an improbable coincidence."

P. 49, l. 35.—Perhaps I should have excluded St. Thomas's fourth " way," the argument from the " scale of perfection," from the scope of this observation.

P. 54, l. 14.—What a " stiff dose of brute fact " the electron is may be seen from Eddington's chapters on " The Quantum Theory " and " The New Quantum Theory " (chs. ix and x) in *The Nature of the Physical World*. A very distinguished scholar now dead once remarked to me : " What I like about Sir Oliver Lodge is that he makes it so plain that a man has to believe some very singular things if he means to believe in science."

P. 57, *n.*1.—*Cf.* the very modest statement of Jeans (in *Evolution in the Light of Modern Knowledge*, p. 29) : " We may reasonably conjecture that planetary systems, *although not the normal* accompaniment of a sun (italics mine), must be fairly freely scattered in space," and the more decided pronouncement of Eddington (*The Nature of the Physical World*, p. 178), " I feel inclined to claim that *at the present time* (italics Eddington's) our race is supreme ; and not one of the profusion of stars in their myriad clusters looks down on scenes comparable to those which are passing beneath the eye of the sun." One cannot, of course, predict what will be the ultimate outcome of the " new physics," but it is notable that, at the present moment, the physicists and astronomers seem to be tending to reinstate the conception of a finite universe, with a first and a last day and a possibly unique earth. Even in my own boyhood this would have been called superstitious " mediaevalism."

P. 67, l. 12.—This " old argument " is *not*, as is sometimes loosely said, that of St. Thomas. His argument turns on very different considerations. Unpardoned " mortal " sin, of its own nature, leads to an eternal penalty because it involves total aversion of the soul from God (*S. T.* Ia IIae q. 87, art 3 *resp.*).

A E. Taylor.

B. Essay 4. The Christian Conception of God

P. 140.—Since the essay was first published, I have come to the conclusion that *actuality* is a better word to employ in reference to the Godhead than *activity*. There seems to be no objection in principle to such a use of the word *activity*. But *actuality* has, through its associations in the history of thought, a wider reference than *activity* and may be held to include it. For fuller statements on this subject I would venture to refer to my recent work *The Incarnate Lord*, especially pp. 109–110 and 415.

L. S. Thornton.

C. Essay 9. The Resurrection

It seems desirable to remove one or two misunderstandings to which my treatment of our Lord's resurrection in this volume has given rise. And, first, something may be said as to the scope of the essay. It was not intended to provide an exhaustive treatment of the subject, but such a treatment as seemed needed in view of the aims of the volume as a whole. An attempt is made, therefore, in the first place, to determine the doctrinal import of the resurrection in the faith and teaching of the Apostolic age, and to show what a large superstructure of beliefs and hopes is built upon the Easter happenings. The central section of the essay is devoted to an examination of a part of these happenings, namely, those connected with the appearances of the risen Lord ; and, in view of the wide vogue of "vision theories" in modern theology, a deliberate endeavour is made to press this line of approach as far as it will go. It may be true, as the Rev. W. J. Peck has said, that I "state the case for mystical experiences too strongly," or, as Dr. Anderson Scott has urged, that at the end of it all "we simply have the old problem under a new name." But at least it seemed to me desirable that, if only as an *argumentum ad hominem*, the "vision theory" should be made to yield up whatever truth it contained ; and I believe that a psychological treatment of the appearances does in fact throw fresh light on their vocational character, and thereby supply fresh evidence for the resurrection itself. I state clearly, however, that I cannot regard the appearances as providing in themselves an adequate basis for the resurrection faith as we find it in the New Testament, which turns less upon the survival of Jesus than upon the reversal and redress of the cross ; and in a brief concluding section reasons are given for belief in the empty tomb as an integral part of the resurrection fact and faith. For a much fuller treatment of the evidence in this connection I will take leave to refer to my article entitled "The Evidence of the Resurrection" in *A New Commentary on Holy Scripture*, pp. 301–315.

There is one particular criticism to which a more detailed reply may be made. In his able and interesting volume, *A Century of Anglo-Catholicism*, Professor H. L. Stewart speaks (p. 216) of "this conjecture by Dr. Selwyn, that the body of our Lord remained in the grave, while the appearances were a series of ' veridical visions ' by which He worked upon the minds of His disciples." Professor Stewart himself does something on a later page (p. 352) to mitigate the force of this statement. But I cannot understand how anyone who had read pp. 318, 319 of my essay in this volume could have attributed to me the belief that " the body of our Lord remained in the grave " ; nor should I be prepared to accept *tout court* his version of my interpretation of the appearances. For this last perhaps I may quote from my article in the *New Commentary*, where it is urged that, " while each appearance to the disciples involved a real presence to them of the risen Christ acting on each occasion upon them in His risen body, this did not involve any such materiality as that an indifferent spectator in the garden or on the way to Emmaus or in the Upper Chamber would have seen any form or heard any words or witnessed any action (such as being touched)."

E. G. SELWYN.

D. ESSAY 12. THE ORIGINS OF THE SACRAMENTS

P. 369.—The justice of the observation with regard to the part played by the sacraments in Protestant Christianity being that of " optional appendages" to religion has been challenged by Dr. Anderson Scott, who points out that the chief official formularies of Protestant Christendom assign a high place and value to the sacraments. But the statement in the text has reference, not to formularies, but to the actual present practice of Protestantism ; and in this connection it is amply borne out by a writer of such unimpeachably Protestant sympathies as Professor H. L. Stewart (*cf.* the passage quoted in the Preface to this edition from his *A Century of Anglo-Catholicism*, pp. 353 f.).

N. P. WILLIAMS.

INDEX